# Consumer Survival

# Consumer Survival

## AN ENCYCLOPEDIA OF CONSUMER RIGHTS, SAFETY, AND PROTECTION

**Volume One**
**A–G**

**Wendy Reiboldt and**
**Melanie Horn Mallers, Editors**

 ABC-CLIO

Santa Barbara, California • Denver, Colorado • Oxford, England

**Library of Congress Cataloging-in-Publication Data**

Consumer survival : an encyclopedia of consumer rights, safety, and protection / Wendy Reiboldt and Melanie Horn Mallers, editors.

    pages cm

  Includes bibliographical references and index.

  ISBN 978-1-59884-936-3 (hardback) — ISBN 978-1-59884-937-0 (ebook)

1. Consumer protection—Law and legislation—United States—Encyclopedias.  I. Reiboldt, Wendy, editor.  II. Mallers, Melanie Horn, editor.

  KF1607.5.C66   2014

  343.7307'103—dc23       2013023279

ISBN: 978-1-59884-936-3

EISBN: 978-1-59884-937-0

18  17  16  15  14    1  2  3  4  5

This book is also available on the World Wide Web as an eBook. Visit www.abc-clio.com for details.

ABC-CLIO, LLC
130 Cremona Drive, P.O. Box 1911
Santa Barbara, California 93116-1911

This book is printed on acid-free paper ∞

Manufactured in the United States of America

# Contents

# List of Entries

# Guide to Related Topics

## Dangers

Affinity Fraud

Bait and Switch

Bankruptcy

Identity Theft: Child

Cosigning

Counterfeiting

Foreclosures and Short Sales

Frauds and Scams

Identity Theft

Levies

Liens

Mechanic's Lien

Multilevel Marketing and Pyramid Plans

Payday Lending

Phishing

Ponzi Schemes

Privacy: Offline

Privacy: Online

Pyramid Plans

Quackery

Rent-To-Own (RTO)

Sexual Harassment

Short Sales

Title Pawn Loans

Usury

Working from Home Schemes

## General

Auto Purchasing

Advertising

Banking

Caveat Emptor

Caveat Venditor

Certified Financial Planners™

Charity and Philanthropic Giving

Consumer Price Index (CPI)

Consumer Reports

Consumer Sovereignty

Credit Cards

Credit Repair Organizations

Credit Unions

Debt Collection

Debt Management

Debt, Student

Discrimination

Extended Warranties

Fair Trade

Fannie Mae

Federal Reserve

FHA (Federal Housing Administration)

Fair Isaac and Company (FICO)

Freddie Mac

Gift Cards

Hazard Analysis and Critical Control Point (HACCP)

Health and Healthcare

Home Equity Loans

Insurance

Investing Regulations

Malpractice

Minimum Wage

Mortgages

Pawn Shops

Penny Stocks

Prepaid Cards

Producer Sovereignty

Social Networking

## Government Agencies

Administration on Aging (AoA)

Attorney General Office (AG)

Bureau of Consumer Protection (BCP)

Bureau of Labor Statistics

Centers for Disease Control and Prevention (CDC)

Commission on Civil Rights

Commodity Futures Trading Commission (CFTC)

Congress

Consumer Financial Protection Bureau

Consumer Product Safety Commission (CPSC)

Customs and Border Protection (CBP)

Department of Agriculture (USDA)

Department of Commerce (DOC)

Department of Defense (DOD)

Department of Education (ED)

Department of Energy (DOE)

Department of Health and Human Services (HHS)

Department of Homeland Security (DHS)

Department of Housing and Urban Development (HUD)

Department of Justice (DOJ)

Department of Labor (DOL)

Department of State

Department of the Interior (DOI)

Department of Transportation (DOT)

Department of the Treasury

Department of Veterans Affairs (VA)

Departments of Consumer Affairs (DCA)

Departments of Insurance

Environmental Protection Agency (EPA)

Equal Employment Opportunity Commission (EEOC)

FDIC (Federal Deposit Insurance Commission)

Federal Aviation Administration (FAA)

Federal Bureau of Investigation (FBI)

Federal Citizen Information Center

Federal Communications Commission (FCC)

Federal Emergency Management Agency (FEMA)

Federal Trade Commission (FTC)

Food and Drug Administration (FDA)

Government Accountability Office (GAO)

Housing and Urban Development (HUD)

Inspector General (IG)

International Trade Commission

National Highway Traffic Safety Administration (NHTSA)

National Institute of Occupational Safety and Health (NIOSH)

OSHA (Occupational Safety & Health Administration)

Patent and Trademark Office

Post Office (USPS, United States Postal Service)

Public Utilities Commission

Securities and Exchange Commission (SEC)

Small Business Administration (SBA)

Small Claims Courts

Supplemental Nutrition Assistance Program (SNAP)

Supreme Court of the United States

Surgeon General

# Legislation

Americans with Disabilities Act (ADA)

Bullying

Checks 21 Act

Children's Online Privacy Protection Act (COPPA)

Cigarette Labeling Act

Clayton Act

Community Mental Health Act

Credit Card Accountability Responsibility and Disclosure Act (CARD)

Credit Practices Rule

Delaney Amendment

Dodd–Frank Wall Street Reform and Consumer Protection Act

Door-to-Door Sales

DREAM Act: Development, Relief and Education for Alien Minors

Equal Credit Opportunity Act (ECOA)

Fair Credit Reporting Act (FCRA)

Fair Debt Collection Practices Act (FDCPA)

Family Educational Rights and Privacy Act (FERPA)

Family Medical Leave Act

Federal Deposit Insurance Corporation Improvement Act

Food Stamps

Food, Drug, and Cosmetic Act (FD&C Act)

## Movements

## Organizations

# Preface

In early 2010, Wendy was approached by an acquisitions editor with ABC-CLIO to write a two-volume encyclopedia that was "cutting-edge" in its examination of major issues in Consumer Affairs. At that time (and until this present work) there was nothing like it on the market, despite the need for a comprehensive reference work on topics that impact consumers. Interestingly, during this time too, Melanie was sharing her thoughts with Wendy about developing a new course in her academic department, Human Services, about advocacy and health. This discussion served as a unique opportunity for the blending of the two fields of Consumer Affairs and Human Services together. Several months later, a joint project ensued. The result became a timely product that combines two academic passions: consumer behavior and well-being. After several editors, conceptual conversations, and working titles, we are pleased to present *Consumer Survival: The Encyclopedia of Consumer Rights, Safety, and Protection*.

The original intended audience of the work was primarily U.S. users of high school, public, and college libraries. Given its evolution however, the work is also suitable for the basic consumer as well. With an expanded emphasis on individual rights, safety, and protections, this work provides an invaluable resource for all to become empowered. Nonprofit directors, social workers, educators, academics, as well as laypersons, in addition to professionals in consumer affairs, law, and policy, can all utilize this resource as a tool for improving the health and well-being of themselves and others. We have provided information on a wide array of pertinent topics, encompassing laws, regulations, personal protections, and more, with topics that address the social, economic, and political arenas, as well as the mental and social well-being of all people. Readers will gain many benefits from reading or referring to this resource. Entries in fact oftentimes include clear instructions and reminders for how to specifically protect one-self from harm. Related sidebar comments provide additional or explanatory information; these have been placed throughout the volumes. These comments often provide personal commentaries, current events, or interesting facts.

To assist readers in navigating through the work, we have designed the encyclopedia to be user-friendly and accessible for all readers. Entries are listed in alphabetical order (A–Z format). For each entry, or headword, we include references as well as suggestions for additional readings, and we also refer to other entries via "see also." At the end of the encyclopedia, we have included a Primary Source Appendix with a few examples of full or partial portions of acts or declarations. All of these resources are intended to assist readers with developing a more fully integrated understanding of topics.

Throughout the text, we have also included "blind entries." These are descriptor words or other common ways that main entry topics are typically referred to in the literature. They are intended to refer readers to the main A–Z entries if otherwise potentially overlooked. For example, a blind entry for the main headword Consumers Union is Consumer Reports, a topic that does not have its own entry, but is discussed in the main headword, Consumers Union. Also note that for ease of reading, and to avoid a repetitive list of United States entries, we have eliminated "United States" in all headwords. For example, the United States Department of Agriculture is listed as Department of Agriculture (USDA).

Overall, entries were selected based on in-depth analysis of media, historical sources, newspapers, websites, journals, and legal documents, and other consumer texts. After several passes at an initial list of topics for entries, we began inviting contributors who are experts in their fields. For the next year and half, the list continued to evolve. Many deletions were made, with realization that the entry really did not fit the scope of our work (nor our assigned allotted word count), such as criminal law and financial investment vehicles. Other decisions were made to add topics, such as social welfare and student debt, in part based on suggestions from contributors, as well as also contemporary events impacting consumer affairs, advocacy, and policy. At the final version of the work, there are over 200 main entries (with over 50 blind entries). Some entries are more comprehensive in nature due to the scope of the book and their impact on and relevancy for the consumer movement and consumer well-being and protection. Overall, entries range between 200 (e.g., Levies) to over 4,000 words (e.g., Privacy: Online) due to their relevance and timeliness. Also, there is minimal attention given to international aspects of consumer rights, safety, and protection, though we did include entries on the World Health Organization, World Trade Organization, Consumers International, the International Trade Commission, and the United Nations. A full discussion on global movements, organizations, and leaders was beyond the scope of this work.

Entries were written by 92 contributors who vary in scope based on their work and involvement in select fields. Contributors were invited to participate based on their expertise, previously published work, or current work in the field. While we suggested word lengths for each topic, as based on our assumptions for the topic's merit and saliency in the field, contributors oftentimes made critical requests to expand or shorten their entries based on their knowledge of the field and relevance to the overall work.

Entries reflect eight subject categories: Dangers, General, Government Agencies, Legislation, Movements, Organizations, People, and Safeguards. A complete list of entries by category is provided to further assist the reader looking for a particular area of interest. One thing to note is that the "General" subject category includes entries that are often multifaceted and could easily fit into several other subject categories. For example, Credit Repair Organizations can be both a "Safeguard" and a "Danger" depending on their legitimacy. Also, many of these entries have subsets of populations as their focus, including older adults, children, women, ethnic minorities, immigrants, and the poor. These entries address the unique needs of each group and on their related rights to advocating for a better quality of life.

Additionally, we took several steps to minimize the contributor's personal "voice" and personal bias; our request was for entries to be written objectively. While this was sometimes difficult to do, as many contributors hold great passion about their topics, all contributors prepared entries based on important and timely information.

Finally, we begin this work with a contextual essay, in which we review factors that drive the consumer movement, provide an overview of what the consumer movement is, including a summary of its history, and discuss future directions of the movement. We also include a presidential chart highlighting all presidential terms and selected consumer-related legislation, as well as a chart of the governmental branches with examples of departments and agencies within each. Overall, we hope that this work advances the understanding of consumer affairs, not just for academics and professionals, but also for individual consumers for whom all of this even matters.

# Acknowledgments

Many persons made important contributions to this encyclopedia. It is our pleasure to acknowledge them. First, we wish to extend our many thanks to the contributors who agreed to provide their expertise and write (and rewrite) their entries. Their contributions were oftentimes completed despite personal loss, injury, illness, and extraordinary work overloads. Several authors also took time to suggest additional entry topics, as well as provide feedback on the title of the encyclopedia. We are deeply grateful to all of them. In particular, we would like to acknowledge Monroe Friedman, who provided additional insight and conceptual direction.

We are grateful to our ABC-CLIO editors, for their thoroughness and patience as we navigated through the editing maze. We are also greatly indebted to Susan Adams and our other dedicated students who provided countless hours of support in conducting research, managing documents, and formatting files. We could not have done this without them.

Finally, we wish to thank our families—Massimo, Reno, and Ambra (Wendy's husband and children), and Danny and Joshua (Melanie's husband and son)—for their ongoing support, encouragement, humor, and understanding. Without them this work would not have been possible.

# Contextual Essay

## Drivers of the Consumer Movement

The American consumer movement has long been characterized by an inherent ebb and flow of marketplace movements and governmental actions. Throughout history, the forces behind the movement have been somewhat predictable. The movement, and attention to it, pick up during poor economic conditions, typically manifested in consumer interest due to such factors as a decrease in disposable income, disillusionment with the government and marketplace, antagonism toward advertising, unresponsiveness on behalf of government, episodes of privacy intrusions, and special problems related to the disadvantaged consumer. Further interest is piqued when charismatic and visionary leaders are prominent, a responsive Congress is in session, and business ethics are in a downturn. Attention to or saliency of the consumer movement, however, loses momentum when the economy is strong, jobs are plentiful, no high-profile cases of wrong-doing against consumers are present, and prosperity abounds. The tide though can easily turn, and it usually does, causing the pendulum to swing back toward a desire for aid and protection of rights whereby consumers want safeguards and they want them quickly. Regardless of the political party of leaders and their respective philosophies, this ebb and flow prevails. Ideologically, many Republicans seek to increase choice and limit governmental restrictions for consumers toward a free market economy, while many Democrats are more paternalistic, believing that too many choices may overwhelm consumers and thus may see the need for providing consumers with more protections and governmental oversight. Despite their ideological differences, both parties seek to provide safeguards for consumers in the marketplace. Likewise, consumers demand these safeguards in their never-ending "consumption quest."

## Consumption as a Driver

Consumption is a powerful factor in driving the economy and the consumer movement. The process of consumption can be as simple as eating a meal, or as complex as buying a house. The concept of consumption also applies to all consumers regardless of income, race, gender, or age. Infants consume food, and utilize diapers, lotions, and clothing; even funeral services are utilized (consumed) by the recently deceased and their families. Consumption is a concept that does not discriminate; indeed all Americans are consumers.

Consumers both spend and earn money that contributes to and stimulates the economy. Most consumers are also producers, participating in the marketplace, earning an income, and generating productivity at the workplace. When consumers spend, they seek low prices on high-quality goods and services. When earning, consumers want the highest possible payment via income at the least amount of effort (which coincidentally helps explain the success of "get rich quick" schemes over the years). However, these marketplace wishes are in opposition to each other and therefore create a continuous tug-of-war that has been operating in the marketplace since its beginning years.

The existence of this tug-of-war eventually led to the formalization of the consumer movement whereby leaders and consumers could speak out against injustices and obtain redress and a presence in the marketplace. Interestingly, businesses viewed this movement as "antibusiness" and devised the term *consumerism* because it was similar to the word *communism*, thus giving it a stigmatized connotation. Manufacturers and retailers did not like the idea of consumers having power, so they hoped that making the concept appear negative would make it disappear. Their plan didn't work.

## The History of the Consumer Movement

In general, the consumer movement is the process by which consumers have power and rights in the marketplace, including the mechanisms by which government supports such rights by enacting legislation, creating protection agencies, and regulating businesses to allow consumers to safely operate and interact in the marketplace. Rights, safety, and protections cross over all areas of the marketplace and economy, touching on a broad array of concepts, including complex consumer issues and basic human and civil rights. To fully understand the consumer movement, it is important to have a foundation and understanding of the consumer movement's evolution.

## The Consumer Movement in Retrospect: The Early Years

There is some debate about the true start of the consumer movement. Was it a group of Denver housewives picketing their local supermarket? Was it the formal announcement of the Consumer Bill of Rights by President John F. Kennedy or the creation of the Office of Consumer Affairs? Could it have been Ralph Nader's publication of *Unsafe at Any Speed?* These highly publicized events marked critical turning points in consumer history, with all events converging in the 1960s, in the midst of a sympathetic president and dynamic, outspoken champions for consumer causes—in the 1960s when civil rights were also on the forefront. In reality, consumer protection efforts have been occurring since America's inception. In fact, the first Congress under President George Washington began protecting citizens immediately through laws ensuring fair trade and the establishment of a banking system. The ebb and flow of consumer and civil rights are depicted in an ongoing series of significant events and dedicated people, which brings us to where we are today.

While early U.S. presidents were busy establishing the nation, laying the government's foundation, and negotiating fair trade, the formalization of consumer-focused legislation as we know it today began one hundred years later. In the late 1800s public figures stood up for consumers and federal laws were enacted to require safe, affordable, and viable products and services desired by American consumers. While Lincoln may be best known for signing the Thirteenth Amendment into law and abolishing slavery in 1865, he also had a considerable hand in stimulating stronger consumer protection. Under his leadership, the U.S. Department of Agriculture was created in 1867, a significant consumer-focused safety organization.

The Mail Fraud Act of 1872 was passed under President Ulysses S. Grant, making it illegal to commit fraud through the U.S. mail. In 1887, President Grover Cleveland passed the Interstate Commerce Act that addressed the monopolistic practices of the railroad industry. Nearly two decades later, a group of middle- and upper-class citizens calling themselves "do-gooders" decided to improve working conditions through education, research, and patronization of stores that treated both workers and buyers fairly. In New York City, these do-gooders created the first Consumers League (CL) that investigated retailers' practices creating "white lists" and "black lists." White listed stores paid fair wages, required reasonable working hours, and maintained sanitary conditions in the workplace, while black listed stores did not. CL urged consumers to utilize these lists, thus starting the concept of "voting with the dollar." The league went national and opened offices in 20 states by 1903, aiding consumer decision-making in the marketplace. These and other protections were emerging on the consumer front.

However, while some conditions were improving, others were not. For example, corruption in medicine became common. "Snake oil" salesmen, such as German immigrant William Radam, sold "microbe killer" in the 1880s, claiming such products could cure all diseases. Additionally, with the advent of unions, wages and working conditions were advancing, but trusts and corporate schemes were also emerging to illegally fix and control prices and thereby eliminate marketplace competition. The Standard Oil Trust was one of the largest, and among the first to be investigated under the Sherman Antitrust Act of 1890 that made these practices illegal. While the Sherman Antitrust Act was passed to protect consumers from price fixing and cartels, it also increased competition, thereby giving consumers more choice in the marketplace.

By 1906, focus had shifted due to portrayals from the book, *The Jungle,* by Upton Sinclair that detailed the deplorable conditions for workers and poor sanitation in meat-packing plants. This expose alerted Americans and leaders that something had to be done on the food safety front. An important figure of the time was Dr. Harvey W. Wiley, who is commonly known as the father of The Pure Food and Drug Act due to his cutting edge work on food safety. As a chemist for the Department of Agriculture, Wiley was famously known for creating the "poison squad," a group of male volunteers who willingly ingested questionable food fillers and additives, kept diaries, and submitted themselves to medical tests that measured the resulting outcomes. As a result of his research efforts and tireless championing, the American Medical Association began analyzing drugs and reporting on their side effects. By the turn of the 20th century, Congress was reviewing bills on the subject, beginning with the Pure Food and Drug Act of 1906 under President Theodore Roosevelt's leadership. Quickly following the Congressional acts, markets opened up on a global level offering more choices, and more potential dangers to consumers; legislators and businesses began to react via legislation and private consumer groups. Most notably, the Better Business Bureau was formed in 1912 to discourage dishonest businesses through promotion of truth in advertising; its work continues today.

In 1914, under President Woodrow Wilson's leadership, the Federal Trade Commission Act was passed, establishing one of the largest consumer protection agencies to date. President Wilson was a champion for consumer causes, and in the same year, the Clayton Antitrust Act was also passed, strengthening the 1890 Sherman Antitrust Act. While consumer issues were prominent under President Wilson, World War I caused a stall in consumer causes under the presidencies of Harding and Coolidge. However, in 1927, the book *Your Money's Worth: A Study in the Waste of Consumer's Dollars* by Stuart Chase and F. J. Schlink focused on economics of the household with particular attention to advertising and high-pressure sales tactics, decreased product standards, and a lack of information provided by producers to consumers. Product testing was inevitable and Consumers Research, the first organization to test products, was founded in 1929. The Great Depression made it critical for Americans to spend their scant dollars wisely thus sparking renewed interest in consumer issues. Sadly, inferior merchandise continued to plague the marketplace that stimulated further product testing and a need for better labeling of consumer products. Because consumers had fewer dollars to spend, they had to make sure that what they were buying was of good quality and would last. Labor organizations and women's groups rallied to encourage then President Franklin Roosevelt to further protect consumers through stricter laws and stiffer punishments for businesses that defrauded consumers. Snake oil salesmen were successful because there was no law to stop them from selling faulty, dangerous, or even deadly products such as cure-alls.

Additional private efforts to protect consumers emerged with the creation of Consumers Union. It was founded in 1935 as part of an employee strike and split-off from Consumers Research, with official incorporation status in 1936. Visionary leader Colston Warne helped form Consumers Union and embraced rigorous product testing, which is still highly regarded and valued by consumers today. President Roosevelt further kick-started the movement by calling for food and drug law revisions. Though many businesses felt additional legislation was "un-American" and "anti-business," the resulting deaths of more than 100 adults and children from elixir sulfanilamide horrified the public and President Roosevelt. As a result, the 1938 Food, Drug, and Cosmetics Act was passed and provided for drug safety testing and federal inspections. When World War II started, consumers were rightfully distracted from consumer issues. However, after the war ended, consumers and legislators refocused on consumer and civil rights. Women and minorities in the workplace stimulated the modern civil rights movement and in 1948, President Harry Truman signed Executive Order 9981, which established equality of treatment and opportunity for all people in the armed services.

President Truman also expanded Social Security, witnessed the signing of the United Nations charter, and passed legislation for fair housing and equal employment. While Truman provided some proconsumer actions, his successor, President Dwight Eisenhower was not an advocate for consumer protection; he opposed truth-in-lending legislation as well as autosafety proposals. In fact, the consumer movement took a hiatus of sorts in the 1940s and early 1950s because there was little support for consumer issues, though significant civil rights actions were transpiring including the 1954 Supreme Court ruling deeming segregation in public schools as unconstitutional.

The consumer movement received a jolt when another book, *The Hidden Persuaders*, by Vance Packard was published in 1957. The book detailed the psychological trickery used in sales, and as a result, it stimulated renewed interest in consumerism. Concurrently, the Civil Rights Act of 1957 was sent to Congress by President Eisenhower, creating the U.S. Commission on Civil Rights and a Civil Rights Division in the Department of Labor. This Act also established a process for investigating civil rights violations.

## The Consumer Movement Formalized

President John F. Kennedy was a true champion for consumers in the post-war era, and his historical speech to Congress in 1962 unveiled the Consumer Bill of Rights that helped to fuel the movement in the 1960s. Later that same year, Rachel Carson's book, *Silent Spring*, revealed the dangers of herbicides and pesticides and added further proof to the arguments made by Kennedy and others that additional safety issues needed to be addressed, in addition to civil rights issues. By 1964, the 24th Amendment abolished the poll tax, which originally had been in place to make it difficult for poor black citizens to vote. During the same year, President Lyndon Johnson signed the Civil Rights Act of 1964, the most noteworthy piece of civil rights legislation since the 1800s. Also of importance under Johnson were the 1965 amendments to the Social Security Act that created both Medicare and Medicaid.

In the 1960s and 1970s, Congress passed significant legislation to protect consumers in the areas of product safety, warning labels, and the credit industry to name a few. Auto safety also experienced significant changes, due in large part to Ralph Nader's 1965 book, *Unsafe at Any Speed*. The book exposed the dangers in the manufacture and design of automobiles both to drivers and pedestrians. Nader was a dogged advocate on behalf of consumers and his legacy perseveres. Much of the legislation of this time is still relevant today, though many laws have been amended and strengthened, further addressing the changing needs of the American people.

President Johnson was one of the most active legislative presidents and a great champion for consumers. Because he was a former Senator and leader in the U.S. Senate, he knew how to work with Congress to pass legislation. He passed significant auto safety legislation and appointed Esther Petersen as the first special assistant to the President for Consumer Affairs (she had been promised the job by President Kennedy, but sadly he was assassinated before it was made official). President Richard Nixon followed Johnson's lead and enunciated a buyer's bill of rights and perhaps most significantly, both the Consumer Product Safety Commission and the National Highway Traffic and Safety Administration were created during Nixon's presidency. Cost-benefit analyses were employed under President Gerald Ford, who passed legislation requiring energy labels on appliances and added the "right to consumer education" to the Consumer Bill of Rights. President Jimmy Carter continued using cost-benefit analyses which was intended to control regulation to some degree. Carter also tackled debt collection abuses and alcohol labeling, and legislatively protected public parks. Perhaps most notable was Carter's creation of the Department of Education in 1980.

## The Modern Consumer Movement

President Ronald Reagan was not a champion for consumers, and like Carter, threatened to abolish the Consumer Product Safety Commission. Unfortunately, Reagan cut many federal programs that assisted consumers and consequently, his measures also weakened consumer agencies through budget reductions and antiregulatory actions. Reagan also demoted the position of special assistant to the president reporting to the White House and moved the position to the Department of Health and Human Services. On the civil rights front, Reagan did, however, designate Martin Luther King Jr. Day as a national holiday.

The deregulation movements of the 1980s that reduced governmental oversight on airlines, trucking, telecommunications, financial institutions, and others created concerns for consumers who were unsure if deregulation would benefit them. In the end, the benefits, in most cases, were greater than expected and consumers enjoyed better prices and service due to the increases in competition. President George Bush was not as detrimental to the consumer movement as Ronald Reagan; he increased the budgets of consumer agencies. Under Bush's leadership, important nutritional food labeling legislation was passed, as was legislation to limit advertising aimed at children. In the mid- to late-1990s, President Bill Clinton worked on health reform legislation, though Congress failed to pass it. He was, however, able to improve meat inspection standards, increase the minimum wage, and strengthen telemarketing rules. Clinton also passed the Family Medical Leave Act in 1993 which provided tremendous flexibility for workers, and he announced the "right to service" as part of the Consumer

Bill of Rights. Near the end of Clinton's presidency, a reluctant consumer advocate, Erin Brockovich, became a household name due to the release of a movie about her life, specifically her 10-year crusade against Pacific Gas and Electric's careless and deliberate pollution of ground water in Hinkley, California. She continues her advocacy work today.

President George W. Bush's legacy, due to the terrorist attacks on America in 9/11, focused largely on legislation related to terrorism, the military, and strengthening homeland security. Bush signed the Patriot Act of 2001 and the Homeland Security Act of 2002 that created the Department of Homeland Security. Bush also enacted the controversial No Child Left Behind legislation, the highly anticipated Do-Not-Call Act, addressed bankruptcy reform (Bankruptcy Reform Act of 2005) as well as class action law suits (Class Action Fairness Act of 2005).

Picking up where Clinton left off, President Barack Obama approved health care reforms in 2010 via the Patient Protection and Affordable Care Act. The Act, which aims to decrease the number of uninsured Americans and health care costs, has been touted as the most significant reform to American healthcare since Medicare and Medicaid were enacted in 1965. Obama has also addressed Federal Aviation Administration (FAA) reform, online shopping (Restore Online Shoppers' Confidence Act of 2010), and he repealed the "Don't Ask, Don't Tell Act" (related to sexual orientation notification in the military). Under his leadership, the Dodd Frank Wall Street Reform and Consumer Protection Act was passed in 2010, which included creation of the newest consumer protection-focused federal agency, the Consumer Financial Protection Bureau. A primary crafter of the Bureau, and a go-to person for Obama, Elizabeth Warren has emerged as a modern day consumer advocate. A Harvard Law Professor and former Assistant to both the President and the U.S. Treasurer, she is now a newly elected U.S. Senator (2013) in a position to positively affect consumer causes in Congress.

## The Consumer Movement: Future Possibilities and Considerations

Irrespective of one's personal political or religious views, Americans desire the pursuit of life, liberty, and happiness, including being protected by democratic procedures addressing changing unfair laws and for improving society. Fortunately, due to consumerism's illustrious past, Americans have more rights today to advocate for themselves than they did 200 years ago. Ironically, at the same time, there is an increase in frauds, scams, illegal practices, and corruption, all aimed at bilking innocent consumers. And the reality is, at any given time, anyone can be a victim of a crime. And so, there will always be a need for advocates who will keep fighting.

So what will consumer champions and Americans face in the future? Paradoxically, many of the things being fought for at the beginning of the consumer movement remain as challenges today, though now the marketplace is more global and multicultural, and certainly more complex. While no one has a crystal ball, major issues that are likely to capture the attention of leaders include technology, demographic shifts, globalization, environmentalism, and human rights, to name a few.

## Technology

With the rapid increases in technology, there are promises for improving health conditions via innovations such as tele-healthcare. Furthermore, there are advances in tracking health and the spread of disease via Google tracking of specific consumer searches. These advances, however, also introduce new challenges. For example, with greater technology, there exists the risk of "Big Brother" whereby criminals can gain access to personal and private information. In fact, the Internet provides scam artists with a new weapon to perpetrate their crimes, especially given U.S. Census estimates that nearly 75% of all households have Internet access. Prosecutors, federal agencies, and others must reframe and retool to keep up with criminals who are perpetuating fraud on the Internet. Despite these efforts, identity theft is the most frequently reported crime to the Federal Trade Commission, with annual loss estimates in the billions (18 billion was the estimate for 2011 according to area experts). New laws and legislation regarding privacy and identity theft will continue to be developed, and, almost as certain, new forms of privacy scams will threaten our well-being.

## Demographic Shifts

Demographic changes also shape the consumer movement. With the "graying of America," paradigm shifts are occurring in the marketplace. Baby boomers and senior markets now greatly influence business behavior, such as the development and delivery of new products and programs. One example is the introduction of cars that park themselves and rearview cameras for better visibility, which serve not only the older adult population, but all drivers. On the other hand, the demographic change also leads to a potential strain on Social Security and Medicare, among other programs, and the imminent challenge of how to ensure quality of life under financial strain. Additionally, legislators report more efforts to harm aging adults, via scams and frauds that prey on the many at-risk adults who suffer from disease or cognitive decline. These issues will need to be tackled and resolved.

## Globalization

Consumer rights, safety, and protection in America do not exist in a vacuum. As a world leader, America is expected to aid the less fortunate. Consumer organizations provide support on a global level through groups such as the United Nations (UN), Consumers International (formerly IOCU), the World Trade Organization (WTO), the World Health Organization (WHO) and the International Trade Commission. As citizens of the world, it is important for Americans to keep a global perspective. Major disasters not only affect the country in which they happen, but repercussions of both the disaster and the recovery often ripple throughout the world. For example, the British Petroleum (BP) oil spill of 2010 caused damage to the U.S. Gulf of Mexico coast and the oceanic ecosystem, not to mention the effect on oil prices and commodity futures domestically and abroad. The terrorist effects of 9/11 resulted in significant and far reaching changes within the United States and the world. The 2011 tsunami in Japan devastated parts of Japan, and also resulted in manufacturing delays, especially for globally traded products. Early after the tsunami, the American auto industry announced difficulties in getting auto parts for repairs of autos made in Japan. While certainly not a life or death situation, it raises a consumer issue nonetheless. Given the significance of taking an international perspective, it is not surprising that Americans today are more aware of sociopolitical issues both locally and worldwide. This has two possible implications, however: it either provides increased opportunities to serve as advocates for injustices or it increases apathy. The historical divide between those who are trying to improve society and those who threaten society today grows deeper. For the former, we still see groups of people who energize and inspire change. Americans and legislators will need to be cognizant about how actions affect others across the globe in addition to reciprocal actions regarding issues such as trade, safety, travel, and immigration to name a few.

## Environmentalism

One of the movements of late that is inspiring change is the "green" movement. Many people today are committed to working hard to preserve and sustain the environment. This has had immediate and direct impact on the marketplace. For example, food today is created, packaged, served, and sold with consideration of its impact on the environment. Alternative fuel sources including solar home options are becoming key priorities for Americans in outfitting their homes. Recycling, repurposing, and composting are becoming more prevalent, affecting the marketplace and the environment. Furthermore, automobiles are now offered in hybrid and electric models in an effort to decrease dependency on oil and to lower emissions. Businesses have also participated in the consumer movement by exercising corporate social responsibility. People care about how businesses respond to them and to the environment and the communities in which they operate. Furthermore, businesses are building relationships with consumers by cultivating brand loyalty and service. Many businesses have buildings that are Gold-certified by the U.S. Green Building Council. Fast-food chains promote healthy lifestyle agendas through consumption of their products. Even the automobile manufacturers are promoting their alternative fuel, electric, and hybrid cars in their campaigns. And the federal government has offered tax incentives for a variety of alternative vehicles, most recently plug-in hybrids. Interestingly, the above-mentioned corporate actions often raise questions regarding corporate motives; is it profit or altruism that drives them? And, in the end, does it matter which is the driver of such actions?

## Human Rights

On the human rights front, there is a growing commitment to destigmatizing or deinstitutionalizing mental illness. Consumer-based organizations, centers, and campaigns are commonplace today and empower persons with mental illness by providing support to one another. Not surprising, the history of the mental health system and its evolution in the United States has strong ties to the general consumer movement and the development of policy-making boards and agencies. For example, organized efforts of such civil rights groups, such as Black/African Americans, women, disabled, and lesbian/gay, grew out of the idea that individuals who have experienced similar life challenges can come together and create necessary change. The United States is ahead on most, but not on all issues. Some basic rights that are enjoyed in European countries are not practiced in the United States. For example, German workers get an average of 35 paid days of vacation each year, compared to workers in America who get only 13 paid vacation days yearly. Swedish parents can share 480 days per child until that child reaches the age of 8 for maternity/paternity leave (with pay) while American workers are entitled, by federal law, to three months' leave, often without pay and usually only for the mother, depending on employee benefits. While some of the above may seem bleak for America, the United States still is a leader in other areas. Women's rights in some poor countries are essentially nonexistent, from disallowing girls to become educated, to sex trafficking, to prosecuting women when they are raped. Quality of life in America is quite good, and despite the recent increase in the number of Americans receiving food stamps, citizens' rights are being upheld. The consumer movement has been well-served over the years by a variety of leaders consisting of outspoken consumer champions who refused to let the American people be taken advantage of by big business, big government, or big brother. Due to efforts of key people like Dorothea Dix, Florence Kelley, Upton Sinclair, Harvey Wiley, Arthur Kallet, Colston Warne, Ralph Nader, Esther Peterson, and many visionary presidential leaders who passed key legislation, major battles were fought and won for consumers. Today, the battle for health and safety continues through promotion of consumer education and knowledge, development of coalitions and legislation to improve rights, and mechanisms to create an inclusive voice for all members of society.

## In Conclusion

The consumer movement is not only an integral part of U.S. economics and its ever-changing ebb and flow, but it is also an essential foundation to American culture. In fact, consumerism has not only helped to shape America's history, it is also helps shape and drive its future. Americans will continue to ask long-standing consumer-based questions such as: "Who deserves help?"; "Who has power or is given power?"; "Should fair exchange or fair deals exist"; "Should we have concern for others?"; "Who is more important, the individual or the group/community?"; "What behaviors are necessary to maintain social order?"; "To what extent are we responsible to help others?"; and "What makes for a good society?" Thus, as noted earlier, consumerism is more complicated than buying a car, paying for services, negotiating prices or engaging in productive activity; it is about how consumers and citizens relate to each other. Indeed, President Obama has managed to focus on a multitude of actions for consumers, but there is always room for more. He can emerge as a champion for the consumer movement and further the consumer cause for the well-being of all Americans, should his agenda call for it. But while America's leader can open the door for the country to move forward, ultimately, it us up to each individual consumer to decide which door to walk through: the one that enacts change and gives voice and power to consumers, or the one that severely limits the quality of life for too many consumers. Consumers deserve fair treatment in the marketplace including a strong future of consumer rights, safety, and protection that will result in safeguards for all consumers. The United States aspires to be a civilized, educated, model nation, one in which peddling faulty and dangerous products and services is not allowed, and ignoring consumers' civil rights is not acceptable. This encyclopedia is yet another tool in the consumer arsenal to help consumers not only to survive, but also to thrive as well.

*Wendy Reiboldt and Melanie Horn Mallers*

# Government Chart

## U.S. Government Summary Table

The federal government is comprised of three branches: executive, judicial, and legislative. These branches were created to ensure the effectiveness of government and the rights of consumers. Each branch operates independently, as well as in cooperation with the other branches. Below are examples of entities within each branch; those in bold are entries in the A–Z index due to their salient role on consumer rights, safety, and protection.

Executive Branch comprised of:
- -Office of the President and Vice President
- **-Executive Departments**
- **-Independent Agencies and Government Agencies**
- -Boards, Commissions, Committees, and more

Judicial Branch comprised of:
- **-The Supreme Court**
- -Lower Courts
- -Special Courts
- -Court Support Organizations

Legislative Branch comprised of:
- **-Congress** (Senate and House of Representatives)
- **-Agencies that Support Congress**

# Presidential Chart

| Term | President (Party/Affiliation) | Important Policies |
|---|---|---|
| 1789–1797 | George Washington (Independent) | 1791 Banking system established by Bank Act<br>1791 Bill of Rights<br>1792 Coinage Act<br>1795 Jay Treaty ratified |
| 1797–1801 | John Adams (Federalist) | 1798 Alien and Sedition Acts<br>1800 Congress established Library of Congress |
| 1801–1809 | Thomas Jefferson (Democratic-Republican) | 1803 Marbury v. Madison<br>1805 12th Amendment<br>1807 Embargo Act<br>1809 Non-Intercourse Act |
| 1809–1817 | James Madison (Democratic-Republican) | 1814 Treaty of Ghent<br>1816 Second Bank of United States chartered |
| 1817–1825 | James Monroe (Democratic-Republican) | 1819 Florida ceded by Spain<br>1820 Missouri Compromise<br>1823 Monroe Doctrine |
| 1825–1829 | John Quincy Adams (Democratic-Republican) | 1825 Erie Canal completed |
| 1829–1837 | Andrew Jackson (Democratic) | 1830 Indian Removal Act<br>1832 Vetoed the rechartering of the 2nd Bank<br>1835 Treaty of New Echota<br>1836 Deposit Act |
| 1837–1841 | Martin Van Buren (Democratic) | 1840 Independent Treasury Act |
| 1841 | William Henry Harrison (Whig) | |

(Continued)

| Term | President (Party/Affiliation) | Important Policies |
| --- | --- | --- |
| 1841–1845 | John Tyler (Whig) | 1841 Pre-Emption Act<br>1842 Webster-Ashburton Treaty<br>1844 Treaty of Wanghia<br>1845 Annexed Texas<br>1845 Signed a bill declared Florida part of the Union |
| 1845–1849 | James Knox Polk (Democratic) | 1846 Treaty of Oregon<br>1846 approved a law restoring the Independent Treasury System<br>1848 Treaty of Guadalupe Hidalgo |
| 1849–1850 | Zachary Taylor (Whig) | 1850 Clayton-Bulwer Treaty<br>Compromise of 1850 |
| 1850–1853 | Millard Filmore (Whig) | 1850 Compromise of 1850<br>1850 Fugitive Slave Act |
| 1853–1857 | Franklin Pierce (Democratic) | 1853 Gadsen Purchase<br>1854 Kansas-Nebraska Act<br>1854 Ostend Manifesto<br>1854 Treaty with Japan negotiated by Commodore Matthew Perry |
| 1857–1861 | James Buchanan (Democratic) | 1857 Tariff Act<br>1808 Congressional act banned the slave trade act |
| 1861–1865 | Abraham Lincoln (Republican/National Union) | 1863 Emancipation Proclamation<br>1865 Thirteenth Amendment (passed after his death) |
| 1865–1869 | Andrew Johnson (Democratic/National Union) | 1868 Purchase of Alaska<br>1868 Fourteenth Amendment |
| 1869–1877 | Ulysses S. Grant (Republican) | 1870 15th Amendment<br>1871 Treaty of Washington<br>1872 Mail Fraud Act |
| 1877–1881 | Rutherford Birchard Hayes (Republican) | 1878 Bland-Allison Silver Purchase Act passed despite Hayes veto. |
| 1881 | James Abram Garfield (Republican) | |
| 1881–1885 | Chester Alan Arthur (Republican) | 1883 Pendleton Civil Service Reform Act |
| 1885–1889 | Grover Cleveland (Democratic) | 1886 Presidential Succession Act<br>1887 Interstate Commerce Act |

*(Continued)*

| Term | President (Party/Affiliation) | Important Policies |
|---|---|---|
| | | 1887 Anti-Polygamy Act |
| | | 1887 Dawes Severalty Act |
| | | 1887 Tenure of Office Act repealed |
| | | 1888 Chinese Exclusion Act |
| 1889–1893 | Benjamin Harrison (Republican) | 1890 Sherman Antitrust Act |
| 1893–1897 | Grover Cleveland (Democratic) | 1893 Sherman Silver Purchase Act of 1890 repealed |
| 1897–1901 | William McKinley (Republican) | 1898 Joint Resolution for annexing the Hawaiian Islands to the United States |
| 1901–1909 | Theodore Roosevelt (Republican) | 1902 Biologics Control Act |
| | | 1903 Creation of the Department of Commerce and Labor |
| | | 1906 Meat Inspection Act |
| | | 1906 Pure Food and Drug Act |
| | | 1908 Federal Employers Liability Act for Labor |
| 1909–1913 | William H. Taft (Republican) | 1912 Sherley Amendment |
| | | 1913 Gould Amendment |
| 1913–1921 | Woodrow Wilson (Democratic) | 1914 Federal Trade Commission Act |
| | | 1914 Clayton Antitrust Act |
| 1921–1923 | Warren G. Harding (Republican) | 1921 Sheppard Tower Act |
| 1923–1929 | Calvin Coolidge (Republican) | 1927 Caustic Poison Act |
| 1929–1933 | Herbert Hoover (Republican) | 1930 Air Mail Act |
| | | 1930 McNary-Mapes Amendment |
| 1933–1945 | Franklin D. Roosevelt (Democratic) | 1933 Established the Anti-Trust Division of the Justice Departments |
| | | 1933 National Industrial Recovery Act |
| | | 1934 Communications Act of 1934 |
| | | 1935 National Labor Relations Act |
| | | 1938 Wheeler–Lea amendment regulating false advertising |
| | | 1938 Federal Food, Drug, and Cosmetic Act |
| | | 1941 Insulin Amendment |
| | | 1944 Public Health Service Act |
| | | 1939 Wool Products Labeling Act |
| | | Established a Consumer Advisory Board |

*(Continued)*

| Term | President (Party/Affiliation) | Important Policies |
|---|---|---|
| 1945–1953 | Harry S. Truman (Democratic) | 1945 McCarran–Ferguson Act<br>1946 Administrative Practice and Procedures Act<br>1946 Lanham Trademark Act<br>1947 Federal Insecticide Fungicide and Rodenticide Act<br>1948 Miller Amendment<br>1951 Fur Products Labeling Act<br>1951 Durham–Humphrey Amendment |
| 1953–1961 | Dwight D. Eisenhower (Republican) | 1954 Miller Pesticide Amendment<br>1956 AT&T Anti-trust Action<br>1957 Poultry Products Inspection Act<br>1958 Food Additives Amendment<br>1958 Automobile Information Disclosure Act<br>1959 Textile Products Identification Act<br>1960 Federal Hazardous Substances Labeling Act<br>1960 Color Additive Amendment<br>1953 Flammable Fabrics Act |
| 1961–1963 | John F. Kennedy (Democratic) | 1962 Established four basic consumer rights: to safety, to be informed, to choose, and to be heard<br>1962 Kefauvar–Harris Drug Amendments<br>1964 White house post of special assistant for consumer affairs<br>Established the Consumer Advisory Council |
| 1963–1969 | Lyndon B. Johnson (Democratic) | 1964 Lyndon Johnson created the post of Special Assistant for Consumer Affairs<br>1965 Federal Cigarette Labeling and Advertising Act<br>1965 Drug Abuse Control Amendments<br>1966 Highway Safety Act<br>1966 Freedom of Information act<br>1966 National Traffic and Motor Vehicle Safety Act<br>1966 Child Protection Act<br>1966 Fair Packaging and Labeling Act<br>1967 Flammable Fabrics Act Amendment |

(*Continued*)

| Term | President (Party/Affiliation) | Important Policies |
|---|---|---|
| | | 1967 Wholesome Meat Act |
| | | 1968 Truth in Lending Act |
| | | 1968 Consumer Credit Protection Act |
| | | 1968 Wholesome Poultry Products Act |
| | | 1968 Pipeline Safety Act |
| | | 1968 Reorganization Plan of 1968 |
| | | Established the President's Committee on Consumer Interest |
| 1969–1974 | Richard M. Nixon (Republican) | 1969 Public Health Cigarette Smoking Act |
| | | 1969 National Environmental Policy Act |
| | | 1970 Postal Reorganization Act |
| | | 1970 Fair Credit Reporting Act |
| | | 1970 Occupational Safety and Health Administration Agency |
| | | 1970 Poison Prevention Packaging Act |
| | | 1972 Motor Vehicle Information and Cost Savings Act |
| | | 1972 Federal Advisory Committee Act |
| | | 1972 Consumer Product Safety Act |
| | | 1972 Consumer Product Safety Commission Established |
| | | 1973 Hobby Protection Act |
| | | Other Accomplishments: |
| | | -Consumer Protection Branch of the Justice Department was created |
| | | -Executive Order 11583- strengthen U.S. Office of Consumer Affairs |
| | | -Nixon's Buyers Bill of Rights |
| 1974–1977 | Gerald Ford (Republican) | 1974 Equal Credit Opportunity Act |
| | | 1974 Fair Credit Billing Act |
| | | 1974 Real Estate Settlement Procedures Act |
| | | 1974 Safe Drinking Water Act |
| | | 1975 Magnuson Moss Warranty Act |
| | | 1975 Energy Policy and Conservation Act |
| | | 1976 Consumer Leasing Act |
| | | 1976 Medical Device Amendment |
| | | 1976 Consumer Product Safety Commission Improvements Act |
| | | 1977 Food Safety and Inspection Service was formed |
| | | Added the "Right to consumer education" to the Consumer Bill of Rights |

(*Continued*)

| Term | President (Party/Affiliation) | Important Policies |
|---|---|---|
| 1977–1981 | Jimmy Carter (Democratic) | 1978 Consumer Product Safety Commission reauthorization<br>1978 Fair Debt Collection Practices Act<br>1978 Eyeglass Rule<br>1978 Deregulation of the Airline Industry<br>1978 Franchise and Business Opportunities Rules<br>1979 Interstate Land Sales Disclosure Act<br>1980 Infant Formula Act<br>Created the Department of Energy and Education |
| 1981–1989 | Ronald Regan (Republican) | 1982 Tamper Resistant Packing Regulations<br>1983 Orphan Drug Act<br>1983 Saccharin Study and Labeling Act<br>1983 Federal Anti-Tampering Act<br>1984 Veterans Compensation and Program Improvements Amendments<br>1984 FTC Funeral Rule<br>1984 Trademark Counterfeiting Act<br>1984 Drug Price Competition and Patent Term Restoration Act<br>1984 Credit Card Fraud Act<br>1984 Toy Safety Act<br>1985 Credit Practices Rule<br>1986 Comprehensive Smokeless Tobacco Health Education Act<br>1986 Amended Wool Products Labeling and Textile Fiber Products Identification Act<br>1986 Childhood Vaccine Act<br>1987 Appliance Energy Standards Act<br>1987 Expedited Funds Availability Act<br>1988 Truth in Mileage Act<br>1988 Omnibus Trade Act<br>1988 Home Equity Loan Consumer Protection Act<br>1988 Fair Housing Amendments Act<br>1988 Fair Credit and Charge Card Disclosure Act<br>1988 Omnibus Drug Act<br>1989 Financial Institutions Reform, Recovery, and Enforcement Act |

*(Continued)*

| Term | President (Party/Affiliation) | Important Policies |
|---|---|---|
| 1989–1993 | George H.W. Bush (Republican) | 1990 Americans with Disabilities Act<br>1990 Smoke-free Environments Act<br>1990 Radiation Exposure Compensation Act<br>1990 Nutrition Labeling and Education Act<br>1990 Clean Air Act Amendments<br>1990 Consumer Product Safety Improvement Act<br>1991 Federal Deposit Insurance Corporation Improvement Act<br>1991 Truth in Savings Act<br>1991 Telephone Consumer Protection Act<br>1992 Americans with Disabilities Act<br>1992 Energy Policy Act<br>1992 Mammography Quality Standards Act<br>1992 Telephone Disclosure and Dispute Resolution Act<br>Advertising regulations on television shows aimed at children |
| 1993–2001 | William J. Clinton (Democratic) | 1994 Telemarketing and Consumer Fraud and Abuse Prevention Act<br>1994 Home Ownership and Equity Protection Act<br>1994 Dietary Supplement Health and Education Act (DSHEA)<br>1995 Seafood Hazard Analysis and Critical Control Point (HACCP) Regulations<br>1996 Communications Decency Act<br>1996 Consumer Credit Reporting Reform Act<br>1996 Telecommunications Act<br>1996 Health Insurance Portability and Accountability Act<br>1996 Credit Repair Organizations Act<br>1997 Volunteer Act<br>1997 Federal Food and Drug Administration Modernization Act<br>1998 Digital Millennium Copyright Act<br>1998 Identity Theft Assumption and Deterrence Act<br>1999 Gramm–Leach–Bliley Act<br>1999 Deceptive Mail Prevention and Enforcement Act<br>2000 Children's Online Privacy Protection Act |

*(Continued)*

| Term | President (Party/Affiliation) | Important Policies |
|---|---|---|
| | | 2000 U.S. Electronic Signatures in Global and National Commerce Act |
| | | 2000 College Scholarship Fraud Prevention Act |
| | | 2001 Crimes Against Charitable Americans Act |
| 2001–2009 | George W. Bush (Republican) | 2001 Patriot Act |
| | | 2002 Best Pharmaceuticals for Children Act |
| | | 2002 Notification and Federal Employee Antidiscrimination and Retaliation Act |
| | | 2002 Dot Kids Implementation and Efficiency Act |
| | | 2003 HIPAA Privacy Rule |
| | | 2003 United States Do Not Call Registry |
| | | 2003 National Consumer Credit Reporting System Improvement Act |
| | | 2003 Pediatric Research Equity Act |
| | | 2003 Fair and Accurate Credit Transactions Act |
| | | 2003 Controlling the Assault of Non-Solicited Pornography and Marketing Act |
| | | 2003 Fair and Accurate Credit Transactions Act |
| | | 2004 Identity Theft Penalty Enhancement Act |
| | | 2004 Food Allergen Labeling and Consumer Protection Act |
| | | 2004 Sports Agent Responsibility and Trust Act |
| | | 2005 Bankruptcy Abuse Prevention and Consumer Protection Act |
| | | 2006 Petroleum Marketing Practices Act |
| | | 2006 Unlawful Internet Gambling Enforcement Act |
| | | 2006 Sober Truth on Preventing Underage Drinking |
| | | 2007 Food and Drug Administration Amendments Act |
| | | 2008 Cameron Gulbransen Kids Transportation Safety Act |
| | | 2008 Children's Gasoline Burn Prevention Act |
| | | 2008 Medicare Improvements for Patients and Providers Act |

*(Continued)*

| Term | President (Party/Affiliation) | Important Policies |
|---|---|---|
| 2009–Current | Barack Obama (Democratic) | 2009 Health Information Technology for Economic and Clinical Health (HITECH) Act<br>2009 American Recovery and Reinvestment Act<br>2009 Credit Card Accountability, Responsibility and Disclosure Act<br>2009 Family Smoking Prevention and Tobacco Control Act<br>2010 Dodd–Frank Wall Street Reform and Consumer Protection Act<br>2010 Truth in Fur Labeling Act<br>2010 Restore Online Shoppers' Confidence Act |

# A

**Abuse, Child**. *See* Public Safety; Social Services

**Abuse, Elder**. *See* Administration on Aging; Older Americans Act (OAA); Public Safety; Social Services

## Activism

Activism is the process in which consumers get involved with creating, developing, and maintaining protections for themselves. Consumers can collaborate with associations, businesses, nonprofit organizations, government agencies, and government officials. Activism can take many forms such as writing letters, campaigning, running in elections, boycotts, or even street marches, sit ins, rallies, and hunger strikes. In some cases individuals may receive a single person whose job is to advocate solely for their well-being, and these people are referred to as advocates. Grassroots movements, nonprofit organizations, and lobbying are three ways in which consumers are able to effectively advocate for themselves and others on a larger scale.

### Grassroots Movements

Grassroots movements are local-level-community-based movements that start without government financing or professional staff. These movements began in the antiestablishment era of the 1960s and 1970s. These movements arise from a need that multiple people in the community are facing. The ideas and force behind this one community then quickly spreads to neighboring communities and towns and from there if the movement is big enough it can go to a national level. Grassroots movements increase community participation in community planning and the development of ways to better meet their needs. This can lead to positive change for local communities and bring national attention to important issues people are struggling with. Communities that experience similar issues can unite and work together toward change on a larger scale. Challenges that these movements experience are gaining the necessary financial funding, community support, and the constantly changing demographics of people's needs. These movements start as the foundation for many larger scale movements and can serve as the launching point for many new organizations. Grassroots movements are illustrated through the formation of battered women's shelters. In the 1970s the first shelter was created to provide a safe place for women that were victims of domestic violence. These shelters started off very small and over time these shelters expanded and were able to offer more advanced services such as employment advocacy, mental health services, and child care. Today battered women's shelters are able to offer a wider variety of services and a higher quality of care to women in need.

Many organizations serve to advocate for vulnerable consumers. For example, the American Bar Association improves access to justice for several underserved and disadvantaged populations, including children, domestic violence, human rights, immigration, aging, homelessness, and disability.

## Nonprofit Organizations

Nonprofit organizations are organizations that redistribute their surplus of funds to reach their goals instead of distributing them as profit. The financial excess is used to sustain the program, expand the program, and develop future plans of the program. Nonprofit organizations began in the United States during the colonial days. In the 1600s, the puritans saw charity and helping others in their community as a duty. Churches often set aside a portion of their collection for the needy in their community. Nonprofit organizations can be at a local, national, or international level. Local-level organizations focus on community building and the empowerment of their members. National-level organizations focus on larger scale issues such as welfare, education reform, and health care. International-level organizations focus on global issues and include the World Health Organization and Doctors Without Borders.

Nonprofit organizations play a huge role in a nation's social, economic, and political development. There are a wide variety of organizations that are considered to be nonprofit. Organizations such as museums, schools, universities, research institutions, foundations, service organizations, labor unions, professional associations, and consumer organizations are all different types of nonprofit institutions. However, when considering nonprofits the most well recognized are those that are involved in charity, philanthropy, giving, or volunteering. Nonprofits are faced with many challenges including efforts to fund services for a large variety of populations and their changing needs, as well as attempts to combine non-profit with for profit services.

Nonprofits can be illustrated by a variety of different organizations. The National Network to End Domestic Violence (NNEDV) is a national nonprofit organization that fights to improve high-profile media coverage of domestic violence cases, provides state-specific legal information for domestic violence survivors, and promotes federal legislation that holds perpetrators accountable for their actions.

Former president of the United States Jimmy Carter has devoted his life toward helping humanitarian efforts and working with nonprofit organizations. In 1982, he and his wife founded The Carter Center in Atlanta, Georgia. This nongovernmental organization focuses on human rights, resolving conflicts, and preventing diseases in more than 70 countries around the world. Another organization that President Carter supports is Habitat for Humanity International. For one week each year President Carter and his wife lead the Jimmy and Rosalynn Carter Work Project in which they help build homes. In 1977, he introduced The Friendship Force, which works in 60 separate countries to increase positive interactions between diverse people and cultures. President Carter also serves on the board for the Millennium Promise, an organization that strives to improve the lives of people living in impoverished countries. The North Korea home-building initiative is also endorsed by President Carter.

*For more information*, see http://www.cartercenter.org/

This program works on the national level by working to increase the nation's awareness of domestic violence, not only in small communities.

## Lobbying

Lobbying is the process in which people take part in any kind of activities to influence the decision of government officials or legislators. Legislators are those who work to write and pass laws at a local, regional, state, or national level. Individuals that take part in lobbying are referred to as lobbyist and they can work together in groups or as individuals. The goal of lobbyists is to bring information they consider to be useful to the attention of policy makers and facilitate the public's involvement and knowledge of government decision making. Lobbyists work to make changes on the state or national level. Activities that people commonly take part in to influence government decisions include writing letters, making phone calls, donating money, urging legislators to prose certain legislation, and voting during elections. Some extreme activities include suing government agencies, making violent threats, and threatening social unrest or revolutions. There are limitations placed on lobbying by Congress such as tax provisions, the Lobbying Disclosure Act, and ethics and laws that govern the members of congress and the executive branch. History has had multiple extremely successful lobbyists. Two of the most well known include Susan B. Anthony who fought for women's rights and Martin Luther King Jr. who fought for equality and civil rights. Challenges of lobbying include illegal forms of lobbying such as bribery, changing political environments from a national to a global level, and oftentimes the cost of hiring a lobbyist to represent an organization.

An example of lobby efforts producing statewide change would be the Sin by Silence Bill passed into California state law in September of 2012. Through phone calls, e-mails, social media interactions, and letters the California state government was made aware of the issues surrounding the evidence restrictions on women who were convicted of murdering their abusive husbands. The new bills will allow these women to have new expert testimony heard concerning their cases and receive more time to gain legal representation.

*Jayna Seidel*

**See also:** Commission on Civil Rights; Congress; Kennedy, John F.; King, Martin Luther, Jr.

### References and Additional Readings

Anheier, H. (2005). *Nonprofit organizations: Theory, management, policy.* Madison, WI: Routledge Taylor and Francis Group.

Hansen, S. (2012). The case for funding grassroots organizing. *Social Policy, 42*(2), 9–13.

Hitoshi Mayer, L. (2009). What is this "lobbying" that we are so worried about? *Yale Law and Policy Review,* 487–490.

Holland, T. P., & Ritvo, R. A. (2008). *Non profit organizations: Principles and practice.* West Sussex: Colombia University Press.

John, S., & Thompson, S. (2006). Lobbying in the 21st century. *Journal of Public Affairs, 3*(1), 9–13.

Kanel, K. (2008). Developments in mental health. In K. Kanel, *An overview of the human services* (pp. 30–32). New York: Houghton Mifflin Company.

Martin, D. G. (2004). Nonprofit foundations and grassroots organizing: Reshaping urban governance. *The Professional Geographer, 56*(3), 394–405.

National Network to End Domestic Violence. (2007). History. Retrieved from www.nnedv.org

Testa, C. (2005). Lobbies and welfare: A common agency approach. *Public Choice,* *125*(3), 305–337.

Walker, E., & McCarthy, J. (2012). Continuity and change in community organizing. *Social Policy, 42*(2), 3–7.

## Administration on Aging (AoA)

With a significant older adult population, protecting the rights of a growing senior population is critical. Funded by the Older Americans Act (OAA), the Administration on Aging (AoA) is part of a federal, state, tribal, and local affiliation entitled the National Network on Aging. Though not officially established until 1965, the U.S. government involvement on behalf of older adults actually began in 1935 with the Social Security Act. In 1950, President Truman held the first National Conference on Aging. Two years later federal funds were set aside for social services programs for older adults. In 1956, President Eisenhower created the Federal Council on Aging. Five years later, the first White House Conference on Aging occurred and by 1965, the AoA began. During this year, Medicare and Medicaid were established. By 1990, the Age Discrimination in Employment Act was established.

Today, the AoA assists about 7 million older adults and their caregivers with 29,000 service providers and thousands of volunteers. Programs include home-delivered meals and nutrition, transportation, adult day care, legal assistance, health promotion, advocacy, elder rights and protection, and much more. Additionally, the AoA supports special projects related to providing older adults with dignity and integrity via opportunities to live independent and productive lives. These programs currently include work related to civic engagement (i.e., volunteer opportunities), global aging (AoA's activities in other countries), and the Home Equity Conversion Mortgages (HECM) program (reverse mortgages insured by Housing and Urban Development, HUD). In a 2012 message from Kathy Greenlee, Assistant Secretary for Aging, during a national aging services network hearing, she articulated how critical it is to enact values that support older adults. She stated, "I have seen firsthand

The AoA explains that "volunteers have been significant contributors to aging services network, serving at every level and in the delivery of all types of services. Each year about 10 million older people use Older Americans Act services, whose delivery largely depends upon the efforts of half a million volunteers."

*Source:* Administration on Aging. (2012). Civic engagement initiative. Retrieved from http://www.aoa.gov

how the Older Americans Act (OAA) and the aging services network support the values I know we all share:

- Helping older Americans and persons with disabilities maintain their health and well-being so they are better able to live with dignity;
- Developing and implementing person-centered approaches;
- Promoting self-determination, respect, empowerment, inclusion and independence;
- Protecting the most vulnerable among us; and
- Providing basic respite care and other supports for families so that they are better able to take care of loved ones in their homes and communities for as long as possible, which is what Americans of all ages overwhelmingly tell us they prefer" (U.S. Department of Health & Human Services, 2012).

Enacting these values is also a core priority for current president, Obama. For example, in 2012 the Obama administration hosted an event to update advocates and stakeholders about the Affordable Care Act, an act that enables older adults and persons with disabilities to transition from institutional settings back to their homes. While the country faces several aging-related challenges, in part due to the increased longevity of older adults, the AoA will continue to work hard to support our aging loved ones and their families.

The United Nations designates October 1 as the International Day of Older Persons.

*Melanie Horn Mallers*

**See also:** Activism; Commission on Civil Rights; Department of Health and Human Services (HHS); Department of Housing and Urban Development (HUD); Equal Employment Opportunity Commission (EEOC); Medicaid; Medicare; Mortgages; Older Americans Act (OAA); Ombuds Offices; Social Security; Social Services; Social Welfare

### References and Additional Readings

AllGov. (2012). Administration on Aging. Overview. Retrieved from http://www.allgov.com/departments/department-of-health-and-human-services/administration-on-aging?agencyid=7391

Department of Health and Human Services. (2012). Statement by Kathy Greenlee. Retrieved from http://www.hhs.gov/asl/testify/2012/02/t20120213a.html

## Advertising

While product safety law tends to focus on product design issues, many product safety standards and makers of risky products include safety information and warnings. Advertising law also addresses safety information primarily to ensure it is not deceptive to consumers but occasionally to make sure advertising doesn't inadvertently cause consumer injuries. There are several sources for U.S. advertising law including the Federal Trade Commission (FTC), competitor lawsuits under the Lanham Act and state attorney general and consumer class actions under state "mini-FTC" acts. Advertising issues involving product safety are relatively rare but when they arise, the FTC has often been the one to address them.

The FTC was established in 1914 as an independent regulatory agency authorized to condemn "unfair methods of competition." Under this authority, it challenged a quack obesity cure that it alleged was unsafe without physician supervision. However, the Supreme Court held the FTC lacked jurisdiction over such misleading advertising claims unless it proved injury to competition. As a result in 1938, Congress expanded the FTC's authority to include "unfair or deceptive acts and practices." It is under this consumer protection authority that the FTC pursues safety practices that are unfair or deceptive to consumers. The FTC most commonly challenges safety claims made in advertising and prohibits them until they can be substantiated. The FTC also may require disclosure of the risks in advertising or on product packaging or both. More rarely, the FTC has requested that products be repaired or refunds be made available and even requested that advertising not depict unsafe behavior.

An early example of persuasive advertising for a popular household item. (*The Designer*, September 1916)

---

**A Classic Case of "Unsafe" Advertising**

A classic case involved bicycle advertising showing unsafe riding, for example, several stunts, riding without a helmet, and riding into a street without looking for oncoming traffic. The advertiser agreed to stop showing unsafe cycling behavior and also agreed to produce safe cycling public service announcements and distribute them to television stations. The Children's Advertising Review Unit of the National Advertising Division (CARU) of the Council of Better Business Bureaus challenged bicycle advertising that showed a helmetless "champion of freestyle riding" doing a handstand on the front tire of an inverted bicycle. The company responded that it did not plan to continue running this ad and it would take safety concerns into account in future advertising.

---

The most common safety case brought by the FTC involves express or implied claims in advertising that a product is safe, when in fact the product is not safe or at least not completely safe. Most of these cases are settled without litigation through a consent agreement where the advertiser does not admit to any wrongful conduct but agrees to be subject to an FTC order. Later violation of that order would lead to fines. Early challenges include deceptive safety claims by drugs, a hair dye, and a water heater. The FTC has pursued misleading safety advertising concerning many products such as paint removers, tanning booths, liposuction, and motorcycles. It successfully challenged advertisements claiming that a product containing radioactive material was "harmless" and it obtained consent orders barring false claims that a playhouse was "flameproof" and a glue was "nontoxic."

In some cases, safety claims cannot easily be proven false, but the FTC requires that advertisers have a "reasonable basis" for factual advertising claims. In the case of safety claims, a reasonable basis would consist of appropriate testing. In a running shoe case where one brand was advertised as preventing more impact injuries than other brands, the FTC's consent order did not ban the claim, but merely prohibited it until the advertiser had appropriate substantiation to support the claim.

Sometimes safety claims are not stated explicitly in advertising but implied visually. A somewhat recent consent agreement with Volvo prohibits false claims or depictions about the structural strength of its cars. Volvo had previously run an advertisement showing all cars but a Volvo being crushed by a "monster" truck. The Volvo's roof had been reinforced for the advertisement. Although Volvo stated the idea came from a consumer letter claiming to have witnessed such an event, it quickly apologized and settled. Similarly in an older case, the FTC challenged advertising for jeep

## Advertising: A critical tool for marketing

Companies are willing to take risks, as well as spend lots of money on advertising in an effort to influence consumer spending. For example, the trend for super bowl advertisements to be quick, one-second intervals is not the case anymore. Many super bowl ads are longer and more of a story.

Super Bowl Advertising Spending Trends:

| Average 30-second advertisement for Super Bowl | | |
|---|---|---|
| | 1967 | $49,500 |
| | 1968 | $54,000 |
| | 1969 | $55,000 |
| | 1970 | $78,000 |
| | 1971 | $72,000 |
| | 1972 | $86,000 |
| | 1973 | $103,500 |
| | 1974 | $107,000 |
| | 1975 | $110,000 |
| | 1976 | $125,000 |
| | 1977 | $162,000 |
| | 1978 | $185,000 |
| | 1979 | $222,000 |

In 1971 the cost of a 30-second advertisement decreased because NBC decided to lower the cost from the previous year to appeal to more advertisers.

| Average 30-second advertisement for Super Bowl | | |
|---|---|---|
| | 1980 | $275,000 |
| | 1981 | $324,000 |
| | 1982 | $345,000 |
| | 1983 | $400,000 |
| | 1984 | $450,000 |
| | 1985 | $500,000 |
| | 1986 | $550,000 |
| | 1987 | $575,000 |
| | 1988 | $600,000 |
| | 1989 | $675,000 |

| Average 30-second advertisement for Super Bowl | 1990 | $700,000 |
| --- | --- | --- |
| | 1991 | $800,000 |
| | 1992 | $800,000 |
| | 1993 | $850,000 |
| | 1994 | $900,000 |
| | 1995 | $1,000,000 |
| | 1996 | $1,100,000 |
| | 1997 | $1,200,000 |
| | 1998 | $1,300,000 |
| | 1999 | $1,600,000 |
| Average 30-second advertisement for Super Bowl | 2000 | 2,100,000 |
| | 2001 | 2,050,000 |
| | 2002 | 1,900,000 |
| | 2003 | 2,100,000 |
| | 2004 | 2,250,000 |
| | 2005 | 2,400,000 |
| | 2006 | 2,500,000 |
| | 2007 | 2,600,000 |
| | 2008 | 2,700,000 |
| | 2009 | 3,000,000 |
| | 2010 | $2,700,000 |

In the last decade the Super Bowl became the highest viewed television program of all time.

Source: Ronstrom, M. (January 29, 2011). Trendski.com. *Super bowl advertising statistics: An overview.* N.p.

vehicles that showed jeeps operating on ordinary roads like ordinary cars. The consent agreement required a warning label be affixed to the vehicle disclosing that it handles differently than ordinary cars because of its high center of gravity. The FTC also obtained a consent agreement with the maker of a high alcohol, fortified wine product prohibiting it from being packaged and displayed in a manner similar to low alcohol, wine coolers. It was concerned that consumers would be deceived about the product's alcohol content.

Safety claims also may be implied by vague advertising statements. One well known case involved Firestone advertising in the 1970s of a tire it claimed to be "The Safe Tire." The FTC argued that this claim communicated to consumers that the tire was both free from defects and safe under all conditions of use, including improper care such as under-inflation or unsafe speeds. Its argument on this latter implied safety interpretation was based in part on Firestone's own consumer survey where 15 percent of consumers interpreted the advertising to have this meaning. Although 15 percent is a relatively small proportion of consumers to perceive an implied claim, the FTC has since stated that it would pursue such small proportions in cases involving safety issues or other relatively large potential injuries.

In addition to prohibiting deceptive or unsubstantiated safety claims, the FTC frequently requires disclosure of safety risks as illustrated by the jeep case discussed earlier. It ordered a silver polish, advertised as "containing nothing harmful" to disclose that its fumes could be dangerous. It also required disclosure of the product risks for a chemical paint remover. The FTC has required disclosure of risks for a wide variety of products and services including tanning booths, descent systems, heat detectors, pesticides, hair implants, eye make-up, weight reduction belts, body wraps, and birth control devices. Occasionally, the FTC has required safety warning for past purchasers. For example, the commission negotiated a consent order with the makers of "Gut Buster" requiring them to notify past purchasers that the spring in the exercise device might overstretch and break.

The timing of safety disclosures can be crucial to consumer safety. Often the FTC requires disclosure in advertising or on product packaging so consumers can learn the safety risks before purchase. For example, in a rental car case, the FTC negotiated a consent agreement that required the company to fix safety defects subject to recall notices or inform customers of the recall and the nature of the unrepaired defect before the rental contract was signed. One commissioner dissented from accepting the agreement arguing that the disclosure should be made before finalizing the reservation. Once informed of the policy, consumers could easily decline the proposed reservation and contact another rental car company. Consumers are less likely to change companies once they arrive at the airport, wait in line, and then discover the safety issue. They won't know if other companies have unreserved cars or whether they have a different policy on safety defects subject to recall notices.

Often the FTC requires information disclosures of shortcomings of safety products. For example, it required that fire escape breathing devices, which filter out many harmful gases, disclose that the mask does not filter out dangerous carbon monoxide, so that users may still perish while trying to escape fires. The commission also announced a consent agreement with the marketer of a radon removal system prohibiting false and unsubstantiated radon removal claims and requiring whenever quantitative radon-decay removal claims are made that the company also disclose that the percentage reduction in the risk of lung cancer is less than the percentage reduction of radon-decay products removal. Finally, the FTC prohibited claims that advertised glasses would protect the wearer from harmful UV rays emanating from computer screens because there was no evidence that computer screens emitted harmful UV rays.

The primary focus of the FTC is safety issues that are explicit or implied in advertising. However, it occasionally pursues safety cases that do not involve any safety discussion in advertising. For example, before the Flammable Fabrics Act, the FTC commonly required warning labels on clothing made from flammable fabrics. Typically, such clothing would not mention safety or flammability in their advertising. Once the Flammable Fabrics Act was enacted, the FTC enforced it until that responsibility was transferred to the Consumer Product Safety Commission.

In an older case involving a toy that consisted of a pair of glasses with a rubber band connected to an inflatable ball, the FTC uncovered three instances where the rubber band broke and consumers were injured in the eye. The package showed the product with yellow lenses. This was deceptive because there were no lenses in the actual product. Aside from this deceptive depiction of lenses, a majority of commissioners held that the product should disclose the risk of rubber band breakage and subsequent eye injury. One commissioner dissented arguing that the product appearance (no lenses) was not deceptively suggestive of safety because consumers should be able to determine the risk of the rubber band snapping into the eyes.

Today an undisclosed safety risk, if severe enough, could be condemned by the FTC as an unfair omission of safety information. In 1984, the FTC pursued International Harvester because if the fuel cap was adjusted while the engine was hot (say for refueling), the fuel might "geyser." This caused severe burns and a few deaths in an extremely small proportion of cases (12 out of a potential of 1.3 million). In order for an omission to be deceptive, the majority stated that it must be in the context of a half-truth or under other circumstances where the silence constitutes an implied misrepresentation. The majority recognized the concept of reasonable fitness for intended use that requires products to be free of "gross" safety hazards, but did not apply it to the "fuel geysering" problem because the problem was so rare. Thus, the majority held there was no consumer deception about the product's safety in International Harvester, because the product was "reasonably safe" (although not perfectly safe) for its intended use. Although one commissioner dissented arguing a lack of information could still be deceptive, all agreed that this omission of safety information was unfair under the FTC Act because it caused an unreasonable consumer injury that could not be reasonably avoided (without information of the risk).

A consent agreement against a plastic surgery center illustrates this dichotomy between deceptive omissions and pure or unfair omissions. The order required the company to disclose the risks of pain and scarring because advertising suggested this would be minimal. This would be a deceptive omission. The center also was required to disclose that breast implants interfere with mammography exams. This was an unfair omission because nothing was said in advertising on this issue but consumers could not choose to avoid this safety risk if they were not informed about it. So this omission of information was unfair.

Prohibiting deceptive or unsubstantiated safety claims and requiring disclosure of safety risks are the two most common FTC remedies in safety cases. However, when necessary, the FTC has imposed more stringent remedies. In two extreme cases, the FTC prohibited not just expressed or implied safety claims in advertising but also prohibited the use of "safety" or similar terms in product names. It felt that the name "Safety Strip" for a hazardous chemical painter remover was deceptive. Similarly, it felt the name "Safti-Brake" falsely suggested to consumers that these automobile brake parts were safer than other brands.

Advertising for safety equipment presents some additional examples of interesting remedies such as repair, replacement, or refund. The FTC ordered the issuance of a repair kit to purchasers of a defective marine survival suit that fails to inflate. In a case involving insulation that was falsely advertised as fire treated, the order requires the provision of free smoke detector in cases where the insulation is not readily removable. In a case involving "the world's best" safety helmet, the commission ordered that a 30-day refund period be established and advertised. The commission also ordered refunds for water purifiers and heat detectors—the latter for not disclosing that people likely will be overcome by smoke before a heat detector sounds the alarm. To correct this omission for past purchasers, the FTC obtained a court order for consumer refunds in the range of $7.59–$49.95 million.

In cases involving nonsafety-related products, the FTC also has ordered product repairs or refunds. The FTC ordered a repair kit for the tractor fuel geysering case discussed earlier. When advertising may have induced wood stove purchasers to install the wood stove too close to flammable walls, the commission ordered respondent to reimburse consumers for moving the stoves or provide free heat shielding.

Before the creation of the Consumer Product Safety Commission, the FTC occasionally would seek the removal of unsafe products from the market or require that an advertiser conduct safety studies. For example, it prohibited placing of razor blade samples in newspapers where they might injure children and also prohibited the sale of a "germ fighter" toothbrush that contained mercury. The FTC also has obtained consent agreements requiring safety studies in a case where bodybuilding was promoted for young children without evidence to support that it was safe and in a case where plastic products were advertised without a warning about their flammability.

Perhaps the most unusual advertising-safety cases brought by the FTC involve advertisements that depict unsafe product behavior that the FTC fears may be imitated. A number of cases condemn unsafe product use behavior in advertising. For example, the FTC obtained a consent order prohibiting advertising depictions of denture wearers using denture cushions for a prolonged, unsafe period of time. Similarly, the FTC challenged newspaper advertising that claimed in a recent clinical test that most people could sleep wearing a particular brand of hard plastic contact lenses and the longer they were worn, the better it was for the user. The commission order prohibited future advertising from making such claims and required that the next four weeks of advertising disclose that a significant number of people could not comfortably wear these lenses while sleeping. Lastly, the commission challenged advertising for an eyelash tint that showed the product being applied without the safety precautions listed in the product directions. While all of these examples regulate information that might influence potential purchasers, the information also appears likely to affect product users as well.

Children are felt to be particularly likely to imitate behavior they see in product advertising. For example, the FTC negotiated consent orders prohibiting depictions of unsupervised children near an active gas stove and children using an electric hair dryer to dry a doll's hair near a bathtub full of water. Similarly, a vitamin company was not allowed to use Spiderman in television advertising for fear that children would take too many vitamins hoping to emulate the superhero.

The potential consequences of advertising are not always agreed upon. For example, a court rejected a common law negligence case against Mountain Dew for showing unsafe bicycling behavior in its soft drink advertising. In *Sakon v. Pepsico, Inc.* (1989), the Supreme Court of Florida affirmed a lower court ruling that a soft drink advertiser had breached no duty of care owed to the 14-year-old plaintiff. The court held it was not foreseeable that the plaintiff would try to copy the stunt, riding a bicycle off an embankment into a body of water to the encouragement and delight of young spectators, depicted in the advertising. Furthermore, the court noted that television often shows activities, such as circus acts, that would be dangerous if untrained viewers attempted them and that the commercial was directed toward encouraging viewers to drink the soft drink, not to undertake the activity.

The FTC did pursue one case where the unsafe behavior did not involve the product being advertised. It obtained a consent order prohibiting depiction of a naturalist eating wild nuts and berries in advertising for Grape Nuts brand cereal. The commission felt viewers, particularly children, might copy this behavior and eat poisonous mushrooms or berries. The most recent FTC case in this category involved a beer advertisement depicting young adults without life jackets enjoying beer while sitting at the edge of a sailing schooner. The FTC obtained a consent agreement prohibiting such depictions. While this case arguably involved unsafe behavior (sailing without life jackets) not directly related to the advertised product, the actors clearly had the advertised beer even if industry self-regulation prohibits actually showing the beer being consumed. While many of these FTC safety-related cases are older, they are still cited today when parties feel advertising depicts an unsafe product or product use behavior. This is particularly true when such advertising targets children.

Adapted with permission from the *Journal of Consumer Policy* (cited below).

*Ross D. Petty*

**See also:** Attorney General Office (AG); Class Action Lawsuits; Federal Trade Commission (FTC)

### References and Additional Readings

Donohue, J.M., Cevasco, M., & Rosenthal, M.B. (2007). A decade of direct-to-consumer advertising of prescription drugs. *The New England Journal of Medicine, 357*, 673–681.

Harris, J.L., & Graff, S.K. (2012). Protecting young people from junk food advertising: Implications of psychological research for first amendment law. *American Journal of Public Health, 102*(2), 214–222.

Liang, B.A., & Mackey, T. (2011). Direct-to-consumer advertising with interactive internet media global regulation and public health issues. *The Journal of the American Medical Associations, 305*(8), 824–825.

Petty, R.D. (1995). Regulating product safety: The informational role of the US federal trade commission. *Journal of Consumer Policy, 18*(4), 387–415.

## Affinity Fraud

Everyone has affiliations with specific groups of people or communities. These connections can be based on a shared language, religion, culture, or ethnicity, profession, location, age (seniors), hobby or interest, or even disability—any trait, status, circumstance, or belief that people use to identify themselves. While such affiliations can be positive and advantageous, they also can be exploited for ill gains and criminal purposes.

The term "affinity fraud" refers to scams that target an identifiable group, exploiting the trust that exists among the group's members. In many cases, the perpetrator of the fraud is actually a member of the group or poses as one. In other cases, the perpetrator befriends or otherwise enlists one or more prominent members of the group, who then become unwitting accomplices. The relationship with the group leader gives the fraudster instant legitimacy with his or her potential victims and prudent skepticism is replaced by misplaced fellowship and blind trust.

Affinity fraud can be particularly problematic for law enforcement. First, it can claim more victims more quickly than schemes aimed at a random population. Word of the "investment opportunity" travels more rapidly within a tight knit group and, with the explicit or implied endorsement of other group members, there are likely to be more converts (in other words, victims). And because victims may, for a variety of reasons ranging from pride to distrust of law enforcement, be reluctant to report the crime, the fraud may be allowed to continue until it is too late to catch the perpetrator or recover funds. Some groups choose to resolve the issue among themselves, particularly when prominent members of the group are involved and the incident might reflect badly on leaders or respected members, or on the group as a whole. This secrecy can make it difficult to detect or prosecute affinity fraud.

In 2006, following a spate of schemes targeting members of particular communities, from Korean Americans to Jehovah's Witnesses, the Securities and Exchange Commission (SEC) issued a warning about affinity fraud in an effort to alert and educate the public. Among its advice, the SEC cautioned investors against making an investment based solely on the recommendation of a member of an organization or religious or ethnic group to which they belong.

Not long after the SEC issued its warning, Bernard Madoff was arrested for carrying out the largest affinity fraud scheme in U.S. history. For more than a decade, until his arrest in December 2008, Madoff ran a massive pyramid, or "Ponzi," scheme. A Ponzi scheme—named for Charles Ponzi, who made the scheme famous in the early part of the 20th century—entails using the money of recent investors to make "earnings" payments to earlier investors, giving the impression that the investment is doing well and thus ensnaring additional investors in the scheme. The scam collapses when the supply of new investors slows down or dries up, or the promoter of the scam vanishes with the money.

The Madoff case is an example of just how successful affinity fraud can be for the perpetrators, even when the target group is made up of experienced investors. Madoff's scam took aim mainly at the Jewish community, of which he is a member. His victims included Jewish federations, hospitals, endowments, philanthropic organizations—the Elie Wiesel Foundation and Steven Spielberg's Wunderkinder Foundation were two of his prominent victims—and many wealthy Jewish individuals. Estimates differ, but victims' actual net losses probably total somewhere between $10 billion and $20 billion.

While some affinity fraud schemes target consumers who are at a disadvantage—they may not speak English well, might not be familiar with their rights, or could be economically marginalized—the Madoff scam hit a group that seemingly had all the resources available to conduct sufficient, independent due diligence and avoid becoming victims. But Madoff, who had been the chairman of NASDAQ and an SEC adviser as well as a trusted member of the Jewish community, escaped any such scrutiny from his investors or even from the SEC. It appears that for some investors a shared affiliation is reasonable justification to lower one's guard. It also makes openly expressing doubt awkward; fraudsters rely on community members' reluctance to ask pointed questions out of social propriety.

Affinity scams, like other types of fraud, have made their way to the Internet, which provides both anonymity and greater reach. Social media, in particular, makes it easy for scammers to infiltrate and claim membership in an online community, and to collect personal information about members of the group. For example, online profiles frequently reveal country of birth, religious affiliation, political views, and other personal information that a con artist can exploit. Online advertisements and websites that display symbols, colors, and logos of a particular group—veterans, for example—are another way scam artists use the Internet to attract members of their target group.

In many cases, victims of affinity fraud do not report the crime because they mistakenly believe that nothing can be done about it since they willingly handed over their money or property. While not every report of affinity fraud results in prosecution or restitution, some do. At the very least, a consumer's report to the SEC or the Federal Trade Commission (FTC) can help prevent other consumers from falling prey to the same scam.

*Monica Steinisch*

**See also:** Frauds and Scams; Madoff, Bernie; Multilevel Marketing and Pyramid Plans; Ponzi Schemes

### References and Additional Readings
Cass, R. A. (2008). Madoff exploited the Jews. *The Wall Street Journal.* Retrieved from http://online.wsj.com/article/SB122956340954216799.html

North American Securities Administrators Association. (2011). NASAA cautions investors about social networking fraud [Press release]. Retrieved from http://www.nasaa.org/5568/informed-investor-advisory-social-networking/

Securities and Exchange Commission. (2006). Affinity fraud: How to avoid investment scams that target groups. http://www.sec.gov/investor/pubs/affinity.htm

**Affirmative Action**. *See* Commission on Civil Rights; Department of Education (ED); Discrimination; Equal Employment Opportunity Commission (EEOC); Roosevelt, Franklin D.; King, Martin Luther, Jr.

## American Council on Consumer Interests (ACCI)

The American Council on Consumer Interests (ACCI) is an organization whose mission is to enhance consumer interests and well-being through advocacy, education, policy development, and research. Established in 1953, ACCI is a nonprofit and nonpartisan organization that caters to individuals with interests in consumer affairs. It focuses on a broad range of consumer issues including financial and consumer product and service safety issues.

ACCI was founded by 22 charter members to contribute to a more effective system for fact finding and consumer information dissemination. Early topics of study included antitrust actions, incorporating consumer views into government legislation, and family financial counseling.

Membership in ACCI has varied from a low of 200 to a high of 2,200. Members are primarily from the United States, although over 30 other countries have been represented in its membership. ACCI is governed by an 11-member board of directors. The board of directors is elected to oversee and make decisions on behalf of ACCI.

ACCI's vision statement, according to the website states that "ACCI is the leading consumer policy research and education organization consisting of a world-wide community of researchers, educators and related professionals dedicated to enhancing consumer well-being. ACCI promotes the consumer interest by encouraging, producing and communicating policy-relevant research." This is reflected in its mission to enhance consumer and family economic well-being by promoting excellence in research and educational programs and through the specific goals of advancing knowledge through research, education, and advocating for policy changes, and providing professional development opportunities to ACCI members.

As part of this mission, and as noted on its website, ACCI conducts a conference that focuses on scholarship and application in the field. They also publish a peer reviewed journal that provides research on consumer and family economic issues, as well as promote projects that exchange ideas between researchers, students, educators, policy makers, and advocates. ACCI created the National Consumer Affairs internship program to place graduate students in consumer offices in government, industry, and nonprofits. Currently, ACCI is focused on reforming financial services regulations and creating more consumer protections for food, housing, financial products, and other services. ACCI was instrumental in the consumer movement by supporting legislation designed to improve the safety of consumer products and services. Its members are consumer researchers and educators, consumer counselors, consumer protection legislators, business consumer affairs personnel, consumer advocates, government officials, and others who focus on creating and disseminating consumer information. Anyone with these interests can join the organization.

ACCI's annual conference focuses on the general topics of consumer advocacy, research, education, and policy. Overarching concepts include consumer behavior, consumer interests, and well-being. Presenters also cover personal finance, including financial education, literacy, and financial decision-making, and bridge consumer and financial topics, addressing subjects such as tax policy, identity theft, pay day loans, and credit cards; they also present information and research on health, employment, and caregiving. A book of proceedings summarizing conference presentations is published each year. ACCI disseminates information through several venues. These include a research journal entitled *Journal of Consumer Affairs* (JCA) and the *ACCI Newsletter*. This journal focuses on consumer issues and problems. It reports current research conducted by ACCI members and others working on consumer issues. Recent issues have focused on topics such as aging consumers, public health issues, and financial literacy. Article titles include "Reading Food Labels, Combined with Exercise, Can Lead to Weight Loss," "Financial Literary Bailout for the Younger Generation," and "Unhappy Customers: Everyone Has a Right to Complain, and Does."

Historical records about ACCI were donated to Kansas State University Libraries in 1988 and are part of the Consumer Movement Archives. These records include information in regard to ACCI's correspondence and newsletters, board of directors, committees, financial documents, and conferences. In conclusion, ACCI continues to be a viable advocate for consumer interests and well-being.

*Cynthia R. Jasper*

**See also:** Peterson, Esther; Society of Consumer Affairs Professionals (SOCAP); Warne, Colston

### References and Additional Readings

American Council for Consumer Interest. (n.d.). Introducing ACCI. Retrieved from http://www.consumerinterests.org/About_Us.html

Delgadillo, L. M., Erickson, L. V., & Piercy, K. W. (2008). Disentangling the differences between abusive and predatory lending: Professionals' perspectives. *Journal of Consumer Affairs, 42*(3), 313–334. doi: 10.1111/j.1745–6606.2008.00112.x.

Makela, C. J., Stein, K., & Uhl, J. N. (1979). The American Council on Consumer Interests: Its activities and future development. *Journal of Consumer Affairs, 13*(1), 117–127. doi: 10.1111/j.1745–6606.1979.tb00133.x.

Silber, N., Merchant, M. M., & Lashway, G. (1987) The American Council on Consumer Interests: An oral history 1954–1984. *The American Council on Consumer Interests.* Columbia, MO: The Council.

Tangari, A. H., Burton, S., Howlett, E., Cho, Y., & Thyroff, A. (2010). Weighing in on fast food consumption: The effects of meal and calorie disclosures on consumer fast food evaluation. *Journal of Consumer Affairs, 44*(3), 431–462. doi: 10.1111/j.1745–6606.2010.01177.x.

Thomsen, P. A. (2009). American council on consumer interests records. Kansas State University Archives. Retrieved from http://www.lib.k-state.edu/depts/spec/findaids/pc1992–02.html

## Americans with Disabilities Act (ADA)

Americans with Disabilities Act (ADA), governed by the U.S. Department of Justice (DOJ), is a civil rights law that ensures equal opportunity and access to participation in the mainstream of American life for persons with disabilities. The first ADA was introduced to Congress in 1988 and was signed into by President George H. W. Bush in 1990. But the ADA story really began well before this when ". . . people with disabilities began to challenge societal barriers that excluded them from their communities, and when parents of children with disabilities began to fight against the exclusion and segregation of their children. It began with the establishment of local groups to advocate for the rights of people with disabilities. It began with the establishment of the independent living movement which challenged the notion that people with disabilities needed to be institutionalized, and which fought for and provided services for people with disabilities to live in the community" (Mayerson, 1992, 1). From a legal perspective, a true impetus for disability policy occurred with the passage of Section 504 of the 1973 Rehabilitation Act. This act banned discrimination based on disability for federal fund recipients, which had already banned discrimination based on race, ethnicity, and sex. For the first time, it was understood that challenges faced by persons with disabilities was not implicitly due to the disability itself, but by limitations in the environment and society.

---

**CASE STUDY:** *Equal Employment Opportunity Commission (EEOC) v. United Airlines*

Attorneys: William R. Tamayo (San Francisco), David F. Offen-Brown (San Francisco) (settlement agreement entered 2009)

United Airlines agreed to settle a federal lawsuit brought by the commission alleging that the Chicago-based company's overtime policy violated the ADA.

The suit arose from a charge filed by Samuel Chetcuti, a storekeeper working for United at the San Francisco International Airport. The commission's suit asserted that United's policy of denying the opportunity to work overtime to anyone placed on light or limited duty had greater repercussions for employees with disabilities, since these workers were more likely to be assigned to light duty. For example, Chetcuti, who has epilepsy, was under medical restrictions that prevented him from operating heavy machinery and working at heights, but did not restrict the number of hours a week he could work. Chetcuti was given light duty for his regular work schedule, and as a result, United had barred him from an overtime schedule despite the fact that he was medically cleared to work overtime.

Under the settlement, United agreed to pay $850,000 to a class of current and former employees with disabilities who were denied employment opportunities at San Francisco International Airport due to this policy. United also agreed not to reinstate the policy, which it had stopped using at the time of the consent decree.

*Source:* U.S. Equal Employment Opportunity Commission. (2009). *United Airlines to pay $850,000 for disability discrimination.* http://www1.eeoc.gov//eeoc/newsroom/release/3-16-09.cfm?renderforprint=1

---

Today, the ADA, after several adaptations since 1988, defines an individual with a disability, as "a person who has a physical or mental impairment that substantially limits one or more major life activities; a person who has a history or record of such impairment; or a person who is perceived by others as having such impairment" (U.S. Department of Justice, 2009, 2). These limitations include physical or mental impairment of one or more major life activities such as walking, speaking, lifting, hearing, seeing, reading, eating, sleeping, concentrating, or working. Major life activities also include the operation of major bodily functions such as brain, immune system, respiratory, neurological, digestive, and circulatory functions. In enacting the ADA, Congress recognized that despite these limitations, all person's should have the right to fully participate in all aspects of society. Unfortunately, many are still precluded from doing so because of prejudice, antiquated attitudes, or the failure to remove societal and institutional barriers.

ADA protections extend to several contexts, including employment, state and local government services, public accommodations, commercial facilities, transportation, and telecommunications.

## Employment

ADA, Title 1, indicates that employers who have 15 or more employees must provide to individuals with disabilities equal opportunities related to all employment-related issues that are typically available to all other employees. For example, activities involving recruitment, hiring, promotions, training, pay, social activities, and other privileges of employment must be enacted as it would to all employees without disabilities. Additionally, employers are not allowed to ask questions regarding an applicant's disability prior to a job offer being made. That is, under the ADA, "employers cannot use eligibility standards or qualifications that unfairly screen out people with disabilities and cannot make speculative assumptions about a person's ability to do a job based on myths, fears, or stereotypes about employees with disabilities (such as unfounded concerns that hiring people with disabilities would mean increased insurance costs or excessive absenteeism)" (U.S. Department of Justice, 2010). Furthermore, upon employment, employers are required to make all "reasonable accommodations" (U.S. Department of Justice, 2010) to the known disability of the employee. Interestingly, employers are not required to provide accommodations unless an employee requests them. This empowers the employee to reveal the disability or not. Examples of accommodations are flexible scheduling; job training or provision of a job coach, specialized equipment, and adapting the work environment (e.g., raise or lower desks). Thus, if a potential employee is qualified, the disability cannot stand in his or her way of getting and keeping the job (U.S. Department of Justice, 2010). If a person believes discrimination on the basis of disability has occurred, that person also has the right to file a complaint with the U.S. Equal Employment Opportunity Commission (EEOC) within 180 days of the date of discrimination, or 300 days if the charge is filed with a designated State or local fair employment practice agency. Additionally, individuals may file a lawsuit in federal court only after they receive a "right-to-sue" letter from the EEOC.

Interestingly, there are sometimes unintended consequences of employment provisions. For example, the CATO Institute, a public policy research institute, has suggested the unemployment provisions of the ADA has harmed the intended beneficiaries of the act, rather than helped them. The apparent decrease in employment rate of disabled Americans, as shown in Tables 1 and 2, is due to the added cost of employing disabled workers to comply with the ADA-required accommodations, which has made those workers relatively unattractive to firms.

**Table 1** Effect of ADA on Employment of Men with Disabilities

|  | Employment rate (percent) and change in employment rate (percentage points) | |
|---|---|---|
|  | **Men with disabilities** | **Men without disabilities** |
| Before enactment of ADA (1985–1990) | 59.8 | 95.5 |
| After enactment of ADA (1991–April 1995) | 48.9 | 92.4 |
| Change in employment rate | –10.9* | –3.1* |
| Employment effect of ADA | **–7.8*** | |

*Change is significantly different from 0 at a 95 percent confidence level.
*Source:* DeLeire, T. (2000.) The Unintended Consequences of the Americans with Disabilities Act. *Regulation (23)* 1, 22. Retrieved from http://www.cato.org/sites/cato.org/files/serials/files/regulation/2000/4/deleire.pdf. Reprinted with permission.

**Table 2** Effect of ADA on Employment Rates of Men with Disabilities by Age, Education, and Type of Disability
(percentage-point differences from rates for men without disabilities)

| Decade of birth | High school dropout | High school graduate | Some college education or college graduate |
|---|---|---|---|
| 1930s | –11* | –2 | –1 |
| 1940s | –16* | –7 | –6* |
| 1950s | –15* | –6* | –6* |
| 1960s | –17* | –8* | –7* |

| Decade of birth | Physical disability | Mental disability | Other disability |
|---|---|---|---|
| 1930s | –3* | –20* | –8* |
| 1940s | –7* | –23* | –11* |
| 1950s | –6* | –22* | –10* |
| 1960s | –7* | –24* | –12* |

*Change is significantly different from 0 at a 95 percent confidence level.
*Source:* DeLeire, T. (2000.) The Unintended Consequences of the Americans with Disabilities Act. *Regulation (23)* 1, 23. Retrieved from http://www.cato.org/sites/cato.org/files/serials/files/regulation/2000/4/deleire.pdf. Reprinted with permission.

## State and Local Government Activities

ADA, Title II, requires that State and local governments give persons with disabilities equal opportunity to participate in and have access to all programs, services, and activities. As described by the Department of Justice (2010), this typically includes public education, employment (as discussed earlier), transportation, recreation, health care, social services, courts, voting, and town meetings. Under this title, state and local governments are also required to follow specific architectural standards for new constructions. Public entities, overall, must make reasonable modification to practices and policies to avoid discrimination. The DOJ hears complaints about title II violations up to 180 days after the time of the discrimination; some cases will be referred to mediation rather than being litigated. Title II may also be enforced through private lawsuits in federal court. It is not necessary to file a complaint with the DOJ or any other federal agency, or to receive a "right-to-sue" letter, before going to court.

## Public Transportation

ADA, Title II, also covers public transportation services, such as city buses and public rail transit systems. Authorities of public transportation are not allowed to discriminate against persons with disabilities, that is, unless it results in undue burden, they may not decrease, remove, or alter their services, but rather, must comply with requirements regarding accessibility, such as good faith efforts to purchase or lease accessible buses. They must also provide paratransit (transportation that picks up and drops off) to persons with disabilities at their destination.

## Public Accommodations

ADA, Title III, covers businesses and nonprofit service providers that are public accommodations or privately operated entities who own, lease, lease to, or operate public facilities. This includes restaurants, retail stores, hotels, movie theaters, private schools, convention centers, doctors' offices, homeless shelters, transportation depots, zoos, funeral homes, day care centers, and recreation facilities including sports stadiums and fitness clubs. This can include modifying no-pets policy to include service animals, membership policies to include bringing in an aide, and modifying procedures at a bank such as if a person can stand for a long period they will not lose their place in line. This title also covers transportation services provided by private entities. Such facilities may not engage in exclusion, segregation, and unequal treatment toward any persons with disabilities. Similar to State and Local Government Activities, under Title II, they must comply with specific requirements related to architectural standards for new and altered buildings; reasonable modifications to policies, practices, and procedures; effective communication with people with hearing, vision, or speech disabilities; and other access requirements. Also, given the availability of resources (e.g., cost) and level of ease, a public accommodation can also include removing barriers in existing buildings that impedes a person with a disability. Commercial facilities, such as factories and warehouses, must also comply with the ADA's architectural standards for new construction and alterations. Finally, all courses and examinations related to professional, educational, or trade-related applications, licensing, certifications, or credentialing must be provided in a place and manner accessible to people with disabilities, or alternative accessible arrangements must be offered. This can include installing ramps to entrances and curbs in sidewalks. Complaints of title III violations may be filed with the Department of Justice. In certain situations, cases may be referred to a mediation program sponsored by the department.

### Telecommunications and Emergency Services

ADA, Title IV, covers telephone and television access for people with hearing and speech disabilities. It requires that telephone companies and other common carriers establish inter- and intrastate telecommunications relay services (TRS) 24 hours a day, 7 days a week. In addition, the ADA requires that emergency preparedness programs be accessible to persons with disabilities. This has become a critical responsibility of local government programs. Persons with disabilities need to be taken into account in order to have effective and safe emergency planning or response activities, especially related to notification, evacuation, emergency transportation, sheltering, access to medications, refrigeration, and back-up power, access to their mobility devices or service animals while in transit or at shelters, and access to information. Examples include providing a transit bus with a wheelchair lift for evacuation, a shelter with accessible features, and using hand gestures or written notes for evacuation to someone who is deaf.

Additionally, there are several other acts that ensure equal opportunity to persons with disabilities: Telecommunications Act, Fair Housing Act, Air Carrier Access Act, Voting Accessibility for the Elderly and Handicapped Act, National Voter Registration Act, Civil Rights of Institutionalized Persons Act, Individuals with Disabilities Education Act, Rehabilitation Act, and Architectural Barriers Act. Finally, there are several federal agencies that have ADA responsibilities. These are the Equal Employment

Opportunity Commission, Department of Transportation, Federal Communications Commission, Department of Education, Department of Health and Human Services, Department of Labor, Department of Housing and Urban Development, Department of the Interior, and the Department of Agriculture. Together, support and advocacy are provided to our nation's population of persons with disabilities.

*Melanie Horn Mallers*

**See also:** Department of Agriculture (USDA); Department of Education (ED); Department of Health and Human Services (HHS); Department of Housing and Urban Development (HUD); Department of the Interior (DOI); Department of Justice (DOJ); Department of Labor (DOL); Equal Employment Opportunity Commission (EEOC); Federal Communications Commission (FCC)

### References and Additional Readings

DeLeire, T. (n.d.). The unintended consequences of the Americans with Disabilities Act. Retrieved from http://www.cato.org/pubs/regulation/regv23n1/deleire.pdf

Department of Justice. (2009). A guide to disability rights laws. Retrieved from http://www.ada.gov/cguide.htm#anchor62335

Department of Justice. (2010). ADA: Know your rights. Retrieved from http://www.ada.gov/servicemembers_adainfo.html

Department of Justice. (2013). Americans with disabilities act. ADA home page. Retrieved from http://www.ada.gov/

Guidotti, T. L. (2011). What options are available for accommodation under ADA?. *Journal of Occupational and Environmental Medicine, 53*(3), 340.

Mayerson, A. (1992). The history of the ADA: A movement perspective. Disability Rights Education and Defense Fund. Retrieved from http://dredf.org/publications/ada_history.shtml

McMahan, B. T., & Hurley, J. E. (2008). Discrimination in hiring under the Americans with Disabilities Act: An overview of the National EEOC ADA Research Project. *Journal of Occupational Rehabilitation, 18*(2), 103–105.

Thomas, V. L., & Gostin, L. O. (2009). The Americans with Disabilities Act. *JAMA: The Journal of the American Medical Association, 301*(1), 95–97.

## Annual Percentage Rate. *See* Banking

## Arbitration

Arbitration is a quasilegal alternative to court litigation that serves to ensure that the rights of consumers to fair outcomes are protected. Since corporations (e.g., credit card, health care) are increasingly requiring that consumers give up their full legal rights and agree to arbitrate all legal concerns by including mandatory arbitration provisions in their contracts with consumers, many advocates are arguing that such requirements are anticonsumer. Consumers are not literally forced to sign such contracts but since they have been adopted widely, within entire industries, finding a healthcare provider or credit card agency not requiring arbitration can be difficult, if not impossible. These contracts are called adhesion. Consumers often feel compelled to accept the provider's terms to receive service.

## Consumer Beware

Consumers are advised to read all the fine print of any contract they sign and thoroughly educate themselves about the rights they are agreeing to relinquish when they sign such an agreement. The National Consumer Law Center has collected a group of legal cases where courts have been increasingly receptive to scrutinizing contracts with mandatory arbitration clauses based on the standard contract defense, or legal attack, that the contract is unconscionable—substantively or procedurally too one sided or unfair. Nevertheless, a consumer can never count on a court siding with the consumer. Many consumers lack the resources needed to launch strong legal cases. A consumer's first recourse should always be doing everything possible to advocate for a contract that they feel good about signing. This may include asking that a mandatory arbitration clause be eliminated or changed and include mediation and other avenues the consumer wants to pursue before arbitrating. It may also require engaging a legal advocate to negotiate the contract on behalf of the consumer.

## Abbreviated Legal Process

At first glance, particularly with an unfamiliar consumer, arbitration might appear to be the same process as that used when a dispute is litigated in a court of law since disputing parties present their case to one or more decision makers who in some ways act like judges. Consumers will often hire lawyers to represent them in these quasilegal proceedings. While arbitration is promoted as less costly than litigation, some complex arbitration can be quite costly. Consumers should fully discuss hourly fees and costs with potential attorneys, seek an estimate of total hours required for their case, and receive a regular (monthly) bill for services rendered to ensure they are comfortable with the price of their representation.

It is important for consumers to understand the rights they waive when agreeing to arbitration. First, there is no right to a jury trial with arbitration. While public opinion and propaganda attack jury decision making, research shows that a jury of 12 can result in higher quality decisions (Jacobstein and Mersky, 2004, 221). There are certain cases, where a consumer has suffered great personal injury, for example, when consumers may prefer the sympathy and judgment of peers who identify with the consumer. While the consumer does not actually waive the right to appeal an arbitration decision, it is difficult to appeal a decision. Review only happens in limited and egregious cases. Arbitrators, the decision makers, are not required to give reasons to support or explain their awards. In many, if not most, cases, consumers essentially give up their rights to public record, appeal, and review when agreeing to arbitrate.

If consumers have suffered legal injury and are concerned about arbitrating that injury, they are advised to consult with a well-respected and trustworthy lawyer with expertise in the subject matter involved. If they innocently agreed to arbitration and are not happy, they are advised to speak with a lawyer with expertise in challenging arbitration awards and clauses.

## Arbitrator Impartiality

The other issue consumers should consider when agreeing to arbitrate is whether they are comfortable with level of impartiality of the potential arbitrators. While arbitrators are ethically bound to make decisions without showing preference, consumers may wish to consider requesting a three-member arbitration panel (Erbe, 2006, 407) in order to increase the likelihood of a fair outcome. The American Arbitration, American Bar, and American Medical Associations have adopted and endorsed due process protocols for the arbitration and mediation of consumer and healthcare disputes, purportedly to ensure fairness. At the very least, consumers should educate themselves about fair arbitration process.

On the other hand, the academy award winning film *Erin Brockovich* is based on a true story where consumers' needs and rights were powerfully served through arbitration. The movie educates consumers about some of the reasons arbitration can be their best alternative.

*Nancy D. Erbe*

**See also:** Mediation; National Consumer Law Center (NCLC); Ombuds Offices

## References and Additional Readings

Erbe, N. (2006). Appreciating mediation's global role in promoting good governance. *Harvard Negotiation Law Review, 11*, 355–419.

Jacobstein, M., & Mersky, R.M. (2004). Jury size: Articles and bibliography from the literature of law and the social and behavioral sciences. Buffalo, NY: William S. Hein Publishing.

Riskin, W., Guthrie, H., & Reuben, R. (1987). *Dispute resolution and lawyers.* St. Paul, MN: West Publishing.

## Attorney General Office (AG)

State Offices of the Attorney General (OAG) are one of the most important ways that consumer protection is provided in the United States. They are the states' law firms, typically serving state government, state agencies, state commissions, and state boards. The roles they play in support of the consumer movement have evolved over time and vary widely. Over time, some states, like New York have taken on strong consumer protection roles and citizens elect office holders who support consumer protection. The political environment in a state and its level of concern about its rating for business friendliness strongly influence the level of activity and the kinds of actions emphasized.

In 43 states, citizens directly elect the leaders of these offices, referred to as the attorney general (AG). Five states (Alaska, Hawaii, New Hampshire, New Jersey, and Wyoming) allow their governor to appoint the AG. The District of Columbia's is appointed by the mayor. Maine's AG is selected by a secret ballot vote of the legislature and Tennessee's is selected by the Supreme Court. Some AGs serve multiple terms, typically four years, while others only serve one term. The AG then appoints leaders of the divisions or sections of the office, each of which specializes in various legal areas that tend to be relatively stable over time. The division or section leaders are often considered to be political appointees and typically change when the AG changes. The staff members who work in the divisions or sections are often career workers and often serve under multiple AGs. Sometimes staff may be located with the specific agency or institution that they serve. For example, if the AG's office is responsible for representing institutions of higher education, state universities' attorneys may be hired and supervised by staff in the AG's office and located on the campuses.

AGs do not represent individual citizens in court or on matters of concern to them as citizens. They typically represent the governor and executive agencies, state boards and commissions, and institutions of higher education. The kinds of issues they deal with for these entities include everything from personnel to real estate.

State legislators and other government officials ask them to provide official opinions on legal issues. These opinions may lead to legislative proposals and they can even influence the decisions made by state boards or commissions. Recently, for example, Virginia's AG informed the state board of health that if it voted to exclude existing abortion clinics from new rules requiring adherence to standards used for hospitals, the AG would not defend members if they were sued. The board reversed its earlier vote so all abortion clinics must meet the standard.

AGs get involved in investigations in specific areas such as Medicaid fraud, computer crimes, environmental crimes, illegal drugs, gangs, sexual predators, human trafficking, bullying, and identity theft. Some states give them responsibility for regulating charities, enforcing freedom of information and open meeting laws, regulating gambling, oversight of the state crime lab, contractors, the division of motor vehicles, or advocating for groups with special needs like children, the elderly, women, veterans, or immigrants. The specific programs may vary based on the concerns and priorities of the office holder and the citizens at a given time and in a given state.

Often asked to review potential legislation, AGs may work with legislators to create and adjust state laws. They represent the state and those doing the state's work when the state or agency must deal with issues in court. When the constitutionality of state law is questioned, they represent the state in court. They may support victims of crime when those victims must deal with appeals of criminal cases or when criminals who harmed them are considered for parole. When those with criminal convictions appeal their conviction or those incarcerated sue the state, the OAG defends the state. Often, these are the cases that get the most media and citizen attention and it is not unusual for people to campaign for the office of AG using their experience and concern about criminals as justification of their suitability for the position. Most AGs are responsible for enforcing the state's consumer laws. Often they supervise the state's office of consumer affairs, which is responsible for receiving, evaluating, investigating, and referring consumer complaints. Thus, the OAG is often consulted when there is a need to understand the trends and the specific consumer issues confronting citizens of a state. Many AGs provide consumer education on issues related to consumer law and sponsor or conduct programs designed to help consumers look out for themselves in the competitive marketplace. They sometimes work with other agencies to reach consumers with educational programs. While most AGs traditionally printed tools to help citizens with consumer issues, the Internet has provided a comparatively inexpensive way to expand consumer education and consumer access to information they need when they need it.

A specific responsibility of most AGs is to represent consumers on utility issues that come before the state's public utility commission (PUC). These highly technical cases result in decisions that affect issues such as how much consumers pay for electricity, when a telephone company must file or have rates approved, and whether a gas company must provide service to a citizen. Some AGs employ large staffs to take care of these matters; others have very small staffs and hire numerous experts and additional attorneys for specific cases. In most states, this representation is focused on residential consumers. In some, the AG considers all businesses and residential customers to be consumers. States vary considerably in how vigorously they advocate for consumers and subgroups of consumers.

AGs typically are responsible for encouraging effective marketplace competition by enforcing state antitrust laws. They may be responsible for taking companies that they believe break the state's antigouging law after a flood or other natural disaster.

Collection of debts owed to state agencies, hospitals, and universities may also be among an AG's responsibilities. The office may lead attempts to collect back child support and other fees owed by parents whose children's care is paid for by the state or who fail to pay the custodial parent. Visiting the websites and news releases of the various AGs reveals that they are involved in quite a wide range of activities on behalf of their citizens. Currently, many are involved in the national foreclosure settlement. An agreement with Ally, Bank of America, Citi, JPMorgan Chase, and Wells Fargo is designed to correct problems caused when loan servicers signed foreclosure-related documents without knowing whether they contained accurate information. In some states at least some of the money will be returned to consumers or used for projects that will support home ownership; however, in many cases, the money will be used for other state needs/goals such as balancing the general state budget or addressing transportation needs. More recently, AGs negotiated a settlement for charges of unlawful conspiracy to set prices that resulted in direct refunds to consumers who purchased e-books from five national retailers. Some AGs focus on involvement in cases that result in money returned to consumers who are victims of scams or fraud. Since payday loans are illegal in West Virginia, the AG has vigorously gone after entities that ensnare West Virginians in payday loan products, whether from brick and mortar sites or via the Internet. Some AGs initiate actions that help citizens of other states as well as their own, such as New York's case against investment brokerage firms that resulted in restitution to consumers and extensive reform of rules governing the industry. Others initiate actions that challenge federal law, such as recent cases asking that the U.S. Supreme Court declare the Affordable Care Act (also known as Obamacare) unconstitutional. Others follow personal agendas, such as Virginia AG's attempts to force a university to turn over e-mail files of a former faculty member in an attempt to prove fraudulent use of research dollars on projects that support global warming. These efforts may be pursued by individual AG or by groups of AGs. The national organization for AGs and their staffs, the National Association of Attorneys General (NAAG), was founded in 1907. It offers three membership meetings per year to conduct business and a assortment of special meetings to help its members, recently including training for new AGs, deposition skills, train the trainer, consumer protection, investigator training, money laundering, and advanced trial techniques. Some parts of some of these meetings may be open to the public. In recent years, states have become more involved in issues that were once the sole responsibility of the federal government, such as trade regulation, environmental enforcement, and criminal justice, so AGs now work with their federal counterparts on these issues. NAAG takes stands on policy and has ongoing projects led by NAAG staff on antitrust, bankruptcy, civil rights, consumer protection, criminal law, cyberspace law, energy and environment, Medicaid fraud, Supreme Court, and tobacco. Individual AGs use this work to support the actions they take in their respective states, making NAAG's perspective on consumer protection extremely important to consumers.

*Irene Leech*

**See also:** Departments of Consumer Affairs (DCA); Federal Trade Commission (FTC); Frauds and Scams; Patient Protection and Affordable Care Act (PPACA); Public Utilities Commission; Supreme Court

### References and Additional Readings

Baker, N. V. (1992). *Conflicting loyalties: law and politics in the Attorney General's office, 1789–1990.* University Press of Kansas.

Furrow, B. (2011). Regulating patient safety: The Patient Protection and Affordable Care Act. *University of Pennsylvania Law Review, 159,* 101–149.

National Association of Attorneys General. (n.d.). About NAAG. Information on the association. Retrieved from www.naag.org

## Auto Purchasing

Buying a new car can be an exciting yet stressful experience for consumers. It is important for consumers to be informed before navigating the

Consumers negotiating a new car purchase. (Andresr/Shutterstock.com)

oftentimes nerve-racking process of finding the right car, negotiating the sales price, and securing financing. Furthermore, the process is complicated by the need to make other major decisions such as buying new or used, buying or leasing, and trading-in an old car or selling it privately; consumers are surely testing their limits.

### Finding the Right Car

The average new car today costs just over $30,000 according to experts' estimates. Consumer should consider several factors before getting a new car, including the type of car one wants, how much one can afford; the transportation needs of self and family, such as type of driving most often done (commuting, long trips, etc.), and the reliability of the car. Consumers are encouraged to consult publications like *Consumer Reports*, car magazines, and car Internet sites. Research on models, prices, incentives, rebates, finance rates, the overall cost of ownership (i.e., gas mileage, maintenance and repairs, insurance costs, and depreciation), and the total cost to own the car (i.e., monthly payment, insurance, gas mileage, and maintenance) is critical.

Other practical strategies for consumers to consider before heading to the dealer:

- *Make sure the dealer has the car.* The dealer will try to sell whatever inventory they have in the lot. Don't settle for a car if you will regret it. If the dealer doesn't have the car, go to another place. The dealer might offer to order or find the car, but this will reduce the negotiating leverage.
- *Make the salesperson get invested.* The dealer needs to spend time with the consumer and realize that the consumer is serious about buying the car if the terms are right.
- *Negotiate the price from the bottom-up, never from the top-down.* Two things the dealer will invariably try to do is have the consumer make an offer starting from the MSRP and focus on the monthly payment the consumer can afford. This is good for the dealer, but bad for the consumer. Don't negotiate around a monthly payment. Instead, focus on the target price, which should have been determined based on the invoice price. Ask the dealer for the invoice price, and verify that the information they give corresponds to the actual car you are buying, as the dealer may end up presenting information that belongs to a higher-priced car. Start by offering the dealer less than the target price. When the dealer makes a counteroffer, the consumer can go up some, but not higher than the target price. Remember, it is OK to haggle long and hard even for a small amount. Even $100 in savings means a nice celebration dinner. It means a lot less for the dealer's overall bottom line. Also, take note that the manufacturers give dealers incentives to move inventory; the dealer will still make money even if they sell the car for the invoice price.
- *Manufacturer rebates and incentives for the buyer, not the dealer.* Rebates and incentives are from the manufacturer to the consumer. Don't let the dealer factor them in while negotiating the sales price. Agree on a sales price first, and deduct the rebates and incentives later. Don't let the dealer make you feel bad that you are offering to pay the invoice price, minus the rebate.
- *Trade-in—don't:* Buyers will not get the best value for their old car at the dealer. This is so because the dealer has to make money in reselling your car. The same person buying the car from the dealer could have been the person buying directly from you. So the profit the dealer makes in reselling your car will come out of the price they pay you for it. This true story illustrates why you should always sell your old car on your own or give it to a loved one:
- Donna decided to buy a new car after she got tired of her 14-year-old car. She went to the same dealer that sold her the old car, and they made her a "great" offer to sell her a new car for $3,000 over MSRP and pay her $1,500 for her old car. Donna walked away. After she and her friend did all the homework listed above, they went to the dealer and negotiated a price on the new car for the invoice price, which was about $1,800 less than the MSRP. And, and at the recom

mendation of her friend, Donna decided not to trade in her old car. Instead, her friend listed on Ebay, where it sold for $5,900. So instead of overpaying for the new car and giving away her old one, Donna saved serious money by being a smart consumer.

- *It's not over until it's over.* You and the dealer have agreed on a sales price. And now is time to write the paperwork. You may feel tempted to lower your guard and relax. Don't. You still have to get through the finance department, where the numbers can change. Many times the numbers change because you ask or are pressured into buying extras like paint protection, GAP insurance, and extended service contracts. Other times, the dealer simply alters the numbers and charges you for things you didn't agree to. So before you sign the contract, review it line-by-line and make sure you understand and agree to every charge made.

- *Extended service contracts (warranties).* One thing the finance manager will most likely pressure you to buy is an extended service contract. Like a warranty, a service contract provides repair coverage for a specific period. But warranties are included in the price of a product. Service contracts cost extra. Generally, you want to pass on service contracts. According to Consumer Reports, extended service contracts don't pay off. If you are concerned about the reliability of the car you are about to buy, consider buying a car with a more reliable track record.

- *Inspect the car before you drive home.* After the dealer cleans the car, do a walk-around inspection to make sure it doesn't have existing damage. Many times new cars are damaged while being transported from loading docks to dealer lots or when taken out on test drives. You don't want to find out the next morning that your new car has a scratch or blemish. Worse, the dealer may claim you damaged the car on your way home and refuse to fix the damage.

*Rigoberto Reyes*

## Buying a New Car

A new car is second only to a home as the most expensive purchase many consumers make. It is important for consumers to compile trusted information from the Internet, friends, and reputable publications. Ultimately, the price one has to pay for a new car depends largely on how much demand and supply there is for the particular model in question. A low-production car that is in high demand will command top dollar, while cars that languish for months on dealer lots often have substantial discounts. But having the right information and knowing some effective negotiation techniques will always make the buyer a stronger negotiator in getting a better deal, regardless of the type of car that is purchased.

**Seven Practical Strategies for Consumers before Heading to the Dealer**

- *Learn the jargon:* Knowing key terms and what they mean will help consumers negotiate a better deal.

- *Invoice price*: The invoice price is allegedly the price the dealer pays the manufacturer for the car. However, this price does not take into effect dealer incentive and discounts given by the manufacturer, but rather lists the manufacturer's suggested price for the car and the features.

- *Get to know specifics about the car:* Doing significant research and collecting good and accurate information is power. Wrong information and bad assumptions can cost money. It used to be that only dealers had information about a particular car, pricing, and accessories; this is no longer the case. Many Internet sites now provide free and current information, including price, accessories, market conditions, rebates, special financing offers, and other incentives. Some reputable sites include Edmunds.com, kbb.com, consumerreports.com, and TrueCar.com. Doing research online saves time and money, and provides peace of mind and avoidance of pressure from overly aggressive salespeople.

- *Get online price offers* for the specific car wanted and from several dealers. Websites like TrueCar.com lets consumers request a quote that can be taken to the dealer for a no-price-haggling experience. Credit unions, membership clubs like Costco, or even employers can also be good sources to obtain quotes and pricing information. When reviewing an offer keep in mind available rebates, special financing, and other incentives.

- *Set a target price and stick to it:* Decide on the budget in advance. Discuss this in advance with anyone else who is going to be involved in the decision-making process, such as a spouse or adult children. Buying a car should be a family decision. Dealers will not hesitate to use the divide-and-conquer strategy to make a sale if they do not see a unified front.

- *Obtain financing in advance:* If a consumer is financing a car, a few higher percentage points in the interest rate can add thousands of dollars to the life of the loan. This can easily happen if the financing terms are not clearly understood. Getting preapproval by a bank or credit union keeps the negotiations at the dealership simpler and removes part of the stress. A consumer can always agree to a dealer's loan if they offer a better rate.

- *Check that the car is reliable and safe:* A consumer can get free information on rankings and safety tests conducted by the *National Highway Traffic Safety Administration*. A division of the U.S. Department of Transportation, NHTSA writes, tests, and enforces auto safety guidelines and regulations. They also maintain recall data that reports if a car has been recalled due to safety concerns. Another good source for auto safety is the *Insurance Institute for Highway Safety*, which compiles personal injury and property damage data resulting from car accidents.

- *Walk away strategy:* Decide when it is time to walk away, especially if the dealer refuses to give the price that is desired. The dealer's claim that their offer is only good that day is rarely true. It is always good to "sleep on" any offer before making a final decision.

## Leasing a Car

A car lease is a long-term rental. In a lease, the consumer does not own the car, they rent it. Most leases allow consumers to buy the car when the lease ends, but consumers are rarely required to do so. Leasing is the easiest way to get a new car every few years, while letting the dealer handle the old one. Payments for a lease are usually lower than payments for a purchase because the consumer is not paying to own the car, but rather is paying for the car's depreciation during the lease term (i.e., rent charges, taxes, and fees). Low leasing payments might be tempting, but leases are not for everyone. There are several things to consider before leasing a car.

It is important for consumers to speak the language. The capitalized cost is the equivalent of the selling price. The residual value is the estimated worth of the car at the end of the lease. The monthly payments are determined by the difference between the capitalized cost and the residual value, plus the money factor, which is the equivalent of the interest rate. A low capitalized cost, high residual value, and low money factor result in lower monthly payments. These terms can be negotiated just as when making a car purchase. Mileage is an important factor to consider in a leasing decision. Leases limit the number of miles allowable, often 12,000–15,000 miles per year. If the consumer goes over the miles allowed, they will be charged for the extra miles at the end of the lease. Be sure that the lease includes the amount of miles that are reasonable for estimated use.

One major drawback with a lease is that the consumer is forced to make a major financial decision when lease expires: return the car or buy it. When buying a car, consumers have more flexibility in deciding when to replace it, hopefully long after the loan is paid off. Another consideration is insurance costs. Insurance costs are usually higher for leased cars. Check with an insurance company to find out if they charge more for a lease than a purchase.

It is important that all promises made by the dealer are in the contract. If there is anything that is confusing, it is important to ask for an explanation. Do not sign anything that is not fully understood; it is difficult and costly to end a lease early. If a lease is terminated before the contract length, early termination penalties are typically applied. Moreover, leases limit the wear on the vehicle. When the vehicle is returned, excessive wear, use, or damage will be charged to the consumer.

Similar to payments, upfront costs can also be lower for a lease than a purchase. At the beginning of the lease, consumers usually pay their first monthly payment, a refundable security deposit, fees for registration, sales tax on the first monthly payment. With a lease, consumers don't pay the sales tax up front for the entire cost of the lease; they pay monthly sales tax on the amount of the payment. Most leases charge an acquisition fee to the bank and a down payment called a cap reduction fee.

The decision to purchase or lease a new car is a big one, typically the second largest purchase made by consumers. Consumers would do well to research and study all aspects of the decision before making a final choice.

---

Learn the jargon to negotiate a better price:

- *Invoice price:* This is supposed to be the price the dealer pays the manufacturer for the car. But the dealer actually pays less for the car because manufacturers give dealers rebates, allowances, discounts, and incentives to move inventory. So even if you offer to pay the invoice price for the car, the dealer would still make money on the sale.
- *MSRP* (manufacturer's suggested retail price): The label affixed to the car's window. It shows the base price the dealer is asking for the car, plus additional options, and any dealer markup.
- *Dealer markup:* Many dealers add thousands of dollars to the MSRP to give you the impression that you are getting a good deal when the dealer offers to sell you the car for MSRP. You should avoid paying a dealer markup, unless there is an unusually high demand and short supply for the car you want. Instead, as mentioned below, you should always negotiate from the invoice price, not MSRP.
- *Accessories:* Things added to the car at extra cost. Some accessories are installed by the manufacturer, such as a sunroof, leather seats, or a navigation system. Other accessories are added by the dealer, including paint protection, upgraded wheels, and anti-theft devices.

Consider this if you are getting a loan to finance the car:

- While dealers and manufacturers often advertise special zero percent and low finance rates, many consumers don't qualify for these subsidized rates that require high credit ratings. And the time to find out you don't qualify for the special rate is not when you are already at the dealer in front of an eager salesperson.

- The dealer is not necessarily going to find you the best alternate rate. So before you head to the dealer check with your credit union or bank for the best loan available. Sites like bankrate.com and Eloan.com are also good sources to find out current interest rates. It's best to get a letter from your own lender that says how much they have approved you for and what the terms of the loan are. Doing so keeps the negotiations at the dealer simpler and removes some of the stress from the car buying experience. When at the dealer, show them the letter and request the best loan they can offer you. If the dealer offers you a better loan, take it.
- In most cases, you can take a rebate in place of any low-rate financing offered by the manufacturer.
- Be cautious about advertisements offering financing to first-time buyers or people with bad credit. These offers often require a big down payment and a high interest rate.
- Know the exact price you are paying for the car, the amount you are financing, how much the finance charges are going to cost you, the Annual Percentage Rate, and the number and amount of payments you'll make.

If you decide to buy a service contract, keep this in mind:

- When does the coverage start and end? Most car manufacturers' warranties provide you coverage for at least 3 years/36,000 miles. It makes no sense to buy a service contract that duplicates coverage you already have. And many manufacturers provide power-train coverage for up to 10 years/100,000 miles. If you buy a service contract that provides similar coverage during this time period, you won't have any use for it.
- Is the vehicle is likely to need repairs and their potential costs? Would the cost of repairing the car be greater than what you are paying for the service contract?
- What does the service contract really cover? Check out all claims carefully as "bumper to bumper" coverage may not mean what you expect.
- Is there a deductible? If yes, how much will you have to pay before the service contract company pays for repairs?
- Will you be required to bring your car to the dealer in order not to void the service contract?
- What is the cancellation and refund policy for the service contract and, are there any cancellation fees?
- Will the service contract company be there for you if you need help?

*Rigoberto Reyes*

**See also:** Department of Transportation (DOT); Consumers Union; Lemon Laws; National Highway Traffic Safety Administration (NHTSA); National Transportation Safety Board (NTSB)

**References and Additional Readings**

Busse, M., & Silva-Risso, J.M. (2010). The "one discriminatory rent" or 'double jeopardy': Multicomponent negotiation for new car purchases. *American Economic Review: Papers & Proceedings, 100*, 470–474.

Ikenson, D.J. (2012). Should new car loans be tax deductible? *The Cato Institute.* Retrieved from http://www.cato.org/publications/commentary/should-new-car-loans-be-tax-deductible

Shay, R.P. (2012). New automobile finance rates, 1924–62. *The Journal of Finance, 18*(3), 461–493.

**Auto Safety Regulations.** *See* Department of Transportation (DOT); National Highway Traffic and Safety Administration (NHTSA); National Transportation Safety Board (NTSB)

# B

## Bait and Switch

Bait advertising, also known as bait and switch, is an illegal advertising tactic in which a product or service is advertised (the bait) at a low price but the seller has no intention of selling it at that price. Once the buyer is lured into agreeing to the purchase, the consumer is then dissuaded from doing so and is offered a higher profit alternative (the switch). As a result of decades of such chicanery, the Federal Trade Commission promulgated the Bait Advertising Rule.

The bait advertising regulation, Section 238 of the Code of Federal Regulations (16CFR.238) is brief and easy to understand. Section 238.1 defines bait advertising; Section 238.2 enumerates the specifics of the initial offer that are fraudulent; Section 238.3 offers examples noting discouragement of the purchase of the offered advertised merchandise; and Section 238.4 explains switching the offer after the "sale."

Examples of Discouragement of the Purchase of Advertised Merchandise, as specified in Section 238.3 include:

the refusal to show, demonstrate, or sell the product offered in accordance with the terms of the offer; the disparagement by acts or words of the advertised product or the disparagement of the guarantee, credit terms, availability of service, repairs or parts, or in any other respect in connection with it, the failure to have available at all outlets listed in the advertisement a sufficient quantity of the advertised product to meet reasonably anticipated demands, unless the advertisement clearly and adequately discloses that supply is limited and/or the merchandise is available only at designated outlets, the refusal to take orders for the advertised merchandise to be delivered within a reasonable period of time, the showing or demonstrating of a product which is defective, unusable or impractical for the purpose represented or implied in the advertisement; and use of a sales plan or method of compensation for salesmen or penalizing salesmen, designed to prevent or discourage them from selling the advertised product.

> One example that was tried on me many years ago was when I attempted to purchase low-cost advertised brakes for my car. The merchant noted that they were too dangerous for him to sell and he offered (switched) to me a great deal on much safer brakes. These were twice as expensive.
>
> *Mel J. Zelenak*

Section 238.4, Switching the Offer After Sale, enumerates:

No practice should be pursued by an advertiser, in the event of sale of the advertised product, in its stead. Among acts or practices of "unselling" with the intent and purpose of selling other merchandise which will be considered in determining if the initial sale was in good faith, and not a stratagem to sell other merchandise, are: (a) accepting a deposit for the advertised product, then switching the purchaser to a higher-priced product; (b) failure to make delivery of the advertised product within a reasonable time or to make a refund; (c) disparagement by acts or words of the advertised product, or the disparagement of the guarantee, credit terms, availability of service, repairs, or in any other respect, in connection with it; (d) the delivery of the advertised product which is defective, unusable or impractical for the purpose represented or implied in the advertisement.

Bait and switch has been a violation of federal and most state consumer protection laws and regulations since the 1970s. Nonetheless, like most other fraudulent practices in the marketplace, the tactic continues because of gullible consumers, greedy sellers, inadequate legislation, and regulations that are not adequately enforced.

---

### Bait and Switch in the News

Groupon is being accused of running false and misleading advertisement. San Francisco Comprehensive tours filed the complaint in a San Francisco court arguing that Groupon has been unlawfully manipulating Google's AdWords advertising systems. The tour company states that Groupon was running text ads that mentioned discounts they were not offering.

*Source:* LA Times Blog. (March 23, 2011). Groupon accused of "bait and switch" advertising on Google.com in lawsuit. Retrieved from http://latimesblogs.latimes.com/

---

*Mel J. Zelenak*

**See also:** Federal Trade Commission (FTC); Frauds and Scams

**References and Additional Readings**

Friedman, D.A. (2012). Explaining bait-and-switch regulation. Retrieved from http://ssrn.com/abstract=2122177

McArthur, D. (2008). How does a $224 flight end up costing $826? *The Globe and Mail.* Retrieved September 17, 2012.

# Banking

Banking is a critical consumer issue, as banking services aid in consumers' cash and credit management through access to safe transaction accounts and credit, and assist in wealth accumulation by providing access to investment vehicles. Some of the important issues related to banking include changes in regulation and fraud protection legislation, safe use of debit cards, and the influence of technology on banking products.

## Deregulation

Regulation of the banking industry has been a topic of debate since before the first major pieces of legislation were passed in the New Deal era. The creation of the Federal Reserve system in 1914 and the Glass–Steagall Act in 1933 signaled the beginning of banking regulation, and several additional pieces of legislation have been passed increasing the regulation of banking and financial markets (i.e., Federal Home Bank Loan Board in 1933, Bureau of Federal Credit Unions in 1934).

The high inflation of the 1970s caused many of the constraints of regulation to become increasingly burdensome to the banking and credit card industries. The elimination of regulation related to usury began at the state

The American Bankers Association (ABA) represents banks of all sizes and charters. It serves as "the voice for the nation's $13 trillion banking industry and its 2 million employees." The ABA believes that "an educated consumer is the best customer." The ABA thus provides information to consumers on several personal financial tips, such as budgeting, credit, mortgages, and saving, as well as provides tips to protect money and identity.

*Source:* ABA. (2012). About the American Bankers Association. Retrieved from http://www.aba.com/

level, and to eliminate interest rate ceilings, the Depository Institutions and Monetary Control Act was passed in 1980. Major deregulation began in the mid-1980s when the Federal Reserve Board began to broaden the interpretation of the Glass–Steagall Act, and increased as the Federal Reserve continued to interpret Glass–Steagall in an increasingly liberal manner. The Riegle–Neal Interstate Banking and Branching Efficiency Act in 1994 decreased restrictions on interstate banking, in 1999 the Financial Modernization Act; these two pieces of legislation essentially eliminated the regulation instituted with Glass–Steagall.

## Debit Cards

### Debit Card Rewards

With the major shift from the use of paper checks for payment to the use of debit cards, commercial banks and credit unions (transaction account granting institutions) have offered debit card reward programs to encourage customer loyalty. These programs operate similarly to rewards programs in other industries, such as airlines and credit card companies, and frequently offer points exchangeable for cash, goods, or travel. Due to the restrictions on transactions fees placed on banks by the Dodd–Frank Act, debit card rewards programs are becoming less common. Research indicates rewards programs rank low in consumers' decision to switch banks. Although most reward program points don't disappear when a rewards program is eliminated, there are programs where accumulated points expire after a certain time, or an account may not have the minimum number of points available for redemption and no additional points may be earned due to the closure of the program.

### Fraudulent Transfers

Debit card (along with credit card) fraud is a major concern in consumer protection. The Electronic Fund Transfer Act (EFTA) provides protection from unauthorized or fraudulent use of debit cards, but contains stipulations on liability for when the card is reported missing. Table 3 displays the relationship between when (or if) the debit card is reported missing and the maximum liability of the cardholder.

Once the card has been reported missing or stolen, the consumer cannot be held liable for any additional fraudulent use of the card. However, because debit card fraud involves the theft of a consumer's own funds (rather

**Table 3**  Liability of debit cardholder based on when they reported their card missing

| When card reported missing | Card was never missing (number used w/o card) | Reported < 2 days | Reported 2+ days but < 60 after statement | More than 60 days after statement mailed |
|---|---|---|---|---|
| Liability | $0 | $50 | $500 | Unlimited |

than funds yet to be paid, as with credit cards) debit card fraud can be more devastating to consumers. To assist consumers, many banks will issue credit in the first 24–48 hours for those who have been victims of fraud, as frequently bank accounts have been drained by perpetrators. In addition, some financial institutions monitor account activity and have made available text or e-mail alerts intended to make accountholders aware of potential fraud. However, careful monitoring of bank accounts is still cited as the most effective method of preventing or detecting fraudulent debit card activity.

### Complaint Filing

The process required for filing a complaint or dispute may vary slightly with each bank, but usually begins by contacting the issuing bank directly. If a debit card is lost or stolen, or if there is a suspicion fraudulent activity, the first step is to call the number provided on the either back of the card (if not lost or stolen), or on banking records. If neither of those is available, the customer service number for the bank may be available online. Due to the restrictions on liability for debit card fraud, it's critical abuses are reported as soon as possible. The issuing bank will typically assist in the processing of fraud claims, but if the financial institution has not handled the complaint satisfactorily, there are additional resources available, including the Board of Governors of the Federal Reserve system and the Federal Deposit Insurance Corporation (FDIC).

### Annual Percentage Rate

The annual percentage rate (APR) refers to the interest rate on a financial account (credit or investment) expressed for one year. The APR is used to make comparison of financial products, including mortgages and other loans, credit cards, and savings vehicles, more feasible, as financial products are frequently provided to consumers with differing terms. The Federal Truth in Lending Act requires that many financial products disclose the APR to consumers, making side-by-side comparison viable, and allowing the consumer to see the actual costs or benefits of the product.

### Technology and Banking

There may be no greater influence on the banking industry than innovations in technology. The availability of online services and virtual banking has become important components in options for consumers. However, these new services have not come without added safety concerns.

### *Electronic Funds Transfer*

Electronic Funds Transfer (EFT) is defined by the Electronic Transfer Act (15 USC 1693a):

> Any transfer of funds, other than a transaction originated by check, draft, or similar paper instrument, which is initiated through an electronic terminal, telephonic instrument, or computer or magnetic tape so as to order, instruct, or authorize a financial institution to debit or credit an account. Such term includes, but is not limited to, point-of-sale transfers, automated teller machine transactions, direct deposits or withdrawals of funds, and transfers initiated by telephone.

This act was passed in 1978 and governs all aspects of EFTs in the United States. EFTs are frequently used by commercial and governmental organizations, as well as consumer and include activities such as direct deposit, wire transfers, electronic bill pay, and most commonly, cardholder-initiated transactions that make use of a payment card (credit or debit). In its issuance of payment checks, the Department of the Treasury estimates that it costs $1.03 to issue a paper check, while an EFT can be issued for 10.5 cents.

### *Online Banking and Safety*

Online banking can provide substantial convenience for consumers. The ability to manage accounts online, transfer funds between accounts, apply for loans and credit, pay bills, and even make deposits saves time and energy for bank customers. However, online banking has also created a host of additional opportunities for fraud. Some of these schemes include phishing e-mail attempting to trick consumers into providing account information and computer viruses that capture this information when consumers enter account details online. Identity theft is an additional method used in online banking fraud; criminals may open accounts with personal information obtained in the identity theft process. As with fraudulent debit card charges, the best methods for preventing online banking fraud are careful monitoring of accounts and carefully guarding account information.

### Virtual Banking

The increase in technology also makes possible banks without brick-and-mortar locations. These virtual or e-banks offer many of the same services as traditional banks, but without physical locations. They exist only on the Internet. E-banks frequently offer the same range of services as traditional banks, and are subject to the same regulations as traditional banks. Because these banks don't have the expense of maintaining brick-and-mortar locations, they are frequently able to offer more competitive prices on financial services and better rates on savings accounts. The major drawback associated with these banks is related to ATMs. As these banks do not have their own machines, making deposits requires mailing deposits to the bank.

*Angela Fontes*

**See also:** Credit Cards; Credit Unions; Debt Management; Dodd–Frank Wall Street Reform and Consumer Protection Act; Privacy: Online

### References and Additional Readings

Bankrate. (2011). Banks offer fewer debit cards with rewards. Retrieved from http://www.bankrate.com/finance/banking/debit-cards.aspx

Federal Reserve. (2010). Board of governors of the federal reserve system glossary. Retrieved from http://www.federalreserve.gov/creditcard/glossary.html

Federal Deposit Insurance Corporation. (2012). Electronic Fund Transfer Act. Retrieved from http://www.fdic.gov/regulations/laws/rules/6500–1350.html

Federal Deposit Insurance Corporation. (n.d.). Federal Deposit Insurance Corporation. Retrieved from www.fdic.gov

Federal Deposit Insurance Corporation. (2012). Depository institutions deregulation and monetary control act of 1980. Retrieved from http://www.fdic.gov/regulations/laws/rules/8000–2200.html

Federal Trade Commission. (2012). Lost or stolen credit, ATM, and debit cards. Retrieved from http://www.ftc.gov/bcp/edu/pubs/consumer/credit/cre04.shtm

Financial Management Service, A Bureau of the U.S. Department of the Treasury. (2012). Electronic funds transfer: Overview. Retrieved from http://www.fms.treas.gov/eft/index.html

Geffner, M. (2011) Are your debit card rewards safe? Retrieved from http://www.bankrate.com/finance/banking/debit-card-rewards-safe.aspx

Sherman, M. (2009). A short history of financial deregulation in the United States. Retrieved from http://www.openthegovernment.org/sites/default/files/otg/dereg-timeline-2009-07.pdf

## Bankruptcy

### What Is Bankruptcy?

Bankruptcy is a privilege based on the U.S. Constitution and the laws passed by Congress. Bankruptcy adjusts the relationship between a debtor (a person who owes money) and creditors (a person/company who is owed money). Under bankruptcy, many debts are forgiven and the debtor is allowed to keep some property known as exempt items. The remainder of the property may be sold and the money used to pay off the outstanding debts. If any property has been pledged as collateral (such as a home for a mortgage, a car for a vehicle loan, etc.), the proceeds from the sale of that item will first go to the repayment of that debt. Any balance will be applied to other debts. Creditors may receive nothing at all, a small amount per dollar owed, or be paid off entirely depending on the value of items sold. The proceedings take place in federal court and are governed by federal law.

Bankruptcy remains on a debtor's credit report for 10 years, making it difficult or very expensive to get future credit. After filing for bankruptcy, the debtor is not legally allowed to file bankruptcy again for six years (except in Chapter 13 filings when repayment of at least 70 percent of the debt is made).

Bankruptcy is not free. Debtors must pay court costs and administrative fees, trustee fees, and, if desired, lawyer fees. In most cases, the fees are due at the time of filing. Bankruptcy should be a last resort, only considered when a debtor cannot see any other way to pay off their debts. Bankruptcy no longer carries the same societal stigma it once did. However, many bankruptcy filers feel hostility from neighbors and business owners who accuse them of "walking away from their debts."

Some of the reasons people file for bankruptcy are large medical bills, inability to pay debts after a divorce, large amount of credit card debt, and consumer attempts to buy time (i.e., to keep a home out of foreclosure or a car from being repossessed while catching up on payments).

### History of Bankruptcy

Bankruptcy dates back to early Rome when creditors who did not have their debts satisfied could either physically cut up the debtor's body and divide the body pieces or, if they preferred, let him live, but sell him into slavery. The cutting up was eventually abolished but the debtor or a family member could be pledged as collateral until the debt was paid, while involuntary bankruptcy dates back to this time. Similarly Roman traders who did not pay their debts were left to the device of their creditors where all their actions for 30 days where presumed fraudulent. The term *bancarotta* was first used in 14th-century Italy. Additionally, Islamic and Jewish laws also have provisions for bankruptcy.

The first bankruptcy law in England was in 1542. The *Statute of Bankrupts* in 1570 was the basis for bankruptcy in the United States in colonial times. This statute was aimed mainly at fraudulent debtors. The act referred to fraudulent merchants who took refuge in their homes, vacated the jurisdiction, and other fraudulent acts to avoid paying their debts.

At the Constitutional Convention in 1787, a clause to establish the uniform laws upon the subject of bankruptcies, Clause 4 of Section 8 of Article 1, was inserted immediately after the power to regulate commerce. Although Congress was given the power at the framing of the constitution, the first bankruptcy statute, the Bankruptcy Act of 1800, was finally passed on February 21, 1800. The act had a maximum life of five years and only covered traders. It was purely involuntary requiring a petition filed by the creditors. No discharge was filed until the "honest debtor" had repaid enough of their debt that two-thirds of the creditors consented to the discharge. The act was repealed in 1803.

Several bankruptcy laws were introduced between 1803 and 1841; however, several were defeated. Some states did manage to pass legislation and have it upheld by the courts. In 1841, a bill was passed that allowed voluntary bankruptcy for individuals and involuntary bankruptcy for merchants, bankers, brokers, underwriters, retailers, and factors. The 1841 act was repealed in 1843. The next bankruptcy bill was passed in 1867. This act allowed for both voluntary and involuntary bankruptcies for all, that state property exemptions would apply, and that no discharge would be allowed unless a majority of the creditors (determined by both dollar amount and number of creditors) agreed to the plan or the debtor's assets would repay 50 percent or more of the total bankruptcy debt.

The first major amendment to the act of 1867 came in 1874. The act of 1874 contained a provision that allowed the discharge of a debtor after paying a pro rata to the creditors over a period of time. This is the first appearance of a rehabilitative notion in bankruptcy. The Bankruptcy Act of 1898 was the next major revision, staying in effect with only minor revisions until the Bankruptcy Reform Act of 1978 was enacted in 1979.

**Types of Bankruptcy**

There are four provisions in the bankruptcy laws:

- Chapter 7—used most often by debtors who are unemployed or deeply in debt
- Chapter 13—used by debtors who have an income
- Chapter 11—for businesses filing for bankruptcy
- Chapter 12—for family farmers and family fishermen

### Chapter 7 Bankruptcy

Chapter 7 is a "liquidation" of nonexempt assets to pay debts. It is also referred to as straight bankruptcy. Through a lawyer, the debtor petitions the court to declare his or her inability to pay debts. A filing fee, an administration fee, and a trustee fee are required.

In filing Chapter 7 bankruptcy, honestly incurred, dischargeable debts—those not incurred by fraud or intentional harm to another person—are forgiven (canceled).

The debtor receives a fresh start without worrying about past creditors seeking payment. The fresh start promised is relief from most debts and the ability to begin rebuilding life with substantially less debt—not a clean credit slate. (See the section on Nondischargeable Debts for a list of debts that are not forgiven.) In exchange, the debtor must surrender all nonexempt property under state law to a trustee who will divide it among the creditors in proportion to what is owed. The trustee will usually abandon property to the extent that it was used as collateral. It may be possible to reaffirm (agree to pay) the debt with the creditor and retain the property. The trustee may also abandon property that is difficult to sell. If this happens, the debtor may keep this property. When considering Chapter 7 bankruptcy, it is necessary to complete an inventory of debts, to determine which can be discharged, as well as an inventory of property to see what must be sold.

### Dischargeable Debts

After Chapter 7 bankruptcy, the debtor will no longer owe money on:

- credit cards
- retail or department store charge cards unsecured loans from banks, credit unions, finance companies, friends, or relatives (an unsecured loan is one in which no item was pledged as collateral)

- unpaid hospital and medical bills
- unpaid utility bills
- unpaid rent (but that means the debtor must move)

Discharge only applies to debts that were incurred before filing and listed on the bankruptcy application. If a debt is not listed, it is probable the debt will not be discharged. Furthermore, if all assets are not reported on the application, debts may not be discharged. Once a debt is discharged, no further payment is required. If there are special reasons to pay a debt that was eligible to be discharged, the debtor can sign a reaffirmation agreement. For example, the debtor may want to keep a car or home. This must be a voluntary agreement that does not place too heavy a debt burden on the debtor. The court must approve any decision to reaffirm a debt. If a debt is reaffirmed, payments must be kept up to date so that the property is not seized when the bankruptcy is discharged. In addition, a debtor may choose to voluntarily repay a debt without signing a reaffirmation agreement.

### Nondischargeable Debts

The following debts are not eliminated by Chapter 7 bankruptcy

- state and federal taxes—unless they are more than three years old
- child support required by law
- spousal maintenance (alimony)
- government-backed student loans (only dischargeable in special circumstances)
- debts due to fraud
- court fines and penalties
- debts due to death or injury caused by the operation of a motor vehicle while intoxicated
- debts due to willful or malicious injury to another person or property.

### Exemptions

Bankruptcy law allows possession of some property for basic survival. In order to take advantage of a state's exemptions, a debtor must live in that state for at least two years (40 months for homestead exemptions) or use the exemptions available in the state of most recent residence. Some states allow the debtor to choose between the federal and state exemptions, however, increasingly, states are allowing only state statutes to determine the exemptions. Exemptions are "per person," so married couples receive two sets of exemptions.

Exemption planning involves deciding what to include in the state exemptions. Nonexempt assets may be converted into exempt assets before filing. An experienced bankruptcy lawyer may provide the most advantageous plan.

In states where there is a choice of federal or state exemptions, both spouses must choose the same type of exemption. In states with this choice, preplanning assistance from a lawyer may be necessary. Under the Bankruptcy Abuse Prevention and Consumer Protection Act of 2005, assets are valued at replacement cost at a retail vendor taking into account the assets' age and use. This is a change from the prior law that estimated value at what items would sell for at a yard sale or auction.

### Chapter 13 Bankruptcy

Chapter 13 is called "Adjustment of Debts of an Individual with Regular Income." It is also known as the debtor-rehabilitation chapter. Under Chapter 13, the debtor who can make regular payments is given the opportunity to propose a realistic plan to pay creditors over three to five years (depending on the results of the means test and the total amount of debt) while supervised by a trustee. A spouse without regular income may file joint bankruptcy with an income-earning spouse. If Chapter 13 is filed, income is used to pay part or all of the debts through a plan filed with the bankruptcy court. The repayment plan must be filed in "good faith" and is designed so that creditors receive at least as much as they would under Chapter 7. Chapter 13 bankruptcy may be used when unsecured debts are less than $290,525 and secured debts are less than $871,550. A secured debt is an asset pledged as collateral that can be sold to repay it, such as a car loan, mortgage, or furniture loan. An unsecured debt has no collateral to secure its repayment, such as credit card debt or medical bills. If the debtor successfully completes the Chapter 13 repayment plan, all debts are free and clear. One exception to the "free and clear" concept is the home mortgage, which must be repaid according to the contract.

To determine whether Chapter 13 bankruptcy is appropriate, the court will use the means test to determine if take-home pay, other income sources, and living expenses will allow repayment of the debts within a reasonable time period. Filing for Chapter 13 forces an automatic end to all credit and contracts with creditors, with the exception of home mortgages. Debtors are allowed to keep property but may sell some of it to help complete the repayment plan.

If a debtor decides to file Chapter 13 bankruptcy, all disposable income (amount left after normal living expenses are paid) is submitted to the trustee who pays the creditors according to the plan. During the repayment period, a debtor is protected from further collection activities by creditors. Little or no sale of assets is required. Once the plan is filed and approved, interest stops accruing on current debts.

Depending on the situation, the income available for debt repayment may be less than the amount of the unsecured debts. If this is the case, the plan reflects a request that debts be discharged (canceled) when the repayment period ends. A court hearing is held after the plan is filed. At the hearing, the court will do the following:

- Decide if the repayment plan is truly a best "good faith" effort
- Determine if unsecured creditors are receiving at least as much as they would have under a Chapter 7 bankruptcy filing
- Analyze if the plan can be feasibly completed in the time allowed
- Give a copy of the repayment plan to all creditors and interested parties
- Require the debtor to pay a filing fee and an administration fee

The court and a trustee (usually a local lawyer appointed by the U.S. Trustee) must approve the debtor's bankruptcy plan; the creditors do not necessarily need to approve it. After the plan is approved, the debtor will make monthly payments to the trustee and pay regular living expenses to him/herself. If there is a mortgage, the debtor must make those monthly payments while the trustee typically pays any amount in arrears before the bankruptcy was filed.

### Chapter 11 Bankruptcy

Chapter 11 was designed by Congress to allow businesses to reorganize their debts and pay what they can without going out of business. Unlike Chapter 13, there usually is no trustee involved in Chapter 11 bankruptcy. Originally, Chapter 11 bankruptcy was designed for large corporate debtors, but it is now available to partnerships, real estate developers, and sole proprietors. Working with creditors, a debtor works out a repayment plan from future earnings of the business. The creditors approve a plan reorganizing any or all other business affairs.

Moreover, Chapter 11 is available to individual debtors whose debts exceed the limits imposed by Chapter 13. However, the filing fee (including the administrative fee) is much higher.

### Chapter 12 Bankruptcy

Chapter 12 was established in 1986 especially for farmers and fishermen. It combines some requirements of both Chapter 11 and Chapter 13. Farmers and fishermen are eligible for Chapter 12 bankruptcy if their debt does not exceed $1,500,000. In addition, 80 percent or more of the debt must be due to operations. At least 50 percent of the stock or equity of the corporation or partnership must be held by one family, with that family conducting the farming operation, and more than 80 percent of the value the corporation or partnership assets must be related to the operation of the business. Finally, if corporate stock exists, that stock must not be publicly traded.

In Chapter 12, the owner is allowed to file a plan for paying off some debts and discharging (canceling) others. Creditors must receive as much as they would have received under Chapter 7 bankruptcy. There is a filing and an administrative fee.

### Deciding to Declare Bankruptcy—Pre-Filing Credit Counseling

When considering bankruptcy, debtors must contact a government-approved provider for a *pre-filing credit counseling* session.

**Table 4**  Bankruptcy timeline

1. Seek pre-filing credit counseling within six months of filing; go to http://www.justice .gov/ust/eo/bapcpa/ccde/ to find a government-approved organization; obtain pre-filing credit counseling certificate.
2. Take the pre-filing credit counseling certificate to the bankruptcy lawyer.
3. Complete means test to determine qualification for Chapter 7 or Chapter 13 bankruptcy.
4. File bankruptcy petition with the clerk of the bankruptcy courts.
5. Pay court costs and administrative fees.
6. Clerk gives petition to U.S. Trustee (bankruptcy trustee).
7. U.S. Trustee takes charge of nonexempt property, reviews petition, and in Chapter 13, reviews repayment plan.
8. Court approval of repayment plan (Chapter 13 only).
9. Completion of plan over 3 to 5 years (Chapter 13 only).
10. Nonexempt property sold to pay debts (Chapter 7 only).
11. Complete the predischarge personal finance class and obtain certificate of completion; go to http://www.justice.gov/ust/eo/bapcpa/ccde/ to find a government approved provider; obtain a Certificate of Debtor Education.
12. Forgiveness of dischargeable debts.
13. End of court proceedings.

A list of approved organizations can be viewed on the Department of Justice website. Debtors must get a Department of Justice Certificate stating that counseling was received. The purpose of the counseling is to determine whether it is possible to work with an informal repayment plan or bankruptcy is really the only option. Debtors are required to participate but do not have to go through with any offer from the provider to manage a repayment plan. If a debtor accepts a repayment plan, bankruptcy will not be filed. However, if a repayment plan is offered and the debtor does not accept, the certificate will need to be submitted to the court. A copy of the pre-filing credit counseling certificate should be made before providing it to the court.

If the counselor approves the decision to file bankruptcy, a lawyer, experienced in bankruptcy, is recommended for the proceedings. The lawyer will require the counseling certificate to pair with other filing documents. The lawyer will also require completion of a means test form to determine if the debtor can qualify to file Chapter 7. If the debtor does not qualify for Chapter 7, the means test will determine how much the debtor must pay for debt repayment under Chapter 13. In addition, the lawyer will help prepare the necessary documents and file with the court. Attorney and court fees should be discussed at the first appointment because costs vary.

### Predischarge Personal Finance Education Class

After filing and receiving a case number, the debtor must take a personal finance class before the petition can be discharged (released from the court). The class must be at least 2 hours long and cover a set of objectives determined by the Executive Office of U.S. Trustees. Classes can be in person, over the phone, or via the Internet. Providers must be approved by the Trustees' Office in a similar manner to those providers offering the pre-filing credit counseling. There is no requirement to use the same provider for both pre-filing counseling class and predischarge education class.

### Automatic Stay Provision

Some people file bankruptcy because of the automatic stay provision, the part of the bankruptcy code that offers legal protection against bill collectors. Even though this sounds inviting, the automatic stay provision should not be the only reason to file. The automatic stay will allow for stops to be made on the following: collection activities, such as calls and letters from creditors; filing of liens, lawsuits, or seizure of property by creditors; utility companies from disconnecting utilities for at least 2 days; foreclosure on a home mortgage; collection of the overpayment of public benefits; wage garnishments.

Under the new law, the automatic stay provision no longer applies to evictions; suspension or restriction of driver's license; suspension or restriction of a professional or occupational license; lawsuits to establish paternity, child support, or child custody; divorce proceedings; lawsuits related to domestic violence; certain tax proceedings; administrative freezes—a bank cannot withdraw money from an account to pay a delinquent loan but they can freeze enough money in the account to cover the delinquency until the court determines what will happen with the debt; and criminal proceedings.

### Income Taxes

Under the new law there is a requirement to provide past tax returns, as follows:

- Chapter 7—the most current year's completed income tax return
- Chapter 13—past four years' tax returns, or
- Proof that income was such that no filing was required

The tax consequences of bankruptcy can vary dramatically depending on the way the bankruptcy is structured. Planning with an experienced tax attorney or accountant can assist in this area.

### Conclusion

A person leaves bankruptcy debt free or with a significantly reduced debt. Bankruptcy is designed to give the debtor a fresh start and a chance to establish sound financial management.

*Celia Ray Hayhoe and Wendy Reiboldt*

*Note: Sadly, Dr. Celia Ray Hayhoe passed away in March 2012. She was an Associate Professor and Family Resource Management Extension Specialist at Virginia Tech. Her research and service centered around the personal finance habits of consumers, with particular interest in savings, credit, and bankruptcy. Celia received numerous professional awards including the 2007 Distinguished Fellow Award from the Association for Financial Counseling and Planning Education and the College of Liberal Arts and Human Sciences Outreach Award in 2006.*

Sections of this entry appear courtesy of Karen Goebel and Virginia Co-operative Extension, Virginia Tech, and Virginia State University.

**See also:** Credit Cards; Debt Collection; Debt Management

### References and Additional Readings

Averch, C. H. (1997). Denial of discharge litigation. *The Review of Litigation, 16,* 65.

Department of Justice. (2013a). Credit counseling & debtor education information. Retrieved from http://www.justice.gov/ust/eo/bapcpa/ccde/

Department of Justice. (2013b). U.S. trustee program. Retrieved from http://www.usdoj.gov/ust/

Frimet, R. (1991). The Birth of bankruptcy in the United States. *96 Com. L. J. 160.*

Leonard, R. (2001). *Bankruptcy: Is it the right solution to your debt problems?* Berkeley, CA: Nolo Press.

Moore, J., & Phillips, W. (1975). *Debtors' and creditors' rights: Cases and materials* (4th ed.). New York, NY: M. Bender.

# Better Business Bureau (BBB)

The Better Business Bureau (BBB) is the common name for a network of local, individually incorporated organizations that operate under the leadership of the Council of Better Business Bureaus (CBBB). Over its 100-year history, the CBBB and its local member BBB have become part of the lexicon of consumer affairs. The CBBB is a nonprofit, nongovernmental umbrella organization for its 116 member BBBs, formed in 1912 by a group of national corporations in response to business sector concerns about the potentially negative effects of then-common advertising practices on consumer confidence in business generally.

Originally formed to promote truth in advertising, the organization went through several iterations through the mid-20th century until 1970, when it came to be known as the CBBB. The CBBB serves as a national network "hub" for the local member BBBs, which cover regional markets by providing local business listings, business ratings, and consumer complaint mediation services. Each local BBB processes complaints, provides complaint reporting and ratings of businesses, and participates in a variety of consumer policy activities. BBBs often work with local governmental organizations, businesses, and consumer advocacy groups to address issues in the marketplace that affect the relationships between consumers and business. The BBB also manages a variety of programs that provide industry with guidance on advertising practices, particularly with respect to advertising to children and pharmaceuticals.

The BBB logo is largely used by qualifying businesses to establish their reliability and to build consumer trust. (AP Photo/Better Business Bureau, Court Mast)

The BBBs have adopted as their motto the slogan "Start with trust," a phrase that flows from the organizations' shared mission " . . . to be the leader in advancing marketplace trust" (CBBB, 2012 online). The efforts of the BBBs to position themselves as unbiased sources for consumer information about businesses and business practices are borne out in national consumer complaint data. According to the CBBB 2011 Annual Report, local BBBs received 927,000 consumer complaints in 2011. In contrast, the Federal Trade Commission's Consumer Sentinel Network, which draws complaints from consumer advocacy organizations, law enforcement, state attorneys general and other sources (including the BBBs), received 1.3 million consumer complaints nationally in 2010 (FTC, 2011). The relative prevalence of consumer complaint reporting to the BBBs reflects the BBBs' position in the consumer marketplace and consumer perceptions with respect to the BBB as a marketplace monitor.

From its genesis, the organization has been funded, managed, and overseen by business interests. Drawing its funding from dues paid by member businesses, the BBB has positioned itself as a consumer advocacy group, yet its primary organizational constituency remains the business sector. The

CBBB has formal partnerships with nearly 200 major corporations, and its leadership and board of directors draw heavily and primarily from business. There are few structural positions in the organizational leadership reserved solely for consumer representatives. This organizational structure and, more importantly, the BBB funding model have together created some challenges for the BBB in its efforts to maintain its position and branding as a resource for consumers.

BBBs have two primary sources of interaction with consumers in the marketplace. The first, and most prevalent, is the provision of information to consumers in response to consumer inquiries about businesses. BBBs handle millions of such inquiries annually, providing consumers with information as to the numbers of complaints received against a business, the nature and status of those complaints, and ratings of businesses that factor complaint information, among other inputs (see Table 5)

The number of inquiries by consumers to the BBB has risen mostly steadily over the past five years, until a nearly 22 percent rise from 2010 to 2011. The number of complaints to BBBs over the same period has not followed the same trend, peaking in 2009, before dipping and rising again. The percentage of complaints considered to be settled by the BBB, however, has remained relatively constant, hovering roughly between 74 and 76 percent.

The BBB, in its March, 2010, press release announcing its annual report, cited the economic upheaval of the recession as a particular challenge to consumers, indicating that the recession could be a driver of its inquiry and complaint traffic. In 2010, however, increasing scrutiny in the media of BBB business rating and complaint process practices provided a counter-narrative to the BBB's claims that it provides objective, unbiased information about the consumer marketplace. While news reports of dissatisfaction with the BBB had been published before (including an *LA Times* article in 2009 questioning the poor ratings given by the BBB to nonmember

**Table 5**    BBB annual inquiries

| Year | Inquiries | Complaints | Settled | Not Settled | Unable to Pursue |
|------|-----------|------------|---------|-------------|------------------|
| 2007 | 52,167,879 | 803,902 | 596,173 | 186,688 | 21,041 |
| 2008 | 60,275,584 | 862,128 | 634,637 | 199,011 | 28,480 |
| 2009 | 62,165,457 | 948,305 | 700,194 | 215,973 | 32,138 |
| 2010 | 67,079,058 | 844,054 | 639,654 | 177,123 | 24,765 |
| 2011 | 97,728,738 | 894,868 | 683,764 | 186,555 | 24,572 |

*Source:* Compiled from data available at http://www.bbb.org/us/2011-complaint-and-inquiry-statistics

businesses including the Ritz-Carlton Hotel and several Wolfgang Puck restaurants), the near-simultaneous investigations into BBB recruitment and ratings practices by national news media and the Connecticut Attorney General's Office presented a more substantial and public challenge to the BBB reputation and brand.

According to a November 10, 2010, letter to the BBB from then-Connecticut Attorney General Richard Blumenthal, the scrutiny of BBB practices by the Connecticut Attorney General's Office began in 2009 with an investigation into the 2008 awarding of the Connecticut BBB's Torch Award to a business that subsequently "defaulted on consumer obligations and filed for bankruptcy." The letter notes that the investigation grew beyond its initial review of "the criteria and judging process for the TAP award. . . . to the BBB's new letter grade, or 'alpha,' rating system . . ." Blumenthal (2010) expressed concern with the assignment of points within the rating system for payment of membership dues, calling it "a 'pay-to-play' system, rather than a transparent and equitable 'rating' system."

Blumenthal also expressed concern about the use of the term "rating" to describe the system used by the BBB to grade businesses. Specifically, Blumenthal raised concerns about the resources required to verify information submitted by businesses, licensing and compliance information, "outstanding lawsuits, time in business and financial stability."

On the same day Blumenthal's letter was released, national news network ABC News aired a story in which it claimed that its investigation revealed pay-to-play sales practices by the BBB in Los Angeles. In its story, ABC cited as examples two incidences at which their cameras were present where local business owners were reportedly told that they could only improve their rating by agreeing to pay membership dues. ABC News reported that in both the cases, the ratings for the businesses increased immediately after the payments were made.

The BBB responded to the coverage by convening a special meeting of the CBBB Executive Committee, saying that the practices reported were not in compliance with its sales and recruitment standards. On November 16, 2010, within a week of Blumenthal's letter and the coverage by *ABC News*, the BBB announced that it was amending its rating system to remove payment of dues from having any role in the ratings. The press release identified specific steps the BBB was taking to address the concerns raised by the ABC News story and the Connecticut Attorney General. In a message delivered on November 18, 2010, the President of CBBB stated:

By next week, the BBB ratings system will no longer give additional points to accredited businesses because of their accredited status. While we believe that businesses that have been approved for accreditation and commit to abide by these standards warrant additional points, we have acknowledged that others view this as creating an appearance of unfairness. What matters most now is to make changes to address those concerns—which is exactly the steps we have taken. BBB will continue to issue ratings based on the other 16 factors currently used. Immediately, BBB will make available on its website a streamlined process for receiving complaints on BBB sales practices and will implement procedures for investigating each complaint. BBB will conduct a review of its process for accrediting businesses, and as soon as possible, make changes that will apply system-wide. BBB will engage an independent third party to assist us in our review process. (Anders, 2010)

Despite its acknowledgment of the concerns raised, the press release also stated clearly that the BBB stood firmly by the information and services it provides to consumers:

We are taking these steps to better serve consumers and small businesses and eliminate any attempts to question BBB's fairness. Any attempt to question the integrity of the entire BBB organization is completely without merit.

If consumer inquiries to the BBB can be considered any indicator, the controversies surrounding BBB practices do not appear to have dampened consumer reliance on BBB information. From 2010, when the controversy broke, through 2011, the CBBB reported a roughly 22 percent increase in consumer inquiries—an increase nearly 7 percent higher than the largest prior year-to-year increase since 2007.

The Federal Trade Commission (FTC) and state attorneys general continue to rely on the BBB for information and complaint data to support law enforcement efforts. According to the FTC Consumer Sentinel 2010 databook, the BBB is the largest nongovernmental contributor to the FTC's Consumer Sentinel Network. Consumer Sentinel is the FTC's national complaint database available to law enforcement agencies seeking consumer fraud data.

While both of the two primary BBB services to consumers in the marketplace (business ratings and information and consumer complaint mediation) have relatively strong records of consumer utilization, questions as to the objectivity of BBB services are not restricted to the ratings systems. Consumer advocates and news media have also expressed concerns as to the efficacy and fairness of the BBB mediation services. David Segal, in his *New York Times* column "The Haggler," devoted two columns to concerns with

BBB complaint resolution practices in February and March 2011. Segal described complaints against the company PC Driver Headquarters, in which consumers reported that the company did not provide refunds as they expected. According to Segal, at the time of the article, PC Driver Headquarters had 312 complaints lodged with the BBB, nearly all for refund issues, yet it had a rating of "A-plus" due to the BBB's assessment of the company's efforts to resolve complaints.

Segal's report included an interview with a consumer whose complaint against the business had been closed as "administratively resolved," reportedly as the BBB "determined that despite the company's reasonable effort to address complaint issues, the consumer remains dissatisfied." Segal reported that, in his interview with the consumer, the consumer said that the software product he had purchased had not functioned, and that the company had refused to provide any refund. Segal also reported that reviews of the company on other third-party websites were generally poor. In a follow-up column, Segal reported on another instance in which a consumer complaint about a business was not included in the BBB reports about the business until the organization was contacted about the issue for the article. Segal questioned the BBB's resolution statistics, as well as the fairness of the services it provides to consumers.

The BBB's complaint services are multilayered. Consumer complaints generally are processed through what the BBB refers to as its "common sense approach," in which the organization attempts to resolve complaints through dialog with the parties. In addition to this basic service, the BBB also offers more formal mediation and arbitration services, whereby consumer complaints are considered in a more formal hearing process. CBBB standards allow for member BBBs to charge fees for these services, which can vary depending upon the service and the policy of the local BBB. In the case of the software company complaint reported in Segal's column "The Haggler," the cost of a consumer appeal to mediation would have been $70, while the refund amount requested was $39.

For decades, the BBB has been an active participant in shaping policy and perceptions in consumer affairs. Despite controversy regarding its complaint processing and ratings practices, its nongovernmental status, membership-funded business model and leadership comprised primarily of business representatives, the BBB continues to maintain a unique position in the consumer marketplace. A consistent source of information for consumers, government regulators, and law enforcement, the BBB has applied a model of business self-regulation to the marketplace that did not exist in an organized fashion prior to its inception. Though a number of publications have questioned the BBB's ability to persist as a trusted repository of unbiased business information for consumers, consumer complaint and, perhaps more importantly, business inquiry behavior statistics indicate that consumers continue to turn to the BBB for these services at an increasing rate.

*Jason M. Duquette-Hoffman*

**See also:** Corporate Social Responsibility; Federal Trade Commission (FTC); Government Accountability Office (GAO)

### References and Additional Readings

Anders, E. (2010). BBB revises rating system to regain consumer trust. Retrieved from http://reloroundtable.com/blog/how-to/moving-tips/consumer-help/bbb-revises-rating-system-to-regain-consumer-trust/

Blumenthal, R. (2010). Letter to the Connecticut Better Business Bureau. Retrieved from http://abcnews.go.com/Blotter/page?id=12132519

Council of Better Business Bureaus. (2009). Complaints to Better Business Bureau up nearly 10 percent in 2009. Retrieved from http://www.bbb.org/us/article/complaints-to-better-business-bureau-up-nearly-10-percent-in-2009–18034

Council of Better Business Bureaus. (2011). Annual report, 2011. Retrieved from http://www.bbb.org/us/cbbb-annual-reports/

Council of Better Business Bureaus. (2012). About us. Retrieved from http://www.bbb.org/us/cbbb/

Federal Trade Commission. (2011). Consumer Sentinel Network databook for January–December, 2010. Retrieved from http://www.ftc.gov/sentinel/reports/sentinel-annual-reports/sentinel-cy2010.pdf

Lazarus, D. (2009). Better Business Bureau grades companies on a peculiar curve. *Los Angeles Times*, January, 21, 2009. Retrieved from http://articles.latimes.com/2009/jan/21/business/fi-lazarus21

Rhee, J., & Ross, B. (2010). Terror group gets 'A' rating from Better Business Bureau? *ABC News*. Retrieved from http://abcnews.go.com/Blotter/business-bureau-best-ratings-money-buy/story?id=12123843#.UIiuMW_A_wk

Segal, D. (2011a). Complaint resolved'? Well, not exactly. *The New York Times*. Retrieved from http://www.nytimes.com/2011/03/13/your-money/13haggler.html?_r=0

Segal, D. (2011b). But who will grade the grader? *The New York Times*. Retrieved from http://www.nytimes.com/2011/02/27/your-money/27haggler.html?pagewanted=all

## Bicycle Safety Standard

While state design safety requirements date back to the late 1800s when bicycles were commonly required to be equipped with audible warning devices such as bells or horns and the District of Columbia banned drop handlebars for fear it would encourage "scorching" (speeding), the development of the federal safety standard by the Consumer Product Safety Commission (CPSC) is a relatively modern development. The standard (16 CFR 1512), and indeed the CPSC itself, had its origin in the President's 1970 Commission on Product Safety. The commission condemned children's high-rise bicycles in its *Final Report.* The report noted that accessories then available such as steering wheels instead of handlebars, large protruding gear shifters, banana seats, and "wheelie" wheels, promoted injuries and unsafe practices such as riding double and performing "wheelies." It further announced that high-rise models accounted for 45 percent of all bicycles but were associated with 57 percent of all injuries. The report condemned the industry for not developing product standards including ones for lights and reflectors.

Later that same year, the Bicycle Manufacturers Association (BMA) responded by adopting a safety standard that served as a basis for the Food and Drug Administration's (FDA) 1973 proposed bicycle safety standard under the Federal Hazardous Substances Act. The 1972 20-page staff report by the FDA's Bureau of Product Safety identified foot slippage off the pedal and failure of the brakes, pedals, and gearing as causes of accidents. The proposed standard sought to address these issues as well as poor night visibility. The notice further noted the problem of protruding hardware, sharp edges, and sharp points.

Four days after the rule was first proposed, authority to enforce the Federal Hazardous Substances Act was transferred to the newly created CPSC. The CPSC was created with jurisdiction over some 10,000 consumer products that were not otherwise regulated for safety. It was empowered to collect information, recall unreasonably dangerous products, and enact

---

The U.S. Bicycle Safety regulations are concerned with standardization (regulating bicycle safety standards) and operation and safety (light, reflectors, helmets); regulations do not apply to motorized bicycles with the ability to go 20 mph or more. While operating a bicycle you must obey lights, signs, and lane markings on roadways to prevent serious injuries. The U.S. Consumer Product Safety Commission helps to regulate laws on bicycle safety standards of the bicycles that you purchase. Furthermore, the CPSC reports that deaths, injuries, and property damage from incidents with consumer products cost the United States more than $900 billion on an annual basis.

*Sources:* U.S. Consumer Product Safety Commission. (2013). CPSC overview. Retrieved from http://www.cpsc.gov

mandatory safety standards for potentially dangerous products. The CPSC favored regulation by mandatory safety standards at this time and began work on several proposals beyond bicycles. The CPSC's interest in bicycles is based on the fact that bicycles are associated with more consumer injuries than nearly any other consumer product. For example, in 1981, the only product associated with more injuries than bicycles were steps and stairs. In 1994, the CPSC estimates the cost of bicycling-related injuries and deaths to be in the order of $8 billion annually.

The CPSC announced that 17 percent of all bicycle-associated injuries are related to product failure and the risk of these injuries would be addressed by its standard. However, the 17 percent estimate was derived from a sample of bicycle injuries designed to over represent product-related injuries. The CPSC consultants who analyzed this biased sample estimated that the proportion of product-related injuries for the population as a whole was 8 percent. Furthermore, most product-related problems occur to bicycles that are at least three years old. Product standards covering new products cannot prevent eventual product failures from worn components or poorly maintained bicycles. Many bicycle components such as brakes and gearing require periodic maintenance and the replacement of worn parts. Thus, the actual proportion of injuries which the CPSC could have possibly affected through a product standard is probably less than 2 percent—far below the CPSC's 20 percent stated goal across all products.

A number of parties that eventually ended up as two individual consumers and one consumer group challenged the legality of the rule itself and 16 of the standard's provisions. On June 1, 1977, the Court of Appeals for the District of Columbia upheld the promulgation and most of the challenged provisions. It upheld the CPSC's authority to issue standards covering nearly all bicycles under the Federal Hazardous Substances Act that only applied to articles intended for use by children. The court also upheld the commission's notice of rulemaking and its authority to issue design as well as performance standards. With four exceptions, the court upheld the commission's support for specific provisions stating that it was not required to develop a precise body count.

The court only remanded a broad prohibition of "protrusions," handlebar width restrictions, a brake system heat test which only applied to hand brakes, not to foot brakes, and a provision on pedal threads for which the court did not understand the commission's justification. The commission later republished its regulation with these four provisions deleted. This standard is 20 pages long and took over five years to promulgate. There is no doubt that this extremely technical standard is very comprehensive. It imposes significant compliance costs on both manufacturers and consumers.

The CPSC standard covers all bicycles, not just children's bicycles, unless specifically exempted (custom-built bicycles, track, and sidewalk bicycles are exempted from at least some requirements). It is important to note that CPSC requirements fall on bicycle sellers, typically the manufacturer, not on bicycle owners or riders. In contrast, most state requirements apply to bicycles being operated on roadways and do not directly impact bicycle merchants.

The CPSC generally requires that bicycles be able to be assembled by ordinary people, include complete assembly instructions, and contain no sharp edges, no fractures, no loose hardware, or other problems that could cause injury or product failure. Bicycles must be subjected to a road test over regular and cleated roads, a dropping test, a protective cap removal test, drive chains must be tested for strengthened numerous other tests. The package must picture the tools needed for assembly and indicate the minimum leg length of the intended rider. The bicycle must have a tag indicating that it meets CPSC requirements. Interestingly, no safety warnings such as use lights at night, or wear a helmet are required on the package or product, although the instruction manual must include information on safe operation.

The CPSC standard has numerous specific requirements. It requires forks to be tested for both deflection and its ability to withstand a front impact. Hubs must securely lock on the frame or fork, but may have quick releases. Rims must satisfy top and side load tests and hubs tested for secure retention. Wheel rims also must be aligned to have at least 1/16 in clearance with the frame or fork. Tires must have the recommended inflation pressure molded on the side and remain intact and on the rim after being inflated to 110 percent and load tested. Seat posts must have a permanent minimum insertion mark at least two diameters up from the end of the post and post strength must be maintained at least one diameter below the insertion mark. Seats may not have any parts 5 inches above the top of the seat above the seat post shaft. The CPSC requires strength testing of the seat adjusting clamps, fork clamps, and handlebar stems. Handlebar stems must have a permanent mark of the minimum insertion depth and may not be extendable more than 16 inches above the highest seat position. Bicycles with both single front and rear sprockets must have a chain guard and derailleur guards must prevent the chain from accidentally stopping the wheel.

The bicycle standard has been criticized as both an attempt to keep out lower-priced foreign manufactured bicycles and as merely being a standard for design and assembly without much consideration of factors that actually cause bicycling-related injuries. It does seem clear that most of its provisions regulate the bicycle design rather than bicycle safety per se. For example, the CPSC standard is silent on audible signaling devices that are arguably a safety device for riders even though such devices still are required in about 10 states. Those involved with the BMA suggest the real goal of its support of a standard was to bolster the position of bike makers in product liability lawsuits and to forestall state-by-state safety standards that would inevitably conflict and raise costs to make bikes compliant with individual state laws. However, a CPSC advisory letter refused to endorse federal preemption. There are two areas where the CPSC standard clearly differs from state law—braking and nighttime equipment.

The CPSC standard requires at least rear wheel brakes and allows front wheel brakes as well. Sidewalk bicycles must have footbrakes. Handbrakes must be secure and are subject to both braking and rocking tests. Brakes must be able to stop a 150 pound rider within 15 feet from a speed of at least 10 mph within a specified limit on the force applied to the hand levers. Footbrake and handbrake forces also must be tested. This standard is tougher than that in the Uniform Vehicle Code (11–706) that requires brakes that enable the rider to stop within 25 feet from a speed of 10 mph on dry, level, clean pavement. The most common state requirement is vague but easy to test: the brake must enable the operator to make the braked wheels skid on dry, level, clean pavement. A few states simply require bicycles be equipped with an adequate brake when used on a street or highway.

The CPSC standard requires that all bicycles for sale be equipped with special reflectors in the front, rear, sides, and pedals. These reflectors must satisfy very specific mounting requirements as well as performance tests. These reflectors were touted as having a 50 percent increase in performance over conventional reflectors, but while the required rear reflector, for example, does have a broader range of reflectivity, the Society of Automotive Engineers (SAE) conventional reflector is 7–10 times more bright when illuminated directly.

Contrary, to the CPSC standard, the Uniform Vehicle Code continues to recommend laws requiring a front head lamp at night visible for a distance of at least 500 feet and a rear reflector at all times visible for 600 feet to the rear when illuminated by motor vehicle low beams. Presently, all 50 states and the District of Columbia have adopted this recommendation although they vary in their definition of night and performance requirements for front lights and rear reflectors.

There is little doubt that the CPSC reflector standard is less safe than state law headlight requirements. The CPSC itself has noted that in 1975, nighttime deaths accounted for 30 percent of all bicycle fatalities, but in 1982, the figure had risen to 42 percent. By 1994, the CPSC found that 46 percent of bicyclist fatalities may be related to riding at night, but that nearly all bicycles had CPSC-mandated reflectors. In contrast, less than 8 percent of bicycles were equipped with lights. The report states: ". . . it is possible that some people perceive reflectors as adequate protection at times when they may not be sufficient." As early as 1982, the CPSC had urged cyclists to use front and rear lights (and leg lights and reflective clothing) when riding at night, but it has not changed its rule to require lighting systems on new bikes being sold.

Despite the rule's lengthy gestation period, studies disagree on whether it has proven or could prove to significantly reduce bicycling-related injuries. Nevertheless, it has remained in force for over 30 years with only a few minor updates. The most recent revision was in the summer 2011. At that time, the CPSC stated its intention to undertake a comprehensive review of the rule in the future. Given the age of the rule and the existence of more up-to-date voluntary industry standards (ASTM Subcommittee F08.10 on Bicycles), a comprehensive review is overdue.

Adapted with permission from *Risk-Issues in Health and Safety* (cited below).

*Ross D. Petty*

**See also:** Consumer Product Safety Commission (CPSC); National Highway Traffic Safety Administration (NHTSA); National Transportation Safety Board (NTSB)

### References and Additional Readings

Bureau of Product Safety Food and Drug Administration. (1972). *Staff analysis of bicycle accidents and injuries.* Washington, DC: Department of Health Education and Welfare.

Epperson, B. (2010). The great schism: Federal bicycle safety regulation and the unraveling of American bicycle planning. *Transportation Law Journal, 37,* 73–118.

*Forester v. Consumer Product Safety Commission.* 559 F.2d 774–798 (D.C. Cir. 1977).

Magat, W. A, & Moore, M.J. (1996). Consumer product safety regulation in the United States and the United Kingdom: The case of bicycles. *Rand Journal of Economics, 27,* 148–164.

National Commission on Product Safety. (1970). *Final Report.* Washington, DC: U.S. Government Printing Office.

Petty, R.D. (1991a). Regulation vs. the Market: The case of bicycle safety [Part I]. *Risk-Issues in Health and Safety, 2,* 77–88.

Petty, R.D. (1991b). Regulation vs. the Market: The case of bicycle safety [Part II]. *Risk-Issues in Health and Safety, 2,* 93–120.

Rodgers, G. B. (1988). Reducing bicycle accidents: A re-evaluation of the impacts of the CPSC Bicycle Standard and Helmet Use. *Journal of Products Liability, 11*, 307–317.

Viscusi, W. K. (1985). Consumer behavior and the safety effects of product safety regulation. *Journal of Law & Economics, 28*, 527–533.

## Boycotts

Consumer boycotts have occurred in the United States throughout history. They have involved a wide range of protest groups, target organizations, and social concerns in virtually all regions of the country. Of interest is the use of boycotts to serve not only consumer economic objectives, such as lower prices, but also the political objectives of various special interest groups outside the consumer movement. Included here are groups representing animal welfare and environmental protection, as well as the rights of women, gays, African Americans, Mexican Americans, Chinese Americans, Jewish Americans, and various labor organizations. At one time or another since 1970 all of these groups have called for boycotts of consumer products or services in an effort to help realize their organizational objectives.

In an interesting twist on the concept of "boycotts," a "girlcott" was started in 2005 by teenage girls across the country. Their target? Popular youth retailer Abercrombie & Fitch. The girls, and others, were offended by the company's production and selling of T-shirts saying such things as "Who needs brains when you have these?" and "I had a nightmare I was a brunette" on the front. Their claim was that such T-shirts are degrading to women and lead to potentially unhealthy body image concepts for girls. While in an attempt at humor, Sarah Gould, president of the Ms. Foundation for Women, said that the T-shirts stated the slogans to "reinforce the message that girls are only as good as what their bodies are, and that's very undermining to a girl's healthy development." In response, Abercrombie & Fitch removed the T-shirts from stores. This is not the first time the popular retailer was under fire from consumers. They also received complaints about caricatures of Asians with slogans reading "Two Wongs Can Make it White" (referring to drycleaning) and "Get Your Buddha On The Floor." Though, the later cases did not result in boycotts or girlcotts.

For more information, see Karnasiewicz, S. (2005). Teens launch "girlcott" against Abercrombie. Retrieved from www.salon.com

Consumer boycotts have also had an important social justice role in American history. Since the Revolutionary War it can be argued that the boycott has been used more than any other organizational technique to promote and protect the rights of the powerless and disenfranchised segments of society. Indeed, one scholar (Scott, 1985) who has studied the efforts of peasants to resist oppression by the use of the boycott, referred to it as a "weapon of the weak."

Some highly publicized examples from the post-World War II era are the United Farm Workers boycotts of grapes and lettuce led by Cesar Chavez from the late 1960s through the 1990s, and the Montgomery, Alabama, bus boycott led by Martin Luther King Jr. in the 1950s. Historically significant earlier efforts include the anti-Nazi boycott of German goods called by the American Jewish community in the 1930s and early 1940s, and the late 1890s and early 20th-century initiatives of the Knights of Labor and other fledgling members of the trade union movement of that time. Moreover, the period of the American Revolution witnessed boycotts of British goods in Boston, New York, and Philadelphia following the passage of the Stamp Act in 1765.

## A Definition of Consumer Boycotts

Before analyzing consumer boycotts it is necessary to define the term. A working definition used by the author in earlier publications referred to a consumer boycott as "an attempt by one or more parties to achieve certain objectives by urging individual consumers to refrain from making selected purchases in the marketplace." Readers should note three characteristics of this definition. The first is the focus on individual consumers rather than organizational entities such as professional associations or business firms. A second characteristic concerns the goals of boycotts. Consumer boycotts are viewed herein as marketplace means to secure what may or may not be marketplace ends.

In addition to such common marketplace concerns of consumer boycotts as lower prices and higher quality goods, a multitude of factors external to the marketplace, such as environmental quality and labor union recognition, have assumed significant roles in boycott actions. A third characteristic of the definition is its emphasis on urging consumers to withdraw selectively from participation in the marketplace. This urging or lobbying may be direct and immediate, as when retail stores are picketed by boycott groups (*a marketplace boycott*), or it may be indirect and gradual, as when boycotters focus on creating dramatic demonstrations to attract the attention of the news media (*a media boycott*) in the hopes that the resulting news coverage will alert consumers to the problem being addressed by the boycott and gain their support for the boycott solution.

## Marketplace Boycotts and Media Boycotts

The distinction just noted between these two types of boycotts is so funda-mental that it became an important focus of the author's 1999 book on con-sumer boycotts. Often it seems that consumer activists are forsaking direct action in the form of marketplace picketing and demonstrations against retail stores aimed at decreasing consumer purchases of boycotted prod-ucts. And instead of the marketplace their focus has become the media. To illustrate why marketplace boycotts have dropped in number, look at a result from an interview the author conducted with a boycott leader for Rainforest Action Network (RAN), an activist ecology group that was criti-cal of a major corporation (Mitsubishi) for extracting tropical timber from third-world rainforests. The leader claimed that her group never consid-ered launching a marketplace boycott against the firm because the mem-bers all knew that the group was too small and its members too busy to place many pickets at the entrances of retail stores selling the firm's prod-ucts. The group's members were largely female and many of them had both work and home responsibilities, leaving little or no time for participation on a picket line.

Interestingly, this description is in marked contrast to what the writer found a generation earlier when he conducted a study of a 1966 national boycott against supermarkets that had sharply raised their prices; he surveyed leaders of 64 boycott groups and found that the leaders and all but a few of the boycott participants were housewives not working outside the home. So circumstances changed from the late 1960s to the early 1990s, and with the change, boycott leaders found that they had largely lost the availability of foot soldiers to devote long hours to walk-ing picket lines, even for a cause in which they strongly believed. It was a new generation of boycotters, an electronic generation raised first on television and then computers, which has largely transformed the boy-cott today to respond to changing societal needs as well as new media opportunities.

Regarding the RAN media boycott, it was found that the organization decided to create a dramatic demonstration in downtown San Francisco, which two RAN members did by unfurling a giant cloth sign from the top of one of the city's tallest buildings, a sign consisting simply of two words in very large letters, that is, BOYCOTT MITSUBISHI. RAN's goal in launch-ing the demonstration was to get the giant sign depicted on the evening news shows for local major TV channels, and to encourage this to occur. RAN personnel contacted all the major news media stations in advance to invite them to be present for the unfurling of the sign. RAN's plan was to embarrass Mitsubishi by the negative publicity seen by a multitude of local viewers of evening news programs. The boycotters hoped that this step, by itself or in combination with others, would lead the corporation to stop the clear-cutting of third-world rainforests.

## The Consumer Boycott Record

While some consumer boycotts have been successful, it seems clear that many more have not. And some of the reasons for the frequent failures are clear to outside observers. Chief among them is the lack of funding and leadership experience for many boycott efforts. It's relatively easy for an individual or organization to call for a boycott, but without a substantial budget and experienced leaders who are prepared to mount a boycott campaign that could continue for months or even years, the effort is not likely to succeed. Moreover, the consumer product or service to be boycotted must be carefully selected in that the demands made of the boycott target should be cognitively simple for consumers to understand and the "wrong" to be righted by the boycott action should be one that consumers find to be emotionally compelling.

Sometimes, however, the boycott success picture is muddied by "bogus boycotts" called by individuals seeking a news media headline associating them with the politically correct side of a public issue, for example, calling for a boycott of a movie theater chain for raising its prices, an announcement that the boycott caller has no plans to pursue with a boycott campaign. And for this reason and others, it is often difficult to arrive at a fair assessment of the success rate for consumer boycotts.

## The Future

The first decade of the new century has brought with it many new developments that may well affect the role of organized consumer action in the United States. The first and least surprising are the major advances in communication technology that facilitate group action, and on a much larger scale through the use of Internet websites and e-mail mailing lists. While these group actions might well be consumer boycotts, a new emphasis in social and clinical psychology, called "positive psychology" may be awakening consumer interest in rewarding businesses for "good behavior" through "consumer boycotts," in contrast to the current practice of initiating punitive boycott campaigns in response to "bad behavior." And the combination of these two developments (better communications among activists and a new interest in boycotts) is beginning to be seen in "carrotmobs," dramatic group actions by consumers for rewarding the environmentally beneficial actions of urban retailers (Hoffmann and Hutter, 2011).

Adapted with permission from the *Journal of Social Issues* (cited below).

*Monroe Friedman*

**See also:** Activism; Commission on Civil Rights

## References and Additional Readings

Friedman, M. (1971). The 1966 consumer protest as seen by its leaders. *Journal of Consumer Affairs, 5,* 1–23.

Friedman, M. (1991). Consumer boycotts: A conceptual framework and research agenda. *Journal of Social Issues, 51,* 197–215.

Friedman, M. (1999). *Consumer boycotts: Effecting change through the marketplace and the media.* New York: Routledge.

Garrett, D. E. (1987). The effectiveness of marketing policy boycotts: Environmental opposition to marketing. *Journal of Marketing, 51,* 46–57.

Hoffmann, S., & Hunter, K. (2011). Carrotmob as a new form of ethical consumption. (Published online in *Journal of Consumer Policy.* DOI: 10.1007/s10603-011-9185-2).

Scott, J. (1985). *Weapons of the weak: Everyday forms of peasant resistance.* New Haven, CT: Yale University Press.

# Brockovich, Erin

## The Early Years

Erin Brockovich was born Erin Pattee in Lawrence, Kansas, on June 22, 1960. Her father, Frank Pattee was an industrial engineer and her mother, Betty Jo O'Neal-Pattee, a journalist. She was the youngest of four children with a disciplinarian father whom she greatly admired. Erin went to high school in the same small town attending Lawrence High School for four years. After high school, Erin attended Kansas State University in Manhattan, Kansas, but ended up graduating from Wades Business College in Dallas, Texas, with an Associate Degree in Applied Arts. She went through a management training program for Kmart in the early 1980s but left that position after only a few months as it didn't seem to be a fit for the young woman. Erin moved to Newport Beach, California, with a girlfriend and ended up entering a Beauty Pageant and winning the title of Miss Pacific Coast. Erin was glad to be on the West Coast as her brother Tommy lived in Southern California as well. However, by 1982 Tommy moved away and Erin was left to make it on her own accord.

Environmental activist Erin Brockovich. (AP Photo)

Erin met her first husband, Shawn Brown, while roller skating near the beach one afternoon and moved quickly into a serious relationship. The two married in April of 1982 and decided to settle in Kansas City, just 40 miles from Erin's hometown. In May of 1983, Erin had her first child, Matthew. Although, her marriage was beginning to feel the strain of daily life, she hung in there for the sake of her first born. Soon after, she and Shawn welcomed their second child into the world, a baby they named Katie. The family of four moved around for Shawn's job, first to St. Louis and then to Lodi, California. Erin felt unsure about the marriage and before long panic attacks began, leading to a diagnosis of anxiety. When another move, due to Shawn's job, was inevitable, Erin decided it was too much. In 1987, Shawn and Erin divorced. Erin was 26 years old at the time.

Erin secured her children in a day care setting and started a secretarial position to support her two children. She was making progress getting her life back to normal and by the spring of 1988, she began dating her boss, Steve Brockovich. Steve, a stockbroker, and Erin decided to marry in 1989; the second marriage for Erin. The relationship was short lived and Erin soon found herself in a failing marriage. Steve Brockovich and Erin divorced in May of 1990 when Erin was just 29 years old. Erin reportedly kept the last name Brockovich only because she was not able to come up with the $675 needed to legally change back to her maiden name. Soon after, however, Erin received surprising news. She was expecting her third child with her ex-husband, Steve. Although Erin was financially unsure of her ability to provide for her children, she decided to keep the baby and unfortunately at four months along, was in a major car accident. Due to the pregnancy, no medical imaging was taken of her injuries and it was unknown that her spinal cord had herniated and caused unbearable pain. Suffering from financial and physical challenges, Erin reached an emotional low.

In 1991, Erin welcomed her baby girl, Elizabeth, to the world. After having Elizabeth, Erin moved back to Southern California. She fell for a local biker, Jorge Halaby, who introduced her to attorney Jim Vititoe for help with filing a case concerning her automobile accident. The firm of Masry & Vititoe filed a lawsuit that resulted in funding the neck surgery Erin needed as a result of her injuries in the accident. While Erin recovered from the surgery, Jorge Halaby moved into her home to help care for the children. Erin's suit was finally settled and resulted in much less compensation than Erin had expected. Her father encouraged Erin to move home for support, but Erin wouldn't be defeated. In desperation, she went to the one place that had helped her before, the Law Firm of Masry & Vititoe. Erin began answering phones for minimal pay and distinguished herself in the office through her manner of dressing and noticeable cleavage. Her boss, Ed Masry came to her one day with a pro bono case that needed filing and Erin took an interest. Investigating the details of the lawsuit she soon found the case with Pacific Gas and Electric Company (PG&E) to be one she couldn't let go. Her intuition led her to discover all was not right with the details in the suit.

### PG&E and Hinkley, California

The PG&E case centered around alleged contamination of the drinking water with hexavalent chromium in the small town of Hinkley, California. The Hinkley Compressor Station was utilized by PG&E as part of a natural gas line that connected into the San Francisco area. From the early 1950s to the mid-1960s, hexavalent chromium was used to decrease corrosion of the pipeline system. The run-off from the cooling towers was leaked into unlined ponds at the PG&E site. This contaminated water seeped deep into the groundwater used by local residents in an area covering 3.2 by 1.6 kilometers. Local residents exhibited symptoms affecting their health and suspicions grew as to the source of so many ills. Erin Brockovich played an instrumental role in pushing the lawsuit, digging up truths, and advocating for the rural residents so deeply impacted by the contaminated water. Many believe without her tenacity to uncover the details of the case, the residents would have continued to suffer and would not have been compensated for illnesses attributed to the water source. In 1996, $333 million was awarded in a settlement between PG&E and the residents of Hinkley, California. The law firm received 133.6 million dollars and Erin was awarded 2 million dollars as a bonus from the firm.

### *The Movie*

A movie about Erin Brockovich's life, entitled *Erin Brockovich*, was released in 2000 and dramatizes the fight between Erin and PG&E in the town of Hinkley, California. In the plot, Erin (Julia Roberts) is an unemployed mother of three children who can only find work as a file clerk in a law firm and eventually noses around the pro bono case of PG&E and the small town of Hinkley, California. Discovering that many of the citizens of Hinkley have medical anomalies, she suspects the chromium-tainted water supplied by PG&E might be a cause of so many illnesses. Eventually, Erin's boss, Ed takes the case to binding arbitration and Erin convinces 634 plaintiffs in Hinkley to agree to a judge's decision in the matter without putting the case in front of a jury. The judge orders PG&E to pay $333 million to be divided among the plaintiffs and Erin earns a bonus of 2 million dollars as compensation from Ed for her efforts to bring justice to the victims. Directed by Steven Soderbergh and starring Julia Roberts as Erin Brockovich, the movie turned into a box office hit and secured many notable awards including Best Actress at the Academy Awards, Best Actress at the Golden Globe Awards, Best Actress at the Screen Actors' Guild and Best Actress for BAFTA (British Academy for Film and Television Arts) for Julia Roberts. Also voting Julia Roberts Best Actress for the year were The National Board of Review, the Los Angeles Film Critics Association, and the Broadcast Film Critics Association. The film received four Golden Globe nominations for Best Director (Steven Soderbergh), Best Dramatic Motion Picture Actress (Julia Roberts), Best Supporting Actor (Albert Finney), and Best Dramatic Motion Picture. The Golden Globes awarded only the Best Dramatic Motion Picture Actress award. The Academy Awards brought five nominations including Best Supporting Actor, Best Original Screenplay, Best Actress, Best Director, and Best Picture. The Academy awarded only Best Actress to Julia Roberts for her role as Erin Brockovich. The movie secured not only the accolades of film critics, but also the hearts of Americans as the story of a small-town girl doing good through her passion to help others hit home for many moviegoers. The film went on to win critics' reviews not only domestically but worldwide as well.

### Erin Today

After the grand success of the movie, *Erin Brockovich*, Erin hosted ABC's 2001 television show, *Challenge America with Erin Brockovich*. The show inspired Americans to help rebuild a dilapidated park in downtown Manhattan. She also went on to host three seasons of the Lifetime series, Final Justice with Erin Brockovich where she highlighted common American women who triumphed over adversity in their lives. She also wrote a book, *Take It From Me. Life's A Struggle, But You Can Win* and continues to write responses to the many e-mails from fans and folks that seek help and advice from Erin. Erin now presides over Brockovich Research & Consulting and has several environmental projects across the country and abroad. She travels nationally to attend speaking engagements and to help in ground water contamination cases around the globe. Erin has settled in Southern California with her husband, three children and continues to work on advocating for injustices of the American people.

*Zoe Bryan Engstrom*

**See also:** Activism; Corporate Social Responsibility; Environmental Protection Agency (EPA)

**References and Additional Readings**

The Biography Channel. (2011). Erin Brockovich biography. Retrieved from http://www.thebiographychannel.co.uk/biographies/erin-brockovich.html

Brockovich, E. (2001). *Take it from me: Life's a struggle but you can win.* New York: McGraw-Hill Companies.

Brockovich, E. (2010). Official website of Erin Brockovich. Retrieved from: http://www.brockovich.com/articles.html

*Chasing the frog.* (2000). Erin Brockovich true story at reel faces. Retrieved from http://www.chasingthefrog.com/reelfaces/brockovich.php

Los Angeles Times. (2012). All about Erin Brockovich. Retrieved from http://articles.latimes.com/keyword/erin-brockovich

Moisse, K., & Davis, L. (2012). Erin Brockovich launches investigation into tic illness affecting N.Y. teenagers. *ABC News.* Retrieved from http://abcnews.go.com/Health/Wellness/erin-brockovich-launches-investigation-tic-illness-affecting-ny/story?id=15456672

Olson, W. (2000). All about Erin. *Reason.com.* Retrieved from http://www.reason.com/archives/2000/10/01/all-about-erin

Sahagun, L. (October 14, 2012). Pollution issue divides desert town as deadline nears. *Los Angeles Times.* Retrieved from http://www.latimes.com/news/local/la-me-1014-hinkley-buyout-20121014,0,6073012.story

Soderbergh, S. (Director). Sher, S. (Producer). (2000). *Erin Brockovich* [Film]. Hollywood: Universal Studios.

Suderman, P. (May 10, 2012). Environmental crusader Erin Brockovich slams 'Absent' EPA. *The Washington Times.* Retrieved from http://www.washingtontimes.com/news/2012/may/10/erin-brockovich-slams-absent-epa/?page=all

**Buckley Amendment**. *See* Family Educational Rights Privacy Act (FERPA)

## Bullying

Bullying is defined as when a person or group repeatedly attempts to harm another person verbally by saying or writing hurtful things, physically by hurting a person's body or personal possessions, and/or socially by hurting someone's reputation or relationships. Bullying often begins with an imbalance of power such as physical strength, knowledge of embarrassing information, or popularity. The bully uses his or her "power" to control or harm others. For example, bullying may manifest as name calling, teasing, taunting, hitting, breaking someone's personal belongings, spreading rumors, or trying to make others reject someone. The term bullying is typically used to refer to behavior that occurs between school-aged kids. However, adults can be repeatedly aggressive and use power over each other, too as is frequently seen in the workplace.

Bullying can occur any time. For children, bullying is most reported to have happened in the school building. However, a significant amount of bullying also happens in places such as the playground or the bus. Bullying may also happen traveling to or from school, in the youth's

Teens gossip about a classmate at school. (Olaf Speier/iStockPhoto.com)

neighborhood, or on the Internet. However, depending on the environment, some groups such as lesbian, gay, bisexual, or transgendered (LGBT) individuals, individuals with disabilities, and socially isolated individuals may be at an increased risk of being bullied. Children at risk for bullying include those who are perceived as (1) being different from their peers such as being overweight or underweight, wearing glasses, being new to a school, or being unable to afford the latest greatest must have item; (2) weak or unable to defend themselves; (3) depressed, anxious, or having low self-esteem; (4) not popular; and (5) not getting along well with others.

While bullying has been around for a long time, technological advances have likely increased the bully's accessibility to his or her victim. For example, text messages and social media sites have both provided ways to contact a person 24 hours a day, 7 days a week. Cyberbullying takes place using electronic technology such as cell phones and computers. Messages and photo are often posted anonymously by the bully and are quickly distributed. Cyberbullying should be reported to online service providers, law enforcement, and schools as applicable. Children who are cyberbullied are often bullied in person as well.

Bullying is far too often dismissed as a "normal" part of growing up. However, the fact remains that bullying is harmful, having effects that may last a lifetime for both children who bully and children who are bullied. In some cases bullying may end in the death of the victim who commits suicide. Nationally, 20 percent of youth in high school experienced bullying in 2011. The National School Safety Center estimates that over 2.5 million students are bullied each year.

Research has shown that youth who are cyberbullied are more likely to participate in risky behaviors such as using alcohol and drugs and skipping school. The victims are more likely to receive poor grades, have lower self-esteem, and have more health problems compared to youth who are not bullied. Bullies are more likely to participate in other risky behaviors such as abusing alcohol and other drugs as well as engaging in early sexual activity. Even children who witness bullying as bystanders are affected having increased use of tobacco, drugs, and alcohol, increased mental health problems, and increased number of absences from school.

There are many warning signs that a child is being affected by bullying, either being bullied or bullying another child. Signs a child is being bullied include unexplained injuries, lost or damaged personal property, frequently feeling sick or faking illness, changing eating habits, difficulty in sleeping, declining grades, sudden loss of friends, avoiding social situations, running away from home, or having thoughts of harming themselves. Signs a child is bullying other children include instigating physical or verbal fights, increasingly aggressive, having unexplained money or personal items, not accepting responsibility for their actions, competitive and worry about their social standing.

## Preventing Bullying

Parents should talk to their children about bullying and be aware of what their children are doing online. Parents should help their children be smart about what they say or post. For example, parents should tell their children not to share anything that could hurt or embarrass themselves or others. Once something is posted, it is out of the child's control regarding whether or not someone else will forward it. Parents should encourage their children to tell them immediately if they, or someone they know, are being bullied. Children often do not feel comfortable talking to their parents about bullying for many reasons such as a fear of backlash from the bully, feelings of humiliation or social isolation, or fear of being rejected by their peers.

## Consumer Safety and Protection Regarding Bullying

In the early 2000s, an increased focus on school bullying and violence occurred due to several U.S. school shootings, including the shooting at Columbine High School. While, there is no federal law that addresses bullying specifically, the first ever White House Conference on bullying was held on March 10, 2011, coinciding with the release of the updated resource website www.StopBullying.gov.

Through state laws and model policies that provide guidance to districts and schools, each state addresses bullying differently. The first state to enact a bullying prevention law was Georgia in 1999. By 2003, 15 states had enacted laws to address school-related bullying. As of 2012, 49 states have passed school antibullying legislation. There are currently no antibullying laws in Montana. Consumers can view state bullying laws on the website. Many states also have laws that protect again bullying because of sexual orientation. In addition, many state and federal laws address bullying-like behaviors in adults under very serious terms, such as hazing, harassment, and stalking. Adults in the workplace have a number of different laws that apply to them that do not apply to children.

*Martie Gillen*

**See also:** Discrimination; Privacy: Online; Privacy: Offline; Public Safety; Social Services

### References and Additional Readings

Department of Health and Human Services. (DHHS). (2012). Bullying definition. Retrieved from http://www.stopbullying.gov/what-is-bullying/definition/index.html

National Institutes for Health (NIH). U.S. National Library of Medicine. (2012). Bullying. Retrieved from http://www.nlm.nih.gov/medlineplus/bullying.html

## Bureau of Consumer Protection (BCP)

The Bureau of Consumer Protection (BCP) is one of three branches of the Federal Trade Commission (FTC). "The Bureau of Consumer Protection works to protect consumers against unfair, deceptive, or fraudulent practices in the marketplace" (FTC, 2012a). It is charged with interpreting and enforcing jurisdictional legislation in advertising and marketing, financial products and practices, and telemarketing fraud, privacy and identity protection. The BCP develops rules to protect consumers, educates consumers and businesses regarding their rights and responsibilities, and investigates and files litigation against those who violate the rules.

The BCP is also responsible for the National Do Not Call Registry, which blocks unwanted telemarketing calls. It also plays a major role in consumer's being able to exercise their right to receive a free credit report and to refer to product warranties. It is also involved with such activities as care labels on clothing and stickers that show the energy costs of home appliances.

### History

The FTC was created after the enactment of the FTC Act, signed by U.S. President Woodrow Wilson on September 26, 1914. The FTC is an independent agency of the U.S. government. Since its inception, the FTC has enforced provisions of the FTC Act and the Clayton Antitrust Act (U.S. Code Title 15). The structure of the FTC has gone through many changes and revisions over time (Holt 1974) and the BCP has been delegated the authority to enforce several additional business regulation statutes, including:

- The Webb–Pomerene Export Trade Act of 1918, which promotes exports through cooperation with other countries.

- The Robinson–Patman Act of 1936, which regulates the pricing practices of suppliers and wholesalers and strengthens the Clayton Act.
- The Wool Products Labeling Act of 1939, which clarifies and enhances the labeling of wool products in order to increase consumer awareness regarding purity.
- The Lanham Trademark Act of 1946, which requires the registration of trademarks and enforces trademark protection.
- The Federal Cigarette Labeling and Advertising Act of 1965, which requires tobacco companies to inform consumers of the health risks associated with the use of their products and to place warnings on cigarette packaging.
- The Fair Packaging and Labeling Act of 1966, which legislates against unfair or deceptive labeling and packaging.
- The Truth in Lending Act of 1969, which requires that companies provide full disclosure of credit terms, limits consumer liability concerning stolen credit cards, and establishes regulations for advertising for credit services.
- The Fair Credit Reporting Act of 1970, which establishes regulations and fair operating practices for credit reporting agencies.
- The Equal Credit Opportunity Act of 1974, which makes it unlawful for any creditor to discriminate against any applicant with respect to any aspect of a credit transaction.
- The Magnuson–Moss Warranty FTC Improvement Act of 1975, which forces manufacturers to explicitly spell out any warranty limitations.
- The FTC Franchise Rule of 1979, which requires franchisors to provide full disclosure of all relevant information regarding the franchise to franchisees.
- The Telemarketing and Consumer Fraud and Abuse Prevention Act of 1994, which imposes restrictions on fraudulent and/or bothersome telemarketing practices (Labaree, 2000).
- The Gramm–Leach–Bliley Act of 1999, which requires financial institutions to ensure the security and confidentiality of customer information and gives the consumer the opportunity to ensure that their personal information is not shared with certain third parties if so desired (Broome and Markham, 2001).
- The Children's Online Privacy Protection Act of 2000, which protects against the online collection of personal information by persons or entities from children under 13 years of age (FTC, 1998).

- The Fairness to Contact Lens Consumer Act of 2004, which increases the consumer's ability to choose where to shop and forces prescribers to provide a copy of the contact lens prescription to the patient (FTC, 2004).

## Organizational Structure

The BCP is comprised of the director's office and the following seven divisions. These are Advertising Practices, Consumer & Business Education, Enforcement, Financial Practices, Marketing Practices, Privacy & Identity Protection, and Planning & Information. The BCP has offices in seven regions of the United States: (1) East Central Region (Cleveland); (2) Midwest Region (Chicago); (3) Northeast Region (New York); (4) Northwest Region (Seattle); (5) Southeast Region (Atlanta); (6) Southwest Region (Dallas); and (7) Western Region (Los Angeles and San Francisco). A detailed discussion of the responsibilities of each division is provided below.

## Division of Advertising Practices

The Division of Advertising Practices was created in order to help protect consumers against unfair or deceptive advertising and marketing practices related to safety and health concerns. It also helps protect consumers against advertising and marketing practices that cause economic injury. It monitors the advertising and marketing of alcohol, tobacco, food consumed by children, movies, music, and video games. It has the authority to bring law enforcement actions and administrative lawsuits in federal district court to stop fraudulent advertising practices.

The Division reviews and enforces a variety of consumer protection laws and regulations, including the Children's Online Privacy Protection Act, the Fairness to Contact Lens Consumers Act, and the Federal Cigarette and Smokeless Tobacco Acts. It also creates various practical consumer guides such as the Dietary Supplements Guide. The Division of Advertising Practices also coordinates with state, federal, and international law agencies, as well as with industry self-regulation groups. It works with agencies in Mexico and Canada to combat the cross-border marketing of dietary supplements. It participates in an interagency committee to prevent underage drinking. It convenes workshops with other government agencies, consumer groups, businesses, and community-based organizations. In addition, it occasionally files comments with the FDA regarding food and drug labeling issues.

The Division's enforcement priorities include:

- Combating deceptive advertising of fraudulent cure-all claims for dietary supplements and weight loss products;
- Monitoring and stopping deceptive internet marketing practices that develop in response to public health issues;
- Monitoring and developing effective enforcement strategies for new advertising techniques and media, such as word-of-mouth marketing;
- Monitoring and reporting on the advertising of food to children, including the impact of practices by food companies and the media on childhood obesity;
- Monitoring and reporting on industry practices regarding the marketing of violent movies, music, and electronic games to children;
- Monitoring and reporting on alcohol and tobacco marketing practices. (FTC, 2012b)

### Division of Consumer and Business Education

The Division of Consumer and Business Education creates educational material regarding fraud, deception, and unfair practices. It promotes these materials to consumers, businesses, and law enforcement officials through various forms of media. It partners with various consumer groups, businesses, professional associations, and government agencies in order to make this information available to the public.

### Division of Enforcement

The Division of Enforcement litigates FTC consumer protection cases, coordinates FTC actions with law enforcement agencies, enforces rules regarding consumer protection, and represents the FTC in Federal Bankruptcy Court. The Division's Criminal Liaison Unit works with various law enforcement agencies to help prosecute consumer fraud by preparing cases for referral and providing special prosecutors to help with cases involving the worst violators of the FTC Act.

The Division also coordinates initiatives that involve civil litigation against marketers that deceive consumers, disseminates information through workshops set up with various agencies, and analyzes marketplace trends that affect consumers. Examples of these initiatives include the Hispanic Law Enforcement and Outreach Initiative and the Negative Option Marketing Initiative.

Some of the most important consumer protection rules enforced by the Division include:

- Energy Rules, which require the disclosure of energy costs of home appliances (the Appliance Labeling Rule), octane ratings of gasoline (the Fuel Rating Rule), and the efficiency rating of home insulation (the R-Value Rule).

- Green Guides, which provide guidance regarding claims that consumer products are environmentally safe, recyclable, ozone-friendly, or biodegradable.

- The "Made in USA" Enforcement Policy Statement, which provides guidelines for domestic origin claims.

- The Mail or Telephone Order Merchandise Rule, which requires companies to ship goods when promised (or within 30 days if no time is specified) or to give consumers the option to cancel their order for a refund.

- Textile, Wool, Fur, and Care Labeling Rules, which require proper origin and fiber content labeling of textile, wool, and fur products, and care label instructions attached to clothing and fabrics.

- Jewelry Guides, which provide guidance about claims about precious metals, gemstones, and pearls. (FTC, 2012c)

### Division of Financial Practices

The Division of Financial Practices protects consumers from deceptive or unfair practices by financial services companies through education, policy leadership, and law enforcement in both federal and administrative courts. The Division challenges deceptive marketing practices, especially by credit card companies. It also ensures that mortgage lenders do not use deceptive lending practices and that lenders comply with the Equal Credit Opportunity Act. It also helps protect consumers against deceptive or unfair practices by companies that service mortgages and takes action against companies that violate laws when collecting debts, marketing debt reduction or relief services, or offering credit counseling services. Finally, the Division coordinates law enforcement efforts against payment processors who commit unfair practices when processing payments for fraudulent merchants (e.g., telemarketers who deceive consumers into providing their bank account information).

### Division of Marketing Practices

The Division of Marketing Practices enforces the FTC Act and several other federal consumer protection laws by filing FTC actions in federal court to stop scams and to prevent those who execute fraudulent schemes from perpetrating them in the future. The Division also takes action to freeze the assets of those who perpetrate fraud and to seek compensation for victims of such schemes. The Division investigates the use of the Internet and other emerging technologies used to defraud customers. Moreover, it presents Internet investigation training programs for various law agencies, sponsors and conducts symposia on legal issues arising from new technologies, and prosecutes civil enforcement actions to keep those who commit fraud from operating on the Internet and related arenas. Some of the more important rules enforced by the Division include:

- The Telemarketing Sales Rule which prohibits deceptive sales pitches and protects consumers from abusive, unwanted, and late-night sales calls.
- The CAN-SPAM Rules, including the Adult Labeling Rule, which requires warning labels on commercial e-mail containing sexually oriented material.
- The Franchise and Business Opportunity Rule, which requires franchise and business opportunity sellers to give prospective buyers a disclosure document containing specific information about the business and any earnings claims the seller makes, to help them make an informed decision as to whether to purchase.
- The 900 Number Rule, which requires sellers of pay-per-call (900 number) services to clearly disclose the price of their services, prohibits the targeting of most of those services to children, and creates procedures to dispute charges for 900 number services like those available for credit card purchases.
- The Funeral Rule, which requires funeral directors to disclose price and other information about their services to consumers.
- The Magnuson–Moss Act, which requires that merchants make warranty information available to consumers in advance of their purchase. (FTC, 2012d)

### Division of Planning & Information

The Division of Planning & Information measures the impact of activities related to the consumer protection mission of the FTC through data collection and analysis. It is also responsible for the Consumer Response Center, the Consumer Sentinel (a website accessible by various U.S. agencies as well as consumer protection agencies in other countries that contains searchable fraud and identity theft complaints and other useful information), and administrative support of the BCP.

### Division of Privacy and Identity Protection

The Division of Privacy and Identity Protection is responsible for monitoring issues regarding information security, identity theft, consumer privacy, and credit reporting. It investigates breaches of data security, operates the Identity Theft Data Clearinghouse, and aids consumers whose identities have been stolen. It also implements laws and regulations for the credit reporting industry. The Division enforces Section 5 of the FTC Act, which prohibits unfair or deceptive practices and deceptive statements involving the use or protection of consumers' personal information. It also enforces the Fair Credit Reporting Act and the Gramm–Leach–Bliley Act.

### Controversial Legislation under Consideration

On May 23, 2007, the House introduced a bill "Energy Price Gouging Prevention Act" (H.R. 1252), which was to provide immediate relief to consumers by giving the FTC the authority to investigate and take action against those who artificially inflate the price of energy. It was created to give the federal government tools to adequately respond to energy emergencies and prohibit price gouging by refineries and large oil companies. However, the Bill was opposed by several groups including the U.S. Chamber of Commerce on the grounds that the penalties being considered were too arbitrary, subjective, and extreme (U.S. Chamber of Commerce, 2007). The Bill ultimately failed to pass into law by a narrow margin.

In October, 2011, House lawmakers introduced a bill "Stop Online Piracy Act" (H.R. 3261) that would expand the ability of federal law enforcement to shut down foreign websites and services that use counterfeited or pirated content created by U.S. firms. Proponents of the bill state that it would protect the intellectual property market and corresponding industry, jobs, and revenue, and is necessary to bolster enforcement of copyright laws. Opponents argue that the proposed legislation threatens free speech and innovation, and enables law enforcement to block access to entire Internet domains due to infringing material posted on a single blog or website. On January 28, 2012, several websites coordinated service blackouts in an effort to raise awareness of the proposed legislation. On January 20, 2012, the House Judiciary Committee Chairman postponed plans to draft the bill. Some opponents of the bill have proposed the Online Protection and Enforcement of Digital Trade Act as an alternative (Kang 2011).

*Troy G.Schmitz*

**See also:** Children's Online Privacy Protection Act (COPPA); Cigarette Labeling Act; Fair Credit Reporting Act; Federal Trade Commission (FTC); Food and Drug Administration (FDA); Magnuson–Moss Warranty Act; National Do Not Call Registry; Privacy: Offline; Privacy: Online; Sherman Antitrust Act; Truth in Lending Act

### References and Additional Readings

Broome, L. L., & Markham, J. W. (2012). The Gramm–Leach–Bliley Act: An overview. Retrieved from http://www.symtrex.com/pdfdocs/glb_paper.pdf

Chamber of Commerce. (2007). Letter opposing the Federal Price Gouging Prevention Act sent to Committee on Energy and Commerce. Retrieved from http://www.uschamber.com/issues/letters/2007/letter-opposing-federal-price-gouging-prevention-act-sent-committee-energy-and-c. May 3

Federal Trade Commission. (1998). Children Online Protection Privacy Act. Retrieved from http://www.ftc.gov/ogc/coppa1.htm

Federal Trade Commission. (2004). FTC issues final rule implementing fairness to Contact Lens Consumers Act. Retrieved from http://www.ftc.gov/opa/2004/06/contactlens.shtm

Federal Trade Commission. (2012a). Bureau of Consumer Protection official government website. Retrieved from http://www.ftc.gov/bcp

Federal Trade Commission. (2012b). Division of advertising practices official government website. Retrieved from http://ftc.gov/bcp/bcpap.shtm

Federal Trade Commission. (2012c). Division of enforcement official government website. Retrieved from http://ftc.gov/bcp/bcpenf.shtm

Federal Trade Commission. (2012d). Division of marketing practices official government website. Retrieved from http://ftc.gov/bcp/bcpmp.shtm

Holt, W. S. (1974). *The Federal Trade Commission: Its history, activities, and organization.* New York, NY: AMS Press.

Kang, C. (2011). House introduces internet piracy bill. *The Washington Post with Bloomberg*. Retrieved from http://www.washingtonpost.com/blogs/post-tech/post/house-introduces-internet-piracy-bill/2011/10/26/gIQA0f5xJM_blog.htm

Labaree, R. V. (2000). The Federal Trade Commission: A guide to sources. *Garland*. U.S. Code Title 15 (2011). Retrieved from http://www.law.cornell.edu/uscode/usc_sup_01_15.html

**Bureau of Labor Statistics**. See Department of Labor (DOL)

# C

**CARD Act**. *See* Credit Card Accountability Responsibility Disclosure Act (Credit CARD Act)

## Carson, Rachel

Rachel Carson (born May 27, 1907, deceased April 14, 1964) was an American author and biologist. Her books include *The Sea around Us* (1951), which was awarded the National Book Award, and *Silent Spring* (1962) which is often cited as one of the fundamental works of the American ecology movement.

Carson graduated in Biology at the Pennsylvania College for Women in 1929 and continued graduate studies at John Hopkins University, where she acquired a master's degree in Zoology in 1932. She enrolled in the doctoral program of Johns Hopkins University, but had to drop out of the program for economic reasons a few years later. In 1936, Rachel Carson was appointed a full-time position as junior aquatic biologist at the U.S. Bureau of Fisheries, Division of Scientific Inquiry. In the following years she made a notable career at the U.S. Fish and Wildlife Service and finally became editor-in-chief, but gave up her appointment at in 1952 to become a full-time writer.

The earlier books by Carson thematically centered on the sea and maritime life. In 1941, she published *Under the Sea Wind*, followed by *The Sea around Us* (1951), and *The Edge of the Sea* (1955). *The Sea around Us* was a huge commercial success; it received enthusiastic reviews and won several prizes (among others the National Book award). A movie adaptation of *The Sea around Us* won the Academy Award for the best documentary in 1953.

The long-term fame as well as most of Carson's political and social impact, however, is due to her book *Silent Spring* (1962). In *Silent Spring* Carson critically examines the use of synthetic herbicides and pesticides like dichlorodiphenyltrichloroethane (DDT) and other chlorinated hydrocarbons and organophosphates. She strongly argues that pesticides

Rachel Carson before a Senate Government Operations subcommittee, discussing pesticides. (Library of Congress)

have many adverse effects on animals, plants, and the human health that massively outweigh their benefits. Important adverse effects include the low selectiveness of the chemicals and most notably the property of DDT and other pesticides to accumulate through the food chain. Parts of the book were prepublished in *The New Yorker. Silent Spring* provoked a controversial public debate—which included attacks based on Carson's style of writing, her person and gender, and the scientific bases of the book. In spite of the criticism, Carson's book managed to start an important public and scientific debates that ultimately led to substantial policy changes, including the ban of DDT. In addition to this direct effect, Rachel Carson and her work influenced the emerging environmental movement and thereby had and still have manifold effects on environment and society.

Rachel Carson died from cancer at the age of 56. For her achievements as a scientist, nature writer, conservationist and political agenda setter, Rachel Carson received several honorary doctorates and was posthumously awarded the Presidential Medal of Freedom in 1980.

*Henning Best*

**See also:** Environmental Protection Agency (EPA); *Silent Spring*

### References and Additional Readings

Brooks, P. (1972). *The house of life. Rachel Carson at work.* Boston, MA: Houghton Mifflin.

Lear, L. (2009). *Rachel Carson. Witness for nature.* Boston, MA: Mariner.

Lytle, M.H. (2001). *The gentle subversive. Rachel Carson, silent spring, and the rise of the environmental movement.* Oxford: Oxford University Press.

## CARU (Children's Advertising Review Unit). *See* Better Business Bureau (BBB)

## Caveat Emptor

Caveat emptor is a Latin term that means "let the buyer beware." As a principle of commerce, the buyer assumes all risk in situations where a warranty does not exist; essentially becoming an "as is" purchase. Ultimately, it implies that the buyer should always be on guard while purchasing a product or service. In fact, the marketplace virtually demands it, despite the myriad protections that exist to protect the consumer. The caveat emptor doctrine implies that the seller knows more than the buyer and that at a point of sale or in a contract negotiation, the buyer should be in peak awareness. The buyer should study, judge, and critically evaluate a product or service. In effect, the seller is held harmless, yet may still face backlash if the product or service is defective.

In its purest form, under the doctrine, the seller could chose to disclose no information and still be in compliance. More specifically, if the seller is not committing fraud, concealment, or misrepresentation, then the seller has no duty or obligation for disclosure. In this scenario, the buyer has the responsibility to uncover and discover defects and flaws. Nevertheless, in a fair marketplace, the buyer is still expected to make a reasonable effort to produce a product or service free of defects, errors, or usability. This is the principle of an implied warranty of merchantability, or basic understanding that goods in the marketplace are fit for sale. Researchers use the caveat emptor doctrine to analyze a multitude of topics, including internet sales and auction fraud, plea bargaining, disclosure, medical care, among other things.

Real estate and property law are also frequently studied and published topics; in fact in some cases, property law doctrine is synonymous with caveat emptor. The term caveat emptor has another side, which is "caveat venditor," Latin for "let the seller beware." The culture and environment of the marketplace determine the extent to which the pendulum swings toward the buyer or seller.

*Wendy Reiboldt*

**See also:** Caveat Venditor; Warranties

### References and Additional Readings

Bibas, S. (2011). Regulating the plea-bargaining market: from caveat emptor to consumer protection. *California Law Review, 99,* 1117–1161.

Braswell, D. E., & Brody, R. G. (2011). Internet sales and auction fraud—caveat emptor. *Insights to a Changing World Journal, 6,* 34–44.

Johnson, A. M. (2008). An economic analysis of the duty to disclose information: Lessons learned from the caveat emptor doctrine. *San Diego Law Review, 45,* 79–132.

Lehman, A. F. (2006). Treatment guidelines: caveat emptor. *Journal of Mental Health, 15,* 129–133.

## Caveat Venditor

Caveat venditor is a Latin term that means "let the seller beware." It is, in a sense, the opposite of the more commonly known term "caveat emptor" (let the buyer beware). Caveat venditor implies that the seller should watch out for the consumer, because consumers are armed with information, facts, and laws that protect them. Buyers do not always have the skills to successfully evaluate products (caveat emptor), especially in cases of technology and information security. Therefore, he argues, caveat venditor should be in place to balance the power. Sellers are held liable if they are selling products or services that are defective, unfit, or of poor quality. The seller must take responsibility for the products or services they sell and make every effort to inspect and judge their wares before placing them into the marketplace. The specific merchantability rights of consumers are covered under warranties.

The laws and agencies that protect consumers have the caveat venditor doctrine in mind, and lawyers purport the doctrine in their profession. A famous court case, *MacPherson v. Buick Motor Co.* (1916: NYC) is largely considered to be the primary case that sets the precedent for caveat venditor. The case had a man who was injured due to a defective wooden wheel on his Buick; the wheel collapsed and he was thrown from the car. Because the wheel was purchased from another vendor, Buick claimed they were not responsible. However, the judge disagreed and noted that

Buick should have inspected the wheel and known it was defective. The judge held Buick liable and negligent. This finding squarely put the blame on the vendor (seller). The term caveat venditor has a mirror side which is "caveat emptor" for "let the buyer beware." The environmental and political climate of the marketplace greatly influences the predominant thinking toward buyer or seller.

*Wendy Reiboldt*

**See also:** Caveat Emptor; Contract Law; Warranties

**References and Additional Readings**

French, G., & Bond, M. (2010). Caveat venditor. *Information Security Technical Report, 15,* 28–32.

New York Courts. (n.d.). *Donald C. MacPherson, Respondent v. Buick Motor Company, Appellant.* Retrieved from http://www.courts.state.ny.us/REPORTER/archives/macpherson_buick.htm

## Center for Science in the Public Interest (CSPI)

The Center for Science in the Public Interest (CSPI) is a consumer advocacy organization. CSPI has two missions: carry out research efforts and advocacy programs related to health and nutrition, and to distribute information regarding health and well-being to consumers. CSPI's three overarching goals are:

> (1) to provide useful, objective information to the public and policy-makers and to conduct research on food, alcohol, health, the environment, and other issues related to science and technology; (2) to represent the citizen's interests before regulatory, judicial, and legislative bodies on food, alcohol, health, the environment, and other issues; and (3) to ensure that science and technology are used for the public good and to encourage scientists to engage in public-interest activities (CSPI, 2012)

CSPI was founded in 1971 by Michael Jacobson, PhD, and two other scientists. They serve as an organized voice of the American public on issues of nutrition, food safety, and other issues that pertain to consumer and environmental protection awareness. They educate the public, advocate government policies, and counter industry's powerful influence on public opinion and public policy. CSPI is a science-based organization and over the years, its influence has grown along with its reputation.

Over the last 40 years, CSPI has launched numerous campaigns to make our food safer and healthier. Forty years ago, a campaign was launched to bar the use of sodium nitrite in bacon and other cured meats. This led to much lower levels of nitrites in many foods making them much safer for us to eat. Around the same time, CSPI unveiled the *Nutrition Action Health Letter*. It is the largest circulation newsletter in North America on health and nutrition and is published 10 times per year. Examples of topics include snacking, cooking healthy meals, inflammation and disease, and beverages. In the late 1970s and early 1980s, CSPI focused on sodium. In 1978, they petitioned the Food and Drug Administration (FDA) to require sodium labeling of all foods. In 1982, the FDA established sodium labeling of all foods.

The late 1980s and early 1990s were prolific for CSPI. During this time they were successful in campaigning to the FDA to ban sulfite preservatives in most foods. A very important law was passed requiring health warning labels on alcoholic beverages sold in the United States. CSPI was instrumental in swaying major hamburger chains to stop cooking French fries in beef fat. One of the most important laws to benefit consumers in this country was passed in 1990—standard nutrition labeling on all packaged foods and banning deceptive health claims. By the late 1990s, CSPI's efforts to make available healthy food for all persons were impressive. They led the effort to have "organic" federally defined so that consumers could be assured of getting organic foods produced in the same manner. They published reports that identified the nutritional value of restaurant foods. One of the most important efforts of CSPI in this time was the mandatory labeling requirements for trans fatty acids. They also warned consumers about the dangers of the fake fat Olestra and led the effort to require lower-fat meals in schools. CSPI did not let up during the last decade—the 2000s. Bacteria testing for meat was expanded and mandatory nutrition labeling for ground meat and poultry was proposed by the USDA. The Centers for Disease Control and Prevention increased funding to encourage better nutrition and more physical activity in school. The Food Allergy and Labeling Law was passed by Congress during this decade. This law required plain language labeling on foods that all consumers could understand. By the middle of this decade, a new litigation unit was established that led to food manufacturers stopping deceptive ads and labels on foods. They also threatened to sue the soft drink companies that resulted in the removal of soft-drinks from the schools. By the end of the decade, the House of Representatives, with input by CSPI, passed the most comprehensive and sweeping reform the food-safety system has seen in 70 years.

In recent years, Congress enacted mandatory calorie labeling on menus and menu board at chain restaurants in recent years. CSPI is also working to get junk food out of schools nationwide, eliminate trans-fats from all foods, and reduce the sodium in processed and restaurant foods. Through nationwide events, political advocacy, and ongoing education, CSPI is committed to shaping the overall well-being of consumers in the near and distant future.

*Diane E. Carson*

**See also:** Centers for Disease Control and Prevention (CDC); Department of Agriculture (USDA); Food and Drug Administration (FDA); Food Labeling; Food Safety

### References and Additional Readings

Center for Science in the Public Interest. (2012). Mission statement. Retrieved from www.cspinet.org

Elliot, C. (2005). Should journals publish industry-funded bioethics articles? *The Lancet, 366,* 422–424.

Hacker, G. A. (1987). Marketing booze to blacks: A report from the Center for Science in the Public Interest. Center for Science in the Public Interest, Department PD/EDRS, 1501 16th Street, NW Washington, DC, 20036.

Wang, S. S., Wadden, T. A., Womble, L. G., & Nonas, C. A.(2012). What consumers want to know about commercial weight-loss programs: A pilot investigation. *Obesity, 11*(1), 48–63.

## Centers for Disease Control and Prevention (CDC)

The Centers for Disease Control and Prevention (CDC) is one of the major operating components within the Department of Health and Human Services. It oversees several institutes and offices, all with the purpose or mission of protecting and improving the health of citizens. The CDC is in its 67th year of operation and serves as the primary leader in public health efforts. Their primary goals are to prevent and control diseases, hazards in the workplace, injuries, and health threats stemming from the environment. Through health promotion, disease prevention, injury and disability resources, as well as provision of information for health threat preparation, the CDC is a leader in serving the public's health. The CDC accomplishes its goals by collaborating with other agencies nationwide to monitor the health of the nation as well as detect and investigate health problems. The CDC also conducts research on prevention efforts and creates and advocates for better public health policies, including implementation of prevention strategies, and promotion of healthy behaviors. The CDC pledges to provide this to Americans with accountability, respect,

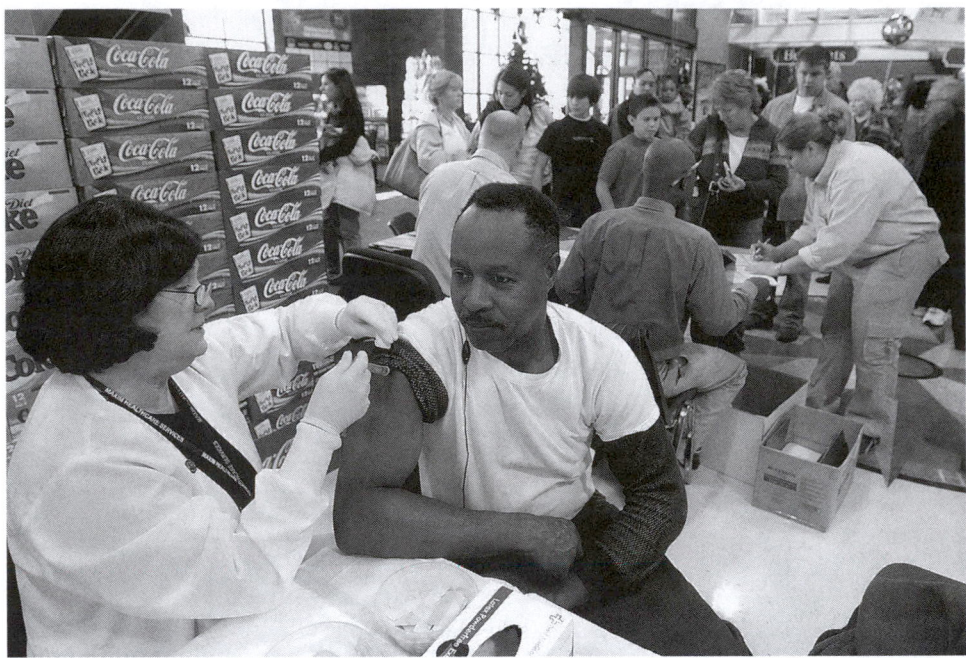

One of the many goals of the CDC is to improve the health and well-being of consumers, including advocating for vaccinations and other forms of preventative care. (AP Photo)

and integrity. This is incredibly important given that, according the CDC, chronic diseases such as heart disease, cancer, and diabetes plague the nation and are the leading causes of death and disability among Americans. Sadly, 70 percent of all deaths in America are due to chronic diseases (about 1.7 million annually). In addition to the deaths, chronic diseases also contribute to major limitations in daily living for nearly 10 percent of people in the United States (about 25 million people).

## The Early Years of the CDC

Descended from the wartime agency Malaria Control in War Areas (MCWA), the CDC initially focused on fighting malaria by killing mosquitoes. Pursuit of malaria was by far the most absorbing interest of CDC during its early years, with over 50 percent of its personnel engaged in it. Among its fewer than 400 original employees, the key jobs at CDC were those of entomologists and engineers. In fact, CDC had only seven medical officers on staff in 1946.

DDT, available since 1943, was its primary weapon, and the CDC's early challenges included obtaining enough trucks, sprayers, and shovels necessary to wage the war on mosquitoes.

In its initial years, over 6.5 million homes were sprayed, and an early organization chart was even drawn—somewhat fancifully—in the shape of a mosquito.

CDC's first budget was under $10 million.

*Source:* Centers for Disease Control and Prevention. (2010). Our history—our story. Retrieved from http://www.cdc.gov/about/history/ourstory.htm

## Overview

The CDC provides information on a range of topics broken down into the following health-related categories:

- Disease and conditions,
- Healthy living, including physical activity, smoking prevention, and immunizations
- Emergency preparedness and response, including bioterrorism and severe weather conditions
- Injury, violence, and safety, including motor vehicle safety and prescription drug overdose
- Environmental health, including toxic substances and air pollution
- Workplace safety, including asbestos and office environments
- Data and statistics, including surveys and vital statistics
- Global health, including global aids and disease detection systems

In addition, the CDC provides information for specific groups, including travelers, with focus on health-related outcomes related to traveling, such as outbreaks and travel vaccinations; persons of all life stages and populations, such as infant and children, minorities, and seniors; and public health professionals who work for state, tribal, local, and territorial entities. Users of the CDC website can also access current health-related publications (e.g., emerging infectious diseases), popular topics (e.g., seasonal flu), and multimedia tools (e.g., body mass index calculator and podcasts). All of this information can also be accessed via an A–Z Index on health-related topics, beginning with Active Bacterial Core Surveillance (ABC) and ending with Zygomycosis (a rare infection). When a consumer clicks on a health topic, more relevant information appears, such as definitions, basic information, frequently asked questions, education resources, relevant data, diagnosis and treatment, fact sheets, and other publications. A person can also access electronic greeting cards to send to loved ones to encourage them to take care of their health. As noted earlier, topics address health issues that impact individuals of all ages, such as child abuse, adolescent health, and menopause. Topics include both physical (such as cancer and flu) and psychological (such as depression) domains of health. Currently on the CDC website are also personal stories from survivors, families, and friends affected by pandemic influenza, including national archives of 1918 pandemic influenza survivors. In addition, the CDC offers information on current, immediate health issues, such as food recalls.

---

Some facts about work-related injuries

In 2007, a total of 5,488 U.S. workers died from occupational injuries. Another 49,000 annual deaths are attributed to work-related diseases each year. In 2007, an estimated 4 million private-sector workers had a nonfatal occupational injury or illness; approximately half of them were transferred, restricted, or took time away from work. An estimated 3.4 million workers were treated in emergency departments in 2004 (the most recent data available) because of occupational injuries, and approximately 80,000 were hospitalized. Work-related injuries and illnesses are costly. In 2006, employers spent nearly $87.6 billion on workers' compensation, but this represents only a portion of total work-related injury and illness costs borne by employers, workers, and society overall, including cost shifting to other insurance systems and most costs of work-related illness.

*Source:* Centers for Disease Control and Prevention. (2011). The National Institute for Occupational Safety and Health (NIOSH). Retrieved from http://www.cdc.gov/niosh/about.html

---

## Organizational Structure

The CDC has a comprehensive, organizational system comprised of its Center, Institute, and Offices (CIOs). These are the Center for Global Health; the National Institute for Occupational Health; Office of Infectious Diseases; Office of Noncommunicable Diseases; Office of Public Health Preparedness and Response; Office for State, Tribal, Local and Territorial Support; Office of Surveillance, Epidemiology, and Laboratory Services; as well as offices for key personnel including the Director of Policy and Office of Minority Health and Health Equity. Each office provides expertise in its respective area, some of which are elaborated here.

*Center for Global Health:* The CDC's Center for Global Health coordinates and manages the agency's resources to address global challenges such as HIV/AIDS, malaria, emergency and refugee health, noncommunicable diseases, injuries, and much more. The CDC has international partners in more than 60 countries. Through its Global Health Initiative (GHI), the CDC works to improve the "health of the poorest families around the world, with a specific focus on improving the health of women, newborns and children through programs that focus on infectious disease, nutrition, maternal and child health, and safe water" (CDC, 2011a). Within this center, International Health Regulations (IHR) are also monitored. Current IHR, or formal guidelines for international-based public health emergencies, require that the United States and other member states of the World Health Organization (WHO) report an outbreak of diseases, including smallpox, cholera, plague, and yellow fever, as well as polio and human influenza. As of 2007, IHR were updated. The United States interprets the new regulations to mean that "countries must report incidents that involve the natural, accidental or deliberate release of chemical, biological, or radiological materials; countries must report, when possible, potential public health emergencies that are occurring in other countries; and there is no separate individual right to legal action against the federal government" (CDC, 2011b).

*National Institute for Occupational Health (NIOSH):* NIOSH is the federal agency "responsible for conducting research and making recommendations for the prevention of work-related injury and illness" (CDC, 2011c). It operates in every state. Its purpose is to collect relevant information and engage in scientific research and from such findings, develop appropriate products and services such as training videos and making recommendations for improving workplace safety and health. The Occupational Safety and Health Act of 1970 created NIOSH. According the Department of Labor's (DOL) website, this act was designed "to assure safe and healthful working conditions for working men and women; by authorizing enforcement of the standards developed under the Act; by assisting and encouraging the States in their efforts to assure safe and healthful working conditions; by providing for research, information, education, and training in the field of occupational safety and health; and for other purposes" (DOL, 2004). Examples of specific activities of NIOSH experts are Prevention through Design, which is working with engineers and architects to create safe working environments and eliminate design flaws that can cause injury; Total Worker Health, which integrates wellness and health promotion into traditional occupational safety and health procedures; and Health Hazard Evaluation Programs, which conducts worksite assessments to determine if workers are exposed to hazardous materials. And while NIOSH serves to protect all workers, particular attention is also given to those who serve, including firefighters, energy workers, and emergency responders.

*Office of Infectious Diseases:* The goal of this office is to engage in activities that lead to the reduction of infectious diseases in both the United States and worldwide. Examples of infectious diseases are zoonotic diseases (those spread from animals to humans), HIV/AIDS, viral hepatitis, sexually transmitted diseases (STDs), and respiratory infections. Interestingly, according to the Center for Disease Control, FastStats, as of 2009, there were nearly 12,000 new cases of tuberculosis, nearly 50,000 new cases of salmonella, 40,000 new cases of syphilis, and over 300,000 new cases of gonorrhea. Additionally, there were nearly 27 million visits to office-based physicians and over four million outpatient hospital visits for infections and parasitic diseases. Data for other infectious diseases are also noted on the CDC website, including details related to emerging infectious diseases (EID). At the time of this writing, this site included information on influenza virus A infections, Creutzfeldt–Jacob variants, and Tick and Tick-borne pathogens. As noted by the WHO, "Today, worldwide, there is an apparent increase in many infectious diseases, including some newly-circulating ones (HIV/AIDS, hantavirus, hepatitis C, SARS, etc.). This reflects the combined impacts of rapid demographic, environmental, social, technological and other changes in our ways-of-living. Climate change will also affect infectious disease occurrence."

*Office of Noncommunicable Diseases:* Within this office, several centers are housed. These are the National Center on Birth Defects and Developmental Disabilities, the National Center for Chronic Disease Prevention and Health Promotion, the National Center for Environmental Health/Agency for Toxic Substances and Disease Registry, and the National Center for Injury Prevention and Control. Together, these serve to reduce the burden and incidence of these forms of diseases. This is done through leadership efforts, promotion of research, policy and programs, and developing inter-agency collaboration. Each center provides specific information on causes and prevention, statistics, state profiles, and resources. At the time of this writing, a current feature exists on Breast Cancer Awareness, with information on general cause, symptoms, and resources for screening.

*Office of Public Health Preparedness and Response:* This center was developed to assist state and local health departments to protect communities from public health threats, such as natural disasters (e.g., hurricanes, floods); biological threats (e.g., flu viruses or bacterial contamination); chemical and radiological materials (e.g., toxic/corrosive gases and substances); and explosions (e.g., as associated with terrorism). The CDC provides funding and technical assistance, surveillance, personnel for emergencies, and assists in logistical designs of emergency responses.

### CDC Features

On the CDC (2013) website there are "current features" that highlights several specific health topics or events. At the time of this writing, these features included "Active Aging," "A Look Inside Food Deserts" (areas that lack access to affordable foods necessary for a healthy diet), "HIV Awareness Day," "World Rabies Day," and "World Heart Day." These features are designed to bring attention to major health issues that affect the nation in ways that promote unity and support among health consumers and advocates. As a result of the CDC, consumers are able to improve their safety, well-being, and quality of life.

*Melanie Horn Mallers*

**See also:** Activism; Department of Health and Human Services (HHS); Environmental Protection Agency (EPA); Health and Healthcare; Public Safety; Social Services; Social Welfare; World Health Organization (WHO)

### References and Additional Readings

Centers for Disease Control. (2011a). CDC and the U.S. global health initiative. Retrieved from http://www.cdc.gov/globalhealth/ghi/

Centers for Disease Control. (2011b). International health regulations. Retrieved from http://www.cdc.gov/globalhealth/ihrMaterial/powerpoint.htm

Centers for Disease Control. (2011c). The National Institute for Occupational Safety and Health (NIOSH). Retrieved from http://www.cdc.gov/niosh/about.html

Centers for Disease Control. (2013). Current features. Retrieved from http://www.cdc.gov/features/index.html

Department of Labor. (2004). OSH Act of 1970. Retrieved from http://www.osha.gov/pls/oshaweb/owadisp.show_document?p_id=2743&p_table=OSHACT

# Certified Financial Planners™

"Certified Financial Planner™" is a trademarked, legal term owned by the Board of Standards for the Certified Financial Planner™, Inc. The designation is allowed to be claimed by individuals who successfully complete the CFPB's initial preparation, examination, and work experience, and then maintains the designation through professional updating.

### Certified Financial Planner™ Designation

The idea of having a professional specializing in helping families with financial well-being began with 13 men gathering in Chicago in 1969. The market for financial products and services had burgeoned after World War II, with the result that the average household money manager was besieged with complex and conflicting information, products, vendors, and procedures having to do with personal finances. The group thought that people could benefit from having an expert help them navigate the marketplace, in addition to alerting them to important financial decisions and products that could help them have financial resources throughout the life cycle. The result of this meeting was that the organization, the International Association for Financial Planners (IAFP) was formed, with an associated educational institution called the College for Financial Planning.

In 1972, the IAFP enrolled its first group of students for the Certified Financial Planning course offered by the newly established college. The first group graduated in 1973. The college continued to operate until 1985, when an announcement was made that a new nonprofit certifying body, the International Board of Standards and Practices for Certified Financial Planners™, Inc. would grant the Certified Financial Planning certification. In 1994, the board was renamed the Certified Financial Planner™ Board of Standards, Inc. Many colleges and universities entered the market, joining the College for Financial Planning, to provide the educational background for individuals to prepare for the CFP exam. Each university or college was and is required for the CFP® preparation courses to be approved by the board as a registered program. This ensures that the students receive an educational preparation in all of the topics covered by the examination for the CFP certification, which translate to the actual areas of expertise in which Certified Financial Planners™ perform professional advice and service for customers.

### Educational and Work Requirements to Become a CFP Professional

The CFP-certified individual has taken courses covering topics such as the time value of money, money management techniques, insurance, investments, employee benefits, retirement, and estate planning. Over 300 academic programs at colleges and universities in the United States offer preparation courses for the CFP examination. Another path to preparation for the CFP certification is through being a certified public accountant, chartered financial consultant, chartered life underwriter, or through holding a PhD in business, economics, or a related discipline. Following the preparation, the individual desiring certification must take a closely monitored 10-hour test consisting of multiple choice questions over the subareas of personal finance, including a case study where all areas are applied to analyzing a family finance situation. The exam is scored using a criterion-based methodology, which means that the individual's performance is scored against an established level of competency.

The competencies are based on 78 topics in the following areas general principles of financial planning, insurance planning, investment planning, income tax planning, retirement planning, estate planning, interpersonal communication, and professional conduct and fiduciary responsibility.

Following the taking and passing the CFP examination, the individual seeking certification must verify that he or she holds a bachelor's degree from an accredited university or college before full certification is allowed. Certification also requires passing the CFP® Board's Fitness Standards for Candidates and Registrants, which consists of upholding a number of ethical and legal requirements. For example, the CFP® candidate must not have declared personal or business bankruptcy within the five years previous to completing the CFP Certification Application.

Three years of full-time work experience in an area of personal financial planning is an additional requirement before full CFP certification is allowed. In addition, the candidate must agree to abide by the CFP® Board's Code of Ethics and Professional Responsibility, Rules of Conduct, and Financial Planning Practice Standards. A full background check is also made on each candidate.

After the education, exam, work experience, background checks, and agreements to ethical and behavioral standards, the candidate may become a full-fledged Certified Financial Planner™. However, the CFP professional must then embark on a continuing education requirement by taking 30 hours of professional development activities (approved by the Board of Standards for the Certified Financial Planner™), each two years.

The Certified Financial Planner™ must uphold a strict fiduciary relationship and adhere to the ethical and professional practices guidelines throughout that person's professional life. If complaints are lodged with the Board of Standards for the Certified Financial Planner™, the board can enforce remediation and even deny the professional the privilege of using the CFP credentials.

## What Certified Financial Planners™ Do

While anyone can advertise themselves to be a financial planner, only professionals who have completed the necessary education, work experience, and activities can advertise themselves as Certified Financial Planners™. The general public has begun to recognize the difference between financial planners and Certified Financial Planners™, understanding the rigorous requirements for CFP® professionals.

Certified Financial Planners™ work in many areas of the financial services sector, but a common characteristic of their work is that they usually have contact with the individual or family members who are responsible for the financial well-being of their household members. One particularly important group of CFP professionals are those who work as fee-only planners. This means that the CFP professionals are not paid by companies to sell products; they are fully employed by the individuals and families for whom they work. The fee-only CFP practitioner examines all facets of an individual or family's desires and goals for the future, since nearly every set of goals has financial underpinnings and requirements. Most families have plans for educating family members, purchasing housing, setting up savings and investing accounts, planning for retirement, understanding and taking advantage of employee benefits, and doing estate planning. Further, these family members may want to go into private business, plan for philanthropic giving, or have special needs, such as disabled family members, who need to be provided for after the deaths of the current main breadwinners. Fee-only planners may meet with an individual or family just once or twice, to set up a plan that can be acted upon by the household members. However, the more usual and desirable arrangement is that the fee-only planner sets up initial planning meetings and then meets on a regular basis with clients to ensure that the plans are being acted upon, and to change plans as circumstances in the family change and/or the marketplace offerings or economic conditions change. In these cases, a Certified Financial Planner ™ becomes part of the client's team of professionals, such as doctors or lawyers, serving an individual or family throughout the life cycle. The fee-only Certified Financial Planner™ is an expert in coordinating the pieces of a comprehensive financial plan for a given client, working in consort with other specialists such as accountants, attorneys, investment advisors, tax specialists, and so forth, as deemed appropriate for the client's needs and goals.

Many financial services businesses hire Certified Financial Planners™ to work with clients as well. Banks, credit unions, investment companies, insurance companies, mortgage companies, real estate companies, and many other financial services businesses find professionals with the CFP® to be well qualified to meet with clients about the company's products and services in the context of the client's overall financial situation. The CFP designation is a signal of the quality of the financial services professional, so from the marketing perspective, any given company may gain more credence with the public by having CFP professionals on staff.

Certified Financial Planners™ who work for sales organizations must adhere to the strict ethical guidelines of the Board of Standards, which state that the most important goal of a CFP professional is to do what is best for the client. While selling products does not violate ethical principles, selling a product to client merely to enrich the planner, without regard for the well-being of the client, is a clear violation of the CFP professional's fiduciary responsibility to the client. Ethical planners will disclose any potential conflicts of interest to the client in order to follow the profession's ethical standards.

### Employment Outlook for Financial Planning Advisers

The U.S. Bureau of Labor Statistics, in the April 2012 *Occupational Outlook Handbook*, paints a fairly rosy picture regarding the demand for financial planning advisers in general, which would include Certified Financial Planners™. The 2010 median pay for advisers was $64,750 per year, or $31.13 per hour. The entry-level educational requirement was a bachelor's degree. In 2010, there were 206,800 jobs in the United States. The job outlook for 2010 to 2020 was for a 32 percent job growth, which was much faster than average. An additional plus is that *CNN Money* named the occupation of "financial adviser" as the third top job in the United States in April 2006. One reason for this ranking was that financial advisers have the opportunity to truly help families achieve their financial goals, which can be psychologically rewarding. A second reason is that babyboomers and younger people are now responsible for their own retirement plans through programs such as Individual Retirement Accounts, 401(k)s, and other self-directed tax-preferred accounts, and many individuals feel unprepared to successfully navigate the products and financial knowledge required to achieve financial success in retirement. The demand for financial advisers was judged to be currently high and increasing in the future due to changing demographics and the demand for individual responsibility throughout the life cycle for one's own financial well-being.

*Deborah C. Haynes*

**See also:** Banking; Consumer Financial Protection Bureau (CFPB); Debt Management; Estate Planning; Investing Regulations

## References and Additional Readings

AlphabetSoup.(October26,2010).*The Wall Street Journal*.Retrievedfromhttp://www .online.wsj.com/public/resources/documents/st_CREDIT1050_20101015.htm.

Bureau of Labor Statistics. (April 26, 2012). *Occupational outlook handbook*. Retrieved from http://www.bls.gov/ooh/business-and-financial/personal-financial-ad visors.htm

Certified Financial Board of Standards, Inc. (2012). CFP board. Retrieved from http://www.CFP.net

Definition of Certified Financial Planner™—CFP®. (2013). In *Investopedia*. Retrieved from http://www.investopedia.com/terms/c/cfp.asp#axzz2HbncJhnl

Kalwarski, T., Mosher, D., Paskin, J., & Rosato, D. (April 25, 2006). 50 Best jobs in America. *CNN Money*. Retrieved from http://www.money.conn.com/magazines/moneymag/moneymap_archive/2006/05/01/8375749/index.htm

## Charity and Philanthropic Giving

Every consumer needs to make decisions regarding the allocation of his or her resources, including time and financial resources. As part of the disposal of these resources, consumers may decide to give to others. Consumers can give both money in the form of donations and time in the form of volunteering. Associated with charitable and philanthropic giving is the idea of altruism, giving of oneself for the benefit of others in a selfless manner, without the receipt or expectation of the receipt of anything valuable in return.

Many beliefs about charitable donation can be traced to ancient times. For example, charity is an important part of most major religions, including Buddhism, Christianity, Islam, and Judaism. In these traditions, sharing of one's resources with those who are less fortunate is encouraged or even obligatory, although what resources are shared and other specifics can vary widely and have been the subject of debate. In the United States in 2010, Americans contributed about two percent of their disposable income to charity.

Many believe that wealthier consumers have a responsibility to share with others. Despite this association, giving time, compassion, and money in small amounts can still make an impact. For example, during then-Senator Barack Obama's campaign for the presidency of the United States in 2008, more than half of the donations collected were of $200 or less. Over the years, many societies, including the United States, have developed strong traditions of charitable giving. No longer associated solely with giving to the poor and less fortunate members of the society, charity and philanthropic giving are defined with a much broader scope than that; in fact, charitable donations fund many programs that form the backbone of American society, including libraries, scholarships for college students, and health services for those without means.

There are several decisions consumers need to make when giving to others. First, they must decide whether to give time or money. Giving time, in the form of volunteering, allows the donor to participate directly and have a personal impact on others. It also allows the volunteer to directly observe conditions and assistance that may be needed. Others find that tax considerations provide an incentive for monetary giving. Beginning in 1917, the U.S. government established tax incentives to encourage philanthropy. Under the current tax code, if a consumer has an income of $100,000 and gives $5,000 to charitable causes, his or her adjusted gross income will be $95,000 for tax purposes.

When giving money, consumers must decide whether to give directly to an individual (e.g., a friend facing cancer treatments), to a cause (e.g., to cancer researchers at a local hospital), or to a charitable organization (e.g., the American Cancer Society). One important consideration is where a gift is likely to have the most impact, although this can be difficult to decide. If they determine to give to an organization, consumers must decide what organization to give to, a question that requires them to ask is which organizations are doing something meaningful in terms of their personal values. Other consumer decisions to be made relate to whether to distribute smaller amounts of money to several organizations or to support fewer with larger contributions.

## Scams

Consumers need to be wise and careful in the ways they decide to donate their time and money. Unfortunately, unscrupulous people find their way into charitable and philanthropic giving with a variety of dishonest methods for bilking donors out of their funds. These include posing as individuals in need when they are not and posing as charitable or nonprofit organizations when they are not. One type of financial scam frequently employed by unscrupulous organizations is to disguise themselves with names similar to those of legitimate organizations to confuse consumers. For example, the Children's Charity Fund and the Children's Defense Fund have very similar names, but very different reputations. The Children's Defense Fund is a well-established organization that allocates 81 percent of its funds to children's programs whereas the Children's Charity Fund allocates only 8 percent of its funds to children's services according to the *Charity Review*. Consumers are often not aware of these differences and they may confuse the two organizations due to the similarity of their names.

Although only about 8 percent of philanthropic giving is done over the Internet, it is a rapidly growing method for giving. However, because the information contained on a single website is all that is available to a consumer, it can be especially susceptible to scams and frauds that misdirect donations.

Another problem involves poorly run organizations that have high administrative costs, so very little funding winds up allocated to the cause. When donating it is important to know about how the charity is managed and how donations are allocated. Consumers need to find out how much is allocated to services or research how much of the administrative costs contribute to the total organizational budget. Most charities now make this information available to consumers; depending on the way the charity is incorporated, it may be required to make this information available in order to comply with state and federal laws.

Although all consumers may be exploited by fundraisers, certain vulnerable groups are often targeted specifically: the elderly, the poor, and the less educated. Several laws have been passed to protect consumers from fraud, some at the state and others at the federal level. In 2009, the FTC launched a crackdown on fake charities that led to 49 states bringing 76 actions against fraudulent organizations, individuals, and fundraising companies. Thus, when giving to charitable causes and nonprofit organizations, consumers need to investigate the status of the organization. Important questions to ask include the following. Is it registered as a nonprofit with a charitable mission? How much of the donated funds are allocated to administrative costs? How much is used for the cause? Who is leading the organization?

To summarize, consumer decisions regarding charity and philanthropic giving involve careful planning, research, and study to allocate and give time and money in a planned and strategic manner. This is necessary for donations to have the maximum impact possible on society and on the lives of others. Thus, wise decision making, from the initial choice to give time or money to the selection of reputable organizations to the size of the contribution, should be practiced by all potential donors. Ultimately, to be successful and meaningful, charitable and philanthropic giving should reflect one's beliefs, values, and have an impact on others.

*Cynthia R. Jasper*

**See also:** Better Business Bureau (BBB); Frauds and Scams

### References and Additional Readings

Federal Trade Commission. (2009). FTC announces 'operation false charity' law enforcement sweep. Retrieved from http://www.ftc.gov/opa/2009/05/chari tyfraud.shtm

Ilchman, W. F., Katz, S. N., & Queen, E. L. (1998) *Philanthropy in the world's traditions.* Bloomington: Indiana University Press.

Isakoff, M. (2008). Obama's 'good will' hunting. Retrieved from http://www.the
dailybeast.com/newsweek/2008/10/03/obama-s-good-will-hunting.html

Jasper, C. R. (2006). The role of women business owners and women executives as
philanthropists. In Shaw-Hardy, S. (Ed.). *New directions for philanthropic fundraising*. San Francisco: Wiley. 55–68.

Jasper, C. R. (2010). Women's Leadership in Philanthropy. *Leadership in nonprofit
organizations: A reference handbook, 1–2*, 242–249.

MacLaughlin, S. (2011). 5 Interesting facts from the giving USA 2011 report. Retrieved from http://www.nptrends.com/nonprofit-trends/5-interesting-facts-
from-the-giving-usa-2011-report.htm

Mathos, M. (2011). Online giving grew 35 percent in 2010 and accounted for 8
percent of all fundraising. Retrieved from http://forums.blackbaud.com/
blogs/blackbaudnews/archive/2011/02/15/online-giving-grew-35-percent-
in-2010-and-accounted-for-8-percent-of-all-fundraising.aspx

## Checks 21 Act

The Checks 21 Act, also known as the Check Clearing for the 21st Century Act went into effect in 2004. The law provided federal legislation
requiring banks to process checks electronically, eliminating the original
paper copies of checks. As a result, redeemed paper checks are no longer
returned to consumers, if paper checks are even accepted by a merchant.
These digital versions of paper checks, also known as "substitute checks,"
are processed in a variety of forms. In fact, a computer scanner or mobile
phone can be used to digitally capture an image of the check, send it to
the bank, and deposit it (aka remote deposit). This process, called trun-
cation, involves both sides of a paper check being scanned to produce a
digital image.

Consumer advocacy groups such as Consumers Union felt that the law
took away rights from consumers and provided savings to banks that
would likely not be passed on to consumers. Consumer advocates also felt
that new fees may be charged by banks that would unnecessarily hurt consumers. Banks saved money by not having to physically ship and circu-
late paper checks. Another concern was that consumers would not balance
their accounts in the same way and might face overdraft fees and bounced
checks. Because consumers were accustomed to a cushion of days before a
check cleared, they may have a habit of depositing money in their checking account after writing the check. With the new law in effect, checks are
processed almost immediately; therefore, the money must be in the account
to cover the balance. To protect consumers, the law provided for a recredit-
ing of funds if the check was paid twice, paid the wrong amount, or other
related errors.

The United States, as well as other countries in the world, has seen a severe decline in check writing. However, with the Checks 21 Act in place, the convenience for banks, coupled with consumer preferences, may preserve the usage of checks in the world banking community. So far, the Checks 21 Act has contributed to the "green movement as well as, maintained the convenience of check writing for consumers."

*Wendy Reiboldt*

**See also:** Banking; Consumers Union; Federal Deposit Insurance Commission (FDIC)

**References and Additional Readings**

Consumers Union. (2011). About us. Retrieved from Consumersunion.org

Starkey, J. (2010). Here to stay. *AFP Exchange, 30,* 16–18.

## Children's Advertising Review Unit (CARU). *See* Better Business Bureau (BBB)

## Children's Online Privacy Protection Act (COPPA)

Among the wide variety of media (e.g., telephones, radios, movies, television, and the Internet), only television and the Internet have been sources of widespread concerns related to children, resulting in regulation at the federal level. For television, there is one federal regulation, Children Television Act of 1990. In contrast, there are four federal regulations concerning children and the Internet: Children's Online Privacy Protection Act of 1998, Neighborhood Children's Internet Protection Act of 1999, Children's Internet Protection Act of 2000, and Deleting Online Predators Act of 2006. These Internet regulations are unprecedented, signifying various serious societal concerns about the negative consequences of the Internet on children and representing governmental strategies to protect children on the Internet. Among them, Children's Online Privacy Protection Act of 1998 (COPPA) is the only federal regulation focusing explicitly on online privacy, a unique, ubiquitous, significant, and complex issue regarding children's personal information online. Here, personal information refers to first and last names, home or other physical addresses, e-mail addresses, telephone numbers, social security numbers, and any other identifiers that permit the physical or online contacting of a specific individual.

A young student uses the computer in class. Congress passed both the Children's Online Privacy Protection Act (COPPA) and Children's Internet Protection Act (CIPA) to allow children to safely navigate the Internet. (morgueFile)

COPPA was enacted as a federal law in 1998 to prohibit unfair or deceptive acts or practices in connection with the collection, use, and/or disclosure of personal information from and about children under 13 on the Internet. The Children's Online Privacy Protection Rule (COPPR) was issued by the Federal Trade Commission in 1999 and became effective in 2000 to implement COPPA. The implementation of COPPA and COPPR was reviewed and reported to Congress in 2005, concluding that COPPA and COPPR have been effective in helping to protect the privacy and safety of young children online.

COPPA consists of eight sections: (1) Short Title, (2) Definitions, Regulation of (3) Unfair and Deceptive Acts and Practices in Connection with The Collection and Use of Personal Information From and about Children on the Internet, (4) Safe Harbors, (5) Actions by States, (6) Administration and Applicability of Act, (7) Review, and (8) Effective Date. It specifies regulations in Section 1303 and addresses procedures of implementing these regulations, including the self-regulatory approach to complying COPPA and COPPR.

Social networking sites are now the mainstream medium, not just for millions of adults, but for our children as well.

The Federal Trade Commission (FTC) offers some guidelines for parents to consider:

- Assist your children in understanding that information like their full names, street address, social security numbers, phone numbers, and other identifying information must be kept private.
- Assist your children in choosing a screen name that does not give away too much personal information.
- Setting up privacy settings to restrict who may access and post on your child's website.
- Explain to your children that they should be aware that whatever they post to these sites may be seen by anyone, and that whatever they may post will not ever completely disappear. Explain that in future years, school administrators, potential employers, and governmental agencies will be able see these postings.
- Be aware of how your children are getting online. As the mobile device continues to grow in popularity, more and more children are accessing the Internet with these devices rather than the home computer. It is important to understand what limitations may be placed on these devices.
- Talk to your kids about online bullying. This can take many forms from spreading false rumors to sending threatening messages. Peer pressure for this age group is significant and can have disastrous results.
- Place the computer your kids use in an open area that you are able to keep an eye on about what is going on online.
- Spend time on the same sites your kids are visiting so that you are aware of the conversations and postings.
- Encourage your children to let you know if they feel threatened. Allow them to trust their own instincts in online encounters and keep you in the loop.

*Source:* Federal Trade Commission. (2012). Safeguarding your child's future. Retrieved from http://www.ftc.gov/

Based on Section 1303, COPPA prohibits websites or other online service providers to collect personal information, such as from children, and has deemed this as an unlawful act. In order to collect, use, and/or disclose such information, websites or other online service providers are required to (1) provide a detailed public notice of collecting children's personal information and a procedure to obtain verifiable parental consent, (2) offer parents specific description and the opportunity to stop the process of collecting and using the information, (3) prohibit any incentives such as participating in a game or offering a prize to collect the information, and (4) establish and maintain reasonable procedures to protect the confidentiality, security, and integrity of the personal information collected from children.

The key features of COPPA can be summarized as (1) the target impact is to protect children's online privacy and online safety; (2) the target strategies are to set forth a set of regulations, primarily parental consent, for operators of websites and other online service providers to comply; (3) the target population is young Internet users under 13; (4) target organizations for implementing the regulations are the Federal Trade Commission (FTC).

Since 2001, the FTC has filed nearly 20 major civil penalty actions against violations of COPPA and COPPR. For example, one of the first cases was *U.S. v. Bigmailbox.com, Inc.* After being issued a warning letter to the website of *Bigmailbox.com,* specifying the compliance problems in 2000, the FTC filed a charge against the website again in 2001 for violating COPPA by collecting children's personal information such as name, home address, telephone number, and e-mail address without parental consent. To settle the charges, the company paid $35,000 in civil penalties and was ordered to delete all information collected from children. One of the recent cases was *U.S. v. Xanga.com, Inc.* The social networking website *Xanga.com* was required to pay $1 million in civil penalties for their failure to notify parents and obtain consent while creating nearly 2 million online accounts for children under 13.

While COPPA and COPPR have been implemented for over 10 years successfully in general, new challenges have been emerging. For example, when COPPA was signed into a law in 1998, Internet technologies mainly concerned websites, e-mails, message boards, chat rooms, and online games. At present, social network sites and smart mobile phones are becoming increasingly popular among young Internet users and thus have created unique challenges in applying COPPA and COPPR. For instance, recently, Danah Boyd, Eszter Hargittai, Jason Schultz, and John Palfrey, a research group in Harvard University's Berkman Center for Internet & Society, conducted a study entitled "Why Parents Help Their Children Lie to Facebook about Age: Unintended Consequences of the 'Children's Online Privacy Protection Act.'" While Facebook complies with COPPA by noticing its *Terms of Service* on its site to prohibit children under 13 from creating an account, their findings suggest that the majority of parents in the study actually knew that their children were too young to be eligible to have an account and often assisted their underage children to join Facebook. They would circumvent the under-13 restriction if it was for educational purposes and communicating with family members and friends. Here, parents' attitudes and beliefs substantially impact how to implement COPPA and COPPR, in addition to technical difficulties for verifying age and various serious legal, economic, and social concerns for verifying age.

*Zheng Yan*

**See also:** Federal Trade Commission (FTC); Privacy: Online; Social Security

### References and Additional Readings

Boyd, D., Hargittai, E., Schultz, J., & Palfrey, J. (2011). Why parents help their children lie to Facebook about age: Unintended consequences of the 'Children's Online Privacy Protection Act'. *First Monday*, *16*(11). Retrieved from http://firstmonday.org/htbin/cgiwrap/bin/ojs/index.php/fm/article/view/3850/3075

Federal Trade Commission. (2010). Implementing the Children's Online Privacy Protection Act: A report to Congress. Retrieved from http://www.ftc.gov/oia/ftccoppareport.pdf

## Cigarette Labeling Act

In 1957, the U.S. Surgeon General announced that "excessive cigarette smoking is one of the causative factors in lung cancer." In response, Senator Wallace Bennett (R-UT) introduced a bill to require health warnings on cigarette packs. This action failed. In January 1964, the Surgeon General's Advisory Committee released its famous report on *Smoking and Health*. By June of 1964, the Federal Trade Commission (FTC) had issued a Trade Regulation Rule on Cigarette Labeling and Advertising. However, regulatory action by the FTC was avoided as hearings before Congress resulted in the Federal Cigarette Labeling and Advertising Act of 1965 (P.L. 89–92). The act required all cartons and packs to carry the message: "Caution: Cigarette Smoking May Be Hazardous to Your Health." According to the act's declaration of policy, the warning was required so "the public may be adequately informed about any adverse health effects of cigarette smoking." Enforcement of the labeling provision was the responsibility of the Department of Justice. The 1965act also required the FTC to submit an annual report to Congress concerning the effectiveness of labeling, methods of cigarette advertising and marketing, and recommendations for legislation. The FTC's first report in 1967 recommended that package warnings be strengthened and extended to advertising, which the 1965 act had prohibited. In 1969, the FTC proposed rulemaking for stronger warnings, which lead to the Public Health Smoking Act of 1969 (P.L. 91–222). The old label was replaced with "Warning: The Surgeon General Has Determined that Cigarette Smoking is Dangerous to Your Health." The 1969 act also banned all cigarette advertising on radio and television, effective January 2, 1971.

During the period 1971–1986, several actions were taken to further strengthen the warning messages. The FTC and the cigarette industry entered into a voluntary plan in 1971 to disclose "tar" and nicotine levels in cigarette advertising in accordance with standardized FTC test results. In 1972, the FTC and the industry agreed to a consent decree requiring all advertising to display the health warning and specifying the size of messages, including billboards. The FTC's 1978 report to Congress recommended adoption of rotating warnings similar to a system used in Sweden. A 1980 report by the surgeon general concluded that more should be done to notify consumers of specific health hazards of smoking, and also recommended rotating warnings. The response by Congress was the Comprehensive Smoking Education Act of 1984 (P.L. 98–474), which mandated four stronger, more specific warning messages for packages and advertisements, each preceded by the phrase "Surgeon General's Warning:"

(1) Smoking Causes Lung Cancer, Heart Disease, Emphysema, and May Complicate Pregnancy; (2) Quitting Smoking Now Greatly Reduces Serious Risks to Your Health; (3) Smoking by Pregnant Women May Result in Fetal Injury, Premature Birth, and Low Birth Weight; and (4) Cigarette Smoke Contains Carbon Monoxide. Legislation enacted in 1986 extended the rotating warnings to smokeless tobacco products.

During the 1980s and 1990s, issues emerged regarding lower tar and nicotine "light" cigarettes, including compensatory behavior by smokers and the adequacy of the FTC's test method. Compensation refers to changes in smoking behaviors, whereby individuals self-regulate their nicotine intake by smoking more, inhaling deeper, and so on. This practice was predicted following the introduction of filtered cigarettes in the early 1950s. In 2000, the FTC abandoned its test method and conceded that "it's impossible to tell from the ratings the amount of tar and nicotine a smoker will get from any cigarette." In 1996, under Dr. David Kessler, the Food and Drug Administration (FDA) unsuccessfully attempted to regulate cigarettes as addictive drugs and impose restrictions designed to reduce the use of tobacco products by children, including additional advertising bans (final rule, 61 *Fed Reg* 44395, August 28, 1996; vacated by *FDA v. Brown & Williamson Tobacco Corp., et al.*, 529 U.S. 120, March 21, 2000). Beginning in 2001–2002, several bills were introduced in Congress to provide the FDA with certain authority to regulate tobacco products. A 2007 report by the Institute of Medicine entitled, "Ending the Tobacco Problem: A Blueprint for the Nation," concluded that FDA regulation would advance tobacco control efforts. The Family Smoking Prevention and Tobacco Control Act (P.L. 111–31), signed into law by President Barack Obama on June 22, 2009, establishes this authority by creating a new chapter in the Federal Food, Drug, and Cosmetic Act. Title II of the Family Smoking Act requires nine larger, stronger warning labels for tobacco packages and advertising, including color graphics depicting health problems that may result from tobacco use. The FDA also can dictate product ingredients and overrule new products through premarket approval. Although cigarette advertising was restricted under the Master Settlement Agreement of 1998, the FDA is authorized to further limit any advertising that targets children or misleads the public, "consistent with and to the full extent permitted by the First Amendment."

Despite a long history, debate continues over warning labels for tobacco products. For example, there is little rigorous evidence on the effectiveness of the regulations. Quasiexperimental studies are difficult to implement, given the uniform nature of the requirements and numerous coincident changes in the marketing and pricing of tobacco products. Two econometric studies of cigarette demand examined the warnings added during 1965–1972, but neither study found a statistically significant effect. Similar findings have been reported for bans of tobacco advertising, where cross-country comparisons are possible. A 1989 report by the surgeon general, "Reducing the Health Consequences of Smoking," concluded that consumers paid little attention to the pre-1985 warnings. Two views have developed about the effectiveness of labels and warnings. The skeptical view is that most individuals are well informed about the potential consequences of smoking, so warning labels are only an incremental addition to health information. The alternative view is that small text warnings placed on the sides of cigarette packs have low levels of salience for many smokers. Studies of Canadian smokers, where large graphic warnings have been required since 2001, suggest pictorial messages have measurable effects on public awareness of the adverse effects of smoking. However, the extent to which increased awareness translates into changes in cigarette consumption and smoking prevalence is more difficult to quantify.

Current demographic-related statistics about cigarette smoking and the U.S. population:

**Overview:**

-More than 80 percent of adult smokers begin smoking before 18 years of age.

-An estimated 45.3 million people, or 19.3 percent of all adults (aged 18 years or older), in the United States smoke cigarettes.

-Cigarette smoking is the leading cause of preventable death in the United States, accounting for approximately 443,000 deaths, or one of every five deaths, each year.

**Gender:**

-21.5 percent of adult men

-17.3 percent of adult women

**Age:**

-19.5 percent of high school students

-20.1 percent of adults aged 18–24 years

-22 percent of adults aged 25–44 years

-21.1 percent of adults aged 45–64 years

-9.5 percent of adults aged 65 years and older

**Race/Ethnicity**

-31.4 percent of American Indians/Alaska Natives (non-Hispanic)

-9.2 percent of Asians (non-Hispanic; excludes Native Hawaiians and Pacific Islanders)

-20.6 percent of blacks (non-Hispanic)

-12.5 percent of Hispanics

-21 percent of whites (non-Hispanic)

**Education**

-45.2 percent of adults with a GED diploma

-33.8 percent of adults with 9–11 years of education

-23.8 percent of adults with a high school diploma

-9.9 percent of adults with an undergraduate college degree

-6.3 percent of adults with a postgraduate college degree

**Poverty Status**

-28.9 percent of adults who live below the poverty level

-18.3 percent of adults who live at or above the poverty level

*Source:* Centers for Disease Control and Prevention. (March 14, 2012). Adult cigarette smoking in the United States: Current estimate. Retrieved from http://www.cdc.gov/

*Jon P. Nelson*

**See also:** Federal Trade Commission (FTC); Food and Drug Administration (FDA); Health and Healthcare; Surgeon General

### References and Additional Readings

Hammond, D. (2011). Health warning messages on tobacco products: A review. *Tobacco Control.* doi: 10.1136/tc.2010.037630.

Nelson, J. P. (2006). Cigarette advertising regulation: A meta-Analysis. *International Review of Law and Economics, 26,* 195–226.

Redhead, C. S., & Burrows, V. K. (2009). *FDA tobacco regulation: The family smoking prevention and tobacco control act of 2009* (R40475). Washington, DC: Congressional Research Service. Retrieved from http://assets.opencrs.com/rpts/R40475_20090528.pdf

## Class Action Law Suits

The Federal Rules of Civil Procedure underwent major revisions in the 1960s, prompting the rise of the modern class action. The class action is, in the words of the U.S. Supreme Court, "an exception to the usual rule that litigation is conducted by and on behalf of the individual named parties only" (*Califano v. Yamasaki,* 442 U.S. 682, 700–01 (1979)). Federal Rule

Several high-profile class action law suits have been filed on behalf of consumers over the years. These include a wide array of issues such as silicone breast implants, financial fraud, sexual harassment, and tobacco-related health hazards. (iStockPhoto.com)

23 provides, "One or more members of a class may sue or be sued as representative parties on behalf of all members only if: (1) the class is so numerous that joinder of all members is impracticable; (2) there are questions of law or fact common to the class; (3) the claims or defenses of the representative parties are typical of the claims or defenses of the class; and (4) the representative parties will fairly and adequately protect the interests of the class" (Fed. R. Civ. P. 23).

The two most commonly pursued types of class actions are known as 23(b)(2) and 23(b)(3) actions. The key differences between these two types of certifications are that 23(b)(2) actions mostly provide injunctive or declaratory relief, in other words, nonmonetary relief. Money damages are sometimes allowed as incidental relief to an injunctive or declarative remedy. Rule 23(b)(3) actions have no limits to their relief. Correspondingly, 23(b)(2) actions do not require notice to all of the potential plaintiffs in the class, nor do such potential plaintiffs have the right to opt out and pursue their own legal remedies. Rather, the court has discretion over whether plaintiffs need to be notified under a 23(b)(2) action. If notice is not given, a plaintiff might be unknowingly barred from bringing suit in an unrelated action arising out of the same facts. A certified 23(b)(3) action, on the other hand, requires the lawyer bringing the action to notify all potential plaintiffs and allow them the choice to opt out of the class and thereby preserve their claims. The notice requirement of a 23(b)(3) action is potentially costly and burdensome for the plaintiff's lawyer, but that burden is weighed against the fact that the remedy includes all types of damages, including monetary damages, so every plaintiff needs to choose whether to join the action or opt out.

The revisions to the Federal Rules of Civil Procedure were based on changing social developments in the 1960s that valued stronger regulation of securities and other financial markets, as well as a more focused attention to civil rights, environmental rights, and increasing attention placed on consumer protection movements. As envisioned, the class action has been a valuable tool for supporting such rights. *Brown v. Board of Education*, the landmark case striking down school segregation, was a class action lawsuit. In fact, according to congressional testimony discussing the original impetus for the reform of the federal rules that ushered in the modern use of the class action procedure, "[i]f there was a single, undoubted goal of the committee, the energizing force which motivated the whole rule, it was the firm determination to create a class action system which could deal with civil rights and, explicitly, segregation." (The Class Action Fairness Act of 1999: Hearing on S. 353 Before the Subcommittee on Administrative Oversight and the Courts of the Senate Comm. of the Judiciary, 106th Cong. 60 [1999] [statement of John P. Frank]).

The lawsuits that inspired the movies *Erin Brockovich* (holding Pacific Gas & Electric accountable for leaking toxic Chromium 6 into groundwater and poisoning town residents) and *North Country* (sexual harassment lawsuit brought by female miners) were both class actions. The toxic tort case portrayed in the book *A Civil Action*, as well as both the Exxon Valdez oil spill litigation and the more recent BP gulf oil spill litigation have been handled through class actions. High-profile financial fraud cases like those brought against Enron and Worldcom were also class actions.

Essentially this type of representative litigation allows citizens to aggregate small individual claims that otherwise might not warrant individual litigation yet arise from some unlawful activity, usually on a widespread scale. Through the class action procedural mechanism, plaintiffs gain access to the courts in cases where a defendant may have gained a substantial benefit through small injuries to a large number of people. By aggregating their individual claims, a group of small injuries takes on the form of a much larger injury. Class actions also allow citizens to be exposed to certain types of widespread abuses through the litigation processes of discovery, grab the attention of the media, and change corporate practices as well as educate other consumers about the possibility of injury. It is, in essence, a tool that was conceived to level the playing field between a large, mostly unorganized citizenry against organized corporate or otherwise powerful interests. However, a combination of recent legislation and Supreme Court decisions has called into question the continuing viability of class action litigation.

In 2005, Congress enacted the "Class Action Fairness Act" (CAFA). CAFA was the centerpiece of a sweeping political agenda of "tort reform" designed to limit people's rights to access the courts. This law limits the rights of class action plaintiffs by transferring many class action cases based on state consumer protection laws from state court to federal court. Proponents of CAFA assumed that the federal court would be more limited in its certification of class actions. Federal judges tend to enforce state laws conservatively when state law-based class actions are removed to federal court under CAFA. Federal courts also are more likely to find that federal regulatory schemes created to protect consumers preempt state consumer protection laws. Such results in federal court would deny a state citizen's right to access its own state laws. Consumer protection is traditionally an area governed by state laws so CAFA has a direct effect on limiting consumer class actions and in fact it was the consumer class action that was most directly targeted by CAFA.

CAFA also gives the court greater scrutiny over class action settlements. By making the procedural hurdles to bringing a class action lawsuit higher, manufacturers are then relieved of what was a powerful incentive to provide safe products, deal fairly with consumers, and curb environmental pollution because they are less accountable through the civil justice system. It is unclear whether CAFA has proved to be the prodefendant tort reform that its proponents advocated for, but it is uniformly agreed that CAFA has resulted in many class actions being transferred from state court to federal court, clogging up the federal docket and delaying judgments for many. At least one empirical study has shown that the majority of judges have not embraced CAFA as its proponents hoped (Kevin M. Clermont & Theodore Eisenberg, CAFA Judicata: A Tale of Waste and Politics, 156 U. Pa. L. Rev. 1553, 1564, 1581–82 (2008)).

With CAFA complicating the ability of citizens to bring consumer protection class actions against a corporate practice causing small harms to large groups of people, state attorneys general have attempted to step in the shoes of their citizen constituents and bring cases on behalf of state citizens harmed under state consumer protection laws. State attorneys general, concerned that federal courts sometimes weaken their state consumer protection laws when interpreting them in federal court, can bring "parens patriae" cases to address widespread consumer injuries in their state. The federal courts are currently split as to whether such suits brought by attorneys general are subject to CAFA. The Fourth Circuit held in *McGraw v. CVS Pharmacy, Inc.* that the lawsuit, brought by the state attorney general of West Virginia alleging certain pharmacies violated state consumer protection laws by selling generic drugs at brand name drug prices, was a classic parens patriae action and not subject to CAFA. The 5th Circuit, however, held in *Caldwell v. Allstate Insurance Co.* that a lawsuit brought by the attorney general of Louisiana alleging insurance companies violated state consumer protection laws by price fixing was a private class action disguised as a parens patriae lawsuit and as such it was subject to the requirements of CAFA.

In addition to the legislative limitations imposed by CAFA, class actions have been weakened further through court decisions. The Supreme Court issued two opinions relating generally to the continued viability of class actions during its 2010–2011 term. The first, *Wal-Mart v. Dukes*, enforced limits on how groups of individuals may be certified as a workplace discrimination class action for purposes of a lawsuit alleging back pay, along with other damages. In that case, plaintiffs attempted to certify a class of 1.5 million female employees of Wal-Mart who were alleging gender discrimination at their employment in violation of Title VII of the Civil Rights Act under Rule 23(b)(2). Specifically the plaintiffs argued that there was a disparate discriminatory impact on female employees at Wal-Mart stores when it came to applying discretion as to pay and promotions. The court held unanimously that the monetary damages requested as a remedy were not incidental to injunctive relief and thus insufficient for a 23(b)(2) action.

A majority of the court went on to hold that there was not a common question of law or fact to allow any class action suit at all in this case because Wal-Mart gave local managers discretion over such employment decisions. According to Rule 23(a)(2), a party seeking class action certification must prove that the class has "questions of law or fact common to the class." A 5–4 majority did not find that the claims of the 1.5 million women gave rise to a common question of law or fact. The court was concerned that although they might share the question of whether they had been discriminated against in their employment, there could not be a common answer to that question given the manager's discretion at the local level. Because each woman could have been discriminated against differently and have a unique remedy, the court felt there was not enough commonality between the claims. The minority disagreed, arguing that only one common issue of fact was required under the federal rules and the claim of gender discrimination was, by itself, enough to pass the Rule 23(a)(2) requirement. The minority then would have remanded the lawsuit to be certified as a Rule 23(b)(3) action, allowing for the monetary damages regarding back pay and denial of employment opportunities and requiring notice and the chance to opt out for the 1.5 million plaintiffs. After *Dukes*, many lawyers expect to see a large drop in Title VII class action certifications and subsequent litigation hurdles for gender discrimination cases against large corporate employers. Gender discrimination class actions against Costco, Best Buy, Goldman Sachs, Toshiba, and Cigna have already been adversely affected by the *Dukes* ruling.

Another recent Supreme Court decision addressing the role of class actions in future litigation was the 2011 decision, *AT&T vs. Concepcion*. In the AT&T case, plaintiff attempted to join a class action complaining that AT&T was charging sales tax on the "free" phones provided with their cell phone contracts. Plaintiff's cell phone contract had an arbitration provision and the issue before the court was whether the arbitration provision was unconscionable because it specifically disallowed for "class-wide arbitration." The Supreme Court ruled that the Federal Arbitration Act of 1925 guides this dispute and the act does not condition the enforceability of an arbitration provision on the availability of class-wide relief.

What this means for consumers going forward is that the arbitration provisions in consumer contracts are binding even if they prohibit class-wide arbitration or other forms of aggregating claims and/or remove the possibility of joining claims with others similarly harmed. Most lawyers expect to see many more arbitration provisions in the coming months and years, and such provisions can be inserted into consumer contracts of any kind. Since these types of consumer harms tend to consist of many very small financial burdens over a large group of people (in the AT&T case, the amount of sales tax levied was roughly $30 for each individual contract holder), in the absence of aggregate dispute resolution, many small claims will go unresolved. The claims that do go to arbitration are likely to not fare well for plaintiffs. For example, California state records showed that plaintiffs won just 0.2 percent of the arbitration cases that went forward through one of the nation's largest private arbitration firms over a four-year period. (*Complaint at 2, People v. Nat'l Arbitration Forum, Inc.,* No. CGC-08-473569, Cal. S. Ct. (2008).)

Criticisms of class action lawsuits are often based on the disputed notion that such cases result in excessive fees for the attorneys. A comprehensive study by law professors Theodore Eisenberg and Geoffrey P. Miller examined 370 class action lawsuits that settled between the years 1993 and 2002. In those cases, the median attorney fee was 21.9 percent of the recovery, significantly less than typical one-third awarded in a personal injury case. In consumer class actions, the median fee was only 13 percent of the recovery.

*Amy Widman*

**See also:** Arbitration; Brockovich, Erin; Department of Education (DOE); Environmental Protection Agency (EPA); Mediation; Supreme Court

### References and Additional Readings

Cornell University Law School. (n.d.). Federal rules of civil procedure. Rule 23: Class actions. Fed. R. Civ. P. 23. Retrieved from http://www.law.cornell.edu/rules/frcp/rule_23

Eisenberg, T., & Miller, G. (2004). Attorney fees in class action settlements: An empirical study. *Journal of Empirical Legal Studies, 1*(1).

GPO. (2005). Class action fairness act of 2005, Pub. L. 109–2, 119 Stat. 4. Retrieved from http://www.gpo.gov/fdsys/pkg/PLAW-109publ2/pdf/PLAW-109publ2.pdf

Supreme Court of the United States. (2011a). *Wal-Mart v. Dukes* (131 S. Ct. 2541). Retrieved from http://scholar.google.com/scholar_case?case=18268052394732696129&q=Wal-Mart+v.+Dukes+(131+S.+Ct.+2541+(2011)).&hl=en&as_sdt=2,5&as_vis=1

Supreme Court of the United States. (2011b). *AT&T v. Concepcion* (131 S. Ct. 17402011). Retrieved from http://scholar.google.com/scholar_case?case=17088816341526709934&q=AT%26T+v.+Concepcion+(131+S.+Ct.+17402011)).&hl=en&as_sdt=2,5&as_vis=1

**Clayton Act**. *See* Sherman Antitrust Act

## Commission on Civil Rights

The modern civil rights movement began in 1948 when President Harry S. Truman signed Executive Order 9981, which established the policy of the president to have equality of treatment and opportunity for all people in the armed services. In 1954, the Supreme Court, in a landmark case known as *Brown v. Board of Education of Topeka, Kansas,* deemed segregation in public schools as unconstitutional. Within a few years following, Rosa Parks, Martin Luther King Jr., and several key others played instrumental roles in launching a year-long boycott, resulting in successful bus desegregation, and essentially kicking off the birth of the Civil Rights Movement. The Civil Rights Act of 1957, as sent to Congress by President Eisenhower, created the U.S. Commission on Civil Rights. This act established the right to investigate civil rights violations and established a Civil Rights Division in the Department of Labor (DOL). Though there were several limitations of the act, it served as the critical foundation for more far-reaching and powerful legislation. By 1964, the 24th Amendment abolished the poll tax, which originally had been in place to make it difficult for poor black persons to vote. During the same year, President Johnson signed the Civil Rights Act of 1964, the most noteworthy piece of civil rights legislation since the 1800s.

Today, the U.S. Commission on Civil Rights is an "independent, bipartisan, fact finding federal agency" whose mission "is to inform the development of national civil rights policy and enhance enforcement of federal civil rights laws." It does this through examination of alleged discrimination and by playing a critical role in the advancement of civil rights. The commission has eight commissioners, each serving a six-year term. Four are chosen by Congress, and four are chosen by the president; Senate confirmation is not required. The president has the power to remove a commissioner for malfeasance in office or neglect of duty, without consultation with Congress. The president also selects the chair and vice chair, with majority approval from the commissioners. Because of the bipartisan nature of the commission, no more than four members may be from the same political party.

In addition to the national office, there are six regional offices, as shown in Table 6.

There are also state advisory committee (SAC) for each state and the District of Columbia. These SACs are comprised of "citizen volunteers" who have experience with and familiarity around civil rights issues. The

**Table 6**    State Advisory Committee (SAC) Regional Offices of the United States Civil Rights Commission

Central Regional Office (CRO): Alabama, Arkansas, Iowa, Kansas, Louisiana, Mississippi, Missouri, Nebraska, and Oklahoma.

Eastern Regional Office (ERO): Connecticut, Delaware, District of Columbia, Maine, Maryland, Massachusetts, New Hampshire, New Jersey, New York, Pennsylvania, Rhode Island, Vermont, Virginia, and West Virginia.

Western Regional Office (WRO): Alaska, Arizona, California, Hawaii, Idaho, Nevada, Oregon, Texas, and Washington.

Southern Regional (SRO): Florida, Georgia, Kentucky, North Carolina, South Carolina, and Tennessee.

Rocky Mountain Regional Office (RMRO): Colorado, Montana, New Mexico, North Dakota, South Dakota, Utah, and Wyoming.

Midwestern Regional Office (MWRO): Illinois, Indiana, Michigan, Minnesota, Ohio, and Wisconsin.

*Source:* These Committees are in addition to the 51 SACs (for each state and the District of Columbia)

commissioners oversee the advisory committees' two-year appointments, with terms of service ranging from 2 to 10 years normally. The commissioners also assure that the composition of the committees is diverse, in terms of skills, backgrounds, experiences, perspectives, and others. As cited on the Commission on Civil Rights website, the volunteer SAC members perform the following functions toward the commission's mission by

- holding public briefings, issuing press releases, making information publicly available on their website, and providing a complaint referral service to promote greater public awareness of civil rights issues, protections, and enforcement;

- conducting hearings on critically important civil rights issues, including issuing subpoenas for the production of documents and the attendance of witnesses;

- publishing significant studies and reports on a wide range of the civil rights issues, that typically include findings and recommendations, to inform and advise policymakers; and

- sustaining advisory committee involvement in national program planning to strengthen fact finding by broadening the scope of the research to include state and local perspectives and data.

The inspector general, from the U.S. Government Accountability Office is also the inspector general of the Commission on Civil Rights. It is the responsibility of the inspector general to conduct "audits and investigations relating to programs and operations administered or financed by the Commission." It is also his or her responsibility to advise Congress and keep them apprised of potential abuses, frauds, or other shortcomings. The inspector general provides recommended actions to correct any issues.

The Commission on Civil Rights has evolved over time, and has seen differing levels of power under different past presidents and key legislators. For example, former Senator Edward Kennedy (Democrat—Massachusetts) introduced the Civil Rights Act of 2008 that proposed several provisions, including ensuring that federal funds are not used to subsidize discrimination and that there exists improved accountability for violations of civil rights among workers. On the Commission on Civil Rights website, there is a complaint referral service procedure for consumers wishing to lodge a complaint. Recent reports and highlights from the commission's accomplishments surround issues such as bullying, redistricting the Census lines, the Black Panthers, immigration, healthcare disparities, among myriad other topics.

*For additional information, refer to the Primary Source Appendix: First session of the 85th Congress of the United States.*

*Wendy Reiboldt and Melanie Horn Mallers*

**See also:** Activism; Boycotts; Department of Education (ED); Department of Housing and Urban Development (HUD); Department of Labor (DOL); Equal Employment Opportunity Commission (EEOC); Sexual Harassment

### References and Additional Readings

Berry, M. F. (2009). *And justice for all.* Random House Digital.

Freedman, S. G. (2009). 50 years of struggle. *The New York Times, B18.*

U.S. Commission on Civil Rights. (2013). About us. Retrieved from http://www.usccr.gov

U.S. Congress. Public Law 85–315, 85th Congress, H.R. 6127 (Civil Rights Act of 1957), September 9, 1957. NAACP Records, Manuscript Division, Library of Congress (111.00.00) [Digital ID # na0111p1]

## Commodity Futures Trading Commission (CFTC)

The U.S. Commodity Futures Trading Commission (CFTC) was founded in 1974 with the passing of the Commodity Future Trading Commission Act, signed into law by President Ford. At that time, agriculture futures trading was the focus. Prior to the act, independent organizations and regulations existed covering a variety of commodities (i.e., wool, eggs, butter, metals, grains, cotton, pork bellies, etc.).

## What Are Commodities?

"A commodity is a good that is normally sold and/or produced by a number of different companies and has the same quality regardless of which company sells it. There are ninety-six different commodities that are traded on commodity exchanges throughout the world. What makes a commodity different from a product is that there is no product differentiation. Things like precious metals, agricultural products, and other raw materials are considered commodities. Commodities are only traded on commodity exchanges, just like stocks are only traded on stock markets, and these exchanges do much more than just facilitate the trade in commodities, they also enforce any regulations and rules in place to govern the trading process involving commodities."

Note: Trading commodities can be risky, just like stock trading. Commodities have different levels of risk and these can fluctuate over time.

*Source:* Biostockspro.com. (2013). What are commodities? Retrieved from http://www. biostockspro.com

Since 1974, the coverage of the commission has changed and evolved with the American market. The mission, according to the website, "is to protect market users and the public from fraud, manipulation, abusive practices and systemic risk related to derivatives that are subject to the Commodity Exchange Act, and to foster open, competitive, and financially sound markets."

The commission is comprised of four commissioners, and the chairman under which other offices operate (i.e., chief economist, clearing and risk, data and technology, enforcement, international affairs, market oversight, swap dealer and intermediary oversight). Regional offices are also operating in Chicago, Kansas City, and New York.

The most recent act overseen by the CFTC is the Dodd–Frank Act, which is a significant reform. CFTC Chairman Gary Gensler noted "The Commission looks forward to implementing the Dodd–Frank bill to lower risk, promote transparency and protect the American public."

*Wendy Reiboldt*

**See also:** Dodd–Frank Wall Street Reform and Consumer Protection Act; Investing Regulations; Securities Exchange Commission (SEC)

### References and Additional Readings

Commodity Futures Trading Commission. (2013). About the CFTC. Retrieved from http://www.cftc.gov/index.htm

Erb, C.B., & Harvey, C.R. (2006). The strategic and tactical value of commodities futures. *Financial Analysts Journal, 62*, 69–97.

Fabozzi, R., Fuss, R., & Kaiser, D. (eds). (2008). *The handbook of commodity investing.* New York: Wiley.

## Community Mental Health Centers (CMHC) Act

The Community Mental Health Centers (CMHC) Act of 1963 is federal legislation that provided funding to communities to create mental health centers. These centers were developed to provide treatment for patients that have been hospitalized. The CMHC Act is a representation of the shift of control over the community mental health system to the federal government from the states. The CMCH was based on the concern of a large population of patients in state hospitals and a need for community-based models that were more humane.

Prior to the development of the CMHC Act of 1963, there were several contributing adjustments made by Congress. In 1946, the National Mental Health Act was passed establishing the National Institute of Mental Health (NIMH). NIMH provided aid to states in order to address mental health, develop and train mental health professionals, as well as to promote and conduct research for mental health.

During a conference on mental health, in 1953, came the recommendation for a study to develop national standards to treat those with a mental illness. Due to concerns about mental health treatment, Congress agreed to sponsor a study and on July 28, 1955, the Mental Health Study Act was passed. The study was conducted by the Joint Commission on Mental Illness and Health. In 1960 the joint commission released the report, "Action for Mental Health," which suggested building on the community clinic model already utilized by the state governments.

In 1963, President John F. Kennedy addressed the findings in front of Congress. During the address, President Kennedy suggested poverty as a cause to mental illness. As a result, he called for community prevention specifically directed toward low-income people. He then motioned that over a 10-year period there would be a reduction in state hospital populations by 50 percent. President Kennedy then formed an interagency task force on mental health.

In 1962, the task force released their findings that proposed to establish a federal grant program to create a national network of community mental health centers. Both President Kennedy and Congress chose to follow the recommendations from the task force instead of those from the Action for Mental Health.

Before the CMHC Act was adopted, psychiatric professionals were divided on how to organize and deliver mental health services. One group preferred to focus on prevention, education, and community care, which was encompassed in the public health model. The first group had the support from the Kennedy administration, the task force, community psychiatrist, and community mental health activist. The group blamed the state government for the failure of the mental health system and the abuse and neglect of psychiatric patients. The second group supported the expansion of state hospital systems and state government control of community services in the medical model. The second group developed an alliance with the American Medical Association (AMA) and state government administrators. Through the support and need for change, the CMHC Act was signed into law on October 31, 1963.

Although, there has been a large regression of CMHC, the goal of servicing low-income patients with serious and persistent mental illnesses has remained. However, CMHCs are often in a bind since they are likely to be understaffed and lack funding. Today CMHC services vary depending on the center. Some examples follow.

The Tri-County Mental Health Services (TCMHS) of Lewiston Main has been operating since 1951. The services provided include outpatient services, substance abuse counseling, specialized children's services, geriatric services, intensive case management, community support service, residential care, community support service, residential care, crisis stabilization, emergency service, day treatment and referrals to inpatient services. Northwestern Mental Health Center (NWMHC) has been providing services in Minnesota since 1958. NWMHC emphasizes services on adults with serious and persistent mental illness and seriously emotionally disturbed children. At NWMHC there are counseling services for children, families, and adults, family-based services, services for adults with long-term mental health needs, mental health services for the homeless, psychological evaluations, intensive treatment for sex offenders that have been sexually abused.

Another state-based example is in California, where the Mental Health Services Act (MHSA), also known as Proposition 63, was passed in 2004. The act provided the California Department of Mental Health (DMH) with increased funding, personnel, and other resources to support county mental health programs and monitor the progress of statewide goals. In order to implement MHSA, DMH has planned to divide the six components of the act into phases of development. The components include community services and supports, capital facilities and technological needs, workforce education and training, prevention and early intervention, and innovation.

The CMHC Act was able to set a foundation for the human treatment of those with mental illness. Although there it has had its faults, it has made a significant contribution to the mental health field.

*Olivia Zavala*

**See also:** Congress; Kennedy, John F.; McKinney–Vento Homeless Assistance Act; Social Services

### References and Additional Readings

Hartley, D., Bird D. C., Lambert, D., & Coffin, J. (2002). The role of community mental health centers as rural safety net providers. Retrieved from http://www.ru ralhealthresearch.org/projects/156/

Kanel, K. (2008). *An overview of the human services*. Boston, MA: Lahaska Press.

Mental Health Services Oversight and Accountability Commission. (2012). About us. Retrieved from http://www.mhsoac.ca.gov

## Complaint Filing

Consumers have the right to know what they will get before they pay for a product or service; to get what they paid for; and to have the seller or service provider listen to their complaints and make good on undelivered promises. While many companies have consumer-friendly complaint resolution processes in place, redress will not occur unless a dissatisfied consumer first complains and demands action. Consumers with legitimate gripes have a far better chance of getting their issues resolved to their satisfaction if they understand how to complain effectively and use the tools at their disposal.

Generally speaking, the complaint process should begin with a phone call, a letter, or an e-mail to the business as soon as possible after the issue arises. Time is of the essence, since in some cases, especially when there is a billing dispute, the business may not be legally liable if the complaint is not made within a particular time period. Also, individual return, exchange and refund policies can vary widely. If a complaint is received after the deadline, the company may be within its rights to refuse to resolve the issue to the consumer's satisfaction. Those who plan to take their complaint to the next level—a small claims lawsuit, for example—will be able to build a stronger case by showing they attempted to contact the company in a timely manner.

It's important that all communications between the consumer and the business—whether electronic, paper, or oral—be tracked. Letters, whether mailed or e-mailed, create a written record that may be useful in the future (e.g., as part of a legal case) and they may even preserve a consumer's rights under the law. Mailed letters should be sent, certified mail or return receipt requested.

A consumer who is aware of his or her rights is in a better position to complain effectively and is more likely to achieve the most advantageous outcome possible. Many states have laws that provide additional or stronger consumer protections than federal law. To learn what their rights are, consumers can conduct an Internet search for key words such as "consumer rights" plus the name of their state. There also are groups that help consumers understand and exercise their rights. They include private companies such as the Better Business Bureau; nonprofit organizations such as Consumer Action and Consumers Union; government agencies such as the Federal Trade Commission (FTC) or a state's public utilities commission or insurance department; each state's attorney general; state and local consumer affairs departments; district attorneys; consumer advocates employed by the media (action lines); and nonprofit legal assistance organizations, private attorneys, and legal self-help resources such as Nolo.

If a consumer is not satisfied with the customer service representative or manager's response to his or her grievance, escalating the complaint to the company owner, the CEO or another high-level executive may achieve better results since these company members may be more sensitive to the firm's image and in a better position to find a resolution. If this doesn't work, the consumer's next step may be to complain to a third party or consider legal action. Businesses that ignore most complaints often resolve issues that are sent to government agencies, consumer groups, business associations, action lines, or other third parties that are likely to have sufficient expertise, sophistication, and resources to cause problems for the business.

Legal action is a last resort. Usually, the money involved in consumer cases is not enough to involve a lawyer, and legal action can take a long time. Small claims court is an appropriate place to settle many consumer cases, and it doesn't require an attorney. Sometimes just notifying the business, by letter, of the intention to sue is enough to change its mind about resolving a complaint. Mediation is another option, but both parties must agree to participate.

Technology has helped level the playing field for consumers. Television, radio, newspaper, and online "action lines," which have become quite popular, are able to pressure a business into resolving a complaint if it doesn't want the issue played out in front of a large audience. Online forums, blogs, review sites, and social media have made it possible for aggrieved consumers to share complaints, write reviews, and shame a business publicly. In response, many companies appear to be more willing to resolve complaints in the consumer's favor in an effort to limit bad publicity.

On the other end of the spectrum are companies that have responded with lawsuits against consumers who wage a public battle. Known as SLAPP suits—strategic lawsuit against public participation—these legal actions have been at least somewhat effective in silencing individuals and groups who fear being sued. To protect themselves from retaliation, consumers should never post anything they cannot prove or defend in court, as they could face legal action from the business if they go too far or make false claims. Even if the consumer wins the case, it can be costly to defend a lawsuit. Adequate liability coverage on a rental or homeowners insurance policy can help protect consumers from such lawsuits.

It's important that consumers be able to recognize when the complaint they have is actually an issue of fraud. In such a case, complaining to the business likely won't get a customer anywhere. However, filing a complaint with the proper authorities—the FTC or the attorney general in the state where the business is located, for example—could result in capture of the fraudsters or financial restitution. While the FTC does not resolve individual consumer complaints, it enters all complaints it receives into Consumer Sentinel, a secure online database that is used by thousands of civil and criminal law enforcement authorities worldwide. At the very least, notifying the FTC and law enforcement agencies can help them educate and forewarn other consumers who could become victims of the same scam.

*Monica Steinisch*

**See also:** Attorney General Office (AG); Better Business Bureau (BBB); Consumer Bill of Rights; Departments of Consumer Affairs (DCA); Federal Trade Commission (FTC); Insurance Commissioners; Nader, Ralph; Public Utilities Commission

## References and Additional Readings

Consumer Action. (2011). *How to complain.* San Francisco: Consumer Action.

Federal Citizen Information Center. (2011). *2011 Consumer action handbook.* Washington, DC: General Services Administration.

Warner, R. (2008). *Everybody's guide to small claims court.* Berkeley, CA: Nolo.

## Confidentiality

Confidentiality relates to the concept of privacy. Siegel (1979) defines it as "the freedom of individuals to choose for themselves the time and the circumstances under which and the extent to which their beliefs, behaviors, and opinions are to be shared or withheld from others" (p. 251). The ethical standard of confidentiality practiced by mental health counselors, social workers, psychologists, and other helpers is meant to reassure clients that they have no fear of disclosure from this helper. It allows clients to open up to helpers. When clients are open and honest, helpers may meet their needs more effectively.

The legal counterpart to the ethical concept of confidentiality is referred to as privilege. This is the term used in court actions, which "refers to a rule in evidence law that provides a litigant with the right to withhold evidence in a legal proceeding that was originally communicated in confidence" (Swoboda et al., 1978, 449). Privileged communication exists in professional relationships that require mutual trust such as that between client and attorney, therapist and client, doctor and patient, and priest and church member.

When confidentiality is broken, a professional may be considered to have engaged in unprofessional conduct and may be subject to disciplinary action such as suspended license or mandatory education courses on ethical standards. Many states have legal statutes that make violation of confidentiality a misdemeanor and if someone is found guilty he or she may be imprisoned or required to pay a fine, or both.

Privacy for people receiving services in any healthcare organization is such an important issue that Congress passed legislation in 1996 designed to standardize exactly how information might be disclosed by healthcare providers nationwide. The Health Insurance Portability and Accountability Act, also known as HIPAA, includes four components that aim to streamline communication among healthcare providers and afford patients more rights. The first component, Privacy Requirements creates rights for patients concerning how their health information is used and disclosed by

---

### Confidentiality in Human Services: Influential Codes of Ethics

- Code of Ethics, the American Counseling Association (ACA, 2005).
- Ethical Principles of Psychologists and Code of Conduct, American Psychological Association (APA, 2002)
- Code of Ethics, National Association of Social Workers (NASW, 1999)
- AAMFT Code of Ethics, American Association for Marriage and Family Therapy (AAMFT, 2001)

healthcare providers. It limits what a healthcare provider can do with a patient's health information without that patient's knowledge and consent. It also sets up standards that require healthcare providers to keep patient information confidential and secure. While most human service and healthcare institutions have been practicing under ethical codes requiring the confidential treatment of patient information, this act ensures that all providers in all states adhere to strict privacy standards. The other three components provide standards regarding security of information, how to secure electronic transactions and sets up National identifier requirements for healthcare providers.

### Exceptions to Confidentiality

While it is true that every attempt should be made to ensure that recipients of human services feel that their disclosures are private, there are some situations in which breeching this confidentiality code is necessary. Some situations require that helpers break confidentiality, others leave it to the helper's discretion. Common sense dictates that confidentiality ends where public peril begins.

Since the passage of the Child Abuse Prevention and Treatment Act in 1974, all states in the nation have been required to set up standards for the identification, treatment, and prevention of child abuse. This created mandatory reporting standards for professionals who engage in the care or treatment of minors. Likewise, after the passage of the Elder Abuse and Dependent Adult Civil Protection Act, states set up mandates that required professionals who intervene with the elderly or disabled adult populations to report suspected instances of abuse to appropriate agencies. Where to make a child abuse report or an elderly or disabled adult abuse report varies from state to state. Urban areas usually have agencies specifically designed to manage abuse reports, while small rural areas may depend on law enforcement agencies to manage them. Child abuse and elderly and disabled abuse are two types of client disclosures that require helpers to breech confidentiality.

Another area in which helpers must breech confidentiality and report disclosures to appropriate agencies is when a client poses a serious threat of physical violence against a reasonably identifiable victim or victims. This exception to confidentiality is known as "Duty to Warn." The helper must report such danger to law enforcement immediately. When a recipient of human services poses a danger to him or herself, a helper is not mandated to report it to law enforcement. Instead, when the danger is to oneself, a helper is permitted to breech confidentiality if it is believed that it is necessary to prevent an act of suicide or self-harm.

Other mandatory exceptions to confidentiality occur when there is a court order, subpoena, or search warrant issued, when a coroner requests records as part of an investigation, and when the client requests that records be shared. The most recent legal mandate that requires exception to confidentiality is contained in The Patriot Act of 2001. This federal legislation prohibits helpers from disclosing to clients that the FBI sought or obtained books, records, papers, documents, and other items as well as requiring them to provide such items to the FBI.

Exceptions to confidentiality are listed in Table 7.

## Summary

Confidentiality is often thought of as the hallmark of any type of therapeutic relationship, including physician/patient, psychotherapist/client, and teacher/student. The clients, patients, and students must often open up to someone they barely know about very personal things that often create feelings of shame and embarrassment. In order for the healer to have access to this material, an atmosphere of trust must be created. Having an ethical standard such as confidentiality allows for this to happen. Of course, there are exceptions to this standard in order to protect people who may be

**Table 7**  Exceptions to Confidentiality

| | |
|---|---|
| Suspected Child Abuse: Physical, sexual, and neglect | Must report to child protective agency or law enforcement |
| Suspected Elderly or disabled adult abuse: Neglect, physical, sexual, or financial | Must report to adult protective agency or law enforcement |
| Duty to Warn: Someone poses a serious physical threat to another person | Must report to law enforcement |
| Danger to Self: someone poses a serious physical threat to himself | Not mandatory to report, though may report to prevent harm |
| Court order or subpoena | Must disclose to judge |
| An investigation into a death of a client | Must disclose to coroner |
| When a client signs a release of information | Must disclose to the person requested by client |
| The Patriot Act of 2001 | Must hand over records to FBI, cannot tell client |

a harm to themselves or others, and most individuals seeking the help of therapists, doctors, and teachers understand these exceptions.

*Kristi Kanel*

**See also:** Federal Bureau of Investigation (FBI); HIPPA (Health Insurance Portability and Accountability Act); Public Safety; Social Services

### References and Additional Readings

American Association for Marriage and Family Therapy. (2005). *AAMFT code of ethics.* Washington, DC: American Counseling Association.

American Psychological Association. (2002). Ethical principles of psychologists and code of conduct. *American Psychologist, 57*(12), 1060–1073.

Benitez, B.R. (2004). Confidentiality and its exceptions (including the US Patriot Act). *The Therapist, 16*(4), 32–36.

Jensen, D.G. (2003). HIPAA overview. *The Therapist, 15*(3), 26–27.

National Association of Social Workers. (1999). *Code of ethics.* Washington, DC. n.p.

Siegel, M. (1979). Privacy, ethics, and confidentiality. *Professional Psychology, 10*(2), 249–258.

Swoboda, J.S., Elwork, A., Sales, B.D., & Levine, D. (1978). Knowledge of a compliance with privileged communication and child-abuse reporting laws. *Professional Psychology, 9*, 448–457.

## Congress

The U.S. Congress was created in 1787 with Article I, section 1 of the U.S. Constitution. The Constitutional Congress provided for a U.S. Senate, comprised of 100 members (two from each state) and a U.S. House of Representatives, based proportionally on each states' census population (comprised of 435 members). In addition, delegates from American Samoa, the District of Columbia, Guam, the Virgin Islands, and the Commonwealth of the Northern Mariana Islands, as well as, a Resident Commissioner from Puerto Rico participate as part of Congress. All representatives are elected for two-year terms, with the exception of Senators, who serve six-year terms. Senators must be 30 years old and been a U.S. citizen for nine years, while Representatives must be 25 years of age and been a citizen for seven years. In both cases, residential status in the representative state must be maintained. There are three classes of Senators depending on the year they were elected, they rotate out (or are reelected) by class. Each state's Senators are from different classes to maintain consistency in representation. Even numbered years bring a presidential election (every four years); in non-presidential election years, 1/3 of the Senate and all of the House members are elected. High reelection rates are enjoyed in both the House and the Senate.

Both Senate and House of Representatives' tasks are divided into committees and subcommittees. Topics covered by these committees include agriculture, banking, pensions, homeland security, small businesses, among numerous others. The vice president presides over the Senate, while a house-elected speaker oversees the House of Representatives. Both may designate a second in charge in their absence. Both chambers of Congress have roles in passing federal laws, declaring war, regulating commerce, controlling taxes and spending

The first African American Senator was Hiram Revels in 1870. The first female senator was elected in 1948, Margaret Chase Smith. She was also the first woman to serve in both the U.S. Senate and House of Representatives. The first African American woman elected to the House of Representatives was Shirley Chisholm in 1969, while the first female Speaker of the House was Nancy Pelosi in 2007.

Meeting in a joint session, members of Congress are joined by a color guard in reciting the pledge of allegiance in the House chambers. (UPI/Bettmann/Corbis)

polices, and serving as a check and balance to the other two arms of government (judicial and executive branches).

*Wendy Reiboldt*

**See also:** Supreme Court

### References and Additional Readings

Schickler, E. (2001). *Disjointed pluralism: Institutional innovation and the development of the U.S. Congress.* Princeton, NJ: Princeton University Press.

Smith, S.S., Roberts, J.M., & Vander Wielen, R.J. (2011). *The American Congress.* Cambridge, UK: Cambridge University Press.

U.S. House of Representatives. (2013). The house explained. Retrieved from http://www.house.gov

U.S. Senate. (2013). Legislation and records. Retrieved from http://www.senate.gov

## Consumer Action

Consumer Action is a nonprofit organization that has championed the rights of underrepresented consumers nationwide since 1971. Throughout its history, the organization has dedicated its resources to promoting financial literacy and advocating for consumer rights in both the media and before lawmakers to promote economic justice for all.

### Financial Education

To empower consumers to assert their rights in the marketplace, Consumer Action provides a range of educational resources focusing especially on financial services and privacy. The organization's extensive library of free publications offers in-depth financial information, while its hotline provides nonlegal advice and referrals. Consumer Action also publishes unbiased surveys of financial and consumer services that expose excessive prices and anticonsumer practices, help consumers make informed buying choices, and elicit change from big business.

### Community Outreach

With a special focus on serving low- and moderate-income and limited-English-speaking consumers, Consumer Action maintains strong ties to a national network of close to 7,500 community-based organizations. Outreach services include training and free mailings of financial education materials in many languages, including English, Spanish, Chinese, Korean, and Vietnamese. Consumer Action's network is the largest and most diverse of its kind.

## Advocacy

Consumer Action is deeply committed to ensuring that underrepresented consumers are represented in the national media and in front of lawmakers. The organization promotes proconsumer policy, regulation, and legislation by taking positions and testifying on key consumer issues, especially in the areas of financial services, housing, and privacy, at the federal and California state level. Additionally, its diverse staff provides the media with expert commentary on key consumer issues supported by solid data and victim testimony.

Consumer Action opened its doors in June 1971, when a few volunteers set up the organization's first office with a phone and some donated space. The group organized its mission around the consumer complaints that began to deluge Consumer Action's first hotline. The individual problems soon revealed a bigger picture: the strong taking advantage of the weak. Adding a mobile complaint unit in an old van and irreverent public protests, such as a "lemonstration" of defective autos, to its arsenal, the feisty group found an eager partner in the press, which helped its influence grow.

In 1973, Consumer Action hit upon an innovative prototype: surveys that compare price and quality in consumer services. "Break the Banks: A Shopper's Guide to Banking Services" was published that year, bringing nationwide recognition. Subsequent surveys have spotlighted the costs of everything from prescription drugs and bank accounts to credit cards and peer-to-peer lending websites.

In the mid-1970s, Consumer Action's work expanded to include not only complaint handling, protests, and surveys, but also reform through legislation, regulation, and lawsuits. The organization published a scathing indictment of the California Consumer Affairs Department in 1974, which forced the agency to become more responsive to the needs of the state's consumers. In 1976, the group filed a false advertising complaint against Bank of America, resulting in a large penalty for the bank. In 1976–1977, it helped the Federal Trade Commission draft new consumer protection regulations.

In the 1980s, Consumer Action began to serve groups—low-income families, seniors, the disabled, immigrants, and limited-English-speaking residents—that were often targeted by unscrupulous businesses. By the early 1990s, Consumer Action was distributing more than one million pieces of information in English and seven other languages at no charge in California each year.

Deregulation of the telephone and banking industries led Consumer Action to a new focus in the fields of banking, finance, and telecommunications. In 1989, the organization's Telephone Information Project was set up to provide community agencies and individuals with free information about telecommunications services. The project was funded through the Telecommunications Education Trust, which resulted from a $16.5 million dollar penalty against Pacific Bell for marketing abuses that occurred in 1985–1986. In its first four years, the project distributed more than three million free publications.

In the 1990s, the organization moved beyond the barricades and into the boardrooms. During the Reagan–Bush years, the group began to work with selected corporations to promote consumer protection. The corporate world responded to Consumer Action's emphasis on consumer education, and corporate-funded national educational contracts became a new source of funding for the group.

In the 1990s, Consumer Action's focus and influence grew steadily on a national level. Expertise in the areas of banking, finance, and telecommunications gave the group an authority that got Congress and federal government agencies, as well as the national media, to listen.

In 1994, Consumer Action presented the first of its annual awards for outstanding consumer protection efforts to California State Senator Herschel Rosenthal. Its Consumer Excellence Awards have become an annual tradition.

In 1996, Consumer Action was one of the earliest groups to establish a presence online, offering its growing library of free multilingual educational materials, newsletters, press releases, and surveys at Consumer-Action.org.

Around the same time, Consumer Action's outreach staff began traveling to different cities to train members of its growing community agency network on how to use the organization's materials to educate their clients. This model of providing free financial literacy materials and trainings nationwide to community-based organizations is still at the core of Consumer Action's multilingual, multicultural education approach.

Consumer Action also launched a unique "mini-grants" program that allows the organization to support innovative education and outreach efforts of select community organizations in its network.

Advocacy remained a priority, with Consumer Action staff regularly speaking out before the media—both mainstream and ethnic—on a wide range of issues. To boost its effectiveness, in 2004 Consumer Action established an office in Washington, D.C.

To further leverage the Internet as a tool to educate and mobilize diverse Americans, Consumer Action built a unique family of websites that includes landing pages, news, and materials in Spanish, Chinese, Vietnamese,

Korean, and several other languages. Updated daily, the main Consumer Action site (www.consumer-action.org) offers a robust visitor experience, including headline consumer news, an online "help desk" and access to the Take Action advocacy database of national, state, and local elected officials. The site gets nearly a million page views per year. Nine topic-specific "subsites" on topics such as privacy, insurance, and housing account for another quarter million page views each year.

In 2008–2009, Consumer Action helped mold the historic Credit Card Accountability, Responsibility, and Disclosure (CARD) Act, which curtailed many of the practices that card companies long relied on to boost profits and keep consumers in debt. The organization's e-advocacy alerts mobilized consumers to send thousands of e-mails to Congress in support of the bill, which ultimately became law in May 2009. Consumer Action maintained the momentum through 2010, when, after actively championing the creation of an independent, proconsumer federal agency to oversee banks and financial companies, Congress established the Consumer Financial Protection Bureau.

At the same time that the organization was making great strides in consumer legislation, the mortgage crisis and "Great Recession" were devastating working families and the American economy. Online and offline, Consumer Action alerted and educated consumers about foreclosure prevention scams, fake check fraud, work-at-home schemes, government stimulus money scams, and other types of fraud that targeted those most desperate for assistance. With the number of foreclosures at record highs, Consumer Action's free national hotline handled a 371 percent increase in calls related to mortgages.

The first decade of the new millennium closed with Consumer Action as outspoken and instrumental as ever in the process to prevent future abuses by financial services companies. The organization became a founding member of Americans for Financial Reform (AFR), a coalition of national and state groups dedicated to improving the financial sector for all Americans. After consistent lobbying, and with great anticipation, the Dodd–Frank Wall Street Reform and Consumer Protection Act of 2010 became law, establishing the Consumer Financial Protection Bureau, forcing mortgage reform and requiring investigation into, among other things, private student loans, binding mandatory arbitration, and remittances.

2011 marked 40 years of Consumer Action's commitment to consumer rights, and an anniversary celebration and awards ceremony in Washington, D.C., propelled the organization into its fifth decade. By the end of 2012, at this writing, Consumer Action had offered 25 multilingual consumer education and training modules, all available at no charge to individuals and nonprofits. The group's hotline staff that year assisted more than 8,500 individuals from all 50 states on a variety of issues, with the top four areas of complaint being retail, automotive, credit/banking, and phone/utility. Its online Take Action center enabled 5,000 subscribers to send messages to their elected officials on a variety of topics, from financial reform to privacy issues. Its third annual National Consumer Empowerment Conference, in November 2012, brought together 75 community educators from close to two dozen states to address critical consumer issues and share best practices in community-based consumer education and empowerment. An update of its *How to Complain* guide, a perennial favorite that has been helping consumers complain effectively and get results for close to 35 years, resulted in widespread renewed interest. A new monthly publication—the Consumer Action INSIDER—was keeping subscribers abreast of the organization's activities. And publication of *Consumer Action News*, the organization's quarterly tabloid newspaper, continued, with surveys on secured credit cards, peer-to-peer lending sites, prepaid cards, and wireless service parental controls.

Looking beyond 2012, Consumer Action is eyeing new methods of evaluating and enhancing its education programs and materials; engaging even more individuals and organizations in our efforts to make the marketplace fairer for all consumers; establishing new supportive relationships and strengthening existing ones; responding swiftly and effectively to emerging consumer issues; and further diversifying our funding. Keep up with Consumer Action at its website, Consumer-Action.org.

*Linda Sherry and Monica Steinisch*

**See also:** Activism; Consumer Financial Protection Bureau (CFPB); Credit Card Accountability Responsibility and Disclosure Act; Departments of Consumer Affairs (DCA)

**References and Additional Readings**

Consumer Action. (2013). Consumer action insider. Retrieved from http://www.consumer-action.org/news/insider/

## Consumer Bill of Rights

President Kennedy was the first president with a vision for consumer rights. In a special message to the U.S. Congress on March 15, 1962, he argued that:

Consumers, by definition, include us all. They are the largest economic group in the economy, affecting and affected by almost every public and private economic decision. Two-thirds of all spending in the economy is by consumers. But they are the only important group in the economy who are not effectively organized, whose views are not heard.

Kennedy was concerned about consumer issues including inferior products, unsafe or worthless drugs, food safety and nutrition, misleading advertising, and consumer credit. He felt that if protected and informed, American consumers would be able to make better use of their incomes and contribute more to their families.

In his historic 1962 speech, President Kennedy outlined his Consumer Bill of Rights (The American Presidency Project, 2012).

(1) The right to safety—to be protected against the marketing of goods that are hazardous to health or life.

(2) The right to be informed—to be protected against fraudulent, deceitful, or grossly misleading information, advertising, labeling, or other practices, and to be given the facts he needs to make an informed choice.

(3) The right to choose—to be assured, wherever possible, access to a variety of products and services at competitive prices; and in those industries in which competition is not workable and government regulation is substituted, an assurance of satisfactory quality and service at fair prices.

(4) The right to be heard—to be assured that consumer interests will receive full and sympathetic consideration in the formulation of government policy, and fair and expeditious treatment in its administrative tribunals.

After defining his vision of the rights of consumers, President Kennedy detailed his plan to act upon his new Consumer Bill of Rights. His plan included increased funding for existing federal consumer programs. He sought staffing at the Food and Drug Administration (FDA) to test the safety of food additives and food colorings. He called upon the U.S. Department of Agriculture (USDA) to regulate pesticides and to increase inspections for meat and poultry. He called upon the Federal Aviation Agency to work toward increased safety and efficiency for flight.

President Kennedy sought tougher laws for cosmetic and drug testing, manufacturing, labeling, and marketing. The Fair Packaging and Labeling Act of 1966, the Cigarette Labeling Act of 1965, and the Wholesome Meat Act of 1967 are examples of legislation that were enacted to address issues with accurate labeling of product content as well as dangers associated with products. Kennedy also sought increased inspections for meat as the current laws only required meat crossing state lines to be inspected, thus leaving 20 percent of all meat sold to consumers uninspected.

The beginnings of the Truth in Lending Act (TILA) of 1968 can also be found in Kennedy's speech. While access to credit helped consumers to plan their purchases, it often came at high costs. Kennedy was concerned that consumer debt had tripled in the 1950s and that consumers were often not aware of interests rates they were being charged on purchases such as used cars. He wanted to require that lenders giver full disclosure of terms, costs, and conditions of credit before consumers entered into a contract. Initially this legislation was focused on protecting consumers with regard to installment loans. Enforcement of this new legislation was to be under the jurisdiction of the Federal Trade Commission (FTC).

Fraudulent business practices were an additional concern. President Kennedy sought to empower the FTC to issue temporary cease-and-desist orders against companies while their cases were being investigated by the commission, thus protecting consumers from potential additional fraud.

Under Kennedy's direction, new programs were developed to assist in protecting consumers including the Office of Highway Safety (now the Federal Highway Administration) that was established to work collaboratively with state and local government, industry, and other agencies to protect consumers through auto accident prevention. The FTC increased its efforts against deceptive practices affecting a wide variety of goods including vacuum cleaners, refrigerators, paint, sewing machines, and carpet. The Federal Communications Commission encouraged an increased development of educational television stations.

A variety of projects were expanded or implemented to increase consumer information including the FDA's Consumer Consultant Program in conjunction with the Agriculture Extension Service's home demonstration program. The Bureau of Labor Statistics conducted a survey of consumer expenditures, income, and savings to update the Consumer Price Index and create model family budgets. The president called upon the postmaster general to display and support the sale of consumer publications.

President Lyndon Johnson, a strong supporter of the consumer movement, built on the consumer foundation that President Kennedy had formed. During his presidency (1963–1969) he introduced and passed more consumer legislation than any other president before him.

In 1965, Ralph Nader began his consumer career with his book *Unsafe at Any Speed* that highlighted the need for increased auto safety including seat belts. Nader is considered to be one of the most influential consumer advocates in U.S. history. He remains active in the consumer movement to this day.

Since President Kennedy outlined his four consumer rights, additional rights have been added. The additional rights include:

- The right to redress for physical damages suffered from using a product
- The right to consumer education
- The right to satisfaction of basic needs
- The right to a healthy environment

On October 31, 1969, President Richard M. Nixon made a special address to the U.S. Congress on consumer protection. In his address, he outlined a new consumer right: the right to redress. He sought to enact a new consumer protection law that would enable consumers as individuals or groups to go to court to obtain compensation for the damages they suffer. He sought to allow individuals suits as well as class action suits access to the federal court system. In addition, he encouraged the states to develop Divisions of Consumer Protection that would function as a part of each state attorney general's office. This consumer right served as an impetus for the development of the small claims court system.

Consumers also have the right to acquire knowledge and skills necessary to make informed, confident choices about goods and services, while being aware of basic consumer rights and responsibilities and how to act on them. President Gerald R. Ford established this consumer right which was the foundation for many consumer education programs in schools and communities across the United States. In continued effort to protect consumers, President Nixon established the Consumer Product Safety Commission (CPSC) in 1972. The CPSC's charge is to protect the public from the unreasonable risks of injury or death from thousands of products that the agency oversees. Cribs, toys, power tools, and household chemicals are examples of products over which the CPSC has jurisdiction.

The right to satisfaction of basic needs and the right to a healthy environment were added by Consumers International. Consumers International, which was founded in 1960, is an organization comprised of over 220 consumer groups from 115 countries that work together to protect the rights of consumers worldwide. The right to satisfaction of basic needs supports the concepts that consumers have the right to basic, essential goods, and services including adequate food, clothing, shelter, health care, education, public utilities, water, and sanitation. The right to a healthy environment acknowledges that consumers have the right to live and work in an environment that is nonthreatening to the well-being of present and future generations. This right was influenced by several presidents, particularly President Lyndon Johnson. In 1964, he appointed Rachel Carson to his newly created post of special assistant for consumer affairs. Carson is considered the founder of the modern environmental movement.

While he didn't establish a specific consumer right, President Jimmy Carter was considered one of the strongest supporters of consumer causes in U.S. history. His consumer advocate appointments included Joan Claybrook (National Highway and Safety Administration), Michael Pertschuk (FTC), Carol Tucker Foreman (Agriculture Department), David Pittle (Consumer Product Safety Commission), and Ester Peterson (special assistant to President Carter for Consumer Affairs).

In recent years, President Barack Obama has enacted legislation to protect consumers including the 2009 Credit Card Accountability, Responsibility and Reform Act (Credit CARD Act). The Credit CARD Act requires credit card companies to provide all forms and statements to consumers in plain language that is in plain sight.

In addition, on February 23, 2012, he unveiled his Consumer Privacy Bill of Rights to help protect consumers while they are online. The aim of the bill is to give consumers more control of how their personal information is being used online as well as helping businesses maintain consumer trust.

From President Kennedy to President Obama, consumer rights have emerged and evolved over time. Government and consumer groups alike work to protect consumers against unscrupulous con men and companies. Despite all the protections and rights provided, consumers still need to be responsible for conducting a thorough review on products and services. The old adage still rings true, if it sounds too good to be true, it probably is.

*Lisa J. Amos Ledeboer*

**See also:** Consumers International; Consumer Product Safety Commission (CPSC); Federal Trade Commission (FTC); Food and Drug Administration (FDA); Kennedy, John F.; Nader, Ralph; National Highway and Safety Administration (NHTSA); Petersen, Esther; Truth in Lending Act

### References and Additional Readings

Consumers International. (n.d.). Consumer Rights. Retrieved from http://www.consumersinternational.org/who-we-are/consumer-rights

Gerald R. Ford Library and Museum. (n.d.) President Ford '76 factbook: Consumer affairs. Retrieved from http://www.ford.utexas.edu/library/document/factbook/factbook.asp

Kennedy, J.K. (1962). Special message to the congress on protecting the consumer interest. Retrieved from http://www.presidency.ucsb.edu/ws/?pid=9108#axzz1qsqOCUB1

Lexington Law. (2011). A history of consumer rights and improvements. Retrieved from http://www.lexingtonlaw.com/blog/credit-repair/history-consumer-rights-improvements.html

Nixon, R. (1969). Special message to the Congress on Consumer Protection. Retrieved from http://www.presidency.ucsb.edu/ws/index.php?pid=2299#ixzz1s8Xd94nZ

The White House, Office of the Press Secretary. (2009). Fact sheet: Reforms to protect American credit card holders. Retrieved from http://www.whitehouse.gov/the_press_office/Fact-Sheet-Reforms-to-Protect-American-Credit-Card-Holders

The White House, Office of the Press Secretary. (2012). We can't wait: Obama administration unveils blueprint for a 'privacy bill of rights' to protect consumers. Retrieved from http://www.whitehouse.gov/the-press-office/2012/02/23/we-can-t-wait-obama-administration-unveils-blueprint-privacy-bill-rights

Zelenak, M., & Reiboldt, W. (2010). *Consumer economics: The consumer in our society.* Sottsdale, AZ: Holcomb Hathaway, Publishers, Inc.

## Consumer Federation of America (CFA)

The Consumer Federation of America (CFA) is an association of nonprofit consumer organizations established to advance consumer interest. The group was established in 1968 to support and conduct research, advocacy, education, and service on behalf of American consumers. Today the organization has over 300 participating groups. The groups participate through representation on CFA's board of directors. The headquarters of the CFA is in Washington, D.C. The CFA website lists 23 employees, including the executive director.

The funding of the organization is provided through dues to CFA paid by member organizations, which include groups such as national advocacy and education groups, consumer cooperative groups (such as credit unions and rural electric cooperatives), public power groups, and other consumer groups. The dues range from $75 to $20,000, depending on the organization size. Consumers Union, a nonprofit organization that publishes *Consumer Reports,* is a large supporter of the CFA, both monetarily and in supporting the direction of the projects.

### Advancing the Consumer Interest through Research

The CFA conducts research in a variety of important topics affecting consumers. These topics include communications, consumer protection and privacy, energy, financial services, food and agriculture, product safety, housing, transportation, and other topics, as they emerge as consumer issues. The organization conducts research through surveys, focus groups, investigative reports, economic analysis, and policy analysis. The information is disseminated to consumer groups, individual consumers, policy groups, legislators, members of Congress, government agencies, and businesses through reports and briefs. Much of the research is also reported through news articles, magazines, other media outlets, and through the CFA's own website. Many of the staff members employed by the CFA are experts in particular areas of consumer interest, such as housing, financial services, and product safety.

### Advancing the Consumer Interest through Advocacy

The CFA staff members are active in advancing policies in the consumer interest through testifying for state legislatures, Congress, the White House, federal and state regulatory agencies, and the courts. Staff members also develop communication linkages in a variety of ways with policymakers at all levels to help provide information on the consumer behalf. This work is important, as individual consumers do not usually have the money or time to represent themselves to policymakers. Business interests are more able to present the business side, therefore resulting in an unbalanced representation of consumer issues. The Consumer Federation Organization seeks to create a more balanced forum of discussions about various aspects of issues affecting consumers. One of the recent successes of the CFA was in providing support for the newly established Consumer Financial Protection Agency.

### Advancing the Consumer Interest through Education

The CFA has an extensive website with materials available to every consumer in the United States. Further, the CFA produces reports, books, brochures, news releases, newsletters, blogs, and a variety of other communication tools to provide consumer education. Yearly conferences bring important, nationally known speakers together with the members of CFA's constituent groups and to consumers interested in the issues being discussed. Three annual conferences are sponsored by CFA—a consumer assembly, a financial services conference, and a food policy conference.

### Advancing the Consumer Interest through Service

One of the major service projects sponsored by the CFA has been the program, America Saves, which they organized in 2000. This project seeks to convince consumers that having savings can result in a more stable, secure, and less credit-dependent lifestyle. Another service project the organization sponsors is the annual Awards Dinner, where CFA honors distinguished public servants, consumer leaders, and media organizations are honored for their work on behalf of the consumer. The CFA website has other service-oriented offerings for individual consumers, such as a credit score quiz, an option to evaluate life insurance policies, identity theft information, and payday loan information.

### Effectiveness of the Consumer Federation of America

The CFA is one of the most effective organizations in the United States, putting quality expertise and knowledgeable strategists together to produce useful and accurate research, advocacy, education and service to advance the consumer interest. The information produced by the CFA is relied upon extensively by government, business, and industry, and nonprofit entities to bring the consumer voice to the forefront. These actions strengthen the marketplace and make the economy more responsive in serving the consumer.

*Deborah C. Haynes*

**See also:** Congress; Consumers Union; Insurance; Payday Lending

### References and Additional Readings

Brill, S. (2010). Government for sale: How lobbyists shaped the financial reform bill. *Time.* Retrieved from http://www.time.com/time/magazine/article/0,971,2001015-1,00.html

Consumer Federation of America. (2013). About CFA. Retrieved from http://www.consumerfed.org

## Consumer Financial Protection Bureau (CFPB)

Controversy surrounded the creation of the Consumer Financial Protection Bureau (CFPB) in the summer of 2010. Toward the end of the first decade of the 21st century, the financial services sector began to collapse, and the United States entered its worst recession since the Great Depression. In late 2008, the situation was considered so dire that Treasury Secretary Henry Paulson (former CEO of Goldman Sachs, a Wall Street investment banking and securities firm), with the full support of Republican President George W. Bush, urged a Democratically controlled Congress to pass the Economic Emergency Stabilization Act of 2008. The 2008 presidential nominees, Republican Senator John McCain and Democratic Senator Barack Obama, also endorsed the bill's passage and voted in favor.

This law, commonly known as the Troubled Asset Relief Program or TARP, authorized $700 billion of government bailout money for financial institutions, segments of the automobile industry and several insurance companies. All had been adversely affected by the collapse of the residential housing market and the derivatives market for residential mortgage-backed securities. Several of the entities that received TARP

Elizabeth Warren was active in the creation and implementation of the Consumer Financial Protection Bureau (CFPB). (Brendan Smialowski/Getty Images)

money were considered too big to fail but were at severe risk because of their investment in these securities, particularly subprime mortgage-backed securities.

Mortgage-backed securities—residential mortgages bundled in various and complex ways and sold as securities—were leveraged on the creditworthiness of the underlying borrowers. Subprime borrowers had a higher risk of defaulting. Bundling the mortgages helped spread the risk of any one borrower's default, but a positive return to the investor required the overall absence of default on the underlying residential mortgages that constituted the security. Some entities receiving TARP monies also invested in credit default swaps. These derivatives functioned like but were not treated as insurance policies—they were issued to hedge the risk of loss associated with the mortgage-backed securities. A positive return for investors on credit default swaps was triggered by the borrowers' defaulting on the underlying residential mortgages in the security the credit default swap was hedging. Many of the entities that received TARP

---

### Case Study: Customers Reap the Rewards of Actions by the CFPB and the FDIC

In late 2012, it was announced that enforcement actions by the Federal Deposit Insurance Corporation (FDIC) and the Consumer Financial Protection Bureau (CFPB) forced Discover Bank to repay customers after engaging in misleading telemarketing campaigns. Discover Bank, the sixth largest credit card issuer in the nation, is now refunding $200 million to 3.5 million customers. The company was also ordered to pay $14 million in penalties and was required to change their telemarketing strategies. Many of the practices employed by Discover Bank used misleading language and deceptive tactics to sell "add-on" products such as identity protection, payment protection, and credit score monitoring. Telemarketers were accused of downplaying key terms, rushing through payment terms, and, in general, speaking in confusing language when reviewing the terms and conditions sections. Moreover, some customers were enrolled in programs and charged enrollment fees, without their consent. Customers who were victimized by any of these actions between December 1, 2007, and August 31, 2011, were reimbursed, without further action on the part of the consumer.

*Source:* Consumer Financial Protection Bureau. (September 4, 2012). Federal Deposit Insurance Corporation and Consumer Financial Protection Bureau order discover to pay $200 million consumer refund for deceptive marketing. Retrieved from http://www.consumerfinance.gov/

monies had invested heavily in both types of derivatives. The market for these derivatives was largely unregulated and opaque. The evolution of the financial services industry during the period between the Great Depression and the 2008 recession helps explain both the absence of a viable regulatory environment for these derivatives and the controversy surrounding the CFPB.

The Banking Act of 1933 (commonly known as the Glass–Steagall Act), enacted after the Great Depression, prohibited banks from offering both banking and investment products and services to their customers. In a 1971 Supreme Court case, *Investment Company Institute v. Camp*, wherein the required separation of these functions under Glass–Steagall was upheld, the Supreme Court noted "Congress [had] acted to keep commercial banks out of the investment banking business largely because it believed that the promotional incentives of investment banking and the investment banker's pecuniary stake in the success of particular investment opportunities was destructive of prudent and disinterested commercial banking and of public confidence in the commercial banking system."

Rulings by the Federal Reserve Board, however, had begun loosening restrictions regarding the separation of banking from investment products and services, particularly after the election of Republican President Ronald Reagan in 1980 and the appointment of Alan Greenspan (former director of J.P. Morgan, a Wall Street investment banking and securities firm) as the chairman of the Federal Reserve Board in 1987 (serving until 2006). In 1999, a Republican-controlled Congress passed the Financial Services Modernization Act of 1999 (commonly known as the Gramm-Leach-Bliley Act), which repealed Glass-Steagall. Democratic President Bill Clinton signed the bill into law. The repeal of Glass-Steagall allowed, among other things, financial institutions to offer banking and investment products and services through one entity, which had previously been prohibited.

The repeal of Glass-Steagall also reflected the prevailing belief in supply-side economics (derided sometimes as "trickle-down economics") and market self-regulation, which took hold with force after the election of President Reagan. In 1981, for example, a Democratically controlled Congress passed the Economic Recovery Tax Act of 1981, which dramatically lowered marginal tax rates, particularly for the top tax brackets on the theory that tax cuts coupled with less regulation would spur investment and economic growth. Tax cuts, particularly for those seen as "job creators" (taxpayers in the top tax brackets), remain a cornerstone of this economic theory and became a mantra for the Republican Party, particularly during the 2012 presidential election cycle. After the 2008 financial collapse, however, even Greenspan, an ardent advocate of supply-side economics, acknowledged a flaw in certain aspects of this economic theory. In October 2008, he stated in testimony before the U.S. House Committee on Oversight and Government Reform that he had "found a flaw in the model that I perceived is the critical functioning structure that defines how the world works, so to speak." That "flaw" was the apparent failure of market players to regulate their own profit-making behavior in the financial services industry.

After the 2008 landslide election of President Obama, a Democratically controlled Congress enacted the Dodd–Frank Wall Street Reform and Consumer Protection Act (commonly known as the Dodd–Frank Act) in July 2010 with bipartisan support and a 60-vote margin. Republicans took control of the U.S. House of Representatives in the 2010 midterm elections, while the Democrats maintained control of the U.S. Senate. Residential mortgage foreclosures hit record highs in 2010 and the number of foreclosures for 2011 was expected to be even higher.

The Dodd–Frank Act was an attempt to regulate previously unregulated sectors of the financial services industry and correct the flaws that led to the recession. Title X of the Dodd–Frank Act also authorized the creation of the CFPB, which is housed in with the Federal Reserve Board and operates with a budget independent from congressional appropriation. The controversy over the CFPB reflects the continued debate about the role of regulation in the U.S. economy. Proponents of the CFPB argued that a lax regulatory environment helped create the conditions leading to the recession. Opponents of the CFPB insisted that principles of supply-side economics remained viable and they were vehemently opposed to the creation of any new regulations, particularly regulatory authority concentrated in one powerful consumer protection agency.

This debate affected even the ability of President Obama to appoint a director to head the CFPB. President Obama initially appointed Harvard law professor Elizabeth Warren, widely considered the architect of the CFPB, as assistant to the president and special advisor to the secretary of the Treasury, a position which did not require Senate confirmation. Her task was to structure the framework and long-term vision of the CFPB. Warren, however, was considered by some as too controversial to be confirmed as the director of the CFPB and President Obama did not nominate her. The CFPB went live on July 21, 2011, without a director. On July 22, 2011, the Republican-controlled House of Representatives passed a bill designed to replace the director of the CFPB with a five-member bipartisan commission, among other things. Warren left her position at the CFPB in August 2011. She ran on the Democratic ticket for the U.S. Senate seat from Massachusetts against Republican Senator Scott Brown in the 2012 election cycle. She was replaced by Raj Date, a veteran of the financial services industry and Warren's top deputy at the CFPB.

The Dodd–Frank Act, however, required the appointment of a director to the CFPB before the majority of the CFPB's authority could be triggered. In July 2011, President Obama nominated Richard Cordray, former Ohio attorney general, to head the CFPB. Senate Republicans blocked consideration of the nomination. On January 4, 2012, while Congress was in recess, President Obama appointed Cordray to the position; under this recess appointment, Deputy Cordray's first term ended at the close of the 112th U.S. Congress in January 2013. He has recently been reconfirmed as the director of the CFPB. On January 5, 2012, Director Cordray appointed Raj Date as the CFPB's deputy director. During the 2012 State of the Union Address to Congress, President Obama stated that "Today, American consumers finally have a watchdog in Richard Cordray with one job: To look out for them."

That charge is echoed on the CFPB's website, which states that the "central mission of the CFBP is to make markets for consumer financial products and services work for Americans—whether they are applying for a mortgage, choosing among credit cards, or using any number of other consumer financial products." Dodd–Frank gives the CFPB extensive rulemaking, supervisory, and enforcement authority. The CFPB's focus includes stopping false, deceptive, and abusive practices in relation to the sale of most consumer financial products and services.

Dodd–Frank accomplishes that task by transferring regulatory authority for most consumer financial protection laws previously scattered among seven regulatory agencies to the CFPB. Scattered regulatory authority undermines a single focus on consumer protection. The CFPB also has the authority to regulate large banks—those with assets exceeding $10 billion—as well as nonbank providers of financial services and products, like residential mortgage brokers, payday lenders, and for-profit educational lenders. Dodd–Frank further empowered the CFPB to supervise and regulate "larger participants" in the consumer financial services market, as defined through the CFPB's rulemaking authority. The CFPB, for example, is currently taking public comment on whether the debt collection and consumer reporting industries should be supervised by the CFPB.

The CFPB also has signed memoranda of understanding with other federal regulators and agencies regarding their activities to avoid overlap and inefficiencies. In late 2011, the CFPB issued a *Supervision and Examination Manual*, which provides guidance to those subject to the CFPB's authority. In December 2011, the CFPB also established a joint task force with the Office of the Special Inspector General for TARP to investigate foreclosure scams. Additionally, the CFPB set up a whistleblower hotline so consumers could warn the CFPB of violations of consumer financial protection statutes. The CFPB appears committed to partnering with local, state, and federal entities to improve consumer protection and to educate consumers about financial products and services.

Specifically, the CFPB is working to provide consumers with complete and understandable information; information they need to shop comparatively for consumer financial services and products. For example, the CFPB quickly initiated a "Know Before You Owe" program, which was geared toward making residential mortgage disclosures, credit card applications, and financial aid offers—and their attendant risks—easier for consumers to understand. The CFPB also focused on outreach to consumers through workshops and programs, and especially through social media. The CFPB has been working to protect members and veterans of the U.S. Armed Services and their family members through the "Repeat Offenders Against Military" database or ROAM, which tracks information on entities that operate to take advantage of these vulnerable groups of consumers. And the CFPB has initiated programs focused on protecting older Americans, consumers who also may be more vulnerable to false, deceptive, or abusive practices in the consumer financial services industry.

The future of the first federal regulatory agency devoted to consumer protection remains to be seen because it largely relies on current and future political climates. The ongoing fierce policy debate on the merits of supply-side economics continues. Republicans have vowed to repeal the Dodd-Frank Act, which would eliminate the CFPB. Republicans in Congress have also made it clear they would work to weaken the CFPB, even if Dodd–Frank were not repealed. While the ultimate outcome remains unclear, the struggle for consumer protection continues and the CFPB will no doubt play a key role.

*Laurie A. Lucas*

**See also:** Banking; Dodd–Frank Wall Street Reform and Consumer Protection Act; Federal Reserve; Securities and Exchange Commission

## References and Additional Readings

Consumer Financial Protection Bureau. (2012). *Semi-Annual report of the consumer financial protection bureau*, 30 Jan. 2012. Print.

*Investment Company Institute v. Camp*, 401 U.S. 617, 634 (1971).

Obama, B. (2012). Remarks by the president in the state of the union address (January 24, 2012). Retrieved from http://www.whitehouse.gov/the-press-office/2012/01/24/remarks-president-state-union-address

Poon, M. (2009). From new deal institutions to capital markets: Commercial consumer risk scores and the making of subprime mortgage finance. *Accounting, Organizations and Society, 34*, 654–674.

Warren, E. (2008). Product safety regulation as a model for financial services regulation. *Journal of Consumer Affairs*, *42*, 452–460.

Wyatt, E. (2011). Dodd–Frank act a favorite target for Republicans laying blame. *New York Times, 21*. Print.

## Consumer Price Index (CPI)

According to the Bureau of Labor Statistics website, "the Consumer Price Indexes (CPI) program produces monthly data on changes in the prices paid by urban consumers for a representative basket of goods and services." Categories of consumer expenditures include, but are not limited to, housing, apparel, transportation, medical care, food and beverage, entertainment, education, and others. Prices for these goods and services are collected from 87 urban areas throughout the United States from nearly 25,000 retailers. Rental prices are gathered from over 50,000 landlords and tenants across the United States. When combined, the items in the CPI create a market basket of products consumers purchase over the course of a year, and are classified by four Census regions, in 26 areas. The most commonly reported CPI is the CPI-U which is All Urban Consumers, covering about 87 percent of the total population. Detailed current and historical data are readily available on the Bureau of Labor Statistics website.

Because data for the United States is available since 1913, consumers can also calculate the cost of an item from any year in the index by using a simple formula provided by the Bureau of Labor Statistics. The CPI is also a commonly consulted statistic to measure inflation or deflation. When there is a significant increase in the CPI in a short period of time, this typically indicates a period of inflation. Conversely, significant drops in the CPI during a short time period typically denote a period of deflation. The CPI is a valuable and consistent tool for consumers, educators, and government officials. See Table 8.

**Table 8** Consumer price index (CPI) history

| Year | CPI | Year | CPI |
|------|-----|------|-----|
| 1913 | 9.9 | 1919 | 17.3 |
| 1914 | 10.0 | 1920 | 20.0 |
| 1915 | 10.1 | 1921 | 17.9 |
| 1916 | 10.9 | 1922 | 16.8 |
| 1917 | 12.8 | 1923 | 17.1 |
| 1918 | 15.1 | 1924 | 17.1 |

*(Continued)*

**Table 8**  (*Continued*)

| Year | CPI | Year | CPI |
|---|---|---|---|
| 1925 | 17.5 | 1958 | 28.9 |
| 1926 | 17.7 | 1959 | 29.1 |
| 1927 | 17.4 | 1960 | 29.6 |
| 1928 | 17.1 | 1961 | 29.9 |
| 1929 | 17.1 | 1962 | 30.2 |
| 1930 | 16.7 | 1963 | 30.6 |
| 1931 | 15.2 | 1964 | 31.0 |
| 1932 | 13.7 | 1965 | 31.5 |
| 1933 | 13.0 | 1966 | 32.4 |
| 1934 | 13.4 | 1967 | 33.4 |
| 1935 | 13.7 | 1968 | 34.8 |
| 1936 | 13.9 | 1969 | 36.7 |
| 1937 | 14.4 | 1970 | 38.8 |
| 1938 | 14.1 | 1971 | 40.5 |
| 1939 | 13.9 | 1972 | 41.8 |
| 1940 | 14.0 | 1973 | 44.4 |
| 1941 | 14.7 | 1974 | 49.3 |
| 1942 | 16.3 | 1975 | 53.8 |
| 1943 | 17.3 | 1976 | 56.9 |
| 1944 | 17.6 | 1977 | 60.6 |
| 1945 | 18.0 | 1978 | 65.2 |
| 1946 | 19.5 | 1979 | 72.6 |
| 1947 | 22.3 | 1980 | 82.4 |
| 1948 | 24.1 | 1981 | 90.9 |
| 1949 | 23.2 | 1982 | 96.5 |
| 1950 | 24.1 | 1983 | 99.6 |
| 1951 | 26.0 | 1984 | 103.9 |
| 1952 | 26.5 | 1985 | 107.6 |
| 1953 | 26.7 | 1986 | 109.6 |
| 1954 | 26.9 | 1987 | 113.6 |
| 1955 | 26.8 | 1988 | 118.3 |
| 1956 | 27.2 | 1989 | 124.0 |
| 1956 | 27.2 | 1990 | 130.7 |
| 1957 | 28.1 | 1991 | 136.2 |

(*Continued*)

**Table 8** *(Continued)*

| Year | CPI | Year | CPI |
|------|-----|------|-----|
| 1992 | 140.3 | 2002 | 179.9 |
| 1993 | 144.5 | 2003 | 184.0 |
| 1994 | 148.2 | 2004 | 188.9 |
| 1995 | 152.4 | 2005 | 195.3 |
| 1996 | 156.9 | 2006 | 201.6 |
| 1997 | 160.5 | 2007 | 207.342 |
| 1998 | 163.0 | 2008 | 215.303 |
| 1999 | 166.6 | 2009 | 214.537 |
| 2000 | 172.2 | 2010 | 218.056 |
| 2001 | 177.1 | 2011 | 224.939 |

Compiled from data available at http://www.bls.gov/cpi/

*Wendy Reiboldt*

**See also:** Bureau of Labor Statistics

---

**The Consumer Price Indexes (CPI) program** produces monthly data on changes in the prices paid by urban consumers for a representative basket of goods and services. Categories of consumer expenditures include, but are not limited to, housing, apparel, transportation, medical care, food and beverage, entertainment, education, and so on. Prices for these goods and services are collected from 87 urban areas throughout the United States from nearly 25,000 retailers. Rental prices are gathered from over 50,000 landlords and tenants across the United States. When combined, the items in the CPI create a market basket of products consumers purchase over the course of a year, and are classified by four Census regions, in 26 areas. The most commonly reported CPI is the CPI-U which is All Urban Consumers, covering about 87 percent of the total population. Detailed current and historical data are readily available on the Bureau of Labor Statistics website.

Because data for the United States is available since 1913, consumers can also calculate the cost of an item from any year in the index by using a simple formula provided by the Bureau of Labor Statistics. The CPI is also a commonly consulted statistic to measure inflation or deflation. When there is a significant increase in the CPI in a short period of time, this typically indicates a period of inflation. Conversely, significant drops in the CPI during a short time period typically denote a period of deflation. The CPI is a valuable and consistent tool for consumers, educators, and government officials.

For more information, see: U.S. Department of Labor. Bureau of Labor Statistics. (2001). Consumer price index overview. http://www.bls.gov/cpi/cpiovrvw.htm

## References and Additional Readings

Bureau of Labor Statistics. (n.d.). Consumer Price Index. Retrieved from www.bls .gov/cpi/

Diewert, W. E. (1993). The early history of price index research. In Diewert, W.E. & Nakaumra, A.O. (Eds.), *Essays in index number theory, Vol. 1* (pp. 33–66). Elsevier Science Publishers.

# Consumer Product Safety Commission (CPSC)

The Consumer Product Safety Commission (CPSC) is a federal administrative agency charged with protecting consumers from unsafe consumer products, an umbrella which encompasses an immense array of wide-ranging products such as cribs and other children's products, all-terrain vehicles, mattresses, pool drains, and sporting equipment. Congress established the CPSC in 1972. Congress envisioned the CPSC as an independent agency led by five commissioners with staggered appointment terms, each nominated by the executive branch and confirmed by the legislative branch. The statute originally creating the commission, the Consumer Product Safety Act (CPSA), transferred from other agencies earlier powers to regulate certain types of products and consolidated these powers at the CPSC. The "transferred acts" as they are known included the Federal Hazardous Substances Act, the Poison Prevention Packaging Act, the Flammable Fabrics Act, and the Refrigerator Safety Act. The CPSC has the delegated authority to ban products, order recalls, require labeling, and set mandatory safety standards as well as control the process by which voluntary standards are set, collect injury data, and inform consumers about product safety issues.

Besides appointing its commissioners, the executive branch also retains control over the work at the CPSC through the Office of Management and Budget's Office of Information and Regulatory Affairs (OIRA). OIRA is tasked with reviewing agency rules for compliance with the sitting administration's policy goals as well as an overall cost–benefit analysis. This less formal control over agency action can greatly affect the particular actions taken (or not taken) by the agency during any given executive administration.

Congress retains control over the actions of the CPSC through both its monetary appropriations and ultimate legislative authority. Congress can and has slashed budgets at the CPSC over the years, in essence rendering the agency impotent at times. For example, in the 1970s, toward the beginning of the commission's life, the CPSC enjoyed a staff of 1,000 employees and an inflation-adjusted budget of roughly $150 million per year. By 2007, the CPSC was down to a staff of 385 employees and an inflation-adjusted

The CPSC is a leader in promoting consumer safety, including standards for baby items such as cribs. Product recall alerts are regularly posted on the CPSC website. (Michael Pettigrew/Shutterstock.com)

budget of $80 million. Obviously such budget restraints have the effect of weakening the agency, and accordingly, by the mid-2000s, CPSC was a very weak agency. However, Congress overhauled the commission's governing legislation in 2008 with the passage of the Consumer Product Safety Improvement Act (CPSIA), discussed in detail later. The commission has since seen steady budget increases in 2009, 2010, and 2011.

Throughout the 1970s, the CPSC focused on unsafe products like asbestos, flame retardant chemicals in children's clothing and mattresses, and bike reflectors. During the 1980s and 1990s, however, the commission struggled with budget and staff cuts. There were examples from this period of lax regulatory action. Such weakened regulatory focus was seen with design flaws that were allowed to continue for too long in three-wheeled ATVs and power lawn mowers, for example. During the years of the Bush administration (2000–2008), the CPSC emerged into the political world, joining with other consumer agencies in a power grab by interpreting its regulations as preempting state common law, and then as a lobbying force against Congress' attempt to pass legislation that would strengthen the commission's budget and authority. These years were ones of a political agenda of less regulation and relaxed oversight of product manufacturing.

Under the Bush administration, federal agencies in general began pushing for preemption of state tort law with the promulgation of new regulatory standards. The CPSC was a part of this movement (along with the Food and Drug Administration, and the National Highway Traffic Safety Administration). Although Congress explicitly inserted a savings clause into the originating Act creating the CPSC, stating that compliance with regulations passed by the CPSC would not relieve common law liability, the Supreme Court read a similar clause in the Motor Vehicle Act as only providing for common lawsuits that do not frustrate the agency goals of uniformity (*Geier v. American Honda*, 529 U.S. 861 (2000)). After *Geier*, Congress reiterated its view that the commission should not be determining the ultimate preemptive scope of its regulations and codified this position in the subsequent passage of the Consumer Product Safety Improvement Act (CPSIA) of 2008.

An example of the strong push for federal preemption that swept through the federal agencies under the Bush administration is seen in the history of regulation updating mattress flammability standards. In 2006, after not mentioning preemption or any possible preemptive scope of the proposed rule during the rule-making processes of notice and comment, the commission then inserted a preamble to the new rule stating that the standard would preempt all inconsistent state requirements, whether created through positive state law or created through the courts. Such sweeping preemption pronouncements were appearing in preambles of regulations from other agencies at the same time. Consumer product safety advocates fought these agency pronouncements of preemption and eventually the Obama administration issued a presidential memorandum condemning "preemption by preamble" and directing the agencies at issue to review their rule-makings for any such pronouncements. Justice Thomas wrote, "implied pre-emption doctrines that wander far from the statutory text are inconsistent with the Constitution . . ." (concurring opinion in *Wyeth v. Levine*, 555. U.S. 555, 583 (2009)).

The 2000s also saw a heightened awareness of the commission's impotence after widespread media coverage of repeated problems of lead in imported children toys and defective cribs. The commission already had a history of slow and ineffective responses to known dangerous products. Moreover, studies showed the commission was reluctant to fine manufacturers for violations of regulations, instead preferring settlements to prosecutions, even for repeat violators. In 2007, Commissioner Thomas Moore issued a statement to Congress detailing his worries about the future of the agency, "[t]he U.S. Product Safety Commission is at a crossroads. Two years of significant staffing cuts and other resource reductions have limited the commission's ability to carry out its mission and have left the agency at a point where it is now doing only what is absolutely necessary for it to do and little else . . . Many employees at the agency are looking for other jobs because they have no confidence the agency will continue to exist (or will exist in any meaningful form) for many more years . . . The commission can either continue to decline in staff, resources and stature to the point where it is no longer an effective force in consumer protection or, with the support of Congress, it can regain the important place in American society that it was originally designed to have" (www.cpsc .gov/pr/moore_proposals.pdf).

Illinois State Attorney General Lisa Madigan was instrumental in shining a light on the weak enforcement at the CPSC, especially regarding dangerous baby cribs. Despite the commission's awareness of multiple deaths and injuries from certain types of crib designs, the CPSC did nothing for over two years. The Illinois attorney general, working in tandem with the *Chicago Tribune*, exposed the dangerous cribs to the general public and the resulting media attention spurred the CPSC to finally investigate and recall the dangerous products. During this same stretch of time, a series of journalist exposes regarding lead paint on imported children's toys were unfolding. Again, the same pattern emerged of a slow and weak agency, reluctant to respond to defective products even after those products had caused multiple injuries. As a direct result of the media coverage of unsafe children's products throughout the mid-2000s, Congress passed the Consumer Protection Safety and Improvement Act of 2008 (CPSIA).

The Consumer Product Safety and Improvement Act of 2008 (CPSIA) overhauled the CPSC. Besides increasing both the powers of the agency and their funding, the act created stricter standards for children's products, granted significant whistleblower protections for those who might alert the authorities to dangerous products or unsafe practices, and it also gave state attorneys general concurrent enforcement authority to enforce some of the commission's powers. The CPSIA addressed the preemption debate directly by exempting certain more stringent state labeling requirements already in existence and allowing states to apply for exemptions from preemption for state legislation going forward. The CPSIA also explicitly disallowed the "preemption by preamble" technique the commission had attempted with its mattress flammability standards and inserted yet another savings clause reiterating the right of state attorneys general to sue under their state consumer protection laws.

The new standards created by the CPSIA originally banned lead and phthalates from all toys and children's products, created rigorous safety testing standards, directed the CPSC to develop safety standards for all-terrain vehicles, and created substantial increases in funding for the commission. The CPSIA also provided for the creation of a public safety database on unsafe products, required new tracking labels on children's products so that a recalled product could be traced back to its factory of origin, and enlarged the commission's authority to recall products and impose larger penalties on manufacturers who violate the regulations.

Parts of these legislative initiatives were controversial. There was large industry pushback to the banning of phthalates, for example. Though Congress had passed the law, the commission itself was reluctant to enforce some of the new provisions. At the time the agency was headed by Bush administration-appointed Acting Commissioner Nancy Nord, who had lobbied against the phthalate ban before the passage of the CPSIA. After the CPSIA was voted into law by an overwhelmingly bipartisan show of support in Congress, Acting Commissioner Nord attempted to delay implementation of both the phthalate ban as well as other new requirements under the CPSIA that were strongly opposed by manufacturers. Eventually a federal district court ruled that the commission's actions in delaying implementation of the CPSIA violated and undermine[d] the purpose of the CPSA and the CPSIA.

Small business owners, book publishers, secondhand retailers, and librarians had initial concern about whether they would fall under the category of children's products that required extensive testing of products. Almost immediately after the passage of the CPSIA, the commission issued a one-year stay on the testing requirements while they formalized guidance as to which products specifically were covered by those provisions. In August 2011, Congress amended the CPSIA to exempt certain types of products and resale organizations from testing requirements. The amendments further lightened the lead and phthalate bans, making the burden to remove small amounts of lead (100 ppm) prospective and relaxing some of the phthalate ban. Small business owners were now provided some leeway in meeting the testing requirements as well.

Even more controversial to many lobby organizations representing manufacturers were the provisions relating to expanding the scope of authority to the state attorneys general to enforce provisions of the CPSIA. The

CPSIA expressly authorized state attorneys general to bring suit in federal court for injunctive relief against the sale of recalled products, uncertified or nontested products violating the act's testing requirements, and products that lack the new tracking labels or otherwise violate the CPSC's regulations and requirements. This expansion of enforcement powers also allowed state attorneys general to determine themselves that a product is a "substantial product hazard" in which case the state may file suit immediately. The state must notify the commission of any suit (and if the product is not a substantial product hazard, the state must give notice to the agency 30 days before filing suit). The commission retains the right to intervene in any state enforcement lawsuit.

Although this provision created a large outcry from industry groups and their representatives, it is not the first time an administrative agency has delegated concurrent enforcement power to the states. Roughly 24 federal laws grant the states concurrent enforcement power, and a great majority of these are in the consumer protection arena. These state enforcement powers are rarely used and recent empirical work has shown that when they are used it is often in conjunction with the federal agency. (Amy Widman and Prentiss Cox, "State Attorneys General's Use of Concurrent Public Enforcement Authority in Federal Consumer Protection Laws," 33 Cardozo Law Review 53 (2011).)

Since the passage of the CPSIA, the CPSC is appearing to gain strength again. Most recently, the commission's involvement with defective Chinese drywall has been robust and thorough. Frustrated with the hurdles of addressing defective products produced in another country, the CPSC set up a field office in China to better position itself to supervise the safety of imported drywall, as well as other imported consumer goods. According to the BBC News, 45 percent of consumer products and 90 percent of toys are imported from China and Hong Kong. Responding to a flood of complaints about the possible health effects on homeowners of structures containing the toxic drywall, the CPSC led one of the largest investigations in the commission's history, which produced a report and comprehensive remediation guidelines for removing the toxic materials. Consumer advocates are waiting to see if the investigation will lead to a formal recall of the toxic drywall.

The CPSC seems to have received a second chance at life after the passage of the CPSIA. In 2011, its increasing budget and staff sets the impression that Commissioner Moore's dire worries of merely five years before have been mostly addressed for now. There is increasing political debate about the value of consumer protection agencies and partisan debates about whether regulation increases cost or whether regulation merely transfers costs from injured consumers to the manufacturers, or even whether costs of dangerous products are ultimately borne by taxpayers regardless of regulation or through the market or through emergency medical care. According to the CPSC, roughly 31,000 people die and 34 million are injured annually from unsafe products. Those deaths and injuries resulted in an estimated $200 billion in costs to consumers. Regulating manufacturers in an effort to keep the dangerous product from resulting in death or injury might increase a manufacturer's costs at least initially, but that cost was not birthed through the regulation, it was merely shifted onto the manufacturer.

*Amy Widman*

**See also:** Attorney General Office (AG); Consumer Safety Product Safety Commission; Bicycle Safety Standard; Customs and Border Protection (CBP); Food and Drug Administration (FDA); National Highway Traffic and Safety Administration (NHTSA); Recalls

**References and Additional Readings**

Adler, R.S. (2011). Safety regulators don't add costs. They decide who pays them. *The New York Times.*

BBC News (2011). US consumer watchdog opens office in China. Retrieved from http://www.bbc.co.uk/news/business-12150355

Callahan, P. (2008). Hidden crib dangers. *Chicago Tribune.* Retrieved from http://www.chicagotribune.com/news/nationworld/chi-081115cribs,0,4984240.story

Center for Progressive Reform. (2008). The truth about torts: Regulatory preemption at the Consumer Product Safety Commission. Retrieved from http://www.progressivereform.org/articles/Truth_About_Torts_CPSC_807.pdf

Consumer Federation of America. (2007). Testimony and comments: Rachel Weintraub, Director of Product Safety and Senior Counsel, Consumer Federation of America. Retrieved from http://www.consumerfed.org/news-room/testimony-and-comments#2007

Consumer Product Safety and Improvement Act of 2008, Pub L. No. 110–314, 122 Stat. 3016. Retrieved from http://www.cpsc.gov/cpsia.pdf

Hearing of the Consumer Product Safety Commission: Hearing Before the Subcommittee on Consumer Affairs, Insurance and Auto Safety of the Senate Committee on Commerce, Science and Transportation, 110th Congress (2007)(Statement of Rachel Weintraub, Director of Product Safety and Senior Counsel, Consumer Federation of America).

Hilsgen, J. (2011). Amendment to CPSIA. In *U.S. Consumer Product Safety Commission.* Retrieved from www.cpsc.gov/businfo/intl/hr2715.pdf

Kids in Danger. (2009). Toxic toys and faulty cribs: An examination of children's product recalls in 2008. Recall effectiveness at the CPSC and the implications for child safety. Retrieved from http://www.kidsindanger.org/docs/reports/ToxicToysFaultyCribsReport.pdf

Possley, M. (2007). Missteps delayed recall of deadly cribs. *Chicago Tribune*, September 24, 2007. Retrieved from http://articles.chicagotribune.com/2007-09-24/business/chi-070922cribs-story_1_simplicity-cribs-liam-johns-full-size-cribs/3

Widman, A. (2010). Advancing federalism concerns in administrative law through a revitalization of state enforcement powers: A case study of the Consumer Product Safety and Improvement Act of 2008. *29 Yale Law & Policy Review, 165.*

**Consumer Reports**. *See* Consumers Union

## Consumer Sovereignty

The concept of consumer sovereignty posits that consumers control the market and ultimately decide what goods and services are provided by purchasing the products they most want or need. In a perfect market, producers respond to consumer purchasing habits by creating more of the desired product. Ultimately, the economic principle of supply and demand implies, in a perfect world, that production is driven by consumption. Because consumers do not always act rationally, this economic assumption is not always upheld.

This idea that consumers are king of the marketplace is grounded in several economic assumptions around the functioning of a perfect market, where consumers instinctively know what they want and need without market input. Consumer sovereignty is threatened by a market situation where producers are perceived to be the kings of persuasion, using advertising techniques to develop new markets and expand old ones through consumer manipulation. This development and expansion arguably would not occur without consumer buy-in, and yet a true test of consumer independence in a perfect marketplace is evermore hindered by rapid development of new products, reduced time to research existing products, and lack of access to all available options.

Rapidly changing technology in the marketplace forces consumers to abandon set preferences and challenges them to constantly adapt. In an era of instant gratification, producers are forced to create products in advance of the need, subsequently requiring them to unload products and reduce rates when market demand changes. This rapid rate of production is further complicated by the rapid pace of product advancement. In this constantly shifting marketplace, products may be purchased solely to keep up with these changes, further diminishing the consumer's ability to be properly educated about each product they purchase. *Caveat emptor* (let the buyer beware) indicates that a certain amount of risk is assumed by the consumer when making a purchase, yet in a global marketplace this risk may be heightened and therefore more critical to acknowledge.

The growth of the Internet makes access to product education more plausible. Therefore, producers may assume consumers have opportunities to be educated and subsequently have the ability to make utilitarian purchase decisions. The reality is, decision makers may not have access to all possible information, may lack the ability to comprehend it, and more frequently, may lack the time needed to process all the information. Vast options available in today's marketplace can overwhelm a consumer searching for a product compelling him/her to make a quick decision to avoid information overload.

Marketers recognize the power of information avoidance in the mind of a busy consumer, often focusing their efforts toward brand recognition rather than consumer education. Even though most consumers desire value, this tactic often leads the consumer to settle for the false security of recognizable brands instead of identifying the most value for the least cost. This market manipulation transfers power away from the consumer into the hands of the producer, further enhancing producer sovereignty, diminishing consumer sovereignty, and disrupting the basic economic principle of supply and demand. This flux between consumer and producer control in the marketplace is further complicated by advancing technology. In a market where the consumer performs duties once assumed to be part of basic customer service and included in the price of a good, the lines between producer and consumer become somewhat blurred. For instance, technology that allows for self-checkout in the online market place is ever more available in physical establishments. The term coined for this movement toward putting the consumer to work for the producer is *prosumerism.* Examples include ATM's, and self-serve filling stations. The lines are even more blurry in consignment situations and community gardens where individuals work in the market, for the market, and consume the product. Consumers are drawn toward prosumerism because it can be personally empowering, more efficient, and perceived to be a more sustainable economic model. The combination of rapidly expanding technology, ever-changing products, and the use of advertising to brand concepts and images into the consumer subconscience make the purity of consumer sovereignty debatable. A newer and better product is almost always available, forcing adaptation and progression. The marketplace has expanded dramatically due to the Internet and globalization of goods through improved transportation, which gives consumers access to more choices. Increased choices initially aided consumer sovereignty, forcing producers to compete on behalf of the consumer. However, these choices have reached a tipping point that has overwhelmed the consumer, subsequently encouraging less informed decisions and decreasing consumer power in the marketplace. As the world economy moves further away from a pure barter economy, it is important to recognize this shift in power from one of consumer sovereignty to a more producer friendly marketplace

*Trena T. Anastasia*

**See also:** Caveat Emptor; Producer Sovereignty

### References and Additional Readings

Keat, R. (1991). Consumer sovereignty and the integrity of practices. In R. Keat and N. Abercrombie (eds.). *Enterprise culture.* London: Routledge, 1–17.

Lerner, A. P. (1972). The economics and politics of consumer sovereignty. *The American Economic Review, 62*(1, 2), 258–266.

## Consumers International

Consumers International is an organizing entity of consumer groups from around the world. Formerly known as the International Organization of Consumers Union (IOCU), it was founded in 1960 by five nonprofit consumer groups from the United States, Europe, and Australia. The meeting that conceived IOCU was the International Conference on Consumer Testing, partially funded by Consumers Union, held in the Hague with 34 people in attendance representing 14 counties and 17 organizations. By the 1990s, the membership had grown to over 250 organizations and 80 nations. It was at that time that the organization underwent a significant restructure, complete with a new vision and mission statement and a name change from the International Organization of Consumers Union to Consumers International. The name was more inclusive, better suiting the organizations growing third-world members, as well as more accurately representing the broader interests and functions of the group.

Today, the organization has grown to 120 countries and 240 member organizations. Registered as a nonprofit organization and a charity in the

United Kingdom, the organization also has offices in Johannesburg, South Africa; Kuala Lumpur, Malasia; London, UK; and Santiago, Chile. The organization announces

World Consumer Rights Day, celebrated since 1983, is on March 15, honoring President Kennedy's historic Consumer Rights speech on that day in 1963.

the following vision as written on its website: "Our vision is of a world where people can make informed choices on safe and sustainable goods and services and in which individual and collective Consumer Rights are secure and respected. We believe that: People: in order to live, all people consume—be it through the satisfaction of the most basic human need, through to considering complex financial products. The fundamental rights of all consumers are upheld and protected by corporations, governments, and international decision-making bodies. We think that consumers should be: provided with the right facts and skills, while being protected from misleading promotion, and be able to make confident and empowered decisions; be confident that the products and services bought are safe to use, and have the minimum impact on social and ecological conditions for both producers and consumers."

## Mission Statement

Its mission, as stated on its website, is "to champion Consumer Rights internationally in order to help protect and empower consumers everywhere. To defend, promote, develop and pursue Consumer Rights as the international basis of consumer protection. To support, develop and work directly with our constituent member organizations, seeking to protect, inform, give a voice to and secure rights for consumers worldwide."

Consumers International is governed by a General Assembly, a Council and an Executive body. The General Assembly is comprised of voting delegates from full members of Consumers International; they meet every four or five years during the Consumers International World Congress. The most recent World Congress, the 19th one, was held in Hong Kong in May 2011. The Council consists of the President of Consumers International, 13 General Assembly elected members and up to six other members representing elected members. All council members serve four-year terms and no limitations exist on terms. The role of the council is to carry out duties as the board, as well as, establishing general policies and strategic planning. The council typically meets once a year. The executive body of Consumers International consists of eight members who meet at least two times each year. They carry out decision-making roles from the council.

Consumer International's strategic plan for 2015 is detailed on the website and covers the following broad topics: consumer justice and protection; food safety, security, and nutrition; financial services; and consumers in the digital age. Part of their work for consumers on an international level involves financial services, climate change, charitable development, sustainable development, and global activity. Their member activity log indicates recent work on defective goods in Singapore, better consumer protection in Hong Kong, Patient Rights in Kenya, Supermarket pricing confusion, carcinogenic Coke products, salt consumption in Africa, interest charges in Tanzania, and low satisfaction with banking in Belgium.

*Wendy Reiboldt*

**See also:** Activism; Consumers Union; Kennedy, John F.; United Nations (UN); World Trade Organization (WTO)

### References and Additional Readings

Brobeck, S. (1997). *Consumers international.* In S. Brobeck (Ed.), *Encyclopedia of the consumer movement* (175–179). ABC-CLIO: Santa Barbara, CA.

Consumers International. (2012a). *Consumer justice and protection strategy 2015.* Consumers International: UK.

Consumers International. (2012b). *Your rights, our mission: Strategy 2015.* Consumers International: UK.

Consumers International. (2013). The global voice for consumers. Retrieved from http://www.consumersinternational.org

Sim, F. G. (1991). *IOCU on record: A documentary history of the international organization of consumers unions, 1960–1990.* Consumers Union: Yonkers, NY.

## Consumers Union

Consumers Union is the world's largest independent product-testing organization. The private, nonprofit organization tests consumer goods and services, serves as an information source for consumers, and advocates for legislative and regulatory reforms through lobbying and consumer activism for the benefit of consumers.

### History of Consumers Union

Consumers Union was founded in 1936 by Arthur Kallet and others who were on strike and ultimately fired from Consumer's Research, an organization similar to Consumers Union. Colston E. Warne, a professor at Amherst College, joined with the others, who were committed to testing products used by consumers, to found Consumers Union. Kallet served as the first director and Warne was the organization's first board chairman, serving for 43 years. The State of New York granted a charter for Consumers Union in February 1936 to provide consumers with "information and counsel on . . . goods and services" and "maintain laboratories . . . to supervise and conduct research and tests." A three-tiered ratings system—"Best Buy," "Also Acceptable," and "Not Acceptable"—was adopted to present the results of scientific tests of products.

In the years since, Consumers Union has tested 155,000 products at its in-house laboratories. In the early years, there was little money available for testers to purchase products for testing. As a result, many early reports were on inexpensive items such as electric fans, hot water bottles, breakfast cereals, Alka-Seltzer, and radios. Televisions were first tested in the late 1940s.

Consumers Union is publisher of *Consumer Reports,* a monthly magazine, which publishes reviews and comparisons of consumer products and services based on reporting and results from its in-house testing laboratories, and numerous other publications and websites. There are nearly eight million subscribers to *Consumer Reports* magazine, its website and two newsletters, *Consumer Reports on Health* and *Consumer Reports Money Adviser*.

The mission of Consumers Union, as written on their website, is to serve as "an expert, independent, nonprofit organization whose mission is to work for a fair, just, and safe marketplace for all consumers and to empower consumers to protect themselves." Approximately 2,000 products are tested annually at the organization's in-house laboratories with the ultimate goal of relaying results to consumers to help them in their decision-making.

To maintain the organization's independence and ensure impartiality, Consumers Union accepts no outside advertising or free samples for any of its publications. A network of mystery shoppers in 65 U.S. cities are employed to buy products that are then tested by technical experts at their laboratories. *Consumer Reports* has a strict policy preventing the use of its name and information for any promotional or advertising purposes by sellers and manufacturers to ensure that there is no appearance of product endorsement for financial gain. The policy also guarantees that consumers have access to the full context of information issued by Consumers Union rather than through advertising by sellers. The company generated nearly $230 million in annual revenue in 2011 from publication subscriptions, newsstand and online sales, and private donations and grants.

Consumers Union is headquartered in Yonkers, New York, which houses the National Testing and Research Center, with 50 state-of-the-art labs for product testing and data collection. It is the largest nonprofit education and consumer product testing facility in the world. An Auto Test Center is situated on 327 acres in East Haddam, Connecticut. Consumers Union has three advocacy offices located in Washington, D.C., San Francisco, California; and Austin, Texas, which are staffed for the purpose of testifying before state and regulatory agencies and filing lawsuits on behalf of consumers relating to pertinent consumer issues. Lawsuits have been filed by Consumers Union on behalf of consumers relating to product safety, housing, the environment, economic discrimination, and telecommunications. Advocates work with members of Congress, state legislators, and government regulatory agencies to ensure consumer product safety in both manufacturing and marketing. The organization employs more than 600 individuals at its various locations throughout the country.

## Product Testing and Research

Thousands of products are tested each year using state-of-the art testing equipment and engineers and technicians employed by Consumers Union. Products are tested based on government and industry standards, as well as standards applied by researchers at *Consumer Reports*. Product testing is supplemented by survey research of subscribers regarding their experiences with products and services. Testing experts work in seven major technical departments—appliances, auto test, baby and child, electronics, foods, health and family, and recreation and home improvement.

In addition to product testing, *Consumer Reports* relies on feedback from subscribers and responses to surveys, including the Annual Ballot and Questionnaire that is sent to all subscribers each spring. The *Consumer Reports* National Research Center is the research arm of Consumer Reports' National Testing and Research Center. More than one million consumers are surveyed each year on a broad range of experiences with products and services. This includes brands of appliances and electronics, cell phone services, travel, and auto and homeowner insurance, to name a few. Consumers also report on the best places to purchase products, both on the Internet and in stores, as well as products they bought and repaired, and on their interactions with major retailers and service providers. The National Research Center further mines data from responses from thousands of car owners to provides auto owner satisfaction information on hundreds of car models. Additionally, *Consumer Reports'* publications include information from consumers on complex healthcare topics and treatments for health conditions. More than 200 qualitative and quantitative projects are conducted annually. Many of those surveys are conducted with random samples selected from subscribers to *Consumer Reports* and/or to ConsumerReports.org. Data also come from the National Research Center, which uses national probability samples to accurately represent the entire U.S. population.

In addition to printed publications, a website (www.consumersunion.org) provides updated news and information regarding consumer issues and current advocacy activities. Additional information on current campaigns sponsored by Consumers Union is also provided.

Consumers Union has helped start several other consumer groups and publications. Consumers International was formed in 1960 with the support of Consumers Union. The organization provided financial assistance to help start Consumers' CHECKBOOK in 1974, an organization similar to Consumer Reports, which provides local services in seven metropolitan areas. The National Commission on Product Safety established in part because of all the products through the years that *Consumer Reports* had found to be unsafe and therefore "Not Acceptable," recommended the creation of the Consumer Product Safety Commission. *Consumer Reports* often shares testing data with the U.S. Consumer Product Safety Commission and has contributed to recalls of numerous consumer products.

### Advocacy and Campaigns

Consumers Union provides unbiased information and advice about products and services, personal finance, health, nutrition, food and product safety, housing, sustainable purchasing, energy and utility deregulation, and other consumer concerns. As part of its advocacy program, there are several websites that inform consumers on specific consumer issues.

- Defend Your Dollars website educates consumers on the efforts to establish reforms to the financial marketplace and curb bad practices by banks and lenders. Topics addressed include credit cards, bank accounts, credit reports, debts and loans, financial reforms, mortgages, and payments.
- Food safety issues are addressed to focus public attention on food safety risks and regulatory deficiencies that can result in harm to the public. "Not in My Food" focuses public attention on food safety risks and regulatory deficiencies that can result in harm to the public. Greenerchoices.

org serves as a guide to environmentally friendly products, and includes coverage of the mercury-in-tuna debate. There is also a guide to environmental labels, such as "USDA Certified Organic," "Fair Trade Certified," and "Rainforest Alliance" (Miller, 2007). Consumers can use the search tools to have labels on food, wood, personal care products and household cleaners evaluated for validity of the products' claims to be environmentally friendly.

- HearUsNow.org educates consumers about communication and media issues involving telephone, cable, Internet, and wireless services and equipment. The objective is to explain increasingly complex communications issues and how consumers are affected, with a special emphasis on local cases.

- CreditCardReform.org educates consumers on proposed reforms to the credit card marketplace and other lenders to curb abusive practices. News of recent legislative events and banking regulations, as well as actions taken by credit card companies, are posted to keep consumers informed.

Consumers Union sponsors several campaigns and initiatives that inform consumers of specific issues and the steps being taken by the organization and its supporters to protect consumers.

- Safe Patient Project is a campaign to eliminate medical harm in the healthcare system. Consumers Union has launched various initiatives within the campaign to promote the safety of patients in their health care. The campaign calls for public disclosure of healthcare outcomes (such as hospital-acquired infection rates and incidents of medical errors) and information about healthcare providers (such as complaints against and license violations of physicians and hospitals). Advocates of the campaign maintain that doctor accountability allows consumers to know the background of their physicians, including number of complaints, malpractice claims, and disciplinary actions. Public disclosure of hospitals and infection rates enables consumers to choose the safest hospitals, and understand the protections afforded to them in the event of mistakes or poor quality care, thereby giving hospitals an incentive to improve. The campaign also works to improve drug safety by ensuring that consumers have full information about prescription drugs (such as in direct-to-consumer ads and access to clinical trial results), by strengthening oversight of the FDA, and by ending practices that create conflicts of interest (such as drug company gifts to doctors).

- Prescription for Change is dedicated to getting affordable, quality health care and coverage for all Americans. Consumers Union supported the passage of the 2010 Patient Protection and Affordable Care Act to increase comprehensive healthcare coverage for more Americans. Initiatives within this campaign address affordable health insurance, improving the purchase and use of healthcare policies, state rate reviews, and safety and quality assurance.

- Buy Safe, Eat Well is a campaign that devotes attention to the safety of the food supply for consumers. The premise of the campaign is that informed consumers should have the right to know where food comes from, what the standards of food quality are for countries that export to the United States and whether foods are safe and free from pesticides and hormones.

- A Greener Energy Future promotes the development of cleaner, renewable forms of energy, such as wind, *solar*, *biomas* and *geothermal*, and better *energy efficiency* in cars, appliances, and buildings. It is the position of Consumers Union that *"greener" choices* offer the opportunity to stabilize consumer energy prices and decrease *water* and *air pollution*. Clean energy initiatives can also reduce America's dependence on foreign oil, and help build an innovative clean energy economy.

### Publications and Digital Media

Consumers Union is the publisher of numerous publications, websites, and digital media. *Consumer Reports* is one of the largest circulation magazines in the United States. The magazine features comparative ratings based on quality evaluation of brand-name consumer products, and offers special features devoted to health, medicine, family expenditures, and other topics. Reviews and comparisons of consumer products and services are based on reporting and results from its in-house testing laboratory. It also publishes cleaning and general buying guides. The annual *Consumer Reports New Car Buying Guide* is typically the magazine's best-selling issue and is thought to influence millions of automobile purchases.

In addition to *Consumer Reports*, there are other magazines published by Consumers Union that cover topics such as kitchen planning and buying, new cars, food and fitness, and shopping smart. Two newsletters—Consumer Reports on Health and Consumer Reports Money Adviser—provide readers with advice and information on personal finance and evaluations of the latest medical trends, procedures, and discoveries.

There are several books and buying guides also in circulation. These include *Electronics Buying Guide, How to Save Protect and Grow Your Money,*

*Consumer Reports Wellness Guide, How to Clean Practically Anything,* and *Best Baby Products.* Other topics covered include new cars, used cars, reducing energy costs, and health.

Consumers can also access *Consumer Reports* online. Additional online services include "Cars Best Deals Plus," "New Car Price Service," and "Used Car Price Service." In 2009, Consumers Union acquired *The Consumerist* blog, targeting younger readers through interactive commentary on pressing consumer issues. Topics include reports on bargains and scams, and updates on consumer news, customer service, and shopping. Versions of *Consumer Reports* for e-readers and tablets are available.

*Consumer Reports* has introduced shopping applications that allow consumers to get ratings and advice at the point of sale. The *Consumer Reports* Mobile Shopper allows consumers to scan an item's bar code and get the latest test results. Build & Buy is a buying service established by *Consumer Reports,* to help car shoppers to purchase new cars at fair prices. Consumers can utilize BillShrink, partnered by Consumers Union, to find better deals on credit cards and telecom services.

In 1953, *Consumer Reports* published the first in a series of reports on the tar and nicotine content of cigarette smoke and health hazards of smoking. There was no information on the contents of cigarettes available from any sources at the time. Ten years later, *Consumer Reports* published a report on smoking and the public interest. As a result, the Surgeon General's Advisory Committee on Smoking and Health used the information from the report to draft the committee's report to caution consumers about the danger of smoking cigarettes.

*Consumer Reports'* testing of safety belts in the mid-1950s showed that two-thirds of seat belts in cars failed to meet modest guidelines, through breakage and failure of simulated crash tests. Consumers' Union called for better seat belts and for federal standards that legislate real-life crash testing simulations. Regular testing of seat belts continued until the federal government mandated, in 1968, that all new cars have belts in the front seats.

*Consumer Reports'* rigorous testing of microwaves in the mid-1970s show that the products leaked radiation at levels that could not be determined to be harmless to consumers. A "Not Recommended" warning was issued for the class of microwave products. Petitions were filed with the federal government. These petitions resulted in improvements in both door interlocks and warning labels on microwaves. As a result, consumers were made aware of precautions to avoid extreme exposure to emitting energy from microwaves.

The Safe Drinking Water Act was passed by Congress in 1974, partly as a result of a three-part series published by *Consumer Reports* on the safety of the U.S. water supply. The reports concluded that many communities' water purification systems were not up to par with appropriate efforts to eliminate high levels of pollution and potential carcinogens in drinking water. In addition to the legislation, these reports also ignited investigations at the local level.

*Consumer Reports* began testing child-safety seats in the early 1970s. As a result of crash testing in 1972, 12 out of 15 seats were rated as "not acceptable." For the next five years, child-safety seats were regularly tested, and results were made available to consumers and government legislators. In 1974, as a result, government leaders proposed stronger child restraints. In 1981, a federal law required all child-safety seat manufacturers to prove, via rigorous crash testing, that their seats were safe.

Consumers Union was selected by the Consumer Product Safety Commission, in 1974, to address lawn mower safety. This was in part due to the fact that each year, hundreds of thousands of lawn mower users experienced injuries related to its use. The standards, which eventually became mandatory by 1983, included a "deadman control," or a mechanism that allowed users to have better control over turning off the blade and reducing unintended injury. Lobbying efforts by the outdoor power equipment industry delayed the standards becoming mandatory for nearly a decade.

In 1988, Consumers Union petitioned the National Highway Traffic Safety Administration (NHTSA) for a safety standard addressing rollover-prone SUVs. Twelve years later, Congress finally mandated that NHTSA conduct dynamic rollover tests. Experts from Consumers Union testified that such information was critical for consumers in order to make informed decisions regarding purchasing safer vehicles. As a result, the federal agency began a more rigorous testing protocol in its rollover information program.

*Mary Jane "M.J." Kabaci*

**See also:** Auto Purchasing; Consumer Product Safety Commission (CPSC); Environmental Protection Agency (EPA); Food Safety

## References and Additional Readings

Archer, R. (2011). Consumers Union: Testing, testing. *Fairfield County Business Journal.* Retrieved from http://www.allbusiness.com/north-america/united-states-connecticut/1086096-1.html

Bounds, G. (2011). Meet the sticklers. *The Wall Street Journal.* Retrieved from http://online.wsj.com/article/SB10001424052748703866704575224093017379202.html

Consumer Reports. (2011a). Retrieved from http://www.consumerreports.org/

Consumer Reports. (2011b). Transformation 2011. *Consumer Reports 2011 Annual Report*. Retrieved from http://www.consumerreports.org/cro/resources/streaming/PDFs/CU_2011AR.pdf.

Consumers Union. (2011). About us. Retrieved from http://www.consumersunion.org/

Gale Directory of Company Histories. (2011). Consumers Union. Retrieved from http://www.answers.com/topic/consumers-union

Leonard, D. (2011). Consumer Reports maintains old-school values. *Bloomberg Businessweek.* Retrieved from http://www.msnbc.msn.com/id/38451478/ns/bsiness-bloomberg_Businessweek

Miller, L. (2007). Consumers Union. *Supermarket News, 55,* 30.

Silber, N. (1983). *Test and protest: The influence of Consumers Union.* New York: Holmes & Meier.

## Contract Law

Every year Americans enter into millions of contracts. Every time consumers engage in a commercial transaction, that is a contract. A buyer agrees to buy a car, a sandwich, a haircut, or a T-shirt by paying money (in some form) for that item to a seller. The buyer assumes that he/she will receive that item or service for the payment, and the seller assumes that he/she will be paid when he/she provides the item or service. Contract law exists to protect individuals who are relying on someone else's consent to engage in some kind of transaction. Both parties to a contract value what they are getting more than what they are giving up; this is called a "value-enhancing" agreement; for example, if a woman is hungry, she values the food she buys more than she values the money she spends on lunch. Contract law takes into account the intentions of the parties and protects their reliance on each other, and it also considers whether the agreement is value enhancing for both parties, although such value need not be measured in monetary value.

### More on Contract Law

A mechanic's lien (or materialman's, supplier's, laborer's, or artisan's lien) is an interest in a property that exists to protect those who have supplied labor or materials to improve that property. The term "lien" comes from the French word for "binding," and such liens date from the 18th century in the United States. All states have them, and they are protections for contractors and subcontractors who build or provide materials for buildings and cars. Liens provide an additional opportunity for contractors who have suffered breach of contract to recover from that breach.

Traditionally, a contract involves a "meeting of the minds" in which two parties agreed to something. The American legal definition, from the *Restatement (Second) of Contracts,* says "a contract is a promise or a set of promises for the breach of which the law gives a remedy, or the performance of which the law in some way recognizes as a duty." Contracts can be *expressed* (written down) or *implied* (inferred from conduct). American contract law has its roots in English common and equity law. Common law is law made by judges; it usually is not written down in any organized way, like a statute might be. Equity law is a type of law that developed when courts and judges decided that the current legal remedies, such as money, for a situation were inadequate.

A key case that illustrates the development of the common law of contracts is an English case called *Carlill v. Carbolic Smoke Ball Company,* decided in 1893. A flu remedy called the "smoke ball" was marketed by the Carbolic Smoke Ball Company, who offered a reward of £100 if someone who used the ball contracted influenza. Mrs. Louisa Elizabeth Carlill used the ball, caught the flu, and tried to claim the reward. The company said that she had not entered into a contract with it because she had not notified the company that she bought and used the ball. The court rejected the company's argument, saying that Mrs. Carlill had entered into a binding contract with the company by purchasing and using the ball, and that she was entitled to the reward.

The *Carlill* case is an excellent example of a *unilateral contract,* where Mrs. Carlill did not need to make a promise of her own to enter into a contract. Many advertisements are unilateral contracts (but they are not considered to be offers). *Bilateral contracts,* on the other hand, are agreements to which each party makes a promise to the other party (or parties).

American contract law comes primarily from three sources. The common law, cases decided in courts, is one primary source. For example, in addition to cases like *Carlill,* English cases like *Hadley v. Baxendale,* decided in 1854, set out many of the primary concepts in American contract law. The *Hadley* case created a basic rule for how to determine damages from a breach of contract. Mr. Hadley and others were proprietors of a mill in Gloucester. The mill broke down, and they needed a crankshaft to fix it, which they ordered from a company in Greenwich. The broken crankshaft had to be delivered to the company so it could be hand-fit to the existing engine. Hadley contracted with Baxendale and Ors, a delivery service, to deliver the broken crankshaft by a certain date. But Baxendale failed to meet the delivery date, so the repair was delayed. Hadley sued for his lost profits, and Baxendale appealed, saying he did not know that Hadley would suffer more damage as a result of the missed delivery date. The court declined to award Hadley the lost profits, saying that Baxendale should not be liable for damages he could not have foreseen or anticipated. The judge wrote, "Where two parties have made a contract which one of them has broken, the damages which the other party ought to receive in respect of such breach of contract should be such as may fairly and reasonably be considered either arising naturally, *i.e.*, according to the usual course of things, from such breach of contract itself, or such as may reasonably be supposed to have been in the contemplation of both parties, at the time they made the contract, as the probable result of the breach of it." American courts still use this principle today to determine damages.

The second major source of contract law is a legal treatise known as the *Restatement (Second) of Contracts.* This is the product of the American Law Institute, a group of select attorneys, judges, and law professors, who have aggregated the issues in many areas of American law and "restated" the legal principles within those areas—including contract law. This document often shapes the ways in which contract law is interpreted and applied by lawyers and judges.

Finally, the *Uniform Commercial Code,* or UCC, is an attempt to harmonize and unify state law in commercial transactions. The UCC covers only sales of goods. So leases, service arrangements like employment contracts, and the like are instead governed by common law. The UCC has been signed by all 50 states (Louisiana was the last state to join, in 1990). Because the UCC is limited only to sales of goods, it is often common law and the *Restatement (Second)* that will govern contracts.

What, then, are the elements of a contract? In the common law, there are generally considered to be four: offer, acceptance, intention to create legal relations, and consideration.

An *offer* is an indication of one party's willingness to enter into a bargain, made so that another party understands that the bargain is invited and will be met. For example, if a boy at school sees a girl with his favorite candy bar at lunch, and he says to her, "Want to trade your candy bar for my cupcake?" that is an offer.

An offer is often followed by an *acceptance,* the second element of a contract. Some showing or manifestation of agreement or assent is necessary. Thus, if the girl replies, "Sure," that is an unconditional acceptance. The terms of the offer cannot change; if they do, the acceptance becomes a counteroffer (e.g., if the girl responds with "Sure, if you give me a quarter too"—and the boy is under no obligation to accept that counteroffer).

But intent (or consent) can be tricky to determine. Meanings of words can be unclear. Contracts Law Professor Randy Barnett suggests that "the meaning that is objectively communicated is the meaning that *a reasonable person* in the relevant community would attach to the other party's words or conduct." So, if the girl's response of "Sure" is understood in her community (her class) by a reasonable person (her classmates) to mean "Yes" (rather than "Maybe" or something else), that would serve as a manifestation of her consent to the boy's offer.

The *intention to create legal relations* element means that the parties cannot contract for illegal purposes or goods. And finally, *consideration* is the legal value of the agreement. It can be money, services, property, or promises of action. Consideration can also take the form of agreeing *not* to do something; this is called forbearance (e.g., if the boy and girl agree that the boy will pay the girl a quarter a week if she does not trade her dessert with anyone else before he gets to decide if he wants to trade for it). Why have consideration? If there is no consideration, there is no contract, because both parties are not bound (e.g., if the boy just gives the girl his cupcake without her agreement to give him the candy bar, he's made a gift to her, and there is no contract). Once the boy and girl have made it clear they agree, he gives her the cupcake, she gives him the candy bar, and the bilateral contract is fulfilled. This consent historically took the form of a wax seal, but can be a handshake, a signature on paper, or a click on an "Agree" box on a website.

Most contracts can be enforceable even if they are not written. But states have enacted "statutes of frauds" that require some contracts to be written to be enforceable, to prevent frauds from happening—for example, prenuptial agreements are required in Texas to be written, and usually contracts that involve selling land or other things for large amounts of money. The name comes from the first such statute, passed in England in 1677.

People below the age of 18 (minors) cannot legally contract (so the boy and girl in the example, assuming they are grade-school age, could not make an enforceable contract). Nor can those individuals who are mentally impaired or incompetent, or under duress of some kind, like danger to one's life. Misrepresentations will void contracts, such as contracting to sell a nonfunctional car by telling the potential buyer that it runs fine. *Illusory promises* also will not be enforced by the courts; these are not considered to be contracts, often because there is no consideration involved. So, if the girl tells the boy, "Tomorrow I will bring you a candy bar," that is an illusory promise because he was not expected to give her anything in return, and because it is really based on her whim.

As noted earlier, contracts exist to protect both parties. But what happens if one party breaches (breaks) a contract? The cause of action is called *breach of contract*, and there are two basic types of remedy: damages and performance. Damages involve financial compensation for loss, and they are usually compensatory damages for actual financial harm incurred (there are punitive damages to punish the breacher for egregious harm, but those are not often assessed in contract law). Performance, an action in equity, is a requirement that a party perform a certain act that was agreed to in the contract and when financial damages would not sufficiently address the harm—for example, an order to paint a house or fix a car or fence. In some cases, simply being able to sue for a breach is not sufficient; for example, if there is a breach of contract in a building project. Mechanic's liens are one way to provide additional protection for these kinds of situations that involve contractors.

In addition to breach of contract, there is another cause of action in contract law: *promissory estoppel.* This is a separate action from breach of contract. It has four elements that must be demonstrated: a promise that is either expressed or implied; detrimental reliance on the promise foreseeable by a reasonable person; actual detrimental reliance by the promise on that promise; and the need for the enforcement of the promise as a remedy. For example, the boy tells the girl that if she brings him a candy bar tomorrow, he will pay her a dollar for it. The girl steals an extra candy bar from home and brings it to school, and the boy then tells her he won't pay her the dollar. Her parents find out about the theft and ground her. She would be entitled to damages because she detrimentally relied on his implied promise.

One area of contract law that has become very important in the age of computers and the Internet are so-called "shrinkwrap" and "clickwrap" license agreements. These terms come from the method by which a user agrees to the contract: by tearing off the shrinkwrap on the software or by clicking on a button that says "Yes" or "I agree" on a website. Generally these are enforceable contracts, even if the user does not read the terms or know what they say. In a 1996 case, *ProCD, Inc. v. Zeidenberg,* a user had purchased a database of information on a CD-ROM, clicked to agree to the contract terms, but then broke them by offering the information on the disk on his own website and charging less than the company did for it. The Seventh Circuit Court of Appeals said that he had been able to read the terms of the agreement before clicking to agree, and so he was bound by those terms. But in one case, *Klocek v. Gateway, Inc.,* decided in Kansas in 2000, a court said that when a user opened the box containing a new computer and that contained contract terms, those terms did not become part of the contract unless the user expressly agreed to them (in this case, a contract term that mandated that disputes with the company be settled through arbitration).

*Genelle I. Belmas*

**See also:** Levies; Liens; Small Claims Courts; Supreme Court

### References and Additional Readings

Barnett, R. E. (2010). *The Oxford introductions to U.S. law: Contracts.* New York: Oxford University Press.

Belmas, G. I., & Larson, B. N. (2007). Clicking away your speech rights: The enforceability of gagwrap clauses. *Communications Law and Policy, 12,* 37–89.

*Carlill v. Carbolic Smoke Ball Company* [1893] Q.B. 256 (C.A.).

Cimeno, C. F. (2009). Virtue and contract law. *Oregon Law Review,* 88, 703–744.

*Hadley v. Baxendale,* 9 Exch. 341, 156 Eng. Rep. 145 (1854).

Hart, D. K. (2011). Contract law now—reality meets legal fictions. *University of Baltimore Law Review, 41,* 1–81.

*Klocek v. Gateway, Inc.,* 104 F. Supp. 2d 1332 (D. Kan. 2000).

*ProCD, Inc. v. Zeidenberg,* 86 F.3d 1447 (7th Cir. 1996).

Restatement (Second) of Contracts. (1981). Philadelphia, PA: American Law Institute.

Uniform commercial code: Official text and comments. (2009). St. Paul, MN: West.

## Cooling Off Rule

Prior to the 1970s door-to-door salespersons were common and the industry was a significant part of commerce in communities throughout the United States. Many home solicitation companies and their employees offered a useful service to consumers. That is, a convenient way for many to purchase products without having to leave their homes. However, as the industry prospered and expanded, a disproportionate number of those in the industry used questionable trade practices to sell their wares. For example, many used high-pressure tactics, for example, intimidation, not leaving the premises until the consumer bought the product The public became increasingly frustrated by these unfair and deceptive trade practices and as a result, the Federal Trade Commission (FTC) promulgated The Cooling Off Rule, also known as the Door-to-Door Rule (16 CFR.429). The Rule, which took effect in 1974, was subsequently amended in 1995.

Since the 1970s many states have enacted a variety of their own "Cooling-Off" type regulations. Originally, the federal Cooling Off Rule applied, for the most part, to home solicitations. However, as states began developing their own cooling off regulations the definition was modified and expanded to include a whole host of industries. Numerous industries that must comply with cooling off regulations in various states are present. Examples include, but are not limited to the following service industries: health clubs, time shares, discount buying clubs, campground memberships, home study or correspondence and vocational school courses, seminar sales, credit repair contracts, weight reduction offers, employment counseling, home equity sales during foreclosures, dating services, health studio, dance studio, job listing services, certain seller-assisted marketing plans, employment counseling, and home repair or restoration contracts following a disaster.

The goal of all cooling off mandates is to combat high pressure and deceptive sales in specified industries where high-pressure tactics are commonplace. All cooling-off rules allow consumers a specified number of days to change their minds. The limit is often from three or five days after signing the agreement to rescind it and obtain a full refund. Additionally, most rules specify the obligations of the seller to comply, for example, summary notices informing the buyer of the right to cancel, the time period in which the monies must be refunded.

The FTC's website regarding the Cooling Off Rule states "The rule, as amended, declares it an unfair and deceptive practice for a seller engaged in a 'door-to-door sale' of consumer goods or services, with a purchase price of $25 or more, to fail to provide the buyer with certain oral and written disclosures regarding the buyer's right to cancel the contract within three business days from the date of the sales transaction." A door-to-door sale is defined as any transaction taking place anywhere (other than the seller's place of business). In this situation, the consumer must be provided with a full and complete receipt or copy of a contract pertaining to the sale at the time of its execution which shall include the "cancellation statements." Additional components of the rule, as noted on the FTC website, are discussed as follows.

The rule stipulates that the consumer has the right to cancel a transaction at any time prior to midnight of the third business day after the date of the transaction. The rule also requires such sellers, within 10 business days after receipt of a valid cancellation notice from a buyer, to honor the buyer's cancellation by refunding all payments made under the contract, returning any traded-in property, cancelling and returning any security interests created in the transaction, and notifying the buyer whether the seller intends to repossess or abandon any shipped or delivered goods.

The rule also requires door-to-door sellers to furnish the buyer with a completed receipt, or a copy of the sales contract, containing a summary notice informing the buyer of the right to cancel the transaction, which must be in the same language as that principally used in the oral sales presentation. Door-to-door sellers also must provide the buyer with a completed cancellation form in duplicate captioned either "Notice of Right to Cancel" or "Notice Cancellation," one copy of which can be returned by the buyer to the seller to effect cancellation (16 CFR.429.1).

The rule provides for certain exemptions and excludes certain transactions from the definition of the term "door-to-door sale" (16 CFR.429.3). According to the FTC (1996), the rule exempts:

(1) sellers of automobiles, vans, trucks or other motor vehicles sold at auctions, tent sales or other temporary places of business, provided that the seller is a seller of vehicles with a permanent place of business; and (2) sellers of arts and crafts sold at fairs or similar places. The Rule also excludes certain transactions. This includes transactions conducted entirely by mail or telephone, and without any other contact between the buyer and seller prior to the delivery of goods or performance of services; transactions pertaining to the sale or rental of real property, transactions pertaining to the sale of insurance, or to the sale of securities or commodities by a broker-dealer whom is registered with the Securities and Exchange Commission (SEC); and transactions in which the consumer has the right to repeal as authorized by the Consumer Credit Protection Act (15 U.S.C. 1635).

The rule does not apply to sales that result from earlier negotiations that have been made at the seller's permanent business. Additionally, sales that are related to an emergency situation are exempt. The rule also ensures that any state laws or municipal ordinances that are directly inconsistent with the rule (16 CFR 429.2) are preempted.

Although the focus of this entry is the specifics of the federal door-to-door sales rule, the prudent consumer should identify and understand the specifics of cooling off rules in his/her state. Generally cooling off laws/ regulations is brief and easy to understand and offer substantive remedies to aggrieved consumers.

*Mel J. Zelenak*

**See also:** Door-to-Door Sales; Federal Trade Commission (FTC)

### References and Additional Readings

Federal Trade Commission. (1996). The cooling-off-rule: When and how to cancel a sale. Retrieved from http://www.ftc.gov/bcp/edu/pubs/consumer/products/pro03.shtm.

Federal Trade Commission. (2009). 16 CFR Part 429. Trade regulation rule concerning cooling-off period for sales made at homes or at certain other locations. Retrieved from http://ftc.gov/os/2009/04/P087109coolingoffrulefrnotice.pdf

Omri, B., & Posner, E. A. (2011). The right to withdraw in contract law. *The Journal of Legal Studies, 40*(1), 15–36. Retrieved from http://home.uchicago.edu/omri/pdf/articles/Right_To_Withdraw.pdf

**COPPA**. *See* Children's Online Privacy Protection Act (COPPA)

## Corporate Social Responsibility

William Clay Ford Jr., former chief executive officer (CEO) of Ford Motor Company, once said a good company delivers excellent products and services, but a great company delivers excellent products and services and strives to make the world a better place. The concept of corporate social responsibility (CSR) refers to practices of operating a business that are committed to accounting for social and environmental impacts that may be created by the business. Often, this means that a corporation will have a commitment to policies that integrate specific practices into daily business operations, as well as a commitment to regularly report on progress toward implementing specific practices. Policies related to CSR impact various areas of operations, including governance and ethics, worker hiring, advancement opportunities and training, responsible purchasing and supply chain policies, and energy and environmental impact. Essentially, social and moral values being infused into business philosophy and business values are key components to CSR. However, CSR might hold different meanings at different times in relation to given societal conditions, traditions, values, cultures, and political influences. Socially responsible companies are expected to integrate economic, social, and environmental concerns into their business strategies and their activities, going beyond simple compliance with the law.

Socially relevant issues such as the improper treatment of workers, environmental damage, and faulty production practices that contribute to customer inconveniences or danger have been highlighted in the media. Additionally, investors and investment fund managers have begun to take account of a company's CSR policies. Finally, consumers are driving the process because they are increasingly sensitive to CSR efforts of companies.

It seems many consumers care about how the companies from which they purchase their goods and services manage social issues. All of these trends have contributed to the growing pressure on corporations to operate their businesses in an economically, socially, and environmentally sustainable way. Thus, when a major corporation like Exxon or Shell Oil is managing an oil spill in the ocean, there is added pressure for a comprehensive and socially responsible strategy.

While initial CSR efforts focused efforts at the head of a given organization, the focus has shifted toward the actions taken by the entire organizations, and not simply by their owners, CEOs, presidents, and others. This transition is recognized as being chiefly responsible for allowing citizens to observe, or evaluate, how involved an organization is in the environment in which it is operating. The shift in focus to the overall organization facilitated the expansion of the concepts of corporate social responsiveness, and then corporate social performance in the 1980s. In the 1990s the concept of corporate sustainability was introduced to address the fact that many consumers believed that companies should increase their awareness of environmental concerns. This further exemplifies the shift in understanding that the companies themselves, and not simply the management, are accountable for being socially active. Most CSR efforts have been focused at larger corporations, but the philosophy behind the movement is intended for all businesses.

CSR has gained an increasingly high profile in recent years. The current practice of CSR has been largely framed and informed by three models: the shareholder value model, the stakeholder model, and the business ethics model. The shareholder and stakeholder models focus on the ways in which a business seeks to align its values and behavior with those of its various stakeholders, or as guided by the shareholders. The business ethics model justifies CSR on three slightly different but interrelated ethical grounds: (1) intrinsic or eternal ethical values; (2) emerging and changing social expectations and social responsiveness to specific social issues; and (3) corporate citizenship, that is, corporation as a good citizen in a society to contribute to social well-being.

Several economic theorists have proffered perceptions concerning what CSR really means. Friedman suggests that CSR is really only a tool to increase a company's profit and that all social and environment activities are actually items for governmental and community management. For Elkington, CSR is best understood to have a threefold set of priorities: to create economic, ecological, and social values. Carroll and Buchholtz expanded on this idea and argued that CSR actually has a fourfold set of responsibilities: economic, ethical, legal, and philanthropic. Most agree, however, that corporations will contribute to CSR only if they believe that CSR will pay off for them in the future.

One of the primary weaknesses of CSR and the sustainability reports that are reported by many corporations is the lack of common measures of performance utilized. Some have suggested that this can lead to hyperbole and *greenwashing*. Greenwashing is a process by which a corporation presents information to the public that infers that the company is more economically friendly than it really is. Thus, the corporation is attempting to gain favor from the growing public concerns for environmental safety and responsibility. In order to address these concerns, supporters of CSR are suggesting that meaningful data gathering will require a multistakeholder process focused on refining a set of common, widely applicable CSR/sustainability reporting guidelines. Such a process would incorporate the participation of representatives from the world of business, investment strategists, economic experts, environment/ecology workers, researchers, advocates for human rights, and labor organizations from around the world. The belief is that in combining the efforts of these varied spheres of influence, corporations would not only feel the pressure to increase responsibility, but would also have the resources necessary to do so, while maintaining profitability.

*James R. Ruby*

**See also:** Activism; Department of Labor (DOL)

## References and Additional Readings

As You Sow. (n.d.). Corporate social responsibility. Retrieved from http://www.asyousow.org/csr/

Boeger, N., Murray, R., & Villiers, C. (2008). *Perspectives on corporate social responsibility*. Cheltenham, UK: Edward Elgar Publishing Limited. Hamburg: Herstellung Diplomica Verlag.

Ford, Jr., W.C. (1999). Ford chairman stresses shareholder value, social responsibility in letter to shareholders: Letter to shareholders from CEO. Retrieved from http://media.ford.com/article_print.cfm?article_id=1283

Mallin, C.A. (2009). *Corporate social responsibility: A case study approach*. Northampton, MA: Edward Elgar Publishing, Inc.

Melis, A., Carta, S., & Del Rio, S. (2009). CSR and integrated triple bottom line reporting in Italy: Case study evidence. In Mallin, C.A., *Corporate social responsibility: A case study approach* (9–10). Northampton, MA: Edward Elgar Publishing, Inc.

Paetzold, K. (2010). *Corporate social responsibility (CSR): An international marketing approach*. Hamburg: Diplomica Verlag

Sun, W., Stewart, J., & Pollard, D. (2010). *Reframing corporate social responsibility: Lessons from the global financial crisis*. WA, United Kingdom: Emerald Group Publishing Limited.

# Cosigning

For some consumers, access to credit may be next to impossible without a co-signer. After reviewing an applicant's creditworthiness and overall credit history, a prospective lender may determine that granting credit to the applicant based on their own merit involves a greater risk than they would like to take. The risk of course, involves lack of repayment and/or timely payments. However, a lender may proceed with granting credit to an applicant if they can get another creditworthy consumer to cosign for them on the line of credit they are applying for. Cosigning for any type of credit is a matter that one should consider with caution.

Cosigning for a loan or any other type of credit involves major responsibility. The role of a cosigner is to guarantee payment. When a consumer decides to cosign for any type of credit for a friend, family member, or loved one, they are agreeing to guarantee a payment should the primary borrow default. Federal laws require that cosigners receive notice of their responsibility. According to the Federal Trade Commission's Facts for Consumers website series, some states may allow creditors to collect debt payments from cosigners first before trying to collect payment from the borrower. A consumer that is considering cosigning should inquire with the creditor whether such law is applicable.

Two business partners signing a document. (Pressmaster/Shutterstock.com)

When it comes to collecting other fees such as late fees, or attorney's fees incurred by a default, a creditor may pursue payment for these fees from a cosigner as well. Cosigners may also be subject to wage garnishment, deficiency balance, and adverse reporting of default on their credit report. A cosigner may always negotiate the terms of their responsibility with a creditor. Some negotiating terms to consider include immediate notice of default and responsibility for principal balance only. Of course, the lender must agree to such terms. Any consumer considering becoming a cosigner should always inquire on the prospective creditor's policies regarding cosigning arrangements.

It is important to note that since the role of a cosigner is to act as a guarantor on a payment, it is unlikely that a cosigner would be released from this responsibility. For example, a cosigner on a mortgage may be released from this liability through refinance. The same is true for automobiles. This is assuming that the primary borrower has not lapsed on any payment and can qualify to refinance on their own. Cosigning for a mortgage or auto loan does not necessarily mean that one will be on title. Being listed on title makes a cosigner an owner whereas simply being a cosigner only makes one liable for the debt. On the other hand, an agreement for a cosigner to be taken off title could be a challenge for the primary borrower if a cosigner decides not to sign off title. In this situation, getting a cosigner is a caveat for the primary borrower.

Finding one's way out as a cosigner on a credit card also proves to be equally challenging. According to the website, Creditcard.com, a bank may refuse to release a cosigner unless the balance is paid if the cardholder does not qualify for a credit account on their own. It is common for parents and spouses with excellent credit to cosign to help their loved ones establish a credit history or to help improve a credit history. One can go about doing this with more ease and control by opting to add them on as an authorized user to their credit accounts instead of cosigning for a credit card. It is a good idea to inquire with the credit card issuer whether an authorized user will have the credit history reported in his or her name as well. Adding a person as an authorized user gives him or her access to a credit card and establishing credit, but does not make him or her responsible for repayment. In this arrangement, the primary account holder is liable for the debt but has control over timely payments.

Financial responsibilities are indeed a major aspect to consider as a cosigner but it is also important to take other impacts into account. For example, the industry standard for credit rating or FICO score is heavily weighted on payment history and outstanding debt. Cosigning is a liability that one assumes and will most often be considered as a debt by any creditor. Thus, cosigning may impede a cosigner's future access to credit and may affect one's credit rating.

The nation's consumer protection agency, the Federal Trade Commission (FTC) reports that three out of four cosigners are asked to repay a loan. Therefore, a consumer who is considering becoming a cosigner should be prepared to repay part or all of a loan, and evaluate his or her own finances to ensure that he or she can afford to repay this debt. It is the author's opinion that as a back-up plan, a cosigner should set up a bank account with at least two payments in reserve. A consumer considering cosigning should also act judiciously in deciding who to cosign for. Inquiring on the primary borrower's financial situation and plans for repayment due to job loss or other life events is essential.

It is recommended that consumers do not cosign for anyone. However, many consumers may still decide to take such risk. Given the responsibility and lack of rights as a cosigner, consumers should use caution and their best judgment before they take action.

*Dolores Robles*

**See also:** Credit Cards; Federal Trade Commission (FTC); FICO (Fair Isaac and Company); Mortgages

### References and Additional Readings

Bankrate.com. (2011). The basics of cosigning a loan. Retrieved from http://www .bankrate.com/brm/news/advice/20020927a.asp

Credit Cards.com. (2011). Escaping cosigning: How to get out of a cosigned loan, credit card. Retrieved from http://www.creditcards.com/credit-card-news/ how-to-escape-exit-cosign-loan-credit-card-1265.php

Federal Trade Commission. (2011a). Cosigning a Loan. Retrieved from http://ftc .gov/bcp/edu/pubs/consumer/credit/cre06.shtm

Federal Trade Commission. (2011b). Credit and divorce. Retrieved from http://ftc .gov/bcp/edu/pubs/consumer/credit/cre08.shtm

Federal Trade Commission. (2011c). Your credit. Retrieved from http://www.ftc .gov/bcp/conline/edcams/gettingcredit/yourcredit.html

Migoya, D. (2010). Parents trap kids into cosigning. *Denverpost.* Retrieved from http://www.moneymanagement.org/About-Us/Press-Room/In-the-News/~/ media/Files/MMI/About/Press%20Room/News/2010/July%202010/Denver% 20Postcom0710.ashx

Smith, A.K. (2009). To cosign or not to cosign. *Kiplinger's Personal Finance.* Retrieved from http://www.kiplinger.com/article/credit/T035-C000-S002-to- cosign-or-not-to-cosign.html

Stern, L. (2010). Should you cosign for your child? *Money.* Retrieved from http:// money.cnn.com/2010/11/04/pf/cosign_for_your_kid.moneymag/index.htm

## Counterfeiting

Counterfeiting is the process of making or selling look-alike goods and services bearing the fake trademarks of the genuine product. This practice is not legal and supports unlawful activities. It is not a new phenomenon. People practiced counterfeiting before the 17th century. However, counterfeiting increased significantly during the past quarter century and remains one of the fastest growing economic crimes of our modern economy. According to the U.S. Customs and Border Protection (CBP) counterfeiting of branded goods costs companies over $720 billion annually. Some estimates report that 7–9 percent of all world trade was counterfeited in 2003, which cost U.S. companies more than $250 billion, or about 2 percent of overall world trade. U.S. companies have $9 billion trade losses for international copyright piracy. Counterfeiting poses a threat not only to the U.S. economy but also to global health and safety. For example, according to the Federal Aviation Administration about 2 percent of the 26 million airline parts installed every year are counterfeit. In addition, in 2003 instances of safety violations due to counterfeit auto parts and transmission fluid made of cheap oil and dyed fluid were reported. Benefits and profits from counterfeiting businesses like these are linked to funding organized crime, global terrorist groups, and drug and human trafficking. These are obviously big threats to global safety. Counterfeiting also directly affects the quality of life for people worldwide. For example, counterfeiters obviously do not pay taxes, thus resulting in less money for schools, hospitals, parks, and various social programs. Those who are involved in counterfeiting practices and production do not pay fair wages or benefits to their employees. They commonly have poor working conditions and often use forced child labor.

### Counterfeiting and Consumers

Counterfeiting of money is one of the oldest crimes in history though with the Secret Service, counterfeiting activity has significantly decreased over time. However, with current technology and ever-evolving counterfeiting production methods, counterfeiting poses a serious threat to consumers.

A great source of information is the U.S. Secret Service. For more information, see http://www.secretservice.gov/

The most commonly counterfeited products are currency and coins followed by intellectual property, postmarks, and mail stamps; manufactured products such as computer software, CDs, DVDs, and aircraft parts; and designer produces like handbags, sunglasses, watches, and clothing. It is believed that during the civil war a third of all U.S. currency was counterfeit. It was difficult to catch counterfeit currency during the 19th century, when most banks were permitted to manufacture a collective 7,000 kinds of coins. Since 1896, when currency was nationalized, counterfeiting currency has decreased significantly. However, the development of advanced technology such as high-resolution printers and copiers in the end of 20th century has again made it easy to counterfeit currency.

Global production and the trade of any kind of goods and services provide opportunity for access to desirable products and technology. Meanwhile, the development of new technology creates new distribution channels such as e-commerce for obtaining these products and technology easily. All these provide unlimited prospects for the diffusion of counterfeit products worldwide. The Internet alone is believed to be a source of over $25 billion counterfeit products. Not surprisingly, it is very difficult to distinguish counterfeit products when shopping online.

---

In 2011, U.S. Immigration and Customs Enforcement's (ICE's) Homeland Security Investigations (HSI) seized 17 websites for selling counterfeit goods over the Internet:

- discountedoakleysunglasses.com
- onlypuma.com
- ralphlauren-polos.org
- solesold.com
- toryburchsoutlets.org
- toryburchsoutletsale.net
- ventma.com
- choosepuma.com
- ebayshoppingjoy.com
- lacosteshoesmall.com
- menlacosteshoes.com
- newerahatsnow.com
- newerahatss.com
- pumaforever.com
- replicaoakleysunglasses.net
- shoplacosteshoes.com
- sneaker-space.com

*Source:* ICE. (July 28, 2011). Homeland Security investigations brings counterfeit designers to heel. Retrieved from http://www.ice.gov/

While providing incredible ease and convenience, shopping online also has many restrictions and limitations such as lack of tangibility, leading to an inability to evaluate and examine products before making a purchase. Perhaps the best way to avoid paying for counterfeit merchandise is to shop from reputable online retailers. According to U.S. Immigration and Customs Enforcement's (ICE's) Homeland Security Investigations (HSI), 17 domain names of websites selling counterfeit goods were seized in 2011. Distribution of counterfeit products may also occur at street carts and flea markets. Every major city in the world nowadays has its district for faux haunts. Canal Street in New York City, Santee Street in Los Angeles, Old City in Shanghai, and Namdaemun Market in Seoul are prime examples.

People's desire of obtaining branded or designer products at lower price levels fuels the distribution of counterfeit products such as apparel, shoes, handbags, watches, sunglasses, belts, and other fashion-related accessories. The most frequently confiscated counterfeit brands in 2011 are known to be Dolce & Gabbana, Gucci, Lacoste, New Era, Nike, The North Face, Oakley, PUMA, Ralph Lauren, Ray-Ban, Sons of Anarchy, Tory Burch, and UGG.

The problem with counterfeits is growing because of consumer demand. People who purchase counterfeit products should know that their money supports unemployment, budget deficits and compromises the global economy, safety, security, and quality of life. The equation is simple—no demand, no supply. Therefore, every single consumer has both the responsibility and power to fight against counterfeiting. The best way to eliminate such a problem is to educate and increase awareness and social responsibility.

Companies and businesses often initiate anticounterfeiting operations. For example, Fortune 500 companies have reported spending from $2 to $10 million a year on anticounterfeiting. Using hi-tech strategies such a holographic marks, technologies similar to those used to protect dollar bills, unique identification numbers, and special package marking are some examples of those strategies. Governments of a number of countries also call for strong legal frameworks and agreements against counterfeiting. For example, in October 2011, a group of countries including the United States, Canada, Korea, Japan, New Zealand, Morocco, and Singapore signed the Anti-Counterfeiting Trade Agreement (ACTA). This was an important step forward in the global attack against counterfeiting and copyright piracy.

The U.S. federal government is currently undertaking an important attempt to reduce and eliminate counterfeiting from the U.S. government supply chain. U.S. Department of Commerce and Government Accountability Office report that counterfeits have penetrated several sectors of the U.S. government supply chain that can result potential serious cause in national defense. Special working group has been created in 2010 to develop anticounterfeiting framework. This includes examinations of current industry standards, creating the ability to authenticate or trace at-risk products, increasing detection capabilities, and encouraging a contractual enforcement of authenticity.

*Mariné Aghekyan-Simonian*

**See also:** Consumer Financial Protection Bureau (CFPB); Customs and Border Protection (CBP); Department of Homeland Security (DHS); Fair Trade

### References and Additional Readings

Intellectual Property Watch. (2010). New US government report on counterfeit, piracy. Retrieved from http://www.ip-watch.org/weblog/2010/04/13/new-us-government-report-on-counterfeit-piracy/

Office of the Federal Register. (2013). Federal register. Retrieved from http://www.federalregister.gov

Perera, D. (2011). Senate approves anti-counterfeiting defense authorization act amendment. Retrieved from http://www.fiercegovernmentit.com/story/senate-approves-anti-counterfeiting-defense-authorization-act-amendment/2011-11-30

## Credit Card Accountability Responsibility and Disclosure Act (Credit CARD Act)

The enactment of the Credit Card Accountability Responsibility and Disclosure Act (Credit CARD Act) was an historic event for American consumers. President Obama signed the Credit CARD Act into law in May 2009. Prior to this enactment, consumers had little protection from the unscrupulous practices of the credit card industry. The PBS Frontline documentary, *Secret History of the Credit Card* released in 2004 revealed that the credit card industry had more complaints than any other industry. The Credit CARD Act has improved the clarity of disclosures on terms and conditions or credit card agreements for consumers.

Many consumer complaints were in regard to fees that the industry was charging. These fees included rising late fees, over the limit fees, return check fees, and any other fees that could be charged. Other complaints were in regard to unfair rate increases or "Universal Default."

This clause in credit agreements allowed creditors to increase the annual percentage rate on a consumer's credit card if they defaulted on *any* account or there was a change in their credit history. According to a 2009 White House press release, every year Americans pay $15 billion in penalty fees. Two-cycle or double billing cycle was another unfair practice employed by the industry. Under this billing method the grace period on new purchases was eliminated thus allowing the companies to collect more in interest fees. These practices were some of the factors in the credit card rising debt levels among American consumers. From 2003 to 2006, profits from late fees alone tripled and contributed 35 percent of bank profits. A report by the Center for Responsible Lending (2011) stated that unclear pricing on credit cards likely led consumers to incur more debt than they otherwise would have (if they had more clarity). It was noted that there were substantial differences in the prices disclosed to consumers and those that consumers actually paid during 2004–2008. For example, the report noted that prior to reform, consumers paid $16.3 billion more than their stated interest rate. The practices related to fees, fee increases, and change in terms and annual percentage rate were disclosed on all credit agreements. The problem was that most, if not all, consumers could not understand the language. Elizabeth Warren, a Harvard law professor and consumer advocate who chaired the congressional panel on how the Troubled Asset Relief Program (TARP) money was spent, and who was appointed by President Obama to create the Consumer Financial Protection Bureau, acknowledged the complicated language used on credit agreements when she was interviewed in 2009. In interview with PBS NOW, Warren stated, "I teach contract law at Harvard Law School and I can't understand my credit contract." Some would find it a bit unsettling to learn that a person of such distinction would not be able to understand a legal contract.

It was speculated by those in the credit card industry that regulation would have a negative effect on consumers. The industry claimed that the end result of regulation would be higher costs and restricted access to consumer credit. However, a report on the outcomes of the reform by the Center for Responsible Lending (2011) refuted those claims. The report revealed that one year after the law was implemented prices for consumer credit by way of credit cards had remained the same, and credit had not tightened to unprecedented levels with respect to the state of the economy.

The Credit CARD Act provides protections for consumers in the following areas:

- Penalty fees: A credit card company cannot charge a late fee of more than $25. Company is allowed to charge a fee of up to $35 if one of last six payments was late. A higher fee may be charged if a company is able to justify costs incurred as a result of a late payment. A late payment fee cannot be higher than the minimum payment.

- Fee protections: Fees associated with any event disclosed on an agreement are limited to one. Inactivity fees are prohibited. Over-the-limit fees may only be assessed if the consumer opts-in to allow transactions that take them over their credit limit.

- Rate increases: The rate for the first 12 months after an account has been opened cannot be changed. The following are exceptions to this rule: a card with a variable interest rate; introductory rate (must be in place for 6 months); late more than 60 days in paying; not making payments in a workout agreement. Advance notice is not applicable here. An explanation for a rate increase must be provided to consumer. A rate increase must be evaluated every 6 months, and if applicable, the rate must be reduced within 45 days. Increased rate only applies to new charges and not previous balance. A 45-day notice must be sent when a company plans to increase rates or other fees.

- Billing and payments: Ends two-cycle billing. Bills must be mailed or delivered 21 days before payment is due and must have the same due date each month. Cut-off time for payment cannot be earlier than 5 P.M. Payments due on weekend or holiday dates may be paid on the following business day before 5 P.M. Payments in excess of the minimum payment must be applied to the balance with the highest interest rate. Exceptions apply to deferred interest plan (no interest if paid by X date).

- Pay-off time table: Bill must include information on how long it would take a consumer to pay-off a balance in 36 months by only making minimum payments. Must also include interest cost for that time period.

- Underage consumers: Consumers under the age of 21 may only be issued a credit card if they can show the ability to make payments or by obtaining a cosigner. A cosigner must agree in writing to a credit limit increase.

The Credit CARD Act is an important piece of legislation to protect consumers against unscrupulous practices perpetuated by the credit card industry. The legislation adds to the long list of credit card legislation that already exists.

*Dolores Robles*

**See also:** Consumer Financial Protection Bureau (CFPB); Credit Cards

### References and Additional Readings

Board of Governors of the Federal Reserve System. (2011). What you need to know: New credit card rules: Effective August 22. Retrieved from http:www.federalreserve.gov/consumerinfo/wyntk_creditcardrules.htm

Consumer Financial Protection Bureau Conference. (2010). The CARD act one year later. Retrieved from http://www.consumerfinance.gov/credit-cards/credit-card-act/card-act-conference-key-findings/

Frank, J. M. (2011). Credit card clarity: CARD act reform works. *Center for Responsible Lending.* Retrieved from http://www.responsiblelending.org/credit-cards/research-analysis/FinalCRL-CARD-Clarity-Report2-16-11.pdf

Garman, E. T. (2006). Banking, credit and housing issues. *Consumer Economic Issues in America, 9th edition.* Mason, OH: Thomson Learning.

Office of the Press Secretary. (May 22, 2009). Fact sheet: Reforms to protect American credit card holders. Press release.

Public Broadcasting System. (2011). Elizabeth Warren on credit card 'tricks and traps. Retrieved from http://www.pbs.org/now/shows/501/credit-traps.html

## Credit Cards

Credit can be traced back to as early as the 1700s as a furniture merchant allowed customers to pay off their debt on a weekly basis. Between the 18th and 20th centuries, clothing was sold by Talleyman by using a stick which was notched on one side to depict credit and the other side to depict payment. During this time, metal tokens, plates, and coins were also used for debt collection record keeping but could only be used at the merchants who issued the credit. By the late 1930s, merchants began accepting each other's debt cards and the first "plastic" money was introduced in the United States in the 1950s where credit could be used between different merchants. The 1950s also brought a new medium for advertising right into the consumer's home—the television. This era was known as "The Golden Age of Television" and provided a prime opportunity to create "needs" for consumers who may not have had the money but had the "plastic" to make the purchases. While the use of credit cards offers several advantages, a number of disadvantages have evolved over the years, including increased personal debt, credit card fraud, and identity theft.

Credit cards have been the most common complaint related to fraud and identity theft over the past several years and this type of complaint continues to increase. It was reported that in 2008, 40 percent of consumers use credit cards as a payment method; therefore, it is critical that consumers are able to recognize credit card fraud and know how to protect themselves from it. While consumers may recognize the obvious forms of fraud as the

Prepaid debit cards and bank account debit cards share some similarities but they also have many differences. A bank account debit card is linked to your checking account whereas a prepaid debit card is paid in advance then loaded onto your card and you use only the amount of money you put on the card. With a bank account debit card you usually have the option of using their overdraft service, where the bank will cover the cost of a purchase if you exceed the amount of money that's in your account. You will have to pay the bank back for the purchase plus pay an additional fee. Many of the federal rules that protect consumers who use bank account debit cards do not apply to prepaid debit cards.

theft of credit card information, this fraud actually derives in several other forms that can have a negative effect on individuals, families, and businesses worldwide.

Credit card fraud comes in variety of forms and unfortunately, consumers are unable to eliminate all risk from becoming a victim. However, cardholders can take precautions to decrease their probability of credit card fraud. It is important for cardholders to keep their cards in a safe place and shred any documents that contain credit card information. Consumers should be cautious with providing credit card or personal information to anyone unless the contact was initiated by the cardholder. If a solicitor contacts the cardholder requesting any form of personal information, it is strongly advised that the information not be provided. The use of pre-paid cards rather than personal credit or debit cards is a viable option for online purchases as this greatly reduces the fraudulent risks. Cardholders should carefully review their credit card statements each month to ensure that unauthorized credit card purchases have not been made. If a credit card is lost or stolen or unauthorized charges have been made, the credit card company should be contacted immediately.

In addition to credit cards being lost or stolen, a well-known scam known as "phishing" is used to entice consumers to reveal credit card information. The scammers direct the consumer to a website that resembles a card issuer's website. If the cardholder logs in to the site, the scammer has access to the consumer's credit card information. A similar scam is used via the telephone as potential victims are contacted and personal information is requested claiming that their records need updated; the unassuming victim innocently shares the information. It is important to note that credit card companies do not call and request such information via the telephone. Another type of scam called "the credit card class action lawsuit" is when a cardholder receives a telephone call or an e-mail claiming that they are entitled to thousands of dollars as part of a credit card lawsuit settlement. In turn, they will be asked to send a legal fee or tax on their portion of the money before they can receive a portion of the settlement. The money is sent, however, a settlement is not received. Scammers are clever and they are continuously developing new strategies to gain credit card information. Consumers cannot be too cautious when using credit card transactions.

In addition to scams and theft, cardholders can also become victims of deceptive practices, although legal, by the credit card issuers themselves. Due to the increase in this type of action by credit card companies, the Credit Card Accountability Responsibility and Disclosure Act (Credit CARD Act) of 2009 was initiated to protect credit cardholders against unfair credit practices. The legislation is designed to terminate unfair, arbitrary interest rate increases and allow consumers to determine their own credit limits. It also ends unfair penalties for cardholders who pay on time, requires fair allocation of consumer payments, and protects against due date issues and confusion. This legislation is important to cardholders because it prevents companies from using misleading terms that can be confusing to the consumer and in turn, ruining a cardholders' credit.

While legislation has been enacted to protect cardholders from deception, misleading information from the credit card companies can still be costly for the consumer. "Teaser rates" are used by card issuers to attract customers with a low introductory interest rate for a specific period of time. After the introductory period expires, the interest rate increases significantly. Cardholders may also be charged an annual fee or a fee for minimal usage of the card; these additional costs can be avoided by spending the minimum yearly amount required or closing the account. The Credit CARD Act of 2009 prevents card companies from issuing late fees for payments that are due on the weekend; however, many companies are still able to issue this charge because they accept weekend payments via online or by phone. The consumer needs to closely investigate the procedures for weekend payments to prevent this added expense. These are commonly used guiles that card issuers may use to charge additional expenses to their consumers; therefore, it is crucial that consumers are aware of these charges so that they can better protect themselves.

Businesses are not immune to the possibility of credit card fraud. It is important for businesses to confirm the customer's identification by examining the signature and photo ID when a customer is using a debit or credit card. Salespeople should be trained to identify suspicious activity carried out by the customer and if in doubt, the recent list of stolen cards should be reviewed to ensure that the card has not been reported stolen.

Credit card skimming involves a portable electronic device that steals data off of a credit card at the point of purchase when the card is swiped through the card reader machine. The data that is collected from the card is then used to manufacture fake credit cards. Any person, including employees, can implement the device that could pose problems for the business owner as the credit card companies may impose fines on the retailer. The retailers may reduce the possibility by monitoring their employees who are handling devices not normally used by the retailer.

Consumer should be cautious of credit card offers. Fraudulent practices used to target consumers include the promise of a credit card even if the consumer has bad credit or charging the consumer a fee to help them qualify for a credit card (except in the case of a secured card). A secured card may be in the consumer's best interest if his or her credit history is less than ideal as this strategy enables the consumer to rebuild their credit. A consumer should work directly with the credit card issuer rather than a second party as this does not improve the chances of being accepted.

A report should be filed immediately if a credit card is lost or stolen, an unauthorized charge on a credit card statement has been found, or if there is any suspicious activity related to fraud. Filing the report is also critical so other consumers are informed of the scams. It has been suggested that one of the best and easiest ways to inform other consumers about a new credit card scam is the Internet. Blogging, Tweeting, or social networking sites such as Facebook. Finally, consumers will less likely become victims of fraud by simply using extreme caution when using credit cards and staying educated and current on emerging scams.

*Linda Simpson and Whitney Paul*

**See also:** Banking; Credit Card Accountability Responsibility and Disclosure Act (Credit CARD Act); Frauds and Scams; Privacy: Offline; Privacy: Online

## References and Additional Readings

Burns, M. (December 13, 2011). Four times more consumers consider mobile payments safer than credit cards. *Market Watch: The Wall Street Journal* (n.p.)

Cartier, C. (2011). Possibly-Everett-based credit card scammers to face internet retribution of the highest order. *Seattle Weekly.* Retrieved from http://blogs.seattle weekly.com/dailyweekly/2011/12/possibly-everett-based_credit-.php

Credit Card Accountability Responsibility and Disclosure Act of 2009, H.R.627, 111th Congress. (2009). Retrieved from http://www.gpo.gov/fdsys/pkg/PLAW-111publ24/pdf/PLAW-111publ24.pdf

Federal Trade Commission. (2010). *Consumer sentinel network databook.* Retrieved from http://www.ftc.gov/sentinel/reports/sentinel-annual-reports/sentinel-cy2009.pdf

Fraud Guides. (n.d.). Credit card skimming. Retrieved from http://www.fraud guides.com/business-credit-card-skimming.asp

Internet ScamBusters. (n.d.). Credit card fraud: 21 tips to protect yourself from being a victim of credit card fraud. Retrieved from http://www.scambusters .org/CreditCardFraud.html

Marquand, B. (2011). Credit card fraud protection: seven instances when you should call your credit card company. *Forbes Money Builder*. Retrieved from http:// www.forbes.com/sites/moneybuilder/2011/12/12/credit-card-fraud-protec tion-seven-instances-when-you-should-call-your-credit-card-company-2/

Marples, G. (2008). The History of credit cards—it all started in the 18th Century. Retrieved from http://thehistoryof.net/history-of-credit-cards.html

National Consumers League's National Fraud Information Center. (n.d.). Bogus credit card offers. Retrieved from http://www.fraud.org/tips/telemarketing/ boguscredit.htm

## Credit Practices Rule

Use of credit has become a standard financial management practice for many consumers to meet daily and long-term financial needs. Financial planners encourage consumers to manage their use of credit in a way that debt ratios remain low and manageable. When consumers become overextended in their use of credit, they need to be protected from unfair practices by creditors so their long-term financial security is not impacted. In 1985, the Federal Trade Commission (FTC) adopted the Credit Practices Rule. The rule protects consumer from unfair treatment by creditors through the use of terms included in credit contracts that allowed creditors to evade rules that are in place to protect consumers/debtors. Creditors included in the ruling are finance companies, retailers, and credit unions that offered consumer credit contracts, which are under the jurisdiction of the FTC. The credit transactions included in the rule are loans made to consumers who purchase goods or services for personal, family, or household use. This does not apply to credit cards but does apply to goods or services sold under lease–purchase plans.

There are three provisions of the Credit Practices Rule. The first prohibits creditors from using confessions of judgment, waivers of exemption, wage assignments, and security interests in household goods, all of which are found to be unfair practices to consumers. The second provision requires creditors to advise cosigners of their potential liability if the debtor fails to make required payments on the loan. The final provision prohibits pyramiding of late.

Keep in mind the Credit Practices Rule is in place to protect the consumer so creditors are expected to comply by the rules. Previous to the implementation of the rule, creditors could require consumers to use certain household items as collateral, permit consumer to agree to wage deductions or seize the item acquired through the loan if payment was not made. Creditors are not allowed to use the practice of "confession of judgment." This practice allowed creditors not to give notice to the debtor if the contract was breached and not to inform the consumer of their rights to appear in court and receive council. Waivers of exemption allowed creditors to seize or threaten to seize property or possessions. This practice is not permissible per the Credit Practices Rule. Finally, wage assignment provision prevents creditors from permitting debtors to use wage deduction to cover default loan payments.

In the situation where a debtor needs a cosigner to secure a loan, creditors are required to provide a notice to explain the potential liability if the debtor defaults on the loan. The notice is required to say:

> You are being asked to guarantee this debt. Think carefully before you do. If the borrower doesn't pay the debt, you will have to be sure you can afford to pay if you have to, and that you want to accept this responsibility. You may have to pay up to the full amount of the debt if the borrower does not pay. You may also have to pay late fees or collection costs, which increase this amount. The creditor can collect this debt from you without first trying to collect from the borrower. The creditor can use the same collection methods against you that can be used against the borrower, such as suing you, garnishing your wages, etc. If this debt is ever in default, that fact may become a part of your credit record. This notice is not the contract that makes you liable for the debt. (Federal Trade Commission, 1992)

The Credit Practices Rule prevents creditors from using the pyramiding method to assess late charges. Late fees can be assessed if a payment is not made on time. Creditors are not allowed to assess late fees on late fee amounts. For example, if a $100 loan payment is not made by the due date, a late fee of $10 is assessed. The loan payment amount ($100) is paid but not the addition amount for the late fee, which is added to the principle. Creditors cannot charge another late fee because the first fee of $10 was not included in the loan payment.

Initially the credit industry was skeptical about the effectiveness of the Credit Practices Rule and predicted the industry would experience a downturn. Since 1985, creditors have developed methods that have circumvented the rule. Saunders penned nine recommendations to address the following unfair practices creditors now have in place. Payday lenders will accept checks as collateral for loans even when the bank account does not have sufficient funds to cover the check. Once property is repossessed, the debtor is required to pay the debt and accumulated fees, but is not able to retrieve the property upon satisfying the debt. Creditors are able to sell or reassign the consumer debt without notifying the debtor and to ignore the exempt status of property. Entering a debtor's home to retrieve property without authorization is allowed by the creditor.

When first adopted, the FTC intended to protect consumers from unfair practices by creditors. No economic impact was experienced by the credit industry and consumers were able to be informed of consumer credit policies. As with any rule, revisions are needed to address evolving credit industry practices.

*Lorna Saboe-Wounded Head*

**See also:** Credit Cards; Debt Management; Federal Trade Commission (FTC)

### References and Additional Readings

Better Business Bureau. (2006). Federal trade commission: Complying with the credit practices rule. Retrieved from http://www.bbb.org/us/article/ftc—complying-with-the-credit-practices-rule-4420

Federal Trade Commission. (1992). The Credit Practices Rule. Retrieved from http://www.ftc.gov/bcp/edu/pubs/consumer/credit/cre12.shtm

Saunders, M. (2010). Time to update the credit practices rule. Retrieved from http://www.nclc.org/images/pdf/debt_collection/credit-practices-rule-update.pdf

## Credit Repair Organizations

Credit repair companies target consumers who have poor credit histories making promises to repair their credit and fix their credit report so the consumer can get a car loan, a mortgage, insurance, or a job, if they pay a fee for the service. Credit repair scams prey on vulnerable people.

Credit repair organizations heavily advertise on television, in newspapers, and on the Internet. However, the Federal Trade Commission (FTC) counsels consumers to beware of these claims because they are most likely signs of a scam. If a consumer responds to credit repair offers, there's a good chance a fraud will ensue. Indeed, attorneys at the FTC report that they have never observed a legitimate credit repair operation making such claims.

According to Consumer Action, some credit repair companies promise a new credit identity or taxpayer ID number, a practice which is illegal. These scams are frequently carried out using forged documents or by applying with false information for a new taxpayer ID number. When false credit history is provided, the law is being broken.

Unfortunately, the reality is that credit repair companies cannot deliver an improved credit report using these tactics; it is illegal. No person or organization can remove legitimate negative information from a credit report. Therefore, after the consumer pays the organization hundreds or thousands of dollars in fees, the consumer still has the same credit report, and they are out the fees they have paid. Experian counselors provide ways to improve a credit report legitimately, without help from others, but it takes time, discipline, and patience to repair damaged credit.

Once negative information is reported to a credit bureau, it may take up to seven years until it is purged from the system. Although consumers can't remove information which is correct, they can fix any inaccuracies. Contact the major credit reporting agencies to fix the inaccuracy. If understanding of the disputed information is different from the creditors and they refuse to remove the entry in dispute, the consumer may include up to a 100-word explanation statement in the credit report. Thereafter, any creditor checking the credit report will at least see both sides of the story.

However, people with legitimate negative information become impatient and want a solution now. This is when the credit repair agency enters the picture. Read a hypothetical account of a typical credit repair experience.

Trent didn't think it was fair that the mistakes he had made when he was young would follow him around for seven long years. He was a college student now and felt much wiser than when he was a teenager. Trent had many late payments, nonpayment of a few accounts, and a repossession of his car all listed on his credit report. He had just gotten off the phone with one of the major credit reporting companies that had explained to Trent that he couldn't just erase negative credit history if it is true.

Unfortunately for Trent, all of the negatives on his credit report were legitimate. But he believed he had learned his lesson and shouldn't have to be penalized for mistakes of the past. Besides, how could he replace his repossessed car if he couldn't qualify for a loan? He worked the night shift at a health club and public transportation wasn't available at that hour. How was he supposed to get to work?

The solution appeared to him in a radio ad promising to repair bad credit. The advertisement guaranteed that for an upfront fee, negative credit entries would disappear. After Trent contacted the "fix-it" company and paid his upfront fee, he was instructed to obtain a tax identification number as if he was going to start a small business. He was to use this number in place of his social security number whenever he applied for credit. Therefore, he would eventually create a brand new credit history in his name.

This tactic succeeded in getting him several credit cards, and soon he was even successful in getting a loan for a used car. Trent would have probably continued on with this new identity if the FTC, who had been compiling evidence against the credit repair firm, had not discovered Trent as one of its customers.

Trent thought that he had found the perfect solution, but had no idea it was illegal. He was falsifying his social security number and living under an assumed number. In fact, Trent learned all this when the FTC and the attorney general's office contacted him after they closed down the fraudulent credit repair company. Trent lost the money he had paid to repair his credit in addition to being a party to an illegal enterprise. Now not only did he have credit problems, but legal ones as well.

If Trent had learned the art of patience, he would have eventually recovered from his negative credit history. True, seven years is a long time for negative credit to stay on a credit report, but many creditors look closely only at the most recent two years. Trent should have concentrated on improving his payment record to provide evidence that his financial management had improved.

Unfortunately, this is a slow process and can't be accomplished overnight. Trent had wanted an improved record immediately and hadn't been willing to wait. This impatience lead to a solution that seemed too good to be true, and it was.

The Credit Repair Organizations Act (CROA) was passed by Congress to guarantee that prospective buyers of credit repair organizations (CROs) are given the information required to make a well-informed decision. Furthermore, the CROA aims to guard consumers from unfair or deceptive advertising and business practices by credit repair organizations. Specifically, the act requires:

> CROs may not receive payment before any promised service is "fully performed." Services must be under written contract, which must include a detailed description of the services and contract performance time. CROs must provide the consumer with a separate written disclosure statement describing the consumer's rights before entering into the contract. Consumers can sue to recover the greater of the amount paid or actual damages, punitive damages, costs, and attorney's fees for violations of the CROA. (Federal Trade Commission, 2007)

In summary, many of the services that a credit report organization offers, can be done by the consumer themselves. If consumers elect to secure their services, they should make sure the organization complies with CROA. The best way to repair credit is to identify those behaviors that contributed to the poor credit history in the first place. The most effective remedy is improved money management and patience. With time, any valid negatives will automatically be removed from the credit report.

*Dara Duguay*

**See also:** Credit Reporting Agencies; FDIC (Federal Deposit Insurance Commission); Federal Trade Commission (FTC)

### References and Additional Readings

Consumer Action. (2012.). Improve your credit: Put bad credit behind you. Retrieved from http://www.consumer-action.org/english/articles/improve_your_credit_put_bad_credit_behind_you_en

Duguay, D. (2008). *Please send money: A financial survival guide for young adults on their own.* Sourcebooks, Incorporated.

Experian. (2009). Basic questions about credit reports and credit reporting. Retrieved from http://www.experian.com/assets/consumer-education-content/brochures/Reports_Issue_1.pdf

Federal Trade Commission. (2007). Credit repair organizations act. Retrieved from http://www.ftc.gov/ro/chro/credit.shtm

## Credit Reporting Agencies

There are three major credit reporting agencies in the United States: Experian®, Equifax®, and TransUnion®.

Experian (2012) is "a global leader in providing information, analytical tools and marketing services to organization and consumers to help manage the risk and reward of commercial and financial decisions. Using [their] comprehensive understanding of individuals, markets and economies, [they] help organizations find, develop and manage customer relationships to make their businesses more profitable." The company helps businesses to manage credit risk, prevent fraud, target marketing offers, and automate decision making. Experian also helps individuals to check their credit report and credit score, and protect against identity theft. Experian employs approximately 15,000 people in 41 countries and has its corporate headquarters in Dublin, Ireland, with operational headquarters in Nottingham, UK; Costa Mesa, California; and São Paulo, Brazil.

Equifax (2012) "empowers businesses and consumers with information they can trust. With a strong heritage of innovation and leadership, we leverage our unique data, advanced analytics and proprietary technology to enrich the performance of businesses and the lives of consumers." It has been in existence for over 100 years. It provides to consumers and businesses with portfolio management, fraud detection, decisioning technology, and marketing tools. Headquartered in Atlanta, Georgia, Equifax Inc. employs approximately 7,000 people in 15 countries through North America, Latin America, and Europe.

TransUnion (2012) "is a global leader in credit information and information management services. For more than 40 years, [they] have worked with businesses and consumers to gather, analyze and deliver the critical information needed to build strong economies throughout the world." Their associates provide solutions to approximately 45,000 businesses and approximately 500 million consumers worldwide.

A credit reporting agency's main function is to gather information from those who supply credit data on individual consumers. These suppliers are usually the lenders that have given loans or approved credit lines to consumers. There are many types of credit reporting agencies. The most well-known are the credit bureaus that are broad based in their reporting. There are also specialty agencies that sell specific information such as check writing histories, medical records, and rental history records.

Before credit reporting companies existed, consumers could obtain credit only in communities in which they were known and had lived for years. In fact, lenders were known to wake up very early and drive by a farmer's property that had made a request for credit. If the farmer's lights were on, they made the assumption that they were industrious and therefore granted the credit request. This method tended to be a judgment call on the part of the lender. However, if the consumer moved to another town, credit was virtually unobtainable since a personal relationship didn't exist yet between the consumer and the lenders. Now credit reporting systems enable a consumer's credit reputation to make credit possible no matter where that consumer resides.

The credit reporting companies collect, store, and keep consumers' financial history. In a matter of minutes, a lender can obtain and review consumers' credit history to assist in making the decision as to whether to grant credit or not. A positive credit history may lead to a lender making an affirmative decision or conversely a negative credit history may cause a lender to avoid offering credit to a consumer who didn't pay his or her bills in a timely or consistent fashion.

Credit reports contain information that fall into five major categories:

- Identification: name, address, telephone number, and social security number.
- Account history: information about credit accounts such as date opened, limit, loan amount, balance, and monthly payment.
- Public records: bankruptcy filings, tax liens, and judgments.

- Inquiries: requests for the consumer's credit report, which includes outside requests and requests by the actual consumer themselves.
- Consumer statements: consumer written statements that dispute or explain circumstances regarding a legitimate debt (e.g., debt related to a medical emergency).

A common misperception is that credit reporting agencies make lending decisions. In fact, they don't. They simply provide credit reports based on the credit grantors' requests. At that point the credit reporting company's job is done. Only the lender makes the credit granting decision and only the lender knows the reasons for granting or denying the credit request.

Companies that supply credit information to credit reporting agencies have to follow specific credit reporting rules, as listed under the federal Fair Credit Reporting Act (FCRA). This act promotes the accuracy, fairness, and privacy of information in the files of credit reporting agencies. The act stipulates who can obtain a copy of the credit report and under what circumstances.

According to the Federal Trade Commission, the FCRA requires each of the nationwide consumer reporting companies—Equifax, Experian, and TransUnion—to provide consumers with a free copy of their credit report, at their request, once every 12 months. Consumers can easily order their credit report online or by phone. They may also opt to pay for more frequent reports or additional services such as to obtain a credit score but, in most cases, it will involve a charge to provide the calculation.

Before the advent of calculation or analysis of their credit score, it is always important to scrutinize the report(s) closely for errors and "red flags."

Another common misperception is that the free credit report will include a credit score. This is not the case. A credit scores, lenders had to go through a process that was very time consuming and often led to arbitrary determinations. This process involved a physical review of each applicant's credit reports. Without a scoring model to assist the lender, decisions often were biased and not based on the most important factor—the applicant's actual ability to repay the loan.

Today, credit scores help lenders assess risk more fairly because they are consistent and objective, not subjective. The primary goal is to attempt to accurately gage the consumer's likelihood to repay debt responsibly based on their past credit history and current credit status. The main factors assessed in the credit report, which ultimately determine the actual score, are total debt; types of accounts; number of late payments; and age of accounts.

Credit scores are three-digit numbers developed by independent companies, credit reporting agencies, and even some lenders. They are used to evaluate creditworthiness and reflect current level of debt, repayment history, and outstanding credit applications. Each score may be different, based on the agency's scoring model.

In 2006, the three major consumer credit bureaus (Equifax, Experian, and TransUnion) announced that they had created a new coordinated scoring system called VantageScore. VantageScore ratings, as shown in Table 9, range from 501 to 990. The rating is similar to the grades one would receive in a school.

Many lenders use scores generated by the Fair Isaac Corporation, or FICO scores, which range from 300 to 850. The higher the score, the lower the risk. The average person scores in the 600s and 700s. The single most heavily weighted factor in determining a credit score is one's payment history (comprising 35 percent of the score).

In addition to payment history, amount owed, and type of credit (mortgage or student loans are considered good) all impact the credit score. Actions like paying bills on time, paying off accounts, and keeping existing balances low improve the credit score. Missing payments and maxing out credit cards will, obviously, make it worse.

The length of the consumer's credit history is also an important factor. According to Duguay (2007), the length of the credit history can either help or hurt you. The average consumer's oldest obligation is 14 years old, indicating that he or she has been managing credit for some time. In fact, Fair Isaac found that one out of four consumers who recently applied for credit had credit histories of 20 years or longer. For those consumers, this longevity will help to increase their scores. "For the one in 20 consumers with credit histories shorter than two years, brevity will pull down their credit scores in the FICO system" (p. 62).

Credit scores are vital to financial health. With the passage of time along with making consistent payments that are never late, consumers can improve their credit report. Most late payments will drop off after two years, with the exceptions of major blemishes like write-offs, repossessions, judgments, or foreclosures which stay on for up to seven years. In the case of Chapter 7

**Table 9** VantageScore Ratings

| Grade | Score | Comment |
| --- | --- | --- |
| A | 901–990 | Strongest |
| B | 801–900 | Strong rating |
| C | 701–800 | On the line |
| D | 601–700 | Weak rating |
| F | 501–600 | Poor credit |

*Source:* Citigroup Financial Education Curriculum.

bankruptcy, the negative mark stays on the credit report for 10 years. However, there are certain exceptions where the credit history can be reported without any time limitations whatsoever. Those instances include when credit history is a determinant for a job with a salary of $75,000 or more and when seeking credit or life insurance valued at $150,000 or more.

*Dara Duguay*

**See also:** Credit Practices Rule; Credit Repair Organizations; Equal Credit Opportunity Act; FICO (Fair Isaac and Company); Federal Trade Commission (FTC)

### References and Additional Readings

Consumer Federation of American & Fair Isaac Corporation. (2005) Your credit scores. Retrieved from http://www.consumerfed.org/elements/www.consumerfed.org/file/finance/yourcreditscore.pdf

Duguay, D. (2007). *Citi commonsense money guide for real people.* Emmaus, PA: Rodale Books.

Equifax. (n.d.). Who are we. *About Equifax.* Retrieved from http://www.equifax.com/about_equifax/en_us

Experian. (2009a). Credit score basics: Tips for unlocking your credit potential. Retrieved from http://www.experian.com/assets/consumer-education-content/brochures/credit-score-basics.pdf

Experian. (2009b). Basic questions about credit reports and credit reporting. Retrieved from http://www.experian.com/assets/consumer-education-content/brochures/Reports_Issue_1.pdf

Experian. (n.d.). About Experian. Retrieved from http://www.experian.com/corporate/about-experian.html

Sprague, Z. (2006). Citi financial education curriculum. Retrieved from http://www.topicseducation.com

TransUnion. (n.d.). Global presence. Retrieved from http://www.transunion.com/corporate/about-transunion/who-we-are/global-presence.page

TransUnion. (n.d.). Who are we. Retrieved from http://www.transunion.com/corporate/about-transunion/who-we-are.page

## Credit Unions

Credit unions are not-for-profit cooperative financial institutions that are owned by its members, and provide many financial services similar to banks, mutual savings banks, and savings and loan institutions. As defined by the Federal Credit Union Act (48 Stat. 1216; 12 U.S.C. 1751 et seq.) a credit union is a "cooperative associate organized in accordance with the provisions of [the Act] for the purpose of promoting thrift among its members and creating a source of credit for provident of productive purposes."

Credit Union National Association (CUNA) and World Council of Credit Unions (WOCCU) are sister organizations, with offices in Washington, DC, and Madison, Wisconsin. Founded in 1934, the CUNA's mission is to be the premier trade association in the financial services arena. CUNA is a nonprofit trade group that is governed by a board of directors (volunteers) elected by their credit union peers. They focus on providing leadership in the credit union movement through research, outreach, and serving as a voice in Washington, DC.

The WOCCU aims to improve people's lives on a global level through credit unions, specifically giving people the right to affordable and reliable financial services. Their mission is to be the world's leading advocate, platform, development agency, and good governance model for credit unions. WOCCU, beginning operations in 1971, is a trade association, like CUNA, but on an international level. Funded by member dues as well as gifts, grants, and governmental support, in addition to the stateside offices, they also operate other offices worldwide.

Due to federal statutes, credit unions cannot serve the general public. Rather, they serve those who share a common bond such as employment, association membership, or residence in a particular geographic area and have elected to join one or more credit unions. The financial institutions are also limited in the products and services offered that are primarily restricted to the consumer credit and savings sector of the financial services market and small businesses. However, credit unions generally offer more attractive savings and loan rates as well as generally lower fees.

Nearly 91 million consumers are member–owners of, and receive all or part of their financial services from 7,535 credit unions in the United States. Credit unions hold about 6.7 percent of household financial assets as of September 2009.

Credit unions differ from other financial institutions, including banks, in several key aspects.

- *Not-for-profit:* Credit unions are not-for-profit financial cooperatives. The mantra of credit unions, as the Credit Union National Association (CUNA) states on its website (2012c), is "We exist to serve our members, not to make a profit." Credit unions do not issue stock or pay dividends to outside stockholders, instead, returning earnings to members in the form of lower loan rates, higher interest on deposits, and lower fees after reserves are set aside. Credit unions apply their "people helping people" philosophy to community involvement through support of charitable activities and community programs.

- *Membership requirements:* Laws require credit unions to have a defined field of membership, which means consumers have to be members of a group to access a credit union and its services. Consumers may qualify for credit union membership through their employer or organizational affiliations (church, school, or social group). Many consumers are eligible for credit union membership at community-chartered credit unions based on their geographic locations within communities or cities. Normally, only a member of a credit union may deposit money with the credit union, or borrow money from it. The rule of thumb for most credit unions is that once a consumer becomes a member of a credit union, he or she can remain a member even after leaving the defined field of membership. Consumers interested in credit union membership can log onto the website developed by the National Credit Union Administration to identify eligible credit unions.

- *Ownership:* Credit union members are also regarded as owners of their credit unions. Each credit union member has equal ownership and one vote—regardless of how much money a member has on deposit. Members elect their boards of directors in a democratic one-person-one-vote system.

- *Volunteer governance:* Boards of directors who are elected by and from the credit union's membership provide governance for credit unions. Board members serve voluntarily to set all credit union policies governing interest rates and other matters. Only members may serve as directors, and directors serve without remuneration. Volunteers also serve on all committees of each credit union, including the supervisory and nominating committees. Approximately 100,000 Americans volunteer for their credit unions, serving as board members, committee members, or providing other assistance.

- *Taxation:* Credit unions are taxed differently from other financial institutions. In 1937, Congress exempted credit unions from federal income taxes. The exemption was affirmed by statute in 1951, and reaffirmed in 1998 in H.R. 1151. The Credit Union Membership Access Act states, "Credit unions, unlike many other participants in the financial services market, are exempt from Federal and most State taxes because credit unions are member-owned, democratically operated, not-for-profit organizations generally managed by volunteer boards of directors and because they have the specified mission of meeting the credit and savings needs of consumers, especially persons of modest means" (CUNA, 2012c).

Early in the history of credit unions, the U.S. attorney general declared state-chartered credit unions exempt from federal income taxes because they were "organized and operated for mutual purposes [in which an organization's members share in the profits and expenses] and without profits" (CUNA Governmental Affairs, 2011). Credit unions are still responsible for other taxes, including payroll taxes, sales taxes, and property taxes.

## Products and Services

Many of the same products and services offered by banks and other types of financial institutions are also offered by credit unions, often using different terminology. For example, savings accounts are known as share accounts, checking accounts are called share draft accounts, and certificates of deposit are called share term certificates. Other services provided by credit unions include credit and debit cards, loans, retirement accounts, and online banking. By law, credit unions can only lend slightly more than 12 percent of their total assets so credit unions normally offer lending services to consumers only.

To enable credit union members to conduct financial transactions at locations other than their own credit unions, many credit unions partner in shared branching networks. Through shared branching, participating credit unions share facilities to give their members access to thousands of convenient locations to perform transactions. There are more than 1,300 credit unions, with 6,000 branches participating nationwide in shared branching. Shared branching gives credit union members more options to conduct their financial business, including more locations, more hours of operation, and more convenience.

Credit unions frequently create cooperatives in an effort to offer services to other credit unions, their members, or both. With a cooperative, more can be accomplished as a group than could be accomplished by a single credit union due to regulatory constraints. A credit union service organization (CUSO) is normally a "for-profit" subsidiary of one or more credit unions. CUSOs have been formed to provide shared branching, payment processing, ATM networks, and call center services. Other examples of cooperatives include credit counseling services, mortgage lending, and insurance and investment services. Most CUSOs are limited liability companies and provide protection to the credit union from their CUSO actions. CUSOs are typically wholly owned subsidiaries of their credit union, and a majority of the profits generated by the CUSO are returned directly to the credit union. CUSOs may also sell stock, normally to other credit unions, in an effort to finance the operation of the CUSO. When this occurs, the profits are converted to dividends and paid to shareholders as stipulated in the CUSO's charter.

## Regulation

As depository institutions, credit unions are regulated by the federal and state governments. The National Credit Union Administration (NCUA) oversees the safety and soundness of all credit unions. Depending on their charter, credit unions are regulated by the NCUA or by state agencies. Credit unions are either federally or state chartered. Federally chartered credit unions are regulated by an independent agency, the NCUA. NCUA is comprised of three board members who are nominated by the president and confirmed by the U.S. Senate. NCUA administers the National Credit Union Share Insurance Fund (NCUSIF) and has the authority to require federally insured credit unions to undergo insurance examinations. Taxpayer money is not used for regulating and overseeing credit unions, because all activities of NCUA and NCUSIF are funded by the credit unions themselves.

Credit unions with state charters are regulated by their states' banking departments. In many states, the agency responsible for commercial bank supervision is responsible for credit union supervision also. State-chartered credit unions must qualify for federal share insurance through the NCUSIF. All federal credit unions and 95 percent of state-chartered credit unions have "share insurance" (deposit insurance) of at least $250,000 per member through the NCUSIF, an amount equal to the insurance protection offered by the FDIC for other types of financial institutions. Generally, if a credit union member has more than one account in the same insured credit union, those accounts are added together and are insured to at least $250,000. Individual retirement accounts are federally insured to at least $250,000.

Consumers who are interested in learning more about the safety and soundness of specific credit unions and look at their finances can search the NCUA website at www.ncua.gov, to review the financial performance reports and official regulatory documents known as 5300 reports. The 5300 reports provide information on the capitalization of credit unions, as well as loan information.

## Credit Union Trade Organizations

Credit unions are represented nationally by the Credit Union National Association (CUNA) (www.cuna.org) and on the state level by credit union leagues. CUNA partners with leagues to provide services to credit unions, including consumer education, continuing professional education, business development, public relations, and representation. Governmental affairs representatives work with Congress, state legislators, and regulatory agencies to improve legislation and regulation favorable to credit unions and their members.

The World Council of Credit Unions (WOCCU) is both a trade association for credit unions worldwide and a development agency. WOCCU is an advocate for the global credit union system and advocates before international organizations and with national governments to improve legislation and regulation. WOCCU also offers technical assistance programs to introduce new technologies to strengthen credit unions' financial performance, increase their outreach, and deliver fairly priced financial services to poor and low-income people. There are 53,000 credit unions in 100 countries serving 188 million people.

## Key Federal Legislation

Congress passed the Federal Credit Union Act in 1934 (48 Stat. 1216; 12 U.S.C. Sec. 1751–1772), which permitted credit unions to be organized anywhere in the United States. The legislation allowed credit unions to incorporate under either state or federal law, a system of dual chartering that persists today. Under the law, credit unions were exempted from taxation. The legislation established the Bureau of Federal Credit Unions, which was the predecessor to the National Credit Union Administration, for the management of federal credit unions, and determined the structure and duties of the federal regulatory agency. The Credit Union Modernization Act of 1977 was a revision of the Federal Credit Union Act, making changes to basic credit union lending and savings programs.

In 1996, the District of Columbia Court of Appeals ruled against NCUA's policy of allowing credit unions to serve multiple common bonds in one field of membership. Consequently, the Credit Union Membership Access Act was passed by Congress in 1998 to allow credit unions to enroll members from outside their membership groups. As a result of the federal legislation, federal credit unions were able to reach out to potential new members, such as small businesses and low-income communities that were unable to previously join credit unions.

## History

Financial credit cooperatives first emerged in Germany in the 1850s as a result of economic depression. The growth of financial cooperatives was widespread across Europe. St. Mary's Bank Credit Union of Manchester,

New Hampshire, was the first credit union organized in the United States in 1908. America's Credit Union Museum now occupies the location from where St. Mary's Bank Credit Union first operated. Key leaders of the early credit union movement included Edward Filene, a Boston merchant and philanthropist, Roy Bergengren, a Massachusetts attorney, and Pierre Jay, Massachusetts Commissioner of Banks. Filene and Jay were instrumental in getting the first credit union law passed in Massachusetts in 1909, which opened the door for further growth of credit unions. The first credit union league, Massachusetts Credit Union Association (MCUA), was organized in Massachusetts by Filene and others. Bergengren headed MCUA, whose purpose was to aid existing credit unions and form new ones. Filene also created the Credit Union National Extension Bureau, the forerunner of the Credit Union National Association, which was formed as a confederation of state leagues, in 1934.

*Mary Jane "M.J." Kabaci*

**See also:** Banking; Federal Reserve; National Credit Union Administration (NCUA)

### References and Additional Readings

Black Hills Federal Credit Union. (2011). National credit union share insurance fund federally insured by NCUA. Retrieved from https://www.blackhillsfcu.org/asp/products/product_1_2.asp.

Credit and Finance Risk Analysis. (2011). Retrieved from http://www.credfinrisk.com/cureg.html.

Credit Union National Association. (2012a). CURIA: Increasing credit union member business loan limits. Retrieved from http://www.cuna.org/gov_affairs/legislative/issues/2008/curia_tp_mbl.html

Credit Union National Association. (2012b). Taxation: Why credit unions are tax exempt. Retrieved from http://www.cuna.org/gov_affairs/legislative/issues/2007/taxexempt_why.html.

Credit Union National Association. (2012c). What is the credit union difference? Retrieved from http://www.cuna.org/gov_affairs/legislative/cu_difference.html CreditUnionsforYou.com.

Kratz, M. (August 29, 2008). How to check the safety of your credit union. *USA Today.* Retrieved from http://www.usatoday.com/money/perfi/columnist/krantz/2008-08-29-credit-union-deposit-insurance_N.htm

Melvin, D.J., Davis, R.N., & Fischer, G.C. (1977). *Credit unions and the credit union industry: A study of the powers, organization, regulation and competition.* The New York Institute of Finance.

National Credit Union Administration. (2011). Share insurance overview. Retrieved from http://www.ncua.gov/ShareInsurance/index.htm.

**CSPI**. *See* Center for Science in the Public Interest (CSPI)

## Customs and Border Protection (CBP)

Customs and Border Protection (CBP) is housed within the Department of Homeland Security as one of its largest and most complex agencies. Their mission is multifaceted; they serve as frontline guardians of America's borders, safeguarding America by protecting against terrorism. They accomplish their mission by enforcing U.S. laws and fostering the U.S. economic security via lawful international trade and travel. Their core values are vigilance, service to country, and integrity. Vigilance involves their continual watch to deter, detect, and prevent any and all threats to the nation. Service refers to their dedicated efforts to uphold the constitution and defend the liberty of the American people. Integrity is the "cornerstone" of the department. They are driven by high ethical and moral standards in their duties.

Duties covered by the currently named CBP began with the second act of Congress in 1789 under President George Washington. The Tariff Act of

A United States Customs and Border Protection agent speaks with a driver entering the United States. (U.S. Customs & Border Protection)

1789 fulfilled the need for revenue for the new country, enacting tariffs on all imported goods. The fifth act of Congress established the U.S. Customs Service and oversight of port entries. This act, and the collection of tariffs provided primary income for the government for over 100 years, including funding the purchase of additional territories such as Oregon, Florida, Louisiana, and Alaska. In fact, because tariffs and customs revenues were so fruitful, the debt of the nation was zero in 1835.

Throughout the years, many duties were placed on the customs service and as a result, the group served as the beginning of what is now known as other major agencies within the federal government. For example, customs officers managed military pensions (now the Department of Veterans Affairs), maintained revenue cutters (ships to protect borders and collect taxes) (now the U.S. Coast Guard), collected and reported import and export statistics (now the Bureau of Census), and had oversight for sick seamen in Marine hospitals (now the Public Health Service).

Following the tragic attacks on America in 2001, President George W. Bush and Congress enacted myriad legislation to counterterrorism and reinforce protection of U.S. citizens. The Terrorism Response Task Force, Office of Anti-Terrorism, Customs-Trade Partnership Against Terrorism (C-TPAT), Federal Air Marshal Program, Container Security Initiative, and the Port and Maritime Security Act all provided U.S. Customs with tools, technology, and oversight to further fight against international terrorism. In 2002, President Bush signed a bill creating the Department of Homeland Security (DHS). In 2003, the bureau of Customs and Border Protection (CBP) was created and placed under the DHS. In 2004, the CBP received the Air and Marine Operations from DHS as part of its operation to further its mission and goals.

Currently, customs activities still provide a major source of revenue for the federal government. According

The Border Patrol's motto "Honor First" dates to the 1930s.

to their website, they provide 16 dollars for every one dollar appropriated by Congress. They are extremely active and pervasive, performing some of the original duties and responsibilities designated at their inception. CBP currently oversees imported merchandise, assures that imported goods are safe, monitors for and counters terrorism, seizes contraband, processes people, baggage, cargo and mail, protects intellectual property rights, and generally protects the welfare of U.S. citizens. Overseeing 326 ports, recent activities of the CBP include launching unmanned Predator B aircraft for border patrol, expanding Operation Against Smugglers Initiative for Safety and Security (OASISS) to counteract smugglers, and deploying Automated

Commercial Environment (ACE), an electronic truck manifest system allowing for quicker processing of trucks and fee collection, to name a few. Several major offices operate under CBP, the complexity and importance of which are evidenced in the organizational chart.

Because of the CBP's role in assuring that incoming products are safe, their employees work closely with the Consumer Product Safety Commission as well as other agencies to monitor products coming into America from abroad. To further their mission to educate their employees and the public, they publish *"Frontline,"* the magazine of CBP. Recent subject matter covered includes protecting livestock, Central America, Global Entry kiosks, trade, and textiles.

*Wendy Reiboldt*

**See also:** Consumer Product Safety Commission (CPSC); Department of Homeland Security (DHS); Department of Veterans Affairs (VA); Public Safety

### References and Additional Readings

Cunningham, M. H. (2009*). In safe hands: True stories about the men and women of United States Customs and Border Protection.* Bloomington, IN: Xlibris, Corp.

Customs and Border Protection. (2012). About CBP. Retrieved from http://www.cbp.gov

Gaynor, T. (2009). *Midnight on the line: The secret life of the U.S.–Mexico border.* New York: Thomas Dunne Books.

# D

## Debt Collection

Complaints about debt collectors top the charts of both federal and state consumer protection agencies. The Federal Trade Commission (FTC) and Consumer Financial Protection Bureau (CFPB), which are responsible for enforcing the federal law governing debt collectors, have reported that the debt collection industry garners more complaints from consumers than any other. In 2011, for example, consumers lodged 142,743 complaints about debt collectors with the FTC's nationwide complaint database, accounting for 27 percent of all consumer complaints received.

The Federal Fair Debt Collection Practices Act (FDCPA) applies only to third-party debt collection companies, not to original creditors. The FTC and CFPB categorize debt collection complaints according to the provisions of the FDCPA that may have been violated. In 2011, 40 percent of the complainants said that they were harassed by debt collectors making repeated phone calls, 14 percent said that collectors had used obscene, profane, or abusive language, and 3.4 percent reported threats of violence if they failed to pay. Allegations that collectors called at inconvenient times (defined in the law as before 8:00 A.M. or after 9:00 P.M., or at other times the collector knew or should have known were inconvenient to the consumer) made up nearly 9 percent of complaints.

The second most common category of FDCPA complaint, also representing nearly 40 percent in 2011, was that collectors were attempting to collect debts that were not owed or were for the wrong amount. And 26 percent of complainants said that the collectors did not provide the FDCPA-required debt validation notice that should include the amount of the debt, the name of the original creditor, and an explanation of the consumer's right to dispute the debt and receive written verification of it. Another 8 percent of consumers stated that collectors failed to provide the requested verification of disputed debts.

Other serious FDCPA violations involve contacting third parties about an alleged debt. The FDCPA generally prohibits third-party contacts for any purpose other than obtaining information about the consumer's location, and collectors are banned from revealing that the contact relates to debt collection. In 2011, nearly 11 percent of complainants reported that debt collectors illegally disclosed a purported debt to a third party, such as employers, relatives, neighbors, and friends. Over 14 percent of complaints that year related to calls to consumers at work, in violation of the FDCPA provision banning such contacts if the collector has been informed that the employer prohibits them.

Other kinds of FDCPA complaints filed with the FTC in 2011 included reports of collectors falsely threatening legal action when they cannot or do not intend to act on it (30 percent); falsely threatening to arrest the consumer or seize property (23 percent); and failing to identify themselves as debt collectors (17 percent).

Numerous consumers told the FTC that they been thwarted in their efforts to take advantage of one of the FDCPA's most important consumer protections by sending a written notice telling debt collectors to stop contacting them. This "cease communications" notice cannot stop collectors from filing suit against the consumer; however, it does prohibit them from continuing to call and send dunning notices. In 2011, 5,922 consumers, or 5 percent, reported that collectors did not honor "cease communication" notices and sustained their collection efforts.

With the recession at the end of the new millennium's first decade and credit card delinquencies at historic highs, reports of debt collection abuses have been steadily increasing. Federal Reserve figures show that consumer credit delinquencies increased over 500 percent from 2004 to 2010, reaching an all-time high of $300 billion in the first quarter of 2010. During that period, the total number of debt collection-related complaints received by the FTC nearly doubled (from 71,000 in 2007 to 142,743 complaints in 2011). Future employment of both bill and account collectors is projected to grow in the next 10 years, sadly this growth is higher than other occupations.

In addition to the recessionary pressures, changes in the debt collection industry have also contributed to the steady upward trend of reported abuses. First, industry consolidation through mergers and acquisitions has produced a different collections culture. In an industry previously dominated by many small businesses, a few large companies now compete for customers and profits.

Second, the "debt buying" business model has been steadily increasing its share of the collection business over that of the contingency market, which collects on behalf of creditors and keeps a percentage of the amount paid. Debt buyers buy uncollected debts for pennies on the dollar and seek to recover as much as they can for themselves, rather than remitting the collections back to the original creditor. Debt-buying firms have been growing at an annual rate of 11 percent, while the contingency market share—though still almost twice as large as that of debt buyers—has been steadily shrinking. Debt-buying companies are thought to be more susceptible to collection abuses than the traditional contingency collectors primarily because the debts are generally older, records are less accurate, and consumer contact information is not as reliable. Also, such collection companies may have less to lose when they employ unscrupulous tactics. Such companies have no creditor clients who might want to preserve relationships with even their delinquent customers, and they are often prone to using aggressive techniques in order to pressure consumers who are more likely to refuse to pay old or questionable debts.

Third, there has been a marked increase in the number of attorneys in the debt collection business. Debt collection law firms' revenue has been growing at a rate of 16 percent a year and is currently at more than $2 billion annually. While complaints against attorney collectors comprise a small fraction of all debt collection complaints, the increasing presence of attorneys in the industry may have expanded the total number of collection accounts and thus the number of problems encountered by consumers.

The FTC has responded to the rise in reported collection abuses by stepping up enforcement of the FDCPA. In 2012, the FTC brought or resolved seven debt collection cases, representing the highest number of debt collection cases pursued by the FTC in one year. In two of the cases from 2012, *United States v. West Asset Management, Inc.* and *United States v. Asset Acceptance, LLC*, and the FTC acquired $2.8 million and $2.5 million, respectively, equaling two of the largest civil penalty cases of record from the FDCPA.

The Asset Acceptance case illustrates the agency's increased focus on abuses in the debt-buying industry. Asset Acceptance, one of the largest such companies in the nation, was charged with continuing collection attempts on disputed debts and failing to provide verification of them when requested to do so in writing by consumers. The case also addressed an increasingly common problem area in debt collection: time-barred debts, which are beyond the applicable statutes of limitation. Companies like Asset Acceptance have been misleading consumers by failing to disclose that they cannot legally be sued for such time-barred debts. Under the settlement agreement, the company is required to disclose to the consumer that due to the age of the debt, Asset Acceptance will not attempt to sue to collect.

A number of the FTC's most recent law enforcement efforts have centered around defendants who collect "alleged debts" related to payday loans. For example, the FTC sued *American Credit Crunchers, LLC* in February 2012, for allegedly making contact with consumers using Indian call centers. Collectors used deceptive and threatening tactics to coerce consumers to make payments on payday loans. The twist was that many of the consumers receiving the calls had never taken out a payday loan. Furthermore, other victims had obtained such loans, but the company was not authorized to collect on them. In another such case, *FTC v. LoanPointe, LLC,* the FTC disputed the practices of wage garnishment and other collection methods of one payday loan operation. The defendants allegedly sent paperwork to consumers' employers that impersonated documents typically sent by the federal government, falsely claiming that they could garnish wages without obtaining a state court order. After the FTC settled against one of the company's owners, in July 2011, the court granted summary judgment against the defendants, and entered a permanent injunction against these practices. Defendants were ordered to pay $294,436 in redress to consumers.

Other recent FDCPA cases have illustrated the trend toward some collectors' increasingly aggressive tactics. The FTC's federal court complaint in a recent case, *FTC v. Forensic Case Management Services, Inc.,* alleged that defendants in the case threatened consumers with physical harm, desecration of dead relatives' bodies, and killing of their pets. Furthermore, collectors allegedly used obscene and profane language, revealed consumers' debts to third parties, and falsely threatened consumers with lawsuits, arrest, seizure of assets, and wage garnishment. In the case, *FTC v. Rincon Management Services, LLC,* the complaint charged that collectors contacted consumers, their employers, family, friends, and neighbors, with false claims of being process servers attempting to deliver legal documents relating to a debt collection lawsuit. In some cases consumers were even threatened with arrest. Even though the FTC charged that the company never brought any lawsuits, it was also charged with demanding that "court costs" and "legal fees" be paid in addition to the alleged debt.

State attorneys general across the country have also been increasingly active in enforcing state laws that provide consumer protections for debtors similar to those at the federal level. For example, West Virginia Attorney General Darrell McGraw announced a lawsuit in March 2012, against Midland Funding, one of the nation's largest debt buyers. The suit accused the company of using false affidavits when obtaining default judgments, among other violations of state law. New York Attorney General

Eric Schneiderman in June 2012, reached a settlement with the Lombardo Davis Goldman Firm, LLC that will permanently ban the owner from the debt collection business for masquerading as a law firm.

In its 2010 report titled "Repairing a Broken System: Protecting Consumers in Debt Collection Litigation and Arbitration," the FTC examined several areas of concern and recommended significant reforms to improve efficiency and fairness to consumers. The study was prompted by statistics showing that over 90 percent of cases (in some jurisdictions) end up in default judgments.

The report, based on information gathered through numerous nationwide meetings and public forums, identified four major consumer protection concerns and offered recommendations:

- The concerns raised about debtors' failure to appear in court to defend against lawsuits led to a recommendation that states adopt actions to increase consumer participation in suits against them, such as taking action against bad actors like "sewer servers" and allowing consumers to participate in proceedings by phone or Internet.

- Debt collection suits frequently do not contain enough information to allow consumers to respond, so the FTC recommended that states require collectors to include additional debt-related information in their court filings.

- Consumers were shown to often unknowingly waive statute of limitations defenses because they do not understand their rights; the commission's recommendations were that the burden of proof be shifted to collectors to prove that debts are not time barred, and that collectors be required to inform consumers in cases where making a payment on a debt could restart the statutory time period.

- Because banks oftentimes freeze bank accounts of debtors, despite the fact that such funds are legally exempt from garnishment, the FTC recommended that federal and state laws be altered to limit the amounts frozen in accounts containing exempt funds.

Following a lawsuit by the Minnesota Attorney General's Office against one of the nation's biggest provider of consumer debt arbitration services for engaging in deceptive practices such as consumer fraud and false advertising, several large banks discontinued the use of mandatory arbitration provisions in their credit card contracts. However, the FTC found in its study that debtors are continuing to encounter the same kinds of problems when facing mandatory arbitration that they do in defending against collectors' lawsuits. They frequently do not receive actual notice of arbitration proceedings, and when they do they cannot afford to participate. They often do not understand what arbitration entails, or what their options are when faced with mandatory proceedings. In its report, the commission recommended several steps that should be taken by arbitration forums to prevent bias and the appearance of bias, to adopt and enforce rigorous ethical standards, and to increase transparency in their proceedings.

The future of consumer protection for debtors will be interesting to watch, as the new Consumer Financial Protection Bureau's (CFPB's) role comes more clearly into focus. The CFPB, which only came into existence in July 2011, has already announced its intention to promulgate the first federal regulations governing debt collectors. As its first foray into that arena, it has proposed a rule that would allow it to supervise and examine large nonbank debt collectors—including third-party collection companies—in a manner similar to the way the Federal Reserve oversees banks. The agency also promises to take appropriate enforcement actions to address consumer harms that are uncovered during the collection agency supervision program. In addition, the CFPB and FTC have published a memorandum of understanding between the two agencies, outlining plans to jointly enforce the FDCPA and promising to work closely together to "create a strong and comprehensive framework for coordination and cooperation" in protecting America's consumers.

*This writing has been done in the author's personal capacity. The author's personal views do not necessarily represent the views of the Federal Trade Commission or any individual Commissioner.*

*Ann M. Stahl*

**See also:** Attorney General Office (AG); Consumer Financial Protection Bureau (CFPB); Debt Management; Fair Debt Collection Practices Act (FDCPA); Federal Trade Commission (FTC)

### References and Additional Readings

Brill, J. (2010). Remarks of Commissioner Julie Brill: Before the ACA international annual convention and exposition. Retrieved from http://www.ftc.gov/speeches/brill/100712aca.pdf

Clark, D.S. (2012). Federal trade commission, letter to the Honorable Richard Cordray. Retrieved from http://www.ftc.gov/os/2012/03/120320cfpbreport.pdf

Consumer Affairs. (2012). West Virginia sues major 'debt buyer'. Retrieved from http://www.consumeraffairs.com/news04/2012/03/west-virginia-sues-ma jor-debt-buyer.html

Consumer Financial Protection Bureau. (2012). CFPB annual report 2012: Fair debt collection practices act. Retrieved from http://www.consumerfinance.gov/ reports/fair-debt-collection-practices-act

Federal Reserve Bank of Philadelphia. (2010). Updated statistics related to consumer credit and consumer payments (credit performance). Retrieved from http://www.philadelphiafed.org/consumer-credit-and-payments/sta tistics

Federal Trade Commission. (2010). Repairing a broken system: Protecting consumers in debt collection litigation and arbitration. Retrieved from http://www.ftc .gov/os/2010/07/debtcollectionreport.pdf

Leibowitz, J., & Cordray, R. (2012). Memorandum of understanding between the consumer financial protection bureau and the federal trade commission. Retrieved from http://ftc.gov/os/2012/01/120123ftc-cfpb-mou.pdf

New York City Press Office. (2012). A.G. Schneiderman shuts down deceptive practices of two western NY debt collectors. Retrieved from http://www.ag .ny.gov/press-release/ag-schneiderman-shuts-down-deceptive-practices-two-western-ny-debt-collectors

## Debt Management

Debt, in its simplest form, is an unmet obligation. In financial terms, debt is money borrowed today to be repaid at a premium at a future date. Yet, the impact of borrowing decisions on consumer financial health and well-being must be understood within the broader economic landscape.

The global credit crisis of 2008 brought attention to the increasing consumer debt in the United States. Consumer debt, on the rise since the end of World War II, picked up steam in the past two decades. Between 2000 and 2007 alone, total household debt nearly doubled, topping $13.9 trillion in 2008. Included in this figure is the amount owed on home mortgages. While increasing home values have historically been regarded as a valuable consumer asset, when the housing bubble burst, many Americans owed far more on their homes than they were worth.

For many consumers, tightening in the availability of credit, the decline in housing values, and the continuing economic recession have contributed to ongoing uncertainty regarding future financial prospects and opportunities. This uncertainty lies in contrast to post-World War II optimism and economic stability in the United States.

The post-World War II economy ushered in a period of prosperity. Job opportunities were plentiful, for those with and without a college

Many consumers struggle with managing their finances, oftentimes due to unexpected expenses, overspending, medical emergencies, or poor wages. (Sebastian Czapnik/Dreamstime)

degree. Across all economic classes, there were substantial increases in net worth, resulting in an increasing, and affluent, middle class that included both white- and blue-collar workers. In addition to a reliable salary, these jobs typically provided generous benefits for their employees, including health insurance and fixed retirement plans. The economic prosperity contributed to a sense of overall well-being, with the majority of Americans enjoying financial stability during their working years, and anticipating financial security when they retired.

Since the mid-1970s, there have been major shifts in the number and types of job opportunities available. The manufacturing jobs decreased by 31 percent, limiting employment opportunities for workers with less education. The chances of experiencing a drop in earnings increased from 7 percent in 1970 to 17 percent in 2002, for those with—and without a college degree. Workers across several industries saw their fringe benefits erode. A primary example was the shift from guaranteed retirement pensions to more risky 401K plans, with values rising and falling along with the fluctuations in the stock market. Compared to 83 percent of employers in 1980 providing fixed-benefit pensions for their employees, by 2003, only one-third did so.

The rising costs of health care, education, child care, limited employment opportunities, and the need for consumers to assume increasing personal responsibility for securing one's financial future, make it challenging to keep up with one's financial obligations. Consumers today need to practice good money management skills to avoid excessive debt.

## Consumer Debt

When a consumer borrows money, a debt is incurred in the form of a *loan*. For the consumer, there is always a cost to borrowing in the form of interest paid to the institution making the loan, called the lender. *Interest* is a fee charged by the lender for the use of funds. Typically, the interest is a percentage of the amount borrowed, called the *interest rate*. The total amount borrowed is referred to as the *principal*. The interest rate is set by the lender and is affected by several factors, for example, the amount of money borrowed, the length of time it is needed, how the money will be used, and the ability of the borrower to repay the amount. Consumer debt arises from many different sources and the cost and consequences associated with inability to repay the debt depend on several factors.

A basic distinction in types of consumer debt regards whether the amount borrowed is secured or unsecured. *Secured debt* refers to loans backed by a tangible asset, also referred to as collateral. Mortgages and car loans are common examples of secured loans. In these cases, the lender places a lien on the title to the collateral (e.g., car, house) until the borrower pays off the loan. The lender retains the legal right to repossess the collateral in the event that the borrower fails to make the payments. If the consumer is unable to make the payments on the loan, it is important to realize that the consumer is responsible for repaying the total amount borrowed, even if the value of the asset falls below the amount owed. Because the consumer offers collateral on a secured loan, and because they are responsible for repaying the entire loan amount, the interest rate charged on secured loans may be lower than the interest rates charged on unsecured loans.

*Unsecured debt,* often referred to as personal loans, is not backed by collateral and is therefore considered more risky than secured debt. A college loan is a common example of an unsecured loan. Because unsecured loans are not backed by collateral, the lender makes the decision to loan money based on the creditworthiness of the borrower, that is, the likelihood that the consumer will repay the loan.

In December 1945, World War II ended and the United States entered a long period of economic growth. At that time, the Federal Reserve reported that total consumer debt outstanding stood at $6.8 billion. By the end of 1968, total consumer debt surpassed $119 billion, and now was reported as two separate components: nonrevolving and revolving consumer credit. *Nonrevolving credit* made up 98 percent of the outstanding total. Nonrevolving credit, also known as term loans, refers to loans with a set principal amount repaid in a fixed number of payments with fixed payment amounts, or *installments.* The installment payment includes both the interest on the outstanding principal amount and repayment toward the outstanding principal amount. The interest rate remained the same throughout the life of the loan, though the proportion of interest and principal changed with each payment; as the outstanding principal amount decreased, the interest rate applied to the outstanding amount decreased as well. Nonrevolving credit includes both secured loans and unsecured loans.

*Revolving credit,* in contrast, does not have fixed payment schedule, but do have a fixed amount, or credit limit associated with the loan. The borrower typically pays a fee to open the account; however, further payments are required only when funds are actually used. Then, regular payments, including interest, are made based on the amount used rather than the amount available. The most common forms of revolving consumer credit are credit cards. At the start of the most recent recession, December 2007, total consumer debt exceeded $1 trillion. At that time, revolving credit made up more than 38 percent of total outstanding consumer debt, compared to 1968 when revolving credit accounted for less than 2 percent of the total. The interest rates on credit cards are higher than on other forms of personal debt. In addition to higher interest rates, interest rates on credit cards are subject to change. There also is the potential for additional fees, for example, late or missed payments and exceeding the credit limit. In many instances, these fees trigger an increase in the interest rate.

In response to public concern over perceived unfair practices and excessive fees associated with credit card use, the federal government passed the Credit Card Act of 2009. The goal of the act is to establish fair and open practices among financial institutions in providing credit card services to consumers. Among the provisions of the act is a ban on increasing the interest rates on existing balances and providing disclosure of credit card terms and conditions in words and format easily understood by the consumer. The act also addresses concern over the increasing credit card debt of young adults requiring credit card issuers and universities to disclose agreements to students regarding marketing and distribution of credit cards and further requiring an adult cosigner on credit card applications for young adults under 21. To hold credit card issuers accountable, the law demands higher penalties for violating the new restrictions.

### Credit Reporting

To evaluate a consumers' creditworthiness and to discern a consumer's pattern of credit and debt management behaviors, the lender will review their *credit history*. Credit history, or a consumer *credit report*, is a record of a consumer's past borrowing and repaying transactions, including the source and amount borrowed, timely or late payment behaviors, and whether the loan was repaid. The information is used by the lender to assess how likely the consumer will repay the loan in a timely manner. Consumer credit history is directly related to whether the lender will approve a loan, and the interest rate that will be charged.

In the United States, information about consumers' borrowing and repaying transactions is maintained by the Federal Credit Bureau though consumer credit transactions reported by firms or institutions to credit agencies. Transactions include loan amounts extended, credit card debt, and payment activity, and in some cases, rental payment history on apartments and other services. The government established the Federal Credit Bureau with the Debt Collection Act of 1982 as a means of improving the federal government's credit management decisions and reducing delinquencies. Consumer credit agencies sign agreements with the government to receive and integrate consumer credit information into their databases. Presently, there are three major credit agencies: Experian, Equifax, and TransUnion.

As information is received, the credit agency integrates the data into the consumer's credit record. The information, or credit report, is provided for a fee to firms and financial institutions with a valid reason for reviewing it. The government establishes and maintains policies governing the reporting and use of consumer credit information, including what information is reported, how long it may be kept, who may see the information, and the fee charged for the information. The government also establishes policies for protecting the consumer against incorrect or fraudulent information recorded in his or her history. The consumer, however, is responsible for the accuracy of the information stored in the report. Thus, it is important for every consumer to monitor his or her credit history on a regular basis. To facilitate this process, the consumer has the right to receive a copy of his or her credit report from each of the three major credit agencies annually.

## Consequences of Debt

Excessive debt increases the risk of bankruptcy. Bankruptcy refers to the legal process whereby an individual or firm who is unable to meet their financial obligations applies to the government for protections or relief from the debts owed. The number of bankruptcy filings, increasing since the mid-1970s, as well as certain loopholes in the law, led to the Bankruptcy Abuse Prevention and Consumer Protection Act of 2005, which eliminated some of the protections afforded to bankruptcy applicants and making it more difficult for debts to be discharged. Despite the new constraints, filings jumped dramatically during the recession, increasing 87 percent nationwide between 2007 and 2010. While filing for bankruptcy may provide the consumer with relief from excessive debt, it is important to realize that it remains part of his or her credit history for several years, making it difficult as well as expensive for him or her to obtain credit for up to 10 years.

In addition to the financial consequences, excessive debt can take a toll on well-being and mental health. Although learning to manage financial obligations during economic ups and down is part of life, economic hardships underscore the need for all consumers to become more knowledgeable about their finances. Financially capable people are better able to manage their income and use credit and debt wisely.

*Joyce Serido*

**See also:** Bankruptcy; Credit Cards; Credit Card Accountability Responsibility and Disclosure Act (Credit CARD Act); Credit Reporting Agencies; Debt Collection; Debt, Student

### References and Additional Readings

Department of Justice. (2006). The Bankruptcy Abuse Prevention and Consumer Protection Act of 2005, Pub. L. 109-8, 119 § 256. Retrieved from http://www.justice.gov/usao/eousa/foia_reading_room/usab5404.pdf

Department of the Treasury. (2013). Guide to the Federal Credit Bureau Program: A companion to the Treasury Financial Manual Credit Supplement. http://www.fms.treas.gov/fedreg/guidance/fedcreditbureauguide.pdf

De Rugy, V. (2011). U.S. manufacturing: Output vs. jobs since 1975. George Mason University. Retrieved from http://mercatus.org/publication/us-manufacturing-output-vs-jobs-1975

Federal Reserve Board. (2013). Consumer Credit G-19 historical data: Consumer credit outstanding. Available at http://www.federalreserve.gov/releases/g19/HIST/cc_hist_mt.html

Flynn, E., & Kearns, T.C. (2011). Filing trends in bankruptcy, 2007–11. *American Bankruptcy Journal, 12*, 71–73. Retrieved on January 9, 2012 from http://journal.abi.org/sites/default/files/2011/september/watch.pdf

GPO. (1982). Debt Collection Act of 1982, 31 U.S.C. 3701 et seq. Retrieved from http://www.gpo.gov/fdsys/pkg/CFR-2011-title11-vol1/xml/CFR-2011-title11-vol1-part8.xml

GPO. (2009). Credit Card Accountability Responsibility and Disclosure Act of 2009, Pub. L. No. 111-24, § 101 et seq. Retrieved from http://www.gpo.gov/fdsys/pkg/PLAW-111publ24/pdf/PLAW-111publ24.pdf

Hacker, J.S. (2007). *The Great American risk shift: Why American jobs, families, health care, and retirement aren't secure—and how you can fight back.* New York: Oxford University Press.

Lotto, D. (2009). Declining fortunes: How the economic crisis affects the future economic prospects of the upper middle income group in America and what changes in political attitudes might follow. *The Journal of Psychohistory, 37*(2), 140–144.

McCloud, L., & Dwyer, R. E. (2011). The fragile American: Hardship and financial troubles in the 21st century. *The Sociological Quarterly, 52,* 13–35.

## Debt, Student

Student debt in 2011 exceeded $1 trillion, an amount greater than what American consumers owe in credit card debt. And of the $1 trillion in outstanding student debt, approximately $150 billion is in private student loans. And while private student loans represent only about 15 percent of total student debt, for-profit schools are costing students and taxpayers too much. For instance, a Senate staff report on private student loans released in July 2012, found that taxpayers spent $32 billion on for-profit colleges in 2009–2010 alone. The same report also found that more than half of the students who enrolled in for-profit schools in fiscal year 2008–2009 dropped out after about only four months. Among other concerns, the report identified inflated tuition, aggressive recruiting practices, abysmal student outcomes, high-taxpayer dollars spent on marketing and pocketed as profit, and regulatory evasion as the main failures of for-profit schools. Perhaps even more harmful for students and their families is the fact that private student loans lack many of the protections federal student loans have, such as repayment deferments, forbearances, and public service debt forgiveness. A report released by the U.S. Department of Education in September 2012, shows that student loan defaults have gone up for the sixth straight year. Of the 4.1 million borrowers who began making payments in late 2009 and early 2010, 9.1 percent defaulted within two years, up from 8.8 percent the year before. The three-year default data showed that nearly half the borrowers had attended for-profit colleges, even though they amounted to only 28 percent of borrowers, and 13 percent of enrolled college students. A recent study by the Pew Research Center found that nearly 20 percent of American households had outstanding student debt in 2010. This is compared to 17 percent in 2007, a percentage already considered too high. Worse yet, student debt is impacting younger Americans the most, with households headed by someone younger than 35 years accounting for 40 percent of those that have student loans.

**Twelve Recommendations for Enhancing Consumer Protection:**

Addressing the student debt crisis requires serious analysis of existing policies and procedures, plus implementation of appropriate solutions. Below are 12 recommendations:

1. Require all for-profit schools to improve their private student loan underwriting, and certify the student's need for financing to prevent over borrowing.
2. Examine whether the bankruptcy code needs to be amended to allow PSL borrowers to discharge student loans when appropriate. The original preferential treatment for PSL obligations dates to 1985 when PSLs were issued mainly by nonprofit schools. Today, PSLs are issued mostly by for-profit lenders. The bankruptcy provisions should be revised to ensure equity for PSL borrowers.
3. Require PSL lenders to provide borrowers with timely and clear disclosures to help them understand their rights and responsibilities.
4. Expand CFPB's role in assisting PSL borrowers who are in financial distress, including addressing abusive debt collection practices.
5. Create an equitable collection system that includes amending the definition of PSLs to provide borrowers with the same rights and responsibilities they get under similar types of unsecured debt, such as credit card debt.
6. Put in place stronger safeguards to reduce collusion and conflict of interest between for-profit schools and PSL lenders.
7. Require borrowers to undergo financial counseling prior to receiving a PSL.
8. Require PSL lenders to adhere to a standard set of rules in setting the interest rates they charge borrowers.
9. Ensure that for-profit schools allocate a greater percentage of taxpayers' dollars to graduating a greater percentage of PSL borrowers, and preparing them for gainful employment.
10. Provide effective relief for PSL borrowers harmed by fraudulent for-profit schools.
11. Improve pre- and post-default programs, including rehabilitation, consolidation and public service forgiveness options.
12. Conduct meaningful research to establish the reasons for-profit schools are failing students, and make recommendations to reverse these results.

Federal aid, in the form of loans, grants, and tax credits, makes up over two-thirds of direct aid to all postsecondary students. Private student loans (PSLs) make up less than 15 percent of total student debt outstanding as of January 1, 2012, and contributed less than 7 percent of the estimated $112 billion in total student loans originated in 2010–2011. But, according to a report by the *LA Times*, the education department "estimates that 96% of students at for-profit colleges take out loans, a much higher percentage than students at community colleges, four-year public universities and nonprofit private colleges. Students at for-profit colleges account for 13% of the nation's college enrollment but 47% of all federal student loan defaults" (Goldberg, 2012).

Moreover, the dropout rate at for-profit colleges is much higher than public and nonprofit colleges and universities. The Department of Education report found correlations between the lack of money spent on instruction at for-profit colleges and high dropout rates. The average marketing expenditure for for-profit colleges was 42.1 percent of their revenue, as compared to 17.2 percent on instruction. And according to the report, many recruiters mislead prospective students about the cost of the program, the availability of federal aid, the job placement rate, and the transferability of credits.

A good college education is still a good investment, as higher education remains the most promising path to a good job and economic advancement. The unemployment rate for younger workers with college degrees is 8.9 percent compared to over 13 percent for those with just a high school diploma. But students and their families must have a better understanding of the lasting harm PSLs can cause them. They also need to know what options they have to obtain and finance a good education at a more reasonable cost. And policymakers and regulators must take stronger action to protect students and their families by curbing some of the most abusive practices for-profit schools engage in.

### Obtaining/Managing Federal and Private Student Loans

*Know the difference between federal and private student loans.* Student loans fall into two main categories: loans issued directly by the federal government and loans issued by banks and other private financial companies. To get a federal loan the student and his or her parents must complete the Free Application for Federal Student Aid (FAFSA). The U.S. Department of Education processes the FAFSA to determine the amount the student and his/her family should pay (expected family contribution, EFC). The Department of Education then sends the application to the schools of interest. The schools calculate the cost of attendance (tuition, fees, room, and board, etc.), and deducts the EFC from it. And after deducting other non-federal aid received, the school awards aid in the form of Federal Pell Grants, work study, and federal student loans to cover the difference.

*Federal loans:* Federal student loans are a form of aid that must be repaid. There are four types of federal student loans, and as of July 1, 2010, they are all issued directly by the government under the Direct Loan program:

- Subsidized Stafford loans: Low-interest, fixed-rate loans based on financial need. The government pays the interest charges while in school and during the grace and deferment periods. (There is no grace period interest benefit for loans made in academic years 2012–2013 and 2013–2014.)
- Unsubsidized Stafford loans: Low-interest, fixed-rate loans available to students regardless of financial need. But the borrower, not the government, pays the interest charges. Borrowers my defer payment of interest as long as they are in school.
- PLUS loans: Available to parents (Parent PLUS) of dependent undergraduate students and to graduate and professional degree students. Generally, the applicants must have good credit to qualify. The borrower pays the interest charges.
- Consolidation loans: Allow borrowers to combine existing loans usually at an overall lower interest rate. Borrowers may also extend the length of the consolidated loan to lower the monthly payments.

*Private Student Loans (PSLs)*: Private institutions such as banks and for-profit schools have been issuing PSLs for many years as a way to supplement federal student loans. However, according to the Consumer Financial Protection Bureau (CFPB), the number of undergraduates who borrowed PSLs nearly tripled between 2003 and 2007. This was mainly due to a high demand for asset-backed securities, which encouraged private student lenders to lower their lending standards and increase direct marketing to students. As a result, PSLs grew from less than $5 billion in 2001 to over $20 billion in 2008. The amount quickly contracted to $6 billion in 2011 as the financial crisis forced lenders to tighten up lending restrictions. But defaults have also increased. According to the CFPB, there are now over $8.1 billion in defaulted private loans, representing more than 850,000 loans. And Congress amended the bankruptcy code in 2005 to make it tougher to discharge PSLs.

*Exhaust federal student loan eligibility before taking a PSLs.* Students repaying PSLs have fewer options than those repaying federal student loans. Federal student loans offer significant consumer protections that PSLs don't. Nevertheless, more than 54 percent of PSL borrowers do not exhaust their federal student loan eligibility before they apply for a PSL.

*PSLs are riskier and more expensive than federal student loans*: From a borrower's perspective, federal student loans and PSLs may look very similar thus creating confusion. But PSLs often lack the repayment flexibility that federal student loans have. For example, Congress and President Bush enacted the College Cost Reduction and Access Act in 2007, which gives borrowers the option to make payments based on a portion of their income. In a tight labor market, this benefit can be very helpful in allowing the borrower to stay current. But this is generally not a benefit afforded to PSL borrowers. And although PSLs are in many ways similar to other forms of unsecured debt such as credit card debt, they are very different when borrowers attempt to modify them or discharge them through bankruptcy. In fact, PSLs are as difficult to get rid off in bankruptcy court as is child support debt or unpaid income taxes. Another key difference is that federal loans have a fixed interest rate, but most private loans have variable rates. And in the current market, most PSLs for undergraduates must be cosigned by a creditworthy person. Another important difference between federal and private student loans is the borrower's ability to repay them. Federal student loans offer several options to borrowers who are unable to repay them. This includes income-based repayment plans, forbearance arrangements that allow for a temporary reduction of payments, and rehabilitation programs that let the borrower remove the default information from his or her credit report. PSLs rarely afford borrowers any of these benefits.

*Know whether your loans are federal student loans or PSL.* This information will come in handy when contacting the servicer (the company that collects the payments) or debt collector to make payment arrangements. If the loan type is unknown, consult the online National Student Loan Database System for Students. The site also lists the loan servicer. Keep in mind that the servicer might be different than the company who originally issued the loan. Federal loans usually go by one of the following names: Stafford, Grad PLUS, Direct, or Perkins. Older federal student loans could be issued by a bank, credit union, the school, or other lending institutions through the Federal Family Educational Loan (FFEL) Program. Federal loans issued on or after July 1, 2010, are funded directly by the U.S. Department of Education. Federal loans are guaranteed by the federal government. PSLs typically use names like "private" or "alternative." They are likely issued by a bank, credit union, the school, or other lending institutions.

*Avoid surprises.* Double check the qualification requirements. Review the current Consumer Guide to Changes in Federal Pell Grants and Student

Loans. On July 1 of each year, planned changes to federal student aid go into effect for the upcoming year. This guide explains important changes to Pell Grant eligibility and the terms of new federal student loans, which apply to new students, students already in college, and borrowers who are repaying their loans. It is important to know what these changes will be to plan how to pay for school and manage existing loans. If enrolling in college for the first time on or after July 1, 2012, a high school diploma or GED, or homeschool verification must be provided to be eligible for federal student aid, including grants, loans, and work-study.

It is also wise to use the CFPB's financial aid shopping sheet, which allows college-bound students to find out the costs of the college they plan to attend before they commit to enrolling. This way students can see clearly which college is more affordable.

*Get help:* There are several things students can do if paying the student loan becomes a challenge. One option is consolidation; students may be able to lock a low fixed rate. For the year 2012–2013, the variable rate for Stafford loans issued between July 1, 1998, and June 30, 2006, is 2.39 percent during repayment and 1.79 percent during in-school, grace, or deferment periods. Furthermore, consolidating loans will allow a single payment instead of separate payments for each existing loans. Consumers can assses if loans qualify for consolidation by examining the "National Student Loan Data System" link offered via the U.S. Department of Education.

The CFPB created the Student Loan Debt Collection Assistant tool to help students get back on track if they are in default. This tool helps students understand their options, communicate with their servicer or debt collector, and bring their loan current.

Another option is Student Debt Repayment Assistant, an online tool that provides borrowers with information on income-based repayment, deferments, alternative payment programs, and much more. If the servicer or debt collector refuses to negotiate, students may file a complaint. In March 2012, the CFPB launched a student loan complaint system. Any consumer with a student loan can file a complaint online at www.consumerfinance .gov for complaints or disputes over federal or private student loans.

All or part of the loan may be waived if the student volunteers or works in a qualified program, such us teaching in economically disadvantaged communities. Information about income-based repayment and Public Service Loan Forgiveness is available at www.IBRinfo.org (income-based repayment).

Students can also consider a deferment. A deferment lets a student stop making payments for a set period of time because of a specific life condition, including going back to school, loss of a job, or economic hardship.

Interest stops accruing for subsidized federal loans during the deferment period. Students may also qualify for a deferment even if they have defaulted on their loan. An application for deferment can be obtained from the federal student aid website www.dl.ed.gov.

A forbearance is yet another option. In a forbearance, the servicer authorizes the student to stop making payments or to reduce payments for an agreed upon period of time. Unlike a deferment, interest charges continue accruing during a forbearance. Common reasons to qualify for a forbearance include health problems, financial hardship, or unforeseen personal challenges. To apply, students can contact their servicer and explain their situation and ask for a forbearance.

An additional option is loan rehabilitation. Loan rehabilitation is a one-time opportunity to a current federal student loan. Participating in loan rehabilitation can allow students to be eligible for federal student aid. However, if a redefault occurs, qualification to rehabilitate the loan again is not possible. The servicer or debt collector may be contacted to make arrangements for a rehabilitation.

A final option may be a "Pay as You Earn." This program caps the amount of payment required on loans at 10 percent of annual income. Servicers have further information.

*Avoid defaulting:* This can ruin the consumer's credit rating for years. And the government can garnish wages, tax returns, and assets without a lawsuit. Defaulting will also prevent a student from borrowing other federal student loans to complete or pursue more education.

*Rigoberto Reyes*

**See also:** Congress; Consumer Financial Protection Bureau (CFPB); Debt Management; Department of Education (ED)

## References and Additional Readings

Adamson, M. (2009). The financialization of student life: Five propositions on student debt. *Polygraph: An International Journal of Culture and Politics, 21,* 107–120.

Baum, S., & Steele, P. (2010). *Who borrows most? Bachelor's degree recipients with high levels of student debt.* Trends in Higher Education Series, College Board Advocacy and Policy Center. Retrieved from www.collegeboard.com/trends

Goldberg, J. (July 30, 2012). For-profit colleges slammed in Democratic Senate staff report. *LA Times.* Retrieved from http://articles.latimes.com/2012/jul/30/nation/la-na-forprofit-colleges-20120731

Reed, M., & Cheng, D. (2009). Student debt and the class of 2008. Retrieved from http://www.projectonstudentdebt.org/files/pub/classof2008.pdf

**Delaney Amendment**. *See* Food Drug and Cosmetic Act (FD&C Act)

## Department of Agriculture (USDA)

The U.S. Department of Agriculture (USDA) is the federal executive department responsible for U.S. federal policy on food, agriculture, natural resources, and related issues to meet the needs of farmers/ranchers, promote agricultural trade and production, assure food safety, protect natural resources, foster rural communities, and end hunger in the United States and abroad.

According to the USDA's website, their mission, is to "enhance the quality of life for the American people by supporting production of agriculture; ensuring a safe, affordable, nutritious, and accessible food supply; caring for agricultural, forest, and range lands; supporting sound development of rural communities; providing economic opportunities for farm and rural residents; expanding global markets for agricultural and forest products and services; and working to reduce hunger in America and throughout the world."

USDA provides financing to create job opportunities; improves housing, utilities, and infrastructure in rural America; improves nutrition for all Americans; supports international agricultural and economic development; provides regulations and inspections of agricultural products to reduce the prevalence of food-borne hazards from farm to table; and manages and protects America's public lands by working cooperatively with other levels of government. The head of the department is the secretary of agriculture, who is a member of the cabinet.

### History

The early economy of the United States was largely agrarian. What was eventually to become the USDA started out as part of the U.S. Patent Office. As U.S. patent commissioner, Henry Leavitt Ellsworth's interest in agriculture prompted Congress to appropriate funds for farming in 1839, used to obtain seeds from foreign countries and allocate them via the U.S. Post Office. By 1845, the U.S. Patent Office was functioning as an agricultural bureau, slating Ellsworth as of "the father of the Department of Agriculture."

In 1849, the U.S. Patent Office was transferred to the newly created Department of the Interior but there was an increasing demand for a separate bureau or department focusing on agriculture. On May 15, 1862, President Abraham Lincoln established what is now known as the Department of

Agriculture, headed by a commissioner without cabinet status. In 1889, President Grover Cleveland made the Department of Agriculture part of the U.S. cabinet.

In 1887, the Hatch Act provided federal land grants to the states to create agricultural experiment stations. These agricultural experiment stations have historically been connected with land-grant state colleges and universities founded under the Morrill Act of 1862. In 1914, the Smith-Lever Act funded cooperative extension services in each state to teach agriculture, home economics, and related subjects to the public. During the Great Depression, when farming was still the major occupation for millions of Americans, USDA provided financial and technical assistances to farmers/ranchers to ensure that food continued to be produced and distributed to those who needed it. Today, USDA assists farmers/ranchers on both the domestic and world markets. To help U.S. farmers, Congress has passed several farm bills, the latest being the Food, Conservation, and Energy Act of 2008 through various means, including price supports. In addition, USDA subsidizes the federal supplemental nutrition assistance program (SNAP) and public school lunch program.

### USDA Organization Chart

USDA is made up of several operating units (Table 10).

As examples of operating units' jurisdictions, the Farm Service Agency administers payments under the 2008 U.S. farm bill. The Foreign Agricultural Service deals with Public Law 480 food shipments, and the Food and Nutrition Service is in charge of SNAP and the school lunch programs.

**Table 10**  USDA organization chart

- United States Secretary of Agriculture
- United States Deputy Secretary of Agriculture
- Under Secretary of Agriculture for Farm and Foreign Agricultural Services
- Farm Service Agency
- Foreign Agricultural Service
- Risk Management Agency
- Commodity Credit Corporation
- Federal Crop Insurance Corporation

*(Continued)*

**Table 10** (*Continued*)

- Natural Resources Conservation Service
- Under Secretary of Agriculture for Rural Development
- Rural Housing Service
- Rural Utilities Service
- Rural Business—Cooperative Service
  - Under Secretary of Agriculture for Food, Nutrition, and Consumer Services
- Food and Nutrition Service
- Center for Nutrition Policy and Promotion
  - Under Secretary of Agriculture for Food Safety
- Food Safety and Inspection Service
- Under Secretary for Agriculture for Research, Education, and Economics
- Agricultural Research Service
- Cooperative State Research, Education, and Extension Service
- Economic Research Service
- National Agricultural Library
- National Agricultural Statistics Service
- Under Secretary of Agriculture for Marketing and Regulatory Programs
- Agricultural Marketing Service
- Animal and Plant Health Inspection Service
- Grain Inspection, Packers, and Stockyards Administration
- Under Secretary of Agriculture for Natural Resources and Environment
- United States Forest Service

## USDA Expenditures

USDA expenditures are given in Table 11.

Expenditures increased from $124 billion in 2007 to $179 billion in 2010. By far, the largest expenditures are for Food, Nutrition, and Consumer Services (FNC). In 2010, USDA's FNC expenditures were $91 billion, which was a sharp increase from the 2007 expenditures of $55 billion. Next in line were the expenditures on farm programs, which have decreased over the past decade. The outlays by the Farm Service Agency were $26 billion in 2010, which were smaller than the 2007 amount of $31 billion and the 2004 amount of almost $25 billion.

**Table 11**  Spending authority, by program area, USDA, 2007–2010 (U.S. million dollars)

| Program Area | 2007 (Actual) | 2008 (Actual) | 2009 (Estimated) | 2010 (Budget) |
|---|---|---|---|---|
| Farm and Foreign Agricultural Services | | | | |
|   Farm Service Agency | 30,832 | 25,422 | 27,885 | 26,451 |
|   Risk Management Agency | 5,654 | 8,074 | 9,633 | 11,453 |
|   Foreign Agricultural Services | 3,987 | 6,222 | 8,529 | 8,204 |
| Total Farm and Foreign Agricultural Services | 40,473 | 39,718 | 46,047 | 46,108 |
| Rural Development | 14,473 | 18,973 | 41,494 | 29,649 |
| Food, Nutrition, and Consumer Services | 54,944 | 60,899 | 79,994 | 90,803 |
| Food Safety | 1,017 | 1,093 | 1,122 | 1,172 |
| Natural Resources and Environment | 8,115 | 9,614 | 10,656 | 9,710 |
| Marketing and Regulatory Programs | 1,770 | 2,151 | 2,123 | 2,899 |
| Research, Education, and Economics | 2,586 | 2,666 | 2,968 | 2,731 |
| Other Activities | 550 | 449 | 561 | 703 |
| Total USDA Spending | 123,928 | 131,451 | 182,276 | 178,650 |

Data compiled from: U.S. Department of Agriculture. 2009. Budget Summary and Annual Performance Plan. (p. 4) Retrieved from http://www.obpa.usda.gov/budsum/FY09budsum.pdf

## USDA Discretionary Spending

The discretionary budget for 2010, which is part of the total budget, totaled $26 billion. The funding highlights are given in Table 12.

**Table 12** USDA discretionary funding highlights

- Provides over $20 billion in loans and grants to support and expand rural development activities, including small businesses, renewable energy, and telecommunications

- Includes a $50 million increase to address deferred maintenance on the most critical health and safety infrastructure within the U.S. national forests

- Supports the implementation of a $250,000 commodity program payment limit to help ensure that payments are made to those who most need them

- Provides for wildfire management and commodity protection by fully funding suppression costs at the 10-year average, establishing a discretionary contingent reserve for wildfires, and includes program reforms to ensure fire management resources are focused where they will do the most good

- Fully funds WIC to serve all eligible individuals

- Includes $1 billion per year for the Child Nutrition reauthorization

- Supports a pilot program to help increase senior participation in SNAP

- Supports independent producers through improved enforcement of the Packers and Stockyards Act and investing in agricultural production diversity, including organic farming and local food systems

- Reduces direct payments to largest farmers, crop insurance subsidies, and overseas brand promotion funding, and eliminates cotton storage credits and Resource Conservation and Development funding

Data compiled from: U.S. Department of Agriculture. 2010. Budget summary and annual performance plan. Retrieved from http://www.obpa.usda.gov/budsum/FY10budsum.pdf

## USDA Selected Agencies/Programs

Selected agency/program costs for 2006, 2008, and 2010 are given in Table 13. For example, Foreign Agricultural Services covers export credit guarantees and foreign food assistance.

**Table 13** Selected agency/program, USDA, 2006, 2008, and 2010 (U.S. million dollars)

| Agency/Program | 2006 | 2008 | 2010 |
|---|---|---|---|
| Farm and Foreign Agricultural Services | | | |
| Farm Service Agency | | | |
| Farm Loan and Grant Program | 3,153 | 3,365 | 6,070 |
| Conservation and Other Programs | 2,102 | 2,025 | 1,904 |
| Commodity Programs | 29,585 | 17,167 | 16,239 |
| Commodity Credit Corporation Programs | 33,285 | 22,721 | 22,390 |

*(Continued)*

**Table 13** (*Continued*)

| Agency/Program | 2006 | 2008 | 2010 |
|---|---|---|---|
| Other Activities | 1,325 | 1,430 | 1,570 |
| Total for Farm Service Agency | 36,165 | 25,422 | 27,719 |
| Foreign Agricultural Services | | | |
| Export Credit Guarantees | 1,363 | 3,115 | 3,090 |
| Market Development Program | 248 | 249 | 253 |
| Export Subsidy Programs | 0 | 0 | 2 |
| Trade Adjustment Assistance for Farmers | 4 | 0 | 90 |
| Foreign Food Assistance | 2,060 | 2,581 | 2,221 |
| Other Activities | 246 | 277 | 187 |
| Total for Foreign Agricultural Service | 3,921 | 6,222 | 5,843 |
| Total for Farm and Foreign Agricultural Services | 40,086 | 30,209 | 31,626 |
| Food, Nutrition, and Consumer Services | | | |
| Food and Nutrition Service | | | |
| Food Stamp Program (SNAP) | 34,576 | 39,451 | 69,459 |
| Child Nutrition Programs | 13,347 | 14,669 | 17,034 |
| Women, Infants, and Children (WIC) Program | 5,363 | 6,400 | 7,257 |
| All Other Programs | 490 | 379 | 423 |
| Total for Food, Nutrition, and Consumer Services | 43,776 | 60,899 | 94,173 |
| Research, Education, and Economics | | | |
| Agricultural Research Service | 1,326 | 1,198 | 1,265 |
| National Institute of Food and Agriculture | 1,207 | 1,227 | 1,486 |
| Economic Research Service | 75 | 78 | 82 |
| National Agricultural Statistics Service | 139 | 163 | 162 |
| Total for Research, Education, and Economics | 2,747 | 2,666 | 2,995 |
| USDA Total | 86,609 | 93,774 | 128,794 |

2006 Data Compiled from: U.S. Department of Agriculture. 2008. Budget Summary and Annual Performance Plan. (p. 4–5) Retrieved from http://www.obpa.usda.gov/budsum/FY08budsum.pdf

2008 Data Compiled from: U.S. Department of Agriculture. 2010. Budget Summary and Annual Performance Plan. (p. 107) Retrieved from http://www.obpa.usda.gov/budsum/FY10budsum.pdf

2008 Data Compiled from: U.S. Department of Agriculture. 2012. Budget Summary and Annual Performance Plan. (p. 119–20) Retrieved from http://www.obpa.usda.gov/budsum/FY12budsum.pdf

## USDA Economic Research Service

The Economic Research Service (ERS) is the main source of economic information and research from USDA. The responsibility of ERS is to provide public policy economic information and to enhance public and private decision-making on economic and policy issues related to agriculture, natural resources, and rural development. ERS economists and social scientists develop and distribute a broad range of economic/social science information and analyses to public and private decision makers (USDA/ERS).

The ERS program is divided among four divisions (Food Economics, Information Services, Market and Trade Economics, and Resource and Rural Economics). The program conducts research and analyses of food and commodity markets, as well as, policy studies, and economic and statistical indicators. Furthermore, the program researches commodity and trade associations, public interest groups, the media, and the general public via agency reports, publications, and data products that are disseminated through the ERS website.

## USDA Nutrition Programs

The USDA's Food and Nutrition Service administers several programs concerned with the distribution of food and nutrition to U.S. consumers. Overseas aid programs that supply surplus food to developing countries operate through USAID and UN/FAO. USDA operates 15 domestic food assistance programs that accounted for over $90 billion of the total USDA budget outlays for 2010 (Economic Research Service, 2011).

## Supplemental Nutritional Assistance Program (SNAP)

SNAP, which is the largest federal nutrition program, provided close to $70 billion in benefits for nearly 45 million Americans in 2010, with children accounting for almost half of the participants. In 2010, SNAP accounted for 72 percent of USDA's food and nutrition assistance expenditures (Figure 1) (Economic Research Service, 2011).

The federal nutrition policy design is based on current dietary guidelines and is updated by law every five years through a collaborative effort of USDA and HHS (Human and Health Services). The 2010 guidelines focus on bringing science-based advice to those older than two years and those with increased risk for chronic diseases related to obesity. The most current guidelines recommend more fruits, vegetables, low-fat milk products, and whole grains for better health (United States Department of Agriculture, Center for Nutrition Policy and Promotion, 2011).

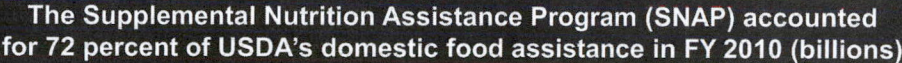

**The Supplemental Nutrition Assistance Program (SNAP) accounted for 72 percent of USDA's domestic food assistance in FY 2010 (billions)**

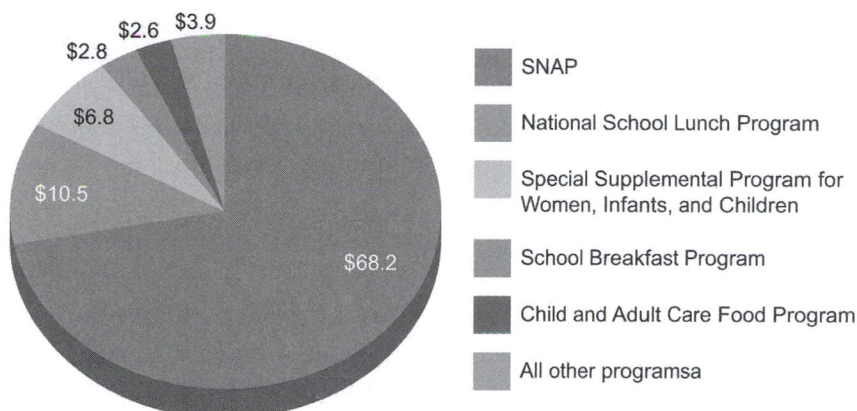

- SNAP
- National School Lunch Program
- Special Supplemental Program for Women, Infants, and Children
- School Breakfast Program
- Child and Adult Care Food Program
- All other programsa

**Figure 1.** Outlays of major food and nutritional assistance programs (USDA/ERS). (*Source: USDA, Economic Research Service using data from USDA's Food and Nutrition Service*)

SNAP costs rose from $35 billion in 2006 to $69 billion in 2010. Participation in the program also increased, with nearly 45 million (one in seven) Americans now receiving federal assistance. In 2010, the average SNAP benefit per family was $133 per month (about 50 percent of the recipients were children and 18 percent were elderly). To be eligible, recipients must earn income at 130 percent or less of the poverty line; in 2010, 41 percent of the recipients earned half that amount or less and 18 percent had no income at all.

### National School Lunch Program (NSLP)

Federal law requires public schools to offer every student hot meals, many of those free or at reduced prices. About half of the children in public schools receive free lunches. The federal subsidy for the school lunch program is $8.2 billion per year, or $2.47 per child. On average, school lunches cost $2.66 to prepare, which means that schools lose nearly 19 cents for every one of the 15 million free lunches they serve daily. As a result, public schools lose nearly $5–$8 million each school day while feeding 30 million children.

Food costs have outstripped federal subsidies for the federal school lunch program, and inflation has driven up the cost of staples such as milk

(12 percent), cheese (15 percent), and bread (17 percent). As a result, the NSLP increased what it pays local school districts by only 3 percent.

### U.S. Biofuels/Ethanol

Since 2005, the United States has been the world's largest producer of ethanol fuel, producing 13.2 billion U.S. liquid gallons (50 billion liters) in 2010, up from 1.6 billion U.S. liquid gallons in 2001 (Lichts, 2011). In the United States, ethanol is used as a gasoline oxygenate in the form of low-level blends (up to 10 percent) and as E85 fuel. Most of the ethanol fuel in the United States is produced using corn as feedstock, roughly one-third of the U.S. corn crop (U.S. ethanol production from corn increased from 2.2 million tons in 1981 to 10.4 million tons in 2010). The market share for ethanol in the United States grew from over 1 percent in 2000 to nearly 10 percent in 2010. Due to the growing demand for biofuels, the 2007 U.S. Energy Independence and Security Act (EISA) requires 36 billion gallons of annual renewable fuel use by 2022, including ethanol from cellulosic feedstock mandated at 16 billion gallons per year (production from corn ethanol is set at 15 billion gallons by 2015), and the Open Fuel Standard Act of 2011 requires that 95 percent of U.S.-manufactured cars be operate on nonpetroleum-based fuels by 2017. Despite these requirements, there is controversy and concerns over ethanol production from corn due to direct and indirect land-use effects, global grain supply, and carbon intensity from biofuels. Part of the controversy is due to the 54 cent tariff on ethanol imports, largely to protect domestic ethanol producers from Brazilian sugarcane ethanol shipments to the United States. Also, since 2004, blenders of transportation fuel have received a tax credit for each gallon of ethanol that is mixed with regular gasoline. Blenders receive a 45-cent tax credit for each gallon of ethanol they blend with gasoline, as of May 2011, regardless of the feedstock. Furthermore, small producers receive an additional 10 cents on the first 15 million gallons produced; and finally, producers of cellulosic ethanol obtain credits up to $1.01. Since the 1970s, tax credits to promote the production and consumption of biofuels have been in effect.

### Agricultural Policy

Modern U.S. agricultural policies have shifted from policies that promote the development of agricultural resources toward the support of agricultural prices. A variety of policy instruments increase agricultural prices by reducing the amount of agricultural outputs available to markets, limiting production using acreage allotments or production set-asides, or acquiring commodities through nonrecourse loans. A variety of policy innovations to make commodity programs more market oriented culminated in the passage of the Federal Agricultural Improvement and Reform Act of 1996, which implemented policy instruments that attempted to decouple commodity supports from production decisions.

Passage of the Food Security and Rural Investment Act of 2002 and the Farm Program of 2008 represented a return to more traditional instruments of commodity programs, including target price and loan rate for basic commodities. For example, the U.S. milk program uses a modified two-price plan that increases the blended price of all milk by restricting the quantity of fluid milk, whereas the U.S. sugar program is supported with a tariff rate quota that restricts the amount of imported sugar. The U.S. peanut and tobacco programs have been terminated by way of buyouts where future rents under the program were purchased by the federal government and paid to farmers, including landowners.

There were very few changes between the 2002 and 2008 U.S. farm bills; specialty crops were included in the 2008 farm bill. The key components, such as loan rates and target prices, remain. Under the 2002 and 2008 U.S. farm bills, the largest USDA expenditures were for SNAP and the federal school lunch program. There have been many issues that USDA has dealt with in addition to price supports. These include the discontinuance of holding government stocks, export enhancement program (EPP), animal food safety issues such as bovine spongiform encephalopathy (BSE), and country of origin labeling (COOL). Prior to 1986, the United States required that the government buy stocks when market prices fell below the loan rate. As shown in Figure 1, because of low market prices, the United States stored large quantities of wheat. However, this is no longer the case as in 1986 the stock-holding requirement was removed. Under EPP, the United States provided massive export subsidies on grain exports, but these have been discontinued. Concerning BSE, although the United States curtailed significantly the importation of beef from Canada, trade has increased significantly since the outbreak in 2001. COOL was made mandatory under the 2008 U.S. farm bill, but the effects are far from clear.

## National Institute of Food and Agriculture (NIFA)

NIFA replaced the former Cooperative State Research, Education, and Extension Service (CSREES). Many research and education activities are under the jurisdiction of NIFA. These include the Hatch Act and the Agriculture and Food Research Initiative. Funding for research has declined significantly. For example, funds under the Hatch Act dropped from $236 million in 2011 to $204 million in 2012.

## High and Volatile Commodity Prices

From 2000 to 2010, there was a significant increase in price volatility and a sharp rise in prices, except for a brief period in 2008. The commodities of corn, cotton, rice, soybeans, sugar, and wheat, market prices have been significantly higher than the U.S. loan rate and target prices. As a result, the cost of the U.S. farm program has been significantly reduced because of the reduction in countercyclical payments. For example, from January 2000 to January 2008, cotton market prices were significantly below the target price and sometimes below the loan rate (Figure 2), but in 2010, cotton market prices were well above the target prices (Figure 3). The subsidization of U.S. cotton created numerous controversies worldwide and resulted in a case against the United States by Brazil to have the U.S. cotton policy changed. Brazil won the challenge against the United States (Powell and Schmitz, 2005).

Beginning in 2007, corn, rice, soybean, and wheat market prices have been significantly above the loan rate and target prices. At the end of 2010, world sugar prices were well above the U.S. support levels. In perspective, world food prices peaked in 2007–2008 and fell sharply in 2009, only to rise again sharply in 2010 (Figure 4). These rises in food prices have created political instability in many countries.

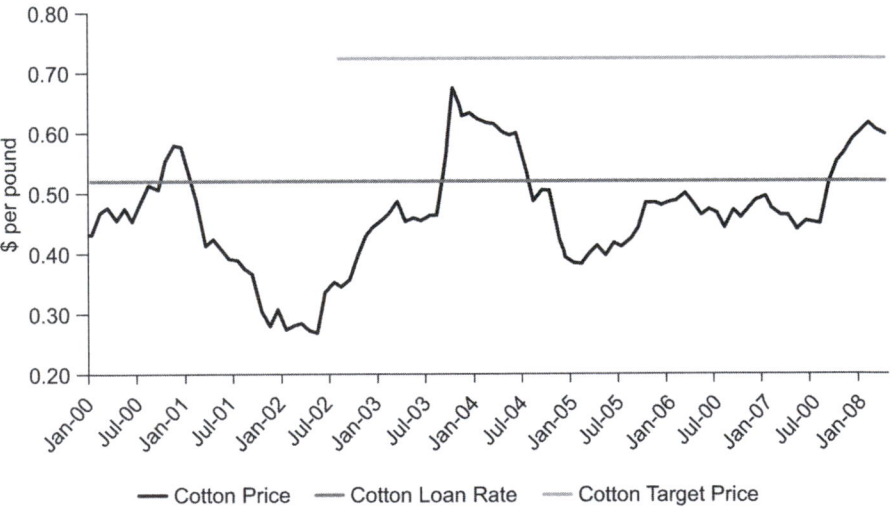

**Figure 2.** Cotton loan rate and target price, 2000–2008. (*Source:* Schmitz, A., C. B. Moss, T. G. Schmitz, H. W. Furtan, H. C. Schmitz, *Agricultural Policy, Agribusiness, and Rent-Seeking Behaviour,* 2d ed. (Toronto, Canada: University of Toronto Press, 2010)

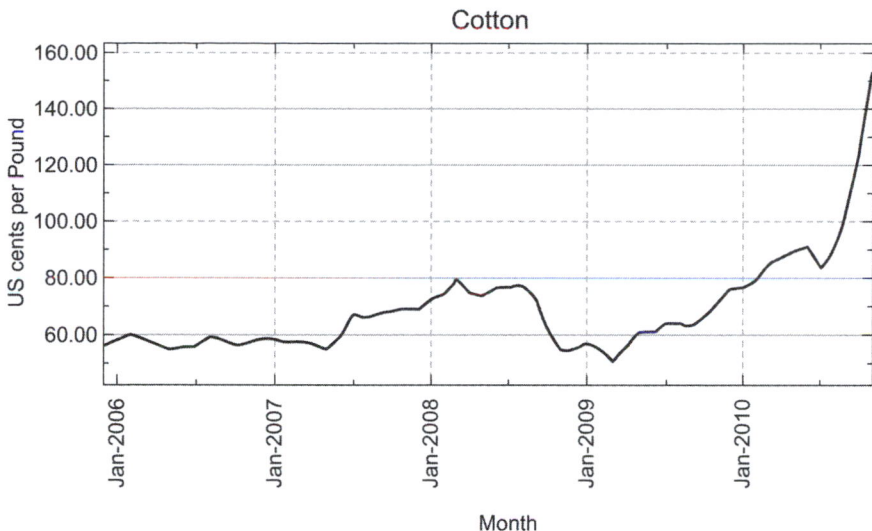

**Figure 3.** Cotton (U.S. cents per pound), 2006–2010. (*Source:* Data Compiled through indexmundi at http://www.indexmundi.com/commodities/?commodity=cotton)

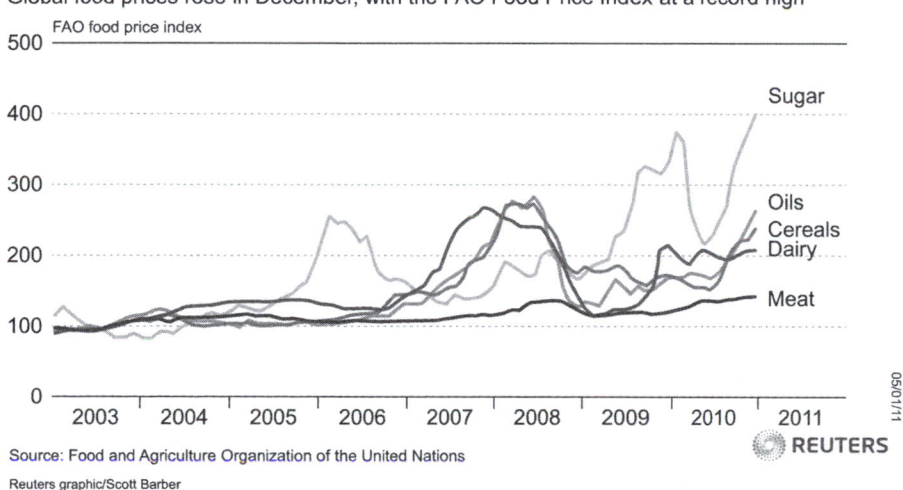

**Figure 4.** World food prices. (*Source:* Food and Agricultural Organization of the United Nations. Data available at http://www.fao.org/worldfoodsituation/wfs-home/foodpricesin dex/en/)

## Conclusions

USDA is involved in a wide range of activities, including administering the U.S. farm program and conducting animal and crop science research. It is important to remember that USDA does not set broad policy goals for agriculture. The U.S. agricultural policy originates with Congress.

*Andrew Schmitz*

**See also:** Americans with Disabilities Act (ADA); Food and Drug Administration (FDA); Food Safety; Patent and Trademark Office; Supplemental Nutrition Assistance Program (SNAP); United Nations (UN)

### References and Additional Readings

Department of Agriculture. (2013). United States Department of Agriculture. Retrieved from http://www.usda.gov/wps/portal/usda/usdahome

Department of Agriculture, Center for Nutrition Policy and Promotion. (2011). Executive summary, dietary guidelines for Americans, 2010. Retrieved from http://www.cnpp.usda.gov/Publications/DietaryGuidelines/2010/PolicyDoc/ExecSumm.pdf

Department of Agriculture, Economic Research Service. (2011). The food assistance landscape FY 2010 annual report (n.p.).

Department of Agriculture, Food and Nutrition Service. (2012). Supplemental nutrition assistance program (SNAP). Retrieved from http://www.fns.usda.gov/snap/

Food and Agriculture Organization of the United Nations. (2012). FAO food price index. Retrieved from http://www.fao.org/worldfoodsituation/wfs-home/foodpricesindex/en/

Johnson, A. (2008). High costs land on school cafeteria trays. Retrieved from http://www.msnbc.msn.com/id/25011096/ns/business-consumer_news/t/high-costs-land-school-cafeteria-trays/

Lichts, F.O. (2011). Industry statistics: 2010 world fuel ethanol production. Retrieved from http://ethanolrfa.org/pages/World-Fuel-Ethanol-Production

Office of Management and Budget. (2010). A new era of responsibility: Renewing America's promise. Retrieved from http://www.whitehouse.gov/sites/default/files/omb/assets/fy2010_new_era/A_New_Era_of_Responsibility2.pdf

Powell, S., & Schmitz A. (2005). The cotton and sugar subsidies decisions: WTO's dispute settlement system rebalances the agreement on agriculture. *Drake Agricultural Law Journal, 10*(2), 287–330.

Schmitz, A. (2011). Agricultural policies in the next decade: A global perspective. *Applied Economics, 18*(1).

Schmitz, A., Furtan, H., & Bayliss, K. (2002). *Agricultural policy, agribusiness, and Rent-seeking behavior.* Toronto: University of Toronto Press.

Schmitz, A., Moss, C., Schmitz, T., Furtan, H., & Schmitz, H. (2010). *Agricultural policy, agribusiness, and rent-seeking behavior, second edition.* Toronto: University of Toronto Press.

Schmitz, A., Wilson, N., Moss, C., & Zilberman, D. (2011). *The economics of alternative energy sources and globalization.* UAE: Bentham Science Publishers.

Teaching with Data. (2011). The rising cost of food stamps. Retrieved from http://teachingwithdata.blogspot.com/2011/07/rising-cost-of-food-stamps.html

## Department of Commerce (DOC)

The U.S. Department of Commerce (DOC) began as the Department of Commerce and Labor. Today, those two entities are separated, and the DOC is comprised of 12 diverse agencies and bureaus:

- Bureau of Economic Analysis (BEA): The BEA provides timely, objective, accurate, and relevant economic data to help in the understanding of the U.S. economy.
- Bureau of Industry and Security (BIS): The BIS works to further national security, foreign policy, and economic objectives by controlling exports and treaty compliance.
- U.S. Census Bureau: The Census Bureau is the primary source of data concerning the U.S. population and economy.
- Economic Development Administration (EDA): The EDA focuses on leading the federal economic development agenda through promotion of innovations and competitive actions. It also prepares America for success and growth in the global economy.
- Economics and Statistics Administration (ESA): The ESA oversees the Census Bureau and the BEA. They also provide economic analyses and publish indicators about the economy.
- International Trade Administration (ITA): The ITA promotes fair trade and investment by strengthening competitiveness in American industry and enforcing trade agreements and laws.
- Minority Business Development Agency (MBDA): The MBDA focuses on creating wealth and entrepreneurship in minority communities. They also seek to ensure success for all U.S. businesses by actively promoting growth and competition in businesses of all sizes.
- National Oceanic and Atmospheric Administration (NOAA): NOAA aims to "enrich life through science" and to keep Americans apprised of changing environmental conditions. They focus on all things atmospheric, from the sun to the ocean floor.

- National Telecommunications and Information Administration (NTIA): NTIA advises the president on information policy and telecommunication issues. They promote programs and policies to expand Internet access and adoption in the United States to stimulate economic growth.
- National Institute of Standards and Technology (NIST): NIST is among America's oldest science laboratories. They support small technologies (nanoscale) as well as large technologies (skyscrapers).
- National Technical Information Service (NTIS): NTIS is the primary resource for government-funded science-, technical-, engineering-, and business-related information. NTIS issues three million publications in over 350 subject areas for businesses, universities, and the public.
- U.S. Patent and Trademark Office (USPTO): The USPTO's responsibility is to stimulate and foster competitiveness and provide high-quality review of trademark applications. The office guides domestic and international intellectual property policies and delivers intellectual property information and education worldwide.

The department's leadership is provided by a secretary of commerce, supported by a deputy secretary of commerce. Similar to other federal agencies and departments, the Department of Commerce has an Office of Inspector General whose job is to assure that the department runs effectively and efficiently with minimal waste, abuse, and fraud. The Office of Inspector General is certified by the Office of Special Council as a Whistle-blower Protection Agency.

The mission statement of the Department of Commerce is to promote the creation of jobs, stimulate economic growth through sustainable development to improve the standard of living for Americans. The department works collaboratively with businesses, universities, communities, and workers. The department also focuses on business development, entrepreneurship, trade, economic development, and related research and analyses The department also works to stimulate international economies to increase trade and open up markets to the United States. With locations across the nation, the department has a $7.5 billion budget and employs 47,000 workers across the nation.

For 2011, the department provided a fact sheet detailing accomplishments over the past year. These are illustrative of the strides made on behalf of consumers by the Department of Commerce, and include connecting U.S. businesses to commerce services, promoting U.S. exports and protecting unfair trade practices, coordinating federal economic development efforts, developing and deploying advanced technologies, expanding broadband Internet access and adoption, realizing a 21st-century patent system, providing accurate and timely economic and demographic data, and protecting lives, property, and the environment. Some of the more recent activities and announcements from the department include the Obama Administration's giving $40 million in an initiative to challenge businesses to "Make it in America," the department's partnership with Cornell to help American entrepreneurs innovate, grow, and create jobs, and National Institute of Standards and Technology's physicist winning the Nobel Prize in Physics.

The future of the Department of Commerce is unknown. Several restructures, movements of agencies, and renaming have occurred over the years, but the department has persisted. As recently as the Obama administration, elimination and restructuring of the department have been proposed as a cost-saving measure. As of this writing, no final decisions were in place.

*Wendy Reiboldt*

**See also:** Patent and Trademark Office; Whistleblowing

### References and Additional Readings

Department of Commerce. (2013). Home. Retrieved from http://www.commerce .gov

Mervis, J. (2012). What would wiping out the commerce department mean for science? *Science Insider.* Retrieved from http://news.sciencemag.org/science insider/2012/01/what-would-wiping-out-the-commerce.html

## Department of Defense (DOD)

The U.S. Department of Defense (DOD) is the largest and oldest government agency, existing before Revolutionary times. The military branches, Navy, Marine Corp, and Army were established in 1775; the War Department (now known as the Department of Defense) was created in 1789. One year later, in 1790, the Coast Guard (now part of the Department of Homeland Security—during times of peace) was established, followed by the U.S. Navy in 1798.

As the branches of military operated on their own, a decision was made to unite them. The National Military Establishment unified the three branches in 1947. That same year, the Air Force was established as an independent branch, becoming a separate entity from the Navy and Army that formerly had Air Corp divisions. The secretary of defense now had oversight of all three military branches, with Senate's confirmation. The National Military

Several days exist to honor the U.S. military and those who support it. May 11th is Military Spouse Appreciation Day, to honor men and women who are married to those serving in the armed forces. The third Saturday in May is Armed Forces Day, honoring the active men and women in the U.S. military. November 11th is Veterans Day, celebrating and remembering former military personnel.

Establishment changed its name to the Department of Defense in 1949 as part of an amendment to the National Security Act.

The secretary of defense operates, with a deputy secretary, as chief advisor on defense policy to the president. The secretary has oversight of the DOD, which includes the military branches, over 1.4 million active duty military personnel, and 718,000 civilian support personnel, covering every time zone, making it the largest employer in the United States. Approximately 450,000 employees are oversees, either ashore or on board on a ship. Additionally, there are more than two million retired military personnel receiving benefits.

The DOD is housed in the Pentagon, which according to the DOD website, boasts 17.5 miles of corridors yet only a 7-minute walk from any two points in the building. The total sum of the installations of the DOD, if combined in one space, would cover 30 million acres of land.

The U.S. military, in line with national health efforts, is focusing on the health and well-being of its service members. In 2008, the Office of Warrior Care Policy was established as a program under the Department of Defense to ensure wounded, ill, injured, and transitioning Service members receive high-quality care and seamless transition support through proactive leadership, responsive policy, effective oversight, and interagency collaboration. The program has the following focuses:

- smoking cessation
- adaptive sports
- health and wellness
- psychological fitness

The program also supports and coordinates with each branch of the military's Wounded Warrior Programs including Army Wounded Warrior Program, Marine Corps Wounded Warrior Regiment, Air Force Wounded Warrior, and Navy Safe Harbor to further assist wounded warriors in their recovery.

The mission of the DOD, according to the website, is "to provide military forces needed to deter war and to protect the security of our country. The mission of Defense.gov is to support the overall mission of the Department of Defense by providing official, timely and accurate information about defense policies, organizations, functions, and operations. Also, Defense.gov is the single, unified starting point for finding military information online. The mission is consistent with the DOD Principles of Information which outline the Department's policy for providing military members, DOD civilians, military family members, the American public, the Congress, and the news media." As of this writing, top issues, as stated on the website included Afghanistan, warrior care, cyber security, and defense strategic guidance.

*Wendy Reiboldt*

**See also:** Customs and Border Protection (CBP); Department of Homeland Security (DHS); Public Safety

### References and Additional Readings

D'Agosino, D. M., Camarillo, Y., Harms, N., Kmetz, L., Perdue, C., Powelson, R., Richardson, T., & Widhagen, J. (2011). *Observations of the costs and benefits of an increased Department of Defense role in helping to secure the Southwest land border.* Washington, DC: Government Accountability Office.

Department of Defense. (2013). Home. Retrieved from http://www.defense.gov

Schwartz, M. (2010). *Department of Defense contractors in Iraq and Afghanistan: Background and analysis.* Darby, PA: Diane Publishing Co.

## Department of Education (ED)

### Overview

The mission of the Department of Education (ED) is to provide students with equal opportunities necessary for success. It prepares students to compete in the global market by stressing the importance of educational excellence, and providing equal access to education despite a student's race, possible handicaps, or income. The ED's $68 billion budget is used to (1) establish policies on financial aid, distribute, and monitor the funds given to students; (2) collect data on American schools and publicize the information found; (3) focus national attention on key educational issues; and (4) stop discrimination and ensure equal access to education. Overall, the ED houses 12 agencies; some of them are Federal Student Aid (FSA), Institute of Education Sciences (IES), National Center for Education

Statistics (NCES), Office for Civil Rights, Office of Elementary and Secondary Education (OESE), Office of English Language Acquisition (OELA), and Office of Innovation and Improvement (OII). Several of these are discussed later.

To serve America's students, the ED engages in four major types of activities. First, the department supports students with financial aid at all levels of education, from early childhood to postsecondary schooling. It hosts a number of special programs designed to support students with particular challenges, including students with disabilities, low-income students, American Indians, immigrants, and English language learners.

The Department of Education houses the National Center for Education Statistics. This provides for FAST FACTS on a range of educational issues, including early childhood learning. For example, approximately 46 percent of fourth graders in the nation read for fun on their own time almost every day in 2011.

Source: National Center for Education Statistics. (2011). FAST FACTS. Retrieved from http://nces.ed.gov/fast-facts/

Second, the ED conducts extensive reviews of research to identify the most effective educational practices and communicate those to teachers, policy makers, parents, and researchers. It regularly publishes reports online and in printed editions. Recent publications have covered critical educational questions such as the advances in education, the condition of education in America amongst many others.

Third, the ED makes suggestions for changes in education at the national level. The ED raises awareness through speeches, published articles, media appearances, and by sending representatives to make personal appearances in schools and other educational settings. It also sponsors a number of national conferences and programs like the monthly television

No Child Left Behind (NCLB) was originally proposed by the administration of George W. Bush. The No Child Left Behind Act of 2001 (NCLBA), which amended the Elementary and Secondary Education Act of 1965 (ESEA), aims to improve student achievement, particularly among poor and minority students. To reach this goal, the law requires states to develop high-quality academic assessments aligned with challenging state academic standards that measure students' knowledge of reading/language arts, mathematics, and science. Student achievement as measured by these assessments is the basis for school accountability, including corrective actions such as removing principals or implementing new curricula.

show, *Education News Parents Can Use*, the Blue Ribbon Schools and Presidential Scholars award programs, and the Teaching Ambassador Fellows Program. It also hosts special events and ceremonies to honor teachers and students.

Finally, the ED enforces civil rights acts to ensure that all children, irrespective of their demographics (e.g., race, national origin, functional ability) receive equal educational opportunity. These laws are followed in all state education agencies that receive ED funds, such as elementary and secondary school systems, colleges and universities, and vocational schools, as well as proprietary schools, state vocational rehabilitation agencies, and libraries and museums.

## History

The ED was created in 1867; it mission was to assist each state to develop effective and strong school systems. In 1890, the Second Morrill Act was passed (the first of which provided funding to establish land-grant colleges and universities) to ensure that race was not used as a criterion for entrance to college. Interestingly, many of the black colleges and universities today evolved from the Morrill Acts. Later, with the passage of the 1917 Smith–Hughes Act (which provided funding to support educational efforts related to agriculture and farming) and the 1946 George–Barden Act (which expanded vocational education such as home economics), high schools received federal aid for educational support related to provision of agricultural, industrial, and home economics training.

Federal support for education was expanded significantly after World War II with the introduction of the GI Bill in 1944. This provided postsecondary education assistance by sending nearly eight million World War II veterans to college. The antipoverty and civil rights laws of the 1960s and 1970s also brought a lot of change in terms of educational support. In 1965, two other acts were passed: the Elementary and Secondary Education Act and the Higher Education Act. The first provided funding for impoverished children in poor rural and urban settings and the latter provided funding for postsecondary education, including financial aid for college students in need of aid.

By 1979, the U.S. Education Department was signed into law by President Jimmy Carter; in 1980 it began operating formally as an established cabinet recognized by Congress. For years thereafter, several more acts were passed, such as the Equal Access Act (1984), No Child Left Behind

(2001), Individuals with Disabilities Education Act (IDEA) (2004), and the Health Care and Education Reconciliation Act (2010). Today, the ED supports programs for over 56 million students.

## Campus Security

The Education Department published *The Handbook for Campus Safety and Security Reporting* in 2011 to guarantee postsecondary institutions' safety. The handbook followed the campus safety and security requirements of the Higher Educating Act of 1965 and includes step-by-step procedures, cases, and references. There is an online tutorial video to help school leaders understand the security-related requirements. The ED provides Campus Crime Statistics online for anyone wishing to review the campus crime statistics for a specific college or university campus.

## Student Financial Aid and Loan Forgiveness

Federal Student Aid, an office of the ED, provides information on several types of aid, loans, scholarships, and grants, for example, Federal Pell Grants. Unlike loans, these are not to be repaid by students. Typically, only undergraduate students can apply for Pell Grants. The amount of monies a student can receive from a Pell Grant depends on several factors, including the actual financial need, amount needed to attend a college, and the student's attendance status (full or part time). Another example of available aid is the Teacher Education Assistance for College and Higher Education (TEACH) grant, designed to support students who are in the process of completing courses that will prepare them for a job in teaching specifically in areas that are low-income and in high-need areas. The Federal Student Aid office also provides information on the Teacher Loan Forgiveness Program. This program is designed to encourage students to become teachers and it assists current teachers with paying back their school loans. Similarly, there is also the Public Service Loan Forgiveness Program that supports students to become professionals in the public service sector by assisting them with loan balances. Other kinds of student loan forgiveness programs include loan forgiveness for volunteer work, military loan forgiveness, and loan forgiveness for legal and medical studies. Some states may offer other federal loan forgiveness. For example, in Maryland, local government employees may be eligible for a loan assistance or repayment program if they are studying in fields such as law, nursing, social work, and education.

## Credible Schools and Degrees

While the ED does not endorse any educational institutions or programs, it is "required by law to publish a list of nationally recognized accrediting agencies that the Secretary determines to be reliable authorities as to the quality of education or training provided by the institutions of higher education and the higher education programs they accredit. The U.S. Secretary of Education also recognizes State agencies for the approval of public postsecondary vocational education and nurse education" (Department of Education, 2013a, 1). The goal of accreditation is to ensure that higher level educational institutions are providing quality education to its students.

## Policies

The U.S. Education Department provides information on several policies and regulations. Many are on a federal level though such policies are oftentimes determined on the state and local levels. Some examples of federal level policies include the Aid for Institutions of Higher Education Impacted by Hurricanes Katrina and Rita; Education for Homeless Children and Youths; No Child Left Behind; Special Education; Veterans Upward Bound Program. Other regulations are discussed such as related to adult education, early childhood education, special education and vocational education.

## NCES Statistics

The ED also houses the Institute of Education Sciences (IES). One of its activities is hosting the National Center for Education Statistics (NCES), whose main task is to collect and analyze educational data on the national level. The NCES explains that its statistics are used for a number of purposes:

- Congress uses them to plan federal education programs, to apportion federal funds among the states, and to serve the needs of constituents.
- Federal agencies, including the Bureau of Labor Statistics, the Department of Commerce, and the National Science Foundation, are concerned with the supply of trained manpower produced by schools and colleges and with the subjects that are being taught.
- State education agencies are both users and suppliers of NCES data.
- State and local officials are concerned with problems of staffing and financing public education.

- Educational organizations, such as the American Council on Education and the National Education Association, use the data for planning and research.

- The news media, such as television networks, news magazines, and many of the nation's leading daily newspapers frequently use NCES statistics to inform the public about matters such as school and college enrollment and expenditures per student.

- Business organizations use trend data on enrollments and expenditures to forecast the demand for their products.

- The general public uses education statistics to become more informed and to make intelligent decisions concerning educational issues (NCES, n.d.).

### Recent Highlights

Recent highlights on the ED website include a new "App" to identify U.S. currency on mobile devices for individuals who are blind or visually impaired; a symposium to discuss innovative resources and technologies necessary to increase postsecondary productivity; and tool kits for teachers to take part in Stop Bullying Prevention programs. In addition, the ED recently issued a directive via its Office of Civil Rights that schools must comply with federal law and ensure that all students with disabilities are given equal opportunities to compete in school athletics. Terri Lakowski, chair of the Inclusive Fitness Coalition, a network of groups that advocate for disability rights, was quoted saying "It's a landmark moment for students with disabilities . . . This is a game changer. I firmly believe this will do for students with disabilities what Title IX has done for women and girls. This gives very clear guidance of what equal opportunity for students with disabilities looks like" (Williams, 2013).

*Shuyi Guan*

**See also:** Americans with Disabilities Act (ADA); Debt, Student; Department of Veterans Affairs (VA)

### References and Additional Readings

Department of Education. (2011). The handbook for campus safety and reporting. Retrieved from http://www2.ed.gov/admins/lead/safety/handbook.pdf

Department of Education. (2012a). About ED: Overview and mission statement. Retrieved from http://www2.ed.gov/about/landing.jhtml

Department of Education. (2012b). The database of accredited postsecondary institutions and programs. Retrieved from http://ope.ed.gov/accreditation/

Department of Education. (2013a). Accreditation database. Retrieved from http://ope.ed.gov/accreditation/

Department of Education. (2013b). Stafford loan forgiveness program for teachers. Retrieved from http://studentaid.ed.gov/PORTALSWebApp/students/english/cancelstaff.jsp

Federal Student Aid. (2013). Home. Retrieved from http://studentaid.ed.gov/

Government Accountability Office. (2009). *No Child Left Behind Act.* Washington, DC: U.S. Government Printing Office.

National Center for Education Statistics. (n.d.). About us. Retrieved from http://nces.ed.gov/about/

Williams, P. (2013). U.S. Department of Education issues 'landmark' directive for disabled student athletes. *The Washington Post.* Retrieved from http://www.washingtonpost.com/sports/highschools/us-department-of-education-issues-landmark-directive-for-disabled-student-athletes/2013/01/25/b03f5cae-6737-11e2-9e1b-07db1d2ccd5b_story.html

## Department of Energy (DOE)

The DOE is a cabinet-level governmental agency designed to "ensure America's security and prosperity by addressing its energy, environmental and nuclear challenges through transformative science and technology solutions." It does this through several programs. For example, the DOE currently has 17 national laboratories and five facilities to implement and conduct research and to develop licensing and patents of laboratory technologies. The overall goal of these efforts is to make the U.S. companies and economy more competitive. The DOE also provides on its website several resources for consumers, including information on tax credits, rebates, and savings programs. For homeowners and renters, information is available for how to make homes more energy efficient, such as via home weatherization, landscaping, and home design. Information about individual state-related developments is also provided. Examples include the city of Los Angeles, the second largest city in the United States, and its efforts to currently working to increase energy efficiency in 30 million square feet of both public and private buildings; and the University of Minnesota, Morris (UMN—Morris) is one of the first schools to be part of the "Clean Energy in our Community" series. This school is using wind turbines to generate enough energy to power nearly 60 percent of the campus's electrical needs. Also, information on how to start a community-shared solar project in one's neighborhood can also be found. A consumer interested in learning more about energy programs in his or her community can search the DOE website by zip code. Another major component of the DOE is its work in National Energy Security, especially as it relates to how the United States is

## Department of Energy (DOE)—Origins

The 1973 oil crisis called attention to the need to consolidate energy policy. On August 4, 1977, President Jimmy Carter signed into law *The Department of Energy Organization Act of 1977* (Pub.L. 95–91, 91 Stat. 565, enacted August 4, 1977), which created the DOE.

taking action to control its energy future as well as the dependence on foreign oil. This is a salient priority of current President Obama. In fact, as of 2011, U.S. natural gas production grew by an estimated 7.4 percent. Overall, the DOE plays an important role in U.S. policies regarding energy and safety, as well as in the development of scientific research and innovation.

*Melanie Horn Mallers*

**See also:** Department of the Interior (DOI)

### References and Additional Readings

Department of Energy. (2012). Increasing energy security. Retrieved from http://energy.gov/articles/increasing-energy-security

Department of Energy. (2013). Mission statement. Retrieved from http://energy.gov/mission

Relyea, H., & Carr, T.P. (2003). *The executive branch, creation and reorganization.* United States: Nova Science Publishers Inc.

## Department of Health and Human Services (HHS)

The U.S. Department of Health and Human Services (HHS) is the federal government's primary agency for promoting health and ensuring that essential human services are provided to all Americans. Particular attention is paid to those Americans who are unable or least able to help themselves. Nearly one quarter of all federal budget expenditures are represented by HHS; it also administers more grant dollars related to service and research contracts than all other federal agencies combined. These grants cover services to the population as well as research efforts designed to improve health. Medicare is one of the primary programs under HHS, representing the nation's largest health insurance program, and handling over one billion claims per year. Medicare and Medicaid, when combined, provide healthcare insurance coverage for 25 percent of all Americans.

State and local governments work in partnerships with HHS and consequently, numerous HHS-funded services are operated at the local level by state organizations, county agencies, or via the private sector by grant recipients. HHS's programs are administered by way of 12 operating divisions, including eight agencies in the U.S. Public Health Service and three human services agencies. The operating divisions include Administration for Children and Families (ACF); Administration on Aging (AoA); Agency for Healthcare Research and Quality (AHRQ); Agency for Toxic Substances and Disease Registry (ATSDR); Centers for Disease Control and Prevention (CDC); Centers for Medicare and Medicaid Services; Food and Drug Administration (FDA); Health Resources and Services Administration (HRSA); Indian Health Service (IHS); National Institutes of Health (NIH); Office of the Inspector General (OIG); and the Substance Abuse and Mental Health Services Administration (SAMHSA).

HHS also manages over 300 programs that provide a wide variety of services designed to address a number of human health challenges. In addition to the services they deliver, these HHS programs provide for various treatments for Americans, and they also enable the collection of national health and other data. Agencies of the department of HHS work to prevent disease outbreaks, assure food and drug safety, conduct health and social science research, and provide health insurance to uninsured citizens of the United States.

The department is led by the Office of the Secretary. Included in the department of HHS are the offices of public health and science, the HHS inspector general, and civil rights. In addition, the Program Support Center provides administrative services for HHS and other federal agencies. The secretary's office of HHS oversees a budget of approximately $700 billion and approximately 65,000 employees.

Three separate functions, service delivery, financing, and research, provide organization for individual program units under HHS. Despite the fact that programs report to an assistant secretary for health, they operate independently. Service delivery functions are a major task of the following: HRSA, the IHS, the SAMHSA, and some parts of the CDC. Functions related to finances are primarily found in the Centers for Medicare and Medicaid Services, emphasizing fiscal duties. The research functions are central to the NIH and the AHRQ, and are also found in the CDC, as well as, the FDA. Experts suggest that not only are the varied functions of HHS somewhat disparate, the program units' accountability relationships should also be viewed as fragmented. Different program units report to different congressional committees and subcommittees. Different programs also address the priorities and perspectives of various interest groups, employing staff members with various training and health backgrounds.

### Historical Developments

In 1953, under President Dwight D. Eisenhower, the Department of Health, Education, and Welfare (HEW) was created, with official opening on April 11. Several years later, in 1965, the Medicare and Medicaid programs were created, making comprehensive health care available to millions of Americans. The Head Start program was also created that year. The Health Care Financing Administration was created in 1977 to separate the management of Medicare and Medicaid from the work of the Social Security Administration. It was during the same year that there was a worldwide eradication of smallpox, led by the U.S. Public Health Service. The Department of Education Organization Act was signed into law in 1979 and this act established an entirely separate Department of Education. One year later, the HEW changed its name to the Department of Health and Human Services (HHS) on May 4, 1980. In 1981, AIDS was identified and in 1985 a blood test to detect HIV was licensed. The JOBS program and federal support for child care was created in 1988, as was the McKinney Act passed to provide health care to the homeless. The Vaccines for Children Program was established in 1993, establishing free immunizations to children in low-income families. In 1995, the Social Security Administration became an independent agency. In 1996, the welfare system was reformed under the Personal Responsibility and Work Opportunity Reconciliation Act. Additionally, the Health Insurance Portability and Accountability Act (HIPAA) was enacted in 1996. In 2002, the Office of Public Health Emergency Preparedness was created to coordinate efforts against bioterrorism and other emergency health incidents. Most recently, in 2010, the Affordable Care Act was signed into law, putting in place comprehensive U.S. health insurance reforms.

The HHS is not immune to controversy. Recent challenges have been experienced related to issues concerning women's health, food safety, care for the elderly, health implications of global warming, substance abuse treatment, mental health services, and programs for children. The wide variety of political and cultural positions in the United States has made it challenging for governmental agencies to be equally representative. Thus, the department will continue to be required to serve Americans in a meaningful way, while operating under the scrutiny of a diverse populace.

*James R. Ruby*

**See also:** Americans with Disabilities Act (ADA); Centers for Disease Control and Prevention (CDC); Community Mental Health Centers (CMHC) Act; Food and Drug Administration (FDA); HIPPA (Health Insurance Portability and Accountability Act); Poverty Guidelines; Public Safety; Social Services; Social Welfare

### References and Additional Readings

AllGov. (2009). Department of Health and Human Services. Retrieved from http://www.allgov.com/Agency/Department_of_Health_and_Human_Services

Department of Health and Human Services. (2011). About HHS. Retrieved from http://www.hhs.gov

Radin, B. A. (2010). When is a health department not a health department? The case of the U.S. Department of Health and Human Services. *Social Policy & Administration, 44*, 142–154.

The White House. (2011a). Department of Health and Human Services: The federal budget, fiscal year 2012. Retrieved from http://www.whitehouse.gov/omb/factsheet_department_health

The White House. (2011b). Executive branch. Our government. Retrieved from http://www.whitehouse.gov/our-government/executive-branch

## Department of Homeland Security (DHS)

The Department of Homeland Security (DHS) was created in 2002 to coordinate federal responses to acts of terrorism and other disasters. Shortly after the September 11, 2001, attacks on the World Trade Center and the Pentagon, President George W. Bush created the Office of Homeland Security within the White House and appointed Pennsylvania Governor Tom Ridge as its director. The next year, Congress passed the Homelands Security Act of 2002, making DHS a standalone department and part of the president's cabinet. The creation of DHS was the largest reorganization within the federal government since the National Security Act of 1947, which created the Department of Defense (originally called the National Military Establishment), the National Security Council (NSC), and the Central Intelligence Agency (CIA).

DHS was formed with the integration of all or part of the following 22 different federal agencies and departments (Table 14).

Because DHS was created in the aftermath of the 9/11 attacks, its initial focus was largely on terrorism. One of the early DHS initiatives was the Homeland Security Advisory system, created by Homeland Security Presidential Directive in March, 2002. The color-coded levels corresponded to the state of terrorism threats to the country, from "green" (low threat) to

Department of Homeland Security agents at work in a forensics laboratory. (Department of Defense)

**Table 14** Federal agencies and departments.

- U.S. Coast Guard
- U.S. Secret Service
- Federal Protective Service
- Federal Emergency Management Agency (FEMA)
- Transportation Security Administration (TSA)
- From the Treasury Department
    - U.S. Customs Service
    - Federal Law Enforcement Training Center
- From the Department of Justice
    - Office for Domestic Preparedness
    - Domestic Emergency Support Teams
    - Immigration and Naturalization Service
- From the Federal Bureau of Investigation (FBI)
    - National Domestic Preparedness Office
    - National Infrastructure Protection Center

*(Continued)*

**Table 14** *(Continued)*

- From Department of Agriculture
    - Animal and Plant Health Inspection Service
    - Plum Island Animal Disease Center
- From Department of Energy
    - Nuclear Incident Response Team
    - Environmental Measurements Laboratory
    - CBRN Countermeasures Department
    - Energy Security and Assurance Program
- From the Department of Defense
    - National BW Defense Analysis Center
- From the General Services Administration (GSA)
    - Federal Computer Incident Response Center
- From Health and Human Services
    - Strategic National Stockpile and National Disaster Medical System

"red" (severe threat). There were no published criteria for the threat levels, and the two lowest levels—"green" and "blue"—were never used. It was only raised to "red" (severe) once, in August 2006, for commercial flights from the United Kingdom. It was raised to "orange" (high) five times on a nationwide basis, including the first anniversary of the 9/11 terror attacks, and three times on a regional or partial basis.

In April 2012, the color-coded system was replaced by a two-level National Terrorism Advisory System (NTAS): imminent threat—warns of a credible, specific, and impending terrorist threat against the United State; elevated threat—warns of a credible terrorist threat against the United States. In addition, NTAS alerts were designed to have an ending date, to avoid the criticisms from the previous system that the threat levels were always high and never changed, causing the public to pay less attention to them over time. In keeping with the advance in social technology, the public could sign up for NTAS alerts directly via email, Facebook, or Twitter.

The DHS's initial focus on the threat of terrorism left little resources available to manage other duties, including customs, border security, and emergency management. This became especially clear when Hurricane Katrina caused massive destruction to the Gulf Coast in August 2005. Although FEMA was still responsible for response and recovery from natural events on paper, their role within DHS had been minimized and resources redirected to other functions. FEMA, as well as the rest of DHS—including former assistant U.S. Attorney General Michael Chertoff who had succeeded Ridge as the Secretary of Homeland Security in February—was heavily criticized for the federal government's slow response.

The U.S. House responded to the national and international criticism of the federal response to Katrina by convening a congressional committee to investigate the charges of misjudgment and mismanagement. Their report "A Failure of Initiative: Final Report of the Select Bipartisan Committee to Investigate the Preparation for and Response to Hurricane Katrina" was released in February 2006. Later that year, in October 2006, Congress passed the Post-Katrina Emergency Management Reform Act, which elevated FEMA to a distinct entity within DHS and returned most of its former responsibilities and resources.

The next year, as part of the Homeland Security Appropriations Act of 2007, Congress mandated a high-level strategic review of DHS, focusing on risk-based performance standards. The Quadrennial Homeland Security Review would review policies and priorities, define DHS mission, and establish goals and objectives every four years. The initiative was modeled after the Quadrennial Defense Review from the Department of Defense. The first QHSR was delivered on Congress on February 1, 2010.

The QHSR was the first of a multistep process that included a Bottom-Up Review (BUR)—which focused on process questions for the mission and goals identified in the QHSR. Both reports were integrated into the Homeland Security Strategic Plan for 2012–2016, which identified a vision, mission, goals, and objectives, and ongoing activities for the department.

The Homeland Security Strategic Plan for 2012–2016 identifies five core missions:

- Preventing terrorism and enhancing security
- Securing and managing borders
- Enforcing and administering immigration laws
- Safeguarding and securing cyberspace
- Ensuring resilience to disasters.

Janet Napolitano, former governor of Arizona, was appointed as secretary for DHS by President Barak Obama in January 2009. She was the first woman to chair the National Governors Association and was named one of the top five governors in the country by *Time* magazine in 2005.

*Valerie Lucus-McEwen*

**See also:** Congress; Customs and Border Protection (CBP); Disaster and Emergency Declarations; Federal Emergency Management Agency (FEMA)

**References and Additional Readings**

Department of Homeland Security. (2007). Appropriations Act, 2007. H.R. 5441. Pub. L. 109 295-120 Stat. 1355.

Department of Homeland Security. (2010a). Quadrennial Homeland Security Review report: A strategic framework for a Security Homeland. Washington, DC.

Department of Homeland Security. (2010b). Bottom-up review report. Washington, DC.

Department of Homeland Security. (2011). NTAS guide—National Terrorism Advisory System public guide. Washington, DC.

Department of Homeland Security. (2012). Strategic plan-fiscal years 2012–2016. Washington, DC.

The Homeland Security Act. (2002). Pub. L. 107-296-116 Stat. 2135. Print.

Homeland Security Presidential Directive 3 (HSPD-3). (2002). Homeland Security Advisory system.

National Security Act. (1947). Pub. L. 235-61 Stat. 496; U.S.C. 402. Print.

The Post-Katrina Emergency Management Reform. (2006). Pub. L. 109-295-120 Stat. 1355.

United States Congress. (2006). A failure of initiative: The final report of the Select Bipartisan Committee to investigate the preparation for and response to Hurricane Katrina. H. Rept 109-377. Washington, DC: GPO.

# Department of Housing and Urban Development (HUD)

The U.S. Department of Housing and Urban Development (HUD) is a cabinet department in the executive branches of the federal government. It was founded as such in 1965 by President Lyndon Johnson as part of the "Great Society" with aim to develop and execute policies on housing. The mission of HUD (n.d.) is:

to create strong, sustainable, inclusive communities and quality affordable homes for all. HUD works to strengthen the housing market to bolster the economy and protect consumers; meet the need for quality affordable rental homes; utilize housing as a platform for improving quality of life; build inclusive and sustainable communities free from discrimination; and transform the way HUD does business.

Inherent in this mission are policies designed to ban discrimination in housing, provide support for low-income families (Section 8, Housing), provide grants for elderly and disabled persons, help communities deal with homelessness, set goals for underserved housing areas, give public housing authorities tools to protect residents from being endangered from other residents who have engaged in criminal or risky behaviors, as well as initiate programs for hopeful homebuyers. HUD also provides consumers information about homeownership (such as via Fannie Mae), rental help, foreclosure, homeless resources, and how to file a housing discrimination complaint. Also offered are local news events, by state, on current HUD events such as planning grants for housing and redevelopment. Additionally, a consumer can look up information on energy, fair lending, Freedom of Information Act (FOIA), homes for sale, home improvements, veteran information, healthy homes and controlling hazards, public and Indian housing, neighborhood stabilization and emergency homeowners loan programs (see Dodd–Frank Wall Street Reform and Consumer Protection Act programs), and finally, sustainable housing and communities. Programs are permanent or temporary and several examples are discussed in greater detail later.

The Federal Housing Administration (FHA) was created by Congress in 1934 and became a part of HUD in 1965. The FHA, in addition to overseeing housing for older adults, also provides mortgages on loans made by FHA-approved lenders. It is in fact the largest insurer of mortgages worldwide. Interestingly, FHA is the only government agency not operated from taxpayers' costs, but is solely funded through self-generated income. FHA was founded in 1934 when the housing industry collapsed. During the 1940s FHA helped finance military housing and homes for veterans. During the next 30 years, FHA helped to provide housing for aged, disabled, and low-income persons. FHA has ensured over 34 million properties.

For more information, see http://portal.hud.gov/hudportal/HUD

## Fair Housing and Equal Opportunity

The Fair Housing Act of 1968 (Title VIII, a permanent program, is applied to almost all housing options in the United States, and it prohibits discrimination in housing based on race, color, religion, sex, national origin, disability, or familial status (including individuals or families with children under 18 years of age and pregnant women). It also protects consumers from discrimination in residential real estate transactions and makes it illegal to coerce, intimidate, threaten, or interfere with people exercising such rights. Thus, a seller, landlord, lender, insurance agent, realtor, or any entity that exercises control over residences of common spaces (such as condominium boards, homeowner associations), or others, may not deny housing or offer different terms based on one's race, color, religion, sex, national origin, disability, or familial status. They may also not use discriminatory advertising.

Consumers who believe they have been discriminated can file a complaint with any HUD office within one year after the alleged discrimination has occurred. An investigation will follow and if it is deemed that discrimination has occurred, HUD law judge will hold a hearing, or the federal court district may get involved. Within the Fair Housing Act there are several coordinating laws and presidential executive orders that govern its orders. This includes, for example:

- Title VI of the Civil Rights Acts of 1964 that prohibits discrimination on the basis of race, color, or national origin in programs and activities receiving federal financial assistance.
- Section 109 of Title 1 of the Housing and Community Development Act of 1974 that prohibits discrimination on the basis of race, color, national origin, sex or religion in programs and activities receiving financial assistance from HUD's Community Development and Block Grant Program.
- Title II of the Americans with Disabilities Act of 1990 that prohibits discrimination based on disability in programs, services, and activities provided or made available by public entities. HUD enforces Title II when it relates to state and local public housing, housing assistance, and housing referrals.
- The Age Discrimination Act of 1975 that prohibits discrimination on the basis of age in programs or activities receiving federal financial assistance.

Another important program is the Fair Housing Assistance Program (FHAP). FHAP "assists state and local agencies that administer fair housing laws certified by HUD as 'substantially equivalent' to the Fair Housing Act or Title VIII of the Civil Rights Act of 1968, as amended. This assistance includes support for complaint processing, training, technical assistance, data and information systems, and other fair housing projects. The program is designed to build coordinated intergovernmental enforcement of fair housing laws and provide incentives for states and localities to assume a greater share of the responsibility for administering fair housing laws" (HUD, n.d.b).

### Single-Family Housing Programs

There are several programs within the single-family housing section, a permanent program. One in particular is One to Four Family Home Mortgage Insurance (Section 203(b)). This is a federal program designed to support purchases of homes, as well as constructions of new homes. Through this program, potential homebuyers may obtain FHA-insured mortgages to buy homes with low down payments. Loan limits change annually and vary on home prices, as guided by Fannie Mae and Freddie Mac. The single-family housing programs also offer direct mortgage insurance for disaster victims (Section 203(h)), such that consumers who become victims in presidentially designated disaster areas recover by making it easier for them to obtain mortgage loans and become homeowners or reestablish themselves as homeowners. Other programs include FHA Home Affordable Modification Programs (FHA-HAMP), Counseling for Homebuyers, Homeowners, and Tenants (Section 106), as well as the Good Neighbor Next Door. Several other programs exist and consumers are urged to peruse the HUD website for more details.

### Multifamily Housing Programs

Similar to the single-family housing programs, there are several sections within the multifamily housing programs, a permanent program. Among these is the Supportive Housing for the Elderly (Section 202) that provides assistance to expand the supply of housing with supportive services for the elderly by providing monies to private, nonprofits, and some for-profit organizations that have been established to provide rental housing to older persons, especially those with very low income. Other programs are Mortgage Insurance for Housing for the Elderly (Section 231) and Multifamily Rental Housing for Moderate-Income Families (Section 221(d)(3) and

(4)) that provide additional housing support for those in need. Several other programs exist and consumers are urged to peruse the HUD website for more details.

### Public and Indian Housing

Several permanent programs are housed within the public and Indian housing programs including voucher assistantships, sections, and activities. One is the Housing Choice Voucher Program that provides rental subsidies as chosen by the tenant, specifically to low-income families. The Family Self-Sufficiency Program is another program within public and Indian housing. Its goal is to give families opportunities to obtain employment and eventually achieve economic independence. Another program is the Loan Guarantees for Indian Housing (Section 184) including Indian families, Indian housing authorities, and Indian tribes to have access to private mortgage financing given several persons of Indian descent could not otherwise acquire housing financing due to the unique legal status of Indian lands. Several other programs exist and consumers are urged to peruse the HUD website for more details.

### Examples of HUD-Related Programs for Specific Populations

The Housing for Older Persons Act (HOPA), signed into law by President Clinton in 1995, amended the Fair Housing Act (FHA), in order to preserve housing specifically designed to meet the needs of older adults. Housing that meets the FHA definition of housing for older adults is exempt from the law's familial status requirements. HUD also offers the Homeless Emergency Assistance and Rapid Transition to Housing (HEARTH) Act of 2009. This act was designed to prevent mortgage foreclosures and increase mortgage credit availability, especially among those that are at-risk of losing their homes, as well as amends the McKinney-Vento Homeless Assistance Act. Among the changes were the addition of a Rural Housing Stability Assistance Program, an increase in prevention resources, and expansion of the definition of homelessness and chronic homelessness. According to HEARTH Final Rule, the following four categories of individuals and families may now qualify as homeless: (1) individuals and families who lack a fixed, regular, and adequate nighttime residence (this includes a subset for individuals who resided in an emergency shelter or a place not meant for human habitation and who are exiting an institution where he or she temporarily resided); (2) individuals and families who will imminently lose their primary nighttime residence; (3) unaccompanied youth and families with children and youth who are defined as homeless under other federal statutes who do not otherwise qualify as homeless under this definition; and (4) individuals and families who are fleeing, or are attempting to flee, domestic violence, dating violence, sexual assault, stalking, or other dangerous or life-threatening conditions that relate to violence against the individual or a family member.

HEARTH is part of larger legislative efforts to prevent and end homelessness in communities across the nation. In particular, efforts are currently targeting the runaway and homeless youth population.

*Melanie Horn Mallers*

**See also:** Americans with Disabilities Act (ADA); Department of Veterans Affairs (VA); Dodd–Frank Wall Street Reform and Consumer Protection Act; Fannie Mae; Freddie Mac; McKinney-Vento Homeless Assistance Act; Mortgages; Poverty Guidelines

### References and Additional Readings

Bostic, R.W., Thornton, R.L., Rudd, E.C., & Sternthal, M.J. (2012). Health in all policies: The role of the US Department of Housing and Urban Development and present and future challenges. *Health Affairs, 31*(9), 2130–2137.

Federal Register. (2011). Rules and regulations. Background—HEARTH Act. Retrieved from https://www.onecpd.info/resources/documents/HEARTH_HomelessDefinition_FinalRule.pdf

Hetzel, O.J., Reno, L., Molseed, S., & Schwarz, L. (2008). Housing and Urban Development. *Dev. Admin. L. & Reg. Prac.,* 309.

HUD. (n.d.a). Mission. Retrieved from http://portal.hud.gov/hudportal/HUD?src=/about/mission

HUD. (n.d.b). Fair housing assistance program. Retrieved from http://portal.hud.gov/hudportal/HUD?src=/hudprograms/fhap

HUD. (n.d.c). Questions and answers concerning the final rule implementing the Housing for Older Persons Act of 1995 (HOPA). Retrieved from http://portal.hud.gov/hudportal/documents/huddoc?id==DOC_7769.pdf

HUD. (2013). Community planning and development. Retrieved from http://portal.hud.gov/hudportal/HUD?src=/hudprograms/toc

## Department of Justice (DOJ)

The U.S. Department of Justice is the foremost organization that enforces U.S. federal laws. The mission statement, as provided on their website is "to enforce the law and defend the interests of the United States according to the law; to ensure public safety against threats foreign and domestic; to provide federal leadership in preventing and controlling crime; to seek just punishment for those guilty of unlawful behavior; and to ensure fair and impartial administration of justice for all Americans." The department is responsible for enforcing the laws of the nation on both a criminal and civil level.

As one of the most influential and important departments in the federal government, the DOJ (also known as the Justice Department) is headed by the attorney general of the United States, and a deputy attorney general and associate attorney general. As of this writing, the attorney general was Eric Holder, a former deputy attorney general under the Clinton administration. Mr. Holder is the 82nd attorney general. Only one woman, Janet Reno, has served as attorney general and head of the DOJ. Attorney General Reno served from 1993 to 2001, the longest of any 20th-century attorney general. Similar to many federal agency heads, the attorney general is appointed by the president, confirmed by the Senate, and serves as a presidential cabinet member.

The department is highly complex with 54 divisions, law enforcement agencies, offices, and programs, including some highly recognized organizations such as the Federal Bureau of Investigation, the Drug Enforcement Administration, INTERPOL, the Office of Tribal Justice, and the U.S. Marshals Service. Total employees number over 100,000, operating with a budget of nearly $30 million, a significant growth from its roots in 1789 with only one employee. The Office of Attorney General (head of the DOJ) was established under the Judiciary Act of 1789, and in the beginning provided advice to Congress and the president. The attorney general became part of the presidential cabinet in 1792. After a failed attempt to establish the department in 1869, an act of 1870, the Act to Establish the Department of Justice, signed by President Ulysses Grant, created the office. The act also transferred power over U.S. attorneys from the Department of the Interior to the Department of Justice. In 1902, President Theodore Roosevelt eloquently proclaimed the importance of the department in the following quote: "The most important department of civilized government is the

---

Department of Justice Motto: For more information, see http://portal.hud.gov/hudportal/HUD

The Common Law is the Will of Mankind Issuing from the Life of the People

Department of Justice. Think of what it means. The Department of Justice! Justice, which means that each man, rich or poor, big or small, shall have his rights and shall not be allowed to do wrong to his fellows."

The department received its current home in 1935, nearly 150 years after its inception. The department is housed in the Robert F. Kennedy Building, often referred to as "Main Justice." The building was renamed in 2001 in honor of the former attorney general who served from 1961 to 1964. In 2003, the functions of the U.S. Immigration and Naturalization Service were transferred to the DOJ after that organization was eliminated. Some other duties were transferred from the DOJ to the Department of Homeland Security when it was established.

The website features recent cases and DOJ news stories and points of interest. In line with their mission and task in the federal government, their strategic plan for 2012–2016, on their website, provides three major goals: (1) prevent terrorism and promote the nation's security consistent with the rule of law; (2) prevent crime, protect the rights of the American people, and enforce federal law; (3) ensure and support the fair, impartial, efficient, and transparent administration of justice at the federal, state, local, tribal, and international levels. Examples of recent news items on the website homepage as of this writing include topics related to a middle school employee pleading guilty for production and distribution of child pornography, a woman pleading guilty to a sophisticated million dollar identity theft scam, and a federal court barring a woman from preparing tax returns. These actions and myriad other investigations by the DOJ on behalf of consumers help to keep Americans safe and protected.

*Wendy Reiboldt*

**See also:** Attorney General Office (AG); Congress; Customs and Border Protection (CBP); Department of the Interior (DOI); Departments of Consumer Affairs (DCA); Federal Bureau of Investigation (FBI); Frauds and Scams; Identity Theft; Supreme Court

## References and Additional Readings

Ashcroft, J. (2009). Reflections on events and changes at the Department of Justice. *Harv. JL & Pub. Pol'y, 32*, 813.

Department of Justice. (2013). Retrieved from www.justice.gov

Kaczorowski, R. J. (2005). *The politics of judicial interpretation: The Federal Courts, Department of Justice, and civil rights* (pp. 1866–1876). Fordham University Press.

Oder, N. (2010). Department of justice criticizes amended Google settlement over copyright, antitrust Issues. *Library Journal, 5*.

Schuh, S., Shy, O., Stavins, J., & Triest, R. (2012). An economic analysis of the 2011 settlement between the department of justice and credit card networks. *Journal of Competition Law and Economics, 8*(1), 107–144.

## Department of Labor (DOL)

The U.S. Department of Labor (DOL) is a federal executive department established in 1913. Initially, the department mediated labor disputes, plus four existing bureaus: the Bureau of Labor Statistics (BLS), the Bureau of Immigration, the Bureau of Naturalization, and the Children's Bureau. When the U.S. entered World War I, issues of working conditions and labor peace became salient priorities. The DOL assumed a significant responsibility for enacting the nation's war labor policies, as well as rights of workers to engage in collective bargaining and to have an 8-hour workday. Years later, when Franklin D. Roosevelt was in office, several New Deal programs evolved the DOL, including a nationwide system of employment offices and placement and recruitment for the unemployed. Later, support for minimum wages and Unemployment Insurance were administered. With President Kennedy, the DOL played a major role in dealing with the new problem of automation and related unemployment. With the passage of the Civil Rights Act, the Equal Employment Opportunity Commission was established. Its mission was to enforce nondiscrimination in the workplace. For years thereafter, under the guidance of several other presidents, the DOL continued to evolve with greater expansion and protection for workers.

Today, the DOL ". . . fosters and promotes the welfare of the job seekers, wage earners, and retirees of the United States by improving their working conditions, advancing their opportunities for profitable employment, protecting their retirement and health care benefits, helping employers find workers, strengthening free collective bargaining, and tracking changes in employment, prices, and other national economic measurements" (United States Department of Labor, n.d.).

As defined by the DOL, a person is considered employed if he or she is working for pay and is over the age of 16. The DOL oversees several federal labor laws designed to ensure the rights of workers to several things, including safe and healthy working conditions; a minimum hourly wage, as well as overtime pay; a workplace free from discrimination; unemployment insurance; and other support for income as necessary. Several divisions are covered by the DOL. These are the Bureau of International Labor Affairs, the Employment and Training Administration, the Pension and

The DOL houses the Bureau of Labor Statistics (BLS). The BLS is "the principal Federal agency responsible for measuring labor market activity, working conditions, and price changes in the economy. Its mission is to collect, analyze, and disseminate essential economic information to support public and private decision-making. As an independent statistical agency, BLS serves its diverse user communities by providing products and services that are objective, timely, accurate, and relevant."

The BLS also provides information on the following categories: inflation and prices, spending and time use, unemployment and employment, pay and benefits, productivity, workplace injuries, as well as international issues. Two interesting findings from the time use category are as of June 2012, on days that Americans provided eldercare, they spent an average of 3.1 hours doing so; in the years 2003–2006, employed, married mothers were more likely to engage in household activities, including childcare, than were employed, married fathers.

*Source:* Bureau of Labor Statistics. (September 15, 2012). About BLS. Retrieved from http://www.bls.gov/bls/infohome.htm

Welfare Benefits Administration, the Employment Standards Administration, the Occupational Safety and Health Administration, the Mine Safety and Health Administration, the Bureau of Labor Statistics, and the Veterans' Employment and Training Service. Within these, several program are implemented, some of which are described later.

The DOL provides support for disaster relief, including Disaster Unemployment Assistance (DUA). DUA supports workers who have lost or experienced interrupted employment due to the occurrence of a major disaster, as declared by the president of the United States. The impact of 9/11, for example, proved to have devastating negative effects on the American economy at local, regional, and national levels. The DOL also provides guidance to consumers about their worker's compensation, pension plans, and health coverage in situations where these have been affected by disaster, such as if records have been lost or if businesses have closed. Under situations where employers and employees are exposed to hazardous materials, such as anthrax, the DOL will also provide support.

Also, the DOL presents information to consumers related to health plans and benefits, including: COBRA (the right to temporary continuation of health coverage at group rates for certain groups of people); Mental Health Parity (MHPA) (provision of uniformity related to mental health benefits); Health Coverage Portability (HIPAA) (provision of protections for both group health and individual policies); Newborns' and Mothers' Health Protection (Newborns' Act) (includes protections for mothers and their newborn children regarding length of stay at hospitals following childbirth); and Women's Health and Cancer Rights (WHRCA) (provides critical protections for individuals who have breast reconstruction as a result of a mastectomy). Information and resources related to jobs and training are part of the DOL role. This includes information for employees and employers on discrimination; hiring persons with disabilities or foreign workers; and receiving training such as among Veterans, older adults, unskilled workers, and disabled persons. The DOL collaborates with *Women Work! The National Network for Women's Employment* and *The Employment and Training Administration.* Disabled persons are protected from discrimination in employment primarily by two federal laws: the Americans with Disabilities Act and the Rehabilitation Act. These acts require that executive government branch agencies take affirmative action in the hiring, placing, and advancing of individuals with disabilities. The DOL provides support for union members too. This is critical for workers involved in labor disputes. Current research indicates that 47 percent of serious labor practice violations occur before a unionization petition is filed. The DOL also publishes a list of various labor-related laws, as listed Table 15.

**Table 15**    Department of Labor: Important Labor Laws

| |
| --- |
| Americans with Disabilities Act (ADA) |
| Black Lung Benefits Act (BLB) |
| Consolidated Omnibus Budget Reconciliation Act (COBRA) |
| Davis–Bacon & Related Acts (DBRA) |
| Drug-Free Workplace Act of 1988 |
| Employee Retirement Income Security Act (ERISA) |
| The Fair Labor Standards Act (FLSA) |
| Family & Medical Leave Act (FMLA) |
| Federal Employees' Compensation Act (FECA) |
| McNamara–O'Hara Service Contract Act (SCA) |
| Occupational Safety & Health (OSH) Act |
| Uniformed Services Employment and Reemployment Rights Act (USERRA) |
| Whistleblower Protections |

**Table 16** The changing mix of the U.S. labor force by age, ethnicity, and sex: 1976–2006

|  | 1976 | 1986 | 1996 | 2006 |
|---|---|---|---|---|
| **Total Labor Force** | **96,158** | **117,834** | **133,943** | **148,847** |
| | **Percentage of the Labor Force** | | | |
| **Age** | | | | |
| 16–19 | 9.4 | 6.7 | 5.8 | 6.0 |
| 20–24 | 14.9 | 13.1 | 10.0 | 10.4 |
| 25–34 | 25.2 | 29.4 | 25.3 | 20.7 |
| 35–44 | 18.0 | 23.1 | 27.3 | 23.8 |
| 45–54 | 17.7 | 15.1 | 19.7 | 23.6 |
| 55–64 | 11.9 | 10.1 | 9.1 | 12.6 |
| 65–74 | 2.6 | 2.2 | 2.4 | 2.2 |
| 75+ | 0.4 | 0.4 | 0.5 | 0.6 |
| **Ethnicity** | | | | |
| White, non-Hispanic | N/A | 79.8 | 75.3 | 72.7 |
| Black | N/A | 10.7 | 11.3 | 11.6 |
| Hispanic | N/A | 6.9 | 9.5 | 11.7 |
| Asian | N/A | 2.9 | 4.3 | 5.4 |
| **Age within Sex** | | | | |
| **Males** | 59.5 | 55.5 | 53.8 | 52.6 |
| 16–24 | 22.3 | 18.7 | 15.5 | 16.4 |
| 25–39 | 35.3 | 42.6 | 39.7 | 32.4 |
| 40+ | 42.4 | 38.7 | 44.8 | 51.2 |
| **Females** | 40.5 | 44.5 | 46.2 | 47.4 |
| 16–24 | 27.2 | 21.2 | 16.2 | 16.4 |
| 25–39 | 33.1 | 42.1 | 38.9 | 31.7 |
| 40+ | 39.7 | 36.7 | 44.8 | 52.0 |

*Source:* Howard Fullerton, A. Labor force 2006: Slowing down and changing composition. *Monthly Labor Review*, November 1997, 23–38. Copyright belongs to the Bureau of Labor Statistics (BLS).

In addition to the aforementioned responsibilities, the DOL monitors workplace safety and health, such as drug-free workplace, hazards, and mine safety. Regarding the latter, workers are entitled, under the Federal Mine and Safety Health Act, to have their worksite inspected regarding mine accidents, miner complaints, criminal violations by mine operators, as well as increased education and training for miners. Under the Office of Worker's Compensation, miners who have been totally and permanently disabled by black lung can receive federal benefits.

Information for youth (those under 16 years of age) is also available. For example, under the Fair Labor Standards Act (FLSA), 14 and 15 years old are allowed to work, as long as guidelines for number of hours, times worked, and school requirements are met. The DOL is heavily involved in the International Labor Organization's (ILO) International Program on the Elimination of Child Labor (IPEC). This includes providing funding to remove children from hazardous work, increase the participation of other countries in the program, and increase awareness about child labor.

Consumers can search on the DOL website the *Occupational Outlook Handbook*, a resource for finding jobs and salaries, as well as information on employment projections and statistics. Such resources are critical for American workers especially given that demographic trends are greatly reshaping the American landscape. With the "graying of America" and increased immigration, projections suggest a major increase in older adults, as well as the Hispanic and Asian populations. Projections from the DOL indicate that over the next decade, 40 million people will enter the workforce, nearly 25 million will leave it, and about 109 million will remain active. Table 16shows the changing mix of the U.S. Labor Force by age, ethnicity, and gender.

Such trends are likely to impact the labor market experience, including unemployment rates, pensions, education and training, and job accessibility.

---

United States Labor Force Statistics

- "In 2009, 72,019,000 women were in the civilian labor force, 66,208,000 of whom were employed."
- As of October 2012, "there were 3.6 million job openings on the last business day of August, essentially unchanged from July, but up over the last 12 months. The hires rate (3.3 percent) and separations rate (3.3 percent) were little changed in August."
- In 2009, there were 27.5 million businesses in the United States. Women owned 7.8 million of these; minorities owned 5.8 million.

For more information, see the U.S. Small Business Administration at http://ww.sba.gov

---

*Melanie Horn Mallers*

**See also:** American's with Disability Act (ADA); Corporate Social Responsibility; Department of Health and Human Services (HHS); Department of Homeland Security (DHS); Department of the Treasury; Equal Opportunity Employment Commission (EEOC); Family Medical Leave Act (FMLA); Federal Emergency Management Agency (FEMA); Roosevelt, Franklin D.; Whistleblowing

### References and Additional Readings

Department of Labor. (n.d.). Frequently asked questions. Retrieved from http://webapps.dol.gov/dolfaq/go-dol-faq.asp?faqid=478

Department of Labor. (2013). A brief history: The U.S. Department of Labor. Retrieved from http://www.dol.gov/oasam/programs/history/dolhistoxford.htm#.UHhRaW9i7b4

Infoplease. (2013). Labor, United States Department of. Retrieved from http://www.infoplease.com/encyclopedia/history/labor-united-states-department-of.html

Lerman, R. I., & Schmidt, S. R. (n.d.). An overview of economic, social, and demographic trends affecting the US labor market. United States Department of Labor. Trends and challenges for work in the 21st century. Retrieved from http://www.dol.gov/oasam/programs/history/herman/reports/futurework/conference/trends/trendsi.htm

Roberts, B. W. (2009). The macroeconomic impacts of the 9/11 attack: Evidence from real-time forecasting. Office of Immigration Statistics, Department of Homeland Security. Retrieved from http://www.dhs.gov/xlibrary/assets/statistics/publications/ois_wp_impacts_911.pdf

## Department of State

The U.S. Department of State's tagline is "Diplomacy in Action." More commonly called the State Department, its mission is to work toward peace and prosperity in the world, using just and democratic methods to create stable conditions and further progress people in America and the world. The State Department partners with a variety of groups to meet its mission, including academics, scientists, innovators, corporations, faith-based organizations, community groups, foundations, and nongovernmental organizations. The secretary of state is the president's chief advisor on foreign affairs and a cabinet member. The secretary is also second in line for succession of the presidency behind the vice president. The secretary of state is appointed by the president with Senate approval, whose duties range from negotiating agreements to supervising immigration laws overseas.

With a vision toward future peace, the Department of State and the U.S. Agency for International Development (USAID) announced the Quadrennial

Diplomacy and Development Review (QDDR) that assessed the two offices' efficiency and accountability. The QDDR plan is to elevate American 'civilian power, advance the national interests, and to be a better partner to the American military. Civilian power leadership involves coordinating resources from American's civilian agencies in an effort to prevent and resolve conflicts. This leadership can assist countries in overcoming poverty and becoming productive democratic states, as well as, to increase global partnerships. Four key outcomes of the QDDR are to:

International Day of the Girl is a campaign that the Department of State unveiled on 10/11/12, in an effort to stop gender bias and promote advocacy for girls and their rights, on a global level. One of the goals of the day is to stop the marriage of girls under the age of 18. In fact, across the world, girls are forced into marriage at ages as young as 7 at a rate of 25,000 each day according to care.org. This leads to children having children, and the perpetuation of gender bias and the degradation of girls and women.

- Build America's civilian power, bringing together the unique contributions of civilians across the federal government to advance U.S. interests.
- Elevate and transform development to deliver results by focusing our investments, supporting innovation, and measuring results.
- Build a civilian capacity to prevent and respond to crisis and conflict and give our military the partner it needs and deserves.
- Change the way we do business by working smarter to save money, planning and budgeting to accomplish our priorities, and measuring the results of our investments (Department of State, 2012).

In 1789, President Washington saw a need for the U.S. government to have a role in foreign affairs, hence the creation of the State Department. Duties and responsibilities have evolved over time and as of this writing, the State Department employed over 50,000 employees in foreign and domestic roles, operating with an annual budget of over $25 billion.

*Wendy Reiboldt*

### References and Additional Readings

Department of State. (2012). *The quadrennial diplomacy and development review.* Retrieved from http://www.state.gov/documents/organization/153109.pdf

Department of State. (2013). Retrieved from http://www.state.gov

Hicks, J. (2010). State department planning and real estate: We don't pick our markets either. *Corporate Real Estate Journal, 1*(1), 53–66.

Koh, H.H. (2012). The State Department legal adviser's office: Eight decades in peace and war. *Georgetown Law Journal, 100*(5), 1748–1781.

## Department of the Interior (DOI)

The Department of the Interior (DOI) is a cabinet-level governmental agency of the U.S. government that houses nine technical bureaus: Bureau of Indian Affairs, Bureau of Land Management, Bureau of Ocean Energy Management, Bureau of Reclamation, Bureau of Safety and Environmental Enforcement, National Park Service, Office of Surface Mining, Reclamation and Enforcement, U.S. Fish and Wildlife Service, and U.S. Geological Survey. Together, these bureaus work to manage America's natural and cultural resources. The DOI manages one-fifth of U.S. land, 35,000 miles of coastline, and 1.76 billion acres of the Outer Continental Shelf. The DOI also upholds the government's responsibilities to over 500 Indian tribes; conserves fish, wildlife and their habitats; and manages water supplies for over 30 million people. Among the programs that the DOI manages and sustains are America's lands, water, wildlife, and energy resources; it also supports and advocates for tribal nations and island communities. Other activities include the America's Great Outdoors (AGO) initiative, launched by current President Obama, to connect American's to national parks and other great outdoor environments and protect our "natural heritage." The DOI has also started a Climate Change Response Council, to coordinate necessary responses to the climate changes and its impact on the natural environment. At the time of this writing, the secretary of the DOI reached President Obama's goal of authorizing 10,000 megawatts of renewable wind power on public lands. Such projects serve as landmark examples for how to conserve energy. Consumers can visit the DOI website for tourist-related information, such as planning a trip to national parks, recreation areas, and wildlife refuges.

According to the DOI website, annually, more than 500 million people visit the national parks and monuments, wildlife refuges, and recreational sites. Our National Park System accommodates approximately 271 million visitors. Another 72 million people visit our National Wildlife Refuge System.

*Melanie Horn Mallers*

**See also:** Americans with Disabilities Act (ADA); Department of Energy (DOE)

### References and Additional Readings

Department of the Interior. (2013a). Climate change. Retrieved from http://www.doi.gov/whatwedo/climate/index.cfm

Department of the Interior. (2013b). Home. Retrieved from http://www.doi.gov/index.cfm

Williams, B.K., Szaro, R.C., & Shapiro, C.D. (2007). *Adaptive management: the US Department of the Interior technical guide.* U.S. Department of the Interior, Adaptive Management Working Group.

## Department of the Treasury

The U.S. Department of the Treasury is one of the 15 departments in the Executive Branch of the U.S. federal government. Each of the secretaries or leaders of these departments make up the president's cabinet, which is the most important advisory body to the president. The members of the cabinet provide an important function to the president by giving the president their expert advice and through running the major federal agencies.

The Department of the Treasury is responsible for ensuring that the federal government's financial systems are sound and secure, not only for the citizens of the United States but also for citizens of all the other countries in the world, as the economies of world's countries are impacted by the economic health of the United States. The mission of the Department of the Treasury, as written on its website, is to:

> Maintain a strong economy and create economic and job opportunities by promoting conditions that enable economic growth and stability at home and abroad, strengthen national security by combating threats and protecting the integrity of the financial system, and manage the U.S. Government's finances and resources effectively.

The department is organized with a secretary of the treasury as the leader of the agency, reporting to the president of the United States. The workforce of the Department of the Treasury is about 102,000 civil servants. The largest part of the workforce in the department is in the 12 bureaus. The bureaus are as follows:

- The Internal Revenue Service, which handles the determination, assessment, and collection of taxes for the United States;

- The Bureau of Engraving and Printing, which designs and manufactures U.S. currency, securities, and other official certificates of the U.S. Treasury;

- The Bureau of the Public Debt, whose job it is to borrow the money needed to operate the federal government;

- The Alcohol and Tobacco Tax and Trade Bureau, which is responsible to enforcing and administering laws related to the production, use, and distribution of alcohol and tobacco products, along with collecting excise taxes for firearms and ammunition;

- The Community Development Financial Institution Fund, which works to expand the availability of credit, investment capital, and financial services to distressed urban and rural communities;

- The Financial Crimes Enforcement Network, whose role it is to support law enforcement investigative efforts regarding financial crimes;

- The Financial Management Service, which receives and disburses all public monies through government accounts;

- The Inspector General's Office, which conducts independent audits, investigations, and reviews of treasury offices and activities;

- The Treasury Inspector General for Tax Administration, which provides leadership and coordination of policies and activities to promote economy, efficiency, and effectiveness in the administration of the internal revenue laws;

- The Office of the Comptroller of the Currency, which charters, regulates, and supervises national banks to support the economy of the United States;

- The Office of Thrift Supervision, whose role is to be the primary regulator of all federal and many of the state-chartered thrift institutions, which are the savings banks and savings and loan association;

- The U.S. Mint, which designs and manufactures domestic, bullion, and foreign coins, and other numismatic items, and also physically houses the nation's silver and gold assets.

---

According to a 2012 CNN news clip, in 2011 the cost to make a penny is 2.4 cents and the cost to make a nickel is 11.2 cents. Due to the high cost of making coins, President Obama has asked Congress to change the mixture of metals that make up pennies and nickels even though this recipe has been unchanged for over 30 years. The U.S. Treasury has yet to come up with a new metal mixture that would be any cheaper than the current mixture.

*Source:* Isidore, Chris. (February 12, 2012). Obama wants cheaper pennies and nickels. Retrieved from http://money.cnn.com/

The primary offices of the U.S. Department of the Treasury are the Office of the Treasurer, the Office of Domestic Finance, the Office of International Affairs, and the Office of Terrorism and Financial Intelligence.

The Office of the Treasurer has oversight of the U.S. Mint, the Bureau of Engraving and Printing and Fort Knox. This office has a key relationship with the Federal Reserve Board, a quasigovernment organization that sets monetary policy for the United States. The role of treasurer is important; not only does the treasurer sign the paper money printed during his or her term of office, but more importantly, the treasurer advices the Secretary of the Treasury on his or her role in community development and public engagement.

The Office of Domestic Finance is headed by the under secretary of the Treasury, and serves as an advisor to the secretary on matters including the domestic financial system, fiscal policy and operations, governmental assets and liabilities and other issues related to governmental finances and the economy. Current work of the office includes work on Wall Street reform, housing finance reform, the small business lending fund, the state small business credit initiative, making homes affordable, and establishing a financial stability plan. This office also houses the Office of Consumer Policy, which ensures that every American has access to safe and affordable financial products and services. The Office of Consumer Policy also endeavors to formulate policy in the areas of consumer financial education and capability, new payment methods, technology designed to improve consumers' financial choices, safeguards for consumer privacy, and other areas.

The Office of International Affairs protects the interests of the U.S. economy by strengthening the economic stability of other countries that impacts the U.S. economy. They are deeply involved in mitigating global financial instability, as the state of the economy of the world has a large impact on U.S. economic well-being. When global economic challenges arise, the staff in this office is deeply engaged in protecting U.S. economic interests.

The Office of Terrorism and Financial Intelligence has the large task of protecting the U.S. economy from illicit and combating rogue nations, terrorist facilitators, weapons of mass destruction proliferation, money launderers, drug kingpins, and other illegal and potentially devastating actions designed to damage the U.S. population and its economy. Any act of terrorism against the United States has an economic impact on the United States and other countries.

The deputy secretary of the treasury, and, ultimately, the secretary of the treasury, also has six other offices reporting to him or her. These are the Office of Economic Policy, General Counsel, Office of Legislative Affairs,

Office of Management, the Office of Public Affairs, and the Office of Tax Policy. The Office of Economic Policy is involved in promoting and protecting the economy of the U.S. states through activities such as the formulation of public policies and positions of the Treasury Department, such as health insurance, terror risk insurance, retirement income security, and long-term care. A large Office of General Counsel is responsible for representing the Department of the Treasury through providing legal advice and doing the department's legal work. The Office of Legislative Affairs advises the secretary of the treasury on congressional relations in order to assist in formulating policy and determining the direction of the overall department. Any interaction the department has with Congress or the White House involves the Office of Legislative Affairs. The Office of Management is in charge of the internal management and policy of the department for budgeting, planning, human resources, and other activities internal to the management of the department. The Office of Public Affairs provides communication strategies for the department. The Office of Tax Policy is involved in developing and implementing federal government tax policies and programs. This office guides the president and Congress on all aspects of taxation, including tax policy decisions between the United States and other countries.

Every citizen in the United States has an interaction with one or more of the U.S. Department of the Treasury activities each year, whether it be to pay taxes, borrow money, or start a small business. The power and the importance of the role of the department are immense and not always appreciated by the average American. However, the department works to support the U.S. economy, which is one of the strongest and most stable economies in history, and therefore provides benefit to every citizen within the United States and to many citizens of other countries around the world.

*Deborah C. Haynes*

**See also:** Congress; Counterfeiting; Department of Justice (DOJ)

### References and Additional Readings

Partnership for Public Service. (2012). The best places to work in the federal government. Retrieved from http://www.bestplacestowork.org/BPTW/rankings/detail/TR00.

U.S. Department of the Treasury. (2013). Organizational structure. Retrieved from http://www.treasury.gov/about/organizational-structure/Pages/default.aspx.

The White House. (2013). The executive branch. Retrieved from http://www.whitehouse.gov/our-government/executive-branch

# Department of Transportation (DOT)

In 1966, by act of Congress, the U.S. Department of Transportation (DOT) was established, opening its doors in 1967. As the primary federal agency overseeing transportation safety, the mission of the department, according to its website is to "Serve the United States by ensuring a fast, safe, efficient, accessible and convenient transportation system that meets our vital national interests and enhances the quality of life of the American people, today and into the future" (DOT, 2012). The department is comprised of 11 administrations (Table 17.

Two other offices were housed under the DOT before the terrorist acts of 2001. When the Homeland Security Act of 2002 was passed, the departmental oversight of the U.S. Coast Guard and the Transportation Security Administration was transferred to the Department of Homeland Security beginning in 2003. Despite the reorganization of the department, in the 2013 budget proposal, the DOT is slated to receive $74 billion toward improving the transportation system in America. Secretary Ray LaHood noted that the money received to invest in the country's infrastructure will not only serve to keep America's "roadways, runways, and railways" strong, but will also stimulate jobs for out-of-work Americans.

Keeping the transportation system in the United States modern through the department's innovative research efforts will assist in keeping America competitive across the globe. One such innovation the department is working on is Vehicle to Vehicle Technology (V2V), which involves the exchange of anonymous information between vehicles on the roadway, to reduce the risk of crashes by notifying drivers of carefully calculated

**Table 17** Department of Transportation Administrations

The Federal Aviation Administration

The Federal Highway Administration

The Federal Motor Carrier Safety Administration

The Federal Railroad Administration

The National Highway Traffic Safety Administration

The Federal Transit Administration

The Maritime Administration

The Saint Lawrence Seaway Development Corporation

The Research and Innovative Technologies Administration

The Pipeline and Hazardous Materials Safety Administration

The Surface Transportation Board

The first Asian-Pacific American to serve as the Department of Transportation's secretary under George Bush was Norman Y. Mineta, a Democrat from California who had been held in a relocation camp for Japanese Americans during World War II. He was 69 years old at the time of his appointment and had previously served in another cabinet position as Secretary of Commerce under President Clinton. Seeing the nation through the 9/11 crisis and beyond; Mr. Mineta served for nearly five and one-half years, longer than any previous Secretary of Transportation, before announcing his retirement in 2006.

threats and risks. Noting the lowest highway death in 65 years, the secretary vows to continue these and other efforts to improve all modes of transportation.

The recently updated website offers links to a variety of things under the DOT jurisdiction such as automobiles, roadways and bridges, pipelines

**Moving Ahead for Progress in the 21st Century Act (MAP-21)** was signed into law in 2012 by President Obama. This law provides multiyear funding of more than $105 billion for transportation projects in 2013–2014. The act, as stated in the overview, is a "streamlined, performance-based, and multimodal program to address the many challenges facing the U.S. transportation system. These challenges include improving safety, maintaining infrastructure condition, reducing traffic congestion, improving efficiency of the system and freight movement, protecting the environment, and reducing delays in project delivery." MAP-21 is focused on investing in U.S. highways, and in the following courses of action:

- strengthen America's highways
- establish a performance-based program
- create jobs and supports economic growth
- support the Department of Transportation's (DOT) aggressive safety agenda
- streamline federal highway transportation programs
- accelerate project delivery and promotes innovation

In addition to the innovations mentioned above, several restructuring efforts within programs, as well as the creation of new programs, exist to address the above goals.

*Source:* http://www.dot.gov/map21

and hazmat, trucking and motor coaches, aviation, public transit, railroads, maritime and waterways, research, and bicycles and pedestrians. Major agendas of the DOT include reducing driving while distracted or under the influence, educating citizens, ensuring air travel safety, and supporting the development of high-speed rail. Of specific importance, given the increased use of technology, is the distracted driving message. A website has been created by the U.S. government called www.distraction.gov, encouraging young drivers in particular to "Stop the texts. Stop the Wrecks." The department reports that drivers who are texting while driving are 23 times more likely to get into a wreck. In fact, the DOT has banned texting and cell phone use for all commercial drivers. These and other efforts will continue as the DOT continues to work toward making transportation safer.

*Wendy Reiboldt*

**See also:** Department of Homeland Security (DHS); Federal Aviation Administration (FAA); National Highway Traffic Safety Administration (NHTSA); National Transportation Safety Board (NTSB)

### References and Additional Readings

Bourne, R. (1995). *Americans on the move: A history of waterways, railways and highways.* Golden, CO: Fulcrum Publishing.

Department of Transportation. (2013a). About Us. Retrieved from http://www.dot.gov/mission/about-us

Department of Transportation. (2013b). Retrieved from http://www.dot.gov.

Dilger, R. J. (2003). *American transportation policy.* Westport, CT: Praeger.

# Department of Veterans Affairs (VA)

Military Veterans are individuals who have completed military service, whether in the United States or overseas, during peacetime or in combat. As a result of their service, Veterans may be entitled to, and in some cases may require, various government services. In 2011, the U.S. Veteran population consisted of approximately 22,234,000 individuals, of whom 9.6 million had served in the army, 5.1 million in the navy, 4 million in the air force, 2.4 million in the marines, 1 million in the reserve forces, and 0.2 million in nondefense functions. Approximately 8.3 percent of U.S. Veterans are women.

A disabled veteran in a wheelchair participates in the dedication day parade for the Vietnam Veterans Memorial. (U.S. Department of Defense)

## Eligibility for VA Benefits

Eligibility for government services and other benefits typically depends on a Veteran's type of military discharge. There are two broad categories of discharge: administrative and punitive. The three types of administrative discharges are honorable, general, and "other than honorable." Punitive discharges come in two forms, bad conduct and dishonorable.

*Administrative:* An honorable discharge is granted when service members complete their tour of duty and meet standards of performance and conduct, which entitles them to full Veterans' rights and benefits. When a service member is not eligible for an honorable discharge (conduct and performance not meritorious, but exit from service was honorable), a general discharge is granted. Veterans may be disqualified from certain benefits when a general discharge is granted (for those benefits requiring an honorable discharge), such as the GI Bill. An "other than honorable" discharge signifies a departure from conduct expected of a service member. Recipients of this type of discharge are typically barred from reenlisting with the armed forces and are ineligible for a majority of Veterans' benefits.

*Punitive:* A bad conduct discharge is also known as a punitive discharge and is provided to an enlisted service member via a court martial. In this case, virtually all Veterans' benefits are forfeited. Similarly, a dishonorable discharge is received through a general court martial conviction, but for offenses such as murder, rape, and desertion as part of the sentence, this discharge results in a loss of all Veterans' benefits.

## Tripartite Organization and
## Its Benefit Programs

The VA is the federal agency responsible for administering programs that provide benefits to military Veterans. It was established as a cabinet-level agency on March 15, 1989 (Public Law 100-527) and is the U.S. government's second largest department. VA is divided into three branches: the Veterans Benefits Administration (VBA), the Veterans Health Administration (VHA), and the National Cemetery Administration (NCA). Each of these three branches provides a defined set of benefits to eligible Veterans.

### Veterans Benefits Administration

The mission of the Veterans Benefits Administration (VBA) is to provide benefits and services to eligible Veterans and their families in recognition of their service to the nation. The VBA focuses on the areas of benefits for education, employment, home loans, and disability compen-sation.

- *Education:* The Servicemen's Readjustment Act of 1944, otherwise known as the GI Bill of Rights (P.L. 78-346), provided World War II Veterans with the opportunity to attend college, vocational education programs, or high school. More recently, Congress passed the Post-9/11 Veterans Education Assistance Improvements Act of 2010 (P.L. 111-377). Effective from October 2011, this act requires VA to provide financial support for education and student housing to Veterans with at least 90 days of aggregate service after September 10, 2001, and an honorable discharge. VA pays full tuition and fees for students attending schools in their states of residence and provides the student with an annual stipend for housing, books, and supplies. The Yellow Ribbon GI Education Enhancement program is a cost-sharing arrangement between VA and participating educational institutions that enables qualifying Veterans to attend private, out-of-state, or graduate schools if the tuition exceeds the amount allowed by the Post-9/11 Bill.

- *Employment:* In 1994, Congress passed the Uniformed Services Employment and Reemployment Rights Act (USERRA 38 U.S.C. 4301–4335), which makes illegal any employment discrimination based on several items, including an individual's prior uniformed service, current obligations as a member of the uniformed services, or intent to join the uniformed services. The law entitles Veterans to be reemployed with the status, seniority, and rate of pay by their preservice employers as if he or she was continuously employed during the period of uniformed service. Veterans are given preference over non-Veterans for many job positions within the federal competitive service. The Office of Personnel Management is responsible for enforcing and interpreting laws pertaining to this Veterans Preference, and includes the three special hiring policies for Veterans. According to the Feds Hire Vets website *(http://www.fedshire vets.gov/)*, the Veterans Recruitment Appointment (VRA) policy allows agencies to appoint eligible Veterans without competition. The Veterans Employment Opportunity Act (VEOA) is used when filling permanent, competitive service positions. Finally, the "30% or More Disabled Veteran" policy allows any veteran with a 30 percent or more service-connected disability to be noncompetitively appointed to a position.

- *VA home loans:* Veterans may apply for a VA home loan, which is a guarantee by the Department of Veterans Affairs to make good to the lender in case the lender defaults. This promise by the government helps many Veterans obtain loans for which they might not otherwise qualify. To be eligible for a VA home loan, the borrower must be within a predetermined debt ratio. The ratio takes into account personal income, credit card debts, car loans, and the new potential indebtedness created by the mortgage. Other benefits of VA home loans include longer terms of repayment, no down payment in certain cases, and accurate appraisal of the property value.

- *VA Disability Compensation:* Military Veterans who are injured during their service, who have a condition that is exacerbated by their service, or who develop a medical illness as a result of their service are entitled to disability compensation from VA. Individuals are eligible for compensation if there is a connection between their service and medical condition and if they did not receive a dishonorable discharge. The VA secretary and Congress have the authority to establish presumptions of service connections and disability for Veterans, and since 1921, nearly 150 health outcomes have been service connected on this basis. VA now provides disability compensation to approximately three million Veterans, spending approximately $41 billion annually for this purpose. Furthermore, the range of pay depends on the extent of disability. Disability compensation is also paid to patients who are rendered disabled because of VA health care.

During the Vietnam War during 1962–1971, the U.S. military sprayed herbicides, consisting mainly of Agent Orange, to destroy the thick jungle canopy in Vietnam that could conceal opposition forces. In 1991, Congress passed P.L. 102-4, the Agent Orange Act that directed the secretary of VA to request the National Academy of Sciences to perform a comprehensive evaluation of the medical and scientific information on the health effects of Agent Orange. Veterans who have conditions related to herbicide exposure are entitled to VA health care and disability compensation. Some of the most prevalent conditions include soft-tissue sarcoma, Hodgkin's disease, lymphoma, skin disorders such as chloracne and porphyria cutanea tarda, respiratory cancer, prostate cancer, multiple myeloma, and acute and subacute peripheral neuropathy.

### Veterans Health Administration

The Veterans Health Administration (VHA) is committed to providing health care for Veterans to improve their health and well-being. The four statutory missions of VHA concern: (1) medical care; (2) education; (3) research; and (4) emergency management. VHA operates 152 medical centers and nearly 1,400 community-based outpatient clinics, community living centers, Vet Centers, and domiciliaries, thus, making it the largest integrated healthcare system in the United States. VA manages the largest medical training program in the United States and has affiliations with over 100 medical schools and 55 dental schools. Furthermore, VHA policy commits the organization to provide needed health care to Veterans, military personnel, and the public during disasters, national emergencies, and, if called upon, times of war. VHA has been involved in the response to every presidentially declared disaster in the United States since 1992.

Eligibility for healthcare benefits is determined by a system of eight priority groups that ensure that certain groups of Veterans are able to be enrolled before others. Higher priority groups include retirees from military service, Veterans with service-connected disabilities, and Medal of Honor and Purple Heart recipients. Veterans without a dishonorable discharge may qualify for VA healthcare benefits. Most Veterans who enlisted after September 7, 1980, or who entered active duty after October 16, 1981, must have served for a minimum of 24 continuous months or the full period for which they were called to active duty to be eligible for VA healthcare benefits. This minimum duty requirement may not apply to Veterans who were discharged for a disability incurred in the line of duty or for a hardship, or to those who served prior to September 7, 1980. Other exceptions to the minimum duty requirements exist. Certain

Veterans, including former prisoners of war, Veterans with service-connected disabilities, and Veterans with household incomes below certain thresholds, among others, may be afforded enhanced eligibility status.

VHA provides enrollees with a VA Health Benefits Package that includes inpatient (i.e., hospital) and outpatient (i.e., ambulatory) care services to promote, preserve, or restore health. The same services are generally available to all enrolled Veterans. Inpatient and outpatient services include, but are not limited to emergency care, general medical services, surgical services, mental health services, acute care, dialysis, substance abuse and mental health services, and chiropractic services. Eligibility for VHA dental care and nursing home care are more restricted than for other health services. VHA patients and nursing home residents are entitled to certain rights during their treatment, including the right to respect and nondiscrimination, disclosure and confidentiality, participation in treatment disclosures and research projects, and complaints.

## National Cemetery Administration

The mission of the National Cemetery Association (NCA) is to honor Veterans and their families with final resting places in national shrines and with lasting tributes that commemorate their service and sacrifice to the nation. Any member of the armed forces who dies during active duty and any Veteran not dishonorably discharged is eligible to be buried in one of the 131 national cemeteries which are managed by NCA.

*This material is based upon work supported by the Department of Veterans Affairs, Veterans Health Administration, Office of Public Health. The views expressed here are those of the authors and do not necessarily reflect the position or policy of the Department of Veterans Affairs or the U.S. government.*

To learn more about the Veteran population, look up the National Center for Veterans Analysis and Statistics, housed within the VA. It is the authoritative clearinghouse for the Department of Veterans Affairs (VA) to collect, validate, analyze, and disseminate key statistics on Veteran population and VA programs to support planning, analysis, and decision-making activities.

*Source:* http://www.va.gov/vetdata/

*Melissa K. Afable and Kevin C. Heslin*

**See also:** Administration on Aging (AoA); Community Mental Health Centers (CMHC) Act; Department of Housing and Urban Development (HUD); Department of Labor (DOL); Funeral Rule; Health and Health Care; Older Americans Act (OAA); Social Services; Social Welfare

### References and Additional Readings

Agent Orange Act of 1991. (1991). *Public Law* 102–4.

Department of Veterans Affairs Act of 1989. (1989). *Public Law* 100–527.

Department of Veterans Affairs. (2013). National Center for Veterans Analysis and Statistics. Retrieved from http://www.va.gov/vetdata/index.asp.

Dobalian A., Callis, R., & Davey, V. J. (2011). Evolution of the Veterans Health Administration's role in emergency management since September 11, 2001. *Disaster Medicine and Public Health Preparedness, 5*(2), 182–184.

Institute of Medicine. (2008). IOM report: Improving the presumptive disability decision-making process for veterans.

Institute of Medicine. (2011). IOM report: Veterans and agent orange: Update 2010.

Koenig, K. L. (2008). Homeland security and public health: Role of the Department of Veterans Affairs, the U.S. Department of Homeland Security, and implications for the public health community. *Prehospital and Disaster Medicine, 18*(4), 327–333.

Post-9/11 Veterans Educational Assistance Improvement Act of 2010. (2010). *Public Law,* 111–377.

Samet, J. M., McMichael, G. H., & Wilcox, A. J. (2010). The use of epidemiological evidence in the compensation of veterans. *Annals of Epidemiology, 20*(6), 421–427.

Servicemen's Readjustment Act of 1944. (1944). *Public Law* 78–346.

Uniformed Services Employment and Reemployment Rights Act of 1994. 38 U.S.C. 4301–4335.

# Departments of Consumer Affairs (DCA)

State Departments of Consumer Affairs (DCA) are offices whereby consumers can seek government help for their problems. Historically, local departments were the first stop, but over the last decade they have almost completely vanished under local budget cuts. State DCA have suffered budget cuts, as well, but they also benefit from advances in computer and Web technology to help balance the loss of personnel. When DCA were created, the primary industry in the United States was agriculture. Thus, DCA were originally placed under state Departments of Agriculture. Today, the majority of DCA are located within Attorney's General Offices. A few are part of the governor's executive offices, several remain in Departments of Agriculture, and several are at other places.

The primary function of many DCA is accepting, sorting, responding to, helping resolve, and when appropriate, referring complaints from individual consumers to other units of government. Most DCA have telephone counselors who assist consumers one-on-one. By tracking the calls, it is often possible to become aware of problems in time to notify other consumers to be vigilant and avoid them. Their first step is collecting and verifying the facts of the situation, often using information provided by the consumer on a specially designed form that may be available online. Traditionally, DCA sent letters to businesses to seek their input and attempt to resolve the problem. DCA's investigators may actively seek the facts around consumer transactions and compile information to settle cases or for the attorney general's use if court action is necessary. Increasingly, DCA rely on mediation rather than litigation to resolve disagreements between consumers and businesses.

DCA staff members have thorough understanding of the state's consumer laws and regulations, often enforcing the state's "Little FTC Act," named for the federal law most state consumer protection laws mirror. Many have expertise in managing a call center, and in some states they serve as the state's primary point of contact with consumers reporting marketplace problems after a natural or other emergency. They may keep the call center open almost 24 hours a day during and after an emergency in addition to handling more normal consumer problems. Consumer education is another typical responsibility of DCA. Offerings range from printed publications to searchable websites. Staff members often speak to groups, partner with community organizations, and other agencies to provide educational events such as fairs, and partner with the media to get information to consumers about relevant scams, frauds, laws, and ways to protect themselves. Several DCA sponsor the LifeSmarts Competition, sponsor state competition for high school students, and support national contests offered by the National Consumers League. They may partner with Cooperative Extension Agents or Educators, Agencies on Aging, public housing managers, and others to reach consumers.

Often DCA have state consumer advisory committees (CAC) whose members represent key constituencies (consumer advocacy groups, groups that support limited resource consumers, groups that represent aging consumers, etc.) or geographic areas. They may work together to set priorities for DCA efforts, design and deliver programs, and coordinate the most effective use of consumer education resources. It is not unusual for CAC to promote National Consumer Week or other focused educational efforts.

Some DCA staff members specialize in areas that draw the most typical consumer complaints. Often new and used automobile sales and automobile repair, home improvement and repair, and landlord tenant issues are included. DCA may handle all complaints or refer some to other state agencies, depending upon how things are set up in the state. Issues related to housing, insurance, utilities, banking, and investments may be the responsibility of other units.

Issues around occupational and professional registration, certification, and licensure and complaints about individuals or businesses offering such services may also be managed by DCA. Consumers may consult DCA-provided Internet databases or call centers to ensure that those offering them services are properly licensed to do business in the state. In some states, DCA are responsible for registering and monitoring organizations that seek charitable contributions from consumers. Documentation of how the funds collected from consumers are used, including the portion that is consumed by the collection process, is kept by DCA so that consumers can know before they contribute and assure that solicitors are legitimate.

State officials who test and certify weights and measuring devices used in the marketplace are often housed in DCA. They generally are responsible for annually testing and tagging the scales, price scanners, and measured product dispensers used in the sale of everything from gravel and coal to fertilizer and gasoline to meat and milk. This core function of state government has been performed since early colonial days and it is crucial that it be done so consumer and business trust devices used to weigh and measure goods in the marketplace. In recent years, state budgetary challenges have led to new fees for businesses providing these devices and to greater privatization of the testing responsibility. In an era when many weights and measuring devices are computerized and easy to adjust, it is vital that consumers and businesses know that a state keeps vigilant watch on the accuracy of weights and measuring devices and aggressively enforces laws and regulations concerning them. Consumers need to be aware of this responsibility and raise questions when tags are dated or missing.

Other responsibilities that DCA have in various states include all registrations, investigations, and related surety management for businesses like charitable gaming, health spas, extended service contract providers, credit service businesses, cemeteries and prepaid funeral plans, travel clubs, membership campgrounds, and prepaid legal services plans.

When DCA are located within an attorney general or governor's office, they are often among the most visible source of citizen service for the office holder. Attorneys general and governors often seek public relations opportunities with DCA to demonstrate their support of citizens. They often participate in DCA events and promote DCA as places that can help consumers resolve challenges in the marketplace.

Because DCA track consumer problems, they are often consulted as legislation and regulations that affect consumers in the marketplace are developed and changed. Staff members may be asked to testify on behalf of consumers before legislative committees and when state legislatures are in session, some staff members may spend most of their time responding to questions and tracking progress of specific pieces of legislation.

The national organization to which staff members of DCA typically belong is the National Association for Consumer Affairs Administrators (NACAA). The organization partnered with the Consumer Federation of America to compile and release annual lists of most frequent consumer complaints. In recent years NACAA has struggled due to falling revenue as state budget cuts reduced membership. Since so many DCA are now located in Offices of the Attorney General, some staff members have chosen to become active in the National Association of Attorneys General instead of NACAA.

*Irene Leech*

**See also:** Administration on Aging (AoA); Attorney General Office (AG); Department of Agriculture (USDA); Federal Trade Commission (FTC); Frauds and Scams

### References and Additional Readings

Fornell, C. (1976). *Consumer input for marketing decisions: A study of corporate departments for consumer affairs.* New York: Praeger.

Fornell, C., & Westbrook, R. A. (1984). The vicious circle of consumer complaints. *The Journal of Marketing, 48,* 68–78.

## Departments of Insurance

The roots of the insurance industry date back to the days of Benjamin Franklin in the 1750s with the rise of the Philadelphia Contributionship for the insurance of homes that burned in a fire. In 1851, New Hampshire appointed the first insurance commissioner and from there the scope of insurance regulation has grown to where it is today. The purpose of insurance regulation is to protect consumers. The government attempted to protect consumers by implementing standards for insurance contracts and premiums in hopes of keeping a fair and just marketplace. In addition, insurance has also been regulated for social and political purposes in addition to economic means with the intervention of Congress. Congress steps in when the marketplace seems to be failing and, as a result, has created programs such as Medicare. Congress, over the years, has implemented the creation of programs such as California's earthquake pool and Florida's windstorm pool that are now mandated benefits within insurance policies for those specific areas. Premium taxation was the first form of government regulation upon the insurance industry. After the trial, *Paul vs. Virginia*, which declared that the insurance industry would be subject to state regulation, state regulators formed the National Association of Insurance Commissioners (NAIC) in 1871. The NAIC is the U.S. standard setting organization that governs the accounting and solvency of the insurance companies. Each insurer must file its financial statement with that state's insurance commissioner and that state's NAIC office. The mission of the NAIC is to assist the state insurance regulators and serve the public by maintaining five goals:

1. Protect the public interest,
2. Promote competitive markets,
3. Facilitate the fair and equitable treatment of insurance consumers,
4. Promote the reliability, solvency, and financial solidarity of the insurance institutions, and
5. Support and improve state regulation of insurance (NAIC, 2012).

The NAIC has an extensive financial database used to analyze the solvency of the carriers.

The turning point with insurance legislation came about in 1945 with the passing of the McCarran–Ferguson Act, which was passed by Congress. Under this act, insurance companies became exempt from federal antitrust legislation and allowed for state regulation of insurance. This prompted the individual states to govern the conduct of the insurance companies within their state.

Postwar and depression eras brought poorly managed insurance companies that led to regulation being handled by each individual state and processed through the three branches of government: legislative, judicial, and executive. On a legislative level, the states set insurance codes regarding the solvency of the carriers, their rates, and investments. The legal branches often provide legal services supporting the fraud divisions in preventing insurance fraud within each state. The judicial branch uses the courts for decisions relating to policy terms and rulings related to the constitutionality of the state insurance laws. The executive branch uses an appointed insurance commissioner who exercises judicial power in interpreting and enforcing insurance codes. The insurance commissioner is appointed by the governor of each state and is the primary figure in the regulation of each state's insurance industry. State legislation has effectively protected the consumer by structuring the regulation around key areas such as company and producer licensing, regulation, of products, market conduct, financial regulation, and consumer services. Under state law, insurers must have a license to selling products or services. Failure to comply with this requirement may result in license suspension, revocation, and fines. Insurance agents and brokers (also known as producers), must comply with state regulations and must have a license to sell insurance products. Producers must continue to educate themselves with continuing education and renewing their license with a minimum of 30 hours of continuing education every two years. Failure to comply can also result in suspension, revocation, and fines on the independent agents themselves. Product regulation protects consumers by having the company's rates submitted for review prior to going into effect. Market regulation takes place in order to keep the insurance companies honest with their trade practices and by investigating and handling consumer complaints. When complaints or violations are caught, the company is given an opportunity to improve their operations and comply within state law. In order to regulate the financial stability of each insurance carrier, each state maintains at least 15 years worth of quarterly filings in a database with the NAIC. Periodic financial evaluations take place by insurance investigators to insure and verify that the insurance companies' annual statements are valid and that the companies remain in good financial standing.

The state's single most important task is to protect the consumer and help the consumer through consumer service programs. States offer toll-free hotlines, Internet websites, and consumer agencies to handle questions, complaints, and educate the consumer about insurance. Many states have published their registered companies' rates, rate comparison guides and offer help for evaluating insurance options. This information is also made public through the NAIC.

Each state has a Department of Insurance and an elected state insurance commissioner. The state insurance commissioner's job is to oversee the regulation of insurance in that particular state, to enforce the consumer protection statutes, to educate consumers, and to support the stability of the insurance marketplace in their state. The Department of Insurance has oversight and authority regarding how the insurance industry conducts business within its state. This authority includes licensing and regulating the rates and practices of insurance companies, agents, and brokers employed in that particular state.

The Department of Insurance assists consumers through regulation of how insurance companies market and administer their policies and ensure that the business conducted within that state is done so in an honest and fair manner. The Department of Insurance is responsible for investigating and arresting any persons involved with insurance fraud. Fraud is investigated and prosecuted though the Department of Insurance and the agencies within it. State and federal laws allow the Fraud Department to pursue its cases on a federal level and in these instances, the insurance fraud cases are usually carried out as "mail fraud," "criminal racketeering," or other federal offenses. Most cases investigated are criminal acts usually involving automobile property and personal injury, worker's compensation, health insurance, and residential and/or commercial property claims.

The Department of Insurance is involved with the consumer and has several departments available to help consumers in need and to educate about insurance. Each state has a toll-free number to call in order to obtain information on insurance issues. The help centers employ knowledgeable insurance professionals who can answer questions, give direction, and provide assistance to consumers with insurance needs and concerns. Consumers can check the licensing status of companies, agents, and brokers and inquire about complaints that they may have outstanding. The agency is also involved with community outreach and offers speakers for community centers, town hall meetings, and business professional events. Each state has a website with information about the department, the commissioner, laws, filings, forms, help, and others.

*Aleta Ostlund*

**See also:** Insurance; Insurance Commissioners; Workers' Compensation

### References and Additional Readings

Baird, W., & Cobb, C. (February 11, 2005). Insurance regulation: History, background, and recent congressional oversight. Congressional research service reports for the people. Retrieved from https://opencrs.com/document/RL31 982/2005-02-11/

National Association of Insurance Commissioners. (n.d.a). About the NAIC. Retrieved from http://www.naic.org/index_about.htm

National Association of Insurance Commissioners. (n.d.b). State insurance regulation: History, purpose and structure. Retrieved from http://www.naic.org/documents/consumer_state_reg_brief.pdf

Randall, S. (1998). Insurance regulation in the United States: Regulatory federalism and the National Association of Insurance Commissioners. *Florida State University Law Review, 26,* 625–699. Retrieved from http://www.law.fsu.edu/journals/lawreview/downloads/263/rand.pdf

## Direct Marketing Association (DMA)

The Direct Marketing Association (DMA) is the largest global trade organization for industries that use direct marketing as a means to make consumers aware of their products and services. The DMA encourages relevance in direct advertising promotions and has been a benchmark for the industry in terms of responsible marketing. The DMA also provides research, educational opportunities, and venues for networking that improve the direct marketing process. Its membership includes many Fortune 100 companies, small and midsize businesses, and numerous nonprofit organizations. Members come from all sectors of the production and service industries, including financial institutions, publishers, retail outlets, manufacturers, and Internet-based businesses. Also included in the DMA membership are the service industries that support these businesses, like advertising agencies, shipping industries, computer support services, and the media.

The DMA has been in existence for since 1917 and currently has over 2,000 members. In 2011, total revenue for the organization was approximately $26 million. The mission of the Direct Marketing Association, as written on its website, is "to advocate for our members' interest, inform and educate for their advancement, and provide opportunities for economic growth throughout our community." DMA headquarters are in New York City, with a branch office in Washington, D.C., that deals primarily with advocacy of issues related to direct marketing. The DMA is considered a leader among marketing organizations in legislative and lobbying efforts for the direct marketing industry.

As of this writing, the chief operating officer of the DMA was Lawrence Kimmel. He took over the leadership in 2011 after the organization suffered a series of setbacks, including member discontent, declining membership, decreasing financial stability, an unclear mission, and numerous layoffs of DMA personnel. Kimmel has defined direct marketing as "the channel-agnostic approach to driving maximum customer satisfaction and optimal marketplace results." In 2010, the DMA started an effort to redefine itself and to help consumers better understand what direct marketing is. For many people, direct marketing is related to just one channel: direct mail advertising. However, the DMA is now placing more emphasis on

social, digital, and mobile marketing. A new website was launched (www
.newdma.org) in 2010 to better serve members and to educate consumers
about direct marketing.

Member benefits of the DMA Association include a variety of educational
opportunities. The DMA offers professional development opportunities,
including seminars, webinars, in-company training, certification programs,
and access to databases related to direct marketing. The DMA holds many
conferences around the country every year for their members to network and interact with industry leaders and government officials. These
conferences include their annual conference, a conference on data and
technology, a conference related to email marketing, an integrated marketing summit held in New York City, and several conferences focusing on
marketing for nonprofit organizations. An annual conference in Washington, D.C., brings DMA members together with policymakers to discuss
concerns related to the direct marketing industry. Speakers at the last Washington summit included representatives from Congress, the Federal Trade
Commission, the Federal Communications Commission, the National Association of Attorneys General, and the United States Postal Service.

The DMA also publishes materials related to direct marketing, including the *DMA Daily Digest* sent to members every day, a weekly publication
called *DMA Marketing Brief,* a monthly e-bulletin titled *DMA Triple Bottom
Line*, and an e-newsletter related to advocacy of the industry titled, *Direct
from Washington.* Members and consumers alike can access these publications on the DMA website.

DMA members can participate in DMA councils, which are committees with shared interests. Currently there are 17 different councils, and
interests include topics such as broadcast marketing, business-to-business
marketing, catalogs, retail marketing, and social media. Members of these
councils receive announcements, news, resources, links, and notice of
events related to their topics of interest.

The DMA has created ethical guidelines for their members related to the
use of direct marketing on consumers. They maintain and update these
guidelines, monitor their members and nonmembers alike in terms of compliance to these guidelines, and address consumer concerns. The DMA ethical guidelines cover all modes of marketing, especially the use of online,
telephone, and mail solicitations. In some cases, the DMA guidelines are
more stringent than laws governing direct marketing. Two examples of
ethical guidelines that have been developed by the DMA include the provision that marketers should authenticate their e-mail solicitations so that
consumers can be sure that the e-mail they send is actually from them, and
marketers should not place a call to a consumer's cell phone where the
called party must pay incoming call charges.

In addition to ethical guidelines, the DMA has developed member principles and commitment to consumer choice guidelines. According to the *DMA Choice Consumer Guide,* principles for member behavior are as follows.

A DMA member

1. Is committed to its customers' satisfaction.
2. Clearly, honestly, and accurately represents it products services, terms, and conditions.
3. Delivers its products and services as represented.
4. Communicates in a respectful and courteous manner.
5. Responds to inquiries and complaints in a constructive, timely way.
6. Maintains appropriate security policies and practices to safeguard information.
7. Provides information on its policies about the transfer of personally identifiable information for marketing purposes.
8. Honors requests not to have personally identifiable information transferred for marketing purposes.
9. Honors requests not to receive future solicitations from its organization.
10. Follows the spirit and letter of the law as well as DMA's Guideline for Ethical Business Practice. (DMA Member Principles, 1)

The Commitment to Consumer Choice (CCC) is a pledge that all DMA members will follow certain practices that address the desires of consumers and policymakers. The CCC was approved by the DMA's board of directors in 2007. Some specific actions required by the CCC include:

- By October of 2009, DMA members had to provide prospective customers and donors with a notice explaining they could modify or eliminate future mailings from their organization or business.
- DMA members must accept and maintain consumer requests to stop sending solicitations.
- Customers must be provided with an annual notice of their ability to opt out of information exchanges.
- Members must honor customer opt-out requests not to have their personal information shared with others for marketing purposes.

- Members must answer a consumer's request as to where the member obtained that consumer's personal information for a direct marketing solicitation.
- Members must access the DMA Choice (see later) suppression files on a monthly basis to determine which consumers have removed their names from national mailers as well as specific organizations or brands they do not want to hear from.

One service provided to consumers that relates to the use of direct marketing is the DMA Choice Name Removal Service. Consumers can access a DMA Choice website where they can sign up to have their names removed from various direct marketing advertising, including credit offers, catalogs, magazine offers, and other mail offers. Consumers who sign up for DMA Choice will have their names removed from the mailing lists they choose for a period of five years. Consumers can opt to receive this service by mailing in a request, but there is a cost of $1 for mailed requests.

The DMA has a self-regulatory program to encourage industries and organizations that use direct marketing to comply with consumer expectations. Consumers concerned with a particular marketing offer can file a complaint with the DMA and a committee of members will investigate and work with marketers to address the consumer's needs and resolve any complaint. This committee will also censure noncompliant companies publicly and will refer possible illegal activities of marketers to the authorities.

Currently, the DMA is concentrating on two recommendations from the FTC: (1) consumers should be able to block direct marketers from tracking what websites they access on the Internet and (2) there should be legislation that allows consumers to see any personal data that brokers may have about them and consumers should be able to correct any held information that they deem incorrect. The DMA has taken the position that the direct marketing industry's attempt to police itself through the ethical guidelines and the CCC are working, and there is no need for government intervention at this point in time.

Recently, the DMA won a court case against the state of Colorado related to disclosure of direct sales for tax purposes. The state was requiring marketers that were shipping orders into Colorado to provide purchase information to the Colorado Department of Revenue, including who the customers were and how much they spent. The court upheld a 1992 ruling that declared a state cannot collect taxes on orders shipped into the state. Therefore, there was no reason the state of Colorado should have access to the commercial transactions its citizens were making from mail order vendors.

Another initiative of the DMA is the DMA Advertising Option Icon. Consumers using the Internet will now see a special icon in the upper right corner of a behaviorally target ad, along with the words "Ad Choices." If a consumer clicks on the icon, a list of ad networks that operate on their browser will appear. With another click, consumers can opt to choose whether they want to receive online behavioral advertising. To date, more than two trillion online ads have displayed a new Advertising Option Icon symbol.

A subsidiary of the DMA is the Direct Marketing Education Foundation. This organization is the only national nonprofit foundation committed to introducing college students to direct/interactive marketing. The foundation provides funding to equip professors with up-to-date education and research resources, encourage creative classroom participation, and prepare students to succeed in today's marketplace. They offer scholarships for college students interested in direct marketing, research opportunities, and databases for professors pursuing new knowledge of direct marketing topics, and awards to both educational and corporate leaders.

*Jean Memken*

**See also:** Attorney General Office (AG); Federal Communications Commission (FCC); Federal Trade Commission (FTC); Post Office (USPS)

### References and Additional Readings

Bush, M. (2010). DMA struggles to reinvent itself as direct evolves in digital world. *Advertising Age, 81*(35), 2–20.

Cerasale, J. (2008). Comments before the Federal Trade Commission. *Federal Trade Commission.* Retrieved from http://www.ftc.gov/os/comments/behavioralad principles/080411dma.pdf

Direct Marketing Association. (n.d.). DMA member principles. Retrieved from http://www.the-dma.org/cgi/disppressrelease?article=656

Direct Marketing Association. (2012a). Commitment to consumer choice and other DMA requirements. Retrieved from https://www.dmachoice.org/dma/static/learn_more.jsp

Direct Marketing Association. (2012b). DMA 2011 annual report. Retrieved from http://www.the-dma.org/annual report/ANNUAL_REPORT-COMPLETE_PDF_WITH_FINANCIALS.pdf

Haire, T. (2012). DMA in DC connects industry, government leaders on March 26–27. *Response, 20*(6), 9.

Hosford, C. (2010). New DMA chair stresses continuity, legislative action. *B to B, 95*(7), 20.

Radelat, A. (2012). Online privacy, postal hikes top list of DMA concerns. *Advertising Age, 83*(17), 3–21.

Tierney, J. (2011). Court sides with DMA in suit against Colorado. *Multichannel Merchant, 7*(2), 7.

# Disaster and Emergency Declarations

The responsibility for issuing "major disaster" or "emergency" declarations within the United States and its territories lies with the president, authorized by the Robert T. Stafford Disaster Relief and Emergency Assistance Act.

Emergency declarations are made in anticipation of a disaster and activate resources to help decrease the threat of an incident becoming a catastrophic event. Emergency declarations are made when a threat is recognized and they help state and local entities coordinate efforts such as evacuation, or relocation. For example, several emergency declarations were issued prior to the landfall of Hurricane Katrina.

Major disaster declarations are the result of a catastrophic event, and allows for federal assistance to help governments and individuals recover. Many major disaster declarations were issued in the wake of the devastation caused by Hurricane Katrina.

Between 1953 and 2011, U.S. presidents declared a total of 2,061 major disasters (averaging 34 per year) and 344 emergency declarations (averaging

---

**Categorizing and Naming Hurricanes**

The Saffie–Simpson Hurricane Scale used wind speed to determine the relative strength of hurricanes. For example, a category 1 hurricane has maximum sustained wind speeds of 74–95 mph, there would be minimal damage expected, storm surges of 3–5 feet. A category 5 hurricane would have maximum sustained wind speeds of over 157 mph, cause catastrophic damage and expect storm surges more than 18 feet.

The National Hurricane Center (part of the National Weather Service) once used latitude–longitude to identify hurricanes, which proved cumbersome for the public. In 1953, it began using short, distinctive female names for tropical storms and hurricanes. The names are established by the International Committee of the World Meteorological Organization. For Atlantic hurricanes, there are six lists of names beginning with each letter of the alphabet, one for each year, and the lists are repeated every 7 years. In 1979, male names were added to the lists. The exception to reusing a name is a hurricane that is exceptionally deadly, costly, or notorious and reusing its name would be inappropriate. In that case, the names are retired and not used again. For example, the name "Katrina" was retired after the 2005 hurricane season, and the name "Irene" was retired after the 2011 hurricane season.

*Source:* Hurricanes: Science and Society. (2010–2011). Hurricane naming and numbering. Retrieved from http://hurricanescience.org

six per year). Shown in Table 18 are major disaster declarations by U.S. states/territories. Table 19 shows the number of presidential declarations between 2000 and 2011.

Two 21st-century disasters are discussed in detail in the following sections.

**Table 18** U.S. states/territories with the most presidential declarations between 1953 and 2011

| State | Major Disaster Declaration | Emergency Declaration |
|---|---|---|
| Texas | 86 | 12 |
| California | 78 | 8 |
| Oklahoma | 70 | 10 |
| New York | 65 | 21 |
| Florida | 63 | 12 |
| Louisiana | 58 | 9 |
| Alabama | 56 | 22 |
| Kentucky | 56 | 4 |
| Arkansas | 54 | 9 |
| Missouri | 53 | 11 |
| Illinois | 51 | 7 |
| Mississippi | 50 | 11 |

Compiled from data available at http://www.fema.gov/disasters

**Table 19** Number of presidential declarations between 2000 and 2011

| | Major Disaster Declarations | Emergency Declarations |
|---|---|---|
| 2011 | 99 | 29 |
| 2010 | 81 | 9 |
| 2009 | 59 | 7 |
| 2008 | 75 | 17 |
| 2007 | 63 | 13 |
| 2006 | 52 | 5 |
| 2005 | 48 | 68 |
| 2004 | 69 | 7 |
| 2003 | 56 | 19 |
| 2002 | 49 | 0 |
| 2001 | 45 | 11 |
| 2000 | 45 | 6 |

Compiled from data available at http://www.fema.gov/disasters

## Hurricane Katrina

Hurricane Katrina was one of the most devastating hurricanes in the history of the United States, causing widespread destruction in August 2005. In addition to the damage and lives lost, the Corps of Engineers came under intense criticism for the failure of the levees surrounding the City of New Orleans; and the poor response to the disaster from all levels of government is widely documented.

The Atlantic hurricane season in 2005 was one of the most active in U.S. history, and Hurricane Katrina was one of the five major hurricanes that season responsible for the majority of the property damage and deaths during the year.

Hurricane Katrina formed over the Bahamas on August 23, 2005. It crossed southern Florida as a moderate Category 1 hurricane on August 26, and rapidly gained strength in the Gulf of Mexico becoming a Category 5 hurricane the morning of August 28. It had weakened to a Category 3 hurricane when it made landfall in southern Louisiana near the City of New Orleans on the morning of August 29, with sustained winds of 125 mph that extended as far as 120 miles inland. After moving over Breton Sound (east of New Orleans), it made a third landfall near the Louisiana/Mississippi border, still a Category 3 hurricane.

Hurricane Katrina has become the most destructive hurricane in U.S. history in terms of economic losses—estimated as high as $125 billion. It also claimed over 1,800 lives and left millions homeless. The Galveston hurricane in September 1900, was the most deadly, claiming more than 8,000 lives.

Most of the destruction from Hurricane Katrina along the Gulf Coast was due to the storm surge—an unusual rise of water generated by a storm, over and above the predicted tides. The worst property damage was along the coastal areas and beachfront towns on the Gulf Coast, where storm surges reached 6–12 miles inland. The destruction was compounded in New Orleans as the levee system built to protect the city from storm surges failed, eventually flooding 80 percent of the city and its neighboring parishes.

On August 28, the National Weather Service field office in New Orleans projected catastrophic damage to New Orleans from the approaching hurricane, predicting much of the resulting destruction, inundations, debris buildups, and lack of clean water. In anticipation of landfall, Ray Nagin, the mayor of the city of New Orleans, ordered a mandatory evacuation of the city. Although 80–90 percent of the population was safely evacuated, many residents did not heed the initial warnings and remained in the city—primarily those with no access to transportation or lacking adequate financial resources.

The Superdome in New Orleans was used as the shelter of last resort, housing and supporting those who were unable to evacuate. The overcrowding and lack of adequate resources led to initial reports of chaos and crime, later found to be exaggerated or rumors. Civil disturbances, including widespread looting, were common and difficult to contain or control because of the attention focused on the initial rescue efforts and lack of executive leadership at all government levels.

The massive rescue effort included military support from the Louisiana National Guard, the coast guard, navy, and marines. Many survivors were bussed to shelters established in Houston and San Antonio, as well as smaller shelters in towns across Texas, Oklahoma, and Arkansas. Disruption of the communications infrastructure complicated coordination efforts, leading to the Internet, blogging, and social networking becoming the means of distributing information—the first public and widespread use of such technologies.

Although FEMA was still responsible for response and recovery from natural events on a federal level when Hurricane Katrina struck, it had been absorbed into the newly created Department of Homeland Security after the 9/11 World Trade Center disasters and its role had been minimized or resources directed to other functions. By the time Hurricane Katrina made landfall, FEMA had lost over half of its employees, affecting its morale and its ability to respond appropriately. Additionally, FEMA had not traditionally responded to local events without a request from the local jurisdiction, which wasn't received until several days after Katrina's landfall.

Following the national and international criticism of the government's response to Katrina, the U.S. House convened a congressional committee to investigate charges of misjudgment and mismanagement. Their report "A Failure of Initiative: Final Report of the Select Bipartisan Committee to Investigate the Preparation for and Response to Hurricane Katrina" was released in February 2006. The report identified failures and lack of leadership at all levels of government that contributed to the loss of life and property before, during, and after Hurricane Katrina. The report reinforced that much of the property damage and loss of lives during Katrina could be attributed to the slow response by government agencies and the neglected levee system.

The levees in the City of New Orleans were designed and built by the U.S. Army Corps of Engineers, as mandated by the Flood Control Act of 1965. Their failure was considered by the American Society of Civil Engineers as the "worst engineering catastrophe" in US History. A Congressional Review of the Corps in September 2005 noted that the initial project was funded in 1965, and when Katrina occurred 40 years later, the project was not expected to be completed until 2015. The Corps had been sharply criticized for its management and lack of accountability before, but the Katrina disaster has led to repeated calls for its reform. In 2008, a US District Court in Louisiana ruled that the flooding during Katrina was a man-made disaster caused by the Corps negligence and gross incompetence, but also found they couldn't be held financially liable because the United States government is immune for legal liability.

## 9/11

On September 11, 2001, four commercial jet planes were hijacked by 19 militants associated with the Islamic extremist group al-Qaeda to carry out suicide attacks against targets on the east coast of the United States. Two of the planes crashed into the twin World Trade Center towers in New York City and one crashed into the Pentagon in Washington, D.C. The destination of the final plane is not known, but theories include the White House, the U.S. Capitol, or one of several nuclear power plants along the eastern seaboard. It crashed into a field outside Shanksville, Pennsylvania, after an attempt by the passengers to regain control.

The attacks resulted in extensive death and destruction, including the collapse of both World Trade Center towers, and 2,992 total dead and missing, including the 19 hijackers and over 400 police officers and firefighters.

In New York City, massive search and rescue operations were initiated within hours of the attacks, although few survivors were found. The rescue and recovery efforts continued around the clock until the clean up was completed in May 2002. During remarks the evening of September, then Mayor Rudy Guiliani said "We will rebuild and be stronger than ever." Plans to rebuild the skyscrapers began soon after. The new 7 World Trade Center building opening in 2006, the others are expected to be completed by 2015. The National September 11 Memorial and Museum was dedicated on September 11, 2011. The memorial was opened to the public the next day; the museum opened one year later.

The Pentagon was severely damaged and one section of the building collapsed, although its structural design prevented worse damage, and unoccupied offices undergoing renovation reduced the number of casualties. The rebuilding was begun immediately, and the offices were re-opened one year later, on September 11, 2002. As part of the reconstruction, a memorial and chapel (the American Heroes Memorial) was included at the point of the plane's impact. A larger, outdoor Pentagon Memorial was dedicated and opened to the public on September 11, 2008.

The Flight 93 National Memorial was dedicated and opened on September 10, 2011, to commemorate the passengers and crew of United flight 93 that crashed into a field in Stonycreek Township, Pennsylvania. The recovered cockpit voice recorder shows that the crew and passengers learned of the hijackers through phone calls to the ground, tried to overwhelm the hijackers. To prevent that from happening, the hijackers intentionally crashed the plane.

Because of the unknown threat from other aircraft, and for the first time in U.S. history, an emergency preparedness plan describing joint action between the Department of Defense, the Federal Aviation Administration and the Federal Communications Commission to control air traffic during emergency conditions was invoked. The Plan for the Security Control of Air Traffic and Air Navigation Aids (SCATANA) allowed the federal government to close all air space and grounded all nonemergency civilian aircraft in the United States, stranding thousands of passengers across the world. Projects like Operation Yellow Ribbon in Canada were established to host stranded passengers until the embargo was lifted three days later.

The media and governments worldwide denounced the attacks, and nations across the globe offered support and solidarity to the U.S. government and the American people. A United National Security Council Resolution condemned the attacks and numerous countries passed antiterrorism legislation to freeze bank account of suspected al-Qaeda.

The 9/11 attacks also triggered serious damage to global economic markets, closing stock exchanges in the United States until September 17. When they reopened, the Dow Jones Industrial Average fell 684 points, the third largest drop in the Dow Jones Industrial Average (DJIA) history, following the global economic crisis in 2008.

The hundreds of thousands of tons of toxic debris from the collapse of the World Trade Center towers contained over 2,500 contaminants, including known carcinogens like asbestos, benzene from jet fuel, mercury from fluorescent lights, led and cadmium from computers, and crystalline silica from the concrete and glass. Subsequent illnesses, particularly respiratory-related conditions, led to a hearing in the U.S. House Committee on Homeland Security investigating claims the Environmental Protection Agency issued false statements regarding air quality.

As a response to the attacks, the United States launched its War on Terrorism, triggering several major initiatives to combat terrorism. Congress rushed through the USA Patriot Act and it was signed by President George

W. Bush on October 26, 2001. The bill reduced restrictions on gathering of intelligence, expanded authority to regulate financial transactions, and expanded the ability to detain and deport immigrants suspected of terrorism activities. The next year, Congress passed the Homelands Security Act of 2002 and created the Department of Homeland Security to coordinate federal responses to acts of terrorism, absorbing 22 executive branch organizations related to terrorism response.

The War in Afghanistan began on October 7, 2001, with the intention of deposing the Taliban, an Islamist militant movement ruling Afghanistan; The Taliban were known to harbor al-Qaeda operatives. Initial suspicion of Saddam Hussein and Iraq's involvement in the attacks—later disputed—led to the second invasion of Iraq on March 20, 2003. The Guantanamo Bay detention camp was established in 2002 to hold detainees from those wars.

The 9/11 terrorist attacks helped define the presidency of George W. Bush as protecting Americans from another terrorist attack and destroy Islamist terrorists and their supporters. Most of the policies he enacted during the rest of his terms as president stemmed from his response to those attacks.

Al-Qaeda and its leader, Osama bin Laden, initially denied involvement in the 9/11 terrorist attacks on the United States. In 2004, they claimed responsibility and cited the presence of U.S. troops in Saudi Arabia, the sanctions against Iraq, and the U.S. support of Israel as their motives. After escaping detection for years, Osama bin Laden was located and killed during a raid on his residence in Pakistan on May 2, 2011.

The National Commission on Terrorist Attacks Upon the United States—also known as the 9/11 Commission—was established on November 27, 2004, and charged with delivering a thorough report of the circumstances surrounding the attacks. Their report was issue on July 22, 2004. The report detailed the events of that day, confirmed the attacks were carried out by members of al-Qaeda, and examined the coordination between security and intelligence agencies. They summarized their findings with this comment: "Across the government, there were failures of imagination, policy, capabilities and management." They also made numerous recommendations to prevent future attacks. In a follow-up assessment on the 10th anniversary of the attacks, the former chairs found many of those recommendations had not been implemented.

*Valerie Lucus-McEwen*

**See also:** Department of Homeland Security (DHS); Federal Emergency Management Agency (FEMA)

**References and Additional Readings**

American Society of Civil Engineers (ASCE). (2012). Hurricane Katrina investigative team report.

Judge Stanwood R. Duval, Jr. In Re: Katrina Canal Breaches Consolidated Litigation, No. 05-4182 E.D. La.

McCarthy, F. X. (2011). FEMA's disaster declaration process: A primer. Retrieved from www.fas.org/sgp/crs/homesec/RL34146.pdf.

National Commission on Terrorist Attacks Upon the United States (2004). *The 9/11 Commission report*. New York: W.W. Norton & Company.

National Weather Service. (n.d.). National Hurricane Center. Retrieved from http://www.nhc.noaa.gov

Plan for the Security Control of Air Traffic and Air Navigation Aids. (1976). 41 FR 9322.

United States Congress. (2005). *Testimony: Army Corps of Engineers, Lake Pontchartrain and Vicinity Hurricane Protection Project*. GAO-05-1050T. Print.

United States Congress. (2006). A Failure of initiative: The final report of the Select Bipartisan Committee to investigate the preparation for and response to Hurricane Katrina. H. Rept 109–377. Washington, DC: GPO.

Uniting and strengthening America by providing appropriate tools required to intercept and obstruct terrorism (USA Patriot Act) ACT of 2001. Pub. L. 107–56.

The Flood Control Act of 1965. Pub.L. 89–298. 17 October 1965. Print.

The Homeland Security Act of 2002. Pub. L. 107–296-116 Stat. 2135.

**Disaster Recovery**. *See* Federal Emergency Management Agency (FEMA)

# Discrimination

## Definition, Theory, and Measure of

Discrimination in the labor market can be defined as treating two individuals who are *equally* productive unequally on the basis of some (demographic or other nonpecuniary) characteristic, such as sex, race, national origin, age, or religion. Nobel Laureate economist Gary S. Becker was the first to develop a theory that explains how discrimination can persist in a competitive labor market. His theory is based upon the existence of a "taste for discrimination," whereby employers, employees, or consumers have a dislike for associating with a certain group. That reduces the demand for workers in that group. It leads to a wage differential in the labor market whereby white workers are paid more than equally productive black workers, for example, and to segregation of blacks and whites among firms. Becker's theory was developed with racial discrimination in mind (the first edition of his book was published in 1957), and it explained that very well. It was not as effective in explaining sex discrimination in the labor market, where men do want to work in the same firms as women, but perhaps find it socially unacceptable to be in the same jobs.

Barbara R. Bergmann developed an alternative to Gary Becker's theory, the theory of occupational crowding. According to that theory, employers exclude blacks and women from certain occupations, but not from others. In the ones where they face exclusion, they will be unable to obtain many jobs. Thus, they will be crowded into those occupations that do not discriminate against them, such as teaching and nursing in the case of women. The crowding results in excess supply to these occupations, thereby lowering the wages in them. Thus, women end up in female-dominated occupations with wages that are artificially lower than those in male-dominated occupations and lower than what would exist in the absence of discrimination. Discrimination can have a pernicious effect on women's choices. If current market discrimination exists, the resulting lower wage for women strengthens the incentives for them to be the ones to engage in household production. These feedback effects of labor market discrimination also limit women's incentives to invest in human capital that will prepare them for more challenging careers because they will not obtain as high a rate of return as men will for such an investment.

How large is market discrimination and what impact does it have on earnings differentials? This has been studied empirically. But, it is difficult to determine because there is no one single accepted measure of discrimination. The method most often used by economists is to estimate the contribution to the differential of all the human capital factors that affect earnings that can be measured, and then to attribute the unexplained remainder to discrimination. According to these types of estimates, discrimination is believed to account for up to about 40 percent of the overall difference in earnings between men and women.

Discrimination against women in the labor market has been declining since the 1970s, but it has by no means disappeared. It is, however, much less blatant now as there are laws enforced against it and firms can pay a substantial penalty if found to be discriminating. Moreover, women have begun to invest more in their human capital and to take less time out of the labor force for childbearing and rearing as their aspirations have changed in response to the reduction in discrimination. This should reduce the employer's tendency to engage in *statistical* discrimination, a type of discrimination that exists due to imperfect information. As a result, employers assume that *all* women will behave in a way that is less beneficial to the firm than men, but when enough women are observed not behaving this way, employer opinions should change. Employment discrimination can also take the form of a glass ceiling curtailing women's upward progress, sexual harassment, and unequal allocation of nonpecuniary benefits, such as office space, overtime, and the like.

## Laws Against Employment Discrimination

The centerpiece of the federal government's antidiscrimination enforcement efforts is Title VII of the Civil Rights Act of 1964 (Pub. L. 88–352). Known as the Equal Employment Opportunity title, Title VII prohibits discrimination in hiring, firing, discharge and recall, and compensation on the basis of race, color, religion, sex, and national origin. The law created the Equal Employment Opportunity Commission (EEOC). This commission operates mainly by investigating charges of discrimination against firms filed by individuals or groups of individuals.

The Equal Employment Opportunity Act of 1972 strengthened and expanded coverage of Title VII by granting the EEOC the right to sue private sector respondents, and by including state and local governments and educational institutions under the law. Another way the federal government fights employment discrimination is with Executive Order 11246, enacted in 1965 by President Lyndon B. Johnson, and amended in 1967 to include a consideration of person's gender. This order created the Office of Federal Contract Compliance (OFCC) in the U.S. Department of Labor. Under this order, any federal contractor with 50 or more employees had to take affirmative action to make their workforce reflect that of the community in which they operated, or risk losing their contracts although that has actually happened in very few cases. This policy, known as affirmative action, was intended to redress disadvantages resulting from previous discrimination. The OFCC required firms to develop affirmative action plans that set goals and timetables. This policy has become controversial because it is believed to require quotas, particularly when utilized in college or law school admissions. In fact, it has led to charges of "reverse discrimination."

As of October 2012, the U.S. Supreme Court is considering the case of *Fisher v. University of Texas*, in which a 22-year-old Texan claims she was denied admission to the school's flagship campus in Austin because she was white.

Title IX of the Education Amendments of 1972 was the first legislative enactment to move beyond sex discrimination in employment: it prohibited discrimination on the basis of sex in educational programs or activities receiving federal financial assistance, with some exceptions. Title IX prohibits discrimination by educational institutions in providing any aid, benefit, or service including, but not limited to admissions, financial aid, courses, testing, athletics, housing, and employment.

Equal opportunity laws impose the expectation of incurring costs upon discriminatory firms or educational institutions. Under Title VII, these may include attorney's fees, court costs, and possible back-pay settlements, while under Executive Order 11246, the federal contract compliance program (FCCP) and Title IX, they include the withdrawal of federal contracts or assistance.

Most of the research evaluating the effectiveness of federal EEO policies concentrated on minorities, and found mixed results. For example, the dramatic increase in black employment in South Carolina manufacturing that occurred in the mid-1960s has been attributed to federal government civil rights and affirmative action policy. Enforcement of sex discrimination charges has also been somewhat effective. This is ironic though as it was never intended to be included in the act. In fact, it is believed that sex was put into the bill by a southern representative under the assumption that that would lead to its defeat. Today the EEOC also enforces the Age Discrimination in Employment Act of 1967, and its amendments, that prohibits employment discrimination against individuals 40 years of age or older, and the Americans with Disabilities Act of 1990 that covers discrimination against the disabled.

Along with the Equal Pay Act of 1963 that prohibits discrimination in compensation on the basis of gender for substantially similar work performed under similar conditions, Title VII prohibits unequal pay for equal work. However, it does not address the problem of occupational segregation, whereby women are employed in different occupations from men, the wages of which have been artificially depressed by occupational crowding. An effort was made to redress this problem through the policies of Comparable Worth or Pay Equity, which advocated equal pay for work of *comparable* value. But this policy, although in effect in some small local areas, never gained widespread acceptance.

## Discrimination in Other Domains

Discrimination also exists in the housing market, leading to neighborhood segregation. This type of discrimination, however, applies more to race and national origin than to gender. Experts know that this type of discrimination exists through audit studies, where people with the same qualifications but a different race are sent out to the same places, and race is clearly seen to be a factor in determining whether the person is offered an apartment to rent or whether they get a loan to buy a house.

*Andrea H. Beller*

**See also:** Americans with Disabilities Act (ADA); Department of Labor (DOL); Equal Employment Opportunity Commission (EEOC)

### References and Additional Readings

Becker, G.S. (1971). *The Economics of discrimination*, 2nd ed., Chicago: University of Chicago Press.

Beller, A.H. (1978). The economics of enforcement of an anti-discrimination law: Title VII of the civil rights act of 1964. *The Journal of Law and Economics, 21*, 359–380.

Beller, A.H. (1982). The impact of equal opportunity policy on sex differentials in earnings and occupations. *AEA Papers and Proceedings, 72*, 171–175.

Bergmann, B.R. (1971). The effect on white incomes of discrimination in employment. *Journal of Political Economy, 79*(2), 294–313.

Blau, F.D., & Beller, A.H. (1988). Trends in earnings differentials by gender: 1971–1981, *Industrial and Labor Relations Review, 41*, 513–529.

Blau, F.D., Ferber, M.A., & Winkler, A.E. (2010). *The economics of women, men and work*, 6th ed., Upper Saddle River, NJ: Prentice Hall.

Heckman, J.J., & Payner, B.S. (1989). Determining the impact of federal anti-discrimination policy on the economic status of blacks: A study of South Carolina, *American Economic Review, 79*, 138–177.

Wolff, E.N. (1997). *Economics of poverty, inequality and discrimination*. Cincinnati, OH: South-Western College Publishing.

## Dix, Dorothea

Born in Maine in 1802, Dorothea Dix was well known for crusading on behalf of the mentally ill. At the age of 39, she became part of the social welfare movement that was systematically developing during this time. She championed the causes of prison inmates, the mentally ill, and the destitute. This work began when she began to volunteer to teach Sunday School class for women inmates at the East Cambridge Jail. She noticed horrific experiences for the inmates, which included crowded, unheated, unfurnished, and despicable smelling quarters. Many of the inmates, aside from being criminals, were mentally ill, and when she asked why the jail was in its current state of conditions, she was told the insane do not feel heat or cold. This ignited Dorothea to take action; she visited jails and almshouses (where the mentally ill where typically housed) throughout Massachusetts and eventually submitted a document to the Massachusetts legislature about the nature of ill care provided to the mentally ill. Eventually, due to Dorothea's conviction and passion, the legislature agreed to pro-

Dorothea Dix was world-renowned for her work on behalf of the mentally ill and for her services as a nurse during the Civil War. (Library of Congress)

vide support and set aside funds for the expansion of a state hospital. She took her crusade to other states, persuading other state governments to take better care of and responsibility for their mentally ill citizens. In this way, she became the "voice for the mad." As a result of her work, by 1843 there were 13 mental hospitals in the country; by 1880, there were 123. She was also critical in establishing libraries in prisons and mental hospitals. Her work also changed the thinking of the time. While most people during this time believed that the mentally ill could not be treated, Dorothea understood that people could get better if their environmental conditions got better.

Dorothea, at the age of 59, then volunteered her services to the Union Army. In 1861, she was appointed the Union's Superintendent of Female Nurses, and was in charge of over 3,000 women nurses working in army hospitals. Under her leadership, the welfare of nurses, who oftentimes experienced brutal environments, had improved substantially, as did the soldiers that the nurses care for. Dorothea Dix died in 1887. Her skill and passion as a lobbyist made Dorothea Dix one of the most politically active women of her time.

## Jane Addams

Another famous woman during the late 1800s, Jane Addams, also advocated for the social welfare rights of people. She founded the Hull House, a settlement house created to assist immigrants to adjust to their new homeland. Many European immigrants lived in crowded, dirty tenements, with little money to improve their quality of life. The Hull House provided the necessary foundation for these families to have a safe, clean environment. The Hull House also provided child care, which allowed mothers to work, and for children to be off the streets. Addams also launched a campaign against sweatshops and for better working conditions for laborers, as well as for a stop to the exploitation of minors. Addams' efforts also led to the first juvenile court in the United States. In 1931, Addams was awarded the Nobel Peace Prize for her work on the Women's International League for Peace and Freedom.

A contemporary advocate for people's rights is Erin Brockovich. Erin began her consumer advocacy career working on a case involving Pacific Gas & Electric, and how they poisoned the water in a small town named Hinkley for over 30 years. Residents of Hinkley suffered health ailments ranging from chronic nosebleeds to cancer. Pacific Gas & Electric was forced to pay $333 million in damages to over 600 people, which is the largest toxic injury settlement in U.S. history. Erin continues to focus on cases involving environmental issues, such as the case in Cameron, Missouri, involving a hide tanning plant called Prime Tanning, and its consumers developing brain tumors because of sludge containing a toxic chemical called hexavalent chromium. She has another case in Kingston, Tennessee, where arsenic levels are more than 100 times than the acceptable level in a river near a massive coal ash spill. She continues to fight for the rights of consumers' health and to improve their quality of life.

*Melanie Horn Mallers*

**See also:** Activism; Public Safety; Social Services; Social Welfare

### References and Additional Readings

Brown, T. (1998). *Dorothea Dix: New England reformer.* Boston, MA: Harvard University Press.

Gollaher, D. (1995). *Voice for the mad: The life of Dorothea Dix.* New York: Free Press.

LeVert, S. (2013). The civil war society's "Encyclopedia of the Civil War." Retrieved from http://www.civilwarhome.com/dixbio.htm

Marshall, H. E. (1937). *Dorothea Dix, forgotten Samaritan.* Chapel Hill, NC: University of North Carolina Press.

Mass Moments. (2013). Retrieved from http://www.massmoments.org/moment.cfm?mid=96

The Social Welfare History Project. (2013). Dorothea Dix. Retrieved from http://www.socialwelfarehistory.com/people/dix-dorthea-lynde/

**DMA**. *See* Direct Marketing Association (DMA)

**Do Not Call Registry**. *See* National Do Not Call Registry

# Dodd–Frank Wall Street Reform and Consumer Protection Act

The Dodd–Frank Wall Street Reform and Consumer Protection Act of 2010 (S.3217), signed by President Barack Obama on July 21, 2010, is considered landmark consumer legislation. It is named for its patrons Senator Christopher Dodd (Connecticut) Senate Banking Committee Chair and Congressman Barney Frank (Massachusetts), House Financial Services Committee Chair. A new coalition, Americans for Financial Reform, consisting of over 250 national, state, and local organizations took the lead supporting this legislation for consumers. The key areas covered by the law include creation of the Consumer Financial Protection Bureau (CFPB), new oversight of credit rating agencies, and derivatives trading, investor protection, and systemic risk regulation.

## Consumer Financial Protection Bureau

Many consumers consider creation of the CFPB the most significant achievement of the law. For the first time, consumers have one independent agency whose primary focus is consumers rather than a plethora of agencies with primary focus on the marketplace or businesses and low priority on consumers. The CFPB is housed in the Federal Reserve; its director is appointed by the president and confirmed by the Senate. Like other financial agencies, the CFPB's budget is granted through a percentage of the Federal Reserve's total operating expenses and up to $200 million more through the appropriations process. Thus, like related agencies, its work cannot be completely undermined by appropriations decisions. However, the CFPB has a limitation not borne by others, its rules may be overridden by a new Financial Stability Oversight Council if it determines they threaten the safety, soundness, or stability of the U.S. financial system.

The CFPB's primary tasks are (1) educating consumers, (2) enforcing federal consumer financial laws, and (3) gathering information through studies. Its website has been designed to make it easy for consumers to obtain and share information with the CFPB. Through the "Know Before You Owe" effort it regularly seeks consumer responses to drafts of forms designed to help consumers understand financial products and make the best decisions possible. CFPB leadership is spending much of its time interacting with consumers all over the country by visiting localities and through the use of technology.

Specifically, the CFPB describes its responsibilities, as written on its website as: "Conduct rule-making, supervision, and enforcement for Federal consumer financial protection laws; Restrict unfair, deceptive, or abusive acts or practices; Take consumer complaints; Promote financial education; Research consumer behavior; Monitor financial markets for new risks to consumers; and Enforce laws that outlaw discrimination and other unfair treatment in consumer finance."

Advocates never considered small banks and financial institutions a target for the new regulations and did not expect Dodd–Frank to harm them. However, they won exclusion from CFPB examination and enforcement authority. Also, the CFPB was not given authority over automobile dealers that finance the vehicles they sell. However, the Federal Trade Commission utilized quicker and simpler processes for auto-financing-related-rulemaking so that such problems could be addressed.

After the 2007 financial meltdown, Elizabeth Warren, a law professor at Harvard, was appointed by President George W. Bush to lead the Congressional Oversight Panel and was given the task of managing the Troubled Asset Relief Program that rescued failing financial institutions. As her work continued into President Barack Obama's term, she suggested creation of the CFPB to help consumers. She was instrumental in passage of the Dodd–Frank legislation and widely favored to lead the new CFPB. However, Republicans in Congress, strongly supported by financial institutions, refused to approve her. Thus, President Obama made her a special advisor for the Financial Protection Bureau and she led the effort to establish it. The CFPB was not allowed to claim all of its power until it had a director so President Obama nominated Richard Cordray, a former Ohio state treasurer, in July 2011. When Congress still refused to act, Obama appointed Cordray during a Congressional recess.

The CFPB has taken major steps to fulfill its mission. However, its continued existence may be challenged depending upon the governmental politics, including future presidential and congressional elections.

### Credit Rating Agencies

Prior to the 2007 financial meltdown, credit-rating agencies were assumed to be neutral entities whose ratings were unbiased and based on complete and accurate facts. However, it became clear that in too many cases, they gave customers ratings they wanted. Dodd–Frank created an Office of Credit Ratings in the Securities and Exchange Commission (SEC) and new rules for oversight of credit-rating agencies. The SEC is studying the issue of customer shopping for the rating agency that will give it the best rating and conflict of interest rules will be developed and enforced in the future.

### Derivatives Trading

Because derivatives, financial tools whose value is based on another asset, have been traded on an unregulated market and many financial institutions now use them, they were of great concern as Dodd–Frank was developed. New third-party clearinghouses are now required and there will be more oversight.

### Investor Protection

The battle over whether to require strict fiduciary duty of financial advisors—meaning that they always put the consumer's interest first (not theirs)—was not settled under Dodd–Frank. The SEC continues to work on this issue. Investors can expect better disclosures on financial products, a new investor advocate position at the SEC, and strengthened SEC enforcement tools such as the ability to impose sanctions on individuals who violate rules even after they leave the entity where they committed the violation.

### Systemic Risk Regulation

In the future, there will be less risk that financial entities will be "too big to fail" and the amount of capital they are required to hold in relation to their debt will increase. The Federal Deposit Insurance Corporation has gained resolution authority to more quickly close banks that are endangering the economy. While the extensive audit of the Federal Reserve some parties wanted will not occur, the Government Accounting Office gained authority for some review.

*Irene Leech*

**See also:** Commodity Futures Trading Commission (CFTC); Congress; Consumer Financial Protection Bureau (CFPB); Dodd–Frank Wall Street Reform and Consumer Protection Act; Federal Deposit Insurance Commission (FDIC); Federal Trade Commission (FTC); Government Accountability Office (GAO); Investing Regulations; Securities and Exchange Commission (SEC)

**References and Additional Readings**

Americans for Financial Reform. (n.d.). Home. Retrieved from www.ourfinan cialsecurity.org

Consumer Financial Protection Bureau (n.d.). Home. Retrieved from www.cfpb.gov

Consumer Protection Act. (2010). *Public Law, 111,* 203.

Cook, R. A., & Musselman, M. (2010). Summary of the mortgage lending provisions in the Dodd–Frank Wall Street Reform and Consumer Protection Act. *Consumer Fin. LQ Rep., 64,* 231.

## Door-to-Door Sales

Door-to-door sellers were once a common feature in American life. Sellers of a variety of items, including encyclopedias, magazines, beauty supplies, cameras, and food made "cold calls" on families in an attempt to persuade them to purchase their wares. In 1968, Paul Rand Dixon, chairman of the Federal Trade Commission (FTC), estimated that the nation had about two million door-to-door salesmen. They were offering products of nearly 1,500 direct selling companies with multibillion-dollar sales.

Door-to-door sellers are rare today, probably because alternative personalized marketing methods, such as telemarketing and spam, are far less costly. Thus, the Bureau of Labor Statistics estimated that as of 2010, the country had fewer than 7,600 door-to-door sellers.

Beginning in the 1960s, consumer advocates argued that door-to-door sales should be subject to "cooling-off period" laws. These laws gave consumers time—typically, three days—to rescind a purchase made at the home. The first such law appears to have been enacted in England in the Hire-Purchase Act of 1964. Michigan was the first state in the United States to adopt such a law, but other states soon followed. Though Congress contemplated a door-to-door cooling-off law, it did not enact one. Instead, in 1972, the FTC promulgated a cooling-off period trade regulation rule for door-to-door sales (the FTC Rule), which continues in effect today, with amendments.

The FTC Rule applies to sales, leases, and rentals of consumer goods of services costing at least $25 and in which the seller solicits the sale personally and the agreement is made at a place other than the seller's place of business. It obliges sellers to furnish buyers with a notice of the right to cancel. The rule has several exceptions, including for transactions conducted entirely by mail or telephone; for certain emergencies; and if the buyer has both initiated the contact and invited the seller to visit the home to repair something or perform maintenance.

Advocates for cooling-off periods made several arguments for the laws. One was that consumers needed to be protected from so-called "hard sells." Advocates testified before the FTC that some sellers even resorted to fraud, claiming to be building inspectors, survey takers, or offering gifts to gain entry to the home. Consumer advocates also pointed out that in conventional sales situations, consumers choose to visit a brick-and-mortar establishment, but that door-to-door sellers selected the consumers to whom their sales pitches were addressed. Thus, these solicitors could target consumers who might be less well equipped to evaluate their products, as for example, when sellers of educational materials targeted poorly educated parents in the hope of selling them materials that were portrayed as helpful to their children, but in fact were not. Similarly, door-to-door sellers were thought to prey on the host's obligation to a guest.

Consumer advocates also wished to protect consumers from making impulse purchases that they might later regret; they believed that the three days would give such consumers an opportunity to back out of the sales. In addition, because consumers buying at their homes lacked the opportunity to comparison shop, consumer advocates hoped that the three days would enable them to compare prices of other sellers.

Industry representatives opposed cooling-off periods for a number of reasons. Some reported that they already had refund policies. Others reported that door-to-door sales generated few complaints and that the cooling-off periods were intended to fix a problem that did not exist. Some argued that the rules would destroy the door-to-door industry (while the industry is indeed smaller than it once was, it seems unlikely that the cooling-off periods caused that decline, though it may have contributed to it, as opposed to the economic factors mentioned earlier). Some critics complained that cooling-off periods would dilute individual responsibility for decisions, invite permissiveness, and undermine the law of contracts.

Little empirical evidence suggests that consumers take advantage of cooling-off periods. A 1969 study on the efficacy of a one-day cooling-off period found that the right to rescind benefits consumers very little. In this study, it was suggested that a longer period is unlikely to result in a significant impact on consumers.

In 1981, the FTC commissioned two studies of its then seven-year-old rescission rule for door-to-door sales. One of the studies surveyed consumers while the other queried businesses subject to the rule. The survey of consumers found that not one of the more than 1,400 respondents had used the cooling-off period to rescind in the previous year, though many had made purchases subject to the cooling-off rule during that time (the rule applies not just to door-to-door sales, but also to purchases in the buyer's workplace and at "product parties," so that many of the buyers had not actually bought anything from a door-to-door seller). The study noted, however, that few consumers became dissatisfied with their purchase within the three days.

In the second study the FTC commissioned, Walker Research, Inc. interviewed 112 executives of companies involved in door-to-door sales. Nearly a fifth said their customers had not cancelled contracts within the three days, while only two percent reported that the rule had increased the number of cancellations of their company's sales. Among those reporting cancellations within three days, the average cancellation rate was six percent. When asked whether the rule had imposed costs on them, 45 percent replied that it had not; 52 percent said it had. More than two-thirds of the respondents said that the rule had no effect on their company while 16 pecent found the rule harmful.

In short, the limited available evidence suggests that consumers rarely take advantage of the right to rescind. It thus appears that the rule has neither lived up to its sponsors' hopes nor caused the damage its opponents feared.

*Jeff Sovern*

**See also:** Cooling Off Rule; Federal Trade Commission (FTC)

### References and Additional Readings

Davis, G. E. (1981). Final report of an impact evaluation of the cooling-off period for door-to-door sales trade rule. Submitted to Bureau of Consumer Protection, Federal Trade Commission.

Department of Labor. (2012). Bureau of Labor Statistics, Occupational employment and wages. Retrieved from http://www.bls.gov/oes/current/oes419 091.htm

Federal Trade Commission. (1968). Hearings on S.1599, Before the Consumer Subcomm. of the Senate Comm. on Commerce, 90th Cong. 2d Sess. 14. Statement of Paul Rand Dixon, Chairman.

Federal Trade Commission. (1971). In re Public Hearing on a Proposed Trade Regulation Rule Concerning a Cooling-Off Period for Door-to-Door Sales Before the Federal Trade Commission.

Federal Trade Commission. (1972). Rule concerning cooling-off period for sales made at homes or at certain other locations, 16 C.F.R. § 429.0 et seq. Retrieved from http://www.law.cornell.edu/cfr/text/16/429

O.Net Online. (2010). Door-to-door sales workers, news and street vendors, and related workers. Retrieved from http://www.onetonline.org/link/sum mary/41-9091.00

Walker Research, Inc. (1981). Three-day cooling-off period trade rule evaluation study. Walker Research.

The Yale Law Journal. (1969). Notes and comments. A case study of the impact of consumer legislation: The elimination of negotiability and the cooling-off period. *Yale Law Journal, 78*, 618–661.

## DREAM Act: Development, Relief and Education for Alien Minors

More commonly known as the Federal DREAM Act the bipartisan proposal was first introduced in the Senate on August 1, 2001, by Senators Dick Durbin and Orin Hatch (Bill Summary & Status 107th Congress (2001–2002) S.1291). This legislation is intended to provide a path to legal residency and citizenship for children of parents who illegally entered the United States. Most of the eligible children were brought to the United States at a very young age and are required to have lived in the United States more than five years to qualify. Children in this category make up approximately 15 percent of undocumented immigrants in the United States. While these children were not born in the United States, they have received a majority of their primary and secondary school education in the United States. Due to the status of their parents, they have limited avenues through which to become citizens. Most of these children are not able to afford college, cannot obtain driver's licenses, and cannot work legally in the United States. While they can legally attend most colleges, they are not eligible for a majority of financial aid including federal and state financial assistances.

A potential waste of talent, the United States is at a loss economically when students who have been educated in U.S. schools and are eligible for college are not able to pursue a professional career and contribute to society. The United States estimates that approximately 65,000 undocumented children who have lived in the United States for five years or longer graduate from high school each year; only about 10 percent continue to higher education. Of these students, only about 18,000 undocumented students enrolled in postsecondary institutions in the United States. Supporters of the DREAM Act have argued that eligible students have an allegiance to the United States and hope for an opportunity to gain legal status so they can become contributing members of U.S. society. Research has indicated that students who often refer themselves as "dreamers" are highly motivated to succeed and have the potential of contributing to the increasing demands for an educated workforce. Under the most recent version of the DREAM Act proposed in 2010 to be eligible students must:

(a)   have entered the United States more than five years ago;

(b)   have entered the country at age 15 or younger;

(c)    be able to demonstrate good moral character;

(d)    graduated from a United States high school, or have obtained a GED, or have been accepted into an institution of higher education (i.e., college/university); and

(e)    be between the ages of 12 and 35 at the time of application.

If the DREAM Act passes, an undocumented person who meets the conditions mentioned earlier could be eligible to apply for the DREAM Act. If the person is approved and given conditional permanent residency, they must either enroll in a college or university to pursue a degree (associate's or bachelor's) or enlist in the U.S. military. Within six years and completion of at least two year of education or military service, and after 5½ years of the six years have passed, Legal Permanent Residency may be sought, followed by an application for U.S. citizenship. Individuals who have already completed at least two years of college education will still have to wait the 5½ years in order to apply for Legal Permanent Residency even though a degree is already obtained.

Some states like California have enacted similar legislation at the state level. While this type of legislation provides for financial assistance for eligible undocumented students it does not include provisions for a path to citizenship. Nonetheless this legislation will assist students who cannot afford to attend a college or university.

*Esiquio Ramos Uballe*

**See also:** Activism; Department of Education (ED); Discrimination; Family Educational Rights and Privacy Act (FERPA)

### References and Additional Readings

Around the Capital. (2011). California legislation: AB 131. Retrieved from http://www.aroundthecapitol.com/Bills/AB_131/20112012

Bill Summary & Status 107th Congress (2001–2002). S.1291.

Dream Resource Center. (2012). The Federal D.R.E.A.M Act. Retrieved from http://www.dreamresourcecenter.org/federal-dream-act.html

Gonzales, R. G. (2009). Young lives on hold: The college dreams of undocumented students. Retrieved from http://professionals.collegeboard.com/profdownload/young-lives-on-hold-college-board.pdf

## Drug Safety and Clinical Trials

Drug safety is clearly an important consumer safety and protection issue. The origins of the consumer movement in the United States and elsewhere were tied in large part to drug safety issues. Herrmann and Mayer described the U.S. consumer movement as occurring in three "eras." In the first era (the 1900s), an increasing incidence of addiction to patent medicines led to the Pure Food and Drug Act of 1906, and in the second era (the 1930s), the 1937 sulfa drug tragedy, in which 107 people died, led to the Food, Drug, and Cosmetic Act. In the third era of the consumer movement (the 1960s and 1970s), Frances Kelsey's refusal to give the U.S. Food and Drug Administration's (FDA) approval of thalidomide, a drug that resulted in birth defects among children outside the United States whose mothers had taken it, lowered political resistance to required drug testing.

Today, the FDA requires extensive clinical trials before drugs are approved for sale. After lengthy in-house research and development, which includes laboratory as well as animal studies, pharmaceutical companies submit their data along with an Investigational New Drug Application to the FDA for permission to take the testing to another level. A team of physicians, statisticians, chemists, pharmacologists, and other scientists in the FDA's Center for Drug Evaluation and Research (CDER) reviews the applications. Approval gives the company permission to proceed to clinical trials

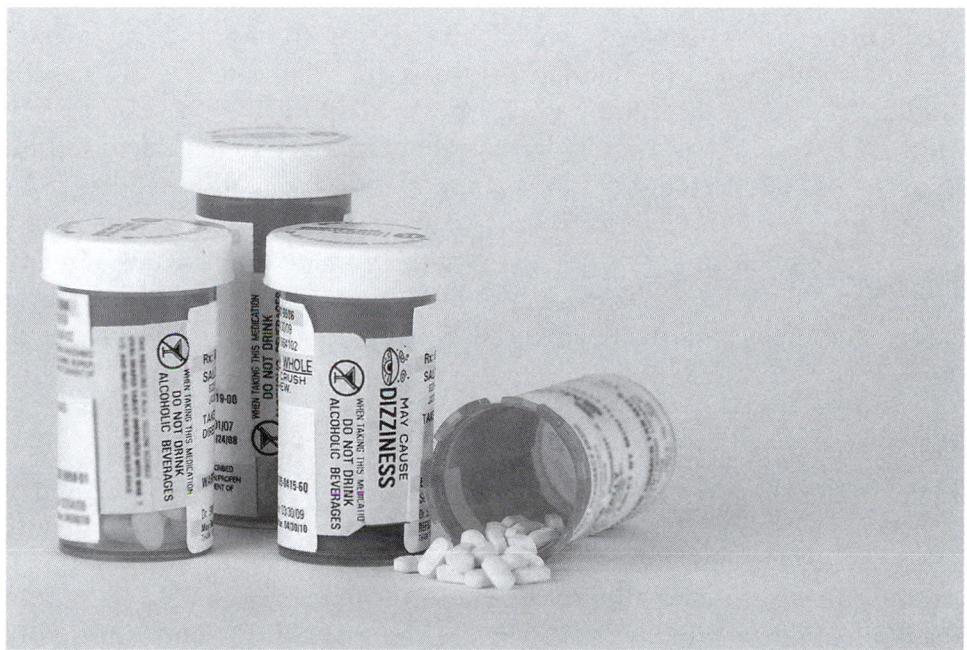

Among other things, the federal government regulates and oversees drug safety and clinical trials to provide assurances regarding efficacy of medications and generic equivalencies. (Sheli Spring Saldana/Dreamstime.com)

with humans. In Phase I of clinical trials, the objective is to identify any adverse reactions or side effects that occur when humans take the drug. A relatively small number of people (typically 20–80 people) participate in Phase I clinical trials, usually for a period of a few months. An estimated 70 percent of drugs "pass" the Phase I trials. In Phase II, the objective is to examine the drug's activity in the human body as well as its safety. A larger number of patients (100–300) participate for a longer period of time (six months to two years) in Phase II studies. Phase II studies often are randomized (patients assigned to the control group receive a placebo) and "blinded" (patients do not know if they are receiving the drug or a placebo). One estimate is that only about 30 percent of drugs "pass" both Phases I and II. Phase III testing involves even larger numbers (thousands) for longer periods of time (one to four years); the emphasis in Phase III testing is safety as well as a more thorough understanding of the drug's benefits and adverse effects. Once a drug successfully "passes" Phase III trials, the company can request FDA approval to market the drug; an estimated 70–90 percent of drugs that enter Phase III testing ultimately are approved.

FDA's drug-testing policy is not without criticism. Patient advocates as well as medical professionals have alternately criticized the FDA for delaying the introduction of new drugs to the market *and* for allowing companies to make new drugs available before they have been thoroughly tested. To address the first concern, in 1993, FDA began to permit companies to apply for permission to market drugs based on the outcome of Phase II clinical trials with the condition that postmarketing trials be conducted. However, several high-profile drug safety cases have called into question the FDA's ability to manage postmarket safety issues and to require companies to conduct and report postmarket trials. In particular, the Vioxx controversy made many people question how many other drugs, already approved for sale, also needed to be reevaluated. After the FDA approved it for sale, Vioxx, an arthritis medication, was found to increase heart risk and its manufacturer subsequently withdrew it from the market. In testimony before the U.S. Senate, Dr. David Graham, a reviewer for the FDA, called into question the safety of three other drugs that had already passed rigorous testing before receiving FDA approval.

Eight major problems with the current FDA system of assessing the safety of drugs have been identified by researchers. This includes FDA's inability to control postmarketing safety studies. Another problem focused on insufficient information about Adverse Drug Reactions (ADRs), primarily because the information comes largely from a voluntary reporting system rather than through clinical trials. Critics believe information from trials is limited because too many trials are short term and involve a small number of low-risk patients. Other problems are the use of subjective thresholds to determine when action is required in response to ADRs; internal conflicts of interest within the FDA because FDA's CEDR both reviews and approves drugs *and* takes regulatory actions when safety issues emerge against drugs it previously approved; the lack of direct legal authority to hold drug companies accountable for actions; FDA's dependence on pharmaceutical industry funding paid as "user fees" to the agency; and a shortage of drug safety and public health expertise on FDA's advisory committees. The authors' recommendations for improvements ranged from expanding FDA's legal authority, including giving the agency the authority to suspend marketing of a drug and to require changes to a drug label, including warnings; to following the path of other countries by having a "conditional approval" policy for new drugs; to increasing the FDA's resources for improvement of the ADR reporting system and establishment of a network of drug safety centers across the United States. Another recommendation addressed the composition of FDA's advisory committees that review drug applications. Currently, the composition of the committee is mostly subspecialty experts, who often receive significant financial support from pharmaceutical companies. The authors recommended that at least one-half of each committee should be composed of experts with diverse perspectives who can be more objective and balanced in their recommendations.

While many of the problems cited earlier continue, a few have been addressed. The FDA Amendments Act of 2007 created the Drug Safety Oversight Board that advises FDA's CDER on emerging drug safety issues. DrugWatch.com, created in 2009, which describes itself as "the Internet's chief resource about a variety of medications including prescriptions, over-the-counter drugs and certain medications no longer in use," makes additional information about drug safety available to consumers. Other issues, including efforts to balance safety with making drugs available when patients need them and balancing objectivity with the expertise needed by members of FDA advisory committees continue to seek long-term solutions.

*Brenda J. Cude*

**See also:** Food and Drug Administration (FDA); Food, Drug and Cosmetic Act (FD&C Act); Wiley, Harvey

### References and Additional Readings

Bouchie, A. (2003). Industry reneges on postmarketing trial commitments. *Nature Biotechnology. 21*, 718.

Drug Watch. (2010). About us. Retrieved from http://www.drugwatch.com/about.php

Food and Drug Administration. (2010). Drug Safety Oversight Board. Retrieved from http://www.fda.gov/AboutFDA/CentersOffices/OfficeofMedicalProd uctsandTobacco/CDER/ucm082129.htm

Furberg, C. D., Levin, A. A., Gross, P. A., Shapiro, R., & Strom, B. L. (2006). The FDA and drug safety: A proposal for sweeping changes. *Archives of Internal Medicine, 166*, 1938–1942.

Genzyme. (n.d.). An introduction to the clinical research process. Retrieved from http://www.genzyme.com/research/clinical_trials/trialprocess.asp

Government Accountability Office. (2007). Drug safety: FDA needs to further address shortcomings in its postmarket decision-making process. Bibliogov Project

Herrmann, R. O., & Mayer, R. N. (1997). U.S. consumer movement: History and dynamics. *Encyclopedia of the Consumer Movement*, 584–601.

## Durable Power of Attorney

When handling one's own affairs becomes difficult or impossible, a power of attorney (POA) can be helpful. A POA provides written authorization for a trusted person called an agent (also attorney-in-fact) to handle the creator's (principal's) financial, health, and other legal affairs either temporarily or permanently starting immediately or when the principal becomes unable to make such decisions. Power of attorney designations are an important part of an estate plan, and should be put in place to ensure that personal affairs are managed by a trustworthy representative who can act on the consumer's behalf with personal values and best interest in mind. A special power of attorney can focus on a specific responsibility. Consumers have the ability to update or change the power of attorney designations as needs change over time. For example, power of attorney could be assigned to a spouse during early years, but with age may be better designated to an adult child or an attorney.

A POA document is commonly nondurable, ending after a specified time or when a responsibility is completed. Unless the document is designated, a springing durable power of attorney (DPA), which becomes effective when a certain event (usually incapacity) occurs, a DPA document becomes effective when the principal signs it; it remains in effect until the principal changes, it is revoked, or the principal dies. The document can focus on health care or finances, but it often includes both.

DPA was enacted primarily in response to estate-planning lawyers who felt there should be an effective and flexible alternative to a court-appointed guardian that involves a time-consuming, expensive, and an embarrassing process of declaring the principal legally incompetent. Before 1954 POA was based on the principle of agency found in common

## Examples of Types of Power of Attorney
## Financial Power of Attorney

A financial power of attorney gives the agent decision-making authority in terms of conducting business and managing finances. When choosing your financial power of attorney, consider your choices: a spouse, another relative or close friend, or perhaps a hired professional such as an accountant or an attorney. It is recommended that the consumer appoint an alternate agent as well, just in case the first chosen representative is unable to act when the need arises. Whomever is chosen should be trustworthy, able to manage finances competently, and willing to take on the role, as needed.

The terms used in a financial power of attorney document can grant full or limited powers to the agent depending on personal circumstances and current or foreseen needs. Broad terms may authorize the agent to handle your affairs however he or she sees fit, or the terms can be very specific in the powers assigned. Some financial powers might include abilities to: file and sign tax returns; open or close accounts in your name; buy, sell, rent or manage your property; give gifts, make donations or collect debts owed to you; sign or terminate contracts; and manage cash flow, budgets, bills, and any other business transactions. Terms should also define when the power of attorney goes into effect. While some are effective immediately, others require written certification from a physician declaring that the principal is incompetent, and still others may further define the conditions of effectiveness timeframes around the agent's powers. The agent's powers terminate at the time of the principal's death. For decisions or business that needs to be conducted after death, a will should appoint an executor of the estate.

## Healthcare Power of Attorney

Similar to a financial power of attorney, a consumer can also designate a person to be a healthcare agent to make health care decisions on the consumer's behalf if the consumer is unable to speak for him or herself. It is also critical to select someone that will empower the choices of the consumer, irrespective of the health care agent's personal views or wishes. Once the healthcare power of attorney document is executed and delivered to the agent, it is deemed valid and effective unless it contains a termination date, it is revoked, or the consumer (principal) becomes competent. The agent's decision making power may also be specified. Given that consumers have a right to take an active role in their health care, they are encouraged to also have a living will, as well as advanced directives, which are legal documents specifying one's wishes for end-of-life care.

law, which is the ancient English law based on societal customs recognized and enforced by court decisions. This case law, differentiated from legislative enactments, governed England and the American colonies before the American Revolution. This early POA terminated if the principals became incapacitated because they would not be able to monitor their agents and intervene if agents abused their authority. Therefore, it was used for specific and temporary purposes such as recuperation periods or to conduct business when the principal was not physically available to sign documents.

Because POA was useless as a long-term planning instrument for elders, the Model Special Power of Attorney for Small Property Interests Act of 1964 was passed, defining POA as a relatively inexpensive alternative to guardianship for estates under a certain value. It required a judge to witness the principal's signature, an estate asset inventory, an annual income statement, and an accounting. The POA document had to be filed and recorded.

In 1969, the Uniform Probate Code introduced the principle of durability, replacing the common law rule. Unlike the initial POA, a Durable Power of Attorney (DPOA or DPA) remains valid even if the principal loses the legal capacity, making it useful for planning for possible incapacity. Because DPAs are used to enable an agent to act on behalf of an incapacitated principal, they usually are written very broadly, giving the agent extensive authority. It was assumed that risks associated with a POA were reduced because the principal's assets were small and family members (most likely appointed as agents) would be more trustworthy than mere acquaintances or those without a relationship to the principal.

Therefore, this 1969 version removed the provisions limiting the POA to small estates and 1984 and 1987 revisions also removed the agent accounting requirement (liability). Between the 1960s and 1990s, the focus was on developing the POA into a convenient estate planning tool. By 1984 every state had adopted DPA laws, helping to make it very popular. None of these early versions of the POA allowed third parties such as banks, attorneys, social service professionals, and family members to draw attention to agent abuse.

These changes loosening the requirements seem to parallel increasing POA financial exploitation since lack of oversight and broadly written powers make it very easy for attorneys-in-fact to abuse their authority. Because exploitation is difficult to prove and to prosecute, DPA has been called a "license to steal" despite the legal requirement to act as a fiduciary. This means the agent is "required to act in a trustworthy manner and to make decisions that are in the principal's best interest or that are consistent with decisions that the principal made for himself or herself before losing decision-making capacity" (Stiegel, 2008, 2).

Clearly the POA was being used to facilitate financial exploitation. Consequently by the 1990s states began to implement reforms. The model Uniform Power of Attorney Act of 2006 included 21 provisions intended to prevent financial exploitation, but not healthcare powers of attorney, already addressed in the Uniform Health-Care Decisions Act of 1993. The 2006 act was designed to address three primary problems: (1) breadth of authority an agent has over the principal's assets, (2) lack of third-party oversight, and (3) lack of legal standards and clarity related to an agent's conduct. For these provisions to apply in a particular state, that state's legislature must adopt all or part of the act into law.

Others have argued the following relatively inexpensive reforms are needed that better educate principals and agents; discourage agent fraud; protect third parties (such as lay persons, financial institutions, and healthcare professionals), and require them to prevent apparent fraud; and create additional redress for victims. She also suggested mandating that agents keep receipts, document costs, and provide accounting when demanded by a principal, third party, or a relevant government agency; requiring medical professionals to assess an elder's competence before signing a POA to prevent undue influence; reinstating requirements that POA documents be signed in front of a judge and then recorded; and financial institutions holding an elder's assets be made mandatory reporters.

Additional improvements came in the Elder Justice Act, part of the 2010 Affordable Health Care Act, that previously had been proposed unsuccessfully. It now provides funding for research on elder financial exploitation and additional caseworkers for Adult Protective Services to investigate reported cases. The Affordable Health Care Act also includes the Patient Safety and Abuse Prevention Act, establishing a national criminal background check system for nursing home and long-term-care facility employees, who sometimes become exploitive POA agents.

Despite these attempts to reduce abuse, the ongoing lack of oversight or supervision of a POA agent when the principal becomes incapacitated and the extensive powers granted, this crime of theft and other misuses of authority are difficult to prove and prosecute. It is easy for vulnerable persons to be manipulated and exploited for the benefit of the agent, instead of themselves.

*Virginia B. Vincenti*

**See also:** Administration on Aging (AoA); Durable Power of Attorney; Estate Planning; Health and Healthcare; Public Safety; Social Services

**References and Additional Readings**

Dessin, C. L. (1996). Acting as agent under a financial durable power of attorney: An unscripted role. *Nebraska Law Review 75*, 574.

Dessin, C. L. (1999). Financial abuse of the elderly. *Idaho Law Review, 36*, 203.

Gallo, N. R. (2009). *Elder Law.* Clifton Park, NY: Delmar.

Ramnarace, C. (March 25, 2010). Congress passes Elder Justice Act. *AARP Bulletin.* Retrieved from http://www.aarp.org/politics-society/advocacy/info-03-2010/congress_passes_elder_justice_act.html

Steigel, L. A. (2008). Durable power of attorney abuse: It's a crime too: A National Center on Elder Abuse1 fact sheet for criminal justice professionals. American Bar Association Commission on Law and Aging. Retrieved from http://www.ncea.aoa.gov/ncearoot/main_site/pdf/publication/DurablePowerOfAttorneyAbuseFactSheet_CriminalJusticeProfessionals.pdf

Vu-Dinh, K. (2010). Reforming power of attorney law to protect Alaskan elders from financial exploitation. *Alaska Law Review, 27*(1), 1–25.

# E

## Environmental Protection Agency (EPA)

The U.S. Environmental Protection Agency (EPA) is a single, independent agency of the federal government of the United States. It is charged with protecting human health and safeguarding the environment, by writing and enforcing regulations based upon laws passed by the U.S. Congress. The agency was signed into law on December 2, 1970, by President Richard Nixon.

EPA is headquartered in Washington, D.C., under the direction of an administrator who is appointed by the U.S. president and approved by the Senate. Approximately 18,000 people are employed nationwide by EPA in DC program offices, and regional offices, and laboratories. Its staff includes engineers, scientists, and specialists in the field of environmental protection.

The agency is responsible for implementing and enforcing environmental statutes. Its duties include regulating and enforcing environmental laws, setting and monitoring standards for pollutants, administering environmental permitting programs, and providing oversight of state environmental laws. EPA enforcement powers include fines, sanctions, and criminal prosecution. The EPA has 12 national offices (see Table 20) and 10 regional offices (see Table 21), with each regional office being responsible for implementing the agency's programs within its region, except those programs that have been specifically delegated to the states, U.S. territories, or tribal authorities.

In 2011, there were seven key themes as the focus of the work of EPA as identified by Lisa Jackson, EPA administrator:

- *Taking action on climate change:* Climate change affects all parts of EPA's core mission to protect air and water quality. EPA has created greenhouse gas reduction initiatives and clean energy and climate legislation through the Clean Air Act, and uses ENERGY STAR to expand cost-saving energy conservation and efficiency programs.
- *Improving air quality:* Improved monitoring, permitting, and enforcement are critical for air quality improvement. With U.S. communities

facing serious health and environmental challenges from air pollution, EPA has proposed stronger ambient air quality standards for air toxics and pollutants to help Americans breathe easier and live healthier lives.

- *Assuring the safety of chemicals:* The Toxic Substances Control Act needs to be modernized to assure the safety of chemicals in our products, our environment, and our bodies. EPA is shifting its focus to address high-concern chemicals and filling data gaps on widely produced chemicals in commerce. Using a streamlined Integrated Risk Information System, EPA will work toward rigorous, peer-reviewed health assessments on dioxins, arsenic, formaldehyde, TCE, and other substances of concern.

- *Cleaning up our communities:* To clean up U.S. communities, EPA accelerated its superfund program to confront local environmental challenges through stricter rules and stronger partnerships with stakeholders affected by cleanup activities. The Brownsfield program is used to spur environmental cleanups and to create jobs in disadvantaged communities.

- *Protecting America's waters:* EPA water quality and enforcement programs face complex challenges, from nutrient loadings and storm water runoff to invasive species and drinking water contaminants. These challenges demand both traditional and innovative strategies. Measures are being initiated to address stronger water quality protection and greater compliance with the Clean Water Act.

- *Expanding the conversation on environmentalism and working for environmental justice:* Environmental justice principles are to be included in all EPA decisions to safeguard the health of everyone in the United States, especially children.

- *Building strong state and tribal partnerships:* EPA is committed to bolstering state and tribal efforts and to building stronger partnerships to ensure that EPA programs are consistently delivered nationwide.

**Table 20** National Offices of the EPA

- Office of Administration and Resources Management (OARM)
- Office of Air and Radiation (OAR)
- Office of Chemical Safety & Pollution Prevention (OCSPP)
- Office of the Chief Financial Officer (OCFO)
- Office of Enforcement and Compliance Assurance (OECA)

*(Continued)*

**Table 20** *(Continued)*

- Office of Environmental Information (OEI)
- Office of General Counsel (OGC)
- Office of Inspector General (OIG)
- Office of International and Tribal Affairs (OITA)
- Office of Research and Development (ORD)
- Office of Solid Waste and Emergency Response (OSWER)
- Office of Water (OW)

**Table 21**  Regional Offices of the EPA

- Region 1 (Boston) includes Connecticut, Maine, Massachusetts, New Hampshire, Rhode Island, Vermont, and 10 tribal nations
- Region 2 (New York City) includes New Jersey, New York, Puerto Rico, U.S. Virgin Islands, and eight tribal nations
- Region 3 (Philadelphia) includes Delaware, District of Columbia, Maryland, Pennsylvania, Virginia, and West Virginia
- Region 4 (Atlanta) includes Alabama, Florida, Georgia, Kentucky, Mississippi, North Carolina, South Carolina, Tennessee, and six tribes
- Region 5 (Chicago) includes Illinois, Indiana, Michigan, Minnesota, Ohio, Wisconsin, and 35 tribes
- Region 6 (Dallas) includes Arkansas, Louisiana, New Mexico, Oklahoma, Texas, and 66 tribes
- Region 7 (Kansas City) includes Iowa, Kansas, Missouri, Nebraska, and nine tribal nations
- Region 8 (Denver) includes Colorado, Montana, North Dakota, South Dakota, Utah, Wyoming, and 27 tribal nations
- Region 9 (San Francisco) includes Arizona, California, Hawaii, Nevada, Pacific Islands, and 147 tribes
- Region 10 (Seattle) includes Alaska, Idaho, Oregon, Washington, and 271 native tribes

### Environmental Laws and Executive Orders (EOs)

Many laws serve as a foundation for EPA's protection of public health and the environment. EPA is authorized by Congress and Presidential Executive Orders (EOs) to write regulations to implement environmental laws. Regulations are mandatory requirements that can apply to individuals, businesses, nonprofit institutions, local, and state governments, and others. As shown in Table 22, the following are among the more than 40 laws and EOs that EPA is charged with administering to help to protect human health and the environment.

**Table 22** EPA Oversight

- Clean Air Act (CAA)
- Clean Water Act (CWA)
- Comprehensive Environmental Response, Compensation, and Liability Act (CERCLA, or Superfund)
- Emergency Planning and Community Right-to-Know Act (EPCRA)
- Endangered Species Act (ESA)
- Energy Independence and Security Act (EISA)
- EO 13045: Protection of Children From Environmental Health Risks and Safety Risks
- EO 13175: Consultation and Coordination with Indian Tribal Governments
- Federal Insecticide, Fungicide, and Rodenticide Act (FIFRA)
- Food Quality Protection Act (FQPA)
- National Environmental Policy Act (NEPA)
- Occupational Safety and Health (OSHA)
- Pollution Prevention Act (PPA)
- Privacy Act
- Resource Conservation and Recovery Act (RCRA)
- Safe Drinking Water Act (SDWA)
- Shore Protection Act (SPA)
- Toxic Substances Control Act (TSCA)

As an example, under the Clean Air Act (CAA), the EPA is supposed to review the national air quality standards for six major air pollutants every five years: ground-level ozone, particulates, sulfur dioxide, nitrogen oxides, carbon monoxide, and lead.

### EPA Controversies

Some of the many controversies about the EPA are as follows:

- Air quality standards: According to Hogue (2006), the Bush Administration altered the EPA process for reviewing and setting health-based air quality standards. There is ongoing criticism that the new process will diminish the role of agency scientists in favor of political influences.
- Fuel economy: In 2007, the state of California was denied the right to raise fuel economy standards for new cars (*LA Times*, 2007). EPA Administrator Stephen Johnson claimed that the EPA was working on its own standards, but the move was highly criticized as an attempt to

shield the auto industry by setting lower standards at the federal level that would then preempt state laws.

- Global warming: EPA has been lax in regulating global warming and has established few, if any, national mandatory global-warming regulations.

- Greenhouse gas emissions: EPA regulates greenhouse gases (GHGs) from mobile and stationary sources of air pollution under the CAA, but controversy exists over the degree to which these regulations are effective.

- Mercury emissions: In 2005, several states sued EPA, contending that EPA's regulation of mercury emissions did not follow the CAA, and that the regulations were influenced by top political appointees (Vedantam, 2005). The EPA rule allows illegal exemptions and pollution credit trading to bypass required mercury emission standards.

- Airborne particulates: Due to criticisms, EPA modified its national regulation of airborne particulate standards, regulations, and enforcement (states currently bear this responsibility). In 2006, EPA strengthened the air quality standards for particle pollution (EPA, 2006).

- Environmental justice: EPA has no comprehensive strategic plan or standards for environmental justice in its daily operations, and is lax in enforcing its Superfund program (O'Neil, 2007).

## Examples of EPA Involvement

### Everglades Restoration

The Florida Everglades restoration is part of the Water Resources Development Act and the Clean Water Act. Because the Everglades restoration was not meeting the requirements of either Act, EPA demanded in 2010 that the South Florida Water Management District (the state agency responsible for construction in the Everglades) to build new storm water treatment projects. In April 2011, Judge Gold (Florida) entered an order giving EPA the authority to take over control of Florida's water quality permitting program if Florida continued to delay implementing needed improvements. EPA has specifically directed that the South Florida Water Management District (SFWMD) construct 42,000 acres of Stormwater Treatment Areas (STAs). EPA outlined the steps to reach this goal as follows: (1) complete the purchase of land from U.S. Sugar Corporation and begin seeking additional land acquisition in the Everglades Agricultural Area; (2) either construct STAs on land acquired from U.S. Sugar Corporation or initiate a trade for other land on which STAs will be built; and

(3) utilize the 16,000 acres of formerly A-1 Reservoir land to construct a large STA.

### Genetically Modified (GM) Crops

Since the 1980s, U.S. agriculture has adopted genetically modified (GM) crops for food (e.g., corn and soybeans) and fiber (cotton). In 2006, an estimated 10.3 million farmers worldwide grew GM crops in 22 countries, with the United States being the world leader at 54.6 million hectares. In 2008, 92 percent of all soybeans, 86 percent of all cotton, and 80 percent of all corn grown in the United States were GM varieties. There is considerable global controversy concerning the public health and environmental safety of growing and consuming GM crops. The controversy surrounds mainly food crops. For example, even though the United States has adopted GM soybeans, the adoption of GM wheat is still on hold. There is added pressure to adopt GM wheat in view of rising food prices and extreme famine in parts of the world, such as Africa. The U.S. regulatory framework is founded on the concept of substantial equivalence in which agricultural products produced using biotechnology do not have greater risks than do agricultural products grown without using biotechnology. Moeller and Sligh (2004, 8–9) discuss Federal agencies involved in GM regulation:

> Federal regulation of GM crops involves primarily three federal agencies: the United States Department of Agriculture (USDA), the Environmental Protection Agency (EPA), and the Food and Drug Administration (FDA), with each agency having regulatory authority over different parts of the development, production, and marketing of genetically modified organisms (GMOs). Sometimes these agencies' authorities overlap, and sometimes there are gaps in federal regulatory authority, including regulation of what happens after GMOs are marketed . . . EPA has the authority to regulate pesticides under the Federal Insecticide, Fungicide, and Rodenticide Act (FIFRA).
>
> Under FIFRA, EPA regulates GMOs containing pesticides to ensure that they do not harm the environment by requiring GMO developers to obtain registration of their pesticide-containing products after EPA has determined that a pesticide is not "unreasonably" harmful to the environment. EPA also sets tolerance levels for pesticides that end up as residues in foods, which includes some GM crops since pesticides are incorporated into the seeds. In practice EPA almost always issues exemptions from pesticide tolerance for GMOs. (Moeller and Sligh, 2004, 9)

## Benefits and Costs of the CAA

Section 812 of the CAA Amendments of 1990 requires EPA to periodically assess the effect of the CAA on the public health, the economy, and the environment in the United States, and to report its findings to the U.S. Congress (EPA, 1999). The first report, which covered the period 1970–1990 but not the CAA amendments of 1990, was published in 1999. EPA (1999) results showed that the nation's investment in clean air greatly benefited public health and environmental quality. The addition of the CAA Amendments of 1990 helped improve the nation's air quality through implementing stricter requirements, revamping the hazardous air pollutant regulatory program, streamlining permitting requirements, and introducing new programs for the control of acid rain precursors and stratospheric-ozone-depleting substances (EPA, 1999). EPA's study was based on the improvements made by the CAA Amendments of 1990. EPA estimates included air pollutant emissions in 1990, 2000, and 2010; the cost of emissions reductions arising from the CAA Amendments of 1990; and the economic value of cleaner air (EPA, 1999). The EPA concluded that the net benefit (benefits minus costs) over the entire 1990–2010 period of the additional criteria pollutant control programs was $510 billion with the monetizable benefits exceeding the direct compliance costs by four to one (EPA, 1999). EPA recognizes the controversies that persist regarding model choices and valuation paradigms, and it stresses the new for new and continued research efforts (EPA, 1999).

## Costly Benefits

Some studies are critical of EPA's findings on environmental issues. For example, EPA's positive net benefit assessment of its arsenic rule that reduced the maximum allowable level of arsenic in drinking water has been called into question (Burnett and Hahn, 2001). While the Safe Drinking Water Act, as amended in 1996, leaves a certain amount of discretion to EPA when setting arsenic standards, the Act does instruct EPA to use economic analysis to choose the standard (Burnett and Hahn, 2001). Burnett and Hahn argue that EPA's cost-benefit analysis was flawed as it did not discount the value of the benefits in light of the lag time between the rule's implementation and the time in which the benefits would begin to emerge.

According to Burnett and Hahn, in many cases, drinking water issues are not national in scope because most of the costs and benefits are borne by local communities. Therefore, EPA should play a limited role by providing information on the risks and benefits of having different chemicals in drinking water and applying different control strategies (Burnett and

Hahn, 2001). "The task of setting drinking water standards could be left to either the states or municipalities" (597).

## Conclusions

The many issues with which EPA has to deal (e.g., clean water and air) are by their very nature controversial. Often, there is disagreement among scientists over environmental issues and their solutions (e.g., the European Union is much more stringent on the adoption of GM foods than is the United States). In the context of rent-seeking behavior by special interests, politics instead of science is often used as the basis for decision-making. When science is used in benefit-cost analysis, it is surrounded by controversy. This led to the creation in the United States of the Benefit-Cost Society, founded in 2007, to strengthen an agreed upon benefit-cost framework. Hopefully, this will help the much needed future work to be carried out by EPA. As Lewis (1988) states:

> The American people are as firmly committed as ever to the fulfillment of EPA's public health and environmental goals. Unfortunately, in many cases, the public's evaluation of what most needs fixing—an opinion EPA must under law solicit and consider—does not always square with expert scientific analyses of the most pressing dangers confronting the health of the nation's citizens and their natural environment. As a result, controversy continues over the appropriate direction and scale of EPA's future regulatory mission . . . .
>
> Ingenious adaptation to administrative challenges will become ever more imperative in the years ahead. EPA's legally assigned tasks have always seemed to dwarf its resources. As the nation's lawmakers strive to resolve the problem of the deficit, EPA managers will have to make sure they and their co-workers learn new ways to improve their effectiveness as regulators.

## Air Quality: An EPA–Consumer Concern

Water quality can be affected by airborne pollutants that oftentimes are deposited back into land and water bodies. Two major contributors of airborne pollutants are human and natural sources. Atmospheric pollutants that can contaminate water bodies include nitrogen compounds, sulfur compounds, mercury, pesticides, and other toxics.

Air quality, too, can be contaminated by both human and natural processes. The combustion of fossil fuels from power generation, the fossil fuels from transportation, and incineration of waste are human sources that contribute to poor air quality. Natural sources that release pollutants and affect our quality of air include volcanoes and forest fires.

*Source:* U.S. Environmental Protection Agency. (March 6, 2012). Air pollution and water quality. Retrieved from http://water.epa.gov/

*Andrew Schmitz*

**See also:** Centers for Disease Control and Prevention (CDC); Department of Agriculture (USDA); Food and Drug Administration (FDA); Organic Foods

## References and Additional Readings

Burnett, J.K., & Hahn, R.W. (2001). A costly benefit: Economic analysis does not support EPA's new arsenic rule. *Regulation, 24,* 44–49.

EPA. (1999). Executive summary. In *The benefits and costs of the Clean Air Act, 1999 to 2010: EPA Report to Congress.* United States Environmental Protection Agency, Washington, DC (November). Reprinted in EPA, 2008, *Applied benefit-cost analysis,* edited by A. Schmitz and R.O. Zerbe Jr., 399–404, Cheltenham, UK: Elgar Publishing.

EPA. (2006). PM standards revision. Retrieved from http://www.epa.gov/oar/particlepollution/naaqsrev.2006.html.

EPA. (2010). Executive summary of amended determination concerning Everglades restoration. Retrieved from http://www.epa.gov/region4/water/wqs/documents/1_AD_final_version_09_03_10.pdf

EPA. (2013). Retrieved from http://www.epa.gov

Hogue, C. (2006). Change in the air. *Chemical and Engineering News,* 84(51), 15.

Lewis, J. (2008). Looking backward: A historical perspective on environmental regulations. *EPA Journal.* Retrieved from http://www.epa.gov/aboutepa/history/topics/regulate/o1.html.

Moeller, D.R., & Sligh, M. (2004). Farmers' guide to GMOs. Famer's Legal Action Group, St. Paul, MN and Rural Advancement Foundation International, Pittsboro, NC. Retrieved from http://www.rafiusa.org/pubs/Farmers_Guide_to_GMOs.pdf.

Moss, C.B., Schmitz, A., & Schmitz, T.G. (2006). First generation genetically modified organisms in agriculture. *Journal of Public Affairs,* 6(1), 46–57.

O'Neil, S. (2007). Superfund: Evaluating the impact of Executive Order 12898. *Environmental Health Perspectives,* 115(7), 1087–1093.

Schmitz, A., Kennedy, P.L., & Hill-Gabriel, J. (2011). Restoring the Florida Everglades: Benefits, costs, and legal challenges surrounding the purchase of U.S.

Sugar Corporation land. FRED Working Paper, Food and Resource Economics Department, University of Florida, Gainesville, FL (July).

Schmitz, A., Moss, C. B., Schmitz, T. G., Furtan, H. W., & Schmitz, H. C. (2010). *Agricultural policy, agribusiness, and rent-seeking behavior* (2nd ed.). Toronto: University of Toronto Press.

Simon, R., & Wilson, J. (2007). EPA denies California's right to mandate emissions. *LA Times*, December 20.

Vedantam, S. (2005). EPA inspector finds mercury proposal tainted. *Washington Post*, February 4, A04.

## Equal Credit Opportunity Act

Enacted in 1974, the Equal Credit Opportunity Act, known also as Regulation B, is intended to prevent credit discrimination against consumers based on race, color, religion, national origin, sex, marital status, or age; regardless of whether all or part of the applicant's income source is from a public assistance program; and even if the consumer, acting in good faith, has exercised any right under the Consumer Credit Protection Act. The Consumer Credit Protection Act supports government's desire for consumers to be informed of their use of credit. Discrimination specifically targeting women, elderly, and religious and racial minorities prompted the need for equal credit regulations. Responsibility for implementation of this act was initially under the jurisdiction of the Federal Reserve Board but the authority was transferred to the Consumer Finance Protection Bureau with the passage of the Dodd–Frank Wall Street Reform and Consumer Protection Act of 2010.

All financial institutions that are in the business of lending money to consumers are responsible for upholding the Equal Credit Opportunity Act. These institutions include banks, small loan and finance companies, retail and department stores, credit card companies, credit unions, and real estate brokers who arrange financing. Anyone who participates in the decision to lend credit, including setting terms, referring applicants to creditors, selecting creditors, or assigning and/or transferring credit are to comply with Regulation B. For consumers, discrimination should not occur during any aspect of acquiring and using credit, such as setting the terms of the loan (interest rates, length of loan, payment period, calculation of interest charges) receiving an extension of credit, reapplication for credit, loan modifications, or deferring debt payments. Advertising and promotions presented either orally or in written by a financial institution describing terms of a credit service that would discourage prospective applications from applying are also prohibited through the Equal Credit Opportunity Act. Additionally, applicants must receive in writing the terms and conditions of either approval or denial of the credit application within 30 days of the decision.

The Equal Credit Opportunity Act has two principal theories of liability which are disparate treatment and disparate impact. Disparate treatment is intentional discrimination of an individual who has a disability or belongs to a group based on age, ethnicity, race, or sex. The creditor is liable for discrimination if treatment is considered to prohibit the consumer based on the group membership or classification from being considered for acquisition of the credit. Disparate impact is using information other than determinants of credit worthiness to assess eligibility for the credit. For example, marital status, number of children, or type of employment is information that is not needed to determine credit worthiness. Information requested on a credit application that may classify a consumer in a distinguishable group cannot be used to determine credit worthiness.

Credit and terms of the credit should be equally available for all consumers who are considered to be creditworthy. Financial institutions or creditors need to assess the creditworthiness of a consumer who is applying for the credit without relying on discriminatory or prejudicial biases. A creditworthy individual has an acceptable or satisfactory credit rating and can take out loans or obtain credit. Additional characteristics that bolster creditworthiness are earning power, a record of debt repayment, or a history of being a responsible borrower. These characteristics are determined based on information provided by the applicant through sources such as furnished credit information from other credit accounts, credit reports, and bank information.

Creditors need to carefully balance the need to acquire enough information to make an informed decision in regard to granting credit and with the need to respect applicants and refrain from unnecessary discrimination. As previously stated, creditors cannot use information related to race, color, religion, national origin, marital status, or sex to determine credit worthiness to not only grant the credit but to also set the terms of the credit. It is likely the information may be observed or inadvertently learned by the creditor when meeting with a potential applicant. The creditor needs to act objectively and use only the applicant information that signifies credit worthiness and not be swayed by an applicant's mannerism, speech, dress, or personal possessions. The process to determine credit worthiness needs to be consistent for all applicants.

Spousal information, marital status, joint credit, alimony, child support, and residency status can be obtained through the application process and used under certain circumstances to assess credit worthiness. Spousal information can be requested when the nonapplicant spouse will be a permitted user of the account, the spouse will be contractually liable for the account, spousal income will be used to repay the credit, the applicant lives in a community property state, or the applicant is relying on alimony, child support, or separate maintenance income as a basis to secure the credit. In assessing marital status, only the terms "married," "unmarried," or "separated" can be used. Age can be considered in determining credit worthiness only if the applicant is under age 18, and therefore too young to sign contracts, or conversely, a person may be favored if they are at least 62 since credit has been established, although this may hurt them if retirement and a drop in income is pending.

Section 701(d) of the Equal Credit Opportunity Act identifies the actions a creditor must take in the case of adverse action, a credit application has been denied. A statement within 30 days needs to be issued from the creditor indicating an application's status or acceptance or rejection. Also, a consumer may request, within 60 days, information regarding why the application was rejected. The purpose of this is for creditors to remain transparent in their decisions when denying credit and to keep the consumer informed.

To further reduce potential discrimination for women and minorities, Section 704B of the Equal Credit Opportunity Act was added by the Dodd–Frank Act of 2010. Section 704B requires financial institutions to collect and report credit applications received by women and/or minority-owned businesses and small businesses. The collection of this information is intended to facilitate the enforcement of fair credit practices for these groups to further economic development.

If discrimination is suspected, the applicant should exercise their right to take action. First, complain to the creditor and ask for a reconsideration of the application. Contact the state's Attorney General's office to report the situation and determine if the creditor has violated the law. Consider suing the creditor in federal district court to recover the actual damages.

The Equal Credit Opportunity Act has been in effect since 1974; unfortunately, incidences of credit discrimination still persist in the marketplace. Credit discrimination prevents women, minority groups, and the elderly from having access to affordable credit. These actions impact consumers' financial stability because of the difficulty in building assets, paying for college, and purchasing a home or a reliable vehicle for transportation.

Consumers need to understand their rights and responsibilities to ensure enforcement of credit rules.

*Lorna Saboe-Wounded Head*

**See also:** Consumer Financial Protection Bureau (CFPB); Consumer Protection Act; Credit Cards; Discrimination; Dodd–Frank Wall Street Reform and Consumer Protection Act

**References and Additional Readings**

Consumer Financial Protection Bureau. (n.d.). Consumer laws and regulations: Equal credit opportunity act (ECOA) and regulation. Retrieved from http://www.cfpaguide.com/files/Uploads/Documents/Manual%20-%20ECOA.pdf

Credit worthiness. (n.d.). In Dictionary.com. Retrieved from http://dictionary.reference.com/browse/creditworthiness

Federal Deposit Insurance Corporation. (2012). Consumer protection. FDIC law, regulations, related acts. Retrieved from http://www.fdic.gov/regulations/laws/rules/6500-200.html

Federal Reserve System. (2011a). Equal credit opportunity. Retrieved from https://www.federalregister.gov/articles/2011/03/15/2011-5417/equal-credit-opportunity

Federal Reserve System. (2011b). Regulation B; equal credit opportunity. Retrieved from https://www.federalregister.gov/articles/2011/06/23/2011-15654/regulation-b-equal-credit-opportunity

Federal Trade Commission. (2009). Equal credit opportunity: Understanding your rights under the law. Retrieved from http://www.ftc.gov/bcp/edu/pubs/consumer/credit/cre15.shtm

Garman, T. E. (2005). *Consumer economic issues in America* (9th ed.). Mason, OH: Thomson.

National Consumer Law Center. (n.d.). Credit discrimination. Retrieved from http://www.nclc.org/issues/credit-discrimination.html

# Equal Employment Opportunity Commission (EEOC)

The U.S. Equal Employment Opportunity Commission (EEOC) is responsible for enforcing federal discrimination laws. Specifically, it is illegal to discriminate based on the following: race, color, religion, sex (including pregnancy), national origin, age (40 or older), disability, or genetic information. Furthermore, it is illegal to retaliate or discriminate against someone who has complained about possible discrimination, or has filed a charge related to discrimination, or participated in a discrimination lawsuit or investigation.

Seal of the Equal Employment Opportunity Commission. (Corel)

Most employers with at least 15 employees are covered by EEOC laws (20 employees in age discrimination cases). Most labor unions and employment agencies are also covered. The laws apply to all types of work situations, including hiring, firing, promotions, harassment, training, wages, and benefits.

Laws enforced by the EEOC include:

- Title VII of the Civil Rights Act of 1964 (Title VII)
- The Pregnancy Discrimination Act
- The Equal Pay Act of 1963 (EPA)
- The Age Discrimination in Employment Act of 1967 (ADEA)
- Title I of the Americans with Disabilities Act of 1990 (ADA)
- Sections 102 and 103 of the Civil Rights Act of 1991
- Sections 501 and 505 of the Rehabilitation Act of 1973
- The Generic Information Nondiscrimination Act of 2008 (GINA)

Additional regulations are also enforced by the EEOC, too numerous to mention here, but are listed on the website. Headquartered in Washington,

**Case Study: EEOC *v. Starbucks Corp.***

A barista with mental impairments (including bipolar and attention deficit disorders) performed well when she was accommodated with extra training and support, but a new manager stopped accommodating her. When her performance suffered, he cut her hours, berated her in front of customers, placed her on a performance improvement plan, and discharged her.

The case settled for $75,000 in monetary relief to the barista and an additional $10,000 to the Disability Rights Legal Center. The employer was also required to purge the barista's employment file of all reviews and notes written by the new manager and to post its EEO policy and a notice of the settlement at all area stores.

*Source:* U.S. Equal Employment Opportunity Commission. (n.d.) The U.S. Equal Employment Opportunity Commission: Twenty years of ADA enforcement, twenty significant cases. Retrieved from http://www.eeoc.gov/eeoc/history/45th/ada20/ada_cases.cfm

D.C., the EEOC also operates 53 field offices throughout the United States, to protect the rights of workers. The commission is a bipartisan body with five members who are appointed by the president. Leadership is provided by the chair, with a vice chair as second in charge. There are an additional three commissions that comprise the commission's leadership, as well as, a general counsel also appointed by the president.

The commission may investigate and assess charges of discrimination and conclude whether discrimination occurred. If they find that discrimination occurred, the commission will attempt to settle the complaint. If a settlement is not achievable, a lawsuit may be filed by the commission on behalf of the public interest. The commission also has oversight into hiring practices and policies. An employer may not enact hiring practices that might disadvantage a particular group. Additionally, employers cannot issue a job announcement that favors or disfavors a particular group. An example of an illegal practice might include an ad for a job that specifies "recent college graduates" (dissuading potential applicants of 40 and over). Furthermore, discrimination is prohibited during recruitment procedures, when administering job screening tests, when considering pay and benefits, when establishing dress codes, when providing a reference, and when reasonable accommodations must be made, including for those applicants with disabilities.

As part of their education efforts, the commission tries to alert the public (including employers), of the laws surrounding discrimination so that it will not occur in the first place. The website lists recent and past cases in which the EEOC, including cases involving a Wendy's franchise, the Hampton Inn, Regions Bank, O'Reilly Auto Parts, and many others.

*Wendy Reiboldt*

**See also:** Americans with Disabilities Act (ADA); Department of Labor (DOL); Sexual Harassment

### References and Additional Readings

Alper, J.S., Alper, J.K., & Natowicz, M.R. (2011). *EEOC compliance manual for the ADA and genetic discrimination [letter].* Georgetown University Library. Retrieved from http://hdl.handle.net/10822/528766

Equal Employment Opportunity Commission. (2013). Home. Retrieved from http://www.eeoc.gov

Hodgson, M.D., & Cooper, R.S. (1997). Federal regulations update: EEOC enforcement guidance on ADA issues and waiver of right to sue; counting employees under title VIII; proposed legislation on nondiscrimination. *Employment Relations Today, 24* (2), 77–86.

**Equifax**. *See* Credit Reporting Agencies

## Estate Planning

Estate planning is a process of setting up legal effective arrangements to ensure that family, health, and financial wishes and goals are met in the event of disability or upon death. The process involves considering a range of issues including the control and management of assets, identifying individual(s) to handle financial and health affairs, and giving legal power to distribute property and possessions upon death with the least amount of complication and cost. Estate planning is for everyone, regardless of age or wealth. Estate planning is essential if minor children are present, if real or personal property is involved, and if specific wishes are made about health-care treatment options. What is an estate? An estate is everything owned or in control by name, everything owed, and anything held in partnership with others. Typically, the first step of planning your estate is to inventory what is owned and minus what is owed. An estate inventory includes:

- Liquid assets—cash, savings accounts, checking accounts, money market accounts, certificate of deposits, mutual funds, stocks and securities, and government bonds.
- Personal property—automobiles and other vehicles; cameras, computers, and other electronic equipment; precious metals; household goods

and furniture; clothing; jewelry; furs; tools and equipment; artwork, collectibles and antiques; livestock/animals; money owed (personal loans, etc.); limited partnerships; retirement plans, IRAs, death benefits, annuities; life insurance; frequent flyer miles

- Business personal property—patents, copyrights, trademarks, and royalties; business ownerships (closely held stock, stock options, partnerships, sole proprietorships, limited liability companies, corporations); and miscellaneous receivables (mortgages, deeds of trust, any rent due from income property owned, payments due for personal or professional services or property sold)
- Real property—land and buildings
- Liabilities—personal property debt (personal loans, credit card balances, automobile loans, student loans); other personal debt; current tax debt; other liabilities (legal judgments, child support, alimony, etc.)

---

**Estate Planning Definitions and Requirements:**

- **A Will**, often called a "Last Will and Testament" is a legal, witnessed document that specifies how you would like your assets, property, and possessions distributed after death. A will should indicate an executor for your estate, as well as appoint personal guardians for minor children. Wills must go through the probate process.

  - An executor is the person with legal authority and responsibility for representing your estate and carrying out the terms of the will. The duties of the executor include: arranging probate; manage will property during process; set up estate bank accounts for paying bills and incoming money to the estate; pay taxes; and supervise the will property transfer to beneficiaries (primary beneficiaries are people or institutions named in a will to receive specific property)

- Legal requirements for wills include:

  - You must be at least 18 years old.
  - You must be of "sound mind."
  - The document should be typed or computer printed.
  - The document must state that it is your will.
  - You must leave some property at least to one beneficiary and/or appoint a guardian for minor children. (Tip: since one's exact estate value is calculated from the date of death and the worth is figured by finding the fair market value of all property, it is suggested that when leaving monetary property in a will to use percentages rather than exact amounts.)
  - You must appoint an executor.

- You must date the will.
- There must be at least two witnesses to your signing of the will, and they must sign as well. Notarization is not mandatory, but can eliminate problems that may arise. In addition, witnesses must be at least 18 years old and of "sound mind," and not a beneficiary of the will.

The next step to successful estate planning is to document details in writing. Documents commonly used in estate planning include Wills, Living Trusts, Durable Power of Attorney for Health Care, Living Will/Advanced Health Care Directive, and Power of Attorney for Finances. There are various types of wills. Dying without a will is called "intestate." Statistically, only one in three persons has a will when they die. If one dies intestate, then the state steps in and distributes the estate according to a property-distribution formula which divides the property among family members based on family hierarchy. There are several basic types of wills that consumers hear about most, other than a formal will executed by a legal representative or lawyer. These include handwritten, oral, statutory, electronic, video, or film. Once a

Proactive consumers reviewing their estate plan with their financial advisor. (Andy Dean Photography/Shutterstock.com)

will has been executed, it is important to follow guidelines and specific rules to making changes and maintaining the validity of the document. In some states, a divorce will revoke a will, and moving to another state might present complications due to marital laws, out-of-state executor issues, or differences in allowable statutory forms.

The one thing that is certain about a will is that it must go through the process of probate. Probate is the legal clerical and administrative process that includes (1) filing the deceased's will with the local court; (2) identifying and inventorying the deceased's property; (3) having all property appraised; (4) paying all estate debts and taxes; (5) having the will proved valid; (6) distributing the contents of the will to beneficiaries, and so on. The probate process has earned a bad reputation because it can take up to a year or more to complete and fees associated with the courts, lawyers, appraises, and executors can add up to a sizable amount of the estate. In reaction to the bad rap of probate, many legal alternatives have been developed to avoid probate including pay-on-death accounts (bank accounts or certificates of deposit that have been set up to pay-on-death to a designated beneficiary), and joint tenancy or ownership (when one owner dies, their share automatically transfers to the joint survivor).

Another step to planning one's estate is to establish a trust. Unlike a will that is only a statement of desires and who should carry them out, a trust is a legal vehicle that manages property, distributes assets to the beneficiaries, and avoids probate. Another advantage to having a trust is privacy. A will is a public document, whereas a trust is private and cannot be viewed by the public.

How does a trust work? The first step is to create the trust. This is handled by the trustor, grantor, donor, or creator (interchangeable terms that refer to the person who sets up the trust) who decides the terms of the trust, names the beneficiaries (those that are to receive the benefits of the trust according to the terms stated), names the trustees (responsible for maintaining any property in the trust, managing trust investments and overseeing payments), and sets up the transfer of property (the estate) to the trust. All of this information is contained in the trust document set up by a lawyer to meet federal and state requirements and restrictions.

There are many different types of trusts available, each designed to achieve certain goals and all are created in a variety of ways. Testamentary trusts are created by a will. This type of trust is funded by the estate upon death and administered by the named trustee. One of the primary goals to setting up a testamentary trust is to have the ability to name a responsible adult to manage the trust for loved ones until they are old enough or capable to handle it on their own. Some examples of popular testamentary trusts are "special needs trusts" set up for a child or loved one with a disability; "spendthrift trusts" often used for unreliable beneficiaries with poor money management or beneficiaries that may waste the trust monies on drugs, alcohol, and gambling; and "sprinkling trusts" in which the property is not specifically stated to go to a particular beneficiary, but rather names a group of beneficiaries and it is the responsibility of the trustee to determine the sprinkling allocation of payments from the trust.

Living trusts are created and go into effect when the trustor/grantor is still alive and can act as the trustee, and names a successor trustee to allocate the property upon your death. Living trusts can be set up by the trustor as either "revocable" or "irrevocable." Revocable trusts are those that can be amended, revised, or changed before one's death (as long as the trustor still has "sound mind"). The maintenance and control of the trust remain with the trustor who is acting as the trustee. When the trustor dies or becomes mentally incapacitated, the role of trustee is passed on to the successor trustee. All of the trust property, principal, and estate remain as part of the trustor's assets. The primary goal of a revocable trust is to manage assets and transfer property outside of probate. Irrevocable trusts are those that cannot be amended or revised once they are created and must remain in effect until the terms of the trust have been carried out. All of the trust property, principal, and estate in the trust are no longer a part of the trustor's assets and the trustor has no legal control of the property. A primary goal of an irrevocable trust is to avoid probate and reduce the size of one's estate for tax purposes. Generally, irrevocable trusts are utilized by families or persons with wealth. One of most common irrevocable trusts are "charitable trusts" in which one creates and gives property to an irrevocable trust, gifts the trust to a tax-exempt charity that is approved by the IRS, and receives income or a deduction on income taxes. The most popular charitable trust is the charitable remainder trust where one establishes a trust, names an income beneficiary (generally the trustor), and a final beneficiary (which is generally the charity). The trust provides the income beneficiary with a set payment for a designated period of time (generally, the charity acts as the trustee) and upon death of the income beneficiary, the final beneficiary gains control of the trust property.

Pour-over trusts are created when the trustor is alive, but funded after death. The primary purpose of a pour-over trust is to receive one-time payouts after death, such as life insurance proceeds or pension annuities. Pour-over trusts can be either revocable or irrevocable, and like other trusts, pour-over trusts avoid probate and reduce the size of taxable estates.

In addition to creating a will and possibly a trust, most estate plans include documents for medical care and incapacity. There are two documents that are commonly used to direct medical care: a Healthcare Declaration and a Durable Power of Attorney for Healthcare. A Healthcare Declaration (also called a "Living Will," Medical Directive, Advanced Healthcare Directive, or Directive to Physician) is a document in which an individual states the medical care he or she wish or do not wish to receive in the event he or she become incapacitated and cannot speak for himself or herself. A Healthcare Declaration provides a straightforward statement of one's wishes about his or her own medical treatment involving prolonging life and withholding or withdrawing treatment. In addition, a Healthcare Declaration document can include choices for pain management, organ donation, spiritual concerns, and emotional issues.

Although all states now recognize the legality of living wills, it is a fairly newly established estate planning document. Living Wills first came into public awareness in the 1960s and were not legalized until California became the first state to legally sanction them in 1976. At the same time, the first highly publicized case of Karen Ann Quinlan was heard by the New Jersey Supreme Court. Karen Ann Quinlan, after consuming alcohol and valium a night, ended up in a "persistent vegetative state" and was placed on life-sustaining equipment. Her parents fought to have the authority to make medical decisions on Karen's behalf, ultimately winning the right to remove her from breathing ventilation. The 1976 court decision allowed for several new medical provisions to be afforded to patients. For example, if patients are mentally unable to participate in health treatment decisions, another person may do so for them. Also, if healthcare decisions result in the death of a mentally incompetent person then the decisions can be made by families and their physicians, not the courts. Furthermore, decisions must consider the invasiveness of the proposed treatment, and whether the patient ultimately recovers. And finally, all patients have the right to refuse treatment, even if their decision hastens their death.

Since a Healthcare Declaration involves wishes for life support treatment, it is generally advisable to also complete a Do Not Resuscitate (DNR) form as well. A DNR order is commonly used to alert emergency medical personnel and hospital clinicians that one does not want to receive cardiopulmonary resuscitation (CPR) to restart their heart or breathing in the event of an emergency.

Often, a Healthcare Declaration is combined with a Durable Power of Attorney for Healthcare (a legal document used to name someone, a "healthcare agent," to act on or make decisions regarding health care when an individual cannot speak for himself or herself). When both of these documents are combined, it is called an Advance Healthcare Directive. An advance directive can be made by anyone over the age of 18 (consenting adult), and becomes operational when a physician determines that one is not of "sound mind" and/or incapacitated and unable to speak on his or her own behalf about medical decisions. It is required that medical and healthcare providers abide by the wishes one has declared in the advance directive. An advanced healthcare directive stays in effect until it is either revoked by the creator, a court invalidates the document, or a court revokes the agent's authority, and eventually terminates upon death. In addition, if one names a spouse to act as agent, and a divorce occurs, the directive is automatically revoked as well.

Some people procrastinate, never take the opportunity or become incapacitated before they are able to create any estate-planning vehicles. When this occurs and one is either mentally or physically unable to make medical or financial decisions on his or her own behalf, the court system steps in and appoints a guardian or conservator to make such decisions. When the court begins guardianship or conservatorship proceedings, the first step of the process is to determine if a person is "incompetent" and deemed unable to manage his or her own affairs. Generally, the role of guardian or conservator goes to a family member; however, when individuals do not have loved ones to act on their behalf, a judge will appoint a nonrelative acting on behalf of the court. Guardians and conservators are held accountable to the legal system of the state and are responsible for handling affairs and liable for any misconduct or abuse of a person and his or her property.

During the guardianship or conservatorship process, individuals have the right to appear in court and dispute or agree to the recommended appointed authority. Guardians and conservators can have varying degrees of authority in dealing with a person's affairs. Some are appointed to only handle the financial obligations of paying bills, while other guardians and conservators may have full legal control over decisions regarding health, financial, and even institutionalization.

---

**Types of Wills:**

- *Handwritten wills* (called "holographic" wills) do not have to be witnessed, but must be written, dated, and signed in the handwriting of the person creating the will. Many states and courts will not accept handwritten wills for fear they were forged or coerced.
- *Oral wills* (called "nuncupative" wills) are only valid in a few states and under special highly unusual circumstances (i.e., death on a battlefield or as a victim of a deadly criminal act).

- *Statutory wills* are preprinted, fill-in-the-blank, or check-the-box format. A statutory will is only authorized in a limited number of states and are not an ideal choice or frequently used because you cannot legally change or alter the form to meet specific needs.
- *Electronic wills* are original wills that are created and stored in electronic format. This type of will must use an electronic signature and one additional positive identifier (retina scan, fingerprint, voice, or facial recognition), however, to date, there is no adequate method for executing an electronic will and they are only accepted in Nevada. Advancement in technology will certainly help this method expand.
- *Video or Film wills* are not valid in any state. They can be produced to document a person reading their own will arrangements, thus proving that they were of "sound mind" or not under extreme manipulation from outside sources.

*Cynthia Schlesinger*

**See also:** Confidentiality; Contract Law; Durable Power of Attorney; Health and Healthcare; Legal Aid; Long-Term Care; Mandated Reporters; Older Americans Act (OAA); Ombuds Offices

### References and Additional Readings

Schoenblum, J. A. (2007). *Multistate and multinational estate planning* (Vol. 1). New York: CCH.

**Experian**. *See* Credit Reporting Agencies

## Extended Warranties

Extended warranties, often called service contracts or by some other proprietary name, are a type of insurance intended to cover repair costs for an array of goods. Although extended warranty is the most popular descriptor, federal law does not define these contracts as warranties and the Federal Trade Commission (FTC) prefers "Service Contract or Agreement." Although it typically uses the term extended warranty, *Consumer Reports. org* states they are neither insurance nor a warranty.

Extended warranties are not covered under the Magnuson Moss Warranty Act of 1974 or specifically under other federal law. However, the FTC becomes involved when marketing schemes for extended warranties are deceptive or fraudulent. Many states have laws specifically aimed at extended warranties, while some regulate them as insurance. In other states, the regulation of extended warranties falls between the cracks. California, New York, and Florida have the most stringent regulations. Although this is a popular consumer product, there is a relative paucity of empirical research on this topic. Most data are proprietary and when available, the sources are typically the popular press, trade journals, and are in online press releases from *ConsumerReports.org*.

These so-called warranties may cover a single product or an array of the durable household goods under single policy. The popularity of extended warranties has increased in recent years. Extended warranties, although typically acquired at the time of purchase of the good, may also be purchased as an aftermarket ad on. These aftermarket extended warranties are sold by direct mail, Internet advertising, and robo calling. Extended warranties offers abound on the Internet; just keying "extended warranty" will reveal dozens of sellers.

There are three types of insurers for extended warranties: manufacturers, third-party insurers, and retailers who sell and back their own product insurance. Manufacturers are more likely to cover new cars sales although they sometimes cover other durable household goods. The extended warranties for many goods, when sold by retailers, are often underwritten by third-party insurers that work through administrators. In a few cases, the retailers themselves underwrite the extended warranties. Often consumers do know the firm with whom they have an extended warranty and mostly believe it is provided by the manufacturer even when it is not.

Retailers offering extended warranties have increased dramatically over the decades. These products not only build customer loyalty and repeat purchases but generate a lucrative profit stream. Although company profits from extended warranties are generally proprietary, persons familiar with the field estimate that profit margins of 50–70 percent are not uncommon. One reason why extended warranties are so profitable is that for many products, they cover a period when it is least likely to break down. There is such a profit margin built into extended warranties that the pricing is often *not* based on the probability of malfunction of a product, but on "price point," the retail price of the product.

Most consumer reporters and educators advise against purchasing extended warranties. The reasons abound with the most common—*they are overpriced.* Regulations regarding pricing are nonexistent with sellers often charging whatever the market will bear. For some sales of durable goods, especially electronics, more profit is made from the sale of service contracts than the sale of the goods. Salespersons receive commissions and other incentives which often results in the use of high-pressure tactics to entice the consumer to purchase this "extra protection." An extensive survey conducted by the Better Business revealed rampant problems with automobile extended warranties with one conclusion being that extended warranty trade associations have done little to police the industry.

Because of the high profit margins and consumer ignorance, deception in the sale of extended warranties is rampant with incentives to overstate the need and the coverage of the contract. For example, the claim may be that there is a three-year extended warranty when it is actually a two-year because the first year is covered by the manufacturer's limited warranty. This leads consumers to believe the warranty has greater time coverage than in actuality. Some extended warranties may offer added coverage during the period of manufacture's limited warranty by offering exchanges, giving added technical assistance, and other services.

Consumers often experience problems that result from exclusions in the extended warranty contract. These are usually included in the fine print and in technical jargon that the consumer may not understand. For example, even though a claim was made for a covered repair, the contract may state that if the problem was caused by a noncovered part, the claim is void. Even when a supposedly covered malfunction is encountered, the insurer may dispute the claim by falsely saying the problems is not covered by the contract or that the claim was improperly submitted. In many cases, especially when the extended warranty is sold by direct mail, phone, or Internet, the consumer is not privy to the contract and all the exclusions until after the sale.

A major problem occurs when the insurer becomes insolvent and the consumer is left with no recourse for his or her warranty claims. The largest seller of automobile extended warranties declared bankruptcy in 2010 with the premiums going to the Cayman Islands and the principles indicted for fraud. Several other extended warranty companies have also become insolvent. In many cases retailers who have backed their own extended warranties have gone out of business leaving the consumer with a worthless piece of paper.

Does the availability of extended warranties discourage manufacturers from offering more generous limited and full warranties? A large retail chain that wishes to sell its own service contracts has disincentives for offering products with generous manufacturer warranties. *Consumer Reports.org* has found that manufacturers' warranties have declined in coverage in recent years while products have fewer break downs. Two studies found that manufacturers' warranties decreased due to extended warranties.

Are extended warranties a prudent purchase for a consumer? It all depends. As stated earlier, extended warranties offer large profit margins and when this consistently occurs in a competitive market, it is often indicative of imperfect information for the buyer. In their minds, consumers inflate the cost and frequency of problems that may occur. However, many buyers of extended warranties are purchasing "peace of mind." Risk adverse consumers may not fully factor monetary costs and benefits, but base their decision to purchase on the fear that there may be a catastrophic breakdown and that they may not have the resources to cover. This fear is often reinforced by the salesperson and sales literature. Chen, Kalra, and Sun (2009) found that consumers are more likely to buy extended warranty for hedonistic goods rather than utilitarian items partly to assuage guilt and/or they are likely to purchase extended warranties for items that are sold at a discount.

Even though extended warranties are gaining popularity, *Consumer Reports.org*, based on reader surveys and its own testing, generally recommends foregoing this purchase. Among the reasons given are that repairs are often covered by the manufactures' warranty, products seldom breakdown in the extended warranty period, and when electronic and appliances do break, the cost does not exceed the price of an extended warranty. In several articles concerning extended warranties, *Consumer Reports.org* finds the marginal cost far exceeds any marginal benefit.

A viable alternative to an extended warranty is to self-insure. Rather than purchase service contracts in the event a good requires repairs, a person may wish to generate an account with the money saved by not buying an extended warranty. The probability is high that this account will not become exhausted and the excess will be available for other purposes.

However, for a big ticket item that has a history of malfunctioning and the consumer does not have the resources to repairs, a service contract may be in order. Also, there is the issue of "adverse selection." If a consumer is really hard on a product, he or she may find a service contract advantageous. If the consumer does wish to acquire an extended warranty, he or she may wish to get advice from websites of the Better Business Bureau, *ConsumerReports.org*, and the FTC.

*John R. Burton*

**See also:** Better Business Bureau (BBB); Consumers Union (CU); Federal Trade Commission (FTC); Magnuson–Moss Warranty Act

### References and Additional Readings

Albaum, G., & Wiley, J. (2012). Consumer perceptions of extended warranties and service providers. *Journal of Consumer Marketing, (27)*6, 516–523.

Bo, J., & Zhang, X. (2011). How does a retailer's service plan affect a manufacturer's warranty? *Management Science, 57*(4), 737–740.

Burton, J.R. (1996). Warranty protection: A consumerist perspective. In W.R. Blischke & D.N. Prabhakar Murthy (Eds.), *Product warranty handbook* (719–757). New York: Marcell Dekker.

Carrick, K. (2012). More consumers choosing warranties to fend off repair costs. Retrieved from http://www.bloomberg.com/apps/news?pid=newsarchive&sid=aGhfo4NMwU74

Chen, T., Kalra, A., and Sun, B. (2009). Why do consumers buy extended service contracts? *Journal of Consumer Research, 36*(4), 611–623.

ConsumerReports.org. (2008). Extended warranties: A high priced gamble. Retrieved from http://www.consumerreports.org/cro/2012/05/extended-warranties-a-high-priced-gamble/index.htm

ConsumerReports.org. (2009). Why you don't need an extended warranty. Retrieved from http://news.consumerreports.org/money/2009/11/why-you-dont-need-an-extended-warranty.html

ConsumerReports.org. (2012). Extended warranty buying guide. Retrieved from http://www.consumerreports.org/cro/extended-warranties/buying-guide.htm

Federal Trade Commission. (2012). How to steer clear of auto warranty scams. Retrieved from http://www.ftc.gov/bcp/edu/pubs/consumer/alerts/alt155.shtm

Heese, H.S. (2012). Retail strategies for extended warranty sales and impact on manufacturer base warranties. *Decision Sciences, 43*(2), 341–367.

Henry, J. (2011). Addictive warranties big factor in Fidelis Indictments. *Automobile News.* Retrieved from http://www.autonews.com/article/20110629/FINANCE_AND_INSURANCE/110629865

Maronick, T.J. (2007). Consumer perceptions of extended warranties. *Journal of Retail and Consumer Services, 14*(2), 224–231.

Popken, B. (2011). The insider debunks the 9 extended warranty sales pitches. *The Consumerist.* Retrieved from http://consumerist.com/2011/02/24/9-extended-warranty-myths-debunked-by-a-guy-who-sells-them/

Tao, C., Kalra, A., & Sun, B. (2009). Why do consumers buy extended service contracts? *Journal of Consumer Research, 36*(4), 611–623.

Teucher, R.H. (2011). Vehicle service contract industry: How consumers lost millions of dollars. Report of the Better Business Bureau of Eastern Missouri and Southern Illinois. Retrieved from http://stlouis.bbb.org/Storage/142/Documents/VehicleServiceContractStudy2011.pdf

Warranty Week. (2005). Though the federal government has been quiet, there are plenty of laws and regulations governing product warranties and service contracts. Retrieved from http://www.warrantyweek.com/archive/ww20050802.html

# F

## Fair Credit Reporting Act (FCRA)

The Fair Credit Reporting Act (FCRA) is a federal law that gives consumers the right to see their credit reports and to dispute inaccurate information in them. Enacted in 1970, the federal law was prompted by complaints about the lack of consumer access to data collected and sold by consumer credit reporting agencies. The law has been amended several times to provide consumers with additional rights to review and correct their credit reports.

The three major consumer credit reporting agencies—Experian, Equifax, and TransUnion—collect data from creditors on how consumers pay their bills and then sell that information to their subscribers. Subscribers such as credit card issuers, landlords, insurance companies, and employers can then access a consumer's credit history when deciding whether to grant them credit, provide insurance, or consider them for a job. The FCRA also covers companies that provide tenant screening, medical information, and check approval services.

The FCRA was enacted to (1) improve the accuracy of credit reports, and (2) prevent the misuse of consumers' credit information. The Fair and Accurate Credit Transactions Act of 2003 amended the law to give consumers the right to annually receive a free copy of their credit report from each of the credit reporting agencies, as well as to provide additional protections for consumers.

The amended FCRA includes several provisions that are designed to improve the accuracy of credit reports. The law gives consumers the right to know what is in their credit reports and to dispute inaccurate information. In addition to the free annual credit reports that consumers are entitled to, they may also obtain free reports if they (1) have been denied credit, insurance, or employment based on a credit report; (2) have been a victim of identity theft; (3) receive public assistance; or (4) are unemployed but expect to apply for employment within 60 days. Any business that takes an adverse action against a consumer—such as denying an application for credit, insurance, or employment—based on his or her credit report must provide the consumer with the name, address, and phone number of the credit reporting agency that provided the information.

The FCRA does not require that consumers be provided with their credit scores for free. Consumers may request their scores, which are numerical summaries of their credit-worthiness based on their credit histories, but may be charged a fee by the provider. Under the Dodd–Frank Wall Street Reform and Consumer Protection Act of 2009, consumers who are denied credit or insurance because of a credit score are entitled to a free copy of that score.

Negative information such as late payments, charge-offs, and judgments may be included in credit reports for no more than seven years (except for bankruptcies, which may be reported for 10 years). The law gives consumers the right to dispute information on their credit reports that is inaccurate or past the seven-year reporting period. The credit reporting agencies must correct or delete information that cannot be confirmed as accurate within 30 days of receiving a consumer dispute.

The FCRA also contains a number of protections designed to prevent the misuse of information in consumers' credit reports. Only those with a valid business need can access a consumer's credit report information. Consumers may also limit "prescreened" offers of credit and insurance that are based on information in their credit reports by calling 1-888-5-OPTOUT (jointly operated by Experian, Equifax, and TransUnion pursuant to an FCRA requirement).

Consumers are provided special protections under the law regarding the use of their credit information for employment purposes. Consumers must give their written consent for reports to be provided to employers or prospective employers. Anyone who is denied a job or promotion based on information in a credit report must be provided with a copy of the consumer report relied on to make the decision, a notice of their rights under the FCRA, and the opportunity to review and respond to the report.

Enforcement of the FCRA is accomplished through individual lawsuits, as well as federal and state enforcement actions on behalf of all consumers. Consumers may sue violators of the FCRA—including consumer reporting companies and the creditors who furnish information to them—in state or federal court. The Federal Trade Commission (FTC), Consumer Financial Protection Bureau (CFPB), and state attorneys general have authority to enforce the FCRA. The CFPB announced in February 2012 that it plans to directly supervise the consumer reporting agencies under proposed new regulations.

The FTC has brought cases against each of the three national credit reporting agencies, Experian, Equifax, and TransUnion, for violations of the FCRA. For example, the three companies agreed to settlements in 2000 resolving charges that they failed to maintain a toll-free telephone number accessible to consumers. According to the FTC's U.S. District Court complaints, the three companies blocked millions of calls from consumers who wanted to discuss the contents and possible errors in their credit reports and kept some consumers on hold for unreasonably long periods of time. Experian and TransUnion agreed as part of the settlements to pay $1 million each in civil penalties, and Equifax paid $500,000.

Consumers who discover errors in their credit reports should send a letter to the credit reporting company with any evidence they have demonstrating the error. It is important to send the disputes in writing, via certified mail, and to keep copies of all relevant correspondence with credit reporting companies and creditors. Then, if the credit reporting company does not resolve the error, the consumer can sue either the credit reporting company or the creditor for FCRA violations. They may file their lawsuit in Small Claims Court, or may want to consider hiring an attorney who specializes in FCRA litigation. Consumers can sue for monetary losses incurred as a result of such problems as having been denied credit or having to pay higher interest rates on credit cards or mortgages. Settlements of such lawsuits typically also include an agreement by the company to correct the disputed error in the consumer's credit report. If the consumer's lawsuit is successful, the FCRA permits recovery of legal fees.

Consumers should continually monitor their credit reports for errors by accessing their free annual reports online or via phone. They can file complaints about possible FCRA violations or obtain further information about their rights by contacting the FTC or the Consumer Financial Protection Bureau.

*This writing has been done in the author's personal capacity. The author's personal views do not necessarily represent the views of the FTC or any individual commissioner.*

*Ann M. Stahl*

**See also:** Consumer Financial Protection Bureau (CFPB); Credit Reporting Agencies; Dodd–Frank Wall Street Reform and Consumer Protection Act; FICO; FICO (Fair Isaac and Company); Federal Trade Commission (FTC)

### References and Additional Readings

Cali Credit Law. (n.d.). Your rights under the fair credit reporting act. Taking action. Retrieved from http://www.califcreditlaw.com/lawyer-attorney-1474780

Consumer Financial Protection Bureau. (n.d.). Consumer finance. Retrieved from http://www.consumerfinance.gov

Federal Trade Commission. (n.d.). Credit. Retrieved from http://www.ftc.gov/credit

Sullivan, B. (2009). How to complain about: Credit report errors. Retrieved from http://redtape.msnbc.msn.com/_news/2009/04/28/6345763-how-to-complain-about-credit-report-errors

## Fair Debt Collection Practices Act (FDCPA)

Congress passed the federal Fair Debt Collection Practices Act (FDCPA) in 1977; President Jimmy Carter signed the bill into law. The FDCPA outlines three purposes: eliminate abusive practices against consumers by third-party debt collectors; insure that those debt collectors who refrained from abusive collection practices were not competitively disadvantaged because others did not; and, promote consistency in the states' regulation of the debt collection process. Initially, the authority to enforce the act was scattered among seven federal agencies, but the primary regulatory authority was assigned to the Federal Trade Commission (FTC). Although the FTC was the primary agency in charge of the act, Congress intended that consumers acting as private "attorney generals" and using civil litigation would provide the primary means of enforcement. The act, like most consumer protection statutes, allows for the recovery of statutory damages, attorney's fees, and costs in the event of a successful action.

Over the years, the volume of FDCPA litigation has increased exponentially. The FTC routinely receives more complaints about debt collection than any other consumer statute under the FTC's authority. In 2010, Congress passed the Dodd–Frank Wall Street Reform and Consumer Protection Act (Dodd–Frank), which created the Consumer Financial Protection Bureau (CFPB). Dodd–Frank transferred the power to enforce most of the consumer protection statutes under the FTC's authority to the CFPB, including the FDCPA. Dodd–Frank also gave the CFPB the authority to promulgate regulations for the FDCPA, authority Congress had declined to give the FTC.

The creation of the CFPB and the authority to promulgate FDCPA regulations will alter the regulatory landscape for those covered by the act. These regulations are needed. The debt collection industry has changed dramatically in the 35 years since the act's passage. Debt collection has become a highly profitable industry for debt buyers. Indeed, the prevalence of debt buying has been one of the most significant changes to affect the industry. Debt buyers purchase large portfolios of charged-off debt at pennies on the dollar making the collection of even a small percentage of the debt highly profitable. This profitability has attracted the attention of venture capitalists and several of the largest debt collection agencies are now publicly traded. Debt buying also allows for easy entry into the market by smaller sometimes less scrupulous and more transient debt collection operations undermining the efforts of debt collectors attempting to comply with the act's provisions.

Additionally, changes in technology have changed the ways in which consumers communicate. More than a quarter of U.S. households have abandoned their landlines in favor of cellular mobile phones. Electronic mail and social media also play a large role in the lives of many consumers and these new technologies have changed the way debt collectors collect debts. Debt collectors' strategies are no longer limited to telephone calls or the postal service. Debt collectors now have automatic dialers, electronic mail, sophisticated voice analytics software, and websites where consumers can make arrangements to electronically pay their debts. The increased use of consumers' credit scores and the sheer volume of information credit bureaus have available to compile them have made information about consumers more accessible and comprehensive—increasing the odds of a successful collection attempt but also the potential for abusive collection tactics.

For example, the FDCPA regulates communication between debt collectors and consumers and between the debt collector and other parties besides the consumer. The act specifically limits whom the debt collector may contact for location information about the consumer, including a consumer's employer. Prior to the act, it was not uncommon for a debt collector to call a consumer's neighbors or coworkers in an effort to shame the consumer into paying a debt. While the strategies may have changed because of new technologies, the problem remains: some debt collectors have begun to use social media sites to obtain information about a consumer as well as to post information about debts a consumer allegedly owes. These technological and social changes could not have been anticipated when the FDCPA was enacted.

As enacted, the FDCPA imposes several affirmative obligations on the debt collector as well as prohibiting certain types of behavior. Most importantly, the debt collector must inform the consumer of his or her rights in the debt collection process. For example, the debt collector must inform the consumer that the consumer has a right to specific information about the debt, including the following: the amount of the debt allegedly owed; the name of the creditor who owns the debt; instructions on how to dispute the validity of the debt; and, instructions indicating which requests for action by the debt collector must be made in writing. Additionally, the act allows the consumer to request that the debt collector not contact the consumer at work or that the debt collector cease communicating entirely with the consumer.

The act also prohibits conduct that results in the harassment or abuse of the consumer, including things like threatening force or violence, using profane or obscene language, or repeatedly calling the consumer. The act further forbids the use of false or misleading representations to the consumer about the nature of the debt or the consumer's rights in the process, including things like threatening action that cannot be legally taken, indicating that the consumer has committed a crime, or falsely implying or stating that the communication is from an attorney. Finally, the act prohibits the use of unfair practices, like attempting to collect more than what is owed or allowed to be collected by law, threatening to take possession of the consumer's property when no legal right to the property exists, or the failing to inform the consumer that every communication with the consumer is an attempt to collect a debt and any information the debt collector obtains will be used for that purpose.

Consumers who are unable to pay their debts—or do not actually owe the debt—are particularly vulnerable to abusive collection tactics. Likewise, debt collectors attempting to work in an industry that has changed so dramatically but is regulated by an act that has not kept pace with technological changes face difficulties trying to comply with the act. Congress did not intend either circumstance. Guidance from the CFPB is sorely needed in this area of consumer protection.

---

### FDCPA Violation

*The following is a fictitious story based on the first editor's experience with the types of behaviors in which bill collectors engage. Most of these actions are in violation of the FDCPA.*

Mr. Smith, who is behind on his car payments, hears a series of angry knocks at his front door at 3 a.m. He listens to the yelling and vulgar language that is occurring on the other side of the door and recognizes the voice as that of the collection agent who has been harassing him by telephone. While he sadly understands that he is behind on his car payments, he is unsure of what to do in this situation. He is scared and feels very violated and harassed.

Finally, the knocking and yelling end, and two minutes later, his home phone rings. He decides to let the answering machine pick up. The same collector is now in his car on his cell phone calling Mr. Smith, it is 3:08 a.m. The collector leaves a two-minute recorded voice message peppered with profanities saying that he will wake up the entire neighborhood if Mr. Smith does not answer his door and pay his car payment. He proceeds to call Mr. Smith names, and demeans him and his character repeatedly with statements like "Either pay your bill or return the car you obviously cannot afford." Finally the call ends. Just three minutes later, a second call comes in and again, Mr. Smith lets the answering machine record the call. The collector leaves another condescending, offensive message before hanging up.

The next day, Mr. Smith's neighbor tells him that a man came to his door the previous day to announce to him that Mr. Smith is behind on his car payments. The neighbor told Mr. Smith that the collector was going around the neighborhood telling anyone who would listen, that Mr. Smith was a deadbeat debtor.

*Laurie A. Lucas*

**See also:** Consumer Financial Protection Bureau (CFPB); Debt Collection; Debt Management; Dodd–Frank Wall Street Reform and Consumer Protection Act; Federal Trade Commission (FTC)

### References and Additional Readings

Federal Trade Commission. (n.d.). Federal trade commission annual report 2011: Fair debt collection practices act. Retrieved from http://ftc.gov/os/2011/03/110321fairdebtcollectreport.pdf.

Federal Trade Commission. (2009). FTC workshop transcript: Debt collection 2.0: Protecting consumers as technologies change. Retrieved from http://www.ftc.gov/bcp/workshops/debtcollectround/091204-DC/transcript.pdf.

**Fair Isaac and Company (FICO).** *See* FICO (Fair Isaac and Company)

# Fair Trade

## Background Information

People, nations, and countries have engaged in trade from ancient times. The origins of trade coincide with the early development of communication systems. Trading was a main and very important provision of ancient peoples. Since currency was invented later, people bartered goods and services.

We live in an era of relatively free and global trade. Free trade can be simply defined as an act of opening up economies. Global trade refers to the process of buying, selling, and producing goods and services between countries. As a result, products exist (e.g., fruits, vegetables, and other grocery products, automobiles, TVs, clothing) from all over the world in our stores. Even services such as banking customer service are offered from overseas. It is believed that countries and people mutually benefit from free trade by consuming goods and services that are not available locally because trade is considered as a primary means to develop countries' economies and wealth. The question follows—do trading countries equally benefit from these activities?

The proponents of fair trade believe that trade between countries with different development levels takes place on uneven terms, and there is a need for mechanisms to protect weaker, less developed countries. Who makes and promotes trading rules? The World Trade Organization (WTO) is the main and only global international organization that creates rules and agreements between nations. Under the WTO agreements, countries generally cannot discriminate between their trading partners, though some exceptions exist. The common criticism of WTO concerns its role in fair trade. Fair trade supporters believe that WTO should consider social and environmental international standards, agreements, and conventions in creating trading rules. To continue this discussion, we must fully understand the concept of fair trade.

Fair-trade-labeled coffee, tea, and cocoa certifies that fair prices were paid for the product. (Transfair USA)

### Definition and Concept

Fair trade is a social movement and approach that strives to help producers in weak, developing counties make better conditions and promote sustainability. The main tenets upheld by this movement are the payment of fair prices to producers and increases in social and environmental standards in trade. The main focus is on exports from economically weaker countries to strong, more developed countries; and exports that themselves mostly consist of hand craft, cocoa, coffee, sugar, tea, honey, cotton, fruits, chocolate, flowers, and gold. The main concept and principles of fair trade are the following: Fair trade (1) creates opportunities for small producers in developing countries; (2) promotes transparent relationships between all members of the supply chain; (3) supports the ability of individual artisans or small producers; (4) pays fairly and in a timely manner; (5) builds and promotes healthy and hazard-free working conditions; (6) supports children's rights; (7) fosters environmentally friendly and sustainable production; and (8) respects cultural identity of producing part. There is no universally accepted definition of fair trade; however, it can simply be defined as a trading partnership between sellers, producers, and consumers from all over the world based on openness, transparency, and mutual respect with the goal of creating greater equity in international trade.

In the fair trade system, the buying party (a person oftentimes from a developed country) agrees to pay a slightly higher cost to help producers maintain reasonable standards of living. However, the higher cost paid for fair trade products increases the final price of these products. Why, then, should people buy fair trade products and pay higher prices? By purchasing fair trade products, people are getting the satisfaction of knowing that they supported an individual or even a family to have a better life. It is common practice by fair trade partners to invest in local communities such as educational, agricultural, health, and other projects. Hence, the benefit from fair trade extends from individuals to a wider range of people and fields. Therefore, fair trade is more than just commerce—it relates to moral and ethical issues.

## History

Some sources indicate the 1940s and 1950s as the origins of the fair trade movement. During this period, the U.S.-based religious group Ten Thousand Villages and nongovernmental organizations (NGOs) Mennonite Central Committee and SERRV International became pioneering fair trade supporters. Most academics believe that Edna Ruth Byler was the first fair trader in the world. During her travel to Puerto Rico in the 1940s, she met women in villages who produced quality linen needlework despite living in a state of poverty. Byler took those items to a Mennonite conference in Switzerland, selling them to participants and visitors. Today, this is recognized as the first fair trade act.

A more notable movement of fair trade was documented in Europe in the 1960s. The main vehicle of this movement was a negative attitude against neoimperialism. Slogans like "Trade, not Aid" are just one indicator of popular discontent with multinational corporations. In 1968, the United Nations (UN) Conference on Trade and Development adopted this approach and view. The UN initiated a new approach to the creation and support of fair trade relations among nations.

Alternative Trading Organization, the first organization focused on the fair trade concept, was created in 1965. During the same year British NGO OXFAM (Oxford Committee for Famine Relief, created after World War II) initiated the "Helping-by-Selling" program, which promoted sales of imported handicraft in its stores in the UK. Later, in 1968, newsprint publication *Whole Earth Catalog* connected a large number of merchants, artisans, and producers directly with consumers, focusing on those who share concerns with supporting independent small producers. This way, they bypassed large retail corporations and firms. The target countries were America, Canada, Latin America, and South America.

During the same general period, in 1969, the store World Shop opened in the Breukelen, Netherlands, and offered fair trade products from underdeveloped countries. Volunteer organizers and managers of this store inspired similar concept stores in many other Western European and Benelux countries such as Western Germany and Belgium. Between 1960 and 1970, fair trade movers started to focus on finding new producer markets of fair trade products. By selling fair trade products in stores, churches, and public events, volunteers of the fair trade movement vocalized their message to support artisans and producers from underprivileged countries and sustainable development. By this time, this movement was commonly labeled as alternative trade. Many support organizations and stores focusing on fair trade products were established in the United States and Western Europe. These organizations successfully arranged campaigns against human exploitation and the domination of developed countries in the world trade arena.

The term "fair trade" was first introduced in 1985 during the Trade and Technology Conference in London, U.K. The fair trade-certified label itself was born in 1989, during a crisis in the coffee market. During that time Max Havellar (Dutch organization) and Father Franz Vandelhoff (a Dutch missionary) worked with coffee producers from southern Mexico trying to eliminate middlemen and provide farmers fair wages. As a result, the fair trade certified label was born.

Later, several fair trade organizations and fair trade towns were created throughout the world (e.g., EFTA—European Fair Trade Association;

NEWS!—network of European World Shops; and Fair Trade Labeling Organization). The first fair trade town campaign was initiated in the U.K., and the first fair trade town was recognized Garstang, Lancashire, in 2000. After this successful campaign, several other cities started to adopt the concept. As a result, over 800 countries worldwide followed this movement and promoted fair trade. Media, Pennsylvania, became the first recognized fair trade town in the United States in 2005. This increased awareness and interest in fair trade towns initiatives, and the movement became more formal with the support of Fair Trade USA, OXFAM America, and the Lutheran World Relief. Between 2005 and 2008, Brattleboro, Vermont; Milwaukee, Wisconsin; Amherst, Massachusetts; Taos, New Mexico; Northampton, Massachusetts; San Francisco, California; Montclair, New Jersey; Ballston Spa, New York; Chico, California; and Bluffton, Ohio, were declared fair trade towns.

In addition to NGOs and international and national federations and associations, there is an increasing number of college students and youth who actively support the fair trade movement. Students' independent organizations supporting fair trade are mostly located in Canada and the United States and are affiliated with major fair trade networks. See Table 23 for a timeline of the fair-trade movement.

### Challenges

Globalization and free trade topics are hot topics of discussion today. There are many who either actively support or critique the concepts of

**Table 23**  Fair-trade movement history

| | |
|---|---|
| 1946: | First movement—Ten Thousand Villages organization initiative; linen needlework of Puerto Rican women. |
| 1965: | Establishment of the first Alternative Trade Organization; OXFAM initiation of "Helping-by-Selling" program. |
| 1968: | Newsprint publication of the *Whole Earth Catalog*. |
| 1969: | Fair trade concept adopted during United Nations Conference on Trade and Development. |
| 1969: | First European store opens in Breukelen, Netherlands. |
| 1985: | *FairTrade* term introduced. |
| 1989: | The first Fair-Trade-Certified label, Max Havelaar, created in the Netherlands. |
| 2000: | First Fair Trade Town was recognized to be Garstang, Lancashire, UK. |
| 2005: | First U.S. based Fair Trade Town was established in the United States—Media, PA. |

free and global trade. The major concerns about free and global trade are that not all participating countries benefit equally. Accordingly, questions arise regarding the exact fairness of trade when both selling and buying parties have opposing goals and lack equality in economic power.

Current trade agreements and regulations often give too much power to some corporations or entire countries. This situation can lead multinational corporations to violate basic human and social rights, ignore the environmental harm of production, and neglect accountability. However, the right balance is difficult to attain because there are several natural conflicts between various members of supply chain. Accordingly, there is an inherent unfairness in trade. The growing fair trade movement throughout the world has many challenges, as globalization in its existing forms does not favor those who want to trade equally and fairly.

Views and approach toward fair trade in the political spectrum are not uniform. For example, some see fair trade as a marketing strategy that slows down global economic growth. Others criticize the concept for not sufficiently challenging the modern trading system.

## Some Statistics

Despite the challenges fair trade movement faces, the sales of fair trade-certified products increase worldwide. For example, in 2008, the movement was reported to have sales amounting to approximately $1.98 billion, which is 22 percent more compared to the previous year. Though this is a tiny proportion of overall world trade, the Fair trade Labeling Organizations International reminds us that over 7.5 million producers and families were benefitted from fair trade in the year of 2008.

## Organizations and Labeling Initiatives

Fair trade organizations are certified by one or several national or international federations. There are number of federations, and following are some of the largest:

- The Fair Trade Labeling Organization International (FLO): This organization was created in 1997 and currently promotes and markets the Fair Trade Certification Mark. FLO examines and certifies products in over 50 countries in Africa, Asia, and Latin America.

- The World Fair Trade Organization (formerly known as International Fair Trade Association): This is a global organization created in 1989. The World Fair Trade Organization initiated the FTO Mark, which registers fair trade organizations, not product as FLO does.

- The Network of European World shops (NEWS!): This network organization was created in 1994 in 13 different countries in Europe.

- The European Fair Trade Association (EFTA): This network was created in 1990 among alternative trading organizations in Europe. These organizations import products from about 400 developing countries in Africa, Asia, and Latin America. The major goal and mission of EFTA is to promote fair trade by supporting producers from developing countries and various publications on fair trade-related issues. There are 11 members from 9 different countries in the EFTA.

Canadian and American fair trade wholesales, importers, and retails created the Fair Trade Federation in 1994. This organization connects its members to fair trade producers in various countries, controls information on fair trade, and provides resources to its members. Perhaps the most notable recent step was the creation of the Fair Trade Action Network in 2007. This is an international network completely operated by volunteers from European and North American countries with the goal of supporting global fair trade movements and the Fair Trade Towns program.

To improve the visibility of the Fair Trade Mark in supermarkets and other retail channels, the Fair trade Labeling Organization International introduced the International Fair trade Certification Mark in 2002.

This initiative makes import–export related procedures simple for both producers and importers. Currently, over 50 countries worldwide use this fair trade mark for products such as coffee rice, bananas, cocoa cotton, tea, and honey.

*Mariné Aghekyan-Simonian*

**See also:** World Trade Organization (WTO); United Nations (UN)

### References and Additional Readings

Bassett, T. (2009). Slim pickings: Fairtrade cotton in West Africa. *Geoforum.*

Fairtrade Labelling Organizations International (2007). FLO International: Annual report 2007. Retrieved from http://www.fairtrade.net/uploads/media/FLO_AR2007_low_res_01.pdf

Kilian, B., Jones, C., Pratt, L., & Villalobos, A. (2006). Is sustainable agriculture a viable strategy to improve farm income in Central America? A case study on coffee. *Journal of Business Research, 59*(3), 322–330.

Moseley, W. G. (2008). Fair trade wine: South Africa's post apartheid vineyards and the global economy. *Globalizations, 5*(2), 291–304.

Valkila, J., Haaparanta, P., & Niemi, N. (2010). Empowering coffee traders? The coffee value chain from Nicaraguan fair trade farmers to Finnish consumers. *Journal of Business Ethics, 97,* 257–270.

## Family and Medical Leave Act (FMLA)

In the United States, the Industrial Revolution in the early 1800s prompted an increased need for workers outside the home and farm, which led to the development of culturally and legally sanctioned separate spheres. For women it was an unpaid, homemaking private sphere and for men, bread-winning in the public sphere. However, over time, a single wage-earner family became less viable as the purchasing power of wages diminished, more jobs became temporary or part-time, and fewer offered benefits. These economic factors, plus the influence of the women's movement, have dramatically increased women's employment since the 1960s.

Public policy in this country has granted employers lower taxes in exchange for administrative responsibility for social welfare benefits (unrelated to work or production) compared to some other developed countries where such benefits are administrated publically. In the 1970s and early 1980s in response to sex discrimination law, many employers adopted maternity leave and related benefits including work leave to manage certain health and family needs. However, workplace policies, upheld by the Supreme Court in 1976, still discriminated against women, who are more likely to prioritize family over work because of pregnancy, childbirth, and primary caregiving. These policies made women's long-term workforce participation difficult and increased employee turnover and a gendered wage gap.

In 1978, Congress passed the Pregnancy Discrimination Act (PDA), which mandated equal treatment for workers unable to work regardless of the reason for the disability. Building on Title VII of the 1964 Civil Rights Act, employers must treat pregnancy and related conditions the same as nonpregnancy conditions. However, such legislation and related policies limited maternity leave to birth mothers because they needed to physically recover. The length of maternity leave was determined by women's ability to return to work, usually 6–8 weeks (the average time for a woman's uterus to return to normal size and position after childbirth). This made it unlawful for employers to discriminate in hiring and retention decisions based on pregnancy. In 1987, the Supreme Court affirmed the PDA, guaranteeing "women the basic right to participate fully and equally in the workforce, without denying them the fundamental right to full participation in family life" (Teehan, 2007, 659). In 1990, the Americans with Disabilities Act (ADA) required employers with 15 or more employees to grant medical leave to employees in certain circumstances not including normal pregnancy, but including pregnancy complications that substantially limit a major life activity requiring reasonable accommodation to perform a job. Although these laws contributed to workplace gender equality, they left unaddressed many other issues including federal employment leave rights for care of children or sick relatives, paternal leave, and gender stereotyping of work and family roles. Some states attempted to correct this problem and after a 20-year legislative negotiation Congress passed the Family and Medical Leave Act (FMLA) in 1993, signed by President Bill Clinton, who said, American workers, "will no longer need to choose between the job they need and the family they love." FMLA went into effect August 5, 1993, with the FMLA final rule, enforced by the U.S. Department of Labor (DOL), in effect April 6, 1995. Until 1993, the United States was the only industrialized country without job-protected family leave.

The FMLA defined eligible employees as entitled to leave for childbirth; and parental care of the newborn child within its first year; adoption or foster care within one year of a child's placement; care of a spouse, child, or parent with a serious health condition; and one's own health conditions making the employee unable to perform essential job functions. Acknowledging the increase in dual-earner households, the law explains that to avoid the serious potential of employer gender discrimination in treatment of employees and in hiring, its language had to be gender neutral. It challenged expectations about unbroken attendance records as a measure of a good worker and the necessity of employer control over work schedules.

The act's main purposes are to (1) promote gender equality in the workplace; (2) resolve work/family conflicts; and (3) better ensure job security for men and women. Congress hoped FMLA would standardize family leave policies by providing employer guidance about employee leave and equal opportunities for women and men to address family and employment responsibilities.

According to the DOL, the FMLA considers employees eligible when they worked at least 1,250 hours within the last 12 months, for a private employer with 50 or more employees within a 75-mile radius. They then can take leave intermittently or work on a part-time basis until they used up the equivalent of 12 workweeks in a 12-month period. A serious medical condition is defined as an illness, injury, impairment, or physical or mental condition that involves inpatient care or continuing intervention by a healthcare provider which is medically necessary for treatment or recovery. This is unpaid, job-protected leave for specified family and medical reasons with continuation of group health insurance coverage and other benefits under the same terms and conditions as if employees had not taken leave. Employees must continue to pay their share of the health insurance premiums. An employer has the right to know why an employee requests a FMLA leave, but FMLA and ADA medical information must be kept in a separate, confidential file. If an employee, returning to work with a physical or mental condition, is unable to perform an essential function of the same or equivalent position, the employer is not required to reinstate the employee into another job.

Although the FMLA is an unpaid job protection law, it granted workers the choice to use, or employers the right to require that employees use, paid accrued sick or medical leave, vacation, family, or personal leave instead of unpaid leave. However, after legal challenges and calls for clarification, the DOL in 2008 revised the regulations to eliminate workers guaranteed right to substitute accrued paid leave for unpaid leave unless they complied with the employer's normal leave-taking policies. This gave employers more flexibility, but made the Act useless for many low-income workers Congress intended to protect.

In 2009, FMLA was further clarified to include employees who are parents or a person standing in loco parentis of biological, adopted, or foster children, stepchildren, legal wards, or children under 18 years old or 18 years old or older who are incapable of self-care because of a mental or physical disability(29 U.S.C. §2611(12).

In 2008 and 2010, the Family and Medical Leave Act was amended by the National Defense Authorization Act to provide two important leave benefits for military families of active duty, reserve, or veteran service members. First the amendments provide up to 26 workweeks of military caregiver leave during a single 12-month period for their spouse, son, daughter, parent, or next of kin to care for their serious injury or illness when the service member is undergoing medical treatment, recuperation, or therapy, is otherwise an outpatient, or on the temporary disability retired list for a serious injury or illness incurred or aggravated in the line of active duty. Second, these amendments permit the spouse, son, daughter, or parent of a military member to take up to 12 weeks of leave during any 12-month period to address the most common issues arising from a military member's deployment to a foreign country, such as attending military sponsored functions, making appropriate financial and legal arrangements, and arranging for alternative child care.

Since 1993, FMLA has stimulated debate among scholars and policymakers concerning its impact on U.S. gender roles and stereotypes. Some argue it provides men and women more opportunity to manage work and family obligations and improves gender equity. Others argue it has paradoxically reinforced culturally defined women's caregiver role since women use it disproportionately, while men continue to focus on work rather than family obligations, unless they are primary caretakers like single fathers. When men do take FMLA leave, it is primarily for their own illness. Consequently leaves, part-time and intermittent employment, and job changing to fulfill caregiving responsibilities have impacted women's long-term occupational and economic attainment and contributed to their higher rates of participation in female-typed occupations and underrepresentation in managerial positions.

FMLA best serves people with access to resources, especially white, middle-class, and married workers, while those most in need, such as low-income mothers and low-skilled workers, are least likely to receive its benefits. Partly because of previous maternity leave policies, employer noncompliance, and narrow definition of family limited to heterosexual, nuclear family relationships, FMLA and similar state laws (California, Connecticut, Hawaii, Maine, Minnesota, New Jersey, Oregon, Rhode Island, Vermont, Washington, Wisconsin, and the District of Columbia) have had little effect on women's leave taking and negligible impact on men's use of leaves. Its lack of pay provisions and the 12-month and 1250-hour work requirement limit a disproportionate percentage of women and low-income workers, including family-oriented ethnic groups disposed to family caregiving, but less able to afford paid caregiving. Wage disparity discourages men from taking FMLA leave because it would often result in greater income loss for the family. Lack of knowledge about their eligibility for FMLA leaves is yet another reason for nonuse.

Compared to other countries, such as Scandinavian countries, FMLA benefits for American parents are quite modest. Also, they are quite easy to administer as compared to other employment rights in this country. However, only about 6 percent of all employers and 60 percent of American workers are covered. Analysis indicates continuous and significant noncompliance with FMLA from not providing leave and providing less than the required length. Some noncompliance reflects failure to update old policies and practices from unintentional oversight and ambivalence about some requirements such as the law's support of men's caregiving. This informally encourages short paternity leaves even when 12 weeks are officially available. In small organizations, lack of human resources professionals contributes to noncompliance. When employers have linked maternity leave to disability benefits, they tend to have illegally short maternity leaves. Supportive top management has reduced the likelihood of more extreme FMLA violations, but has not increased required maternity leaves of compliant length.

With regard to paternity leave, the more work–family policies, especially gender-neutral policies that employers have, the more likely they are to have paternity leave. Financial resources seem to be affecting whether an organization has compliant paternity leaves. Management behaviors reinforcing gender norms can discourage long paternity leaves regardless of the official policy.

Other conditions that contribute to noncompliance include (1) requirements that affected employees file complaints or lawsuits to start an investigation rather than having an agency inspect or audit employers; (2) confusion about employer action regulated by both state and federal laws and by multiple federal laws such as FMLA regulated by Department of Labor and ADA regulated by the Department of Justice; and (3) when the social safety net is delivered through employers rather than through public programs.

More public education would draw attention to FMLA provisions and may reduce noncompliance. However, policy changes are needed to reduce barriers by incorporating paid leave and pay equity that would make family work more socially and economically valued and men's caregiving more socially acceptable. The federal 1996 Defense of Marriage Act (DOMA) prevents legally married same-sex couples from taking FMLA leave to care for their sick spouse. Also, providing short-term leave for family members to care for relatives with mild illnesses and flextime for family responsibilities like appointments with doctors, teachers, and learning specialists (shown to affect children's educational performance), is also needed.

*For additional information, refer to the Primary Source Appendix: Family and Medical Leave Act (1993).*

*Virginia B. Vincenti*

**See also:** Americans with Disabilities Act (ADA); Congress; Department of Justice (DOJ); Discrimination; Equal Employment Opportunity Commission (EEOC); Supreme Court

## References and Additional Readings

Anthony, D.J. (2008). The hidden harms of the family and medical leave act: Gender-neutral versus gender-equal. *Journal of Gender, Social Policy & the Law, 16*(4), 459–501.

Department of Labor. (2012). Americans with Disabilities Act. Retrieved from http://www.dol.gov/dol/topic/disability/ada.htm

Department of Labor. (2013a). Wage and hour division, Family and Medical Leave Act. Retrieved from http://www.dol.gov/whd/fmla/

Department of Labor. (2013b) Wage and hour division, Family and Medical Leave Act, Military Family Leave Provisions. Retrieved from http://www.dol.gov/whd/fmla/MilitaryFLProvisions.htm

Department of Labor. (2013c). Wage and hour division, Federal vs. State Family and Medical Leave Laws. Retrieved from http://www.dol.gov/whd/state/fmla/index.htm

Equal Employment Opportunity Commission. (2012). Notice concerning the Americans with Disabilities Act Amendments Act of 2008. The U.S. Equal Employment Opportunity Commission. Retrieved from http://www.eeoc.gov/policy/docs/fmlaada.html

Family and Medical Leave Act of 1993. (1993). Retrieved from http://www.harvardlawreview.org/media/pdf/vol123_%20FMLA_final_rule_73.pdf

Family and Medical Leave Act of 1993, as amended. Retrieved from http://www.dol.gov/whd/fmla/fmlaAmended.htm.

Healey, M.T. (2012). LGBT rights. Toward a more perfect union. A state's challenge to DOMA. Federalism and constitutional Rights. *Albany Government Law Review, 5*(2), 422–439.

Kelly, E.L. (2010). Failure to update: An institutional perspective on noncompliance with the family and medical leave act. *Law and Society Review, 44*(1), 33–66.

Teehan, J. (2007). Family and Medical Leave Act. *Georgetown Journal of Gender and the Law,* VIII, 657–668.

# Family Educational Rights and Privacy Act (FERPA)

The Department of Education oversees the Family Educational Rights and Privacy Act (FERPA), a federal law which governs all schools who receive funds under an applicable program from the Department of Education. The entity under the Department of Education that implements FERPA (also known as the Buckley Amendment) is the Family Policy Compliance Office (FPCO). The FPCO also implements the Protection of Pupil Rights (PPRA) law that further protects the rights of parents and students through oversight of instructional materials and parental consent. The goal of FERPA, passed in 1974, is to provide and protect the privacy of students and their personally identifiable education records. For students under the age of 18, parents have specific rights to educational records. However, after the student reaches the age of 18, these rights transfer to the student, now called "eligible students." Parents and eligible students are provided the following rights:

- The right to inspect and review the student's education records maintained by the school. Schools are not required to make copies of the records, unless necessary and then may charge a fee for copies.
- The right to request that a school correct records which they believe to be inaccurate or misleading. If not corrected, the parent may request a formal hearing, and may place a statement in the records.
- Schools must have written permission from the parent or eligible student to release any information from the education record. However, schools may release records under several conditions:
  - School officials with legitimate educational interest
  - Other schools to which a student is transferring
  - Specified officials for audit or evaluation purposes
  - Appropriate parties in connection with financial aid for a student
  - Organizations conducting studies on behalf of the school
  - Accrediting organizations
  - To comply with judicial orders or lawfully issued subpoenas
  - Appropriate officials in cases of health and safety emergencies
  - State and local authorities within the juvenile justice system pursuant to state law

Information for a directory may also be disclosed without consent; however, parents and eligible students must be notified so that they may choose not to be included in such a directory. Furthermore, as part of the law, schools are required to notify parents and eligible students of their FERPA rights on an annual basis. The format for this notification is not regulated, and is up to the judgment of the school itself.

In 2000, two amendments, the Foley Amendment and the Warner Amendment were enacted to allow university administrators to notify parents and/or the public when a student commits a crime such as substance abuse or other illegal acts that are perpetrated. Regarding alcohol, the age of the student must be under 21 (hence the reason for the crime).

> ## Example of FERPA Violation
>
> *Gonzaga University v. Department of Education (ED):*
>
> A student at Gonzaga University was working on becoming an elementary school teacher. All new teachers are required to get an affidavit of good moral character from their graduating college. The teacher certification specialist overheard one student tell another that they had engaged in sexual misconduct and contacted the state agency to report the student by name. Because of this, the student was not allowed to get their certification affidavit and decided to sue the school for violating the Family Educational Rights and Privacy Act. The student was awarded compensatory and punitive damages by a jury.
>
> *Source:* Oyez. (2013). *Gonzaga University v. DOE*. Retrieved from http://www.oyez.org/cases/2000–2009/2001/2001_01_679

In April 2011, a "Notice of Proposed Rule Making" (NPRM) was released from the Department of Education amending FERPA; it became final rule and was published in the Federal Register in December 2011. The amendment provides states with the ability to share student data from the statewide longitudinal data systems (SLDS) for the purpose of guaranteeing that tax funds are invested in the best possible way, while still maintaining privacy and accountability for student records. Under this clarification, states would be better able to evaluate programs for the benefit of students while increasing transparency and accountability. Furthermore, the NPRM extends FERPA coverage and protections to entities who do not enroll students but collect student data from schools. If these entities do not properly protect the information, the department can bring action against them.

The directory exclusion discussed earlier was also mentioned in the NPRM, stating that schools much disclose to parents if they are creating a directory and must limit its distribution. This is also true for directories such as yearbooks or graduation programs. Because "directories" potentially open students to increased risks, the department notes that most have gone to limited directory information.

A second change from the NPRM addressed the use of ID badges, allowing schools to require wearing of a badge if they feel it aids in ensuring the safety and security of students. According to this ruling, parents may not "opt out" of such an action.

Another change involved the defining of an education program and an authorized representative. These clarifications were made to ensure the protection of records by authorized individuals at the state and federal level and to study the effectiveness of specific programs receiving funding. Research studying effectiveness of these programs is also covered under the NPRM and must meet several requirements spelled out in the rule.

The Department of Education has created a Privacy Technical Assistance Center (PTAC) which, according to their website, "serves as a one-stop resource for the P-20 education community on privacy, confidentiality and data security." The PTAC receives data from the National Center for Education Statistics (NCES) and is further overseen by the Privacy Advisory Committee and the Chief Privacy Office from the department. As evident here, several entities and acts of legislation are involved in the protection of student records.

*Wendy Reiboldt*

**See also:** Confidentiality; Department of Education (ED); Privacy: Offline

### References and Additional Readings

Department of Education. (2011). The Family Educational Rights and Privacy Act guidance for eligible students. Retrieved from http://www2.ed.gov/policy/gen/guid/fpco/ferpa/for-eligible-students.pdf

Kaufman, A.B. (2012). The new Massachusetts miracle: How a recent state law motivated one college to improve its FERPA compliance. *College and University, 87*(3), 41–43.

O'Donnell, M.L. (2003). FERPA: Only a piece of the privacy puzzle. *Journal of College and University Law, 29* (3), 679–717.

## Fannie Mae

Fannie Mae was established in 1938 by the federal government as part of Franklin Roosevelt's New Deal, as a way to keep funds available or liquid to mortgage lenders to keep the housing market strong and provide a way that would allow for home ownership as the United States was coming out of the Great Depression. Federal National Mortgage Association is the actual name, but the acronym FNMA, when pronounced is "Fannie Mae," and the organization became known by that name.

Fannie Mae does not provide or originate home loans or mortgages, but purchase loans from mortgage brokers or lenders. This provides money for the mortgage lender to replenish their funds and loan money to other potential homeowners. The ultimate outcome is to provide the possibility of affordable home ownership to more people. When Fannie Mae purchases mortgage loans from a mortgage lender, the original lender will continue to service the loan and take payments, and then he or she would pass the payments along to Fannie Mae.

Today, as a means to keep homeowners from losing their homes to foreclosure, Fannie Mae has several programs that work with homeowners. Home Owner Advance is for homeowners who more than two months late, possibly are facing foreclosure, but are able to make some payment, but not the full monthly payment. Home Affordable Refinance Program (HARP) is for homeowners whose homes have lost value but have had an increase in the mortgage payment, making it possible for them to keep their homes and make lower monthly payments.

Providing loans for affordable rental properties is also part of the Fannie Mae program. Affordable, low interest loans are made to those who supply multifamily housing and apartments to senior citizens, working families, members of the military, and students at lower rental rates.

In 1968, Fannie Mae became a private, shareholder-owned company, but is still a GSE, government-sponsored enterprise meaning they are protected financially by the federal government. With the downturn in the economy over the last couple of years, Fannie Mae has focused on keeping funds flowing to the mortgage market, helping distressed homeowners, and encouraging sustainable lending.

*Elowin Harper*

**See also:** Banking; Department of Housing and Urban Development (HUD); Federal Housing Administration (FHA); Freddie Mac; Mortgages

### References and Additional Readings

Fannie Mae. (2012). Fannie Mae responsibilities. Retrieved from http://www.fanniemae.com/portal/index.html

History News Network. (2008). George Mason University, Fannie Mae. Retrieved from http://hnn.us/articles/1849.html

# FDIC (Federal Deposit Insurance Commission)

In 2008, a global credit crisis erupted in the United States, fueled by the collapse of the U.S. housing market, bringing with it the worst economic downturn in the United States since the Great Depression. Reminiscent of the aftermath of the stock market crash of 1929, hundreds of U.S. banking institutions disappeared and consumer confidence in the financial services industry plummeted. The extent of the collapse of financial institutions during the Great Depression was epic. Between 1921 and 1929, more than 600 banks per year failed. In 1933 alone, 4,000 banks failed.

Desperate depositors rushed to withdraw their money from their savings accounts. A "run on the bank" became a common occurrence, as bankrupt banks closed their doors unable to meet customers' demand for the money deposited in them.

Although bank closings were a recurring problem since the mid-19th century, the suddenness of the withdrawal demands ignited a nationwide banking panic. By March 4, 1933, every state in the Union had declared a bank holiday. The magnitude of the banking crisis, and the commercial disruption it caused, pushed the federal government to take action, establishing the Federal Deposit Insurance Corporation (FDIC). Federal deposit insurance was an important factor in restoring public confidence in the banking system during the 1930s and continues to maintain stability and confidence in the nation's financial system.

### The Organization

Despite earlier attempts to establish banking deposit insurance, it was the collapse of the banking system in 1933 that provided the necessary impetus to move Congress to action, passing the Banking Act of 1933. Signed into law by the newly inaugurated Franklin Roosevelt on June 16, 1933, Section 8 of the act created the FDIC through an amendment to the Federal Reserve Act.

As an independent U.S. federal executive agency, the FDIC provides insurance coverage for bank and thrift deposits secured by the treasury, promotes sound banking practices through regular examination of banking operations. Moreover, the FDIC has authority to dissolve, restructure, or otherwise dispose of insolvent or unsound banks. Following the global financial crisis of 2008, the powers of the FDIC has been expanded to take over and liquidate failing nonbank financial firms (Dodd–Frank Wall Street Reform and Consumer Protection Act).

### Initial and Ongoing Funding

The initial funding to establish the FDIC came from loans provided by the U.S. Treasury and the Federal Reserve. The repayment of the loans and ongoing financing of the FDIC come from ongoing assessments of insurance premiums. Banks and financial institutions may apply either to become members of the Federal Reserve System (Member FDIC) or to be insured by FDIC (FDIC insured). Members and insured institutions are required to pay premiums at the end of each quarter. Assessment rates are set semiannually, and modified from time to time in response to changing economic conditions and reserve amounts. In addition to insured premiums, the FDIC is also funded by earnings from investments in treasury securities, the only investments allowed by law.

In return for the premiums paid, the FDIC guarantees payment on deposits held in member and other insured institutions. In addition, member institutions are afforded additional benefits including direct access to the national payments system through the Federal Reserve's check and electronic clearing facilities.

Management of the FDIC is conducted by a five-member board of directors, appointed to six-year terms by the president of the United States, and confirmed by the senate, with a maximum of three appointees from the same political party.

Following the restabilization of the banking system, the FDIC developed permanent policies and procedures for conducting ongoing oversight of the nation's banking operations.

## FDIC Coverage

Deposits made in national banks, in state banks that are members of the Federal Reserve System, and other qualified state banks are guaranteed by the FDIC up to the limits set by law.

The original 1933 banking amendment stipulated temporary insurance coverage up to $2,500 for each depositor which took effect on January 1, 1934. Effective July 1, 1934, the amount increased from $2,500 to $5,000. During the post-World War II growth and relative economic stability, FDIC insurance protection amounts were raised three times: from $5,000 to $10,000 in 1950, to $15,000 in 1966, and to $20,000 in 1969.

The economic volatility in the 1970s and 1980s, including the move to a floating exchange-rate system from a fixed-rate system (1973), multiple oil embargos (1973, 1978), the dissolution of the Soviet Union (1990) coupled with increased risk-taking among banking institutions, prompted more dramatic increases in deposit insurance coverage. In 1974, deposit insurance coverage was increased from $20,000 to $40,000, with coverage increased to $100,000 for IRA and Keogh accounts in 1978. Then, in 1980, deposit insurance coverage was increased to $100,000 in recognition of the increasing number and amounts certificates of deposit (CDs) outstanding among insured banks.

Savings, checking, and other deposit accounts, when combined, are now insured to $250,000 per depositor in each FDIC-insured bank or thrift. Retirement accounts, such as individual retirement accounts (IRAs) and Keoghs, are separately insured up to $250,000.

*Joyce Serido*

**See also:** Consumer Financial Protection Bureau (CFPB); Dodd–Frank Wall Street Reform and Consumer Protection Act

### References and Additional Readings

Federal Deposit Insurance Corporation. (1998). A Brief History of Deposit Insurance. Retrieved from http://www.fdic.gov/deposit/insurance/history.html

GPO. (2010). Dodd–Frank Wall Street Reform and Consumer Protection Act, Pub. L. No. 111–203, § 211. Retrieved from http://www.gpo.gov/fdsys/pkg/PLAW-111publ203/pdf/PLAW-111publ203.pdf

Halpert, S.K. (1988). The separation of banking and commerce reconsidered. *Journal of Corporate Law, 481,* 495–496.

Hynes, R.M., & Walt, S.D. (2010). Why banks are not allowed in bankruptcy. *Washington & Lee Law Review, 67,* 985–1051.

Kaufman, G. (2007). Some further thoughts about the road to safer banking. *Federal Reserve Bank of Atlanta Economic Review, First and Second Quarters,* 135–138.

McKay, P., & Seale, C. (2000). FDIC (Federal Deposit Insurance Corporation). *Journal of Business & Finance Librarianship, 5,* 63–73.

## Federal Aviation Administration (FAA)

The Federal Aviation Administration (FAA) is an agency within the Department of Transportation whose purpose is to regulate and oversee all aspects of civil aviation within the United States. According to their website, the FAA's official mission is to, "provide the safest, most efficient aerospace system in the world." The FAA's vision is to "strive to reach the next level of safety, efficiency, environmental responsibility and global leadership (while being) accountable to the American public and our stakeholders." There is no facet of aviation in the United States that the FAA does not affect in one way or another.

The first human attempt to conquer the skies took place successfully on December 17, 1903. Despite the rapid advancement in aviation that took place following this momentous day, 23 years passed before aviation had any government regulation. The first set of procedures, rules, and action was the Air Commerce Act of 1926. This act created the Aeronautic Branch in the U.S. Department of Commerce and was the official agency with regulating powers over all nonmilitary aviation. The Aeronautic Branch was responsible for pilot testing, the creation of pilot licensing, creating standards of airworthiness, and issuing certificates, and the overall job of safety. Additionally the Aeronautic Branch had the challenging task of creating airways and navigational aids. Since this new form of technology was still being developed, incidents and accidents were commonplace. The Aeronautic Branch was responsible for investigating them and ensuring the technology was properly maintained thereby allowing aviation to evolve into a more safe form of transportation.

As aviation became more advanced and complex, the government was forced to rename the Aeronautics Branch to the Bureau of Air Commerce and expand its role. The bureau added air traffic control to its responsibilities and established the first official air traffic control system. Prior to this, air traffic control was conducted by commercial airlines. In order to move forward and advance, the government needed to take over air traffic control and provide consistent and reliable service.

A short time later the Civil Aeronautics Act of 1938 created the Civil Aeronautics Authority which assumed responsibility for all nonmilitary aviation. CAA, as it was known, began to regulate fare and route structures for all commercial airlines. When this became too burdensome and broad for one organization, the CAA established the Civil Aeronautics Board or CAB. The CAB was responsible for all safety regulations, accident investigations, and pricing for commercial airlines.

The 1940s and 1950s brought tremendous advancements in aviation technology, including the development of radar and pressurization. It was the birth of jet aircraft, however, that changed the entire industry. Soon the airspace became congested with aircraft putting pressure on a system that was unable to handle this rapid growth. Two major aircraft accidents occurred

> According to the FAA website, as of 2009, there were 594,285 total pilots holding licenses in the United States. Over 70,000 were students and nearly 3,500 flew planes for recreation or sport. Over 200,000 held private licenses and over 125,000 had commercial licenses.
>
> *Source:* Federal Aviation Administration. (n.d.). US civil airmen statistics. Retrieved from http://www.faa.gov

and it became apparent that the system needed to be enhanced. President Dwight D. Eisenhower quickly created a commission to analyze the aviation infrastructure and determine a plan to deal with the congestion issues that plagued the system.

The commission proposed creating a new federal agency that would combine the CAA and CAB. This new agency, the Federal Aviation Agency, consolidated civil operations, created safety rules and standards, and modernized the infrastructure so it could better handle the growth of the industry. In 1966, the Federal Aviation Agency was transformed and became the Federal Aviation Administration within the Department of Transportation. The FAA is responsible for the management and oversight of all aspects of civil aviation, which includes the development of regulations, encouraging development of new technologies, operation of the national airspace and determination of flight standards. Above all, their main focus is on passenger safety.

Today one of the most contentious issues facing the FAA is the seating rights of passengers and the relative implications these rights have on airline operations. One perspective assumes the passenger, who has purchased the ticket, must be guaranteed certain rights and expectations from a particular airline. The other perspective, however, suggests the FAA must promote the industry and provide airlines the authority to establish their own regulations to satisfy the demand of their passengers. While the FAA's purpose is to promote the industry, it is also accountable to the American people who rely on the system as a form of transportation.

Certain rights are assumed for every person on every flight regardless of that flight's purpose. Because aviation must be a safe method of transportation steps need to be taken by the airlines to guarantee safety and maintain this as their highest priority. If the safety of an individual, or flight, is in question, the airline is held responsible and expected to take all appropriate measures to ensure that safety is restored.

Delayed and canceled flights are fairly common and can easily disrupt passenger travel. Many times issues are outside of the airlines' control, like weather and air traffic. Other issues, such as mechanical concerns and overbookings, can be the fault of the airlines and in these cases, certain rights are promised to the passenger. Surprisingly, however, there are no federal laws on what an airline must do if a flight is delayed. According to the Department of Transportation's flyrights publication, "Contrary to popular belief, airlines are not required to compensate passengers whose flights are delayed or canceled." Most airlines do attempt to accommodate the passenger by offering vouchers for future travel, a hotel stay, or reaccommodation on another carrier. The only time airlines are required by law, per Title 14 Part 250.8, to compensate a passenger is when the flight is overbooked and they are subsequently involuntarily bumped. In 2010, 65,000 passengers were forcibly bumped from flights and 681,000 voluntarily gave up their seats, in exchange for deals or offers from the airline. It is encouraging to note that these passenger counts represent only one percent of all airline travelers in the United States.

The most recent change to passenger rights came by way of the new tarmac delay rules. These new rules, which took effect at the beginning of 2011, require airlines to limit the amount of time passengers are kept on board an aircraft waiting at the gate or on the tarmac. The maximum number of hours a passenger can be kept on board, per Title 14 Part 359, is three hours for domestic flights and four hours for international flights. If the airlines disregard this, they are subject to a fine of $27,500 per passenger. These rules are a result of passengers being held on on-board an aircraft while on the tarmac for six, eight, even ten hours, in extreme cases. The suspected outcome of this new ruling is expected to be the cancellation of flights so that the airlines can avoid payment of these fines.

Another rule that has recently been implemented, Title 14 Part 399.84, is that airlines must disclose to customers all fees related to the purchase of a ticket. In addition to the base fare, airlines also include 9/11 security fees, baggage fees, passenger facility charges (PFC), as well as numerous taxes and surcharges. Additionally, per Title 14 Part 374, passengers may also encounter fees for changing reservations or upgrading seat assignments. Due to numerous complaints by the flying public and the need for more accuracy in pricing, the DOT implemented these new rules in an effort to force the industry to be more transparent and provide customers the ability to reliably comparison-shop.

All passengers, regardless of their physical abilities, have certain guaranteed rights. The Air Carrier Access Act, created by the DOT, details the procedures designed to ensure that passengers with disabilities have the same opportunity as every other customer to have a pleasant and enjoyable flight. Title 14 from CFR Part 382 states in depth the rights guaranteed to passengers with disabilities. The main components of this rule include prohibition of discriminatory practices; accessibility of facilities; administrative provisions; and other related services and accommodations.

The prohibition of discriminatory practices section is intended to provide consistent service to all passengers, regardless of their physical abilities. The exception to this standard is if a particular passenger would endanger the overall safety of the flight, as prescribed in Title 14 Part 382.7. If this expectation is acted upon, the airline must provide a written explanation of that decision. Unless certain preparation time is required—as in the case of an electric wheelchair transportation or respirator hook-up—airlines cannot require advance notice of a person with disability on a flight, per Title 14 Part 382.39. Along these same lines, airlines may not limit the number of persons with disabilities on a particular flight. Title 14 Part 382.7 states that no seat may be reserved or restricted from a person with disabilities, with the exception of an exit row seat. The overall message of this section is to ensure that all persons are treated fairly and equally.

In terms of accessibility of facilities, all aircraft (including ramps, lavatories, and exits) must be accessible by all passengers. Priority boarding is required for all persons with disabilities so they can have time to get arranged and prepared for the flight per Title 14 Part 382.38. Wheelchairs and other assistance devices have priority over standard items in the baggage compartment per Title 14 Part 382.41. Additionally, all employees must be trained with how to deal with the traveling public. The airlines must also make available specially trained personnel to help mediate any conflict that may arise with passengers with disabilities. Regardless of what the needs of each specific customer may be, to a reasonable point, all airlines are required to accommodate the needs of their passengers.

The airline industry has gone through significant transformations since its genesis. From 1938 to 1978, the airlines operated under the regulations specified by the Civil Aeronautics Act. While this act detailed many operational constraints for the industry, possibly the most impactful was the regulation of routes and fares. Before flying a route, airlines would have to file a formal request to the Civil Aeronautics Board, which would only approve it after considering the relative competition and need for service capacity. Interestingly, during this era, the airlines were mostly profitable because the approved fares usually included a percentage of profit that was guaranteed to the airline.

Over time this system began to show its weaknesses and on October 24, 1978, President Carter signed the Airline Deregulation Act. This act removed all governmental interference in regards to determining routes and fares allowing the airlines to operate in a free-market environment.

The impact on the industry was substantial with new airlines seemingly starting up almost weekly and as they became more successful, the legacy carriers slowly started to suffer. It was too difficult for them to adjust from operating with an almost guaranteed profit to competing for customers with new airline entrants that were operating with more efficient aircraft and lower overall costs. Shortly after deregulation took effect, many of the legacy carriers disappeared from the horizon, such as Braniff, Eastern, and Pan Am, to name a few. The industry was evolving into one that included air carriers like Southwest Airlines, whose core competency focused on good service at a low fare.

The aviation industry plays a significant role in the world's economy and is the platform from which the growth of other industries becomes possible. As new technologies are developed and implemented, such as NextGen, the industry will continue to flatten the world. Reflecting back on the short 100 years since the first aircraft flew, aviation has had an impact on various aspects of human life. The future promises much of the same with unparalleled growth, new and unimaginable possibilities, while maintaining the safest form of transportation in the world.

*George Richard-Thomas Stahle and Mary Niemczyk*

**See also:** Americans with Disabilities Act; Department of Transportation (DOT)

### References and Additional Readings

Department of Transportation. (2011). U.S. Department of transportation expands airline passenger protections. Retrieved from http://www.dot.gov/affairs/2011/dot5111.html

Department of Transportation Aviation Consumer Protection Division. (2012a). Passengers with disabilities. Retrieved from http://airconsumer.dot.gov/publications/disabled.htm

Department of Transportation Aviation Consumer Protection Division. (2012b). Rules. Retrieved from http://airconsumer.ost.dot.gov/rules/rules.htm

Department of Transportation Aviation Consumer Protection Division. (2013). Fly rights. Retrieved from http://airconsumer.dot.gov/publications/flyrights.htm

Federal Aviation Administration. (2013a). FAA regulations. Retrieved from http://www.faa.gov/regulations_policies/faa_regulations/

Federal Aviation Administration. (2013b). NextGen implementation. Retrieved from http://www.faa.gov/nextgen/implementation/

Federal Aviation Administration. (2013c). Mission. Retrieved from http://www.faa.gov/about/mission/

Government Printing Office. (2012). Electronic code of federal regulations. Retrieved from http://ecfr.gpoaccess.gov/cgi/t/text/text-idx?c=ecfr

New Rule to Limit Airline Tarmac Delays. (2011). CBS News. CBS Interactive, April 20, 2011. Retrieved from http://www.cbsnews.com/2100–500395_162–20055556.html

## Federal Bureau of Investigation (FBI)

The Federal Bureau of Investigation (FBI), an agency under the Department of Justice (DOJ), is focused on protection and defense of the United States. Their priorities, listed on their website, are to:

1.  Protect the United States from terrorist attack.
2.  Protect the United States against foreign intelligence operations and espionage.
3.  Protect the United States against cyber-based attacks and high-technology crimes.
4.  Combat public corruption at all levels.
5.  Protect civil rights.
6.  Combat transnational/national criminal organizations and enterprises.
7.  Combat major white-collar crime.
8.  Combat significant violent crime.
9.  Support federal, state, local, and international partners.
10. Upgrade technology to successfully perform the FBI's mission. (Federal Bureau of Investigation, 2012)

To carry out those priorities, with a budget of over $8 billion, the bureau employs nearly 36,000 employees, including nearly 14,000 special agents, and 22,000 support professionals. The bureau currently has 56 field offices and 380 smaller offices called resident agencies. Internationally, there are attaché' offices in 60 countries across the globe.

The core values, spelled out on the website are as follows:

*   Rigorous obedience to the Constitution of the United States;
*   Respect for the dignity of all those we protect;
*   Compassion;
*   Fairness;

- Uncompromising personal integrity and institutional integrity;
- Accountability by accepting responsibility for our actions and decisions and the consequences of our actions and decisions; and
- Leadership, both personal and professional. (Federal Bureau of Investigation, 2012)

The values are evident in all of the duties and responsibilities overseen by the bureau. They work on many fronts, as defined by their history. The most requested services, according to the website, are crime statistics, criminal background checks, criminal justice information services, laboratory services, name checks, security clearances for law enforcement, sex offender registry, and training. They offer resources for a variety of groups from business, to crime victims and law enforcement.

## History of the "Bureau"

The FBI began as a force of special agents in 1908 by then Attorney General Charles Bonaparte during Theodore Roosevelt's presidency. The creating of a federal investigative service was controversial at the time, because states, cities, and counties fulfilled the law enforcement duties that were required; federal oversight was not highly valued. In the early years only a few agents were needed to oversee interstate law enforcement activities. However, within 10 years, over 300 agents were hired, with an additional 300 support agents.

When the United States entered World War I under President Woodrow Wilson, the FBI's responsibilities increased to investigating espionage allegations, acts of sabotage, and enemy aliens. After the war ended, the bureau again focused on federal crimes. Prohibition, in the 1920s brought gangster-related activities and illegal bootlegging. However, the jurisdiction for most of the related criminal activity fell largely under the Department of the Treasury.

The true shaping of the FBI came under J. Edgar Hoover, a highly qualified law school graduate with vast experience in the field. During his tenure as director, he established standardized training for agents,

The motto of the FBI was coined in 1935 and is "Fidelity, Bravery, Integrity" and is attributed to W.H. Drane Lester, a former editor of their employee magazine, The Investigator. It is a clever reinterpretation of the acronym FBI.

and recruited specialized agents with particular skills such as accounting and law. He institutionalized much of the system that is in place today.

The stock market crash of 1929 brought a new wave of desperate criminals. Using the media to his advantage, and to assist local law enforcement agency efforts, Hoover began publicizing a list of "Fugitives Wanted by Police." Congress passed laws to enhance the bureau's jurisdiction as the positive public perception and appreciation of the FBI increased. Additional resources were provided by Congress, allowing for state-of-art training laboratories and hiring of forensic experts. In the 1930s, the number of employees had grown to 654 agents and 1,141 support employees. There were field offices in 42 cities, up from 30 just a decade earlier.

Despite the growth and success of the bureau, the growth of communism and fascism around the world threatened the democracy of America. World War II, combined with the effects of the depression on the American people spawned in-country groups of fascists and communists which were closely watched by the FBI. The FBI was given power to investigate subversives by Congress, with a law making it illegal to overthrow a government. Once again, the FBI was charged with tasks related to sabotage, espionage, and subversion. The FBI is credited with uncovering significant spy operations in Germany and other countries. After the United States joined the war, the FBI was also charged with draft dodgers and deserters.

Following the Japanese attack on Pearl Harbor, the FBI's role increased yet again, including receiving specific war-related training. The number of employees rose from 7,400 to more than 13,000. With increased pressure from African American groups, the bureau was given oversight of the Fair Employment Practices Commission (an antidiscrimination entity with no enforcement power) as it related to the war. Moreover, with increased fear of Japanese living in America, internment camps were ordered for American citizens of Japanese descent. Though Hoover found the internment actions unnecessary, the FBI was charged with overseeing the operation.

In the mid-1940s, counteracting communism was a priority for America. The FBI once again was given authority to investigate threats to national security including espionage, conducting background checks on suspected individuals, and determining loyalty of individuals, specifically related to topics of Atomic energy. In the 1950s, after the Korean War, the number of employees was around 6,200 in 58 field offices. Also, around this time, the FBI announced its "Ten most wanted fugitives" list, to help local law enforcement.

By the 1960s, civil rights were at the forefront of the FBI's duties. They conducted important investigations on assassinations of Martin Luther King Jr. and Medger Evers (NAACP representative). They also turned their attention to racketeering and gambling, overseeing laws passed by Congress to stop such actions. During the Vietnam War era, the bureau's role shifted back to investigating antiwar sentiments and acts of violence, including the shooting at Kent State University and the bomb explosion at the University of Wisconsin.

In the mid to late 1970s, the FBI was addressing antiwar movements just as they had in the past, with counterintelligence and traditional investigative techniques. In 1972, Hoover died after serving nearly 48 years as the FBI director. He was given a highly honored state funeral. The newly appointed Acting Director, L. Patrick Gray, had, near the beginning of his appointment, the Watergate scandal to contend with. The bureau investigated the scandal and revealed suspicion surrounding Gray himself; he subsequently withdrew his name for consideration for the permanent role. William Ruckleshaus served in an acting role until Clarence Kelly was appointed as director. After President Ford took office following Nixon's resignation, the FBI worked to restore trust in the bureau and law enforcement in the wake of the Watergate scandal. Director Kelly also worked to hire more women and people of color. Field offices numbered 59 with 8,000 agents and 11,000 support employees.

In the 1980s, the FBI focused largely on espionage cases, as international terrorism incidents emerged. The new Director, William H. Webster announced four priorities for the FBI: foreign counterintelligence, counterterrorism, organized crime, and white-collar crime. Illegal drug trade also grew significantly in the 1990s such that the attorney general gave FBI jurisdiction with the Drug Enforcement Administration (DEA) over narcotics trafficking violations. Because the bureau's antiterrorist activities were so successful in the United States, Congress expanded their jurisdiction outside U.S. borders. In the late 1980s, the bureau received another Director, William Steele Sessions. During this time, the white-collar crime investigations continued in an effort to combat the resultant fraud, including banking fraud, and other large-scale financial crimes.

Two major events in the 1990s put a mark on the reputation of the FBI. A standoff in Idaho that ended in the fugitive's wife being accidentally shot by FBI agents, and a 51-day Waco Texas compound standoff that ended in the 80-person cult setting the compound and themselves on fire, led to questions about the bureau's ability to react to crises. In 1993, Sessions was removed from office and Floyd I. Clarke was appointed as acting director. A permanent director was later appointed, Louis J. Freeh. One of Freeh's priorities was to increase international law enforcement efforts and expand the bureau's international presence; he opened 21 new atta-ché' offices abroad.

With computers and the Internet becoming more common and accessible in the United States, the FBI began to look at crimes in cyberspace. Efforts to stop pedophiles, viruses, and frauds became a priority. In 2001, Robert S. Mueller III became the bureau's current director. One of his directives was to address information technology, management of records, as well as en-hance counterintelligence efforts. After only one week in his post, the 9/11 attacks were perpetrated, significantly shifting efforts of the bureau. The Patriot Act signed by President George W. Bush gave the bureau further responsibility to protect America from another attack. As a result, counter-terrorism efforts were revisited and revised. These efforts remain in place today.

*Wendy Reiboldt*

**See also:** Department of Justice (DOJ); Frauds and Scams; King, Martin Luther, Jr.; Public Safety

### References and Additional Readings

Burrough, B. (2005). *Public enemies: America's greatest crime wave and the birth of the FBI, 1933–34.* New York, NY: The Penguin Press.

Cunningham, D. (2004). *There's something happening here: The new Left, the Klan, and FBI counter intelligence.* Berkeley, CA: University of California Press.

Federal Bureau of Investigation. (2012). Quick facts. Retrieved from http://www.fbi.gov/about-us/quick-facts)

Federal Bureau of Investigation. (2013). Home. Retrieved from www.fbi.gov

Zegart, A. B. (2007). *Spying blind: The CIA, the FBI, and the origins of 9/11.* Princeton, NJ: Princeton University Press.

## Federal Citizen Information Center

The Federal Citizen Information Center (FCIC) has been a one-stop source for answers to questions about consumer problems and government services for more than 40 years. It was originally the Federal Consumer Information Center, a distribution outlet that sent out free and low-cost consumer publications on a variety of topics from the Government Printing Office. The site was located in Pueblo, Colorado, and the web-site was Pueblo.GSA.gov. Today's FCIC has expanded the effort to serve the public through technology. The FCIC began and remains a part of the U.S. government's General Services Administration (GSA).

## History of the Federal Citizen Information Center

The FCIC has a 40-year history of providing U.S. government information and services directly to the public. The FCIC, and subsequently USA.gov (the official web portal of the U.S. government), began long before the information age was in full swing. In 1970, an executive order of the Nixon administration created the Consumer Product Information Coordinating Center, and the GSA was charged with finding more effective ways to disseminate information to the public.

In 1994, GSA launched one of the first government websites, Pueblo. GSA.gov. It was named after the Government Printing Office's Pueblo, Colorado, facility. Online versions of government publications were offered immediately from this site.

In the year 2000, six years later, Internet entrepreneur Eric Brewer built for the government a search engine, at no cost. President Clinton approached the GSA and asked them to collaborate with Brewer, which resulted in FirstGov.gov. The site was later renamed USA.gov and went live in September 2000—just 90 days after its start.

During the 2000's, the GSA transformed itself to enter the 21st century by utilizing new technologies, launching electronic government initiatives, and helping to develop a means of doing government business on the Internet. In July, 2002, GSA established the Office of Citizen Services and Communications. This office was designed to house all citizen-centered activities in one place. Its mission was to help the public, media, and private corporation to interact with the federal government online or through other telecommunications networks. This effort was later bolstered by a new Office of Citizen Services and Innovative Technologies, created in 2009. This new office engaged the public by using innovative technologies to connect the public to government information and services. It was important to President Obama's administration to also expand the effort to serve the public through technology.

The FCIC in the Office of Citizen Services and Innovative Technologies currently offers a variety of information channels, including websites, web chat, telephone, print, social media, and e-mail.

## Website Management and Content Program

FCIC programs include the following website management and content programs.

- USA.gov connects people with government information, benefits, and services. It is the official web portal of the U.S. government, and also features a mobile version and an apps gallery.

- GobiernolUSA.gov is the Spanish-language counterpart to USA.gov. It has a mobile site and apps gallery.

- Blog.USA.gov showcases the helpfulness and practicality of federal, state, and local government information.

- Kids.gov was designed especially for kids and educators and is a portal to government websites.

- Social media in English is helpful for up-to-the-minute information on Facebook, Twitter, YouTube, e-mail alerts, updates, and Scribd RSS feeds. (RSS stands for Really Simple Syndication and is an easy way to keep up with news and information without browsing or searching on websites. It can allow you to scan headlines from a number of news sources in a central location.)

- Social media in Spanish is written especially for the U.S. Hispanic community, and includes Facebook, Twitter, YouTube, RSS feeds, and email alerts and updates.

### Contact Center Services Program

The Contact Center Services Program provides direct contact through the telephone at 1-800-FED-INFO, and it also provides web chat and email services to the public through the National Contact Center (NCC). The NCC answers 1.5 million inquiries a year. The Contact Center Services Program also organizes communication services for government agencies through USA Contact. Last, it manages the Government Contact Center Council (G3C). G3C is a group of federal call center managers that share industry best practices, emerging technology, and collaborate during national emergencies.

### Publication Services and Citizen Outreach Program

Today, even as the FCIC has embraced new technologies, it continues to provide materials at publications.usa.gov. The FCIC site still offers important consumer information and publications to help people make important life decisions. The new site provides better navigation, search, shopping experience, and some of the favorite publications in popular e-reader formats. Social media channels are also used to keep consumers informed about new consumer publications.

The mission of FCIC is to get accurate, complete, and concise government information into consumers' hands when, where, and how they want and need it to make important life decisions. The Publication Services and Citizen Outreach Program have several functions.

- It coordinates outreach and delivery of FCIC services to both the public and federal agency customers.
- The Citizen Outreach team produces educational promotions and public service advertising that inform citizens about the FCIC websites, National Contact Center services, and consumer publications.
- The Information Program Managers team assists federal agencies with warehousing, promoting, and distributing publications through the Pueblo, Colorado, publications distribution facility, which is FCIC's Consumer Information Catalog and online information. The team manages the website Publications.USA.gov (formerly Pueblo.gsa.gov), providing access to hundreds of the best federal publications, including the popular FCIC-published *Consumer Action Handbook* and its Spanish counterpart *la Guía del Consumidor*.

### Exploring the Website

The publications.USA.gov website offers a variety of categories to search for consumer and safety information. Numerous subtopics and publications can be found under each category. Some major categories include animals, cars, computers, consumer protection, education, employment, family, federal programs, food, going green, health, history, housing, money, small business, travel, and Español. Subcategories include government publications on a variety of topics related to each category. For example, under cars, you might find consumer information on fuel savings, warranties, buying new and used cars, child passenger safety, distracted drivers, green vehicles, scams, motorcycle safety, lowering auto insurance, renting a car, tire safety, and vehicle financing. Consumers will find a list of popular publications and a publication of the week. The site also offers the capability to (1) subscribe to free e-mail updates on a favorite topic; (2) get mobile text updates on consumer publications and promotions; (3) receive monthly e-newsletters; and (4) participate in live chats.

Two publications, the *Consumer Information Catalog* and the *Consumer Action Handbook* appear on the website with instructions for ordering. The *Consumer Information Catalog* lists approximately 150 free and low-cost publications available from various federal agencies. The *Consumer Action Handbook* provides information to help with consumer purchases, problems, and complaints. It also provides information to help consumers contact hundreds of companies and trade associations, local, state, and federal government agencies, national consumer organizations, and more.

*Joanne Bankston*

**See also:** Consumers Union; Public Citizen

### References and Additional Readings

Federal Citizen Information Center. (n.d.). Publications.USA.gov. Retrieved from http://publications.usa.gov/

General Service Administration. (n.d.a). USA.gov. Federal Citizen Information Center makes government easy. Retrieved http://www.gsa.gov/portal/content/101085

General Service Administration. (n.d.b). A brief history of GSA. Retrieved September 11, 2012, from http://www.gsa.gov/portal/content

USA.gov. (n.d.). What is RSS? Retrieved from http:www.usa.gov/Topics/Reference-Shelf/Libraries/RSS-Library/What-I

## Federal Communications Commission (FCC)

### History of Communication

Communication serves as the foundation to a society's ability to function as a civilized community. It is believed the Phoenicians developed an alphabet in the year 3500 BC, the Greeks started the first library in 530 BC, the first movable type was invented in the year 1049 in China, and in 1450, newspapers first appeared in Europe. In 1835, Samuel Morse invents Morse Code, in 1861, the United States begins the *Pony Express*, and in 1902, Guglielmo Marconi transmits radio signals from Cornwall to Newfoundland, the first radio signal across the Atlantic Ocean. In 1926, movie studios figured out a way to record sound separately from film and synchronized the sound for the beginning of motion pictures. This was an improvement on work done previously by Thomas Edison. In 1927, NBC started two radio networks and CBS was founded. In 1951, computers were first sold commercially and in 1972, HBO invented a method to pay for television service through cable. In 1976, Apple's home computer was invented and in 1985, cellular telephones became widespread in automobiles. By 1994, the World Wide Web was released in America and communication was changed forever. From cave paintings, petroglyphs, to writing with the alphabet, and now mass communication through the Internet, communication has evolved with political and economic systems to a power-filled force in the global setting today.

**Government Entities Housed Under the Consumer & Government Affairs Bureau**

- The Reference Information Center (RIC)—the official FCC records custodian Enforcement Bureau
- The Office of Intergovernmental Affairs (IGA)—provides two-way communication for consumers and the FCC through federal regulatory agencies, state, local, and Tribal governments
- The Disability Rights Office (DRO)—responsible for disability-related telecommunications matters including telecommunications relay service (TRS), access to telecommunications equipment by persons with disabilities, access to emergency information, and closed captioning
- The Consumer Policy Division (CPD)—oversees the development of policy for regulated entities such as common carrier, broadcast, wireless, satellite, and cable companies and responsible for the Telephone Consumer Protection Act (TCPA), CAN-SPAM Act, Slamming (the unauthorized use of changing telecommunications carriers), truth in billing, and advertising
- The Consumer Inquiries and Complaints Division (CICD)—mediates individual consumer inquiries and complaints falling under the jurisdiction of FCC regulations
- The Consumer Affairs and Outreach Division (CAOD)—conducts outreach and establishes education goals and ensures the commission has a wide spectrum of public viewpoints for decision-making, informs the public of FCC regulatory programs
- The Web and Print Publishing Division (WPPD)—oversees consumer content the commission develops for its website and print publications, writes blogs, consumer guides, and consumer documents, also performs foreign-language translation
- The Office of Native Affairs and Policy (ONAP)—maintains outreach to tribal governments for understanding of FCC programs, policies, rules, and decisions

## Communications Act of 1934—The Need for the FCC

Franklin D. Roosevelt prompted the study of electronic communications through Daniel C. Roper, secretary of commerce, in 1933 citing communication as an interstate good. The impetus for the study was the idea of regulating telephone and broadcasting with similar jurisdiction the Interstate Commerce Commission (ICC) had over regulating railways and interstate commerce. The ICC was created by the Interstate Commerce Act of 1887 and regulated railroads, trucking, fair rates, bus lines, and telephone companies. The study concluded communications services should be regulated by a single body of government. A new agency was needed for regulation of all interstate and foreign communication by wire and radio, telegraphy, telephone, or broadcast. Congress was summoned to create the Federal Communications Commission (FCC). Senator Dill and Representative Rayburn introduced the bill and eventually Senate Bill (S.3285) passed the House and was on its way to the beginning of the FCC. Franklin D. Roosevelt signed into law the Communications Act of 1934. This federal law was enacted as Public Law Number 416 by the 73rd Congress and began its effectiveness on July 1, 1934. The FCC was born. The Communications Act of 1934 is an important piece of legislation. It replaced the Federal Radio Commission with the FCC. The new law also transferred the regulation of telephone services from the ICC to the FCC. The purpose of the act was to regulate interstate and foreign commerce in communication so it was accessible to all people of the United States. The goal of the act was to have quality wire and radio communication service at reasonable charges. The newly formed FCC was to be utilized for a more effective execution of communication involving a centralizing authority. Recently talks of an Internet kill switch have been discussed challenging the original powers of the Communications Act of 1934. The idea is the president of the United States needs authority to stop the Internet in the case of a cyberattack threatening national security.

## The Telecommunications Act of 1996

The first substantial amendment to the Communications Act of 1934 occurred through the 104th Congress of the United States and the passage of the Telecommunications Act of 1996. It was the first major change to the communications policies in more than 60 years. President Bill Clinton signed the Act that included for the first time the Internet as part of the broadcasting services the FCC would cover. The controversial signing included Title 3 allowing cross-ownership of media sources and cable services. The FCC cited the purpose of the law was to allow for free competition in the communications arena. Coupled with a free competitive market, the Act also provided for deregulation of the broadcasting industry.

## The Federal Communications Commission

The FCC is an entity of the U.S. government and acts as the premier agency regulating communications across the country. Established by the Communications Act of 1934, the agency oversees regulation of interstate and international communications by radio, television, wire, satellite, and cable. The FCC not only covers the 50 United States, but also the District of Columbia and any U.S. possessions. The FCC has an estimated budget of $354.2 million for 2012 and employs 1,898 federal employees. Five commissioners are appointed by the president and are confirmed by the Senate for five-year terms. The chairman of the FCC is designated by the president of the United States. Three of the five commissioners can be members of the same political party and none of the five can have financial interests in commission related business. Three commissioners currently sit on the FCC with Julius Genachowski serving as the chairman since June 2009. His focus has been digital communications, specifically wireless broadband and empowering consumers in the digital age. Commissioner Robert M. McDowell was appointed to the FCC by President George W. Bush and was reappointed to the commission in 2009. He became the first Republican to be appointed to an independent agency by President Barack Obama. Finally, Mignon Clyburn was also appointed to the FCC by President Barack Obama in June 2009 and confirmed by the Senate in July of that same year. As chief executive officer of the FCC, Chairman Julius Genachowski oversees the management and administrative responsibilities of the managing director. The commissioners oversee seven bureaus and 10 offices organized by function in the organization.

## Seven Operating Bureaus and Ten Staff Offices

The seven bureaus of the FCC function according to varying responsibilities including consideration of applications for licensing, handling complaints, investigating current affairs, fostering regulatory programs, and participating in hearings pertinent to specific bureau subject matter. Although the bureaus and offices have individual responsibilities based on specified function, they coordinate resources and expertise for common issues. The bureaus are described here.

### *Consumer and Governmental Affairs Bureau*

This bureau oversees consumer policies, notably disability access. Self-described as the "public face" of the FCC they boast outreach education as well as consumer inquiries and complaints. The bureau works with state, local, and tribal governments in such areas as emergency preparedness and implementation of new technologies.

### Enforcement Bureau Organization

The Office of the Bureau Chief and four divisions of the Enforcement Bureau Organization are located in Washington, D.C., at the FCC headquarters. Three regional offices and 24 field offices are across the country as well as the Equipment Development Group. Components of the Enforcement Bureau Organization include the Investigations and Hearings Division (IHD), which investigates telecommunications violations, The Market Disputes Resolution Division (MDRD), which mediates business disputes, The Spectrum Enforcement Division (SED), which enforces rules relating to equipment marketing, hearing aid compatibility, unauthorized operations, and public safety issues, and the Telecommunications Consumer Division (TCD), which focuses on telemarketing, consumer privacy, prepaid calling, and closed captioning. The Enforcement Bureau Organization utilizes personnel in the field to conduct on-site investigations, inspections, audits of radio facilities, and aid in disaster recovery support. The enforcement bureau also works with the Department of Justice in seizing equipment used by unauthorized users.

### International Bureau

The International Bureau works globally on telecommunications, FCC policies, licensing, promotes regulatory functions, advocates for interests of the U.S. government, and promotes an international visitors' program.

### Media Bureau

The Media Bureau administers licensing and regulates radio and television stations, cable television, satellite services, and handles questions regarding the processing of complaints of cable services, loud commercials, cable signal quality, and placement of dishes and antennas.

### Wireless Telecommunications

The Wireless Telecommunications Bureau oversees policies and procedures for wireless services including microwave links, amateur radio, mobile broadband services, including the needs of businesses, aircraft, ship operators, and individuals.

### Public Safety and Homeland Security Bureau

The FCC's Public Safety and Homeland Security Bureau (PSHSB) oversees the agency's policies relating to public safety in communications, including

9-1-1 and E9-1-1, disaster response, network security, and enabling smooth assistance for first responders, law enforcement, and hospitals in the event of a natural disaster, pandemic, or terrorist attack. The PSHSB consists of the Emergency Response Interoperability Center (ERIC) and three other divisions, including the Cyber Security and Communications Reliability Division, the Operations and Emergency Management Division, and the Policy and Licensing Division. Notable functions of the PSHSB include 911 centers, emergency outreach, alert of U.S. citizens, and continuity of government operations (COG), disaster management, and network security.

### Wireline Competition Bureau

The Wireline Competition Bureau works to provide all Americans access to affordable broadband and voice services, ensure access to affordable communications for schools, libraries, healthcare providers, and low-income consumers, protects fair competition, and ensures availability of utility poles and rights of way, oversees telecommunication services through corded and cordless telephones.

---

**The Ten Offices of the FCC**

- The Office of Administrative Law Judges—presides over hearings
- The Office of Communications Business Opportunities—advices small, minority, and women-owned communications-based businesses
- Office of Engineering and Technology—provides leadership for competitive technologies
- Office of The General Counsel—serves as chief legal advisor to the FCC
- Office of Inspector General—provides investigations, audits, and reviews of the FCC's programs and operations
- Office of Legislative Affairs—is the FCC's liaison to Congress
- Office of the Managing Director—manages the FCC's budget, financial programs, human resources, and contracts, serves under the Chairman
- Office of Media Relations—releases the FCC's announcements, takes media requests for interviews on FCC activities
- Office of Strategic Planning and Policy Analysis—develops strategic plans and identifies objectives for the agency
- Office of Work Place Diversity—advises the FCC on employment opportunities for all persons regardless of race, color, sex, national origin, religion, age, disability, or sexual preference

---

## Current Events of the FCC

The FCC is a complex network working on countless telecommunications-related issues at a given moment. Some of the notable issues currently and recently in the news are discussed here.

### Cell Phone and Telemarketing Calls

Irritating cell phone and landline telemarketing calls from solicitors are seemingly controlled by the FCC through registration on the national Do Not Call list. However, aggravating automated solicitations are still bothering consumers. In February 2012, the FCC's Chairman, Julius Genachowski, acknowledged the need for deeper regulation of the automated calls with prerecorded messages and more control by consumers as to whether or not they want to receive them. Although the FCC and Congress have rules to control telemarketing calls, consumers still receive the unwanted solicitations. In a 3–0 vote, the FCCs approved moving forward with adopting changes to the rules that include requiring telemarketers to obtain prior written consent, eliminate the exemption for companies that have an established business relationship, require an opt out mechanism during the call, and limit dead-air calls where consumers answer phones and hear nothing. Exempt from the new rules are informational calls, charitable calls, and political solicitations.

### Cussing, Indecency, and the Airwaves

There has long been a debate as to whether the FCC should relax the original rules of the 1930s of what can or cannot be seen or heard on television. In January 2012, the Supreme Court heard arguments pertinent to Fox Television issues involving potential fines for the F-Word used by Cher Bono and Nicole Richie during live broadcasts. The justices noted they want television to be a "safe haven" for children and families without profanity and nudity. Chief Justice John G. Roberts Jr. mentioning there are 800 other channels where people can go for that. Cable television, satellite television, and the Internet are sources where consumers can view nearly anything as they do not fall under these FCC regulations. Heavy fines can be imposed on broadcasters not adhering to the FCC's rules. ABC was recently fined for an episode of *NYPD Blue* featuring nudity of a woman entering a shower in one of its scenes. Some argued the rules are arbitrary due to a recent allowance by the FCC for Steven Spielberg's, *Saving Private Ryan,* with soldiers cussing as they fight on the beaches of Normandy.

Members of the Supreme Court argued the time of day and context in which the expletives air on television make a difference in the regulation of airtime by the FCC.

Another notable incident involving the FCC is that of Janet Jackson and the halftime show at the 2004 Super Bowl. Fellow performer Justin Timberlake pulled off a portion of Janet Jackson's costume exposing her breast (with a nipple shield) on live television. The incident occurred on CBS television and was explained as a wardrobe malfunction by promoters. The media coverage and outrage by some led to a debate of the standards in live broadcasts. The FCC fined CBS $550,000 but was voided in 2011 by a legal ruling in favor of the television network. The fine for indecency violations was raised to $325,000 after the incident and the Super Bowl promoters vowed MTV, the producers of the halftime show, would never do a halftime show again.

In February 2012, British rapper M.I.A. once again pushed the limits of live broadcasting while performing in the halftime show on NBC for the Super Bowl. She gave the audience the middle finger while singing her solo portion of the performance. Reminiscent of Janet Jackson's stunt, the FCC is reviewing the incident and is expected to fine NBC for the live telecast. The FCC received letters and complaints from viewers while the NFL and NBC apologized. NBC seemed to blame the NFL for hiring the talent while others complained NBC should have censored the incident on a 5-second delayed broadcast.

### NFL Blackouts during Home Games

In an effort to give football promoters the opportunity to sell as many tickets as possible during a home game, the FCC policy holds that an NFL home game must be sold out 72 hours before kickoff to air on television. Creative ticket sales have occurred to skirt the issue including the Cincinnati Bengals giving fans a buy-one-get-one-free deal and the Miami Dolphins securing purchases by Anheuser-Busch and other sponsors of tickets before the deadline. In 2011, 16 blackouts of NFL home games occurred, preventing local fans from viewing the game from the comfort of their homes. In January 2012, the FCC opened their doors to public comment for another review of the rule as NFL league officials insist it helps keep all of its games on free television. Richard M. Nixon supported a bill eliminating blackouts in professional sports before Congress passed the current legislation in 1973. NFL supporters of the bill report sales of tickets for home games have increased since the passage of the bill and want the rule to remain in place. Opponents of the rule claim the

FCC's blackout rule is antifan and anticonsumer, citing television pulls in the financial resources for support of local televised games while the NFL charges exorbitant prices for game tickets. The issue remains in debate.

*Zoe Bryan Engstrom*

**See also:** Advertising; Americans with Disabilities Act (ADA)

### References and Additional Readings

Aufderheide, P. (1999). *Communications policy and the public interest: The Telecommunications Act of 1996.* New York: The Guilford Press.

Bellis, M. (n.d.). The history of communication. Retrieved from http://inventors.about.com/library/inventors/bl_history_of_communication.htm

Einstein, M. (2004). *Media diversity: Economics, ownership, and the FCC.* Mahwah, NJ: Lawrence Erlbaum Associates, Publishers.

Federal Communications Commission. (2005). History of communications. Retrieved from http://transition.fcc.gov/omd/history/

Federal Communications Commission (FCC). (n.d.). Federal communications commission. Retrieved from http://www.fcc.gov/

Flint, J. (2011). CBS beats FCC again in Janet Jackson 'wardrobe malfunction' case. Retrieved from http://latimesblogs.latimes.com/entertainmentnewsbuzz/2011/11/cbs-wins-again-over-fcc-in-janet-jackson-case.html

Granelli, J.S. (2012). Regulators hang up on robo-calls. Retrieved from http://www.latimes.com/business/money/la-robo-calling-rules-20120215,0,3017021.story

Klinenberg, E. (2007). *Fighting for air: The battle to control America's media.* New York: Metropolitan Books.

Lynch, R. (2012). Super bowl fallout: Will M.I.A.'s middle finger draw FCC fine? Retrieved from http://latimesblogs.latimes.com/nationnow/2012/02/super-bowl-fallout-will-mia-middle-finger-draw-fcc-fine-.html

Palazzolo, J. (2012). A gesture to the Supreme Court as it mulls indecency case. Retrieved from http://blogs.wsj.com/law/2012/02/06/a-gesture-to-the-supreme-court-as-it-mulls-indecency-case/

Ray, W.B. (1990). *FCC: The ups and downs of radio-TV regulation.* Iowa: Iowa State University Press/Ames.

Sandomir, R. (2012). F.C.C. may move to end N.F.L. blackouts. Retrieved from. http://fifthdown.blogs.nytimes.com/2012/01/12/f-c-c-may-move-to-end-n-f-l-blackouts/

Savage, D.G. (2012). Supreme Court appears unlikely to ease broadcast decency rules. Retrieved from. http://articles.latimes.com/2012/jan/10/business/la-fi-court-indecency-20120111

**Federal Deposit Insurance Corporation**. *See* FDIC (Federal Deposit Insurance Corporation)

**Federal Deposit Insurance Corporation Improvement Act**. *See* Banking

## Federal Emergency Management Agency (FEMA)

The Federal Emergency Management Agency (FEMA) is an agency within the Department of Homeland Security (DHS) and is responsible for coordinating federal disaster response and recovery in the United States and its 14 territories.

### The Phases of Emergency Management

Emergency management is an interdisciplinary field, utilizing management principles to develop a structure that will address risks that threaten a community, business, or government jurisdiction. Emergency management has a strategic—not a tactical—purpose and generally resides in or close to the executive level in an organization.

The plans and procedures generally take an "all-hazard" approach, rather than focusing on a specific threat. The process is divided into four overlapping phases, designed to create resiliency within an organization.

**Mitigation** addresses risk reduction or prevention. Hazards are identified (earthquakes in California), the risk from those hazards are quantified (major damage to infrastructure), and strategies are developed to prevent the hazard or reduce the effect of it (seismic retrofitting homes). The strategies can be structural or nonstructural. An example would be land-use planning to prevent homes from being built in flood plains.

**Preparedness** includes building capabilities and changing behavior to affect a successful response and recovery. This phase involves planning, training, and conducting exercises. Plans are developed to include special needs populations, animals, cultural artifacts, and vital records. Public education campaigns, to encourage individuals to become more prepared, is part of the preparedness phase, as is encouraging and training volunteers. Examples of responding volunteer groups are the American Red Cross, search and rescue teams (SAR), community emergency response teams (CERT), and amateur radio clubs.

**Response** addresses the efforts to respond to an incident and limit further damage. These actions are primarily carried out by public safety (fire, police, EMS, public works). Although response is the most recognized phase of emergency management, it is the shortest. It begins when the event commences and ends when the immediate dangers to life and property are controlled.

**Recovery** begins as the response phase is winding down and the immediate life safety needs are addressed. Recovery plans focus on returning the entity as close as possible to the state it was in prior to the disaster. Most recovery plans focus on rebuilding in a manner that would reduce (mitigate) the hazards that pose inherent risks to the community.

**Prevention** was added as a fifth element in 2007 to help resolve conflicts between emergency management and homeland security. Prevention means actions taken to avoid an incident or stop it from occurring. Examples would include surveillance, intelligence gathering, and general deterrence operations.

As the emergency management profession has moved away from its early civil defense, response-oriented past, the opportunities within the field have increased. During the past 15 years, advanced degree and certificate programs in some aspect of emergency management have proliferated. In 2012, FEMA's higher education website listed over 250 different programs within colleges and universities, and others that were proposing or developing from sort of hazard, disaster, or emergency management program.

Disaster relief was considered a local government function until the Congressional Act of 1803 was passed to provide assistance to a New Hampshire town following a major fire. From that time until FEMA was created, federal disaster relief was provided through ad hoc Congressional Acts and related to a specific event. Concurrently, specific authority was granted to more than 100 federal agencies, creating a piecemeal approach to federal disaster response.

During the 1940s and 1950s, the Cold War and its potential for nuclear war and subsequent fallout were considered the major risk to the United States. Civil Defense programs flourished in local communities, and community volunteers were responsible for helping educate citizens about protecting themselves from nuclear weapons. International events, including a successful nuclear bomb test in the Soviet Union, prompted Congress to pass the Federal Civil Defense Act (FCDA) of 1950. The FCDA defined "civil defense" very broadly, including rescue, emergency medical services, health and sanitation services and emergency welfare. Again, there was very little funding provided to the volunteers who carried out these duties. It did help to establish the concept of community emergency responders, the early forbearers of today's professional emergency managers.

During the 1960s and 1970s, massive natural disasters (e.g., the 1964 Prince William Sound Earthquake in Alaska) brought attention to the fragmented and informal approach to federal disaster relief efforts. With no single entity directing federal disaster response, and duplicative state and local programs, the National Governor's Association asked President Jimmy Carter to consolidate and centralize federal emergency management functions.

FEMA was established in April 1979 by President Jimmy Carter in his Executive Order 12127and 12148 to resolve the fragmented federal approach to disasters. President Carter created FEMA by merging disaster-related responsibilities nestled within other federal agencies.

Agencies that were absorbed into FEMA in 1979 included the Federal Insurance Administration, the National Fire Prevention and Control Administration, the Community Preparedness Program (National Weather Service), the Federal Preparedness Agency of the General Services Administration, and the Federal Disaster Assistance Administration activities from HUD. FEMA was also given responsibility for overseeing the nation's Civil Defense, a function that had previously been performed by the Department of Defense.

In the years between 1979 and 2003, responsibilities were gradually added to FEMA by legislation, including earthquake preparedness and mitigation (Earthquake Hazards Reduction Act of 1977), emergency food and shelter (McKinney Homeless Assistance Act of 1987) and dam safety (National Dam Safety Program Act of 1996). Following the Alfred P. Murah Federal Building bombing in Oklahoma City in 1995, FEMA was also given authority for coordinating federal response to counterterrorism in the Nunn-Lugar-Domenici amendment within the Weapons of Mass Destruction Act of 1996.

The most wide-reaching responsibility given to FEMA is in the Robert T. Stafford Disaster Relief and Emergency Assistance Act of 1988, which gives FEMA the responsibility for coordinating all federal disaster relief efforts. The Stafford Act provides a structure for the president to make a formal declaration of an emergency, which opens the way for federal resources and assistance to state and local governments.

FEMA responded well to disaster, but there were problems and inefficiencies inherent in any new government agency. The FEMA administrator was a political appointee of the president until it was absorbed into DHS, and it was rare to find an administrator who had any previous emergency management experience.

In 1993, President Bill Clinton appointed James Lee Witt to be the FEMA administrator. Witt had been the head of the Arkansas Office of Emergency Services since 1988. Witt was able to overcome FEMA's previously poor reputation by bringing his experience as an emergency manager for numerous disasters in Arkansas, directing attention to state/local government agencies, promoting individual preparedness, and focusing on disaster mitigation as the primary method of reducing the soaring costs of disasters.

After the September 11, 2001, attacks, Congress passed the Homelands Security Act of 2002 and created the DHS to coordinate federal responses to acts of terrorism. FEMA was one of the 22 executive branch organizations (which included the U.S. Customs Service, the Transportation Security Administration, and the Office of Domestic Preparedness) that were absorbed into DHS and its mission was restricted to emergency preparedness and response.

DHS was focused on counterterrorism, border security, and immigration. Threats posed by natural and other manmade hazards, previously the purview of FEMA, did not receive the same level of attention. The resulting dismantlement of FEMA was instrumental to the poor federal response to Hurricane Katrina in 2005.

Following the national and international criticism of the government's response to Katrina, the U.S. House convened a congressional committee to investigate charges of misjudgment and mismanagement. Their report "A Failure of Initiative: Final Report of the Select Bipartisan Committee to Investigate the Preparation for and Response to Hurricane Katrina" was released in February 2006. The report identified failures and lack of leadership at all levels of government that contributed to the loss of life and property before, during, and after Hurricane Katrina.

As a result, Congress passed the Post-Katrina Emergency Management Reform Act in October 2006 that restored FEMA's role in disaster management, required that FEMA remain a distinct entity within DHS, and defined the requirements for any future FEMA administrators to include crisis management experience.

In 2009, President Barak Obama appointed W. Craig Fugate to be the first administrator of FEMA since the Katrina Reform Act. Fugate was well known in the emergency management community as the director of the Florida Division of Emergency Management since 2001. Shortly after he was confirmed in his appointment, he defined FEMA's mission:

> FEMA's mission is to support our citizens and first responders to ensure that as a nation we work together to build, sustain and improve our capability to prepare for, protect against, respond to, recovery from and mitigate all hazards.

Fugate's tenure as FEMA administrator is built around a "whole community" concept, emphasizing the importance of engaging all community partners—public, private, tribes, educational, nonprofits, and citizens in meeting the needs of the entire community, including children, pets, and people with disabilities.

---

## FEMA and Disaster Declarations

The responsibility for issuing *major disaster* or *emergency* declarations within the United States and its territories lies with the president and is authorized by the Robert T. Stafford Disaster Relief and Emergency Assistance Act.

*Emergency* declarations are made in anticipation of a disaster and activate resources to help decrease the threat of an incident becoming a catastrophic event. Emergency declarations are made when a threat is recognized and help state and local efforts coordinate efforts such as evacuation, or relocation. For example, several emergency declarations were issued prior to the landfall of Hurricane Katrina.

*Major Disaster* declarations are the result of a catastrophic event, and allows for federal assistance to help governments and individuals recover. Many major disaster declarations were issued in the wake of the devastation caused by Hurricane Katrina.

Between 1953 and 2011, U.S. presidents declared a total of 2061 "major disasters" (averaging 34 per year) and 344 "emergency" declarations (averaging six per year).

*Source:* McCarthy, Francis X. (May 18, 2011). FEMA's Disaster Declaration Process: A primer. Congressional Research Service 7-5700, RL 34146.

---

*Valerie Lucus-McEwen*

**See also:** Department of Housing and Urban Development (HUD); Department of Homeland Security (DHS); Disaster and Emergency Declarations; Frauds and Scams; McKinney–Vento Homeless Assistance Act; Social Welfare

### References and Additional Readings

A Century of Lawmaking for a New Nation: U.S. Congressional Documents and Debates, 1774–1875. House of Representatives, 7th Congress, 2nd Session. (Congressional Act of 1803, Bill 11 of 54). Washington, DC, Library of Congress. Electronic.

Congressional Research Service. (2011). FEMA's disaster declaration process: A primer. Francis X. McCarthy, Analyst in EM Policy, 7-5700, RL 34146. Retrieved from www.crs.gov

Defense Against Weapons of Mass Destruction. (1996). 50 USC Sec.2301–2368.

Defense Against Weapons of Mass Destruction. (2007). 50 USC Sec.2301–2368.

Disaster Relief Act of 1974. (1974). Pub. L. 93–288. 24.

Earthquake Hazards Reduction Act of 1977. Pub. L. 95–124. 42 U.S.C. 7701 *et. seq.*

Executive Order 12127 of March 31, 1979. 3 CFR. 1979. Print.

Executive Order 12148 of July 2, 1979. 3 CFR. 1979. Print.

Fugate, C.W. (2009). Memorandum. Federal Emergency Management Agency. Retrieved from http://www.6pinternational.com/news/fema's%20mission%20statement.pdf

The Homeland Security Act of 2002. Pub. L. 107–296 Print.

McKinney–Vento Homeless Assistance Act of 1987, as amended, Title VII, Subtitle B; 42 U.S.C. 11431–11435.

National Dam Safety Program Act of 1996. (1996). 104th Cong. Pub. L. 104–103. Print.

The Robert T. Stafford Disaster Relief and Emergency Assistance Act. Pub. L. 100–707. November 23, 1988. Print.

United States. Cong. House. (2006). *A Failure of initiative: The final report of the Select Bipartisan Committee to investigate the preparation for and response to Hurricane Katrina.* H. Rept 109–377. Washington, DC: GPO.

United States. Cong. Senate. (1950). *The Federal Civil Defense Act of 1950.* 81$^{st}$ Cong., 64 Stat. 1245. Washington, DC: GPO. Print.

## Federal Reserve

In 1913, Congress initiated the Federal Reserve System to function as the central bank of the United States. While originally tasked with providing a safe, flexible, and stable monetary and financial system, the Federal Reserve's tasks have expanded since its inception. Today the Federal Reserve is tasked with conducting monetary policy, the supervision and regulation of banks, protecting the credit rights of consumers, and maintaining the country's financial stability.

### History

The Federal Reserve System was created, in part, because of the bank failures that occurred in the 19th and at the beginning of the 20th century. In 1907, Congress established the National Monetary Commission, which proposed creating an institution that could help avert and restrain banking crises in the future. This proposal was referred to as the Glass–Willis proposal, after Virginia Representative Carter Glass, who was the chairman of the House Committee on Banking and Finance, and after H. Parker Willis, who was an expert advisor to the committee (http://www.federalreserve education.org/about-the-fed/history/).

After much debate, Congress passed the Federal Reserve Act, which President Woodrow Wilson signed in to law on December 23, 1913. The

The Federal Reserve System is headquartered in the Eccles Building on Constitution Avenue in Washington, D.C. (iStockPhoto.com)

Federal Reserve is considered to function as an independent central bank, but is often called a system that is "independent within the government." Its decisions are not ratified by anyone in the executive branch; however, the Federal Reserve is subject to oversight by Congress and is tasked with working to achieve economic and monetary policy that is set by the government.

### Organizational Structure

The Federal Reserve System is supervised for the board of governors (composed of seven members, each with staggered 14-year terms), located in Washington, D.C. A board member may not be reappointed to the board after serving a full 14-year term. The chair and vice chairman of the board have four-year terms and must already be members of the board of governors. They are appointed to the position by the president and confirmed by the senate.

The Board of Governors supervises the 12 Federal Reserve Banks, which are the operating divisions of the central bank, and 25 branch banks that make up the Federal Reserve System. Each Reserve Bank is identified by a number and is responsible for a specific region or district in the United States. The banks are located in Boston, New York, Philadelphia, Cleveland, Richmond, Atlanta, Chicago, St. Louis, Minneapolis, Kansas City, Dallas, and San Francisco. Each bank has its own board of directors, consisting of nine persons chosen from outside the Federal Reserve Bank, with the intent of representing economic and public interests within the Reserve Bank's region. There are three Class A directors. They represent commercial banks that are members of the Federal Reserve System, while three Class B and Class C directors represent the public interest. The banks in the region that are members of the Federal Reserve System elect the Class A and Class B directors. The board of governors appoints the Class C members and selects from them the chairman and vice chairman.

There are currently 24 Federal Reserve Branch Banks. Each branch bank also has its own board of directors, composed of no less than three and no more than seven members, most of whom are appointed by the district bank while others may be appointed by the board of governors.

The Federal Reserve Bank also has member banks, which are banking institutions throughout the United States that have been selected to join the Federal Reserve System, and that meet the membership requirements issued by the board of governors. National banks, by law, are members of the Federal Reserve System, while state banks may or not be members.

### Scope of Responsibilities

The board of governors is responsible for the supervision, regulation, and operation of the Federal Reserve Banks, as well as setting requirements for financial institutions with regards to deposits and discount rates. The board also plays a large part in administering the nation's payment systems and the laws that regulate consumer credit protections. One of the most important functions of the board of governors is its participation in the Federal Open Market Committee, also known as the FOMC. The FOMC sets and manages the nation's monetary policy by supervising open market operations, a function which is dictated by law. The FOMC is composed of the seven members of the board of governors and five votes cast by five Reserve Bank presidents, and the members are tasked with forming economic policy that promotes economic growth and stable prices.

The Federal Reserve district banks are responsible for administering banking and credit policy within their region, being a depository for banks in its region, supervising banks in the region, and conducting research on regional, national, and international economic issues. The banks also interact with the U.S. Treasury, assist with payments, manage cash flow, and help sell government securities. Finally, the Federal Reserve Banks have three advisory councils that work directly with the board of governors.

*Erin S. Cikanek and Angela Fontes*

**See also:** Banking; Congress; Department of the Treasury

**References and Additional Readings**

Bernanke, B.S., & Kuttner, K.N. (2005). What explains the stock market's reaction to Federal Reserve policy? *The Journal of Finance, 60*(3), 1221–1257.

Greider, W. (1989). *Secrets of the temple: How the Federal Reserve runs the country.* New York, NY: Simon & Schuster.

Federal Reserve Education. (n.d.). The structure of the Federal Reserve System. Retrieved from http://www.federalreserveeducation.org/about-the-fed/structure-and-functions/

The Federal Reserve System. (n.d.). Overview of the Federal Reserve System. Retrieved http://www.federalreserve.gov/pf/pdf/pf_1.pdf#page=4

# Federal Trade Commission (FTC)

President Woodrow Wilson signed the Federal Trade Commission Act (FTC Act) into law in 1914 enabling the Federal Trade Commission (FTC) to go live in 1915. In 1937, President Franklin D. Roosevelt himself laid the cornerstone for the FTC's building in Washington, D.C. The FTC occupied the offices in 1938. Nearly 100 years after the FTC Act was passed, in 2011, Republican Representative John Mica introduced a bill in the U.S. House that would have moved the FTC out of and the National Gallery of Art into this historic building. A similar bill was introduced that year in the U.S. Senate by Republican Senator John Boozman. Neither bill passed, but the struggle over even a physical space for the first administrative agency charged with the protection of consumer welfare seems indicative of the struggles the FTC has endured throughout its history.

This struggle stems in part from the FTC's dual mission to protect the interests of both consumers and businesses and the differing ideological perspectives at play during any historical moment regarding the appropriate role of regulation in a market-based economy. Consumers tend to favor a regulatory response during or immediately following times of social or economic unrest. Consumers are generally more accepting of regulation to try and resolve or ameliorate market problems when those problems immediately affect them—whether that unrest is grounded in the anticompetitive effects precipitated by the large trusts of the late 19th and early

20th centuries, the collapse of the financial services industry near the beginning of the 21st century, or just an increase in telemarketing calls during dinner prior to the enactment of the FTC's do-not-call list. Conversely, the relative lack of enthusiasm among business leaders for the regulatory apparatus has remained fairly consistent. Opposition to regulation, however, reached a new peak in the 30 years since the election of President Ronald Reagan in 1980 and the widespread embrace of the theoretical precepts of supply-side economics and limited government.

The statement of purpose on the FTC's website reflects this dual focus indicating that the FTC's mission is "to prevent business practices that are anticompetitive or deceptive or unfair to consumers; to enhance informed consumer choice and public understanding of the competitive process; and to accomplish this without unduly burdening legitimate business activity." To achieve this complex mission, the FTC works through three bureaus: the Bureau of Competition, the Bureau of Consumer Protection, and the Bureau of Economics. The Bureau of Economics' mission includes engaging in independent economic research to support the FTC's competition and consumer protection missions; this bureau's research also is used to help educate consumers about the benefits to society that flow from the competitive process.

Historically, the FTC was primarily focused on its competition mission through the enforcement and prosecution of America's antitrust laws. The passage of the Sherman Antitrust Act in 1890 forbade any commercial contract in restraint of trade; it also authorized the regulation of monopolies and cartels, as well as trusts (large corporations). In *Standard Oil Company*, a famous trust-busting case involving the petroleum industry, the U.S. Supreme Court upheld the constitutionality of the Sherman Antitrust Act under the Commerce Clause. The court, however, also held that the Sherman Act's language applies only to those commercial contracts that "unduly" burden interstate commerce—this ruling established the "rule of reason" in antitrust law. Some violations, like agreements among competitors to fix prices for goods and services, are considered per se illegal. Other business practices must be considered under the rule of reason. A court will weigh the value of the business practice at issue against the anticompetitive effects of the practice for consumers and only those practices considered unreasonable will constitute a violation. After the *Standard Oil* case, many trust-busting lawsuits followed involving the railroad, petroleum, and meatpacking industries.

Under its competition, or antitrust mission, the FTC is responsible for the enforcement of several statutes that allow the FTC to regulate business activities in the following areas: prohibiting unlawful tying contracts, monitoring corporate mergers/acquisitions and interlocking corporate directorates; premerger notification requirements for businesses; regulating and investigating export trade associations; licensing for deep-water ports; oil company agreements regarding domestic oil shortages; oil and gas exploration on the Outer Continental Shelf; licensing for deep seabed mineral extraction; establishing protections for joint research, including the development of industry standards; cooperation with foreign authorities in relation to antitrust violations; rate agreements among common carriers; pharmacy services in group health plans; crab fisheries; exemptions from antitrust laws primarily for biodefense drugs and vaccines; and, the U.S. Postal Service in relation to unfair methods of competition.

Under its consumer protection mission, the FTC has been charged with enforcing several statutes that also allow the FTC to regulate a wide range of business activities. As noted, these statutes tend to be enacted in response to technological and other changes in society that adversely affect consumers and their ability to engage in meaningful comparative shopping for goods and services—an ability necessary for a competitive market to function as conceived. For example, the FTC has authority to regulate the following: misbranded wool products; the labeling and advertising of fur products; labeling and advertising of textile fiber products, including designations regarding where the product was manufactured; cigarette warnings; and, the labeling and packaging of food, drugs, therapeutic devices, and cosmetics.

The FTC also regulates in a wide range of other business activities—again with a focus on protecting consumers and the competitive process—including the following: numismatic and collectable political items and how they may be manufactured or imported; gasoline octane ratings and how they are posted by retailers and distributors, including alternative fuels and their labeling requirements; using the mails to send unordered merchandise to consumers; marketing and labeling tuna as "dolphin safe": disclosure of information to consumers about light bulbs and labeling requirements for plumbing fixtures; the prohibition of advertising and marketing smokeless tobacco on television or radio; pay-per-call telephone services; restrictions on telephonic marketing; regulating contact between sports agents and student athletes; the prevention of underage drinking; preventing fraud in college education financial assistance services; and, the regulation of prices and services in the funeral industry.

The FTC also has historically regulated broad aspects of the consumer financial services industry including the following: disclosures related to consumer credit finance charges, including disclosing the annual percentage rate paid for the credit extended; consumer credit card billing procedures; consumer credit reports; prohibiting discrimination based on certain characteristics in the extension of credit; the collection of consumer debts by third-party debt collectors; the use of electronic fund transfer systems; consumer leases; establishing standards for warranties and service contracts, including how to disclose and designate such warranties and what remedies must be made available to consumers; abusive practices in high-cost consumer mortgages; requiring that consumers have access to free yearly credit reports; requiring credit card issuers to disclose information to consumers about minimum monthly payments; requiring disclosure to consumers when a financial institution is not federally insured as well as regulating and auditing those institutions insured by private carriers; identity theft; and, the protection and regulation of consumers' private financial information.

Changes in technology—including in computers and the Internet—also have necessitated regulation of the following: the privacy of children online; fraudulent charitable solicitations; unsolicited commercial email and labeling of pornography; regulating Internet gambling; imposing procedures for data breaches and inadvertent disclosure of consumers' personal health records; regulating online consumer transactions; and, implementing and enforcing the very popular do-not-call registry, which protects consumers from unwanted telephone marketing calls. Since 2010, the FTC also has had its own Facebook and Twitter pages.

Additionally, the FTC enforces various statutes that pertain to both its consumer protection and competition missions. For example, the FTC regulates certain aspects of compensation and sponsorship in professional boxing; consumers' rights to control their contact lens and eyeglass prescriptions; spam, spyware, and misleading advertising on the Internet; energy efficiency ratings for household appliances; market manipulation of petroleum products; businesses' trademarks; and, working to help coordinate federal administrative efforts under the 2010 Patient Protection and Affordable Health Care Act.

One of the most powerful statutory tools for the FTC is Section 5 of the FTC Act. Section 5 allows the FTC to prevent unfair competition and unfair or deceptive acts or practices that affect commerce, a broad charge. In 2010—in response to the collapse of the real estate and financial markets that occurred in late 2008—Congress passed the Dodd–Frank Wall Street Reform and Consumer Protection Act (Dodd–Frank Act). The Dodd–Frank Act, among other things, created the Consumer Financial Protection Bureau (CFPB), the first administrative agency devoted solely to consumer welfare in relation to consumer financial products and services. The CFPB went live in 2011 and its authority extends to banks with assets exceeding $10 billion, nonbank providers of financial products and services, and larger participants in that market. The FTC's jurisdictional authority under the FTC Act to regulate the consumer financial services market has been to some extent preempted by the jurisdictional authority of the CFPB in the financial services sector. Regulatory and enforcement authority that under many of the statutes related to consumer financial services industry have been transferred to the CFPB. The Dodd–Frank Act also augments the FTC's existing authority under Section 5 of the FTC Act.

For example, the Dodd–Frank Act requires the FTC and CFPB to coordinate their work under federal financial consumer protection statutes. The CFPB's charge also expands the scope of prohibited conduct beyond Section 5 of the FTC Act's "unfair or deceptive acts or practices" to also encompass and prohibit "abusive acts or practices," at least in relation to consumer financial products and services. How the CFPB ultimately interprets "abusive" remains to be seen. The FTC and CFPB entered into a 2012 Memorandum of Understanding and are now working together and sharing consumer complaints and other information in order to leverage each agency's efforts. Dodd–Frank also gave the CFPB authority to draft regulations for some of the consumer protection statutes that the FTC previously did not have the authority to issue. The two agencies also are working together on these efforts. In this sense, although the Dodd-Frank Act transfers much of the FTC's regulatory authority for consumer financial services to the CFPB, the CFPB's mission also complements and extends the existing authority of the FTC.

Generally, the FTC's enforcement authority includes the authority to initiate broad investigatory proceedings, issue preliminary and permanent injunctions, and prosecute civil actions against offenders as allowed under the relevant statute. The legislative histories of many of the statutes under the FTC's consumer protection mission indicate that Congress intended consumers, acting as private attorney generals using private litigation, to be the primary means of enforcement. Most of the consumer protection statutes therefore allow for the recovery of attorney's fees and costs in the case of a successful action. Some of the antitrust statutes under the FTC's authority also allow for the recovery of triple damages and attorney's fees. When prosecuted by the antitrust division of the U.S. Department of Justice, some statutes under the FTC's antitrust mission also allow for the imposition of criminal penalties.

The FTC's organization is headed by a five-member bipartisan commission. No more than three of the five commissioners may be members of the same political party, and the president appoints the chair of the commission who serves for a seven-year term. While the CFPB is an independent agency housed in the Federal Reserve with a single director and a budget independent from Congressional appropriations, the FTC's structure makes it more vulnerable to the political processes at play in society. The FTC's funding is subject to the whims of Congressional appropriation and the willingness of Congress to fund the agency has ebbed and flowed since its inception.

The sheer scope and minutia of the FTC's consumer protection mission outlined earlier helps illustrate the central role of the FTC in modern economic activity and the difficulties inherent in trying to promote consumer welfare in a marketplace that changes rapidly. Businesses also have access to armies of lobbyists and may engage in regulatory arbitrage designed to avoid the effects of regulation. There is much to debate regarding the appropriate role of regulation, but the answers to such problems are not always clear—nor are the implications for consumers and society—particularly in the short term.

For example, many businesses and consumers roundly criticized the FTC for its failed attempts to regulate the advertising of sugary foods to children in the late 1970s—a three-year effort known as "kidvid." The opposition was so great that none of the FTC's recommendations were adopted. While the long-term public costs of the FTC's inability to act can never be measured with certainty, in the 30 plus years since that failed effort, obesity rates have more than tripled among children in the United States. In 2012, one-third of the U.S. population was obese. By 2030, estimates are that nearly half the population will be obese. Furthermore, health officials estimate that this public health crisis has resulted in millions of additional cases of diabetes, heart disease, stroke, and cancer, in addition to adding billions to the already staggering cost of health care in the United States.

Some self-regulation by businesses in response to this public health issue has occurred, as well as government efforts to regulate at the municipal level. For example, in 2006, the Better Business Bureau and many food producers started the Children's Food and Beverage Initiative, designed to promote healthy food choices by consumers. In the summer of 2012, Walt Disney Corporation announced that it would no longer run junk food ads on its TV channels, radio stations, or websites that are intended for children. And that same summer, the mayor of New York City, Michael Bloomberg, proposed banning sugary drinks larger than 16 ounces in all city restaurants, stadiums, and movie theaters. These examples show that approaches to effective regulation are many and the debate about how to resolve problems like childhood obesity needs to consider them all, both private and public.

The debate over consumer protection in the 21st century, however, appears to have moved beyond issues about how to regulate effectively toward questions of whether to regulate at all. The efficacy of the regulatory process has continually been questioned and the process has been under attack by those who favor self-regulation and limited government regulation. For example, in 2011, the Republican-controlled House of Representatives passed the Regulatory Accountability Act of 2011, largely along party lines, and the bill was then referred to the U.S. Senate. The bill passed in the House even though it faced strong opposition from the American Bar Association's Administrative Law Section and legal scholars generally. Those opposed to this amendment to the Administrative Procedures Act offered evidence indicating that the amendments would add an additional two to two and one half years to the already glacially slow rulemaking process of five to eight years. President Obama indicated that his administration would veto the bill, but the struggle to define the appropriate role and method of regulation has not ended.

At this writing, the continued viability of the FTC and other administrative agencies like the CFPB appears tied to the outcome of the 2012 presidential election. The Republican nominee, former Massachusetts' Governor Mitt Romney, has vowed to repeal the Dodd–Frank Act, which will affect the mission of the FTC. A Republican president also seems likely to sign the Regulatory Accountability Act into law. And Governor Romney adheres to the principles of supply-side economics, advocating limited or no regulation of the markets. Regardless of whether Dodd–Frank is ultimately repealed or impaired, whoever wins the presidential election will have the opportunity to appoint at least three commissioners to the FTC. The outcome of the 2012 presidential election therefore seems more important than ever for the future of the FTC.

*Laurie A. Lucas*

**See also:** Better Business Bureau (BBB); Consumer Financial Protection Bureau (CFPB); Dodd–Frank Wall Street Reform and Consumer Protection Act; Frauds and Scams; Federal Trade Commission (FTC)

### References and Additional Readings

Federal Trade Commission. (n.d.) Memorandum of understanding between the Consumer Financial Protection Bureau and the Federal Trade Commission. Retrieved from http://www.ftc.gov/os/2012/01/120123ftc-cfpb-mou.pdf.

Majoras, D. P. (2006). The Federal Trade Commission: Learning from history as we confront today's consumer challenges. *UMKC Law Review, 75*(1), 115–135.

Shapiro, S. (2012). The Regulatory Accountability Act of 2011: Way too much of a good thing. *Administrative & Regulatory Law News, 37*, 10–11.

*Standard Oil Co. of New Jersey v. United States*, 221 U.S. 1 (1911).

Winerman, M. (2003). The origins of the FTC: Concentration, cooperation, control, and competition. *Antitrust Law Journal, 71*, 1–97.

**FEMA**. *See* Federal Emergency Management Agency (FEMA)

**FERPA**. *See* Family Educational Rights and Privacy Act (FERPA)

**FHA (Federal Housing Administration)**. *See* Department of Housing and Urban Development; Mortgages

## FICO (Fair Isaac and Company)

FICO, or Fair Isaac and Company, credit scoring is a system that employs statistical analysis to predict probability of default. Thus, a consumer's credit score is a grade on potential risk. The score ranks the consumer on his or her likelihood of repaying a debt if credit is extended. The higher the score the less risk of default, conversely, the lower the score the higher the risk of default. There are many different types of scoring models that measure risk but the industry standard used by most lenders is the FICO score. FICO

configures these scores for the three major credit reporting agencies in the United States: Equifax, Experian, and TransUnion. A consumer's FICO score from each of these agencies will differ as each agency has its own customized FICO-scoring model. A FICO score can range from 300 to 850. A consumer can purchase his or her true FICO score directly from MyFICO. com. One scoring model developed by and used by all three of the credit reporting agencies is the VantageScore. This score falls within a range of 501–990.

For the average consumer, credit scoring is a rather complicated system to understand. Credit scoring entails comparing a consumer's credit behaviors against those of other consumers with similar credit profiles. According to a 2010 article published by the Federal Reserve Bank of Cleveland, credit scoring involves three steps. It is important to note that the following steps have been simplified. In the first step, data on an individual are analyzed. In the second step, consumers are categorized into groups with other consumers who have had similar credit events. As an example, a consumer who has missed a mortgage payment will be placed in a group with

## FICO and Social Networking

A 2012 study published in the *Journal of Consumer Research* found a relationship between time spent on Facebook and (1) lower credit scores (FICO), (2) higher credit card debt, and (3) larger waistlines (i.e., higher body mass index or BMI), regardless of age and gender. The authors of the study, two marketing professors, point out that the effects are subtle and cumulative and reveal interesting information about how social networking is related to personal habits. This study and past studies have found that users of Facebook and other social networking sites tend to have higher self-esteem because they are connected to family and friends and receive affirmation and praise (mostly) based on things they post. This study points out some potential negative outcomes that may occur as a result of social networking, something for users to be aware of.

It is important to note that this study does not imply a cause–effect relationship; using Facebook does not cause consumers to have higher credit card debt, lower credit scores, and larger waists. Experts agree that the topic needs further study.

*Source:* Mecia, Tony. (October 24, 2012). Heavy Facebook use, higher credit card debt go together. Retrieved from http://www.creditcards.com

other consumers who have also missed a mortgage payment. Based on this information, consumers are then assigned into groups that range from low to high scores. In step three, an odds ratio is then translated into a score, a score that puts risk into perspective for the lender. As a consumer's behavior changes so does his or her score. A credit score is a snapshot of risk at a particular point in time.

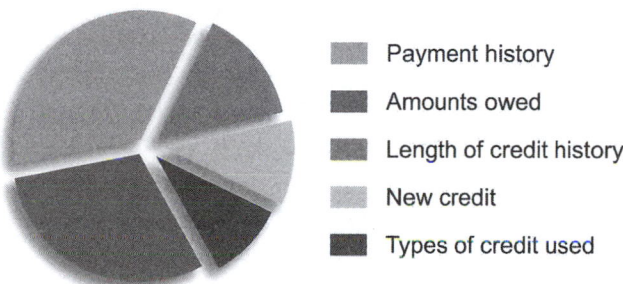

■ Payment history
■ Amounts owed
■ Length of credit history
■ New credit
■ Types of credit used

**Figure 5.** The pie chart shows the weighting of various factors in the FICO calculation. (*Source:* Myfico.com)

A consumer with a score of 750 or higher is considered to be at low risk for defaulting compared to a consumer with a score of 599 or below who would be considered at high risk for default. Creditworthiness and interest rates for mortgage, automobile loans, and credit cards depend on a consumer's credit score as well as other determinates such as income and employment. A credit score greatly impacts a consumer's access to and price of credit. One publication by the Consumer Federation of America illustrated the difference in price of credit based on credit scores. Using 2005 rates, a credit score of 720 would qualify for an interest rate of 5.5 percent on a 30-year loan whereas a score of 580 would qualify for an interest rate of 8.5 percent. A consumer with the lower score would pay $2,400 a year more on interest and $72,000 over the life of a 30-year loan of $100,000.

The Equal Credit Opportunity Act prohibits demographic characteristics such as race, sex, national origin, marital status, or religion to be used as factors while credit scoring. According to the website MyFICO.com credit scores are based on five categories. The chart in Figure 5 illustrates the weight on the score of each of these categories.

One's FICO score is heavily weighted on payment history (35 percent). Timely payments are therefore the key. Negative information such as late payments, collection accounts, judgments, liens, and bankruptcy fall in this category. Negative information is typically reported for seven years from date of delinquency. A Chapter 7 bankruptcy will be reported for 10 years from the date it was reported. A Chapter 13 bankruptcy will be reported for seven years from the date paid. Judgments remain for seven years from the date filed. For California residents, unpaid tax liens will remain for 10 years from the date filed.

The amounts owed (30 percent) on all accounts are also factored into a credit score. In this category, utilization is the term used to evaluate the amount of credit one is using in comparison to debt limit (balance ÷ credit limit). A long history of timely payments and low balances is ideal. The website MyFICO states that a utilization ratio of less than 10 percent per account is an ideal way of helping improve one's score. Another item factored into one's score is the length of established credit history (15 percent). Older accounts will help contribute to one's score, even if they are not actively used.

An application for new credit is an inquiry and falls under the category of new credit (10 percent). Consumers should not apply for credit unless otherwise necessary. Applying for multiple credit accounts can hurt one's score. According to the website MyFICO.com all credit applications for auto or mortgage loans within a 30-day period will only be counted as one inquiry. It is recommended for consumers to be selective of the finance companies that they wish to submit a credit application within this 30-day time period. The last category in credit scoring is types of credit used (10 percent). This takes into account the mix of credit that one is currently using. This includes credit cards, auto, mortgage, student loans, and others.

Consumers should review their credit history from each of the three major credit bureaus (Equifax, Experian, and TransUnion) once per year. Under the Fair and Accurate Credit Transactions Act (FACT) of 2003, consumers are entitled to one free credit report every 12 months from these three major credit-reporting agencies. Consumers can request their free credit report from the website www.annualcreditreport.com. These credit reports do not include a credit score. Consumers can purchase their credit score from each of these three agencies at a reasonable price. However, the credit score that a consumer purchases may not be the same score used by lenders. As noted previously, there are different credit-scoring models that measure risk. The score that a reporting agency selects to sell to consumers may not be the same as the score that they choose to sell to lenders. In a recent 2011 report to Congress, the Consumer Financial Protection Bureau (CFPB) reported that consumers do not have access to the same scores lenders do. This difference in score availability can create inaccurate picture for a consumer. A consumer can purchase his or her score and think he or she is well qualified when indeed a different score can paint a different picture for the lender. The CFPB is working on analyzing the difference between the scores sold to consumers and lenders.

There is no quick fix to improving one's FICO score. Time and timely payments are the key. Recent negative information that is reported on a consumer's credit history will undoubtedly lower his or her score. An effort to make timely payments on all accounts after a credit misstep, and time can help improve a FICO score. Credit repair agencies provide little to no benefit for consumers trying to improve history. In most cases, consumers can contest inaccurate information found on their credit history on their own. A consumer can dispute information he or she feels is incorrect by contacting the bureau that is reporting adverse information by telephone, mail, or the company website.

Understanding and applying the information offered on the website MyFICO.com can be beneficial for all consumers. Federal consumer protection agencies such as the Federal Trade Commission and the CFPB provide educational material and other information in regards to credit scores and scoring.

*Dolores Robles*

**See also:** Bankruptcy; Credit Reporting Agencies; Consumer Financial Protection Bureau (CFPB); Debt Collection; Debt Management, Equal Credit Opportunity Act; Federal Trade Commission (FTC)

### References and Additional Readings

Consumer Federation of America. (2011). New national survey reveals what consumers know and don't know about changing credit score marketplace. Retrieved from http://www.consumerfed.org/pdfs/Credit-Scores-Vantage-PR-2–28–11.pdf

Consumer Federation of America and Fair Isaac Corporation. (2005).Your credit scores. Retrieved from http://www.consumerfed.org/pdfs/yourcreditscore.pdf

Consumer Financial Protection Bureau. (2011). The impact of differences between consumer and creditor purchased credit scores. Retrieved from http:// http://www.consumerfinance.gov/pressrelease/consumer-financial-protection-bureau-report-examines-differences-between-credit-scores-consumers-and-lenders-receive/

Government Accountability Office. (2005). GAO-05–23. Credit reporting literacy: Consumers understood the basics but could benefit from targeted educational efforts. Retrieved from http://www.gao.gov/docdblite/summary.php?rptno1/4GAO-05–223&accno=A19577

MyFICO. (2011). What's in your FICO score. Retrieved from http://www.myfico.com/CreditEducation/WhatsInYourScore.aspx

MyFICO. (2013a). About credit scores. Retrieved from http://www.myfico.com/CreditEducation/

MyFICO. (2013b). Credit missteps-how their affect on FICO scores vary. Retrieved from http://www.myfico.com/CreditEducation/Questions/Credit_Problem_Comparison.aspx

MyFICO. (2013c). Length of time negative information remains on credit reports. Retrieved from http://myfico.custhelp.com

Yuliya D. (2010). Your credit score is a ranking not a score. Research Department of the Federal Reserve Bank of Cleveland. Retrieved from http://www.cleveland fed.org/research/commentary/2010/2010–16.cfm

**FMLA**. *See* Family Medical Leave Act (FMLA)

## Food and Drug Administration (FDA)

The Food and Drug Administration (FDA) is an agency within the U.S. Department of Health and Human Services that is responsible for protecting and promoting public health. It regulates over-the-counter pharmaceutical drugs, vaccines, dietary supplements, tobacco products, veterinary products, and cosmetics. It also regulates medical devices, electromagnetic radiation emitting devices, and blood transfusions and helps promote food safety. It also enforces Section 361 of the Public Health Service Act and other laws related to disease control and sanitation. In addition, the FDA regulates prescription-drug-related advertising and promotion.

The FDA is led by the Commissioner of Food and Drugs, appointed by the president with the advice and consent of the Senate. The commissioner reports to the Secretary of Health and Human Services. It has its headquarters in White Oak, Maryland, and began opening offices in foreign countries in 2008. The FDA has over 200 field offices and laboratories located across the United States (FDA, 2012a).

In 2007, the FDA had regulatory authority over more than one trillion dollars in consumer goods, which included $466 billion in food sales, $275 billion in drugs, $60 billion in cosmetics, and $18 billion in vitamin supplements. This represents approximately 25 percent of all domestic consumption and approximately 33 percent of all imports (Harris, 2008).

The majority of federal laws concerning the FDA are part of the Food, Drug and Cosmetic Act (passed in 1938 with frequent and extensive revisions since). These laws can be found in Title 21, Chapter 9 of the U.S. Code. There are other significant laws enforced by the FDA and, in many instances, the responsibilities for enforcing these laws are shared with other federal agencies. These include the Public Health Service Act, parts of the Controlled Substances Act, and the Federal Anti-Tampering Act (FDA, 2006).

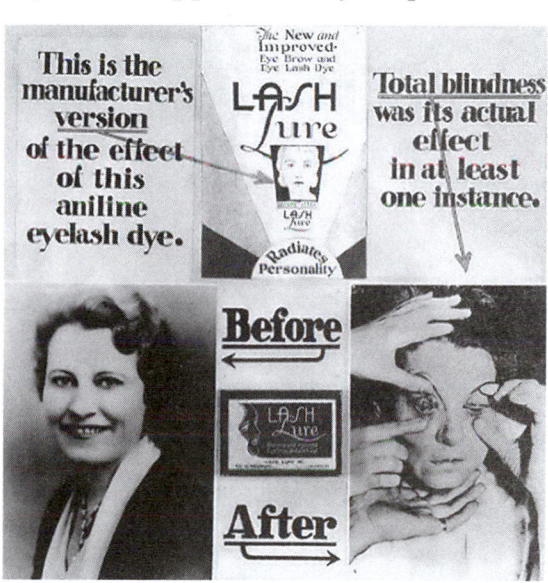

The Food and Drug Administration, in its attempts to persuade a reluctant Congress to make improvements to the Pure Food and Drug Act, assembled examples of products that illustrated shortcomings in the 1906 law. This exhibit shows how an unregulated eyelash dye caused blindness in some of the women who used it. (Food and Drug Administration)

## Overview of the FDA Organizational Structure

The FDA consists of the Office of the Commissioner and four directorates overseeing the core functions of the agency, which are (1) Medical Products and Tobacco; (2) Foods; (3) Global Regulatory Operations and Policy; and (4) Operations. Each directorate is comprised of various operating units. Table 24 provides an overview of the organizational structure of the FDA (2012b):

**Table 24**   FDA: Overview of the organizational structure

Office of the Commissioner

- Office of the Chief Counsel
- Office of the Chief Scientist
- Office of the Counselor to the Commissioner
- Office of the Executive Secretariat
- Office of External Affairs
- Office of Legislation
- Office of Minority Health
- Office of Policy and Planning
- Office of Women's Health
- National Center for Toxicological Research

Office of Medical Products and Tobacco

- Center for Drug Evaluation and Research
- Center for Biologics Evaluation and Research
- Center for Devices and Radiological Health
- Center for Tobacco Products
- Office of Special Medical Programs
- Office of Combination Products
- Office of Good Clinical Practice
- Office of Orphan Product Development
- Office of Pediatric Therapeutics

Office of Foods

- Center for Food Safety and Applied Nutrition
- Center for Veterinary Medicine

Office of Global Regulatory Operations and Policy

- Office of International Programs
- Office of Regulatory Affairs

(Continued)

**Table 24**    *(Continued)*

Office of Operations
- Office of Equal Employment Opportunity
- Office of Finance, Budget and Acquisition
- Office of Information Management
- Office of Management

A more detailed description of the Office of the Commissioner and each of the four directorates, as well as the responsibilities of the major offices and centers is provided in the following pages.

## FDA Offices and Centers

### Office of the Commissioner

The Office of the Commissioner provides leadership for the agency's scientific activities, communication, legislative liaison, policy and planning, women's and minority health initiatives, agency operations, and toxicological research. The Office of the Commissioner also houses the National Center for Toxicological Research.

### National Center for Toxicological Research

The National Center for Toxicological Research (NCTR) supports FDA's mission to promote and protect public health and its strategic plan focuses on three goals: (1) to advance scientific approaches and tools necessary to support public health; (2) to develop new and innovative outreach communications materials, methods, and processes; and (3) to strengthen and modernize administrative management to support FDA science goals. Its current research focuses on bioinformatics, biostatistics, computational toxicology, food protection, imaging, and nanotechnology (NCTR Strategic Plan, 2012).

### Office of Medical Products and Tobacco

The office of Medical Products and Tobacco advises the commissioner regarding all medical product and tobacco-related programs and issues.

### Center for Drug Evaluation and Research

The Center for Drug Evaluation and Research evaluates drug products and first determines if a new drug can be sold with a prescription. It also determines whether a drug can be sold over the counter (OTC) without a prescription. New drugs must first go through a process called a New Drug Application (NDA). Once approved as a "new drug," it is available by prescription only. In order to receive OTC status, the sponsor of a "new drug" must go through a trial period in which the drug is offered by prescription only. The sponsor must report every adverse drug experience of which it learns in a timely manner. Serious and fatal adverse effects must be reported within 15 days, while other adverse effects must be reported every quarter (FDA, 2011a). It can take several years for an OTC drug to be approved. The FDA sometimes grants conditional approval to a sponsor who must then conduct additional Phase IV clinical trials. The FDA may also require an additional risk management plan before it is approved. A drug must finally be considered safe and effective when used as directed before it is approved for OTC status. The FDA has approved approximately 800 ingredients that have been combined to create more than 100,000 OTC drug products. While the FDA has the authority to regulate prescription drug advertising and promotion, the advertising and promotion of OTC drugs are regulated by the FTC (FDA, 1999).

The Center for Drug Evaluation and Research is also responsible for approving less expensive generic drugs that are chemical equivalents of brand-name drugs whose patents have expired. The FDA requires scientific evidence that a drug is interchangeable with or therapeutically equivalent to the original in order to be approved (Cohen, 1990).

### Center for Biologics Evaluation and Research

The Center for Biologics Evaluation and Research (CBER) is responsible for ensuring the safety and efficacy of biological therapeutic agents. These include blood and blood products, vaccines, allergenics, cell- and tissue-based products, and gene therapy products. The Federal Food, Drug, and Cosmetic Act of 2006 expanded the authority of the CBER to include all biologic products. Biologics are derived from living sources in contrast to drugs that are chemically synthesized. Many biologics are manufactured using biotechnology. New biologics are required to go through a premarket approval process similar to that for drugs (FDA, 2012c).

### Center for Devices and Radiological Health

The Center for Devices and Radiological Health (CDRH) is responsible for the premarket approval of all medical devices, as well as overseeing the manufacturing, performance, and safety of these devices. It also oversees the safety performance of nonmedical devices that emit certain types of electromagnetic radiation. Examples of regulated devices include cellular phones, airport baggage screening equipment, television receivers, microwave ovens, tanning booths, and laser products. CDRH has the authority to declare regulated products defective and to order the recall of defective or noncompliant products.

### Center for Tobacco Products

The Center for Tobacco Products oversees the implementation of the Family Smoking Prevention and Tobacco Control Act that became law in 2009. It regulates the manufacture, distribution, and marketing of tobacco products. Its mission is to educate the public regarding the dangers that tobacco products pose to smokers and nonsmokers through second-hand smoke. It is responsible for "setting performance standards, reviewing premarket applications for new and modified risk tobacco products, requiring new warning labels, and establishing and enforcing advertising and promotion restrictions" (FDA, 2012d).

### Office of Foods

The Office of Foods addresses food and feed safety, nutrition, and other related areas to achieve public health goals. The Office of Foods houses the Center for Food Safety and Applied Nutrition, and the Center for Veterinary Medicine.

### Center for Food Safety and Applied Nutrition

The Center for Food Safety and Applied Nutrition (CFSAN) is responsible for ensuring the safety and accurate labeling of most food products in the United States by establishing and maintaining food standards and setting the requirements for nutrition labeling. However, CFSAN does not have authority over beverages containing more than 7 percent alcohol (regulated by ATF) or nonbottled drinking water (regulated by the EPA). Furthermore, meat products derived from livestock fall under the jurisdiction of the USDA. A memorandum of understanding between the FDA and USDA is used to determine which agency has regulatory authority over products that contain small quantities of meat.

CFSAN was also granted the authority to regulate dietary supplements as food rather than as drugs under the Dietary Supplement Health and Education Act of 1994. Manufacturers of dietary supplements are permitted to make specific health claims in advertising and product labels as long as they add a disclaimer that these products have not been proven to treat, diagnose, cure, or prevent disease. Dietary supplements are not subject to the safety and efficacy testing undergone by prescription or OTC drugs (FDA, 1994).

Cosmetics are also regulated by CFSAN but are not generally subject to premarket approval unless they make functional claims that transform them into drugs. However, color additives must be specifically approved by CFSAN before the product containing the additive can be sold and any cosmetics that have not been subjected to rigorous safety testing must contain a warning to that effect.

### Center for Veterinary Medicine

The Center for Veterinary Medicine (CVM) regulates the manufacture and distribution of food, food additives, and drugs that are given to animals. CVM regulates animals from which human foods are derived, as well as food additives and drugs for pets. It is responsible for regulating millions of companion animals, poultry, cattle, swine, and others. Vaccines for animals are regulated by the USDA and not by CVM.

### Office of Global Regulatory Operations and Policy

The Office of Global Regulatory Operations and Policy provides leadership for domestic and international product quality and safety efforts, including development and harmonization of standards and global collaboration. It includes the Office of International Programs and Office of Regulatory Affairs.

### Office of International Programs

The Office of International Programs serves as the primary liaison with respect to other U.S. government agencies and foreign governments and provides leadership in policy formulation and execution of international activities that impact the FDA and/or FDA-regulated products. It includes activities to combat counterfeiting. It also serves as the primary

FDA authority on trade issues involving, for example, North American Free Trade Agreement (NAFTA), World Trade Organization (WTO), Free Trade Area of the Americas (FTAA), Asia Pacific Economic Cooperation (APEC), and United States Trade Representative (USTR). It also works multilaterally through organizations such as the World Health Organization (WHO), WTO, and Organization for Economic Cooperation and Development (OECD).

### Office of Regulatory Affairs

The Office of Regulatory Affairs (ORA) serves as the lead office for all FDA field activities and provides leadership on imports, inspections, and enforcement policy. ORA supports the five FDA product centers through inspection and regulation of manufacturers and also analyzes physical samples of products. It also develops policies on compliance and enforcement and executes the Import Strategy and Food Protection Plans of the FDA, funds grants and cooperative agreements to perform State inspections, and provides technical assistance to the states in such areas as milk, food, and shellfish safety.

## Issues and Controversies Surrounding the FDA

There have been many issues and controversies surrounding the FDA over its history. Some of these issues are described in the following pages including (1) length of the drug approval process; (2) approval of generic drugs; (3) legalization of drugs by state governments; (4) graphic warning labels for tobacco products; and (5) plant-made pharmaceuticals.

### Length of the Drug Approval Process

Concerns regarding the length of the drug approval process were raised early during the AIDS epidemic in the 1980s. The FDA was accused by certain groups of delaying the approval of medications to fight HIV. As a result, the FDA issued new rules that expedited the approval of drugs for life-threatening diseases and expanded preapproval access to drugs for patients with limited treatment options (Mitka, 2003).

### Approval of Generic Drugs

The procedures used by the FDA to approve generic drug sales to the public have been legally challenged on several occasions. For example, the order in which new generic drugs are approved may have been set by

FDA employees even before drug manufacturers submitted applications and the FDA may have given preferential treatment to certain companies. Several manufacturers have also been accused of falsifying data submitted in seeking FDA authorization to market certain generic drugs (Mossinghoff, 1999).

### Legalization of Drugs by State Governments

In two instances, state governments have sought to legalize drugs that have not been approved by the FDA. On several occasions, federal authorities have claimed the authority to seize, arrest, and prosecute for possession and sales of these substances, even in states where they are legal under state law. The first instance was legalization of laetrile in the late 1970s. The second instance is the legalization of medical marijuana starting with California in 1996 (Clark, 2000) and the legalization of marijuana for recreational use in Colorado and Washington State in 2012.

### Graphic Warning Labels for Tobacco Products

Congress passed a law requiring color warnings on cigarette packages and on printed advertising, in addition to text warnings from the U.S. Surgeon General in 2009. Nine new graphic warning labels were announced by the FDA in June 2011 and were set to be required to appear on packaging by September 2012. Several companies filed suit in federal court, claiming that the graphic labels were an unconstitutional way of forcing tobacco companies to engage in antismoking advocacy on the government's behalf and that the labels infringe on commercial free speech. In March 2012, a federal judge ruled tobacco companies do not have to print these graphic warning labels on cigarette packs. In August 2012, a three-judge panel affirmed the lower court ruling blocking the FDA mandate because it violates free speech protections under the First Amendment. In December 2012, an appeals court denied the federal government's request to reconsider the decision (Associated Press, 2012).

### Plant-Made Pharmaceuticals

Plant-Made Pharmaceuticals (PMPs) are plants which are used to produce substances such as antibodies, enzymes, vaccines, other therapeutic drugs for humans and livestock, and materials for research and industry. Either food plants (e.g., corn or rice) or nonfood plants (e.g., tobacco or algae) can be used to produce PMP products. In 2005 alone, 38 new protein-based drugs were approved and more are in the FDA pipeline.

Certain PMPs are considered indirect food additives unless classified by the FDA as "generally regarded as safe" (GRAS). Substances can be classified as GRAS if they were in food prior to 1958 and were safe or they are generally recognized, among qualified experts, as having been shown to be safe food additives through scientific procedures. Since most PMPs are not intended for use as food, most do not have scientific evidence for their safety and are not considered GRAS. The FDA has effectively established a "zero tolerance" level for PMPs not classified as GRAS in food or feed products. Meeting a zero-tolerance level is difficult and essentially impossible to achieve with absolute certainty. Some groups have called for relaxing the zero-tolerance policy for PMP contaminants in the food supply. Several representatives of the food industry have opposed relaxing the zero-tolerance standard, fearful of consumer and export market rejection of food if even low levels of PMPs appear in the food supply (Dumas et al., 2008).

*Troy G. Schmitz*

**See also:** Department of Agriculture (USDA); Department of Health and Human Services (HHS); Environmental Protection Agency (EPA); Food Safety; Generic Drugs; Organic Foods

### References and Additional Readings

Associated Press. (2012). Appeals court won't reconsider graphic tobacco warning labels. Retrieved from http://www.cbsnews.com/8301–204_162–57557300/appeals-court-wont-reconsider-graphic-tobacco-warning-labels/

Clark, P. A. (2000). The ethics of medical marijuana: Government restrictions vs. medical necessity. *Journal of Public Health Policy, 21*(1), 40–60.

Cohen, L. (1990). Government policies and programs—United States—generic drug scandal. The new book of knowledge. *Medicine and Health, 276*–281.

Dumas, C. F., Schmitz, T. G., Giese, C. R., & Sligh, M. (2008). Economic implications of plant-made pharmaceutical production in North Carolina. *Rural Advancement Foundation International* (RAFI-USA). North Carolina.

Federal Drug Administration. (1994). Dietary Supplement Health and Education Act of 1994. Retrieved from http://www.fda.gov/RegulatoryInformation/Legislation/FederalFoodDrugandCosmeticActFDCAct/SignificantAmendmentstotheFDCAct/ucm148003.htm

Federal Drug Administration. (1999). Guidance for industry: Consumer-directed broadcast advertisements. Retrieved from http://www.fda.gov/downloads/Drugs/GuidanceComplianceRegulatoryInformation/Guidances/UCM070065.pdf

Federal Drug Administration. (2006). Federal Food, Drug, and Cosmetic Act. Retrieved from http://www.fda.gov/RegulatoryInformation/Legislation/FederalFoodDrugandCosmeticActFDCAct/default.htm (cited January 10, 2012)

Federal Drug Administration. (2011). Code of Federal Regulations. Title 21 Vol. 5. 21CFR314.80.

Federal Drug Administration. (2012a). FDA globalization. Retrieved from http://test.fda.gov/InternationalPrograms/FDABeyondOurBordersForeignOffices/default.htm

Federal Drug Administration. (2012b). FDA organization. Retrieved from http://test.fda.gov/AboutFDA/CentersOffices/default.htm

Federal Drug Administration. (2012c). About CBER. Retrieved from http://www.fda.gov/AboutFDA/CentersOffices/OfficeofMedicalProductsandTobacco/CBER/ucm123340.htm

Federal Drug Administration. (2012d). FDA Center for Tobacco Products strategic overview. Retrieved from http://www.fda.gov/downloads/AboutFDA/CentersOffices/OfficeofMedicalProductsandTobacco/AbouttheCenterforTobaccoProducts/UCM245518.pdf

Harris, G. (2008). The safety gap. *New York Times Magazine.*

Koppel, N. (2011). FDA defends new graphic cigarette labels. *The Wall Street Journal.*

Mitka, M. (2003). Accelerated approval scrutinized: confirmatory phase 4 studies on new drugs languish. *Journal of the American Medical Association, 289,* 24.

Mossinghoff, G. J. (1999). Overview of the Hatch–Waxman Act and its impact on the drug development process. *Food and Drug Law Journal, 54,*187–194.

NCTR. (2012). NCTR strategic plan. Retrieved from http://www.fda.gov/AboutFDA/CentersOffices/OC/OfficeofScientificandMedicalPrograms/NCTR/NCTRStrategicPlan/default.htm

## Food, Drug, and Cosmetic Act (FD&C Act)

### Overview

The Federal Food, Drug, and Cosmetic Act (FD&C) (also referred to as FFDCA or FDCA) represents the current food and drug safety standards in the United States. Initially signed by President Franklin D. Roosevelt in 1938, it has undergone numerous changes before it took the current form.

The FFDCA authorizes the Food and Drug Administration (FDA) in the Department of Health and Human Services to be in charge of inspecting, sampling, and testing of most food, drug, and cosmetic products marketed in the United States. The only exception is the pesticide chemical residue on food products, for which the Environmental Protection Agency (EPA) is commissioned to set tolerance levels and maximum limits. For all other food, drugs, and cosmetics, the FDA operates and supervises hundreds of laboratories nationwide and sets the national enforcement measures. Violations may result in imprisonment, civil penalties, seizure, debarment, temporary denial of approval, and suspension.

## History

The predecessor of the FFDCA was the 1906 Pure Food and Drugs Act. Prior to 1906, federal laws regarding food and drug safety in the United States were primarily concerned with imports, while domestic food and drug products were left to discretion of each state for the most part. At the turn of the 20th century, however, a number of economic, social, and technological forces called for increased federal control in food and drug safety. For example, the fast-growing interstate commerce in food and drug industries, such as large-scale meat packing businesses, could no longer depend on state laws and piecemeal adoption of federal regulations. Also, household food consumption became increasingly dependent on specialized, urbanized, and impersonalized markets. Technological innovations in food manufacturing also resulted in increased skepticism and distrust about product quality and safety, depriving consumers of the ability to discern product adulteration ex ante.

The Pure Food and Drugs Act was signed by President Theodore Roosevelt in June 1906. It was also known as the Wiley Act named after Harvey Washington Wiley (1844–1930), chief chemist of the Bureau of Chemistry in the Department of Agriculture, who played a major role in passage of the law and later became the first commissioner of the FDA. The 1906 Act defined and forbade "misbranded" and "adulterated" foods, drinks, and drugs from interstate commerce. The Pure Food and Drugs Act was responsible for creation of the FDA as a consumer protection agency and its modern regulatory functions.

Although the 1906 Act was constantly expanded and achieved moderate success especially in product labeling, frustrations had mounted around the early 1930s within the FDA regarding the 1906 Act's legislative deficiencies. One prominent issue with the Pure Food and Drugs Act was the difficulty for the FDA to identify fraudulent therapeutic claims in patent drugs. Another notable problem was that food and drug products that were locally produced and consumed were still governed by state laws, and resultant legislative gaps were exploited by some businesses. Public awareness grew with the success of national bestsellers such as *Your Money's Worth: A Study in the Waste of the Consumer's Dollar* (1927) by Stuart Chase and Fred Schlink and *100,000,000 Guinea Pigs: Dangers in Everyday Foods, Drugs, and Cosmetics* (1933) by Arthur Kallet and Schlink. It is said that the outbreak of a deadly epidemic from an adulterated elixir known as Lindol in the early 1930s also precipitated a major amendment of the 1960 Act. Overhauling the 1906 Act was one of the first initiatives of the Roosevelt New Deal. The major contributor to the initial draft of the new bill was Royal S.

Copeland (1968–1938), a three-term U.S. senator representing New York and former homeopathic physician. In June 1938, the 75th U.S. Congress passed the bill and President Franklin D. Roosevelt signed it into law.

The 1938 FFDCA was far more comprehensive than the 1906 Act. It removed the FDA from the U.S. Department of Agriculture and repositioned it into its current organizational location in the U.S. Department of Health and Human Services, and granted the FDA with greater regulatory power. The FDA's authority was expanded to cosmetic and therapeutic devices; the FDA began to conduct factory inspections; it began to set standards for identity, quality, and fill-of-container for foods; the FFDCA established safety tolerances for unavoidable poisonous substances; it added the remedy of court orders to the previous penalties of seizures and prosecutions, to name a few. Most importantly, the 1938 Act renounced the Sherley Amendment, which had required the FDA to prove the intent to defraud before any accusations of drug misbranding cases were made, and instead shifted the burden to manufacturers and processors by mandating all new drugs to demonstrate they were safe before market release—opening a new era of drug regulation.

### Food Safety Amendments

The FFDCA has undergone numerous incremental changes through legislative actions and adaptations. One of the most debated amendments was probably the Food Additives Amendment passed by Congress in 1958. Also known as the Delaney Amendment named after Congressman James Delaney of New York, the amendment required all new food additives to verify safety prior to marketing and granted the FDA authority to scrutinize premarket dietary and health claims made by food processors. In particular, the part commonly referred to as the Delaney Clause forbade any new food additives that can induce cancer in humans and experimental animals, and required pre-market approval of new food additives for zero carcinogenic risks. The original clause read *"No additive shall be deemed to be safe if it is found to induce cancer when ingested by man or laboratory animals or if it is found, after tests which are appropriate for the evaluation of the safety of food additives, to induce cancer in man or animals."* The Delaney prohibition appeared in three separate parts of the FFDCA then: Section 409 on food additives, Section 512 relating to animal drugs in meat and poultry, and Section 721 on color additives.

The zero tolerance principle in the food safety regulation represented by the Delaney Clause generated much dispute. Chief among criticisms of the Delaney Amendment were (1) it discouraged innovation in food processing technology, (2) it failed to assess the risks of food additives relative to their potential benefits, and (3) it ignored substances that contaminated foods inadvertently such as chemical residues in raw food, only paying attention to chemicals and ingredients that were purposefully used in food production. Also, the concept of zero risk became outdated as innovations in science and technology continuously reduced the smallest measurable unit for substances, and as the complexity of cancer biology was increasingly understood.

The Delaney Clause was repeatedly amended by Congress to allow for exceptions in pesticide residues in foods and was repealed in 1996, when the Food Quality Protection Act (FQPA) was signed into law. Delaney Clause constraints were fully removed from pesticide residue tolerance. Enactment of the FQPA meant a significant transition in U.S. food safety history. Not only the FFDCA's food safety standards have been extended to raw, unprocessed food commodities, it meant a departure from the "zero-risk" standard to the standards that forbid risks of "reasonable certainty." The Pesticide Residue Amendment (Section 408 of the FFDCA) states that legal tolerance levels should account for a balance between the need for the health of consumers and the need for "an adequate, wholesome and economical food supply." It authorizes the Environmental Protection Agency (EPA) to set tolerances or maximum residue limits for pesticide residues on foods based on risk-benefit analyses. The pesticide may still be subject to the Delaney Clause if it is applied to food to be processed. Food products such as dairy, meat, and poultry that do not have any recognized processed food forms are exempted from the Delaney Clause.

## Current Contents

Currently, the FFDCA consists of nine chapters: Chapter I short title, Chapter II definitions, Chapter III prohibited acts and penalties, Chapter IV food, Chapter V drugs and devices, Chapter VI cosmetics, Chapter VII general authority, Chapter VIII imports and exports, and Chapter IX miscellaneous.

Chapter II includes legal definitions of "food," "drug," "cosmetic," "label," "labeling," "pesticide chemical," "food additive," "safe," "animal feed," "infant formula," "dietary supplement," "processed food," and other key terms used in the subsequent chapters. Chapter III defines violations and describes how penalties, seizures, debarment, temporary denial of approval, suspension, and civil penalties are determined and administered. Adulteration and misbranding of foods, tolerances and exemptions for pesticide chemical residues, standards and requirements for dietary supplements, food additives, bottled drinking water, and infant formulas are discussed in Chapter IV. Provisions regarding drugs for rare diseases or conditions, and discussions of the electronic product radiation control program appear under Chapter V. Adulteration and misbranding of cosmetic products are discussed in Chapter VI. Chapter VII includes general administrative provisions, fees, information and education, environmental impact review, national uniformity, and safety reports. Provisions concerning colors and color additives also appear in Chapter VII. Chapter VIII includes regulations regarding imports and exports of food, drugs and devices, and cosmetic products.

*Yunhee Chang*

**See also:** Department of Agriculture (USDA); Department of Health and Human Services (HHS); Food Safety; Wiley, Harvey

### References and Additional Readings

Cavers, D. F. (1939). The food, drug, and cosmetic act of 1938: Its legislative history and its substantive provisions. *Law and Contemporary Problems, 6,* 2–42.

Federal Food, Drug, and Cosmetic Act. (2002). In *P.L. 107–377.*

Merrill, R. A. (1997). Food safety regulation: Reforming the Delaney clause. *Annual Review of Public Health, 18,* 313–340.

Merrill, R. A. (1978). Regulating carcinogens in food: A legislator's guide to the food safety provisions of the federal food, drug, and cosmetic act. *Michigan Law Review 77*(2), 171–250.

## Food Labeling

Early food labeling legislation grew out of food safety concerns and a need for fair competition. Contemporary arguments for labeling have expanded to health claims, production practices, and the amount and placement of label information. Legislative activity has been influenced by consumer–industry–government battles over both mandated requirements for food labeling, industry's freedom of speech in messaging, and consumers' struggle to make informed choices in a complex food environment.

Federal laws with labeling implications were first promulgated in 1906 with the passage of the Pure Food Act, after decades of consumer activism and the exposure of unsafe food processing conditions. As food production became more industrialized, the number of adulterated, mislabeled, or unsafe products available for sale also increased: chocolate adulterated with rice and soap, "factory" farm dairies producing milk from sometimes dying cows fed whiskey swill, butter produced without milk, and margarine sold as butter. During the "pure food movement," consumers and some businesses were concerned about new technologies, but industry and legislators fought against legislation, and lobbyists were hired to oppose the Pure Food Act and obtain exemptions for the industries that they represented. Public outcry generated by journalistic "muckrakers" and Sinclair Lewis' 1906 novel, *The Jungle*, joined with other crusaders and legislators and provided a catalyst for Congress. These events also aided the passage of the Federal Meat Inspection Act. Responsibility for administering the Pure Food Act fell to the Bureau of Chemistry, renamed in 1930 the Food and Drug Administration. Administration of the Federal Meat Inspection Act was allocated to the Secretary of Agriculture.

By the 1930s, consumer advocates lobbied for more stringent legislation. In 1938, Congress passed the Federal Food, Drug, and Cosmetic Act, replacing the Pure Food Act of 1906 and expanding the FDA's regulatory oversight. The growth labeling legislation during the mid-20th century was driven by the same food industry changes that helped to pass the 1906 Pure Food and Drug Act. After World War II, the number of products available for sale and the number of places to buy them grew. The new legislation also closed many of the regulation gaps relating to food quality and packaging. FDA oversight of food labeling grew by the 1960s to include nearly half of the food supply.

While the FDA is responsible for regulating food safety and related labeling, the Federal Trade Commission regulates food advertising and labeling. The majority of labeling initiatives put into place by the Federal Trade Commission prior to 1960 were designed to regulate commerce and not to protect the consumer. Both the FDA and the FTC have long operated in consort, but often at cross-purposes, just as the USDA and Bureau of Chemistry did at the time of the passage of

### Food Labeling Research Study

Marketing professor Aradhna Krishna (University of Michigan) conducted a revealing survey of customer behavior with respect to food labeling in restaurants. Many customer decisions were influenced by product labeling. For example, in a recent study, people were offered cookies of the same size under different labels. People who were offered a cookie labeled "large" usually ate just one cookie, while people who were offered a cookie labeled "medium" usually ate two or more. In other words, product labeling influences consumer decisions.

*Source:* Thompson, H., & S. Vedantam. (September 26, 2012). How food and clothes size labels affect what we eat and what we wear. NPR. Retrieved from http://www.wbur.org/

the Pure Food Act. To protect commerce, FTC language refers to harm to "ignorant" consumers, while the FDA's more stringent criteria refers to the "ordinary person." The FDA had a difficult time enforcing the misleading package size clause outlined in the 1938 Food, Drug, and Cosmetic Act. Wall notes that there were terms such as jumbo, giant, super, and economy, on all types of items found on supermarket shelves. While the agencies tried to provide oversight to protect *both* consumers and business, business had the resources to fight back, while individual consumers, especially women shoppers, lacked any cohesive power. Consumers remained relatively powerless until consumer groups began to represent the public. Consumers' Union received 500 complaint letters about deceptive packaging issues from individual consumers. The Fair Packaging and Labeling bill required a business name and address and the actual quantity contained on packages and producers could no longer sell a large package with little contents that either fooled the customer or allowed sellers to cut their cost of goods compared to other sellers. Legislators, consumer advocates led by Ester Peterson, and President Lyndon Johnson supported new legislation.

Another era of increasing consumer reliance on processed and packaged foods occurred in the 1960s. The number of products on typical supermarket shelves nearly doubled from 5,800 at the end of the 1950s to over 10,000 by 1970. Furthermore, families were eating fewer meals together and snacking or eating away from home more, resulting in nutrition imbalances. Labeling legislation occurred to guide consumer behavior toward healthier choices. A 1969 White House Conference on Food, Nutrition, and Health paved the way for nutrition labeling. The passage of the 1973 nutritional guidelines required the labeling of certain foods: those with added nutrients and those for which a nutrition claim was made on the label, or in advertising. From that "simple" legislation, the regulations have spiraled to hundreds of pages of guidelines for labeling.

Consumer distrust of food advertising and labeling became widespread in the 1980s. There are numerous examples of false label claims from the 1970s and 1980s, including "fruit juicy Hawaiian Punch," which only contained 10 percent juice and "Wonder Bread builds bodies twelve ways," which was no different than any other fortified bread on the market. Pressure on business to increase sales and increasing competition through differentiation of products contributed on the marketing side. Lack of enforcement on the government side gave a green light to businesses to gravitate further into a gray area of label messages that might be considered false or misleading. A comprehensive study of health advertising claims found that the number of health claims grew by 550 percent between 1987 and 1990. During this same period, the state's attorney generals brought many companies to task about their messaging. Kellogg's countered by bringing a harassment suit against the Iowa Attorney General's office. Kellogg's lost its case when it advertised Rice Krispies Cereal as fortified with energy releasing B vitamins, reaching an agreement with the New York Attorney General. This litigation was one of the engines that spurred the Nutrition Labeling and Education Act of 1990 (NLEA). With individual states involved, each with differing laws, industry was faced with mounting court costs and federal regulation would provide consistent rules. The NLEA established standards for health and nutrition claims and mandated most foods to have nutrition facts labels. The number of health claims fell for several categories of processed foods between 1992 and 1999, while the percentage of conforming claims increased. The 550 percent increase in the number of claims during the 1980s fell almost immediately back to pre-1987 levels. However, the 1997 Food and Drug Administration Modernization Act relaxed procedures for proving a health claim. Rules were relaxed further in 2003.

In the first decade of the 21st century, the FDA continued to take a deregulated approach and consumers were faced again with misleading labels similar to those of the 1970s and 1980s. Consumer confusion grew due to an increase in the number of label claims, simplistic front of package label schemes that provide a composite image about a product, and because many claims come in multiples, such as organic *and* low calorie. And, there is a new wave of value-based labeling that threatens to open gaps in consumers' ability to make informed choices. In addition, major food companies including Kraft, Campbell's Soup, Kellogg's, and Hershey Foods started to refocus on the "high-growth" health segment.

The FDA increased enforcement of labeling laws in early 2010. In 2009, Kellogg's labeled Rice and other Krispies cereals with a claim "now supports your child's immunity," and Dannon made exaggerated health claims for Activia yogurt. They settled out of court. In 2010, the FDA sent 17 warning letters covering 22 labeling violations for labels bearing nutrient content claims that did not meet requirements, showing a new emphasis on labeling enforcement under the Obama administration.

Front of package labeling (FOP) composites have been proposed by both industry and government as a method to help consumers navigate the many health claims that have proliferated and decrease the complexity of available information. The first generation of FOP labels was industry developed and proprietary. Several supermarket chains instituted

**Table 25** Summary overview of significant food labeling legislative history

| Year | Legislation |
|---|---|
| 1906 | The Federal Food and Drugs Act and the Federal Meat Inspection Act |
| 1913 | The Gould Amendment requires food packages to state the quantity of contents. |
| 1924 | In *U.S. v. 95 Barrels Alleged Apple Cider Vinegar,* the Supreme Court rules that the Food and Drugs Act condemns every statement, design or device which may mislead, misdirect or deceive, even if technically true. |
| 1938 | The Federal Food, Drug, and Cosmetic Act passed. It requires the label of every processed, packaged food to contain the name of the food, its net weight, and the name and address of the manufacturer or distributor. A list of ingredients also is required on certain products. The law also prohibits statements in food labeling that are false or misleading. |
| 1939 | First Food Standards issued (canned tomatoes, tomato puree, and tomato paste) |
| 1950 | Oleomargarine Act requires prominent labeling of colored oleomargarine to distinguish it from butter |
| 1957 | The Poultry Products Inspection Act authorizes USDA to regulate, among other things, the labeling of poultry products. |
| 1962 | President Kennedy proclaims the Consumer Bill of Rights, including the rights to safety, **information,** choice, and the right to be heard. |
| 1966 | The Fair Packaging and Labeling Act requires all consumer products in interstate commerce to contain accurate information and to facilitate value comparisons. |
| 1969 | The White House Conference on Food, Nutrition, and Health addresses deficiencies in the U.S. diet. It recommends that the federal government consider developing a system for identifying the nutritional qualities of food. |
| 1973 | FDA issues regulations requiring nutrition labeling on food containing one or more added nutrients or whose label or advertising includes claims about the food's nutritional properties or its usefulness in the daily diet. Nutrition labeling is voluntary for almost all other foods. |
| 1975 | Voluntary nutrition labeling, postponed from its originally planned 1974 date, goes into effect. |
| 1990 | FDA proposes extensive food labeling changes, which include mandatory nutrition labeling for most foods, standardized serving sizes, and uniform use of health claims. The Nutrition Labeling and Education Act (NLEA) reaffirms the legal basis for FDA's labeling initiative and establishes an explicit timetable. |
| 1991 | FDA issues more than 20 proposals to implement NLEA. In addition, the agency issues a final rule that sets up a voluntary point-of-purchase nutrition information program for raw produce and fish. FSIS unveils its proposals for mandatory nutrition labeling of processed meat and poultry and voluntary point-of-purchase nutrition information for raw meat and poultry. |
| 1992 | FDA's voluntary point-of-purchase nutrition information program for fresh produce and raw fish goes into effect. |

*(Continued)*

**Table 25** (*Continued*)

| Year | Legislation |
|---|---|
| 1993 | FDA issues the final regulations implementing NLEA. Regulations covering health claims become effective May 8, 1993. Those pertaining to nutrition labeling and nutrient content claims are effective May 8, 1994. |
| 1995 | American Heart Association initiates a food certification program, implementing the Heart Check Symbol for foods that are low in saturated fat and cholesterol. |
| 1997 | Food and Drug Administration Modernization Act marked an official recognition that the FDA would be working with increasingly complex technological, trade, and public health issues. |
| 1997 | FDA authorizes the use of health claims on the relationship between soluble fiber from whole oats and the risk of coronary heart disease. Manufacturers must include the source of the soluble fiber so as not to mislead consumers to think that all soluble fiber prevents CHD. |
| 1999 | FDA concludes that soy protein included in a diet low in saturated fat and cholesterol may reduce the risk of CHD by lowering blood cholesterol levels. To assert this claim a product must contain a minimum amount of soy protein per RACC. |
| 2000 | After receiving petitions from manufacturers, the FDA authorized the food-labeling claim connecting plant sterol/ stanol esters to lower risk of CHD. |
| 2002 | The 2002 Farm Bill requires retailers to provide country-of-origin (COOL) labeling for fresh beef, pork, and lamb. The law goes into effect on October 1, 2008, after 6 years of deliberation. Also in 2002, the National Organic Program (NOP) is enacted, restricting the use of "organic" to certified organic producers. |
| 2003 | FDA requires addition of trans fatty acid to nutrition facts label. Some manufacturers are already in compliance; all manufactures will have until 2006 to comply. |
| 2004 | Food Allergy Labeling and Consumer Protection Act is passed, requiring labeling of food that contains one or more of the following list: peanuts, soybeans, cow's milk, eggs, fish, crustacean shellfish, tree nuts, or wheat. |
| 2006 | Hannaford Brothers Supermarket launches "Guiding Stars" program intended to help customers find healthy foods. Sales increase for foods with high ratings. Similar programs initiated by grocers between 2006 and 2009. |
| 2009 | Smart Choices launches formally in the summer only to suspend itself after the FDA sends "Dear Manufacturer" letter to the board stating concern that the front of package label is misleading. |
| 2010 | The USDA requires cuts of meat to display nutrition as well, starting in January 2012. |
| 2011 | The Grocery Manufacturers Association announces Nutrition Keys, a new front of package labeling system. |

Adapted and updated from http://www.fda.gov/aboutfda/whatwedo/history/milestones/ucm128305.htm

FOP programs, including NuVal, Guiding Stars, Healthy Ideas, and nutrition iQ. The Smart Choices program, a broad industry led FOP initiative, was suspended shortly after its introduction. It was described as an example of the power of joining private and expert groups, including the American Diabetes Association, to foster the development of FOP labels that signal healthier choices backed up by the Dietary Guidelines for Americans 2005. Industry giants were participants. The program provided an icon on the front of packages that met certain nutritional criteria, created to "direct consumers to smarter food choices in the supermarket." The scoring mechanisms that allowed products to be labeled a smart choice were flawed toward highlighting positive benefits and downplaying negative ones. In 2009, both the FDA and USDA stepped in and the Smart Choices program voluntarily shut down. In 2011, while the FDA continued to work on their own FOP initiative, industry was introducing "Nutrition Keys."

An increasing number of credence food characteristics are appearing that have prompted a renewed interest in food labeling. These include a long list of *values* consumers consider in decision making, for example, fair trade, organic, locally grown, no genetic engineering (GE). Value-based decisions make the task of labeling more difficult. Theories are only developing about value-based labels and there is no agreement amongst industry, consumer advocacy organizations, and governments. In addition, the science of product development is progressing more quickly than the science used to test safety, as in the case of GE foods. While European nations have relied on the precautionary principle as a way to address currently unknown harm to society or the environment, the United States relies on "scientific evidence as we know it today" as the benchmark for making labeling decisions. Consumer advocacy organizations lead the crusade for mandatory GE food labeling and include the Truth in Labeling Coalition, Union of Concerned Scientists, and Organic Consumer Association, but currently the U.S. government only allows voluntary labeling of GE-free products.

There are growing numbers of consumers who want to know how their food is produced. Organic, natural, free range, fresh have found their way into the regulatory lexicon. Food safety is one component of this movement, but it also includes sustainability of the planet and support for local economies. U.S. National Organic Standards went into effect in 2002. Products labeled organic must be certified. Organic label regulation did not come without compromise and conflict. Organic farmers worried about losing control over the process fought large agribusiness lobbies that added "loophole" language, which initially allowed genetically modified and synthetic ingredients. Renewed interest in protecting the organic label indicates that there are factions that believe current legislation is not effective and that clearer, trustworthy, and enforceable labeling rules are necessary.

Locally grown claims are another recent example food labeling initiatives. Numerous food borne illness outbreaks have occurred since the 1980s, and both the number and size of recalls tainted foods are increasing. Knowing where food is grown helps identify contamination points. Not since the Pure Food Act of 1906 has the United States faced such a magnitude of food safety issues. Tomatoes, ground beef, hot peppers, peanuts, and spinach have all been implicated on a national scale. Currently, there are no current federal labeling guidelines as to what is local.

At the international level of "local," Country of Origin Label (COOL) was implemented in 2009. This label requires retailers to provide consumers with information about where meats and perishable agricultural items originate. While proponents of this label point to the benefit of consumers knowing where their food comes from and possibly portraying it as a food safety issue, the COOL labeling program is primarily a marketing program since it is under the jurisdiction of the Agricultural Marketing Service, not the FDA or FSIS who handle issues of food safety.

Table 25 shows a summary overview of significant related legislation.

*Jane Kolodinsky*

**See also:** Consumers Union; Federal Trade Commission (FTC); Food and Drug Administration (FDA); Food Safety; *The Jungle*; Organic Foods

### References and Additional Readings

Armstrong, K. (2010). Stumped at the supermarket: making sense of nutrition rating systems. *Nation Policy & Legal Analysis Network to Prevent Childhood Obesity.*

FDA. (2010). FDA history part I–part V. Retrieved from http://www.fda.gov/AboutFDA/WhatWeDo/History/Origin/default.htm.

Gunn, D., & Gray, C. W. (2009). Country of origin labeling (COOL) and livestock producers. Retrieved from http://www.cals.uidaho.edu/edcomm/pdf/CIS/CIS1146.pdf

Ippolito, P. M. (2004). What can we learn from food advertising policy over the last 25 years? *George Mason Law Review, 12*(4), 939–965.

Kolodinsky, J. (April 26, 2012). Persistence of health labeling information asymmetry in the United States: Historical perspectives and twenty-first century realities. *Journal of Macromarketing*. SAGE Publications, Inc., All rights reserved. doi: 10.1177/0276146711434829.

Thomson, H., & Vedantam, S., (2012). *How food and clothing size labels affect what we eat and what we wear*. New York City: National Public Radio.

Wall, E.C. (2002). A comprehensive look at the Fair Packaging and Labeling Act of 1966 and the FDA Regulation of Deceptive Labeling and Packaging Practices: 1906 to today. Retrieved from http://leda.law.harvard.edu/leda/data/444/Wall.pdf

Young, J.H. (1989). *Pure food: Securing the Federal Food and Drugs Act of 1906.* Princeton, NJ: Princeton University Press.

## Food Safety

Food safety issues have plagued people for thousands of years. Sources of food contamination include soil, water, airborne pathogens, dust, wild and domestic animals (feces), and insects. Through time and experience, people gained everyday knowledge to wash fruits and vegetables, use salt, smoke, ice, drying, root cellars, and primitive cooking and canning methods to preserve food and prevent food borne illness caused by microorganisms. As science began to evolve, and through trial and error, Appert won a French prize for his food canning process and wrote one of the first food preservation books, *The Art of Preserving Animal and Vegetable Substances* in 1810. In that same year, Durand developed a method of canning in tins. Later, in 1855 *Escherichia coli* (*E. coli*) was discovered, in the 1860s Pasteur began processing with heat to control bacterial growth. In 1885, Salmon identified what is now called *Salmonella* bacteria, and in 1895, Van Ermengem isolated *Clostridium botulinum*. However, links of these organisms to food borne illness was not immediately uncovered.

Food safety involves more than just contamination by microorganisms. As food production became more and more industrialized in the 19th and early 20th centuries, the number of poorly produced, adulterated, mislabeled, or unsafe products available for sale also increased: chocolate adulterated with rice and soap, "factory" farm dairies producing milk from sometimes dying cows fed whiskey swill, butter produced without milk, and margarine sold as butter. Margarine's ingredients were deemed, "filthy fats." Hartley pointed to distillery milk as destroying the lives of multitudes. Public outcry generated by the muckrakers and Sinclair Lewis' 1906 novel, *The Jungle,* with vivid descriptions of Chicago's meatpacking industry helped the passage of the Federal Meat Inspection Act and the Pure Food Act.

The U.S. Public Health Service started publishing summaries of outbreaks of gastrointestinal illness attributed to milk in 1925 and by 1938 the summaries included all types of food. The 1938 Food, Drug and Cosmetic Act addressed the safety of food additives (such as preservatives and coloring). The GRAS (Generally Regarded As Safe) list is dynamic, and is based on scientific evidence of the time. By the late 1990s Hazard Analysis Critical Control Point (HACCP) systems were required for meat and poultry plants and by early in the 21st century for juice and seafood manufacturers as well. HACCP procedures prevent, eliminate or reduce biological, chemical and physical hazards in food production. The first Food Safety Modernization Act of 1997 did not provide more stringent regulations related to food safety and actually relaxed previous legislation about proof of food claims. President Barack Obama signed the second Food Safety Modernization Act (FSMA) into law in January 2011. The act amends the Federal Food, Drug, and Cosmetic Act with respect to safety of the food supply. The FSMA mandates a science- and risk-based approach to food safety by requiring food facilities to identify potential food safety hazards and develop and implement preventive control plans. This represents a shift from the previous reactionary approach to food safety in the United States.

The 2011 Act comes in response to a rise in food borne illness in the United States, as both the number and size of recalls from tainted foods are increasing. Not since the pure Food Act of 1906 has America experienced a decade with such a magnitude of food safety issues related to food borne illness as occurred at the turn of the 21st century. Tomatoes, ground beef, hot peppers, peanuts, and spinach have all been implicated on a national scale. However, increased surveillance may indicate that a better job of reporting food safety issues is occurring, explaining some of the increase in the count of food borne illness. The Centers for Disease Control (CDC) estimates that food borne infections cause 48 million illnesses (one in six Americans) including 128,000 hospitalization and 3,000 deaths each year in the United States, with an associated cost of 10–83 billion dollars per year. It has been estimated that the multiplier effect of food borne illness is 38; that is, for every illness diagnosed, there are 38 affected individuals who are not reported in the system. *Salmonella, Campylobacter, Shigella, Cryptospridium*, and *E. coli O157:H7* are the leading causes of food borne illnesses.

There are a number of reasons for the increase in food borne illness. With a globalization of our food supply, one cannot assure that foreign producers follow HACCP rules, label ingredients correctly, or follow other safe handling processes. In the United States households now spend almost 50 percent of their food budgets on food away from home. Through its surveillance system the CDC reported that one-half of food borne illness happened at away from home venues. While food handled at home may not be washed, refrigerated, nor cooked to the proper temperature, failing to follow safe food handling procedures in a restaurant can lead to many more illnesses. A third reason for the increase in food borne illness is the genetic variability and emergence of new pathogens. For example, new resistant strains of *Salmonella* have emerged. Finally, there are proportionally more consumers at higher risk for illness. Older individuals are vulnerable, and in the United States the elder population is growing quickly. In addition, chronically ill people are more prone to food borne illness, and the number of people with chronic conditions in the United States has been growing for decades.

Government regulation, surveillance systems, and enforcement can help track food borne illness, but implementation is spotty according to a "report card" issued by the Center for Science in the Public Interest. Therefore, many groups are interested in providing consumer education and outreach to the public. For example, the Partnership for Food Safety Education has a Fight Bac campaign with information for adults and even a video game for children.

There are also whistleblower and watchdog organizations that have evolved to address what they see as lack of leadership and enforcement of food safety regulations by the U.S. government or in other instance of turning the proverbial blind eye to food additives and production techniques that may be hazardous to human health. STOP Food Borne Illness, for example, provides information and raises awareness of the issue. Beyond food borne illnesses, irradiation of food, transgenic crops, and the use of pesticides, herbicides and fungicides in food production are examples that consumer groups believe are under or not regulated by government to protect consumers.

The Food Integrity Campaign is part of the Government Accountability Project (GAP) and focuses on many food safety issues by "strategically working to alter the relationship of power between the food industry and consumers; protecting the rights of those who speak out against the practices that compromise food integrity; and empowering industry whistleblowers and citizen activists." Food and Water Watch includes information about many food safety issues including genetic engineering, toxins in fish (e.g., mercury and dioxins) and provides information on food alternatives. The Organic Consumer's Association "deals with crucial issues of food safety, industrial agriculture, genetic engineering, children's health, and corporate accountability." As with any information, consumers must be informed enough to critically analyze and interpret information from all sources, including governmental, private, and nonprofit organizations. While there is no debate on food safety issues surrounding pathogens that cause food borne illness, there is no consensus on whether genetic modification, chemical residues, or irradiation of food is harmful.

Many nations around the world have adopted what is called the precautionary principle. The principle's premise is that if an action or policy has a suspected risk of causing harm to the public or to the environment, in the absence of scientific consensus that the action or policy is harmful, the burden of proof that it is not harmful falls on those taking the action. The United States, takes the scientific approach to making policy concerning food safety issues. In general, if there is no scientific evidence that a substance or process causes harm, then there should be no policy banning that substance or process.

From a consumer perspective, these types of food safety issues are classified under "credence goods." Credence goods are goods in which a consumer cannot tell their quality even after using the product. Within credence goods, the most government regulations are found. In the case of food safety concerns where the U.S. government does not follow the precautionary principle, consumer groups have mobilized to use their collective voice to increase awareness among our citizenry. If consumer voice, through boycotts or buycotts or media attention, does not catch the attention of regulators, often industry will respond to offer alternatives.

In 2008, the U.S. Department of Health and Human Services drafted a report with the finding that there is no direct evidence that human exposure to bisphenol A (BPA), found in plastic bottles of water and baby formula harms reproduction or infant development. Retailing giant Walmart stopped selling baby bottles produced with BPA plastic in response to public outcry. Water bottle producer Nalgene and baby bottle maker Playtex also pledged not to use the chemical in their production. In 2011, Consumers' Union and others continued to call for government regulation of the use of the chemical, but the U.S. Federal Court of Appeals ruled against the Natural Resources Defense Council's effort to force the Food and Drug Administration to limit (BPA) in food additives.

As the food system becomes increasingly complex and technology continues to advance, food safety issues are not likely to diminish in the coming years. While government regulation and oversight of food safety issues will remain a major line of defense against the outbreak of food borne illness, both industry and consumer groups must remain diligent in their efforts to ensure that consumers have alternative choices to foods, food packaging, and other possible food contaminants that may cause harm, but have not been found to cause harm using current scientific methods. It is quite possible that technology used to create these possible food safety threats is moving more quickly than the science that is able to detect harm.

*Jane Kolodinsky*

**See also:** Centers for Disease Control and Prevention (CDC); Corporate Social Responsibility; Food, Drug and Cosmetic Act (FD&C Act); Hazard Analysis and Critical Control Point (HACCP); *The Jungle*

### References and Additional Readings

Centers for Disease Control (CDC). (2010). OutbreakNet: Foodborne outbreak on-line database. Retrieved http://wwwn.cdc.gov/foodborneoutbreaks/Default.asp

Dodd, C., & Powell D. (2009). Regulatory management and communication of risk associated with *Escherichia coli* O157: H7 in ground beef. *Foodborne Pathogens and Disease 6*(6), 743–747.

Food and Water Watch. (2013). Retrieved from http://www.foodandwaterwatch.org

Food Detectives. (n.d.). Retrieved from http://www.fooddetectives.com/

Government Accountability Project. (2013). Retrieved from http://www.whistleblower.org/

Lynch, M., Painter, J., et al. (2006). *Surveillance for foodborne-disease outbreaks: United States, 1998–2002.* US Dept. of Health and Human Services, Centers for Disease Control and Prevention (CD).

Nyachuba, D. G. (2010). Foodborne illness: Is it on the rise? *Nutrition Reviews, 68*(5), 257–269.

Organic Consumers Association. (2013). Retrieved from http://www.organiccosumers.org

Taylor, M. R. (2011). Will the Food Safety Modernization Act help prevent outbreaks of foodborne illness? *New England Journal of Medicine, 365*(9), e18.

**Food Stamps**. *See* Department of Agriculture (USDA); Social Welfare; Supplemental Nutrition Assistance Program (SNAP); Telephone Assistance Programs

## Foreclosures and Short Sales

While the American Dream of most Americans is to own a home, it can also be a financial burden that results in financial ruin. How much house one can afford is based on a simple mathematical calculation, whereby payments should not exceed 30 percent of pretax household income. Unfortunately many Americans today are paying for more house than they can comfortably afford. Being "house poor" has become a reality for many Americans, and when tough financial times hit, they find themselves unable to make the payments on the home they love but cannot afford now and in reality could not afford when they purchased it. "House poor" is simply a term that is used when someone is using a large percentage of their income to make the mortgage payment and cannot afford other things or must do without. After a prolonged period of time of not being able to make the full payment or any payment at all, the bank starts the process of foreclosure.

When the consumer purchases a home they enter into a contract with a lending institution to make regular payments. If for any reason the person or persons who signed the contract are unable to make the agreed upon payments, the process of foreclosure is started. Foreclosure can occur because of any number of reasons, but the typical reasons are unemployment, divorce, illness, job transfer, excessive debt and credit card bills, or the death of the borrower. Becoming "upside down" in a mortgage loan means that the borrower owes more for the property than it is valued at. This situation occurs when the economy goes into a recession and values drop. The homeowner may have paid $250,000 for a home, borrowed $225,000 plus interest, only to find that when the housing market drops the home is only valued at $175,000. They owe more than the house is worth. Foreclosures also occur when housing prices become over inflated, the economy drops into a trough, and it loses value. In some cases, as prices and values drop, the buyer will find the home is worthless than they owe, walk away and let the bank or lender foreclose, terminating all of their rights to the property. Financial counseling should be a homeowner's first step when they find their selves unable to make the mortgage payment. If done early, steps can be taken to avoid foreclosure and bankruptcy.

Rules on foreclosures vary from state to state. Lenders want to work with homeowners to resolve the situation before it gets to the foreclosure stage. It is important for home/property owners to communicate with their bank or lending institution if they find themselves in a situation where they are unable to make the monthly payments. Homeowners who live in states that use mortgages for home purchases can possibly stay in the home for up to a year before having to vacate. In states that use deeds of trust, the homeowner has 4 months or less before the home is sold in trustee's sale. Buyers need to check the laws in their state before purchasing property, and at the time of purchase read all fine print so they are informed about the process in the event of foreclosure. Most states work with the property owner during the foreclosure process. This means that the property owner/seller has the right during a specific time period to bring the past due payments current and paying all foreclosure costs.

Normally the process is started once the borrower is 3 months delinquent, but can vary depending on the state. The first step in the foreclosure process is for the lender to send a formal letter, known as *Notice of Default*, demanding payment. There are two main types of foreclosures, judicial and nonjudicial. In a judicial foreclosure process, the lender or bank will file a complaint against the borrower, and receive a decree of sale from the court in the county where the property is located. The court will allow the borrower to pay the delinquent amount plus court costs within a specified period of time. If the borrower is unable to pay in the time period given, the court will order the property to be sold. In a nonjudicial foreclosure, there is a "power of sale" clause in the mortgage or deed of trust. A "power of sale" is a clause in a mortgage or deed of trust in which the borrower preauthorizes the lender to sell the property to pay off the balance of the loan in the event the borrower defaults on the loan. While these are the two basic types of foreclosure proceedings, the laws and rules will vary from state to state, with some states having as few as 30 days and others having up to 180 days to bring the delinquent payments up-to-date.

When purchasing a home, buyers may agree to a balloon payment mortgage, where their monthly payments will be low, and after a set number of years of making regular monthly payments, the balance of the loan is due in one large balloon payment. The payments will be set up like another mortgage with the number of years of the loan specified. The difference is that the monthly payments will be lower during the life of the loan with a large payment at the end. Balloon mortgage loans are not for everyone. In fact, research indicates that mortgages with balloon payments are 46 percent more likely to go to foreclosure than loans without balloon payments.

Short sales occur before the property is sold at auction or in a foreclosure sale. In a short sale, the lender will accept a selling price that is lower than what the seller owes on the home. The lender is willing to take less than what is owed because he or she does not want to be in the real estate business with an inventory of foreclosed homes to sell. For the seller, a short sale helps him or her to avoid foreclosure if the lender accepts his or her short sale package. The seller will need to provide documentation to the lender that he or she is unable to make the required mortgage payments and why.

Once the lender has received a notice of default on the property, he or she will discount the property. Until the default on the property is received, the lender will not discount the property. Lenders will agree to a short sale because they know if the home goes to auction they could possibly lose more money. After the lender agrees to the short sale, a real-estate agent will inspect the property and determine in his or her opinion what the property is worth. This price is known as BPO, broker's price option, and the lower the value of the home, the better for the seller because the lender will give a greater discount to buyers

When a buyer puts a contract on a short sale property, the bank can accept or reject it based on what the loan balance is and how much they want to discount the property, but they will need to use the BPO as a guideline. Another factor that can be in favor of the buyer is the condition of the property. If there is a lot of work to be done, especially cosmetic to the home, the buyer may be able to negotiate a deeper discount. For the lender these properties are seen as undesirable by most potential buyers because they need work, but for those that do not mind doing the work or that can afford to have it done, this is a great deal.

Those facing foreclosure must also be aware of scams and rescue schemes. Foreclosure scams can appear legitimate and the person facing foreclosure can be led to believe the person is doing them a favor. Scammers are able to get the name and address from anyone facing foreclosure from the list of properties in preforeclosure listed in newspapers. The scammer will then contact the consumer and tell the consumer he or she will be able to avoid foreclosure if the property is signed over, and mortgage payments are made to the scammer. In turn the scammer says they will pay the past due payments and foreclosure costs, and make the monthly mortgage payments. Unfortunately for the owner this is a scam and the scammer will take control of the property and keep any mortgage payments the owner pays to them. The scammer may also refinance the property since the property owner signed the title over to them, make them move out of the house, or sell the property and keep all of the money, leaving the owner in default owing even more in unpaid payments. Property owners who are scammed in this way are forced into foreclosure, in addition to the monthly mortgage payments they paid the scammer for the period of time the scam took place.

Foreclosures not only hurt the credit of the owner, but the market because when there are foreclosed homes on the market they are in competition with homes that are being sold by real estate agents that are not discounted. According to an article in *USA Today*, "short sales and the sale of foreclosed homes held by banks accounted for 23% of sales in 2011; homes in some stage of the foreclosure process accounted for 9% of total homes sales and sold for 22% less than other types of homes. Sales of new homes make up only 10% of the market, the lowest it has been since 1963" (Viega, 2012). Neighborhoods can also be adversely affected by fore-closures, because buyers might be reluctant to purchase a home in a neigh-borhood with several foreclosed homes or short sales in progress.

*Elowin Harper*

**See also:** Banking; Home Equity Loans; Home Ownership and Equity Protection Act (HOEPA); Mortgages

**References and Additional Readings**

Lewis, H. (2005). Prepayment penalties, balloon repayments increase foreclo-sure risk. Retrieved from http://www.bankrate.com/brm/news/mortgages/20050127a1.asp

Viega, A. (2012). Bank-owned homes and short sales were 23% of all 2011 sales. *Associated Press.* USA Today Money. Retrieved from http://www.usa today.com/money/economy/housing/story/2012–03–01/foreclosures-short-sa les-2011/53314076/1

# Frauds and Scams

Frauds and scams come in a variety of forms and unscrupulous sellers have found ways to enter in almost every product or service available to a consumer. Consumer fraud occurs when lies or tricks are used to get a consumer to part with money for products or services that have little or no value. Technology has allowed seamless international borders and the most common venue for fraud is the Internet. Some of the more common fraud schemes are described later.

Disaster-related and charity scams become popular when disasters occur that have a negative effect on people or the environment. Human nature is to quickly provide financial assistance to the victims; however, a disaster provides a perfect opportunity for scammers to develop fraudulent web-sites, make quick phone calls, or send numerous e-mails to good natured citizens as well as vulnerable victims. Strategies to avoid these scams are to ensure the validity of the charity and only give to the charities that are trustworthy and well known. Be cautious of high-pressure tactics for dona-tions and avoid paying in cash.

The bait and switch scam most commonly occurs in retail sales occurs when a customer is lured into the store via advertising featuring a low price and has a specific product in mind to purchase. The customer finds that the advertised good is not available; therefore, the salesperson "switches" the consumer to higher priced product. The best strategy is to resist the temptation of purchasing the higher priced product and comparison shop prior to making the purchase decision.

---

## Case Study: Nigerian Email Scam

Dear Friend,

I have packaged a financial transaction that will benefit both of us. I got your contact during my search for a reliable person to whom I can confidentially and secretly entrust this huge project with. As the Nigerian regional manager of my bank, it's my duty to send financial reports to my head office during each fiscal end of the year audit. On the course of the last year 2010 end of the of the year audited cash flow statement report, I discovered that my branch in which I am the manager made Four Million Nine Hundred and Fifty Thousand US Dollars (US$4,950.000.00) due to the numerous natural disaster that hit our Asian customers who lost their life during the flood and earthquake.

The good news is that our head office is not aware of the fund and will never be aware of it as I have since then PLACED this fund on a SUSPENSE ACCOUNT without a beneficiary.

As an officer of the bank, I cannot be directly connected to this huge amount of money hence requesting you to stand as the beneficiary of the fund to enable me introduce you to our head office as the beneficiary and you will request our bank to re-transfer the money into your bank account in your country. I want to assure you that there is practically no risk involved in this as it's going to be a bank-to-bank transfer. I will resign and come over to share the money with you once the money is successfully transferred into your bank account.

All I need from you is to stand as the beneficiary of this fund and I will guide you secretly on what to do if you accept this offer. I will appreciate your timely response.

Regard
Mr. Benjamin Debrah
Nigerian Regional Manager

---

Phishing is a scam used by cyber thieves who send a forged email, pop up message, or spam claiming to be from a legitimate organization. These organizations might include the Better Business Bureau, Red Cross, the American Cancer Society, the Federal Trade Commission, banking institutions, to name a few. The perpetrators attempt to gather private information from the victim such as usernames, passwords, bank account numbers, and social security numbers allowing the thief to obtain that person's identity. When using these websites, manually type the address into the address bar rather than using a link from a website.

Home Repair is a common complaint with homeowners. This type of complaint may include phony workers who require a large down payment and then never return to complete the work or start the job and then state that the completion of the job will cost hundreds or thousands of dollars. The phony workers may offer a free inspection to a home and while in the home, will cause damage and claim that there is a safety hazard. The con artist will require a large amount of money to repair the damage that they caused. Oftentimes the older population is a target for home scams as many of them own their home and may live in an older home in need of repairs. Some con artists will actually use the obituary page to find vulnerable seniors who might be living alone. To avoid becoming a victim, it is advisable to get a second opinion from a local, reputable business. In addition, check the credentials and identification. If repair work is to be done, request an estimate in writing and ask for references. If a high-pressure sales tactic with a "now or never" deal is offered, it is best to "pass" on the deal.

Ponzi Schemes were made famous by Bernie Madoff where victims were promised a high rate of return on an investment. The con artist simply pays dividends to the initial investors from funds received from subsequent investors. The scheme fails when the person to pay later investors because enough money is not generated to keep the process intact or the person in charge flees with everyone's money and no more dividends are dispersed. A scam similar to a Ponzi Scheme is a Pyramid Scheme but in this case, the investors recruit further victims to buy in, pushing themselves up the pyramid. Eventually the pyramid collapses as participants drop out and eventually new investors are not joining. Consumers should be wary and avoid any participation with a Ponzi or Pyramid Scheme. Healthcare fraud costs the country an estimated $60 billion a year and with national healthcare spending reaching $2 trillion, fraud in this area is likely to continue to increase. An example of healthcare fraud includes unnecessary or fake tests conducted on patients and then billed to an insurance company or Medicare. Medicare fraud is often targeted toward the older population. Con artists will forge physician signatures to certify that equipment or testing is needed. Once the con artists have the signatures, Medicare is billed for the unnecessary service or equipment. A patient should never sign blank insurance claim forms or give blanket authorization to medical providers.

While technology has allowed the increase in fraud to occur due to the large audience, telemarketing fraud is still very much an avenue used by con artists. Consumers should be aware of various warning signs that can reveal a scam. Scammers often use such language such as act now, free gift, high profit, and no risk. Other red flags include having a check picked up by a courier or stating that reference checks are not necessary. A simple "no thank you" by the consumer and hanging up the telephone will end the conversation and prevent fraud from occurring. Consumers should only buy products from companies whom they are familiar and make donations to reputable charities.

Home-based business scams have become very popular due to the down-turn in the economy. People are trying to supplement incomes to make ends

## Telemarketing Fraud: Two Case Studies

The incidents described here happened to an 81-year-old woman who will be referred to as Jane.

In the first incident, contact was made by a clever con artist claiming to be her great nephew. The questions that were asked were very generic and started with "Do you know who this is?" Jane answered, "Well it sounds like Danny." Right at that moment, the con artist had the "in" as the unsuspecting victim thought that she was talking to her nephew. The con artist proceeded to tell Jane that he was on his way to surprise his parents and his car broke down. He asked her to wire $500 to fix his car so that he would not have to spoil the surprise. The con artist contacted the victim several times throughout the day making arrangements for the money transfer and always ended the conversation with "I love you." The victim fell for the con and wired the money; however, the wire service on the end that received the money refused to give it to the con artist due to not having the necessary identification with the intended recipient's name. Jane received her $500 back.

In the second incident, the same victim was called claiming that she had won $650,000 through Publisher's Clearinghouse. They informed her that they would be coming to her home between 10 a.m. and 2 p.m. the next day for her to claim her prize. She had the option of having the van, balloons, and media present or she could have a private ceremony with family. They also told her that she could choose to have a police officer present. The victim was reluctant due to her previous experience but there was no indication at this point that it was a scam. Family members became involved to assist Jane in researching the call and in the meantime, the scam artists were still in contact making arrangements for the delivery of the $650,000 check. The next day the truth was revealed. Jane was contacted and was told that her check was being held in customs at the Dallas airport and she needed to wire a check for $3,500 for the check to be released. The proper authorities were contacted to report the crime.

In both incidences, Jane was extremely fortunate that no money was lost.

*Linda Simpson and Whitney Paul*

meet or replace a lost income due to company layoffs. Again, con artists see a target market such as this and prey on people who may be down on their luck. These schemes may offer people the opportunity to work from home addressing envelopes, envelope stuffing, home typing, turn-key websites, multilevel marketing, and reshipping to name a few. These so-called opportunities often end up costing money. It is recommended to carefully research any home-based business offers by asking questions, contacting references, and contacting the Better Business Bureau prior to any agreement.

A vacation is a much anticipated time of relaxation and fun but can quickly turn into a nightmare as predators are seeking victims to fall prey to travel scams. The traveler is a lucrative market for a scam artist as pre-payment is usually required and the Internet is a method often used to make travel arrangements. Vacationers should be cautious of free trip offers, especially if the offer is unsolicited, and remember that it is not free if a fee is imposed. While the fine print may be boring and difficult to read, it is the most important document to fully understand prior to purchase. The consumer may have unknowingly signed up for a timeshare presentation or some other sales pitch. The consumer should always review the restrictions that may eliminate travel dates that fall during popular vacation time periods and pay for purchases via a credit card rather than cash. If the charges come under dispute, the credit card provides better protection for the consumer.

Vanity rackets prey on those people wanting to get noticed by publishing a book or song. Publishers encourage submissions with promises of success and of course a fee for "servicing." The agony of trying to publish through normal channels often sends people through this route with hopes of getting a contract. This "quick route" to stardom should be avoided in the publishing world as it will often cost a high price and accomplish nothing.

Knowledge and consumer education is the key to greatly reducing the chances of falling victim to fraud. The Federal Trade Commission website is designed to provide valuable information to help protect the consumer (www.ftc.gov) and the Better Business Bureau (www.bbb.org) monitors the ethical practices in the marketplace. Remember—if it's too good to be true . . . it probably is.

*Linda Simpson and Whitney Paul*

**See also:** Affinity Fraud; Bait and Switch; Better Business Bureau (BBB); Disaster Recovery Scams; Federal Trade Commission (FTC); Madoff, Bernie; Multi-Level

Marketing and Pyramid Plans; Ponzi Scheme; Privacy: Online; Working from Home

### References and Additional Readings

Consumerprotectionlawfirms.com. (n.d.). Home repair fraud. Retrieved from http://www.consumerprotectionlawfirms.com/Home-Fraud.cfm

Federal Bureau of Investigation. (n.d.a). Common fraud schemes. Retrieved from www.fbi.gov/scams-safety/fraud/fraud

Federal Bureau of Investigation. (n.d.b). Health care fraud. Retrieved from http://www.fbi.gov/about-us/investigate/white_collar/health-care-fraud

Federal Deposit Insurance Corporation. (2011). Beware of disaster-related financial scams. Retrieved from http:www.fdic.gov/consumers/consumer/news/cnsum11/bewardofdisaster.html

Fraud Guides. (n.d.). Fraud tip of the day. Retrieved from http://www.fraud guides.com/tips/may6.asp

Illinois General Assembly. (n.d.). Consumer Fraud and Deceptive Business Practices Act (815 ILCS 505/1) (from Ch. 121 1/2, par. 261). Retrieved from http://www.ilga.gov/legislation/ilcs/ilcs3.asp?ActID=2356&ChapterID=67

Rosefsky, Robert (2002). *Personal finance* (8th ed.). New York: John Wiley & Sons, Inc.

USA.gov. (2012). Phishing scams: What you need to know. Retrieved from www.usa.gov/topics/consumer/scams-fraud/types/phishing-scams.shtml

## Freddie Mac

Freddie Mac, officially known as Federal Home Loan Mortgage Corporation, was created by Congress on July 24, 1970, as a federally chartered corporation. On September 6, 2008, Federal Housing Finance Agency (FHFA) was created and appointed as regulator of Freddie Mac. The main headquarters of Freddie Mac is in McLean, Virginia, with offices in Atlanta, Chicago, Dallas, Los Angeles, and New York. While Freddie Mac was created by Congress, it was chartered by Congress as a private company to serve the public. In 1989, Freddie Mac was converted to a stock that could be purchased and traded by all investors.

The purpose of Freddie Mac was to stabilize the nation's residential housing market and expand opportunities for home ownership and affordable rental housing. Freddie Mac does not make loans, but purchases loans from thrift banks, creating low interest loans for the financial institutions. Thrift banks are usually smaller institutions that retail and commercial banks and they tend to be community focused. Access to low-cost funding through Federal Home Loan Banks helps customers reap higher savings yields and greater liquidity for mortgage loans. The goal is that by buying mortgage loans from these financial institutions, it frees up money for the financial institution to make affordable mortgage loans to others seeking home ownership at affordable rates.

When created and still today, the ultimate goal of Freddie Mac is to make not only home ownership, but also rental housing affordable to the working class that may otherwise may not be able to afford to purchase or rent acceptable housing. Working with families that are in danger of foreclosure keep their homes is also a mission of Freddie Mac. By working with families in danger of foreclosure, financial institutions continue to receive payments for those mortgage loans, which can then be purchased by Freddie Mac allowing new loans to be created by the financial institution.

*Elowin Harper*

**See also:** Banking; Department of Housing and Urban Development (HUD); Fannie Mae; Federal Housing Administration (FHA); Mortgages

### References and Additional Readings

Freddie Mac. (2012). About Freddie Mac. Retrieved from http://www.freddiemac.com/corporate/company_profile/

Investopedia. (2012). Definition of a thrift bank. Retrieved from http://www.investopedia.com/terms/t/thriftbank.asp#axzz2AMz5Q1Wm

## Freedom of Information Act (FOIA)

The FOIA Act "provides that any person has a right, enforceable in court, to obtain access to federal agency records, except to the extent that such records (or portions of them) are protected from public disclosure by one of nine exemptions or by one of three special law enforcement record exclusions" (FOIA, n.d.) The FOIA was enacted in 1966, going into effect in 1967, following in the path that Kennedy created, championing consumer rights; specifically the right to information. This act provided consumers the ability to have access to governmental file and records, not of harm to national security (see exemptions and exclusions). Requestors of information do not have to be citizens of the United States. Administration and compliance of the act is overseen by the Office of Information Policy at the Department of Justice.

## Nine Exemptions to the Freedom of Information Act (FOAI)

**Exemption 1:** Information that is classified to protect national security. The material must be properly classified under an executive order.

**Exemption 2:** Information related solely to the internal personnel rules and practices of an agency.

**Exemption 3:** Information that is prohibited from disclosure by another federal law.

**Exemption 4:** Information that concerns business trade secrets or other confidential commercial or financial information.

**Exemption 5:** Information that concerns communications within or between agencies which are protected by legal privileges, that include but are not limited to:

1. Attorney–work product privilege
2. Attorney–client privilege
3. Deliberative process privilege
4. Presidential communications privilege

**Exemption 6:** Information that, if disclosed, would invade another individual's personal privacy.

**Exemption 7:** Information compiled for law enforcement purposes if one of the following harms would occur. Law enforcement information is exempt if it:

- 7(A). Could reasonably be expected to interfere with enforcement proceedings
- 7(B). Would deprive a person of a right to a fair trial or an impartial adjudication
- 7(C). Could reasonably be expected to constitute an unwarranted invasion of personal privacy
- 7(D). Could reasonably be expected to disclose the identity of a confidential source
- |7(E). Would disclose techniques and procedures for law enforcement investigations or prosecutions
- 7(F). Could reasonably be expected to endanger the life or physical safety of any individual

**Exemption 8:** Information that concerns the supervision of financial institutions
**Exemption 9:** Geological information on wells

*Source:* http://www.sec.gov/foia/nfoia.htm

There are three special law enforcement record exclusions, as written on the FOIA website:

The first exclusion protects the existence of an ongoing criminal law enforcement investigation when the subject of the investigation is unaware that it is pending and disclosure could reasonably be expected to interfere with enforcement proceedings. The second exclusion is limited to criminal law enforcement agencies and protects the existence of informant records when the informant's status has not been officially confirmed. The third exclusion is limited to the Federal Bureau of Investigation and protects the existence of foreign intelligence or counterintelligence, or international terrorism records when the existence of such records is classified. Records falling within an exclusion are not subject to the requirements of the FOIA. So, when an office or agency responds to your request, it will limit its response to those records that are subject to the FOIA. (FOIA, n.d.)

Following the Watergate scandal under Nixon's Presidency, the act was amended in 1974, heavily pushed by Congress Watch (a group grown out of Public Citizen). The amendment made information more accessible to consumers, and according to the website, to allow consumers to have an integral role in the Democracy of the United States. Specifically, the amendment required public catalogs of agency information, time lines for responses to FOIA requests, appeals and litigation, cost and fee recovery, and annual reports surrounding FOIA's administration and compliance. The amendment also expanded the definition of "agency" within the law itself.

Under the Obama administration, the act has received attention from both the president and the attorney general. According to the website, the president seeks to be the most transparent president to date. To this end, on his first day as president, he signed the Memorandum on Transparency and Open Government, which called for openness and governmental transparency, stating that "information maintained by the federal government is a national asset." This act will continue to get attention with Obama's reelection for a second term of office.

*Wendy Reiboldt*

**See also:** Department of Justice (DOJ); Kennedy, John F.; Nader, Ralph; Public Citizen

### References and Additional Readings

Feinberg, L. E. (2004). FOIA, federal information policy, and information availability in a post-9/11 world. *Government Information Quarterly, 21*(4), 439–460.

Freedom of Information Act. (n.d.). What is FOIA. Retrieved from www.FOIA.gov

Kreimer, S.F. (2007). Rays of sunlight in a shadow war: FOIA, the abuses of anti-terrorism, and the strategy of transparency. *Lewis & Clark Law Review, 11*(4), research paper no. 08-01.

## Funeral Rule

When a loved one dies, grieving family members are often confronted with several decisions about funerals. Oftentimes, legal requirements and arrangements need to be made quickly and under great emotional distress. Most families want to ensure that their loved one has a dignified and meaningful funeral, but unfortunately, the process of planning can be confusing and overwhelming. And given that most funerals cost, on average, from $6000 to $10,000, having a funeral also becomes a costly decision as well.

According to the latest projections of the National Center for Health Statistics and the U.S. Bureau of the Census, the U.S. death rate, which has been in decline over the last 20 years, will maintain at an average of 8.3 (annual deaths per 1,000 population) over the next 10 years. In years

Headstones at Arlington National Cemetery in Washington, D.C. (Orhan Cam/Shutterstock.com)

to come though, the death rate is projected to increase due to the progressive aging of the U.S. population. As such, funerals have become a large economic business. In fact revenues, from funeral home and funeral home combined with crematories, have steadily increased and are nearly $12 billion yearly.

Though most funeral providers are professionals who work hard to serve their clients' needs, interests and feelings, and all states required they are licensed, the reality is that funerals have become a costly business and some greedy providers have been known to take advantage of their clients by inflating prices, overcharging, or offering unnecessary services. Fortunately, the Federal Trade Commission (FTC) enforces the Funeral Rule. According to the Funeral Rule, people are not legally required to use a funeral home to plan and conduct a funeral. However, given that most people have little experience with funeral planning, most choose to use a funeral director who works for a funeral home. It is important to ensure then too that the funeral director is licensed.

The Funeral Rule is therefore in place to protect such consumers. As written on the FTC's website, the rule supports the following broad rights to clients:

- To choose most of the funeral goods and services they want
- To have the funeral provider state in writing the general price list (such as for cremation, burial, type of burial)
- To be informed, in writing, if their state or local law requires them to buy any particular item (and the funeral provider must disclose it on the price list with a reference to the specific law)
- To have their selected funeral provider use and not charge a fee to handle a casket bought from another funeral provider
- To be provided containers by their funeral provider that offers cremations

Specifically, many funeral providers offer various "packages" of commonly selected goods and services that make up a funeral. And though these are permitted by law, an itemized price list must also be provided. Clients, thus, have the legal right to buy individual goods and services and to reject a package. Further, if the general price list does not include specific prices of caskets or other burial containers, the law requires the funeral director to show the client the price lists for those items before actually showing the items. The Funeral Rule further allows funeral providers to charge a basic services fee for services common to all funerals that customers cannot decline to pay. These include funeral planning, securing the necessary permits and copies of death certificates, preparing the notices, sheltering the remains, and coordinating the arrangements with the cemetery, crematory or other third parties. If optional services or products are desired, such as memorial services, transportation of the remains, use of staff for graveside services, price lists again must be given. The Funeral Rule also requires funeral providers that purchase or pay for outside goods and services, such as flowers, officiating clergy, and organists, to indicate their cost for the items as well as whether they add a service fee. This all needs to be in writing. Funeral providers must also indicate to their clients whether they offer refunds, discounts, or rebates from their suppliers on any cash advance item. Overall, the funeral provider is require to give their clients itemized statements of the total cost of food and services selected, or a "good faith" estimate is required if not all costs are known. This statement also must disclose any legal, cemetery, or crematory requirements related to any specific funeral goods or services. The Funeral Rule does not require any specific format or document for this information.

Additionally, embalming generally is not necessary or legally required if the body is buried or cremated shortly after death. However, many funeral homes require embalming if the family is planning for a viewing or visitation. Under the Funeral Rule, a funeral provider may not provide embalming services without permission, they may not falsely state that embalming is required by law, they must disclose in writing that embalming is not required by law (except in certain special cases), and they may not charge a fee for unauthorized embalming (unless embalming is required by state law). For families that choose cremations, the Funeral Rule also protects consumers. No state of local law requires a casket for direct cremations. Also, the funeral home must disclose in writing the client's right to buy an unfinished wood box or an alternative container for a direct cremation, and as stated earlier, the home must make this available.

Interestingly, veterans (and their spouses and dependent children), some civilians who have provided military service, as well as some Public Health Service professionals, are entitled to a free burial in a national cemetery and a grave marker. Other rights exist as indicated on the Department of Veterans Affairs website.

Finally, most states have a licensing board that regulates the funeral industry. Consumers are encouraged to contact the board in their state. This will help to answer additional issues related to practices for handling funds for prearranged funerals, transferring funeral plans to other geographic areas, interest income on money that is prepaid and put into a trust account, as well as options to cancel contract and get refunds. Consumers are also encouraged to know their rights by gaining more information from the

Better Business Bureau's website, the Funerals Consumer Alliance, and the Cremation Association of North America.

*Melanie Horn Mallers*

**See also:** Better Business Bureau (BBB); Department of Veterans Affairs (VA); Federal Trade Commission (FTC)

## References and Additional Readings

Cremation Association of North America. (2012). Retrieved from www.cremation association.org

Department of Labor. (2012). Funeral directors. Retrieved from http://www.bls .gov/ooh/Personal-Care-and-Service/Funeral-directors.htm

Funeral Consumers Alliance. (2010). Retrieved from www.funerals.org

# G

**General Accounting Office (GAO)**. *See* Government Accountability Office (GAO)

## Gift Cards

A gift card is defined as a preloaded debit card that allows the cardholder to redeem it for goods or services. There are two categories of gift cards: closed loop or private merchant gift cards and open loop or bank gift cards. Closed loop or private merchant gift cards are those that can only be used at a specific store or merchant, such as Walmart, Target, or Starbucks. Open loop or bank gift cards carry the logo of a payment card network such as Visa or MasterCard and can be used at any business that accepts credit card payments. Open loop gift card fees are paid to the issuer, not to the retailer.

Gift cards have replaced gift certificates, which were a part of the American consumer marketplace dating back to the 1930s. Mobil Oil Company used prepaid phone card technology to produce the first retail gift certificate with a magnetic strip in 1995. That same year Blockbuster premiered the modern-day gift card, produced by SSI Technologies. According to Tower Group, in 2012, sales of gift cards reached $100 billion in the United States.

Gift cards are a popular consumer purchase for a variety of reasons. For purchasers, convenience and time saving are advantages. A gift card can be selected from a wide range of stores allowing the giver to somewhat personalize the gift to be a good fit for the recipient. With many family units located far from one another, a gift card is easy to send with negligible shipping charges. Many retailers allow for selection of gift cards from a variety of designs and even offer custom packaging to somewhat individualize the choice. A number of retailers offer incentives to purchasers of gift cards, such as a lower dollar amount gift card in return for each card purchased. A recipient can use a gift card to purchase an item of his/her choosing, thus removing the worry about whether a gift is going to be well liked, a good fit, color, or appropriate. If a recipient decides a gift card is not a good fit, there are many ways to regift the card, including online resale sites.

One drawback for gift cards is the impersonal nature of the gift card. Private merchant cards also force the recipient of a gift card to shop at a specific retailer. A larger concern, however, is the high percentage of gift cards that go unused each year and fees sometimes associated with gift cards. A Consumer Reports survey in 2007 indicated 56 percent of respondents received gift cards in the 2006 holiday season, however, a year later, 27 percent of them had not used their cards. As gift cards evolved into a mainstay of gifting in the United States, there were few state and no federal laws regulating business practices relating to gift cards. Before the Credit Card Accountability Responsibility and Disclosure Act of 2009 (Credit CARD Act) was passed, there were many incidents of consumers trying to redeem their gift cards, only to be dismayed to find the original amount of the card had diminished due to dormancy or service fees.

The Credit CARD Act of 2009 included Regulation E, mandating consumer protections related to gift cards. Both open and closed loop cards are bound by the new regulations. Originally slated to be in practice for gift cards sold on or after August 22, 2010, Regulation E was later delayed and not put into full practice until January 31, 2011. Forty states now have also passed individual legislation related to gift card practices. The requirements of Regulation E include limits on expiration dates, rules related to replacement cards, fee disclosures, and limits on certain types of fees. A summary of Regulation E (Board of Governors of the Federal Reserve System, 2012) includes the following highlights:

- Limits on expiration dates. The money on a gift card will be good for at least five years from the date the card is purchased. Any money that might be added to the card at a later date must also be good for at least five years.
- Replacement cards. If a gift card has an expiration date the customer still may be able to use unspent money that is left on the card after the card expires. For example, the card may expire in five years but the money may not expire for seven. If the card expires and there is unspent money, the customer can request a replacement card at no charge. Check the card to see if expiration dates apply.
- Fees disclosed. All fees must be clearly disclosed on the gift card or its packaging.

- Limits on fees. Gift card fees typically are subtracted from the money on the card. Under the new rules, many gift card fees are limited. Generally, fees can be charged if the consumer has not used the card for at least one year, and the customer is only charged one fee per month. These restrictions apply to fees such as: dormancy or inactivity fees for not using the card, fees for using the card (sometimes called usage fees), fees for adding money to the card, and maintenance fees.

Card disclosures should be read carefully so that related and applicable fees are understood. All of these disclosures must be provided to consumers before the purchase is made. Issuers must also include a toll free phone number or website address consumers can access should they have questions about any of the card features.

With gift cards ranking near the top of many gift request lists and the continuing evolution of the gift card industry, wise consumer practices can increase individuals' satisfaction with both giving and receiving gift cards. If buying gift cards, be sure to buy only from reputable sources. With the downturn of the U.S. economy since 2008 and large numbers of retailers filing for bankruptcy, investigate the financial condition of the business before buying. Chapter 11 bankruptcy laws view unspent gift cards as loans to a company.

When Blockbuster Video filed for bankruptcy in September 2010, the bankruptcy proceedings did not require the company to honor gift cards that had been sold. On March 23, 2011, Blockbuster posted notices to consumers informing them all gift cards would expire on April 7, 2011. This was a two week notice. If a card is purchased and the business goes bankrupt, competitors will sometimes honor the card. When the Sharper Image chain filed for bankruptcy in 2008, rival company Brookstone decided to accept Sharper Image gift cards. However, the conditions did not honor the full dollar value of the card, but allowed the card holder to a 25 percent discount off a purchase at Brookstone. There has been a push for a change in bankruptcy law to require companies to put funds received from the purchase of gift cards into a separate account that could then be accessed in case of bankruptcy. Always be sure to get a receipt for each gift card purchased. Check the amount of the receipt for accuracy with the amount paid for the gift card. Include the receipt when giving the card as a gift. Ask for the terms and conditions for the redemption of the gift card. Be familiar with any fees charged for buying the card, expiration dates associated with the card and fees for redemption. Convey this information to the recipient. Be especially cautious in buying gift cards at online auction sites. These sites consistently rank near the top for consumer complaints. Recipients of gift cards need to be cognizant of any rules related to redemption. Read any terms and conditions attached to the card upon receipt of the card. Keep the card and any receipt for purchase in a safe location until the entire value of the card has been expended. Even without expiration dates or fees, many gift cards are not redeemed due to being forgotten. Consider making a recurring calendar notation as a reminder to use the card. Use the entire value of the card as soon as practical after receiving it. If just a small amount of money remains on the card after use, inquire if that amount can be returned as cash. Treat the card as if it is cash. Retailers have individual rules related to lost or stolen cards. Inquire with the issuer to find out if a lost or stolen card can be replaced. The Federal Trade Commission allows consumer complaints to be filed online or by phone.

A recent variation of gift card usage is the appearance of online swap sites, allowing consumers to buy, sell, and swap unused gift cards. The online retailer Plastic Jungle touts itself as the worlds' largest secured gift card exchange. Consumers can sell unused gift cards to Plastic Jungle for a lower percentage of the unused dollar amount remaining on their card. Plastic Jungle then resells the cards to other consumers at a cost less than the amount remaining on the card. Plastic Jungle will not accept cards with less than $25 remaining on them. Consumers are allowed to receive cash, Amazon.com credit or PayPal payment in return for their unused cards. A competitor of Plastic Jungle, CardPool operates on similar principles. CardPool recently launched its own gift card. This allows shoppers to purchase CardPool gift cards, which then enable the recipient to purchase a resold gift card of their choice. CardPool also recently announced the ability to trade unused gift cards in the online environment, without sending in the original card.

If considering reselling a gift card, a few rules can help consumers from becoming fraud victims. The value of an existing gift card should be determined. Many card companies determine this through their website or by calling a toll-free phone number. Because the offers for buying the cards vary by company, spend some time shopping around. Be sure to investigate the company's reputation before sending in a card. Finally, keep documentation of all transactions until compensation card balance is received.

*Susan Reichelt*

**See also:** Bankruptcy; Credit Card Accountability Responsibility and Disclosure Act (Credit CARD Act); Credit Cards; Federal Reserve; Federal Trade Commission (FTC); Frauds and Scams

### References and Additional Readings

Board of Governors of the Federal Reserve System. (2010). What you need to know: New rules for gift cards. http://www.federalreserve.gov/consumerinfo/wyntk_giftcards.htm

Consumer's Union. (2008). Consumer reports takes on gift cards in second annual public education campaign. Retrieved from http://www.consumersunion.org/pub/core_financial_services/005188.html

Federal Trade Commission. (2011). Buying, giving, and using gift cards. Retrieved from http://www.ftc.gov/bcp/edu/pubs/consumer/alerts/alt010.shtm

Knobbe, C. J., Cook, N. J., & Hanson, L. M. (2011). The new federal gift card regulations. *The Franchise Law Journal, 30*(3). Retrieved from http://www.ballardspahr.com/alertspublications/articles/~/media/Files/Articles/2011–03–16_New_Federal_Gift_Card_Regulations.ashx

## Good Samaritan Law

Generally speaking, a Good Samaritan refers to someone who renders aid in an emergency to an injured person or person in peril on a voluntary basis. In fact, its purpose is to encourage emergency assistance by removing the threat of liability for damage done by the assistance. However, the assistance must be reasonable; a rescuer cannot benefit from the Good Samaritan doctrine if the assistance is reckless or grossly negligent. That is, under this law, the help or aid is intended to be with a duty of being reasonably careful. If a victim is unconscious, a Good Samaritan can help under the premise of implied consent, but otherwise, the person must inquire if they can assist. Good Samaritan laws are meant to protect those who come to the aid of others for no other reason than kindness; if the helper is acting with expectation of reward, such as monetary compensation, the law will not apply. The Good Samaritan Law also generally does not apply to persons rendering emergency care, advice, or assistance during the course or regular employment, such as services rendered by a healthcare provider to a patient in a healthcare facility. Additionally, the Good Samaritan doctrine is also used as a defense by persons who act to prevent or contain property damage while using due caution.

Many states are content to follow the Good Samaritan doctrine; some states have general statutes mandating the doctrine. Utah and Hawaii, for example, have Good Samaritan acts, which provide in part, respectively, that:

> [a] person who renders emergency care at or near the scene of, or during an emergency, gratuitously and in good faith, is not liable for any civil damages or penalties as a result of any act or omission by the

person rendering the emergency care, unless the person is grossly negligent or caused the emergency; any person who in good faith renders emergency care, without remuneration or expectation of remuneration, at the scene of an accident or emergency to the victim of the accident or emergency shall not be liable for any civil damages resulting from the persons acts or omission, except for such damages as may result from the persons gross negligence or wanton acts or omissions. (Justia U.S. Law, 2006; U.S. Legal, 2013)

Other states have enacted statutes that "protect specific emergency care or assistance." Indiana, for example, protects the emergency care of veterinarians. Alabama provides immunity to those who assist or advise in the mitigation of the effects of the discharge of hazardous materials. Some states also provide protection to those participating in the cleanup of oil spills. In 1990, Congress passed the Oil Pollution Act (Pub. L. No. 101–380, 33 U.S.C.A. §§ 2701–2761 [1994]), which gave immunity from liability to persons who participate in oil cleanup efforts. Like all Good Samaritan law, the statute does not protect a person who is "grossly negligent or reckless" (Justia U.S. Law, 2006).

However, because the law is open for interpretation, Good Samaritans may find themselves at risk for lawsuits. For example, in California in 2004, two coworkers, Lisa Torti and Alexandra Van Horn, were driving home in two separate cars after attending a function for Halloween night. The car carrying Van Horn hit a light pole. Torti witnessed the event and feared the car was going to explode. In an attempt to save her life, Torti pulled Van Horn out of the car which rendered Van Horn a paraplegic. Though The Good Samaritan Law was assumingly in place to protect such efforts, Van Horn sued Torti, arguing that Torti's actions exacerbated her injuries, thus leaving her permanently paralyzed. As cited by Mallery (2010), "The California Supreme Court, in a four-to-three decision, construed the state's Good Samaritan Law narrowly and held Torti liable for Van Horn's injuries." The court interpreted the law as protecting only Good Samaritans rendering "emergency *medical* care" (p. 648). Since pulling her friend out of a car was not technically "medical care," the court found Torti civilly liable for Van Horn's injuries. In this case, the California Supreme Court held that, while the California Health and Safety Code provides immunity for any harm caused by those who render emergency services, immunity applies only to volunteers who render traditional medical services, such as CPR.

However, the California Health and Safety Code was amended such that Chapter 77 was created to expand protections afforded to Good

Samaritans in an effort to encourage the public to help one another during emergencies. As summarized by Mallery (2010), it provides "immunity from civil liability for those rendering emergency services at the site of an accident, regardless of whether their actions are considered 'medical' (e.g., performing CPR) or 'non-medical' (e.g., pulling someone out of a burning building). Chapter 77 does not provide immunity for harm caused while rendering emergency services in places that offer traditional medical services. Further, civil immunity does not apply to any person whose acts or omissions while rendering emergency care constitute gross negligence or wanton misconduct. Chapter 77, however, ensures that medical, law enforcement, and emergency personnel who act in good faith will continue to be immune from liability for harm caused while responding to an emergency" (p. 648).

Overall, it is the intention of Good Samaritan laws that community members are encouraged to come to the aid of others.

*Melanie Horn Mallers*

**See also:** Activism; Public Safety

**References and Additional Readings**

Justia U.S. Law. (2006). 2006 Utah code-78-11-22-Good Samaritan Act. Retrieved from http://law.justia.com/codes/utah/2006/title78/78_0f025.html

Mallery, S. (2010). Beyond Seinfeld's Good Samaritan debacle: Protecting citizens who render care at the scene of an accident from civil liability. *McGeorge Law Review, 41*(3), 647–654.

Ridolfi, K. M. (2000). Law, ethics, and the good Samaritan: Should there be a duty to rescue? *Santa Clara Law Review, 40,* 957–70.

White, C. H. (2002). No good deed goes unpunished: The case for reform of the rescue doctrine. *Northwestern University Law Review, 97,*507–45.

# Government Accountability Office (GAO)

The U.S. Government Accountability Office (GAO) received its current name in 2004 with the passing of the Human Capital Reform Act. First known as the General Accounting Office, it began in 1921 with approximately 1,700 employees, when the Budget and Accounting Act moved auditing and accounting functions from the Treasury Department to the newly created GAO. This transfer was performed because wartime spending for World War I was high and drove up the national debt, causing governmental concern. Congress sought better information and control over these and other expenditures during this difficult time. During

World War II, due to military spending, the need for additional workers expanded and employees numbered over 14,000 in 1945. Today, the agency employs just over 3,300 employees, in several cities across the United States including Washington, D.C.; Atlanta, Georgia; Boston, Massachusetts; Chicago, Illinois; Dallas, Texas; Dayton, Ohio; Denver, Colorado; Huntsville, Alabama; Los Angeles, California; Norfolk, Virginia; San Francisco, California; and Seattle, Washington, according to the website. Furthermore, they boast an impressive 81-dollar return on every dollar invested.

The GAO, according to its website is an independent, nonpartisan agency working for Congress. They investigate the federal government's spending of tax dollars and are often referred to as the "congressional watchdog." Their mission is to support and aid Congress in meeting its constitutional responsibilities. These responsibilities involve increasing performance and guaranteeing accountability of the federal government for the betterment of the American people. The GAO supplies Congress with information that is objective, timely, fact based, nonpartisan, non-ideological, fair, and balanced. Accountability, integrity, and reliability are their core values and are part of all tasks they undertake, and they carry out these values with strict professional standards for both facts and analyses performed. The Agency head is the Comptroller General of the United States, and is appointed to a 15-year term by the president from a slate of three candidates proposed by a commission from Congress, and later confirmed by the U.S. Senate. The long term provides for stability and vision for the Office.

The GAO advises Congress on their findings in an effort to make government run more efficiently. Their reports and research often provide the backbone for new legislation, which ultimately saves American taxpayers' money. According to the website, they support Congress in the following ways:

- Auditing agency operations to determine whether federal funds are being spent efficiently and effectively;
- Investigating allegations of illegal and improper activities;
- Reporting on how well government programs and policies are meeting their objectives;
- Performing policy analyses and outlining options for congressional consideration; and
- Issuing legal decisions and opinions, such as bid protest rulings and reports on agency rules.

In addition to its own Office's annual financial auditing report, every three years, the GAO is externally reviewed and audited based on government standards to check for operational accuracy and efficiency. The 2010 results are online, and overall show the Office in good standing with high-quality output.

The Office is productive and visionary, and in the last 20 years, achievements of the GAO include reporting on a broad array of issues including the savings and loan industry's problems, warning about deficit spending, modernizing outdated financial systems, computer security, oil and gas spending costs, healthcare fraud, and nursing home conditions. Goals through 2015 have been listed as part of the strategic plan of the GAO.

*Wendy Reiboldt*

**See also:** Department of the Treasury

### References and Additional Readings

Ashby, C. M. (2006). Higher education: Science, technology, engineering, and mathematics trends and the role of federal programs. Testimony before the Committee on Education and the Workforce, House of Representatives. GAO-06-702T. Government Accountability Office.

Government Accountability Office. (2012). Government auditing standards 2011. Retrieved from http://www.gao.gov/yellowbook

Government Accountability Office. (2013). Retrieved from http://www.gao.gov

## Gramm–Leach–Bliley Act

The purpose of the Gramm–Leach–Bliley Act (GLBA, also known as the Financial Services Modernization Act of 1999) is to protect against the sale of individuals' personal financial information. The GLBA was signed into law by President Bill Clinton on November 12, 1999. This act essentially does three things:

- It repeals key provisions of the 66-year-old Glass–Steagall Act to permit commercial banks to affiliate with investment banks.

- It substantially modifies the 43-year-old Bank Holding Company Act of 1956 to permit companies that own commercial banks to engage in any type of financial activity.

- It allows subsidiaries of banks to engage in a broad range of financial activities that are not permitted for banks themselves (American Bankers Association, 1999, n.p.).

Public concern developed regarding the financial industry's disregard for protecting their customers' personal information. There were a series of domestic and international events that led Congress to include Title V into the provisions of the GLBA. Title V focuses on protecting personal financial information. One such event took place in November of 1997 when Charter Pacific Bank of Agoura Hills, California, sold millions of customer credit card numbers to an adult website company. The website company then began to charge customers for access to their sites that they did not request. "In September 2000, the FTC announced that it has won a $37.5 million judgment against the website company" (Electronic Privacy Center, n.d., para. 7). Despite this judgment, the bank claimed to have done nothing illegal; however, they have stopped selling credit card numbers. A similar event occurred in 1998, when NationsBank was fined for sharing customer information with an affiliate subsidiary, Nations Securities. Nations Securities used this information to convince low-risk customers to invest in high-risk securities. This led to many individuals losing large sums of money, including senior citizens.

Title V of the GLBA provides five main types of privacy protection; the first being developing safeguards to guarantee the safekeeping and discretion of customer information. This prevents any disclosure of information that could potentially harm a customer. A second type of privacy protection that this act ensures is that of mandating financial institutions disclose their privacy policies at the time of first becoming a customer of the institution and then every year thereafter. These privacy policies will include information about the company's restrictions on selling or sharing any of the customers' information to any third party without their prior permission. Thirdly, this section of the act allows customers the chance to "opt out" of offers from these third-party companies before having provided any personal or financial information to them.

Two other important privacy provisions of the GLBA are that it bans financial institutions from disclosing access codes and account numbers to third-party companies and it prohibits certain types of "pretexting"—the act of collecting personal information under false pretenses. However, financial institutions do have the right to share client information with credit reporting and financial regulatory agencies.

There are many loopholes for financial institutions to still find ways of sharing customer information. One problem is with the "opt out" policy. This puts all the weight on the customers to protect themselves. In other words, the institution can share or sell information to any third-party company they desire unless explicitly told not to by the customer. Another way that institutions may get by with sharing information is with their affiliated companies. There is no "opt-out" policy in place for affiliations. Financial institutions can have thousands of affiliations that may have little or nothing to do with financial services.

In addition to financial institutions needing to be in compliance with the GLBA, educational institutions that are in compliance with the Federal Educational Rights and Privacy Act (FERPA) are also considered financial institutions are in compliance with the GLBA. Many higher educational institutions are considered financial institutions based on their activities in areas such as student loans and check cashing services.

*Axton Betz and Whitney Walters*

**See also:** Banking; Family Educational Rights and Privacy Act (FERPA); Federal Trade Commission (FTC); Privacy: Offline; Privacy: Online

### References and Additional Readings

American Bankers Association. (1999). Financial modernization: The Gramm–Leach–Bliley Act summary. Retrieved from http://cyber.law.harvard.edu/rfi/casebook/covington.pdf

Cullen, T. (2007). *The Wall Street Journal complete identity theft guidebook.* New York: Three Rivers Press.

Electronic Privacy Information Center. (n.d.). The Gramm–Leach–Bliley Act. Retrieved from http://epic.org/privacy/glba/

McCoy, M., & Schmidt, S. (2008). *The silent crime: What you need to know about identity theft.* Des Moines, IA: Twin Lakes Press.